ANOTHER KIND

PHOTOGRAPHY ON THE MARGINS

OF LIFE

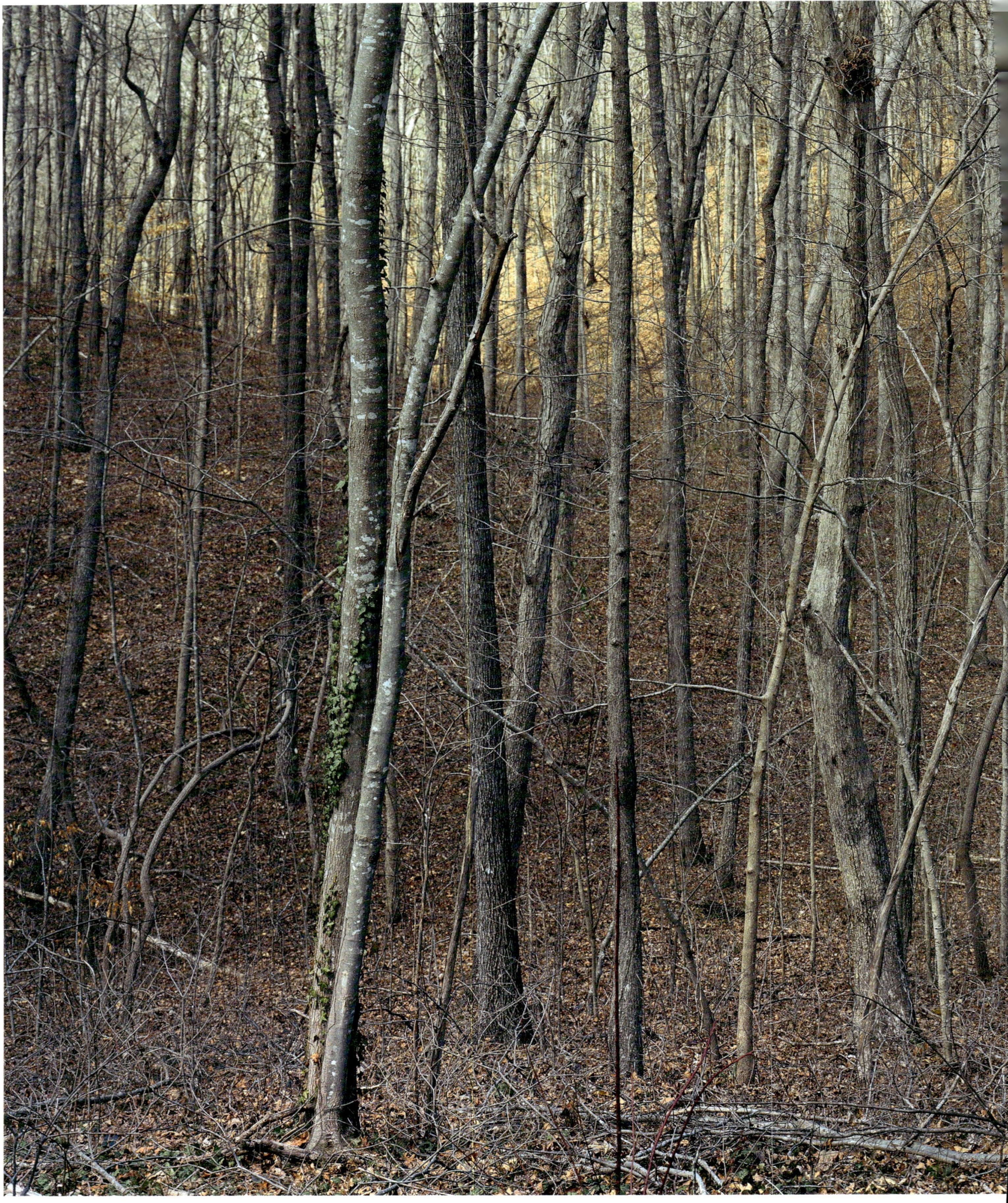

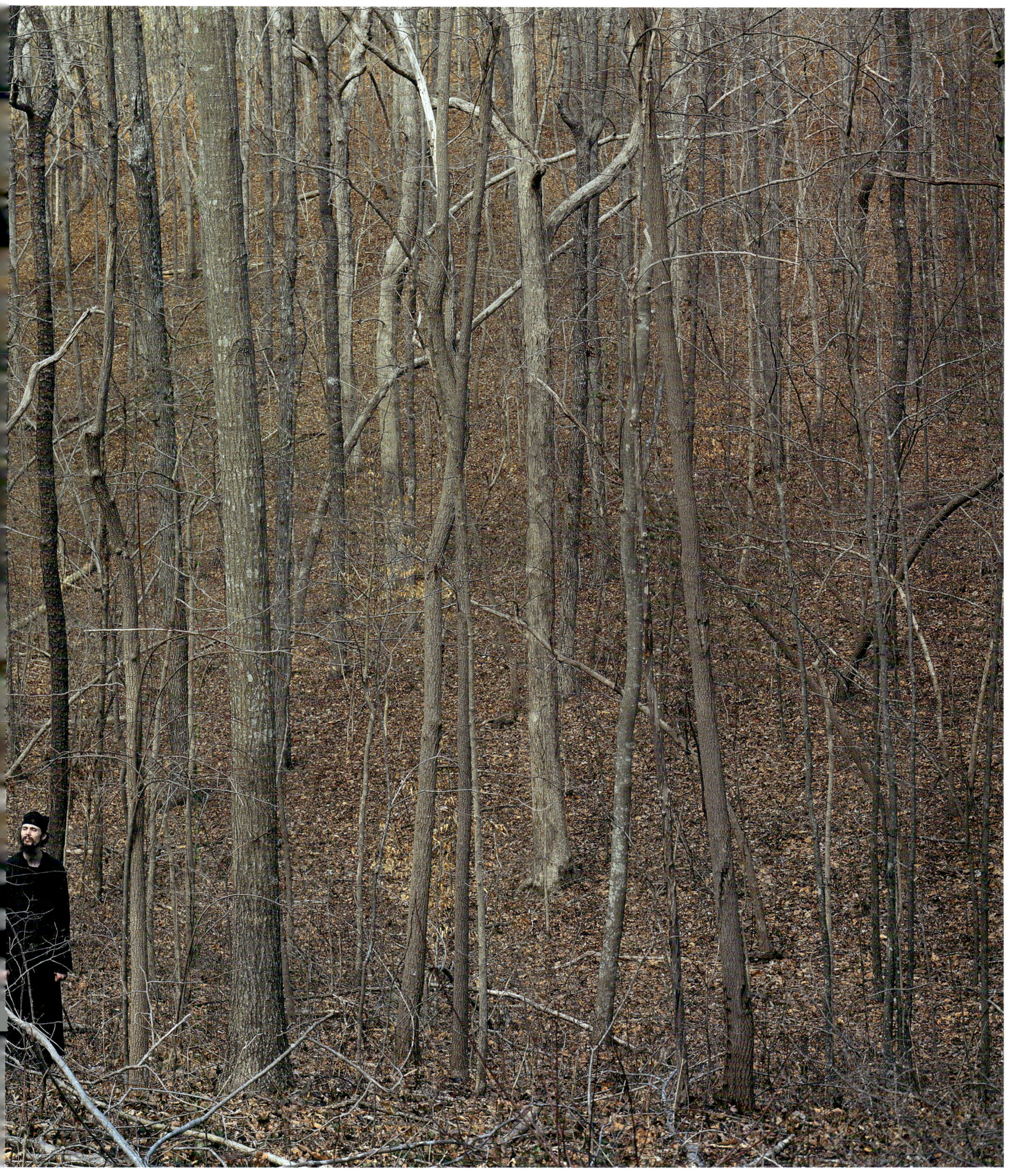

ANOTHER KIND OF LIFE

PHOTOGRAPHY ON THE MARGINS

Edited by
ALONA PARDO

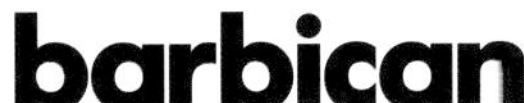

PRESTEL
MUNICH · LONDON · NEW YORK

CONTENTS

Another Kind of Life: Photography on the Margins looks at the continuing fascination of artists with the margins of society through the photographic medium. Indeed many of the most compelling photographic images of the twentieth century have been the result of a determined and often prolonged engagement with communities seemingly at odds with or on the fringes of the mainstream. While the world has changed dramatically over the last sixty years, we are still living in an uncertain world where individual rights are being contested from East to West and those on the fringes feel ever more marginalised from mainstream political and social narratives. *Another Kind of Life* explores photography's relationship with this compelling subject through the work of twenty exceptional image-makers.

As part of the Barbican's 2018 season Art of Change, which reflects on the dialogue between art, society and politics, *Another Kind of Life* directly – and at times poetically – addresses difficult questions about what it means to exist in the margins, the role artists have played in portraying subcultures and the complex intermingling between artistic and mainstream depictions of the outsider.

A rich tradition of American and European social documentary work dominated in the pre-Second World War period, with image-makers from Lewis Hine to Walker Evans preoccupied with documenting the poor and disenfranchised, both urban and rural. More often than not these images – commissioned by organisations such as the National Child Labor Committee or Farm Security Administration, who harnessed the power of photography as a tool for social reform – were by photographers who, while indicting society for its inequities, belonged resolutely to the establishment. The idealistic vision of humanity presented in the legendary *The Family of Man* exhibition held at the Museum of Modern Art in New York in 1955 was the apotheosis of a desire to elevate and empower individuals as a new reality dawned in the post-war era. It was not until the late

1950s that photography in the United States, Europe and to a certain extent Japan underwent a major realignment. The publication of Robert Frank's seminal work *The Americans* in 1959 heralded an era of questioning and self-doubt – particularly in American photography – in which subject matter, composition and style were turned upside down. By the early 1960s, from Tokyo to New York, a much darker and alienating side of society was emerging through the era's race riots and anti-war protests, while gay rights, civil rights and women's liberation movements were simultaneously on the rise. A new generation of photographers emerged ready to respond to the turbulent society of the 1960s and '70s. *Another Kind of Life* charts this exciting chapter in post-war photographic history.

Driven by motivations both personal and political, many of the photographers in the exhibition have sought to provide an authentic representation of disenfranchised communities, often conspiring with them to construct their own identity through the camera lens. Featuring communities of sexual experimenters, romantic rebels, outlaws, survivalists, the economically dispossessed and those who openly flout social convention, the works in the exhibition present the outsider as an agent of change. The non-conventional subject is here a prism through which to view the world afresh. Employing a diverse set of aesthetic strategies, from portraiture to social documentary and from vernacular to street photography, the artists in the exhibition approach their subject with a humanity and empathy that is both empowering and inclusive.

Reflecting a diverse, complex and authentic view of the world, the exhibition touches on themes of gender and sexuality, countercultures, subcultures and minorities of all kinds, and includes bodies of work from Japan, the US, Chile and Nigeria, among other places. By recording and documenting life on the margins, the images in *Another Kind of Life* bear witness to how social attitudes

change across time and space, charting how visual representation has helped shape current discourse in relation to marginalised or alternative communities.

Photography has an unparalleled capacity to reflect and communicate ideas, visually and directly, about the world in which we live. In the hands of great artists, that observation moves far beyond simple description. Our aim has been to seek out those artists and present their work regardless of the tradition from which it has arisen. *Another Kind of Life* not only continues the Barbican's commitment to presenting those artists and photographers but also demonstrates our desire to address issues that stretch beyond art and help us to understand the world from new perspectives.

Rich in thought-provoking material, this book, which is compiled chronologically, includes illuminating texts that shed new light on each artist by some of the most insightful writers and critics working in the field of photography today. The list of authors is expansive, comprising Oriana Baddeley, David Campany, Tim Clark, Lucy Davies, Duncan Forbes, Juliane Fürst, Sophie Hackett, Max Houghton, Sean O'Hagan, Alistair O'Neill, Leo Rubinfien, Aaron Schuman, Stanley Wolukau-Wanambwa and Francesco Zanot. Suffice to say they each entered fully into the spirit of the project and contributed texts that deepen our understanding of every body of work included here, for which we are truly grateful. The book is further enriched by facsimiles of original magazine photo-essays that testify to the considerable influence of the illustrated press. The circulation and dissemination of the work of eminent photographers such as Bruce Davidson and Mary Ellen Mark, to name but two, was instrumental in fostering greater understanding and awareness of the complexity of our world.

Another Kind of Life: Photography on the Margins is the product of collective effort and generosity. Our sincere gratitude goes to the lenders, who parted with works of value or personal significance for the sake of the exhibition. They have been instrumental in supporting our vision for the project. An exhibition of this scale and complexity would not have been possible without the support of international museums, collections and galleries as well as individuals; these include: Art Gallery of Ontario, Canada; ARTIST ROOMS, National Galleries of Scotland, Edinburgh, and Tate, London; Bruce Davidson Studio, New York; Daidō Moriyama Photo Foundation, Tokyo; Fotomuseum, Winterthur, Switzerland; Fraenkel Gallery, San Francisco; Frith Street Gallery, London; Galerie Gregor Staiger Zurich; Galerie Peter Kilchmann, Zurich; Galerie Sultana, Paris; Gavin Brown's enterprise, New York; Howard Greenberg Gallery, New York; Jim Goldberg Studio, California; London School of Economics Library, London; Luhring Augustine, New York; Magnum Photos, London and Paris; Mary Ellen Mark Studio & Library, New York; Melanie Rio Fluency, Nantes; Michael Hoppen Gallery, London; Simon Lee Gallery, London; Sprovieri, London; Stevenson, Cape Town; Taka Ishii, Tokyo; and Zen Photo Gallery, Tokyo.

Our greatest debt, of course, is to the artists and photographers who have generously agreed to participate in this ambitious exhibition, including Philippe Chancel, Larry Clark, Bruce Davidson, Paz Errázuriz, Jim Goldberg, Katy Grannan, Pieter Hugo, Seiji Kurata, Danny Lyon, Teresa Margolles, Boris Mikhailov, Daidō Moriyama, Igor Palmin, Walter Pfeiffer, Dayanita Singh, Alec Soth and Chris Steele-Perkins. Their fervour and dedication to reflecting the complexity of the world through the lens has enriched and shaped our visual landscape beyond the realm of the imagination.

The catalogue has been designed by the immensely talented Melanie Mues of Mues Design, who weaved her innate sensibility for the subject and medium into the fabric of this book. She has brought precision and intelligence to every aspect of its creation. Thanks are also extended to Lincoln Dexter, who handled details large and small with alacrity and good humour and was calm personified throughout.

A defining feature of exhibitions at the Barbican is the ambition of the spatial interventions. As ever, we have reinvented the architecture of the gallery in response to the energy and spirit of the works in the exhibition. We are indebted to Olaf Kneer and Marianne Mueller, ably assisted by Vicente Hernandez, of Casper Mueller Kneer Architects for their vision, sensitivity and commitment towards the exhibition design.

At the Barbican Art Gallery, we would like to thank Exhibition Assistants Charlotte Flint and Tatjana LeBoff for their sustained support of this project; their energy and enthusiasm has known no bounds. Sincere appreciation is also extended to Julie Verheye, Research Assistant, whose passion and diligence cannot be underestimated. Exhibition Organiser Ross Head expertly coordinated all of the myriad details for the exhibition with poise and humour. Production, installation and technical support has been expertly handled by Peter Sutton with support from Bruce Stracy, Margaret Liley and Angus Sanders-Dunnachie. Additional contributions from Ann Berni, Lily Booth and Bréifne Ó Conbhuí in Media Relations; Phil Newby, Charlotte Kewell and Victoria Norton in Marketing; and Lynette Brooks, Camilla Lawson and Cassandra Scott in Development have all played their part in making this exhibition a reality.

We hope that visitors will be moved and enriched by their encounter with this powerful selection of work.

Jane Alison
Head of Visual Arts
Barbican

Alona Pardo
Curator
Barbican Art Gallery

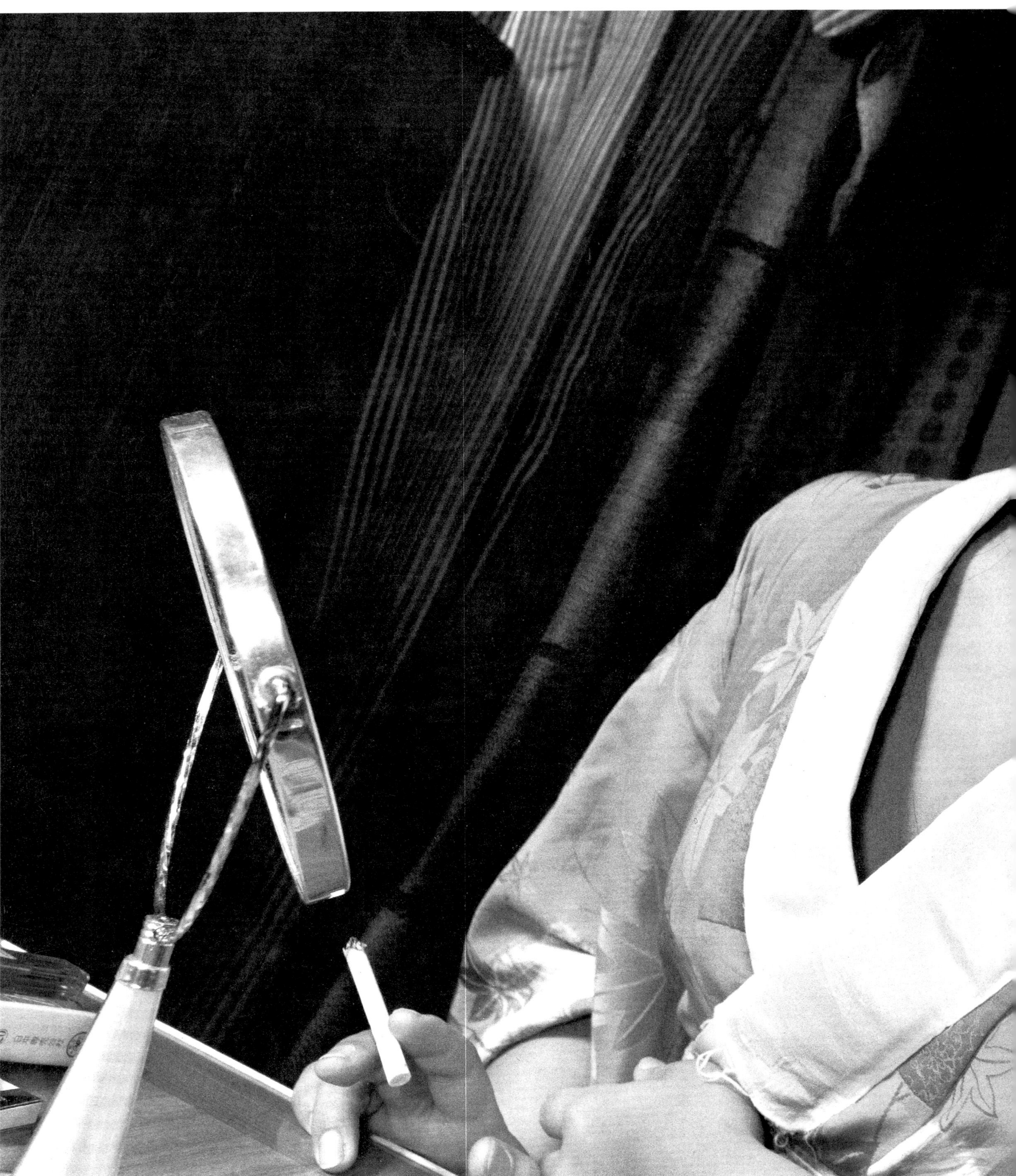

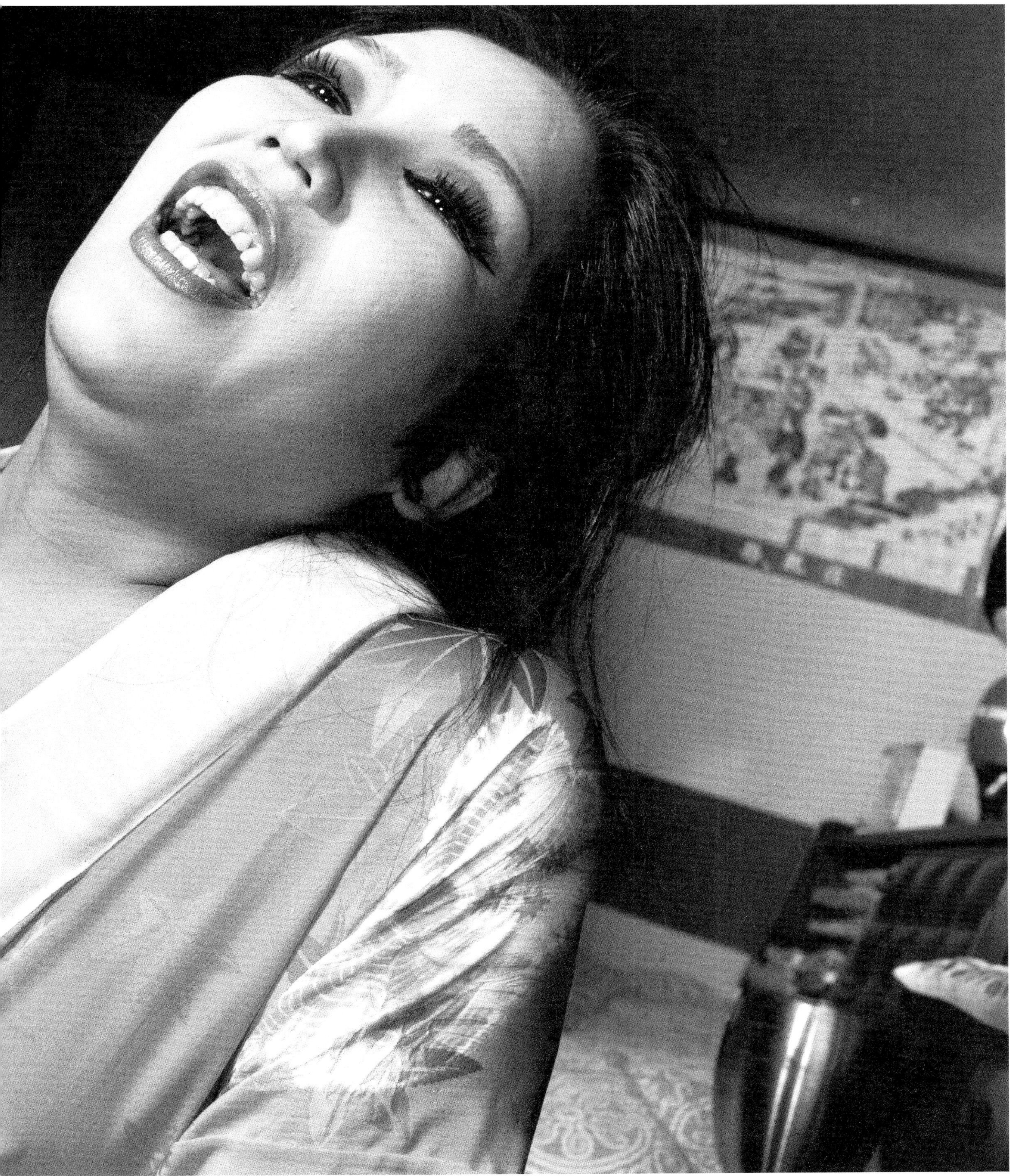

THE LONELY CROWD

Alona Pardo

It seemed funny to me that the sunset she saw from her patio and the one I saw from the back steps was the same one. Maybe the two different worlds we lived in weren't so different. We saw the same sunset.[1]

S. E. Hinton, *The Outsiders* (1967)

Set in Tulsa, Oklahoma, S. E. Hinton's *The Outsiders* is a coming-of-age story that chronicles the adventures of two rival gangs, the Greasers and the Socs, who hail from different sides of the socio-economic track. Published while Larry Clark was in the midst of making his genre-defying work *Tulsa*, Hinton's novel is littered with references to sex, violence, suicide, and underage smoking and drinking, and has at its heart a story about belonging, identity and the desire to foster a community – an *inside*.

Another Kind of Life: Photography on the Margins does not attempt to define 'the outsider'.[2] Rather it sets out to explore photography's endless fascination with those who because of their gender, sexuality, identity, politics, class, geography or simple personal inclination occupy society's hinterlands.

Addressing ideas both of fitting in and standing out, in defiance of cultural conventions as well as the existing visual record, the artists featured in this book – and the exhibition it accompanies – are acutely aware of how their work embodies, performs or documents an authentic experience. While working directly and unobtrusively is paramount to many of the photographers gathered here, maintaining detachment from their subjects is never a realistic objective. By getting close to their subjects, literally and photographically, many of the photographers here have attempted to place themselves in the work, producing penetrating and incisive works that reveal 'new ways to see the world'.[3] What unites all these image-makers – insiders and outsiders alike – is not only a sustained engagement over a period of months, years or even decades between photographer and subject, but more significantly a sophisticated understanding of their respective positions, alongside a genuine willingness to comprehend and share the experiences of those they were seeking to represent.

In her influential essay 'America, Seen through Photographs, Darkly' (1977), Susan Sontag argued that to take a picture is to assign importance. She recognised that this significance varies according to culture and history: while at one time it may have meant the pursuit of 'worthy' subjects, by the time Sontag published her essay it was Andy Warhol's democratic stance of 'everybody is a celebrity'[4] that prevailed. Praising Walt Whitman for his rejection of definitions that divide the world into subjects that are either 'beautiful' or 'ugly', and affirming Alfred Stieglitz's desire to transcend difference and show humanity in the totality of its beauty, Sontag excoriated Diane Arbus as a photographic tourist intent on exploring an 'appalling underworld' whose view was always from the outside.[5]

Contrary to Sontag's treatise, which suggested that documentary photographers cannot transgress the line that divides the world into insiders and outsiders without falling into the violent trap of stealing an unidentifiable *something* from the individuals and communities they are claiming to represent, this essay argues for the necessity of artists to create images that unsettle easy truths. This exhibition and book privilege a form of photography – be it portraiture, documentary or vernacular – that causes clean lines to blur, that in effect forces the viewer to question the comfortable narratives of our world.

This essay borrows its title from David Riesman's era-defining sociological study *The Lonely Crowd: A Study of the Changing American Character* (1950). In the post-war period the 'lonely crowd' became a byword for the increasing alienation of individuals in a capitalist paradigm that demanded their subservience to the status quo. Dealing primarily with the social character of the urban classes, particularly in America, Riesman argued that society could be broken down into 'inner-directed' and 'outer-directed' subjects. In pre-industrial contexts the individual is typically 'inner-directed', their personal values determined by power relations such as class, profession, caste or clan. These values are characteristically passed intact from one generation to another. When the population

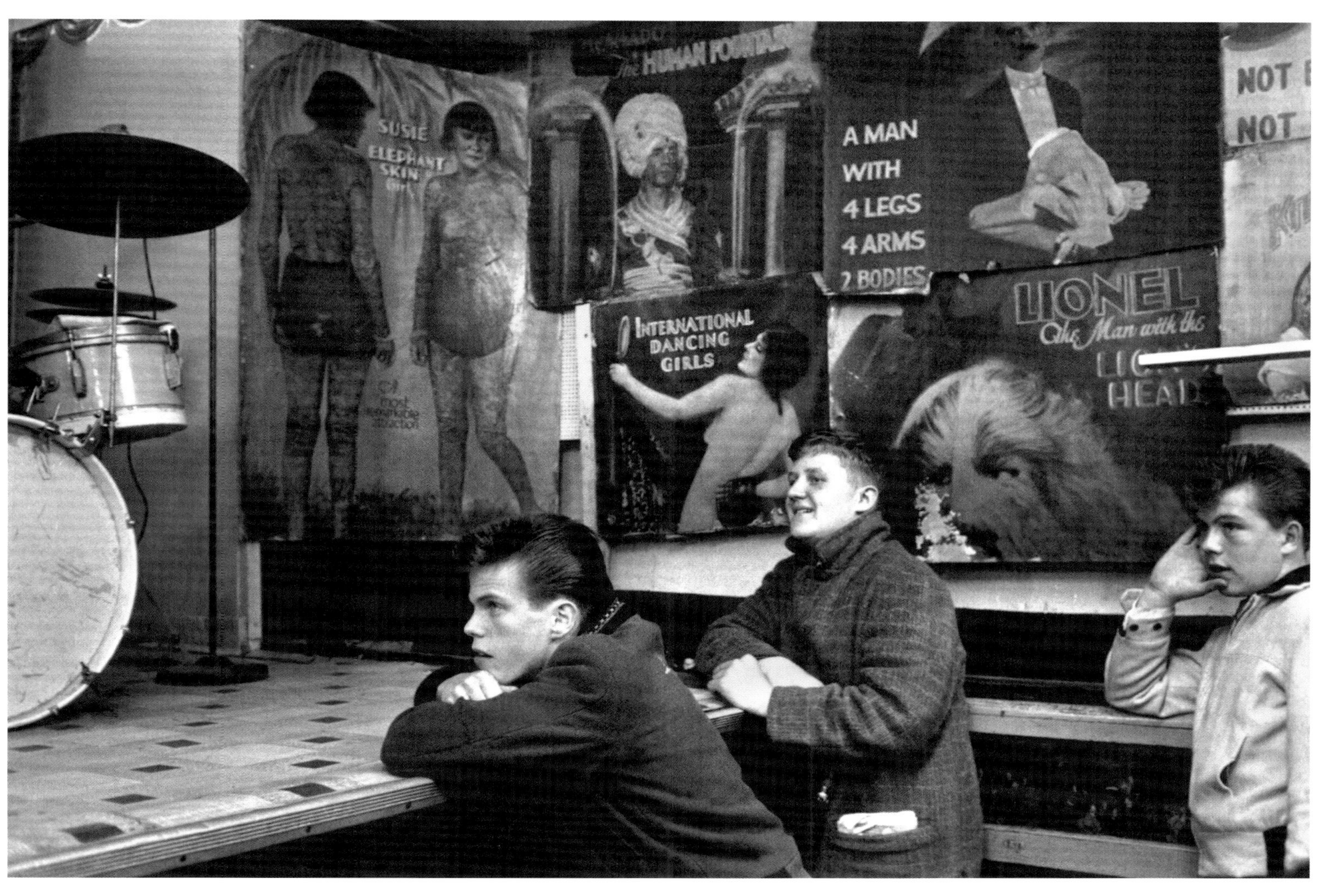

Bruce Davidson, from 'Brooklyn Garg', *Brooklyn, NY*, 1959

is growing but has not reached the stage of crowding (western Europe in the period from the Renaissance to the early twentieth century, for example), the 'inner-directed' individual predominates. Riesman asserted that in post-industrial societies, by contrast, where the population is dense, the 'outer-directed' individual emerges. Their life is in large part shaped by peer groups of persons resembling them in age, social class and other attributes and they adjust their values to conform to those of their group, in a constant process of change.[6]

The Cold War battle between communism and capitalism that came to define the global post-war period created an atmosphere of fear and distrust of the ideological other. It allowed figures such as Joseph McCarthy to protect the status quo by defining themselves in oppositional terms – that is, as the antithesis of 'those damn Soviet commies' and anyone else who strayed from the accepted heteronormative, white, middle-class nuclear family norm. Photography was also used as a propaganda tool in this war of soft power. For instance, the 1955 exhibition *The Family of Man*, organised by Edward Steichen, the noted photographer and director of the department of photography at New York's Museum of Modern Art, presented a singular narrative of human experience as perceived predominantly through a Western perspective.[7]

Responding to this culture of conformity and oppression that had settled, almost imperceptibly, like a fine dust over the new world order that emerged from the ashes of the Second World War, photographers in the late 1950s began to explore the outsiders they found on the margins of their own societies.

———

This exhibition traces a sixty-year arc that charts an exceptionally vibrant period of social change, from the race riots and anti-war protests that dominated the 1960s, to the battles for gay rights and women's liberation of the 1970s, to the decline of socialist values in the post-Cold War era, through to the battleground of today's divisive world where authoritarian regimes are taking hold from India to Turkey, Russia to the United States.

The exhibition starts resolutely in the fecund period of post-war America, which by the late 1960s was marked by a fatalism and weariness – expressed by musicians such as Bob Dylan, Jefferson Airplane, and Lou Reed

and The Velvet Underground, whose searing lyrics meditated on the failed utopianism of the period. By the early 1960s, as the editorial grip on photography began to waver and its social function was replaced by personal statement, photographers working across the United States, Europe and Japan offered new views of the social landscape of their time.

This shift from the social to the personal was championed early on by John Szarkowski, Steichen's successor at MoMA, who introduced the work of three relatively unknown figures – Diane Arbus, Lee Friedlander and Garry Winogrand – in the exhibition *New Documents* in 1967, marking this turning point in photography in its American context. In the exhibition's opening statement Szarkowski wrote: 'In the past decade a new generation of photographers has directed the documentary approach toward more personal ends. Their aim has been not to reform life, but to know it. Their work betrays a sympathy – almost an affection – for the imperfections and the frailties of society.'[8]

Working in New York through the 1960s, Diane Arbus was a trailblazer of a new photographic aesthetic, and her distinctive approach is characterised by the directness of her portraiture as well as her ability to find the familiar in the strange and discover the unusual in the ordinary. Her iconic images of transsexuals, musclemen, nudists, and circus and sideshow performers are by turns raw and unflinching, disturbing and illuminating. Born into a wealthy Jewish family, from the outset Diane and her brother, the poet Howard Nemerov, saw themselves as outsiders, with her schoolteacher going so far as to describe her as being imbued with a 'sense of separateness'.[9] In seeking out her subjects in diaper derbies, nudist camps, circuses, asylums and nightclubs, it has been argued that Arbus – a self-confessed adventurer – was trying to break out of her own notions of propriety and normalcy.

More recently, however, the scholar Philip Charrier has highlighted Arbus's relationship to the New Journalism of the period, most commonly associated with figures such as Tom Wolfe and Norman Mailer. Mailer, in his editorial accompanying Bruce Davidson's *Brooklyn Gang* images in the June 1960 issue of *Esquire*, described his writing as being 'fortified by a message'.[10] Charrier has argued that '[Arbus] should be regarded as someone who formed part of a trend of deeply researched, more "personal" journalism focused upon non-

conventional, "non-authority" subjects.'[11] He
has furthermore linked her working method to
those of Bruce Davidson, Danny Lyon and Larry
Clark, each of whom immersed themselves in
youth subcultures.

Exhausted by the relentless need for photographic
renewal in the realm of high fashion and the
crippling world of photojournalism as dictated
by the likes of *Life* magazine, by the late 1950s
both Diane Arbus and fellow photographer
Bruce Davidson dedicated themselves to
creating photographs that privileged a direct
relationship with the subject. In the case of
Arbus, whose images depended on the 'active
participation of her subjects', she struck up
lasting relationships with gay rights figures
such as Stormé DeLarverie, whom she
photographed backstage, as well as other
'singular people', as she called them.[12] Both
Arbus and Davidson recognised the importance
of the hyper-subjective exchange between
photographer and subject and were rewarded
with the publication of extended photo-essays
in *Esquire* magazine during 1960.

Describing himself as 'an outsider on the inside',
Bruce Davidson has spent the last fifty years
photographing 'isolated, abused, abandoned,
and invisible' worlds,[13] from his breakthrough
project *Brooklyn Gang* (1959) – a portrait of
post-war outsider youth culture in which he
chronicled the Jokers, a gang of teenagers he
spent months befriending and shooting – to
his intimate and powerful portrait of Jimmy
'Little Man' Armstrong in his series *The Dwarf*
(1958). Upon the suggestion of Sam Holmes, an
amateur trapeze artist and librarian at Magnum,
Davidson visited the Clyde Beatty Circus, which
had set up camp at the Palisades Amusement
Park in New Jersey in late 1958, where he was
immediately captivated by Jimmy Armstrong,
a clown who also happened to be a person of
short stature.

Immersing himself into the lives of the
performers, Davidson spent several weeks
travelling around with them photographing the
prosaic reality of circus life, paying particular
attention to Armstrong. Rather than document
the grand spectacle of Clyde Beatty the lion
tamer or Hugo Zacchini the human cannonball,
Davidson's sombre photographs foreground the
daily drudgery of circus life with its collection
of outsiders whose dreams seem to be forever
out of reach. Davidson's images of Armstrong
capture him dressed up, regaling children
with his jokes or at rest in bed, curled up in

the corner listening to the radio as if to protect
himself from the outside world; in each he seems
enveloped in a cloak of solitude and isolation.
In one particularly poignant image, Armstrong
is seen eating a sandwich while subject to the
curious stares and sniggers of his fellow diners,
a marked reminder that beyond his stage
persona of Little Man he is still an outsider.

A decade later in Japan, the young photographer
Daidō Moriyama turned to the back streets
and dark interiors of dressing rooms and small
stages in the districts of Asakusa – famous
for its underworld and theatrical tradition –
and Shinjuku, to photograph performers and
strippers. In pursuit of reality as it unfolded
before his camera, his black-and-white, raw,
grainy and out-of-focus images homed in
on gangsters, nightclub entertainers and
prostitutes to create a steamy portrait of Tokyo,
a city that was witnessing unprecedented
political dissent in response to the ongoing
American occupation, the Vietnam War and
the increasing Westernisation of Japanese
culture. An urban wanderer by nature,
Moriyama embraced the erotic, chaotic and dark
elements of society in his photographs and was
instinctively drawn to the outsiders and outlaws
who prowled Tokyo's narrow back streets.

The photographers active during this period
are united by their need to delve into the
darker aspects of society, and their work can
be characterised by their distance from the
conventionalism and sanctified rituals of the
middle class. Diane Arbus, Bruce Davidson and
Daidō Moriyama went on to influence a younger
generation of artists – including Larry Clark,
Danny Lyon and Seiji Kurata – whose work
continued to explore social margins and break
down the barriers that had kept such groups
away from the camera.

Moriyama's influence over young Japanese
photographers in the 1970s cannot be
underestimated. He demonstrated that it was
possible to go out into the streets and engage
anybody and anything with the camera.
Inspired to take up photography as a direct
result of encountering Moriyama's work, Seiji
Kurata entered the nocturnal underworld of
Tokyo armed with his Pentax 6×7 and a flash.
Kurata, like Weegee before him, followed the
police and the world of gang fights, yakuza,
motorcycle boys and death. His book *Flash
Up*, published in 1980, involved a descent into
the separate clans of Tokyo's underground
network. In the midst of one of the safest cities,

in a society that was viewed as one of the most conformist, Kurata introduced a cast of tattooed gangsters, leather-boys, bar-girls and an emerging queer community that countered the perception of Japan as a beacon of social precision and repression. Kurata's images exposed a side of Tokyo that was steamy, dangerous and at times brutal.[14]

For photographers such as Lyon and Clark, their immersion in the communities they were documenting was critical to their work's faithfulness to reality. Their privileged position as insiders not only granted them unfettered access into these private worlds but more significantly attests to the authenticity of their representation.

In 1964, Lyon joined the Chicago Outlaws motorcycle gang, a motley crew of antisocial, heavy-drinking bike riders. By joining their ranks he demonstrated that he wanted to be one of them and describe their way of life from the inside out. Taken over a period of four years, Lyon's strikingly dynamic images of biker culture served as a clarion call for a style of American liberty that was at the time subversive. Indeed, *The Bikeriders* (1963–67)

was the inspiration for Dennis Hopper's 1969 film *Easy Rider*, a landmark counterculture film that explored the societal landscape, issues and tensions of 1960s America, such as the rise of the hippie movement with its recreational drug use and communal lifestyles. Belonging to the trend of New Journalism as opposed to a photojournalistic tradition, Lyon described his encounter with the Outlaw biker gang as a subject with 'which I could indulge my fantasies and realize my dreams, and develop through my camera new ways to see the world'.[15]

New ways of picturing the world were also critical to the photographic vision of Larry Clark, who had learned the art of photography through his mother, a studio photographer who specialised in mother-and-baby shots. His visceral book *Tulsa*, published in 1971, marked a watershed moment in American photography. A brutally frank personal testament, it chronicled the lives and deaths of a group of high-school drug addicts – with a particular focus on two individuals, Billy Mann and David Roper. Over a period of eight years during the 1960s and '70s, Clark himself was intermittently an active member of this group in Tulsa, Oklahoma, the artist's hometown.

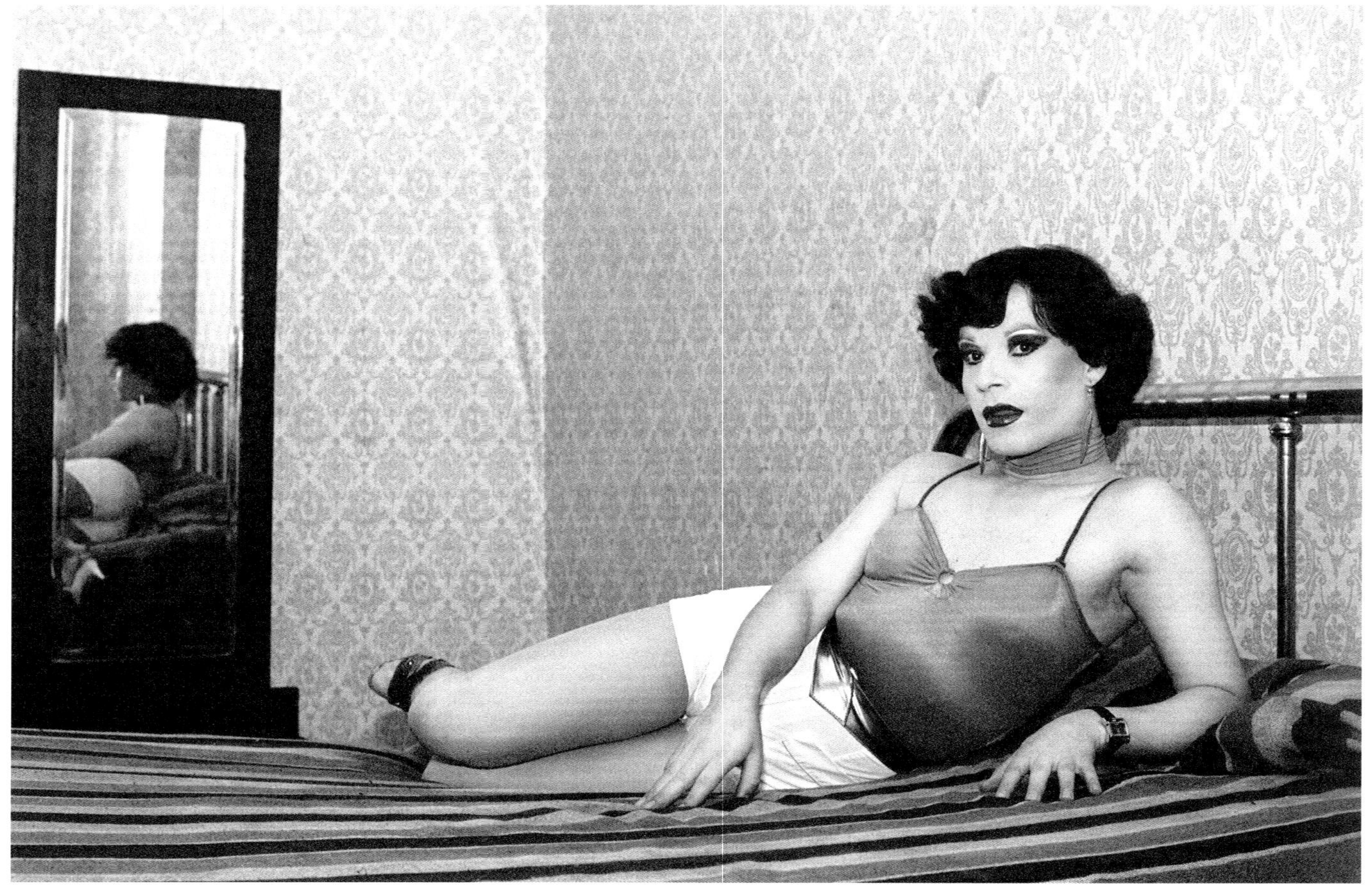

   Paz Errázuriz, from 'La manzana de Adán' (Adam's Apple), *Evelyn, Santiago*, 1983

Sex, drugs and violence were captured in a raw, grainy monochrome that defined the untrammelled confessional style adopted later by the likes of Nan Goldin and Corinne Day.

Writing about *Tulsa* in *The Photobook: A History*, Martin Parr and Gerry Badger suggest that the 'incessant focus on the sleazy aspect of the lives portrayed, to the exclusion of almost anything else – whether photographed from the "inside" or not – raises concerns about exploitation and drawing the viewer into a prurient, voyeuristic relationship with the work'.[16] Yet it is this very dynamic that imbues the images with such disturbing power.

The autobiographical nature of Lyon's and Clark's photography was accentuated by their use of text, an approach first introduced into the field of photography in the 1930s by the likes of Walker Evans and the vernacular architecture, billboards and advertising signage that populated his work for the US Farm Security Administration. By the late 1970s and early 1980s, combining words and photographs had become a genre of art photography with a wide and varied practice, ranging from simply writing on photographs to the first experiments with the digital collaging of word and image. At the same time, the photograph had long since outstripped the word as mass media's preferred descriptive system. As a consequence, artists could no longer rely on the same frames of reference for language as even Evans could in the 1930s.

Incorporating text into his multimedia projects is central to Jim Goldberg's radical style of 'documentary storytelling'. A multi-year exploration into the existence of homeless youths living on the urban fringes, *Raised by Wolves*, published in 1995, is an unflinching and at times shocking portrait of teenage runaways in Los Angeles and San Francisco. Seamlessly intertwining interviews, handwritten notes, Polaroids and photographic remnants of the protagonists' lives – from doctors' reports to doodles to psychiatric tests – the project's gritty street style directly relates the experiences of this loose-knit group of young people who have been effectively written out of mainstream social histories.

Goldberg's work is defined by a collaborative method whereby he actively encourages his subjects to write on his images, while also combining his photographs with other media. The individuals he photographs are given a say not only in the making of the work but also in the construction of the narrative. Recording the teens' most private moments, *Raised by Wolves* narrates the tragic story of veteran traveller, junkie and self-proclaimed rock star Tweeky Dave and recent runaway Echo. Appearing as both photographer and character in this twisted plot, the artist's nuanced role in this constructed narrative disrupts the conventional binary position – as put forward by Sontag – of the photographer as either insider or outsider. The implication here is that these contested positions are not mutually exclusive, complicating accepted photography theory and suggesting that this terrain is full of contradictions that need to be pulled apart and revisited.

In one her most personal projects to date, Dayanita Singh weaves words and images into the very fabric of her 2001 photobook *Myself Mona Ahmed*, a serial portrait of Mona Ahmed, a unique individual who belongs to one of India's many visible yet largely ignored marginal communities. Cutting across social and class boundaries and at once a chronicle and a memoir, the book is narrated through a series of letters written by Mona to the publisher that complicates the idea of authorship.

Another Kind of Life also looks back through the last sixty years to explore how photography has been used as a tool to document, advocate for and spark debate around the representation of gender nonconforming people. This seems particularly current given that, in the UK at least, 2017 marked the fiftieth anniversary of the partial decriminalisation of homosexuality in the Sexual Offences Act. This marks a point in recent history against which we can chart historical progress, survey the present day, and potentially look to a more inclusive and diverse future.

In the early 2000s, 'a hundred loose snapshots, both colour and black and white, and three neatly preserved photo albums'[17] that revealed the existence of a retreat called Casa Susanna were recovered from a New York flea market. First named Chevalier d'Eon after an eighteenth-century cross-dressing spy who lived the second half of their life as a woman, the retreat was later renamed Casa Susanna. Active through the 1950s to the end of the 1960s and run by the formidable Susanna Valenti and her wife, Marie, Casa Susanna operated as a resort in the Catskills for a burgeoning gender nonconforming community.

The resort became a safe haven where cross-dressers from all walks of life could safely shed societally prescribed clothing and behaviour and adopt their preferred identities.

Testifying to an alternative form of kinship, the casual snapshots in this collection, mostly taken by the subjects themselves, portray cross-dressers – their outfits painstakingly assembled and their hair perfectly coiffed – playing to the camera and consciously exploring female stereotypes. These unique vernacular prints, recalling the form of a family album, reveal a hidden community that nonetheless found expression through photography. Instrumental in helping the individual community members construct their own gender-fluid identities, this collection, which served both a private and a social function, attests to the pivotal role photography played in capturing and documenting this hitherto concealed history.

The desire of Casa Susanna's members to affirm their performed identities resulted in the publication of *Transvestia*, a pioneering self-published bi-monthly periodical founded in 1960 by Virginia Prince, a regular visitor to both Chevalier d'Eon and Casa Susanna. A story-driven magazine, it was published by and for the burgeoning transvestite and transgender community with the stated aim to 'serve as a means of gathering information in its chosen field and to aid, by any means available, the dissemination of knowledge'.[18] Offering a safe space for individuals to narrate their own stories without societal judgement, the magazine featured images – often taken clandestinely – of cross-dressers, who found acceptance in its pages from a like-minded community. Ultimately, *Transvestia* broke important new ground in the discussion of gender and dress and played a vital role in calling for self- and public acceptance, awareness and legal protection.

Documenting one of the most obscure and difficult moments in Chile's recent political and sexual history under the brutal dictatorship of General Augusto Pinochet, Paz Errázuriz's series *La manzana de Adán* (Adam's Apple) centres on the lives of Pilar, Evelyn and Mercedes, members of a community of transvestite sex workers working in the 1980s in the brothels of La Jaula and La Palmera, in the towns of Talca and Santiago respectively. Conspiring with them to create their own identities, Errázuriz's intimate colour and black-and-white images portray the protagonists of

this underground world as they go about their daily lives, be it preparing for a night's work or simply finding refuge in their domestic space. The personal struggle they demonstrate in their refusal to conform to accepted notions of gender marks them out as unlikely heroes against a political regime determined to control and regulate every aspect of society. Taken at a time when gender nonconforming people were regularly subjected to curfews, persecution and police brutality, Errázuriz's images of Pilar and Evelyn – which more often than not capture them staring directly into the camera – represented a collaborative and defiant act of political resistance for both the artist and the wider community.

The specificity of the Latin American context is further explored in Teresa Margolles's powerful series *Pista de baile* (Dance Floors; 2016), which exposes the precarious economic position of transgender sex workers in the Mexican border town of Ciudad Juárez. Standing tall and proud under the beating sun and set against a vivid blue sky, the individuals documented here have been excluded from the social order first for their gender and then for the only profession open to them, prostitution. Subject to continued violence, Margolles's figures become part of a landscape in which ruin and devastation are the main protagonists. Despite this, the sex workers show their best face, as if reaffirming their presence in the midst of violence and destruction.

From Errazuriz's and Margolles's defiant representations of transvestite and transgender sex workers to Lyon's and Clark's intimate portrayals of distinct subcultural tribes, what connects these seemingly disparate communities is the idea of agency and consent through the act of photography. Reflecting the plurality of lives lived in fractured post-war societies across the globe, the artists gathered here have through collaboration, dialogue and personal participation turned their lens on anti-establishment, non-conventional communities of all persuasions, to present a more complex, diverse and authentic view of the world.

Taken together, the personal viewpoints presented here are at once empathetic and engaged; they inspire, threaten, shock and empower in equal measure and ultimately force us to look at ourselves and our attitudes towards those on the fringes of society, encouraging us to celebrate another kind of life.

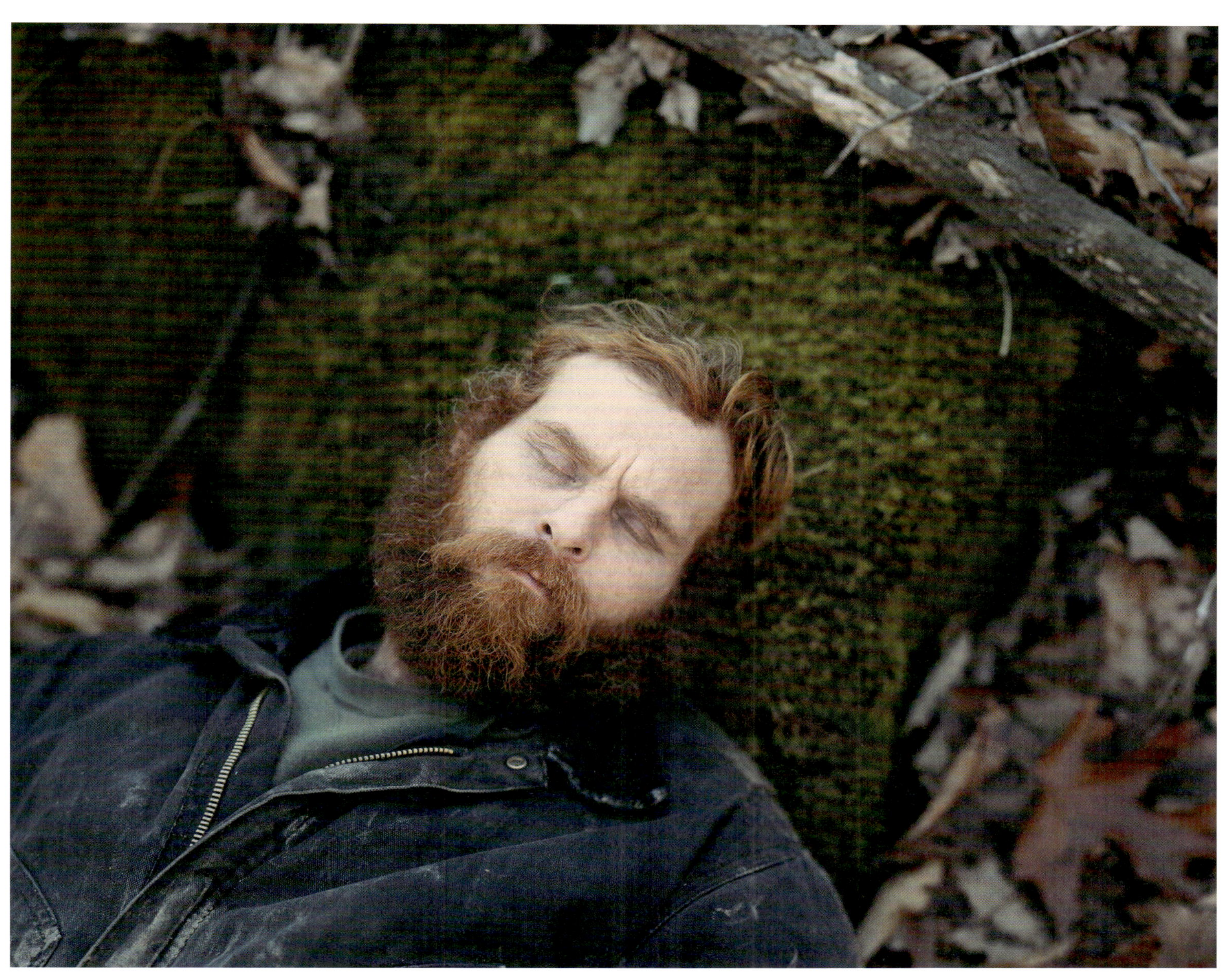

PLATES

DIANE

ARBUS

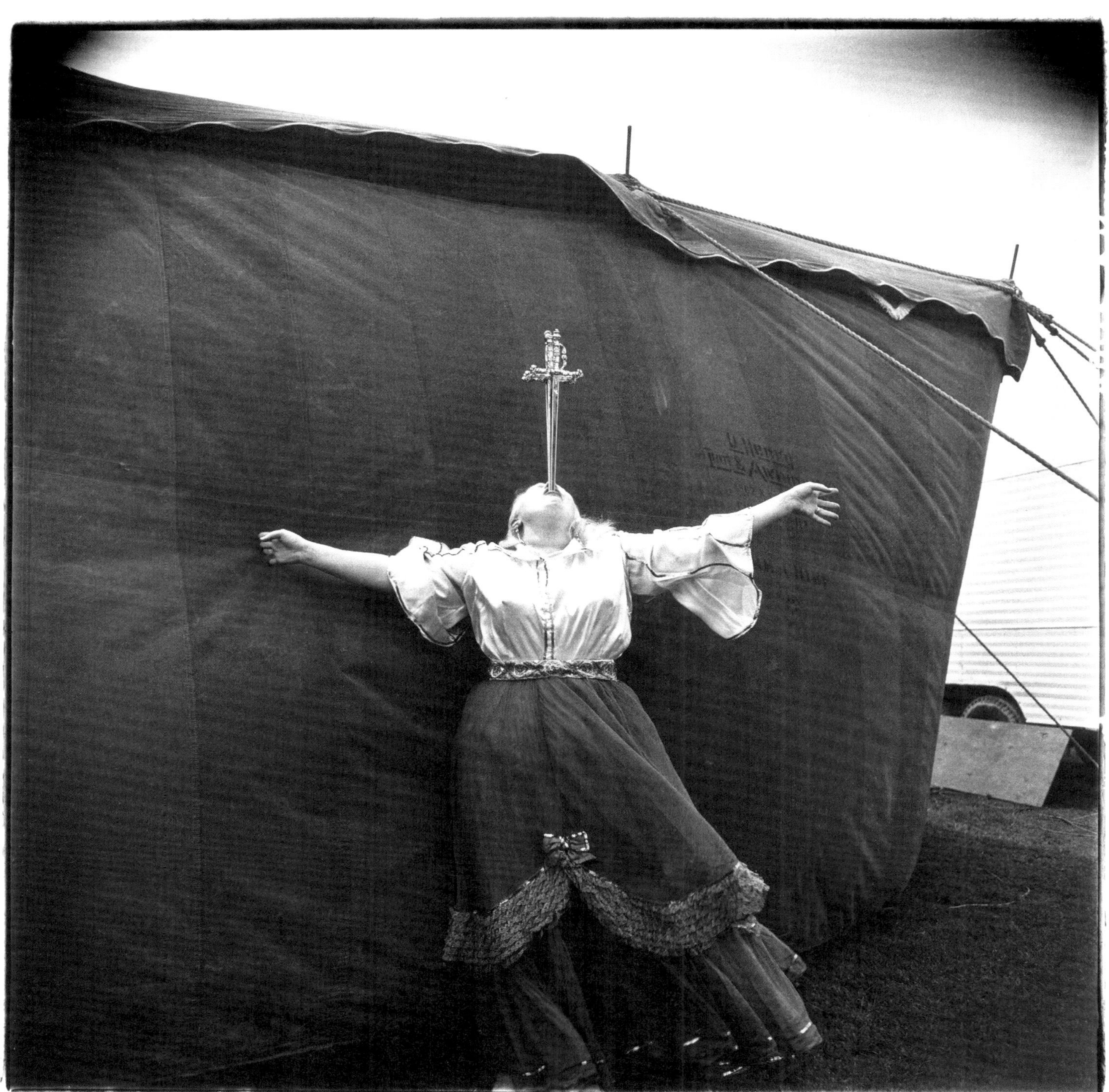

For almost four decades the complex, profound vision of Diane Arbus (b. 1923, USA; d. 1971) has had an enormous influence on photography and a broad one beyond it, and the general fascination with her work has been accompanied by an uncommon interest in her self. Her suicide has been one, but just one, reason for the latter, yet for the most part the events of her life were not extraordinary.

Arbus's wealthy grandparents were the founders of Russeks, a Fifth Avenue department store in Manhattan. Growing up well-protected in the 1930s, Arbus had only a vague sense of the effects of the Depression, and in her generation her family had become greatly cultivated (her brother was the poet Howard Nemerov). She married Allan Arbus at age eighteen and learned her craft with him as they prospered as commercial photographers and raised two daughters, but by the mid-1950s she felt trapped in fashion and advertising. Leaving their business, she dedicated herself to her personal work, and by the decade's end she and her husband separated, though they remained married until 1969 and were close until the end of her life. Her essential interests were clear after 1956, and for the next six years she photographed assiduously with a 35mm camera, in locations that included Coney Island carnivals, Hubert's Museum and Flea Circus of 42nd Street, the dressing rooms of female impersonators, and the streets, cinemas, parks and busses of Manhattan.

Arbus studied with Lisette Model from 1956 to 1957. In 1962 her work changed dramatically when she adopted the square camera and emptied her work of elisions, digressions, evocative shadow and routes of escape. Her subjects would come to include the members of many kinds of subculture – among them nudists and transgender people – and also people with physical impairments. In her new photographs she used a bright flash and let the background go chaotic. They exhibited their subjects like specimens in jars, and forced themselves on the viewer as stubbornly as unwelcome news intrudes into the mind.

Arbus's square photographs speak the language of the 1960s in many ways – through their raw intensity and love of the strange, in asserting that the present moment is crucial, in denying one a mere observer's safe distance – but these are all aspects of their fundamental concern with whether the subject and the viewer admit the truth. In this preoccupation, her pictures belong to the decade's overarching search for authenticity. They retain within their blackness, even now, the exhilaration of a departure upon a ship from which certainty has been flung over the side, and they also touch the decade's torment profoundly.

Arbus took abundantly from literature, movies, the news and popular myth, but if one wanted a purely photographic genealogy for her, one would have to put on one side Weegee, who loved the extreme as she did, and Lisette Model, who passed her a small legacy from the Neue Sachlichkeit and from whom she learned graphic drama and the importance of getting close. On the other side would go Walker Evans, in whom she must have admired the ability to look critically and untangle the contradictory things for which a subject stood, and August Sander. Sander especially seems to have underwritten Arbus's instincts. She saw his work in 1960 in the Swiss journal *Du* (and later studied it at MoMA), and she wrote of one spring day that year when Manhattan's people looked to her like his: 'everyone [on the street] ... immutable down to the last button, feather, tassel or stripe. All odd and splendid as freaks and nobody able to see himself.'[1] She would have understood from Sander how people can conceal and reveal themselves at once, but where this matter was subtle for him, Arbus put it right at the front of her art.

If we can say that their coats, hats, medals, canes and dogs give Sander's strongest subjects screens behind which to hide, almost all the principals in Arbus's finest portraits are also masked. What impressed Arbus the most powerfully, though, was less the mask per se than the discrepancy between mask and face. She seems to have been able to tell from a block away ('you see someone on the street and ... essentially what you notice ... is the flaw'[2]) who would be unable to keep from showing what he or she hoped to protect, and she found an elegant name for this: 'the gap between intention and effect', between 'what you want people to know about you and what you can't help people knowing'.[3] The idea of the gap offers not just a guide to the route Arbus's intuition took; it is also a principle that sets her world apart from the ordinary one.

Position and prestige meant far less to Arbus than the isolated person's yearning – to be glamorous, to be strong, to be fetching, to be lovable, to be female if one was male, male if female, to be, sometimes (as in *Tattooed Man at a Carnival, Md. 1970*), something so indefinable that the unanchored hysteria of pure desire is the point. Where it is conspicuous, the gap between intention and effect is actually one of the main things that distinguishes a strong from a weak Arbus picture.

For all the ardour with which she pursued it, though, the distance between what a person wants to be and is only amounted to her starting place. Her best work supports the Chekhovian idea that even an awful character, if he is worth describing, must display some genuine virtue, and the subject of any strong Arbus picture is never merely ridiculous. When her work is at its most august, Arbus sees through her subject's pretensions, her subject *sees* that she sees, and an intricate parley occurs around what the subject wants to show and wants to conceal.

One particular series of phenomena – the masked subject; the slipping of the mask; the subject's awareness that his or her pride has been exposed *and* that the photographer has seen – was the great discovery of Arbus's strongest years. The *Naked Man Being a Woman, N.Y.C. 1968* (p. 27) should have found it easy to ask Arbus to leave, but instead, like so many others, let her intrusion become, for a moment, terribly important. Each sitter allowed a miniature trial to occur, in which he or she might fend off the photographer's strenuous eye, or sag and reveal the truth. And what would it mean to be courageous? In Arbus, paradox is everywhere. For some of her subjects keeping the mask up would be nobler; for others, letting it drop. We cannot say that she *wanted* to find her people brave – she was impartial on this – but she weighed their courage as minutely as if it had been dust of the purest gold, which in fact it was.

Arbus has been called a voyeur of 'freaks', of 'damaged', 'deviant' and 'fatally flawed' 'objects of revulsion', of the 'horrible' and 'bloodcurdling'. It is often countered that her photographs express a warm compassion for the outcast, yet this is no less simplistic. The distress that her work provokes is real. Its ability to awaken fear, for example, is one of its great strengths, and that emotion is felt by those who cherish it as well as by those who hate it. It is likewise said in her defence that deformity did not really interest her, when of course it did. What is essential to understand is that it interested her not as a blunt, obscene fact, but for how it shaped the psyche of the person who endured it, which is the meaning of her famous comment that 'freaks were born with their trauma. They've already passed their test in life. They're aristocrats.'[4] If to get to the ultimate beauty and tenderness in Arbus's photographs one must abandon the idea that she was an artist of the horrible (as Susan Sontag crudely expressed it in *On Photography*), one cannot do so completely because it is partly true. It does no good to sanitise Arbus's work, but then, one must never fail, either, to see how it shines with wonder. There are loves more complex than that for handsome faces and figures. It was with her characteristic hilarity that Arbus wrote, 'I cannot seem to [make] a person ... look good ... the few times I've made a special effort the photograph was rotten.'[5]

Meanwhile, no other photographer makes viewers feel more strongly that they are being directly addressed, and this must have been another incitement to her opponents. All strong photographs are richly ambiguous from the start, and if anything, they grow even more complex.

———

How people challenge their fates is Arbus's transcending subject – if, and to what extent, they are free. In refusing to assume that they are, or can be, she expresses a vestige, perhaps, of the temper of the vanished Jews of Eastern Europe, who saw inevitability everywhere. Her 'collage wall' included an old picture of some fifty women and children of the Warsaw Ghetto, forced against a building, hands high and heads down, all choosings finished now. And then there was a Jacob Riis that she once hung in her apartment, in which a young girl stands on a box at the edge of the vast Atlantic, under a blank, ungenerous sky; she has a broom in the surf and seems to be working diligently; it is called *Sweeping Back the Ocean*.

I suspect that Susan Sontag really denounced Arbus's work for this – not the freakishness of her characters, but their fatedness. Sontag needed too much to believe that people are the authors of themselves to be able to recognise

the humour and poignancy and strange beauty that Arbus found in acquiescence, and with leaden positivism wrote that Arbus 'undercut politics',[6] as if negotiation and protest could push back the sea. Americans have long been among the most optimistic of people, and the idea that we lead and follow blindly is among us a heresy. Arbus once said, 'I don't like to arrange things. If I stand in front of something, instead of arranging it, I arrange myself.'[7] She was speaking here of the directing of subjects, but the echo of a philosophical position is also there in her words. To call her an all-out fatalist would be wrong, yet a not terribly American fatalism is strong in her, and it is mixed in an extraordinary way with a fully American rationality. She sets forth the obsessions of her characters, and their helplessness before them, with the elegance of a logical problem that can never be solved.

Leo Rubinfien

Adapted by Alona Pardo from the essay 'Where Diane Arbus Went' by Leo Rubinfien, originally published in *Art in America*, October 2005, pp. 65-77

   Naked Man Being a Woman, N.Y.C. 1968

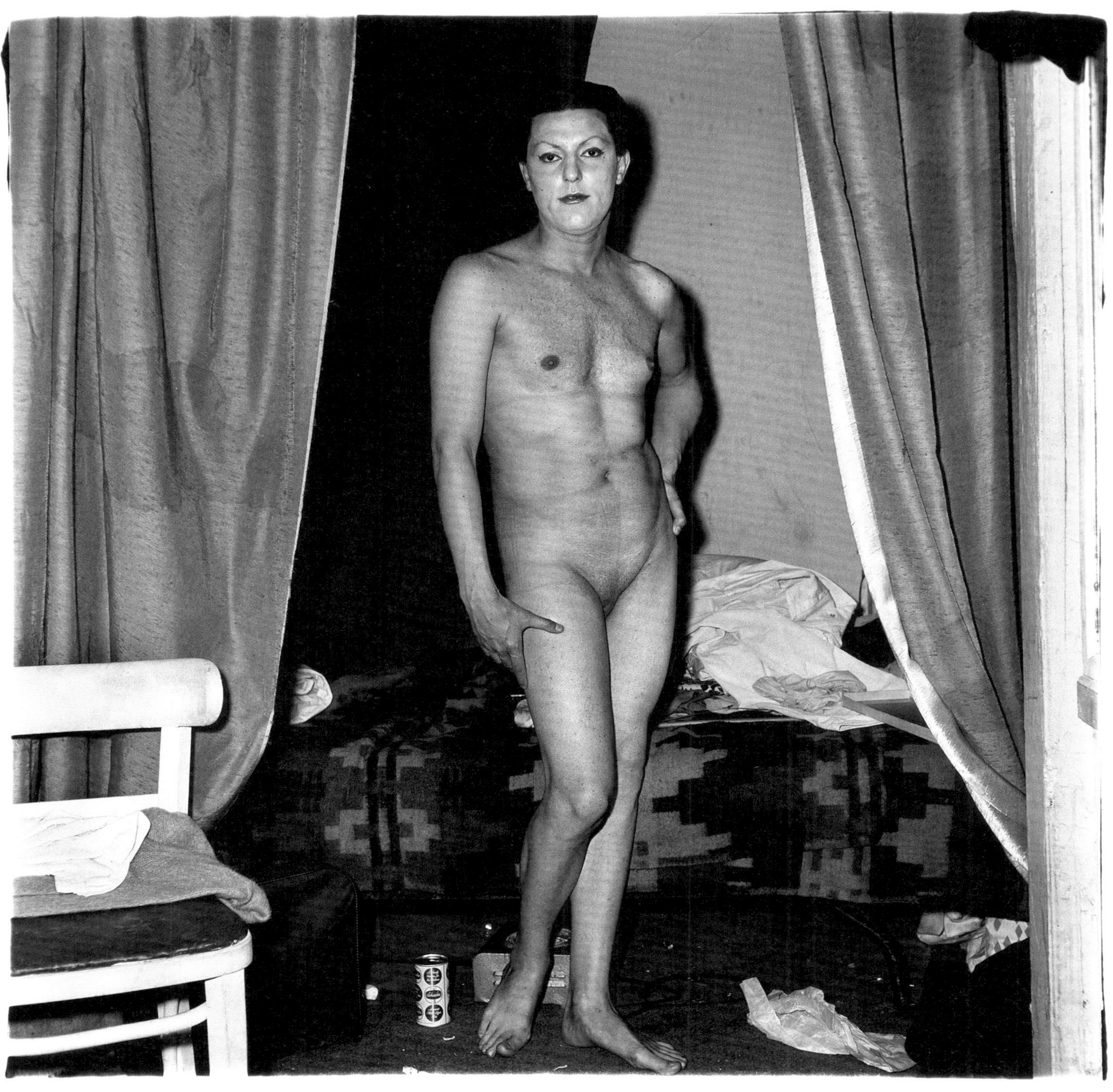

28   Young Man and His Pregnant Wife in Washington Square Park, N.Y.C. 1965

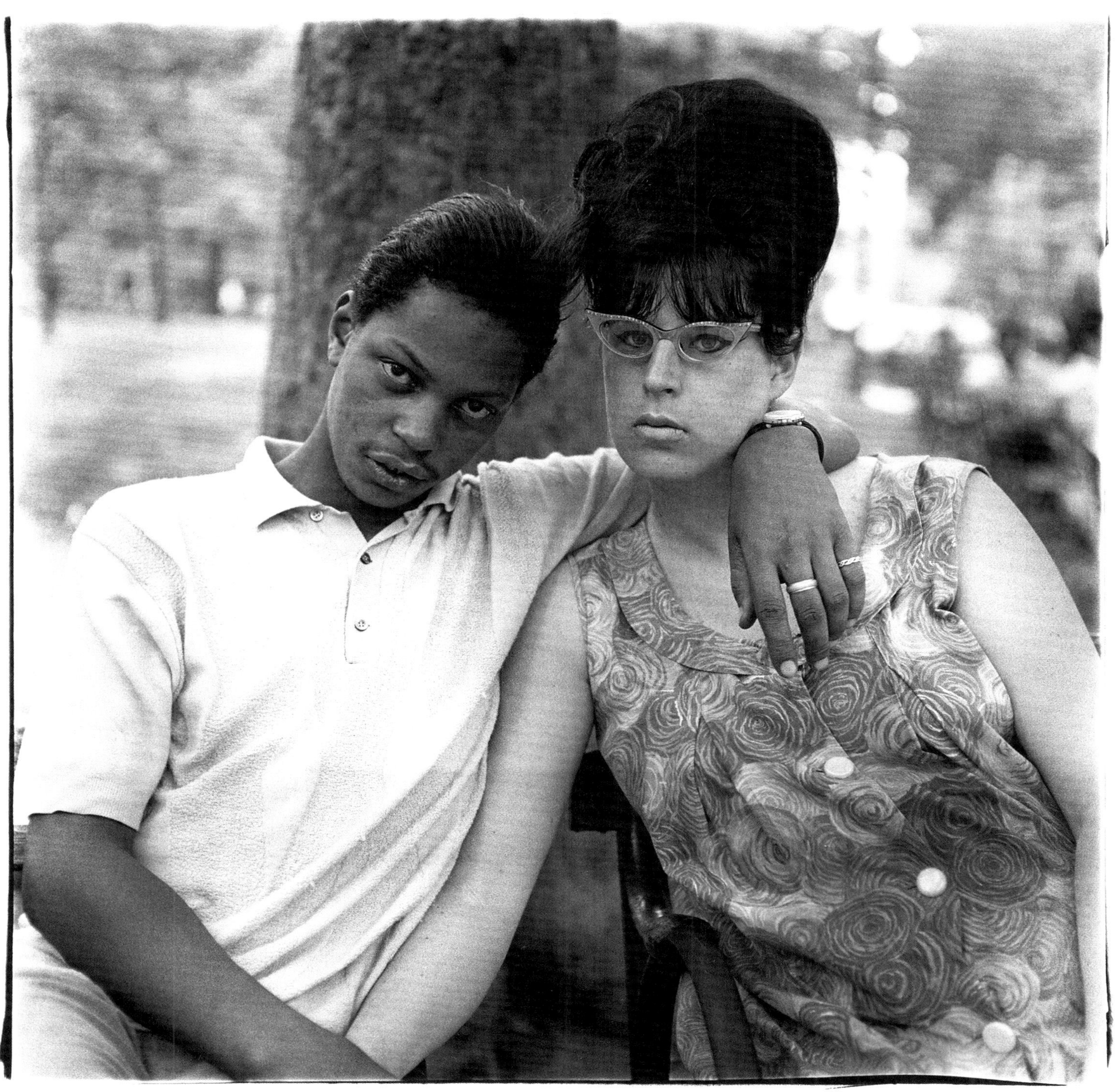

BRUCE

DAVIDSON

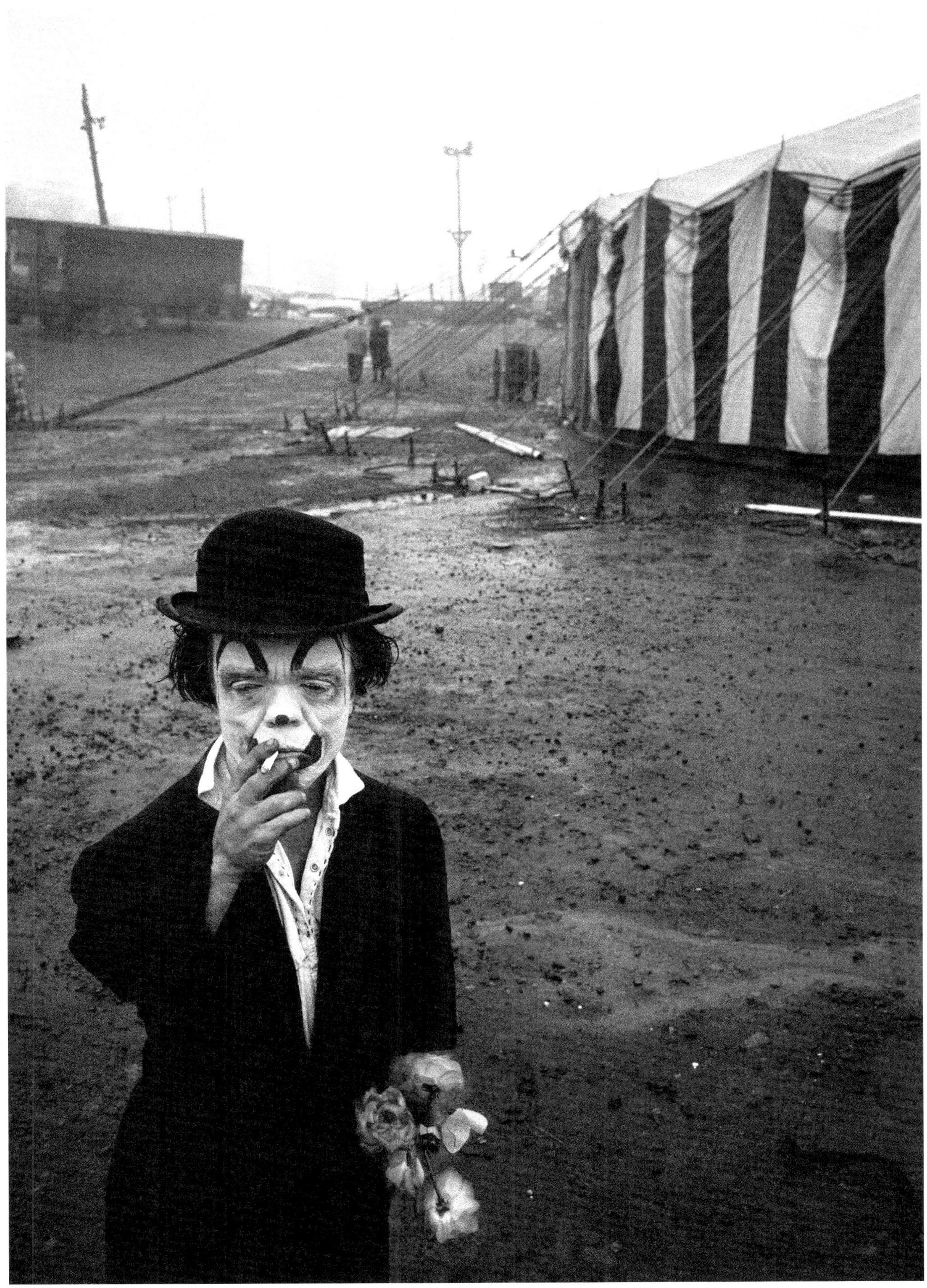

I start off as an outsider, usually photographing other outsiders, then, at some point, I step over a line and become an insider. I don't do detached observation.[1]

Bruce Davidson, 2011

In 1958, aged 25, Bruce Davidson (b. 1933, USA) joined Magnum Photos. When Henri Cartier-Bresson arrived in New York that same year to photograph the city, Davidson accompanied him on a bus ride to Manhattan's Lower East Side, where they each went their separate ways. 'On the bus,' Davidson later recalled, 'he spoke to me about self-discipline, reading and looking at paintings.'[2]

Soon afterwards, Davidson began travelling out to New Jersey every weekday to photograph a circus that had pitched its big top in Palisades Amusement Park. He had absorbed Cartier-Bresson's advice on self-discipline, and when the circus left town he went with it, hitching a ride with the human cannonball and his family on the silver truck that transported the cannon.

'I first saw the dwarf standing outside the tent in the dull mist of a cold spring evening,' he recalled in an illuminatingly honest essay for *Bruce Davidson: Photographs*, a retrospective book published in 1978.[3] 'His distorted torso, normal sized head and stunted legs both attracted and repelled me. He stood, sad and silent, smoking a cigarette outside the tent.'[4] Davidson's images of Jimmy Armstrong, who worked as a clown in the Clyde Beatty Circus, possess a more unsettling undertow than his images of other performers, like the lion tamer or the various acrobats and roustabouts he also photographed. Armstrong's physical otherness, which had 'attracted and repelled the young Davidson',[5] is often portrayed here as a source of often intrusive public curiosity and puerile fascination. More than once, Davidson photographed Armstrong as he was being stared at by groups of onlookers, often children and teenagers, and in one instance when he is being sniggered at by a group of adults in a diner (p. 35).

These moments of casual cruelty, which surely defined Armstrong's outsider life as much as the exaggeratedly grotesque performing persona he adopted nightly, are contrasted with more observational photographs of him as he goes about his daily routine: resting, chatting with his fellow performers, smoking a cigarette, practising the trumpet and applying or removing his circus make-up – his mask. Throughout, Armstrong exudes a complex aura of stoicism, self-containment, dogged professionalism and aloneness.

The stark, high-contrast tones of Davidson's black-and-white portraits emphasise what he later called the 'strange loneliness' of the circus performer's existence. He was chronicling the lives of a community of outsiders at a historical moment when the essentially Victorian collective fascination for the spectacle of the travelling circus, complete with wild animals and so-called human oddities, was on the wane. 'I was chronicling the end of something, the last tent shows,' Davidson told me in 2011. 'Television put paid to the era of the circus performer and you can feel that sense of sadness, of a time passing into history, in the photographs.'[6]

At that moment, too, Davidson's style was changing as he moved away from the kind of traditional photojournalism he had done previously for *Time* magazine towards a kind of immersive documentary that eschewed detachment for emotional engagement. That approach inevitably took its toll. 'One thing I've discovered is that it's easier to get inside a world than it is to leave it,' he said in 2011, referring specifically to his series on Jimmy Armstrong, who came to consider the photographer his best friend. 'The painful part is leaving it. You find you have attachments, bonding.'[7]

In the spring of 1959, having completed the circus project, Davidson returned to his one-room attic apartment in Greenwich Village: 'I had a red light in the fridge so I could eat cold chicken and print pictures at the same time.'[8] It was there that he read an article about the street fights that had erupted over the previous months between rival teenage gangs in Prospect Park, Brooklyn.

At that time, there were about a thousand gang members in New York City, mainly teenage males from ethnically defined neighbourhoods in the outer boroughs. Davidson contacted the New York Youth Board, an organisation formed to tackle the problem. Alongside one of their workers, he took the subway across the Brooklyn Bridge to meet with the Jokers, one of the gangs featured in the article, with the intention of entering what he called 'their cool world'.

When his extended photo-essay *Brooklyn Gang* eventually appeared in book form in 1998, Davidson wrote of his younger self, 'I was twenty-five, they were about sixteen. I could easily have been taken for one of them.'[9] His identification with the volatile teenagers went much deeper than that, though. Their initial indifference gave way to an acceptance of his presence and, over time, to a kind of trust. Davidson trailed the Jokers over several months as they hung out in the neighbourhood candy store, roamed the local streets and travelled on weekends to Coney Island, where they relaxed with their girlfriends on the beach and the boardwalk. The resulting series, grainy, monochrome and yet often surprisingly tender, comprises one of the earliest photographic portrayals of rebellious American youth culture.

Unlike the circus performers he had spent time with previously, the Jokers were self-styled outsiders with little interest in posing for Davidson's camera. The coolness he immediately identified was an attitude as well as a style, and their casually aberrant behaviour, which had already sparked a moral panic in the mainstream media, was a symptom of much deeper discontents.

Amid Davison's intimately observed images of the teenagers drinking beer, dancing and hanging out, you can glimpse a sense of quiet desperation beneath the outward mask of defiance. It is detectable in the dark, grainy images taken in Prospect Park after dark, in which NYPD officers remonstrate with a line of agitated youths. It is there, too, in the glimpses of blonde-haired, fourteen-year-old Bengie, whom Davidson catches more than once lost in brooding self-absorption among his friends, his hand kneading his knitted brow.

In one snatched portrait, Bengie stares down Davidson's camera, his bruised face simmering with anger beneath a wall of adverts for Pepsi, Coca-Cola and Kodak, key signifiers of the post-war American dream of leisure and contentment. (Davidson had initially been commissioned by the Youth Board to 'take

   Previous page: from 'The Dwarf', *Jimmy Armstrong*, Palisades, New Jersey, 1958 pictures of their wounds from a gang war in front of their candy store hang-out'.) In the intervening years, some of these images have gained a kind of iconic status due to their encapsulation of the now familiar iconography of 1950s American youthful rebellion: two young men with rockabilly haircuts, one shirtless, dancing on the boardwalk (p. 42); beautiful Kathy fixing her tumbling blonde tresses in the reflection of a cigarette machine (p. 43); a couple intertwined in the back seat of a car on a freeway (p. 45). (The latter image was used by Bob Dylan on the cover of his 2009 album *Together Through Life*.)

Behind each of these evocative images lies a world of suffering that was yet to fully unfold. They are, in a way, premonitions of the darkness that was to follow. The second edition of *Brooklyn Gang*, published by Twin Palms in 1999, contains an extended afterword by the then 55-year-old Robert 'Bengie' Powers. In it he recalls his damaged childhood: alcoholic parents, grinding poverty, beatings from the nuns who taught him at primary school and the sanctuary and sense of security provided by the Jokers, whose other members were survivors just like him.

At first, they drank, smoked joints and popped pills, but before Bengie had made it into his twenties, many of his fellow Jokers were heroin addicts. 'If you see Jimmie, he's like the Fonz, like James Dean – handsome,' Powers says of Davidson's photographs of one of the older members of the gang. 'Later, though, the whole family, all six of them – Charlie, Aggie, Katie, Jimmie, the mother and the father – died; wiped out, mostly from drugs.'[10] He recalls Cathy, the beautiful young fourteen-year-old girl whom Davidson photographed as she fixed her blonde hair in the reflection of the cigarette machine while waiting for the Staten Island Ferry with her boyfriend, Junior. 'Cathy was beautiful like Brigitte Bardot ... I remember [her] living up 20th Street, in a rooming house with her mother. Cathy would always come out immaculate ... Cathy always was there, but outside ... Then, some years ago, she put a shotgun in her mouth and blew her head off.'[11]

Of his younger self, the self-absorbed, not-quite-at-ease young teenager immortalised by Davidson's camera, Powers writes, 'I see a fifteen-year-old kid who looks like he's in a lot of pain. I see a kid who wished he was dead a million times.'[12]

So *Brooklyn Gang* is a requiem, too, a series steeped in the sadness of all that has happened to Davidson's wayward subjects since. It is a sadness made all the more acute by the unselfconscious energy of the teenagers, who back then lived utterly in the moment, their uncertain lives evoked through the observant, tender gaze of Bruce Davidson's insider's eye.

Sean O'Hagan

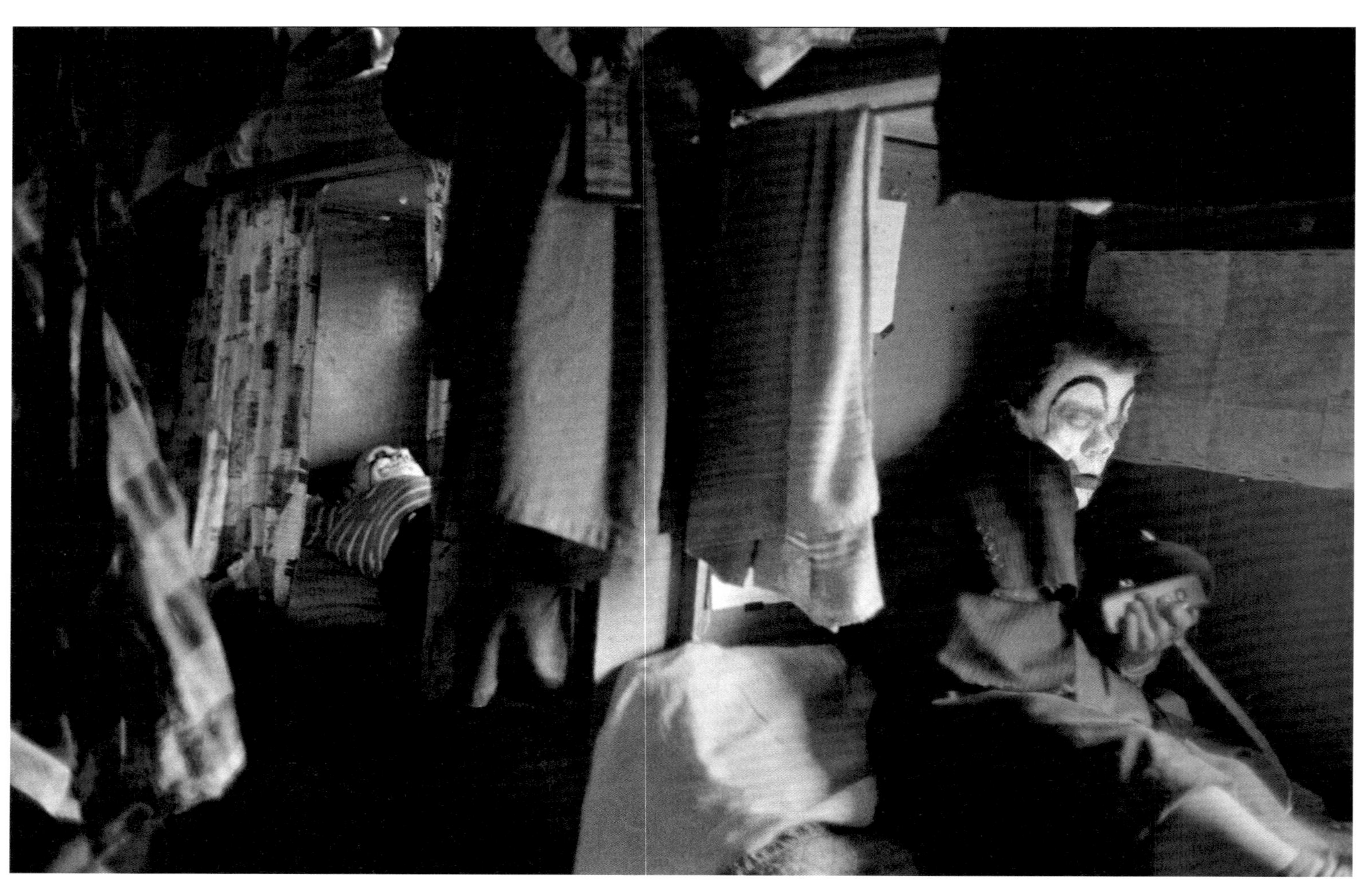

34   This page and opposite: from 'The Dwarf', *Jimmy Armstrong*, Palisades, New Jersey, 1958

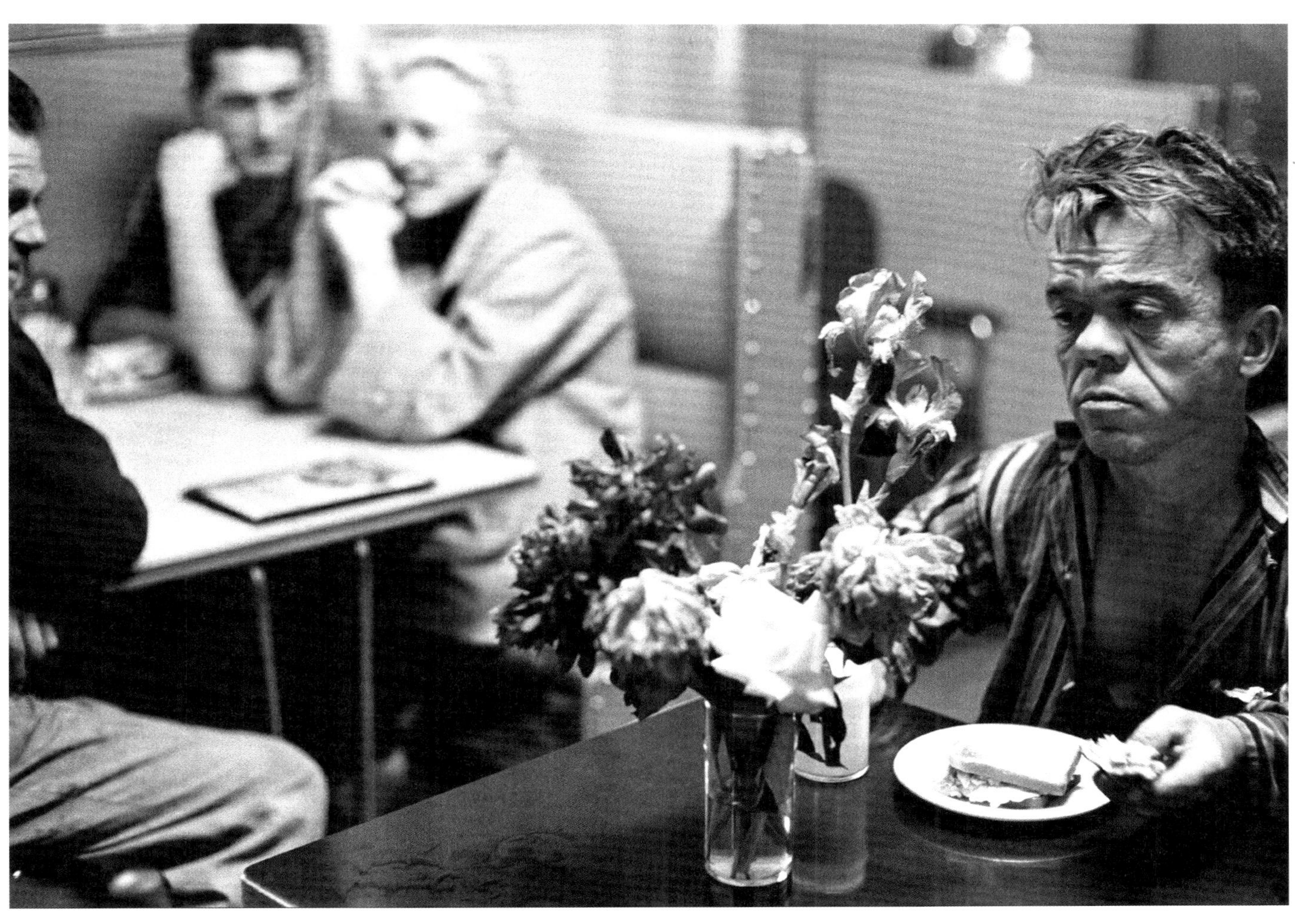

36   From 'Brooklyn Gang', *Lefty Showing his Tattoo*, New York City, 1959

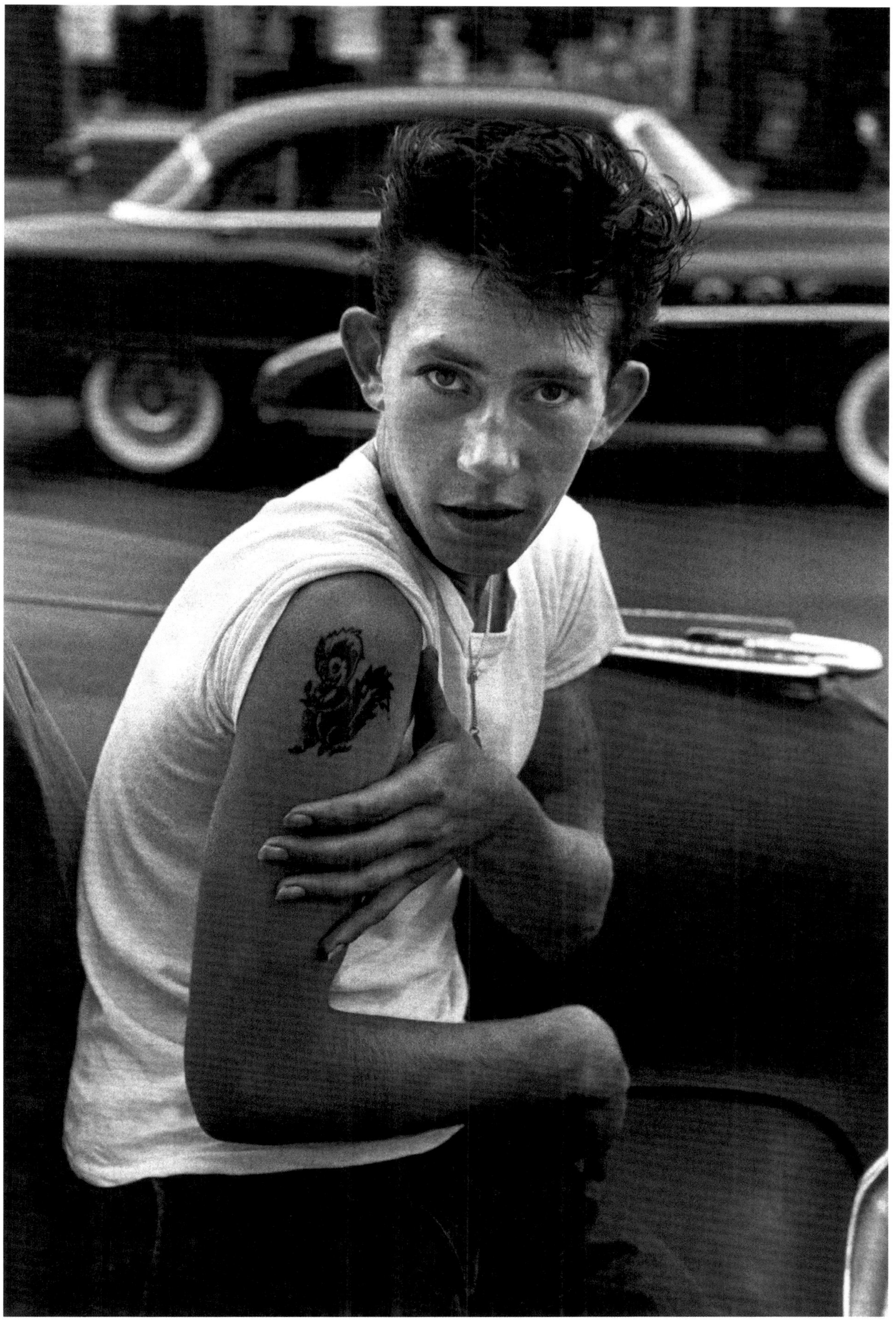

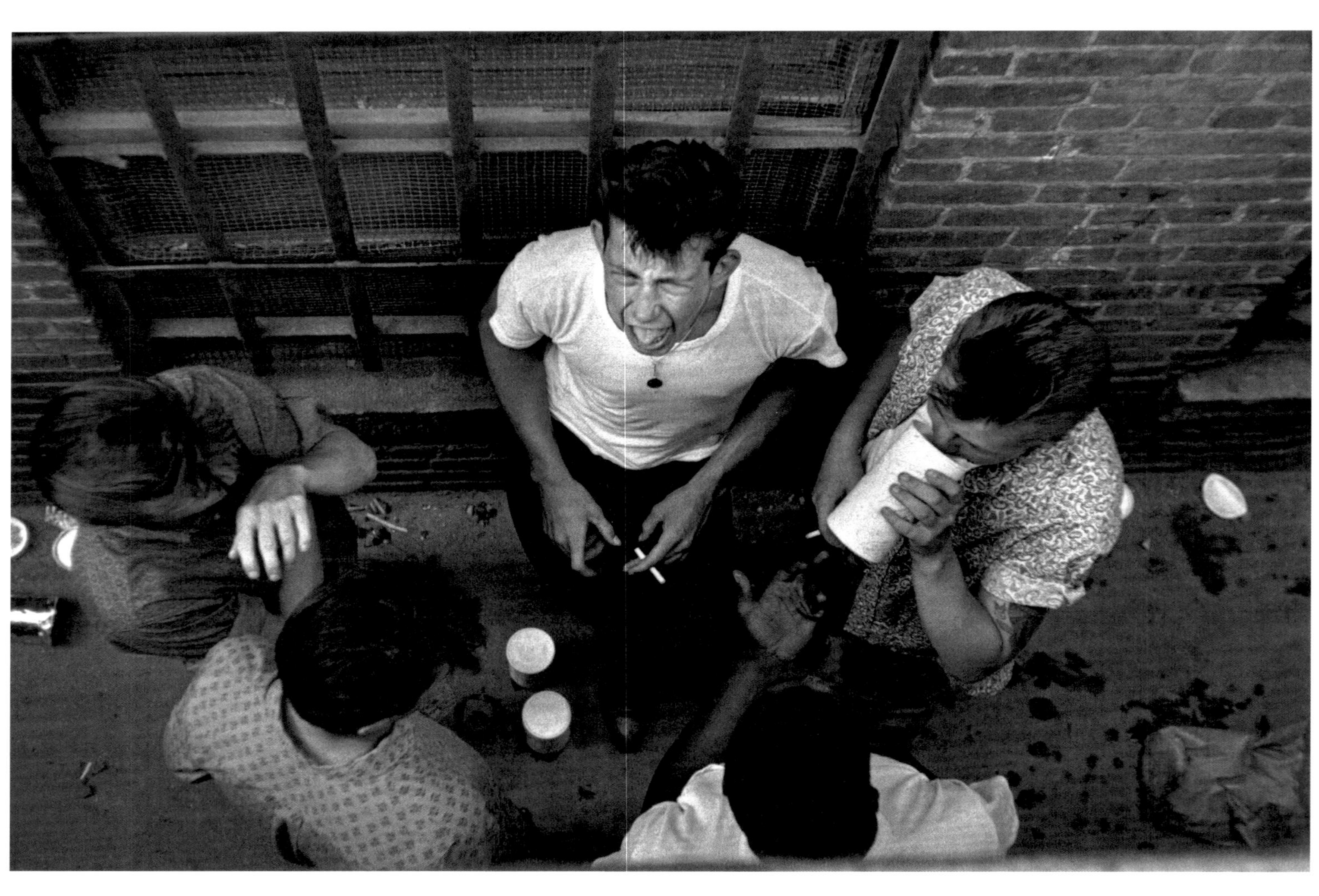

   This page and opposite: from 'Brooklyn Gang', *New York City*, 1959

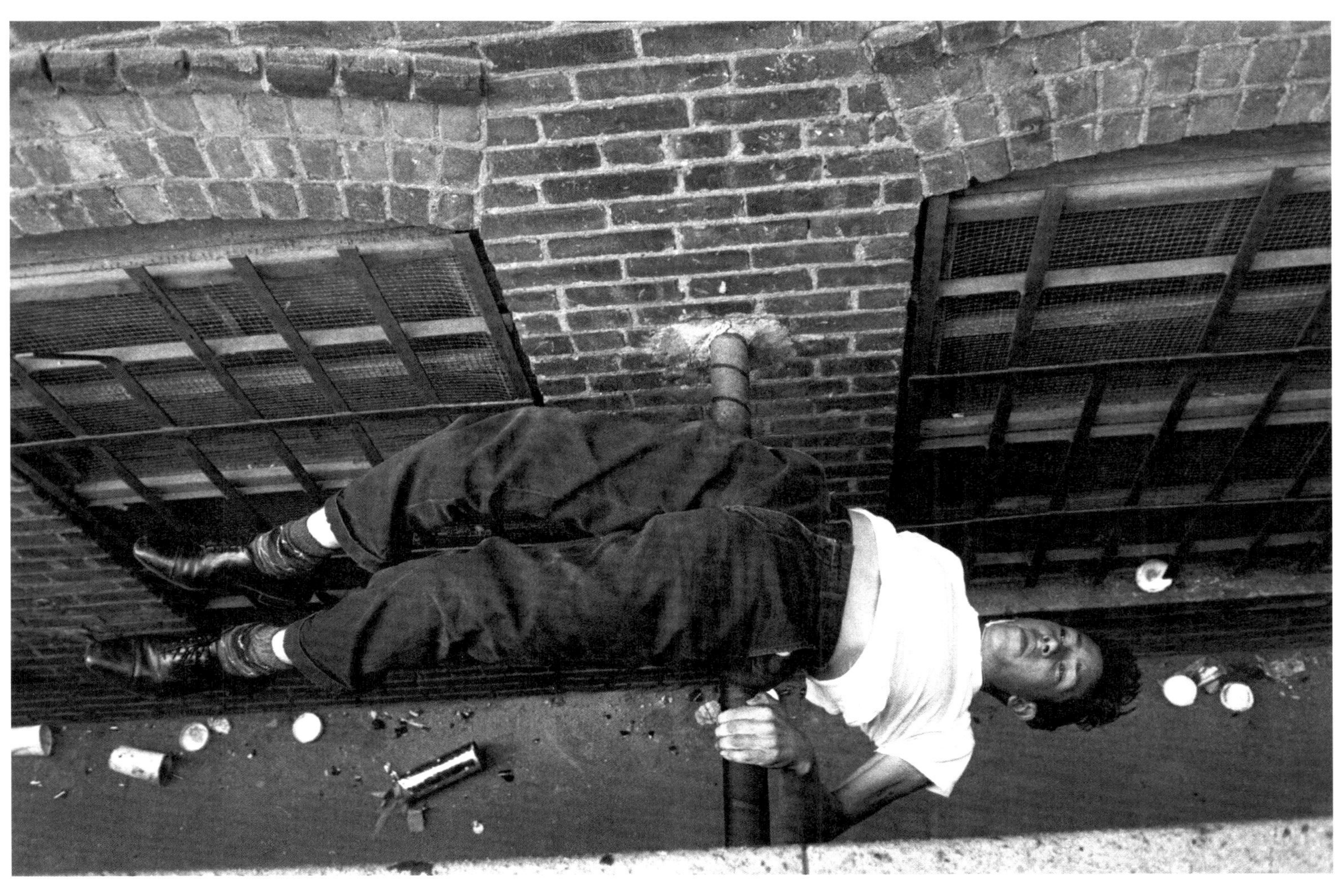

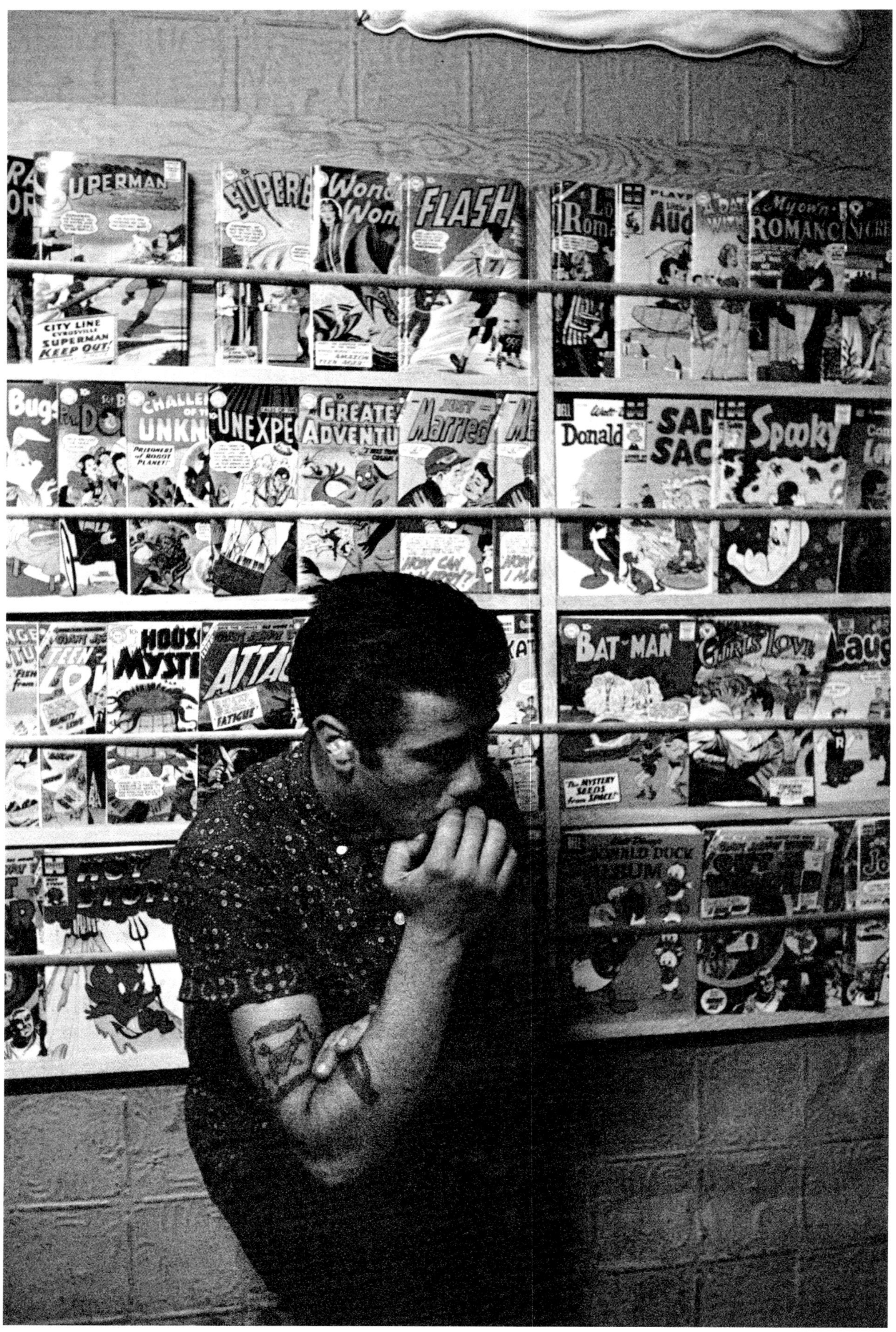

SUPERMAN
SUPERB
Wonder Wom
FLASH
Rom
Aud
My own ROMANCE
CITY LINE
CYRUSVILLE
SUPERMAN
KEEP OUT!
Bugs
CHALLE
UNKN
UNEXPE
GREATE
ADVENTU
Married
Donald
SAD
SAC
Spooky
HOUS
MYST
ATTA
BAT-MAN
GIRLS' LOVE
Laug
TEEN
DONALD DUCK
Jo

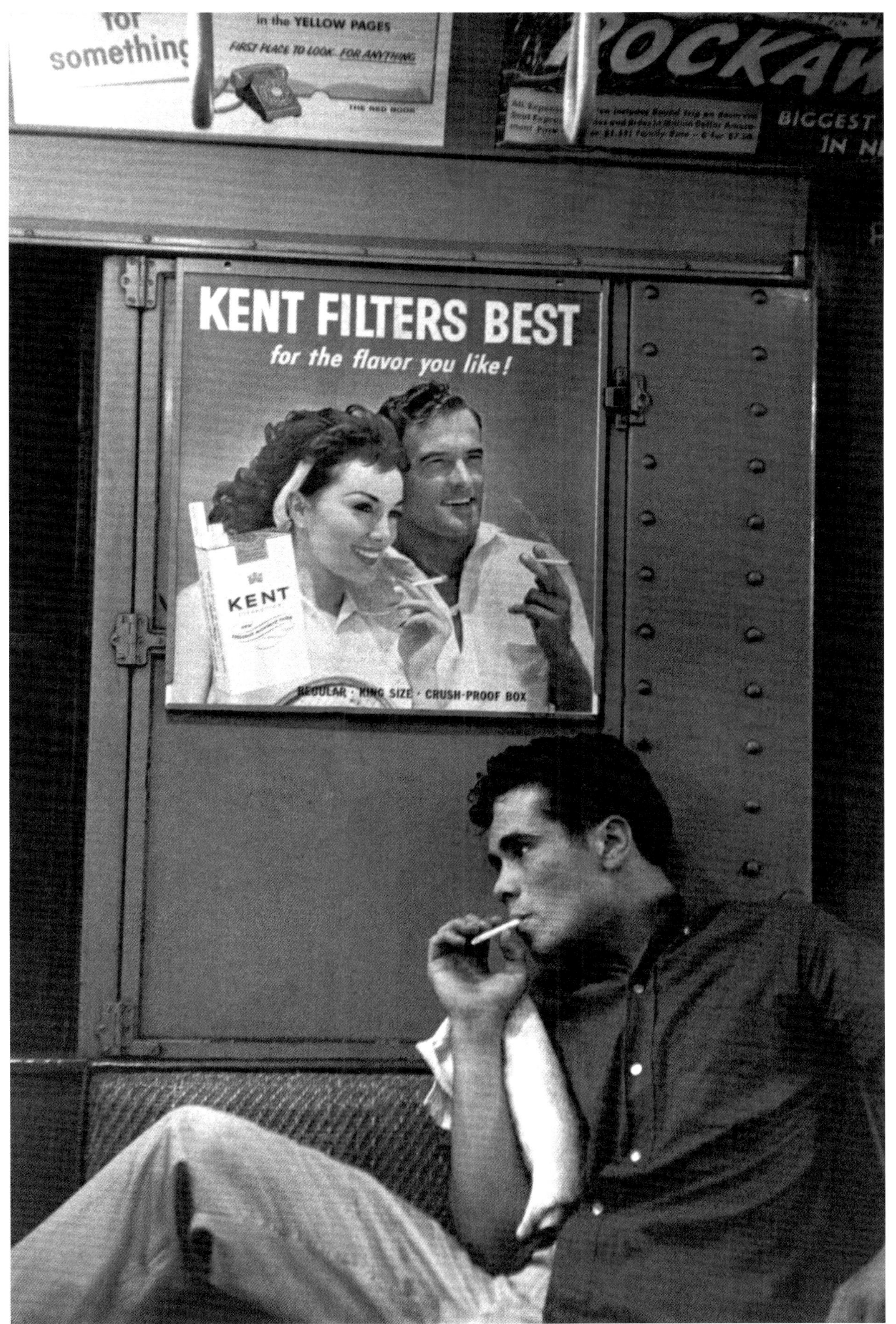

From 'Brooklyn Gang', *Subway, New York City, 1959*

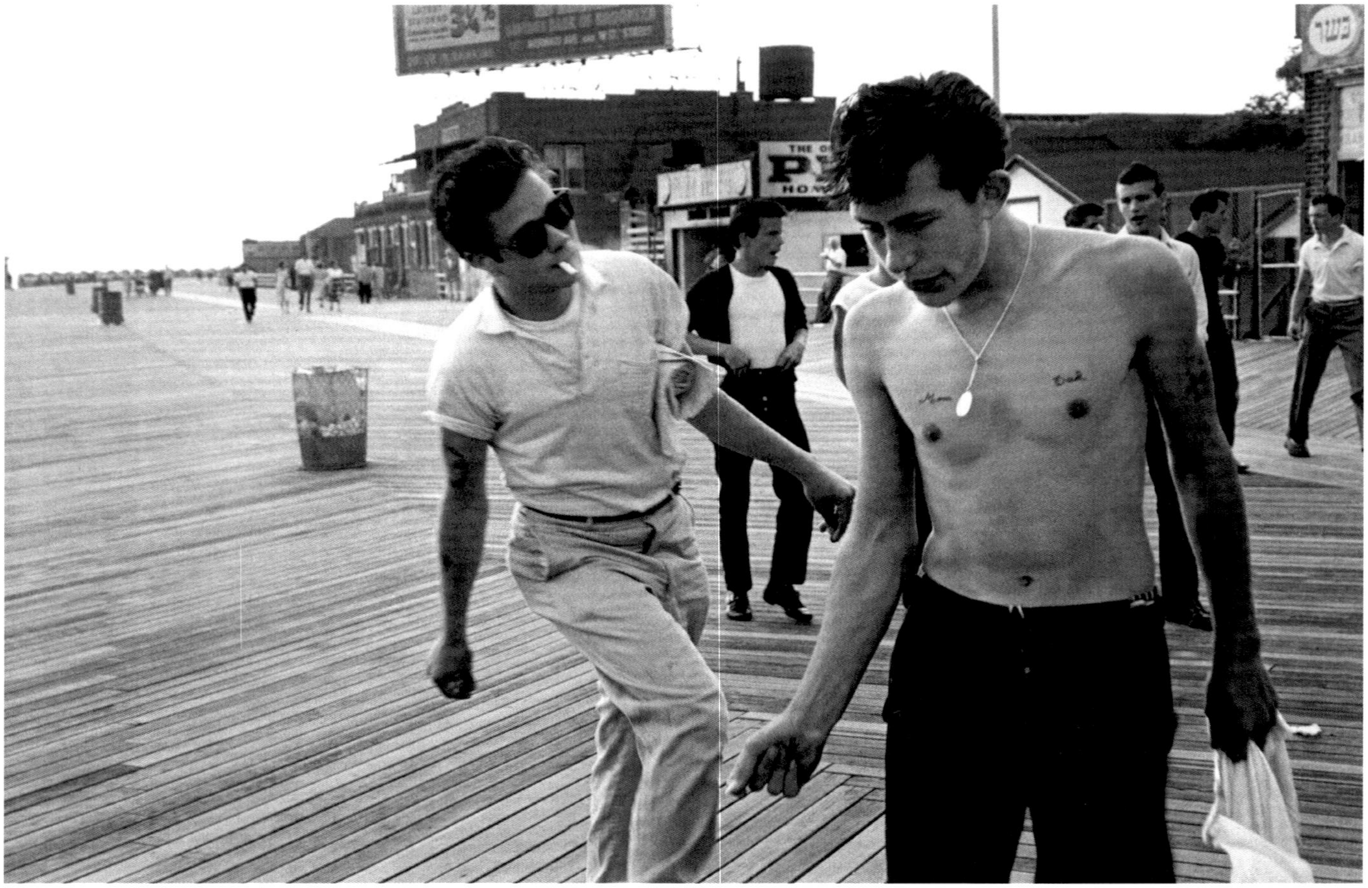

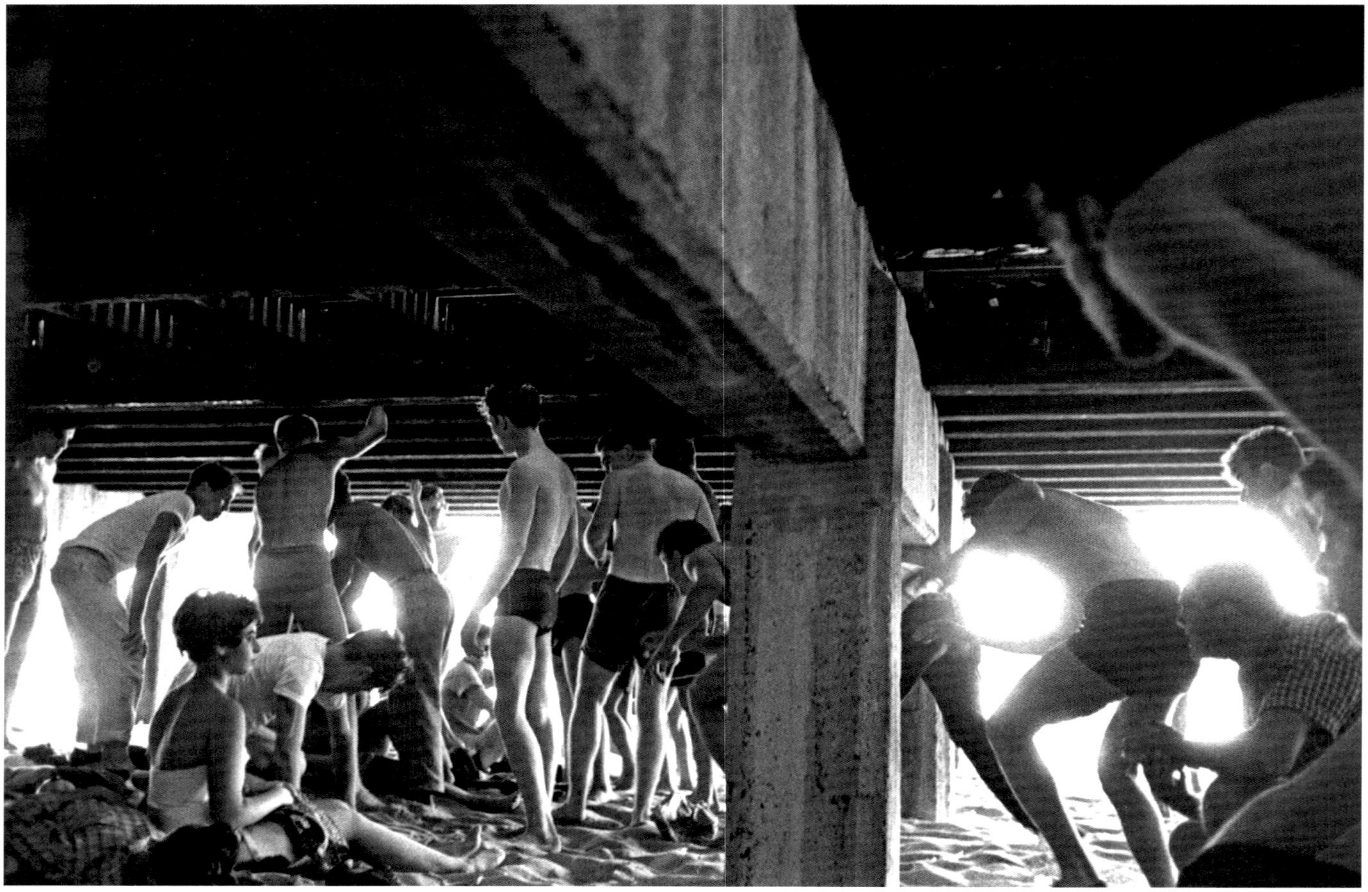

Top: from 'Brooklyn Gang', *On the Boardwalk at West Thirty-third* Street, Coney Island, NY, 1959
42   Above: from 'Brooklyn Gang', *Coney Island*, NY, 1959

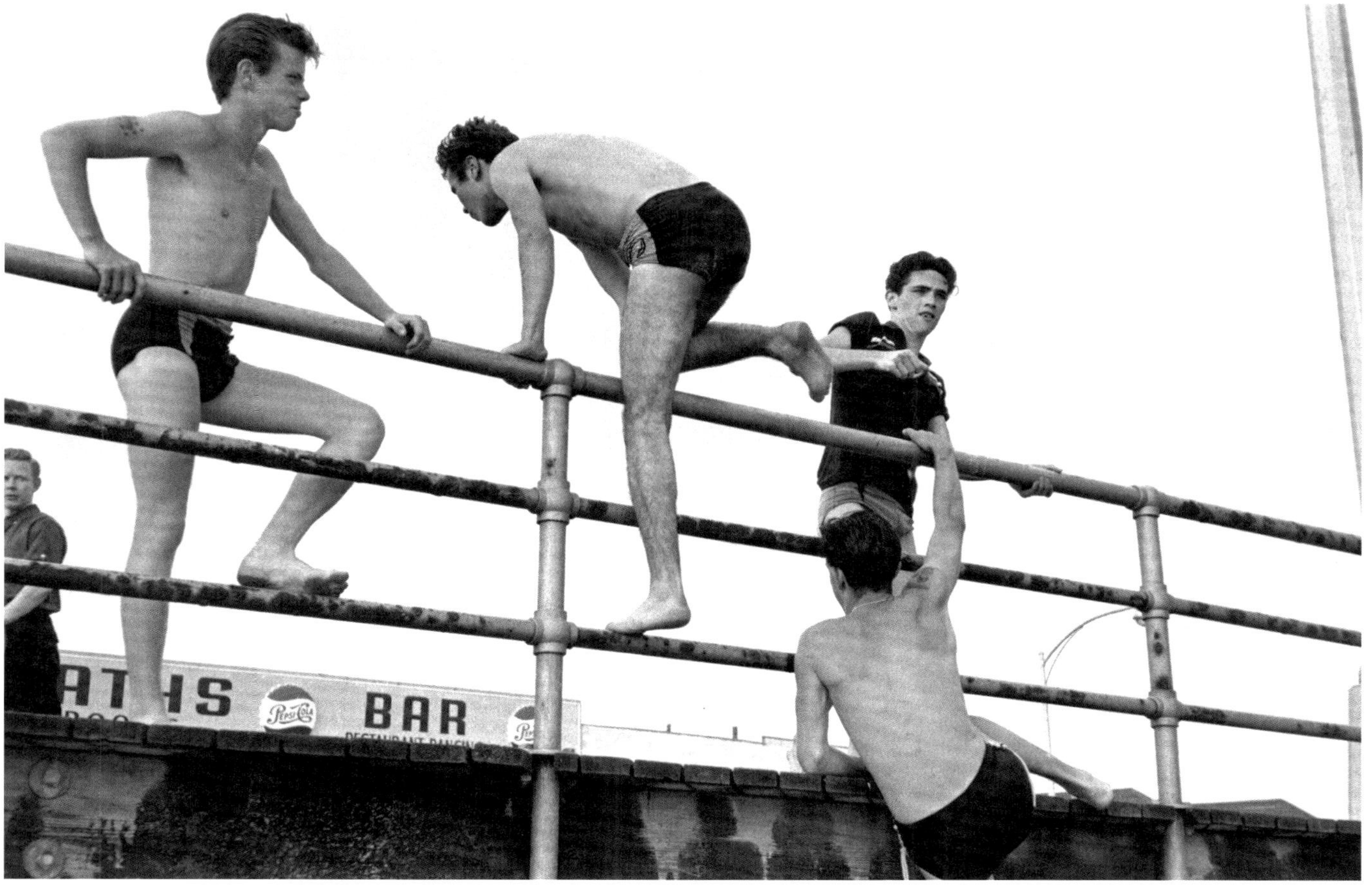

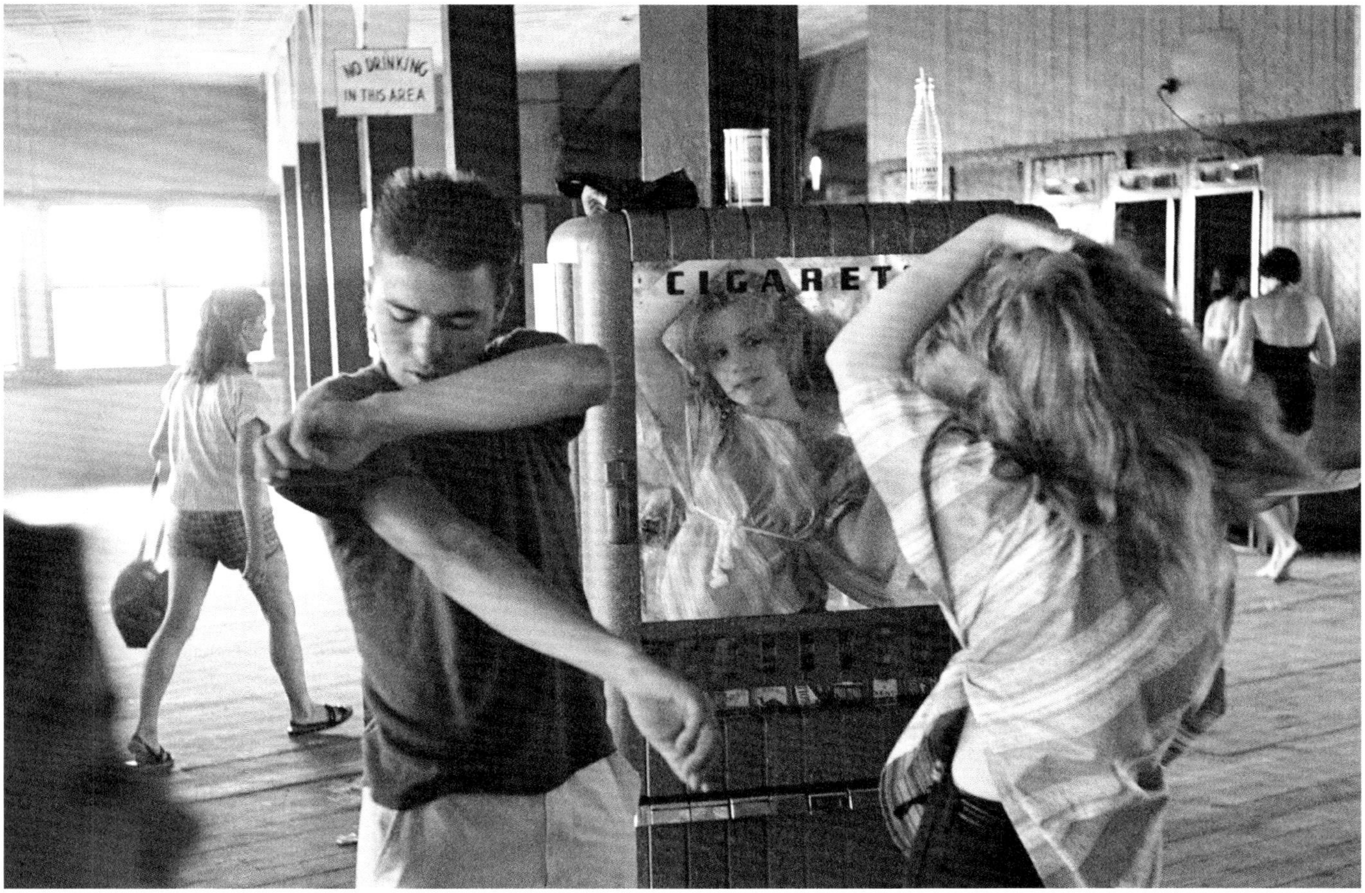

Top: from 'Brooklyn Gang', *Bengie and Friends at Bay Twenty-Two*, Coney Island, NY, 1959
Above: from 'Brooklyn Gang', *Kathy Fixing her Hair in a Cigarette Machine Mirror*, Coney Island, NY, 1959

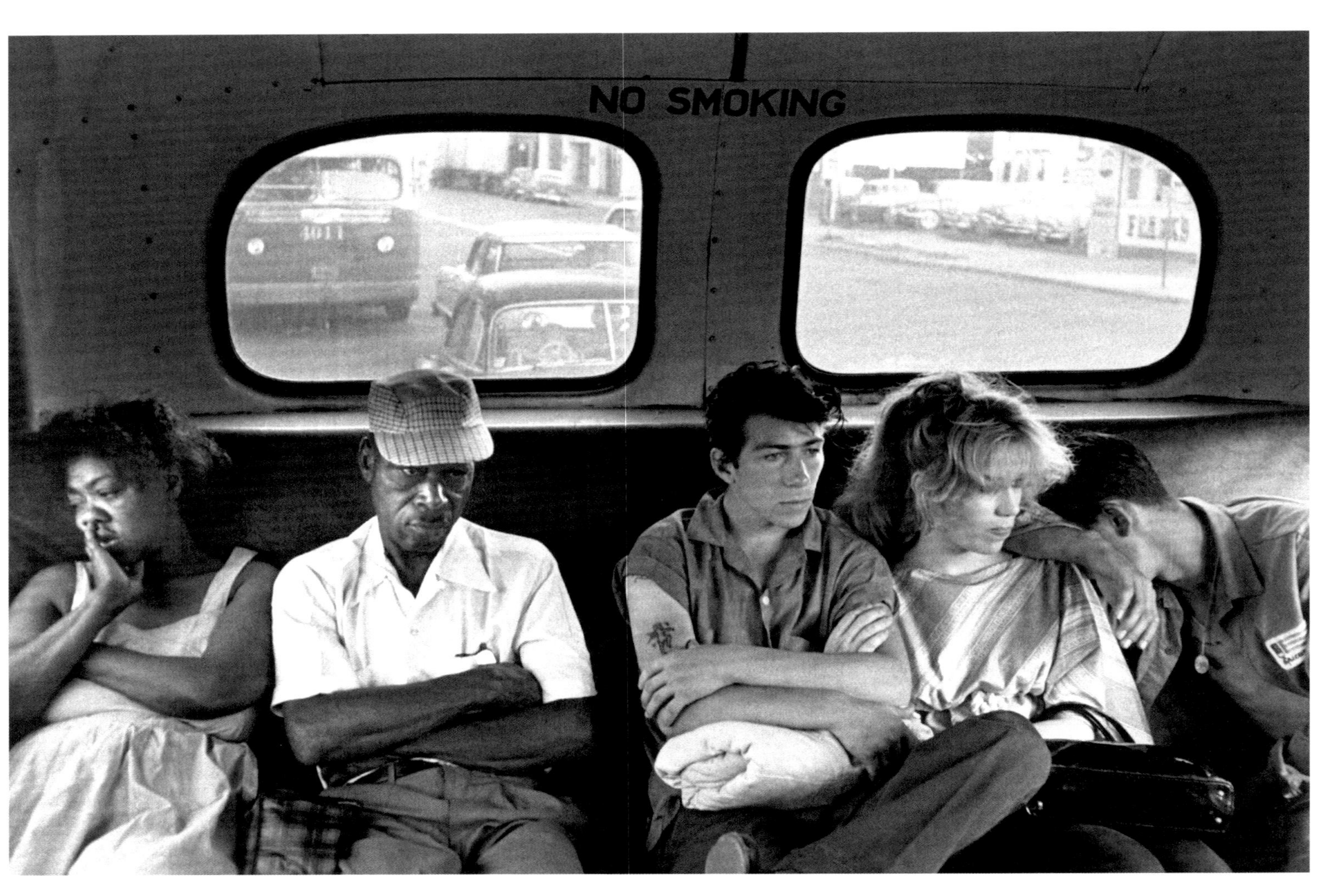

44   From 'Brooklyn Gang', *On the Way Home by Bus*, New York City, 1959

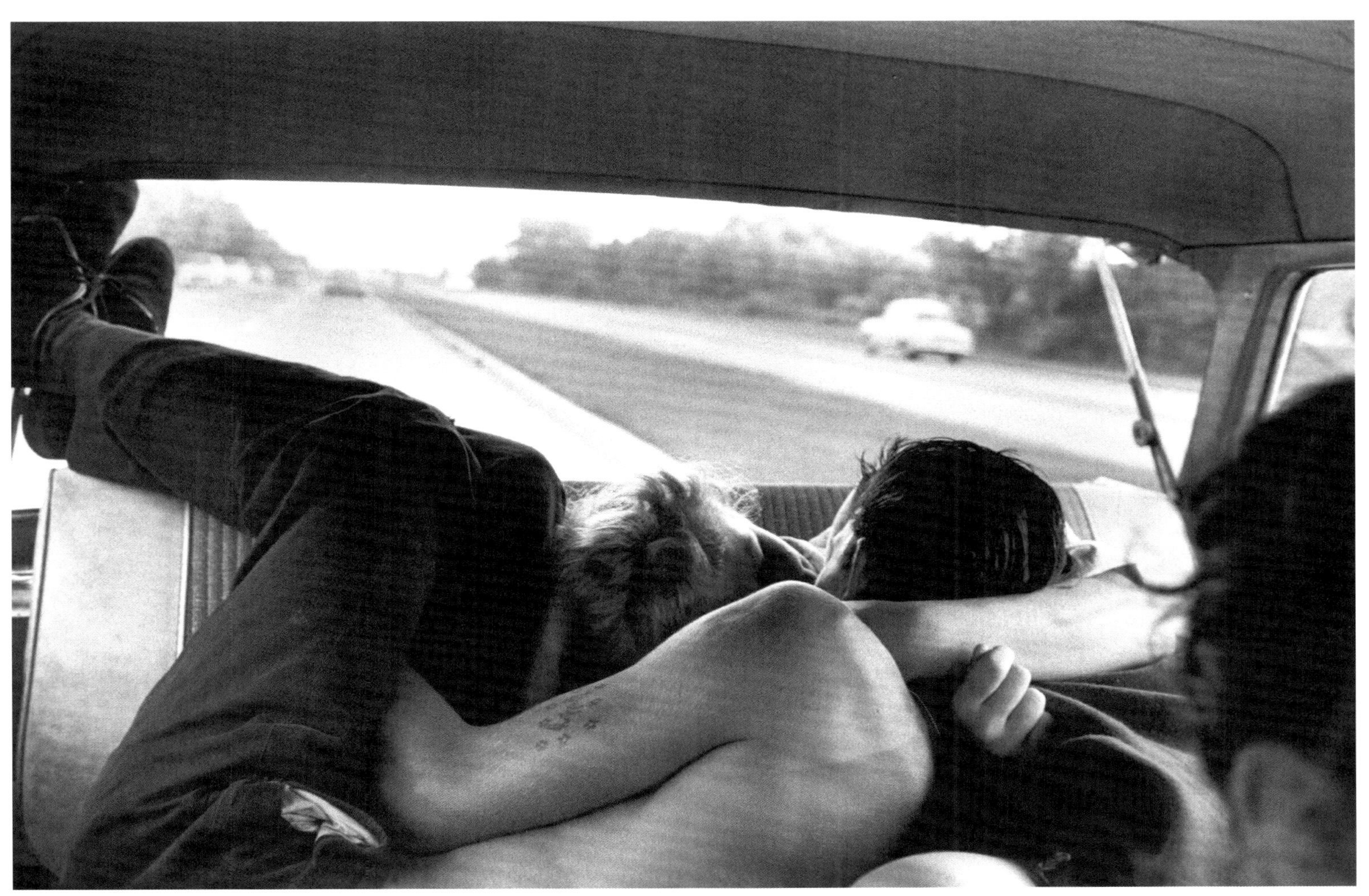

DAIDO

MORIYAMA

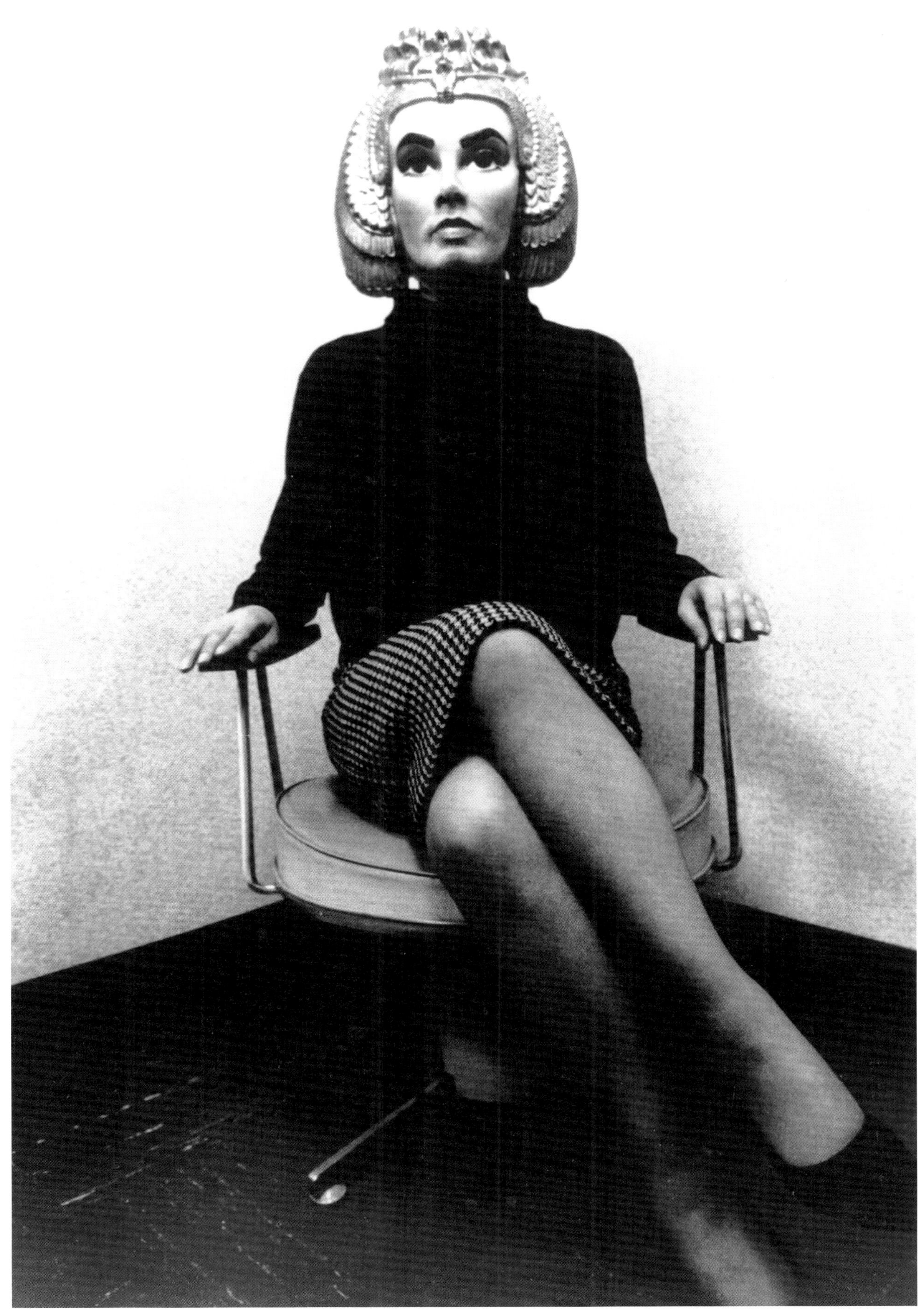

The first photograph in Daidō Moriyama's (b. 1938, Japan) *Japan: A Photo Theatre* shows Shimizu Isamu, an elegant actor of short stature in a dinner suit, a member of a theatre troupe, seated on the edge of a tiny chair. An arm stretched nonchalantly across its rail, he makes room for the viewer to join him, to crouch down and share the spectacle about to unfold. Eliciting our complicity, the photograph stages a fascinating preliminary. It suggests that to read this book means adopting another's perspective. It means submerging ourselves in the performance and abandoning all decorum.

Modestly presented in its slipcase and olive-green cover, *Japan: A Photo Theatre* opens out into an outlandish space of disorientation and display: the shadow of a looming figure flared with light; a lascivious, schematic mouth on a TV screen; a man submissively on all fours glowering back at the viewer (p. 57). Each subsequent image lures us deeper into the weirdness of Tokyo's inky underbelly. Shot with 35mm and 28mm lenses and printed in a grainy, dark gravure, this is a world (as one photograph states) 'off limits', a place where realities collide and life becomes a tenebrous fiction. Theatre is a central theme, combined with street views of working-class Tokyo and Yokosuka, stage sets for murky human interaction. Moriyama's camera equalises and fixates. It obliterates the documentary function of the photograph and finds a mystery in everything. At the same time, it keeps its distance, a voyeurism unprecedented in the history of photography.

In *Japan: A Photo Theatre*, Moriyama is both observer and fabricator of a world of make-believe. This is the underground theatre of his close collaborator the writer and director Shūji Terayama, the *enfant terrible* of Japanese culture.[1] In 1967 Terayama established his theatre company, Tenjō Sajiki, drawing many of its members from the margins of society. He recruited the young Moriyama to document his performances; *Japan: A Photo Theatre*, published in July 1968, is a summation of nearly two years of activity. Moriyama mixes theatre images with his earlier documentary work, restaging both in a phantasmagoric display.[2] Actors rushing through the streets of Tokyo, players in traditional costume, even photographers themselves – all are transmogrified in black and white. Celebrated for its erosion of narrative hierarchy and its heightening of visual pleasures, the book is also

marked by a fascinating ambivalence. Even the monstrous carcass of a dead whale rotting on a beach manages to become a kind of tragic performance.

Moriyama's republic of images is visceral and ill-defined, a loosening of symbolic meaning in favour of a grainy carnivalesque. His pictures issue from the ferment of Japan in the 1960s, but they have little specific to tell us. There is none of the directed anger – aimed at US imperial power – of many of his contemporaries. Social critique is muted, seen instead in the faces of an affected couple on a Tokyo housing estate; the photographic ghosts and shadows of American sailors; or the juxtaposed images of an older, conservative Japan, creating a feeling of unease and generational upheaval in the face of rampant modernisation. Neither is there much overtly sexual imagery, although a vital, charged photograph of a stripper, genitals emitting a flash of light, speaks to the significance of female desire for Moriyama.

On the whole, however, the provocation of *Japan: A Photo Theatre* lies elsewhere. Moriyama doesn't so much rewrite the rules of photography as refuse them altogether, transforming documentary into something more elusive. His pictorial method – blurred, often askew images printed in sooty blacks and bleached with light; disorienting, enigmatic close-ups; the lurid abstraction of black and white – lends vision a stronger, psychological charge. The mechanisms of desire in photography – voyeurism and fetishism especially – become more explicit. The book is a work of symbolic violence akin to Terayama's disruptive energy, its juxtapositions all the more disturbing for their refusal of obvious meaning, their obliteration of the boundary between the fictional and the real. Forged in the shadow of a literary avant-garde, *Japan: A Photo Theatre* served to sharpen its visual politics. It was a formal shock that revolutionised Japanese photography.

How, then, are we to explain this mesmerising display, this flagrant transgression of respectable image-making? My suggestion is that *Japan: A Photo Theatre* is one of the great statements – and perhaps the first really great statement – of perversion in photography. I mean this not in relation to the liberating acts the book portrays, but rather in a structural sense, in the way the volume challenges social norms of identification and desire.

As psychoanalysis tells us, the pleasures of perversion are enabled by a crisis of authority. They are expressed through the inadequacy of the paternal function and a refusal to follow the father's demand that the child sacrifice *jouissance*, the desire associated with the mother's body. The child refuses to hear 'No!' and pleasure is staged, in effect, in defiance of the law. But crucially, the pervert is both the subject and the object of that pleasure, serving the (m)Other's desire by assuming an imaginary position he thinks the (m)Other lacks. Perversion is an exaggerated, instrumental desire, a kind of short-circuited satisfaction untroubled by prohibition or symbolic authority more generally.[3]

My argument is that *Japan: A Photo Theatre* does not merely document the perverse pleasures of the counterculture. It *is* that pleasure. Disavowing any separation, it gives itself over wholeheartedly to that culture's libidinal investments. Terayama's subtle and outrageous influence is crucial here, an impresario of perversion who, as one critic has noted, was 'pathologically mother-centred'.[4] Moriyama, too, ignores paternal injunction, exploiting a wider social breakdown in the regime of the image. The medium itself, the object cause of his desire, becomes his obsession. *Japan: A Photo Theatre* is Moriyama's delirious initiation: it subverts photography's – and especially documentary's – evolved symbolic heritage in an ecstasy of fabulation. Narrative content is deliberately eschewed in favour of extreme formal devices that push perceptibility, above all the erosion of the boundaries of the real, to breaking point. It is not so much what Moriyama photographs that is significant as the excess that shapes its presentation. Nothing much matters beyond this fixation (this, to put it crudely, is how the book gets off). This is an utterly original accomplishment, far exceeding the subcultural longing of those before it.[5] *Japan: A Photo Theatre* is not so much the image of another kind of life as the urge to be that life itself.

To read the book as a perverse production is also to answer a key conundrum: how is it that such a potent testimony to counterculture, published at the height of the revolutionary turmoil of the 1960s, should be so wilfully free from politics? Why is it that the thousands of students who so heroically battled the police at Shinjuku and elsewhere are entirely absent? Even Terayama, whose political allegiances were erratic to say the least, spoke supportively in 1968 to protesting students.

Moriyama's re-visioning of documentary photography is, as Sandra Phillips has politely put it, 'more romantic than critical'.[6] I think this is right, but isn't this political conservatism also typical of perversion and its short-circuited desire? Isn't this characteristic of a drive whose object (paradoxically) is also to bring the law into being, to compel the father to fulfil the paternal function? As Jela Krečič and Slavoj Žižek have recently argued, perversion, far from being subversive, is in fact 'the hidden obverse of power': 'every power needs perversion as its inherent and sustaining transgression.'[7] This, I think, explains both Moriyama's political quietism and his obsessive interest in those living on the margins of Japanese society. The desire to photograph is not social as such (he has no wish to improve his subjects' conditions or comment on their circumstances), but rather lies in the act of voyeurism itself, in the relentless reworking of the object as representation, in the fabrication of the fetish of the imagistic double.[8]

Japan: A Photo Theatre ends with one of the creepiest sequences in the history of photography: eight photographs of dead foetuses in test tubes, reproduced as if on a stage and abstracted in black and white. Drawing from one of Moriyama's earliest series, *Mugon geki* (Silent Theatre), shot in a maternity hospital, it offers an abject conclusion to the book, a shocking parade of preternatural flesh enveloping all that comes before it. This haunting, protoplasmic chorus is the ultimate perversion, the contumacious, swollen underbelly of Japan's now sleek social body. In its absolute, fleshy materiality, in its literal mindlessness, the horror and pleasure of the (m)Other's domain is completely freed from a society demanding conformity, discipline and sacrifice. An exaggerated echo of the book's opening image, this senseless absorption of bodies frames the desire of *Japan: A Photo Theatre*. Not long afterwards, Tadanori Yokoo, a co-founder of Tenjō Sajiki, famously described Moriyama's photographs as taken 'from the point of view of a peeping Tom or a rapist ... a criminal'.[9] He might in all good conscience have added 'pervert'.

Duncan Forbes

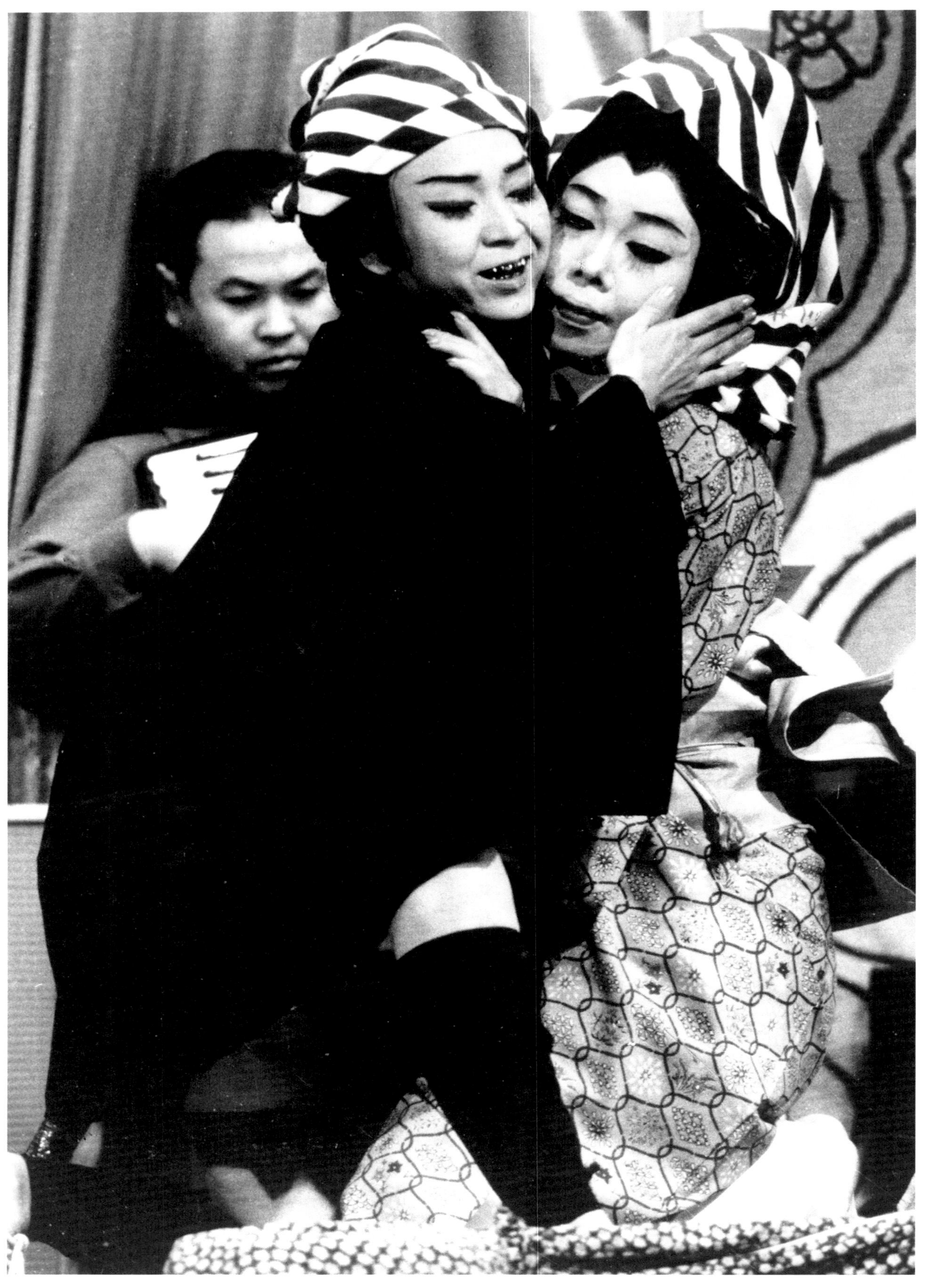

50   This page and opposite: from 'Japan: A Photo Theatre', 1968

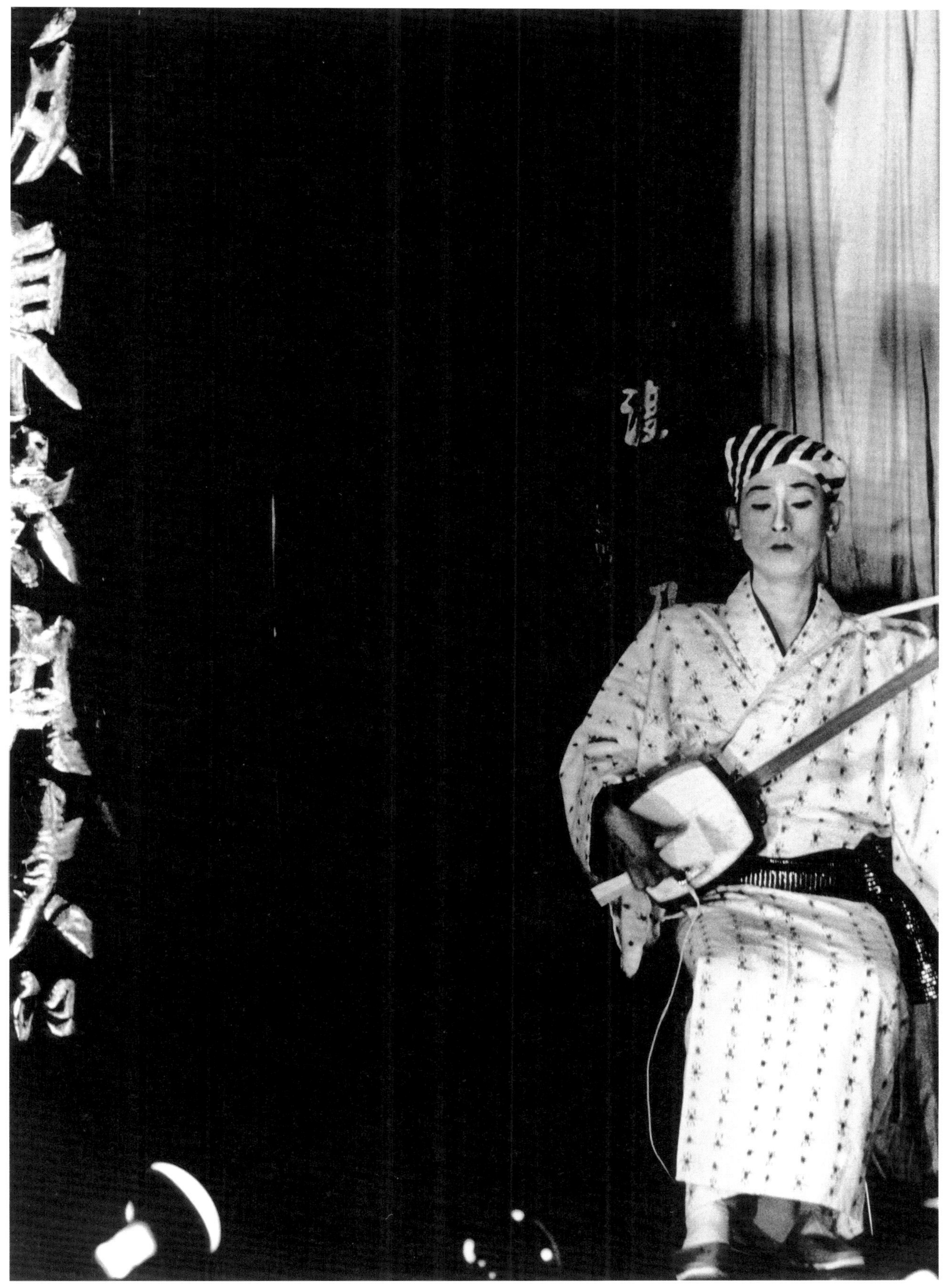

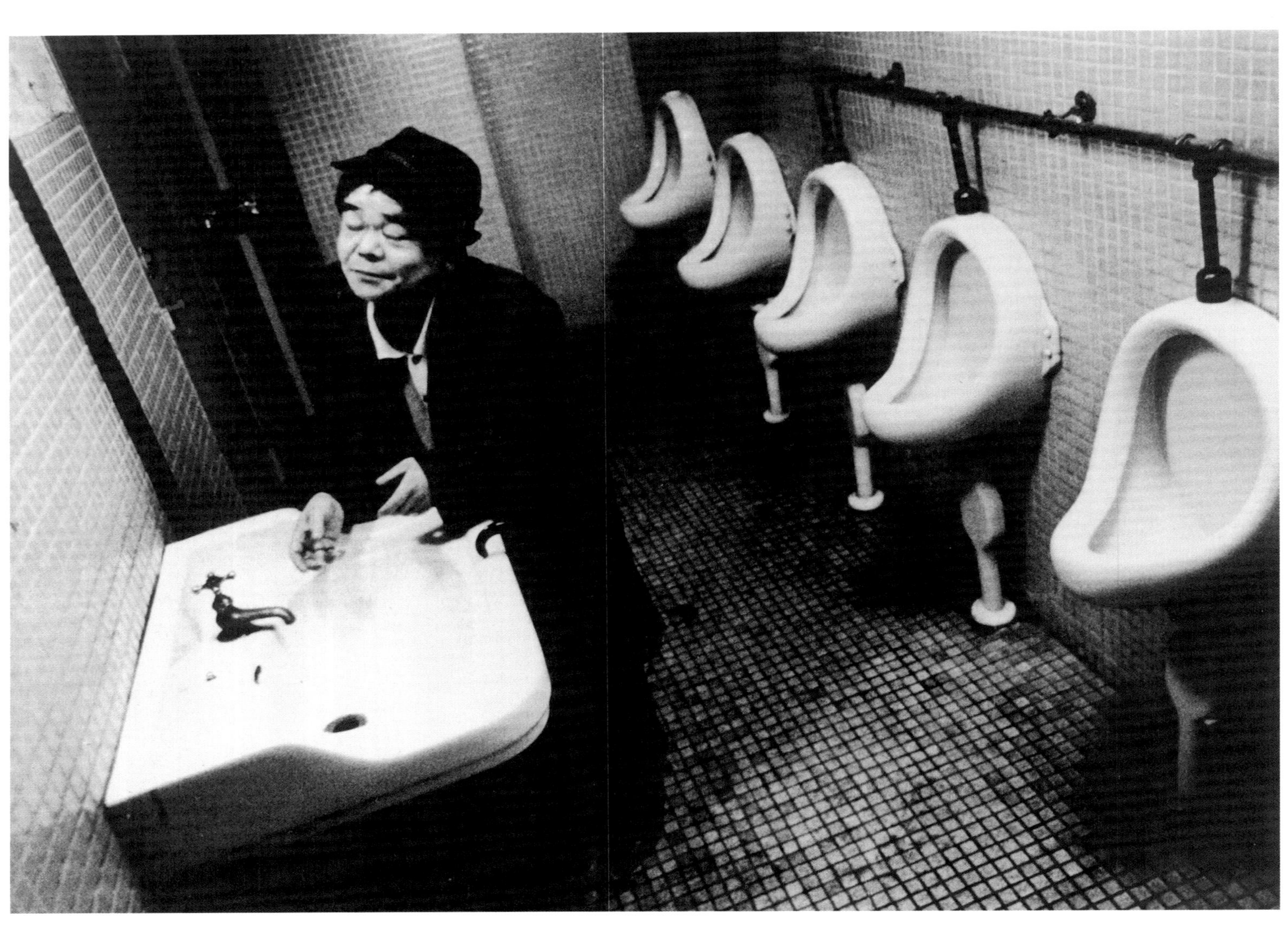

   This page and opposite: from 'Japan: A Photo Theatre', 1968

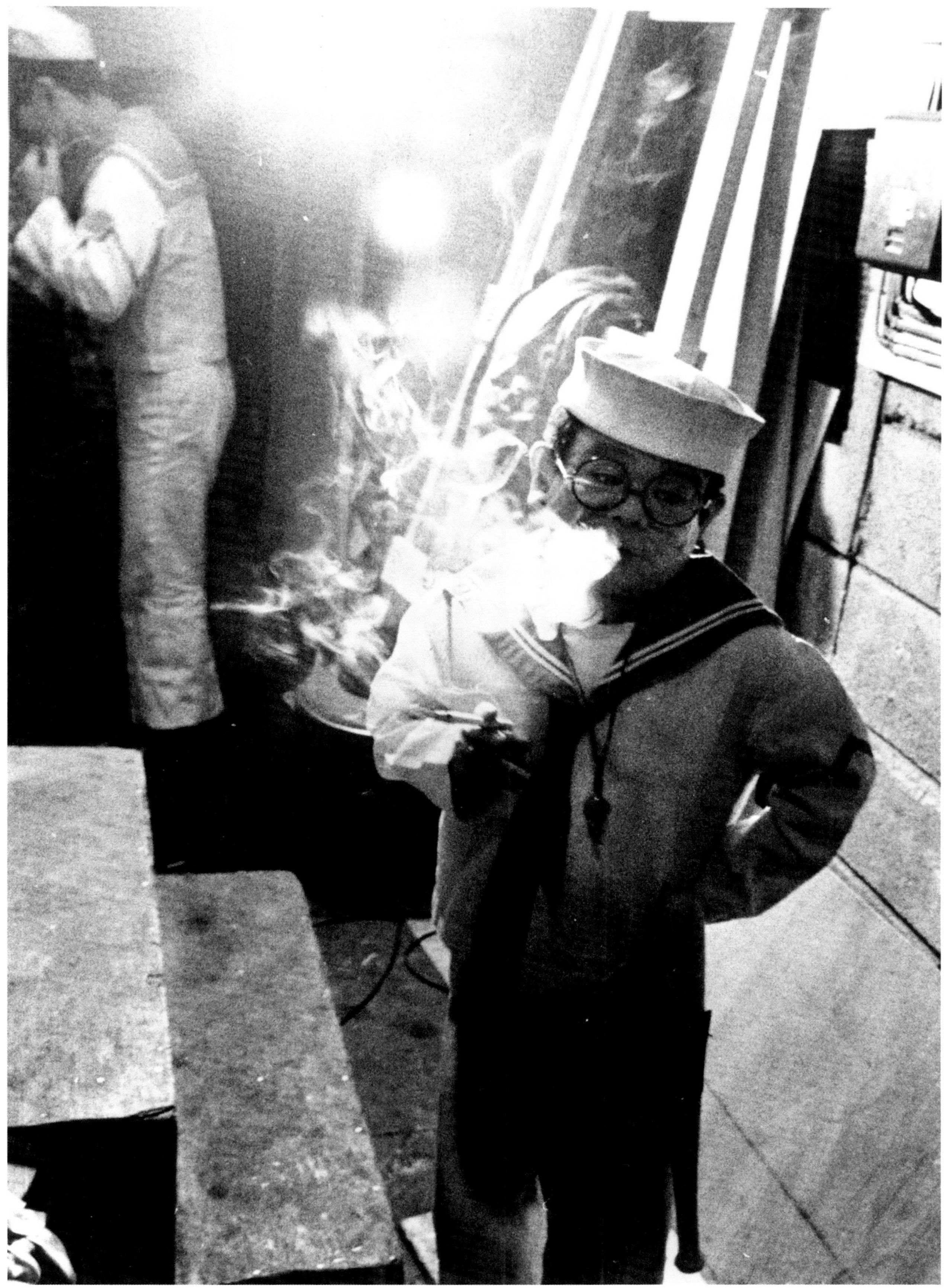

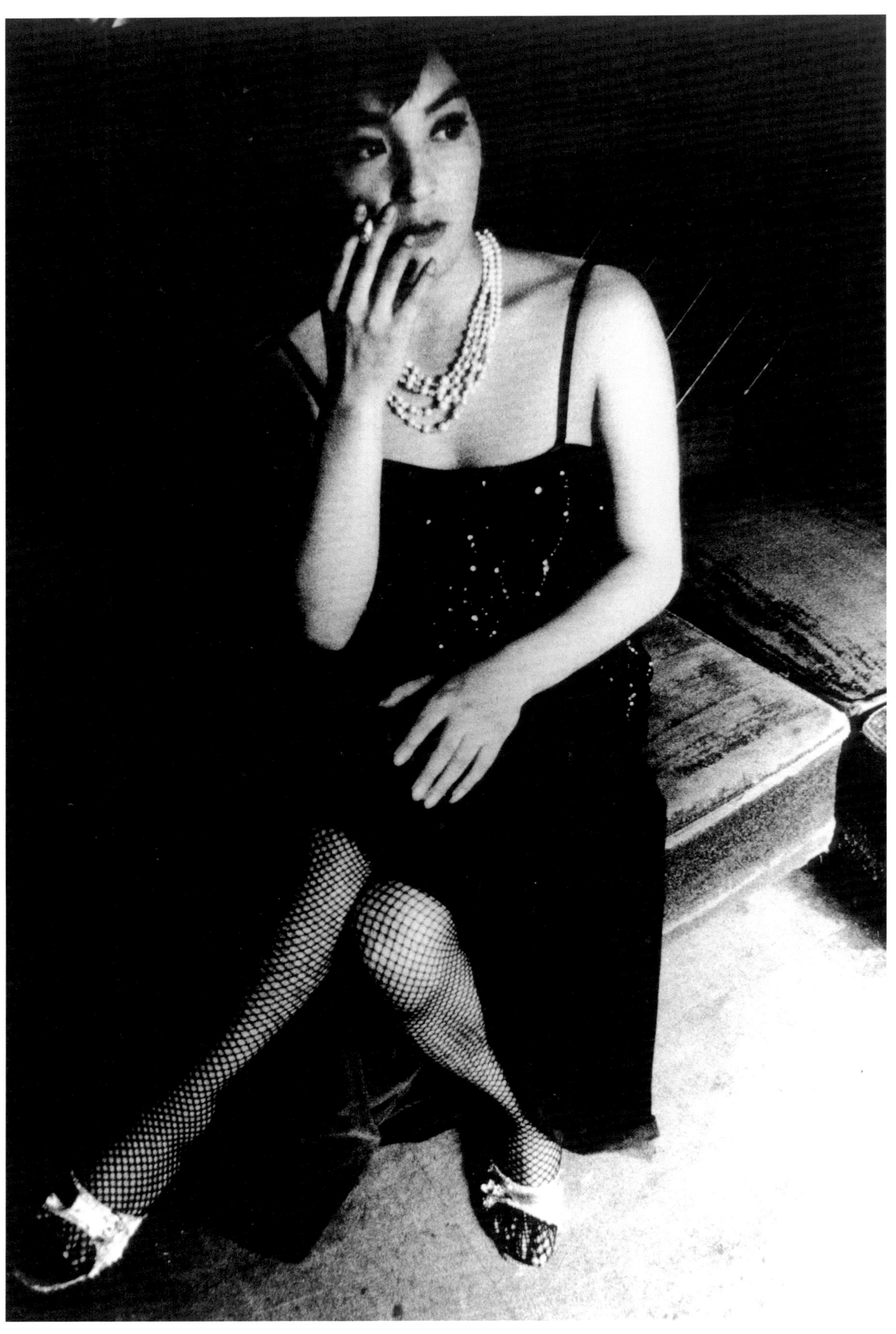

54   This page and opposite: from 'Japan: A Photo Theatre', 1968

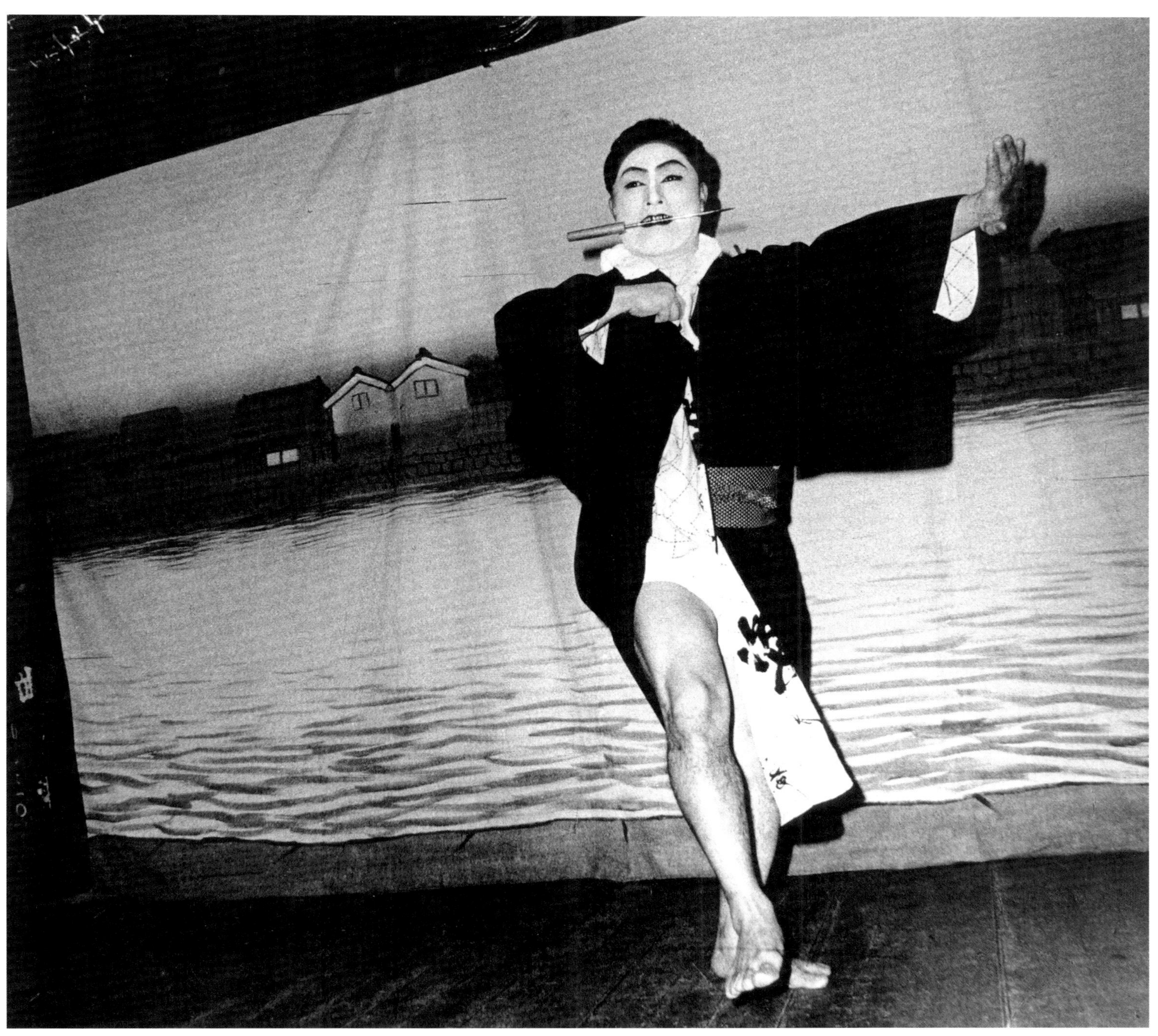

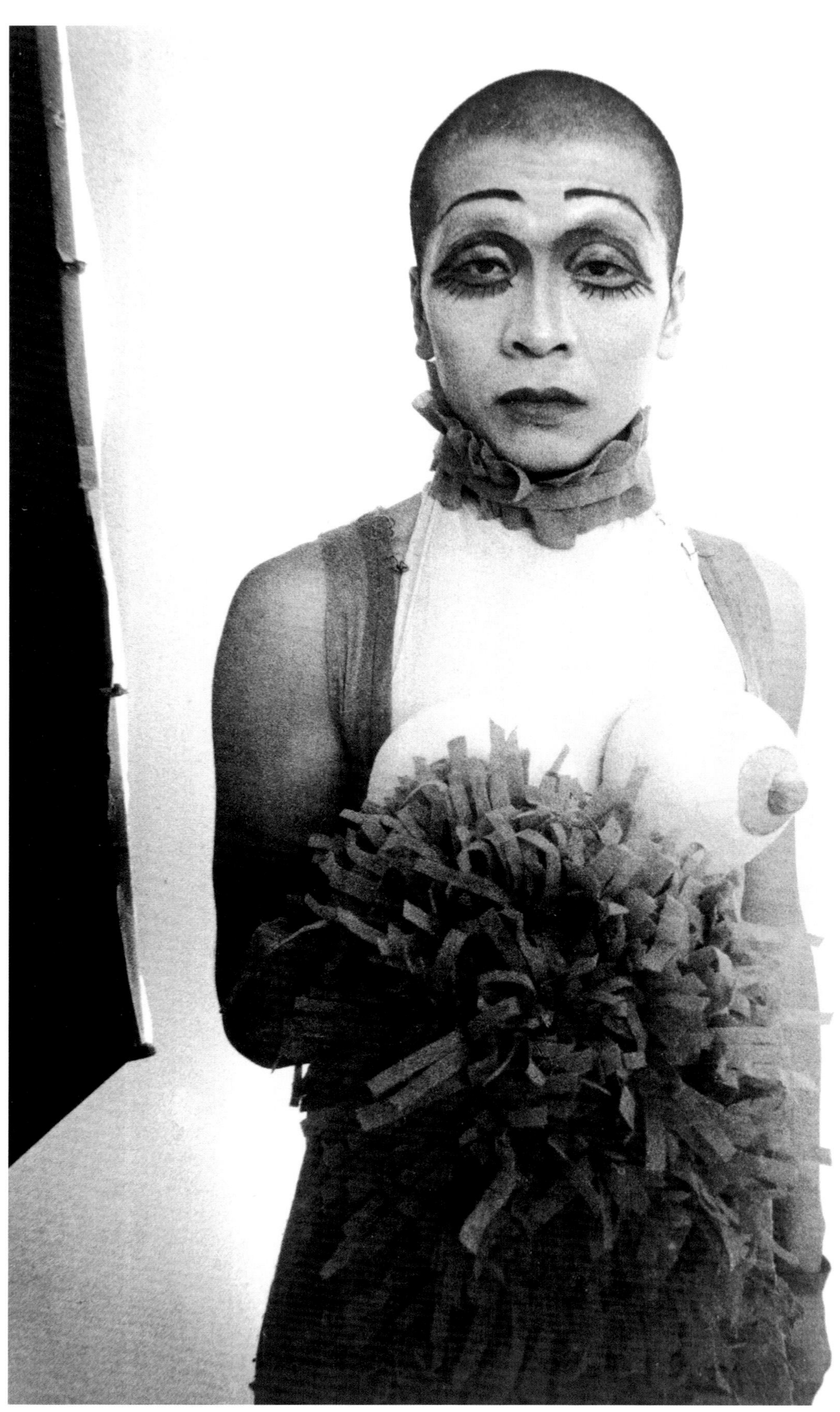

56   This page and opposite: from 'Japan: A Photo Theatre', 1968

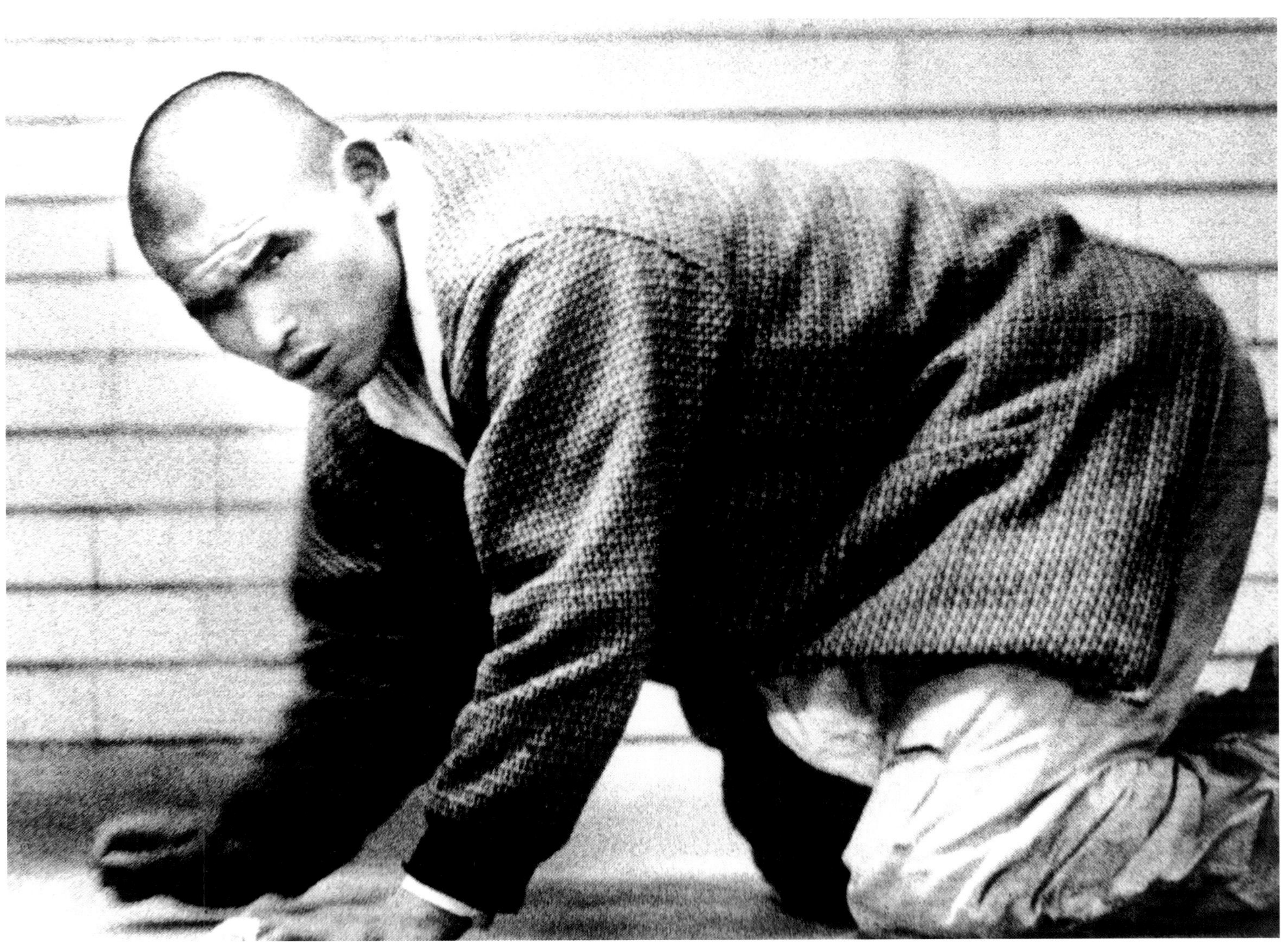

CASA

SUSANNA

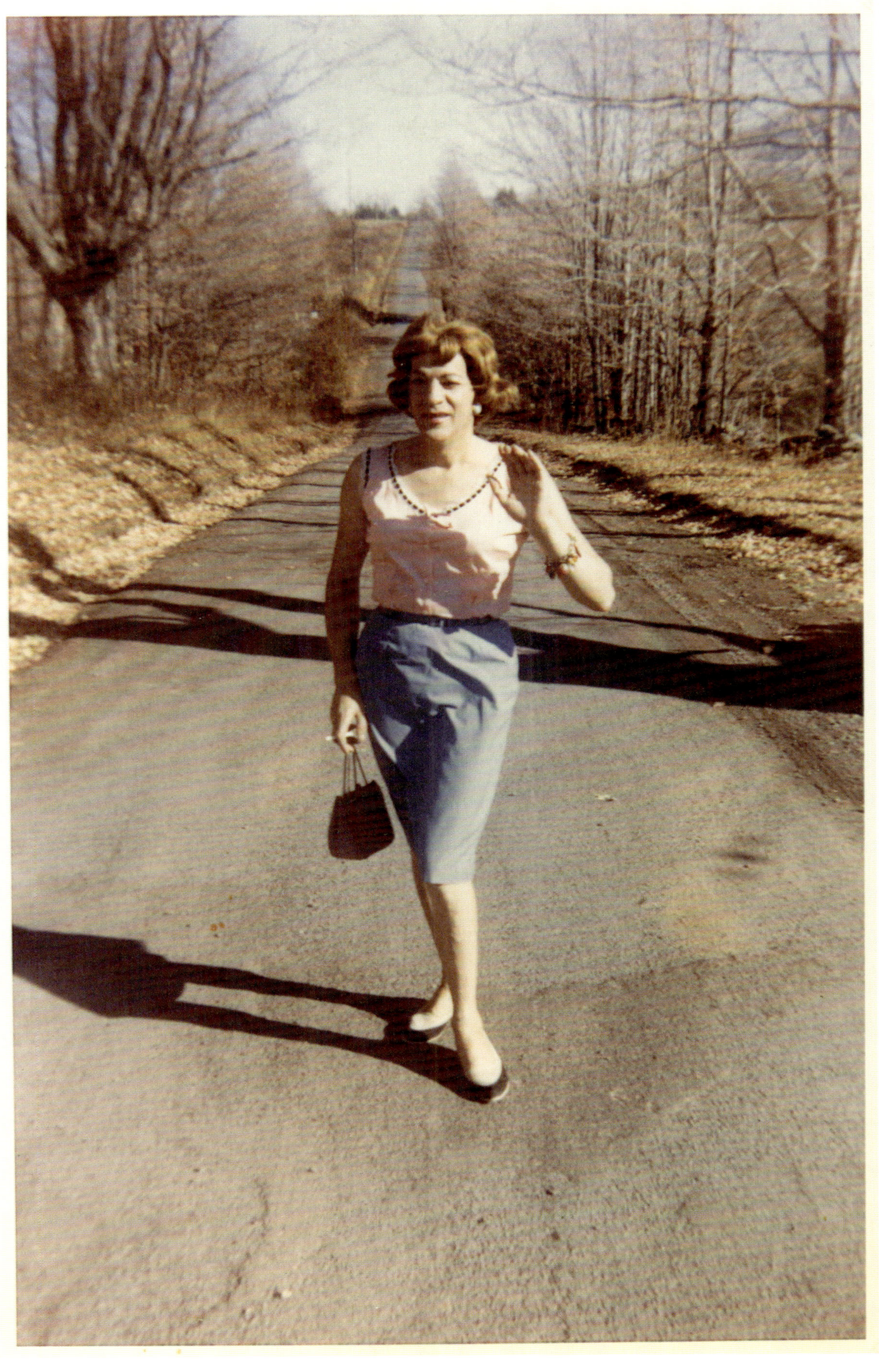

Photographs occupied a central role in the lives of Susanna Valenti and the cross-dressers who formed a burgeoning network in the United States and beyond in the 1950s and '60s. This network was sustained by the bi-monthly magazine *Transvestia*, local chapters of the Foundation for Full Personality Expression (FPE, which in 1976 became part of the Society for the Second Self, or Tri-Ess), and weekends at the Chevalier d'Eon (1955–63) and later Casa Susanna (1964–69), the two resorts that Susanna ran near Hunter, New York with her wife, Marie.

Like any gathering of friends – delighting in seeing each other again, fostering camaraderie, marking the occasion – a gathering of cross-dressers provided a reason to pull out a camera.[1] The freedom of being among cross-dressing peers, however, offered a rare chance to embody one's performed identity and to commit that self to film. The photographs that survive of these occasions not only show off a new dress or wig but a kinship and community. The kinship in question centred on how clothes, accessories and bearing could 'make the woman', as the saying goes. As Virginia Prince, founder of the magazine *Transvestia*, recounted on her first visit to the Chevalier d'Eon resort in 1961, 'We spent a lot of time taking pictures of each other with all kinds of cameras and just having a good time in our party clothes.'[2] But the act of posing for a photograph allowed for something more: a chance to bring that woman to life in the particular way that only photographs can. Is she genteel, coquettish, confident, elegant, sexy? What effect does this turn of the ankle make, this tilt of the chin, this knowing smile, this elongated arm with wrist and fingers poised, mannequin-like? It is both playful play and serious play, a visual journey to discover through these photographs: which self suits best? Which looks most like me? In that way, the photographs also deliver 'photographic

reassurance', as Katherine Cummings described it, a sense that this woman was possible and viable, that she could live.[3]

These photographic explorations reveal what attentive students of femininity the Casa Susanna cross-dressers were. The photographs show us the girl-next-door, the housewife, the lady, the femme fatale, and sometimes more than one role from the same person. Aspiration is evident in the poses drawn from fashion and movie magazines, but also familiarity and decorum.

Beyond making these photographs, there was the act of sharing them. As the many snaps of friends gathered around looking at photographs and holding envelopes from developing labs attest, Casa Susanna clientele brought their photographs with them when they got together. Photographs were also shared by mail – proxies for travel that could not easily be undertaken – fulfilling the promise to send copies of group shots, opportunities to solicit advice on hairstyles or to send festive greetings (Susanna and Marie certainly received photographic Christmas cards). They were shared on the spot, too, once Polaroid cameras became more readily available in the 1960s, the instantaneous thrill as attractive as the fact that there was no need to risk exposure at the developing lab.

Perhaps even more powerful than sharing the photographs with friends in person or by mail, however, was having them published in *Transvestia*.[4] Prince founded the magazine in 1960 and determined from the start that its content would come chiefly from its readers.[5] The photographs they sent in to the magazine, modest though they were, signalled to other subscribers that they were not alone in their desire to explore a feminine gender identity.[6] These images also served to strengthen the sense of a network, to build a sense of consensus around what it meant to cross-dress at this moment and what that in fact should look like, a 'cultural imaginary.'[7]

Ultimately, these photographs became keepsakes. When Robert Swope and Michel Hurst found a collection of snapshots at New York City's 26th Street flea market in 2004 – now in the collection of the Art Gallery of Ontario, Toronto, and from which these works are drawn – most were housed in albums. One even included a business card taped to its front

cover that read: 'Susanna Valenti / Female Impersonation / Spanish Dancing'. That the snapshots were placed in albums reflects yet another kind of work: that of building a personal visual record, the story Susanna wanted to keep for herself – pictures that would spark the memory of moments like the one relayed above, from 1962, in the early years of nurturing a cross-dressing community.

How Susanna's photographs ended up at the flea market remains unknown. Casa Susanna closed in 1969 and Marie died around this time. Susanna wrote her final *Transvestia* column for its 61st issue, in January 1970, after declaring in the prior issue that she had decided to live as a woman full-time. It is possible that Susanna no longer needed the mirror that these Casa Susanna photographs provided, as she made new, non-cross-dressing friends.[8] Someone did manage to keep all the photographs together. Whether this was by design or by neglect, it meant that they could be discovered, collected and preserved as the important pieces of queer visual history that they are.

Sophie Hackett

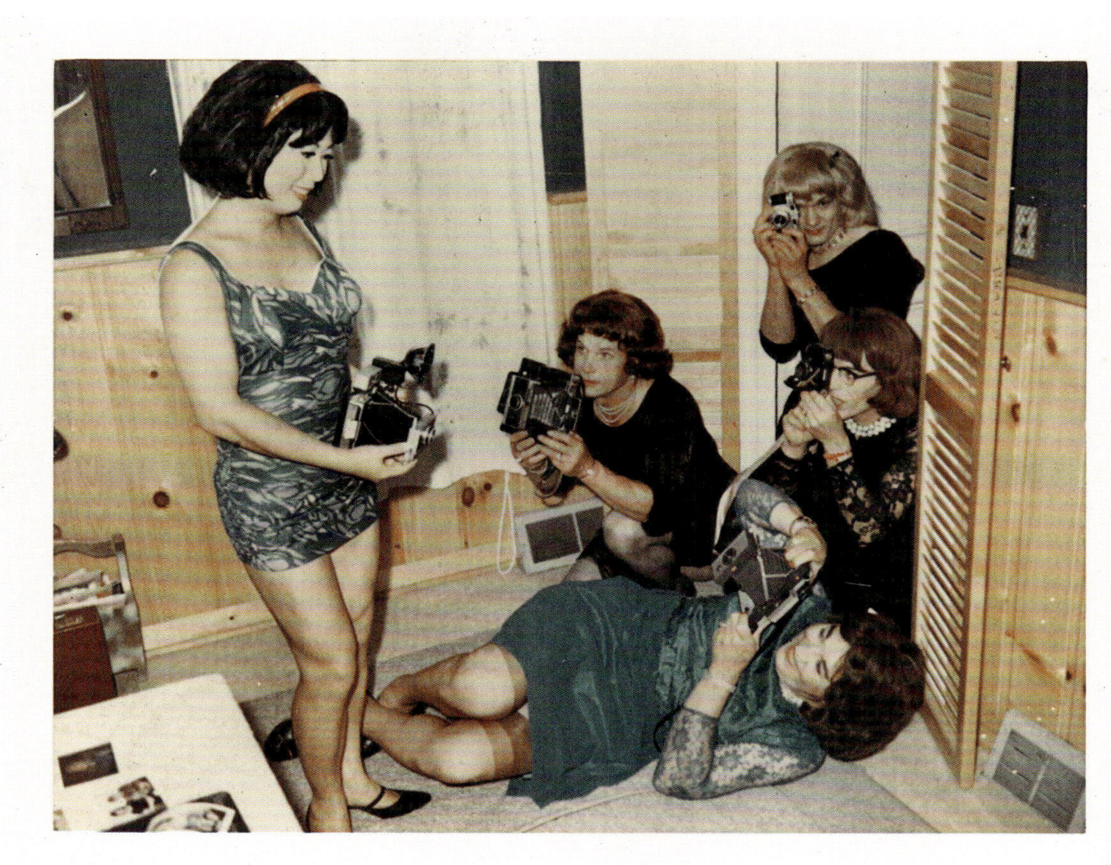

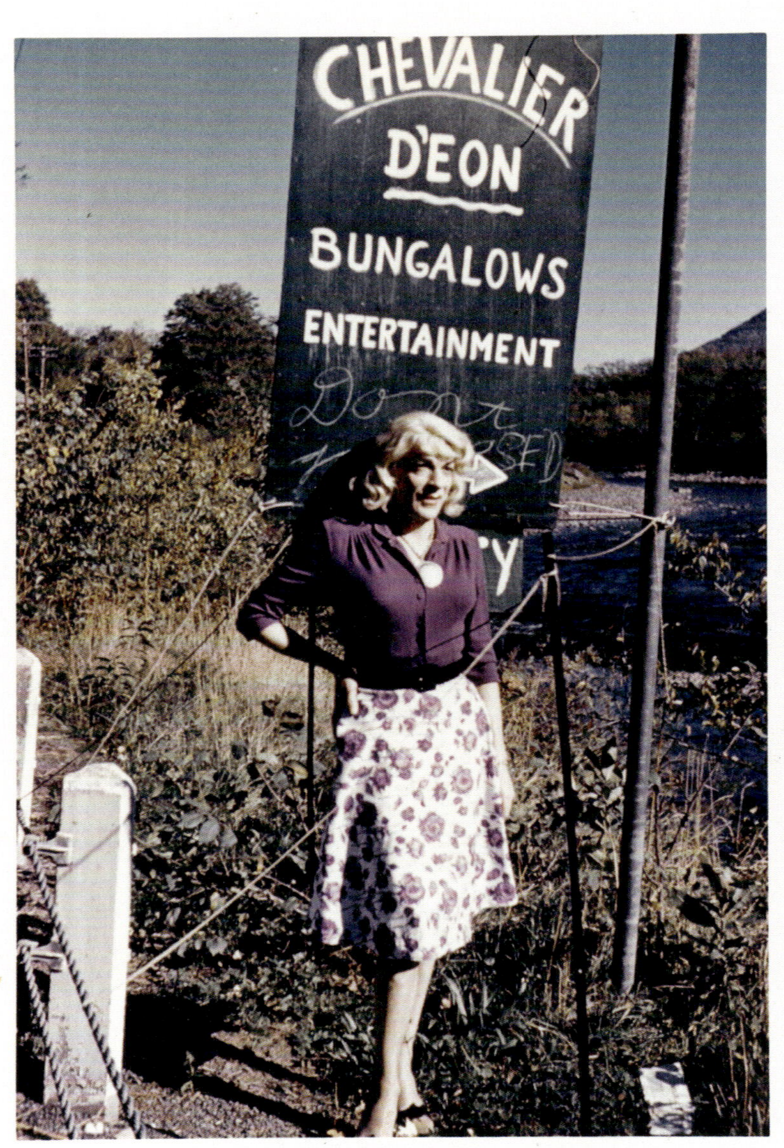

CHEVALIER
D'EON
BUNGALOWS
ENTERTAINMENT

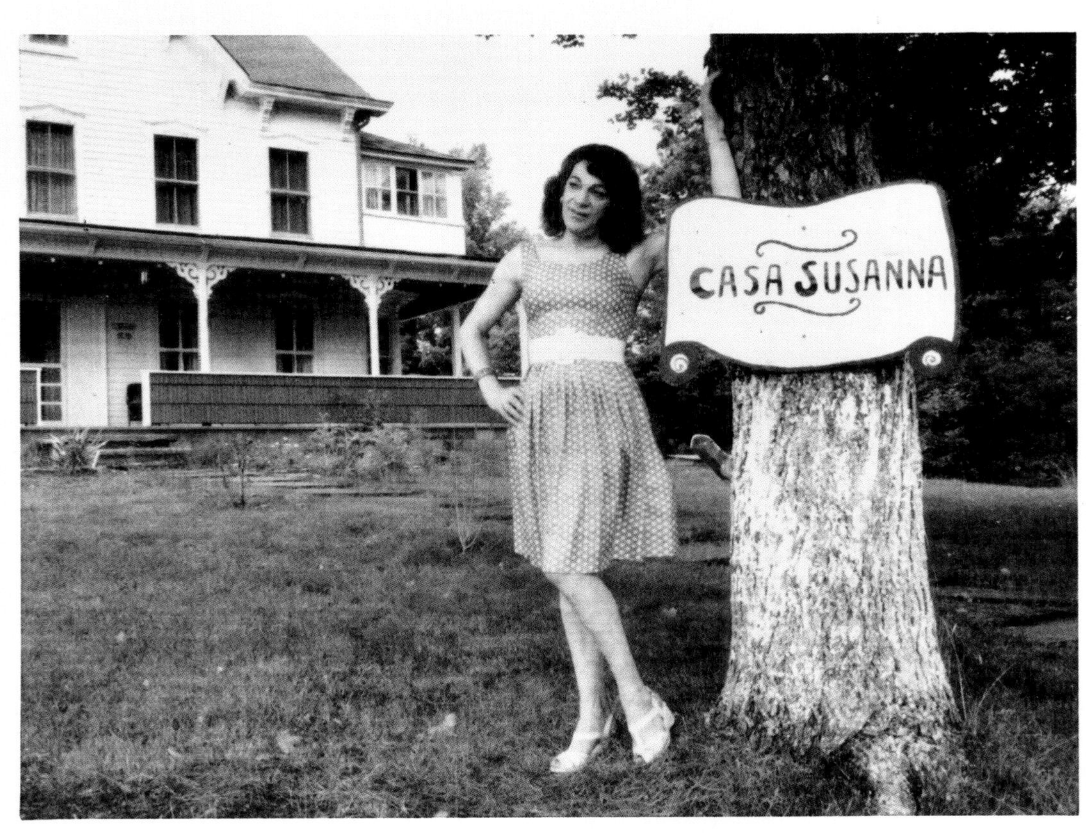

Attributed to Andrea Susan, *[Susanna at Casa Susanna]*, 1964–1969   63

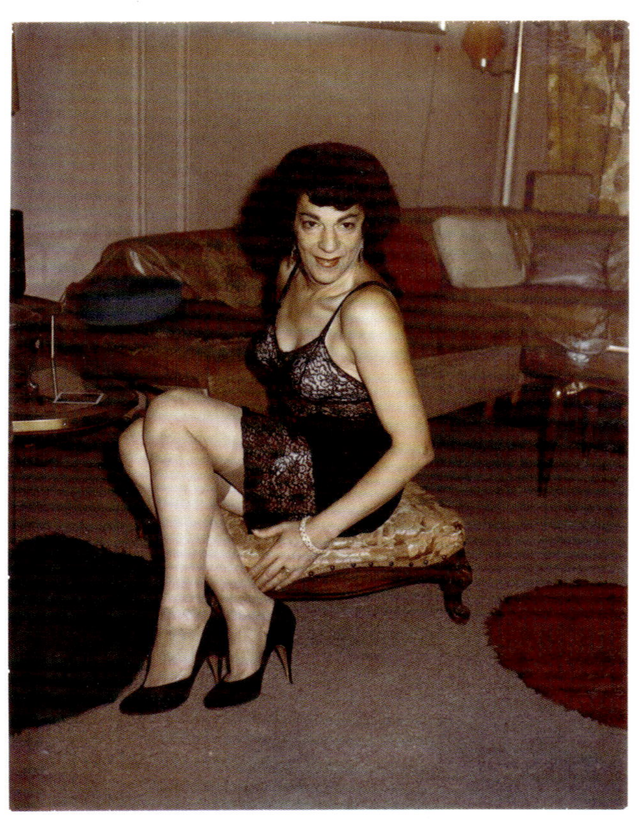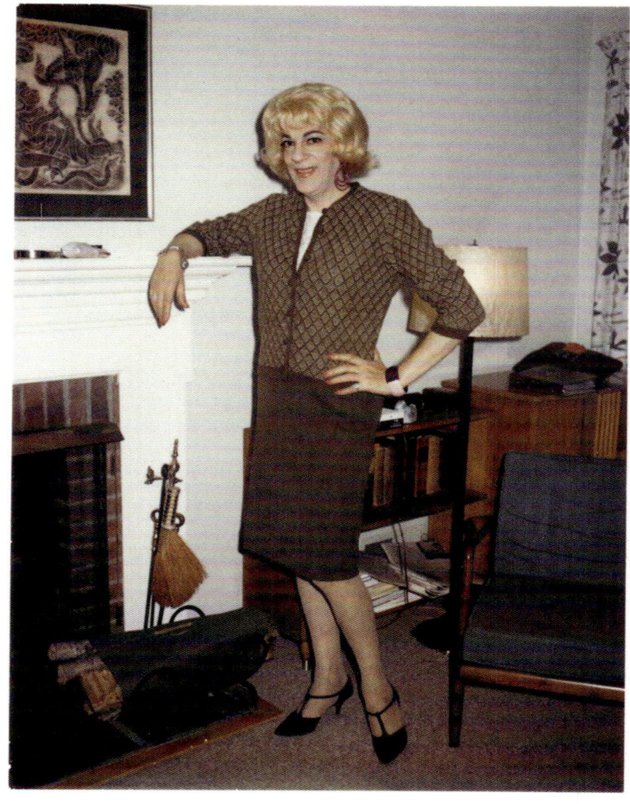

Left: attributed to Andrea Susan, *[Susanna in Black Lingerie]*, 1960s
Right: attributed to Andrea Susan, *[Susanna Standing by the Fireplace]*, 1964–1969

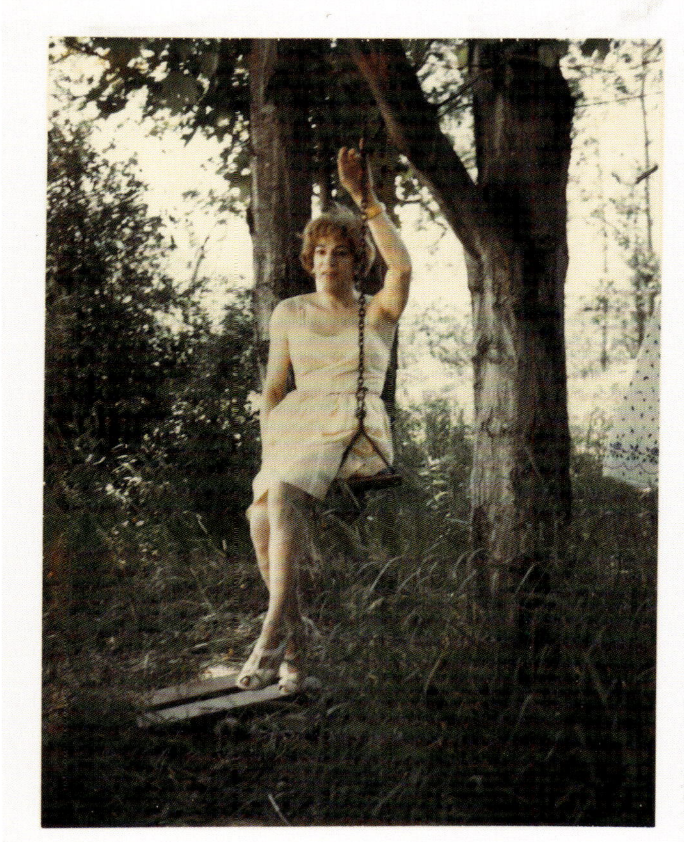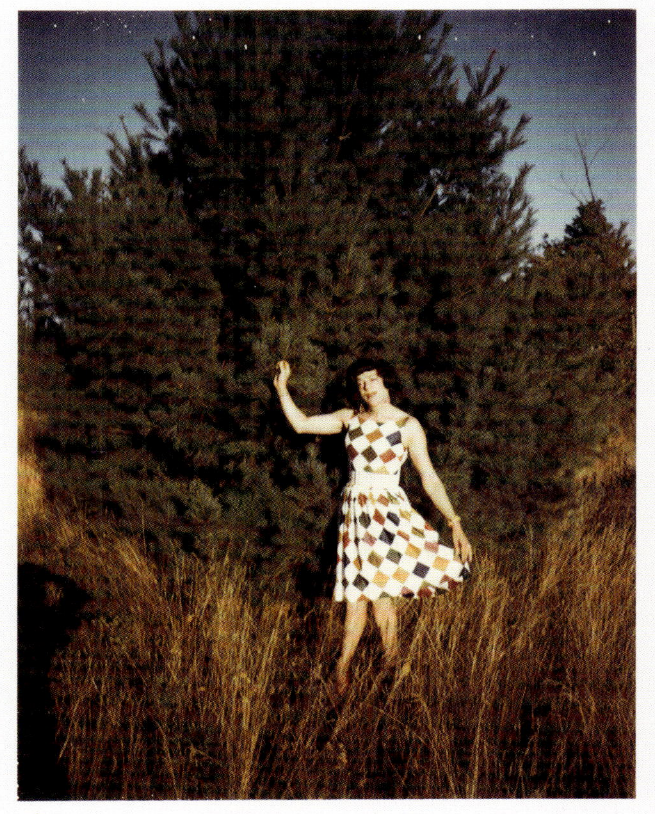

Left: attributed to Andrea Susan *[Susanna on the Swing]*, 1964–1969
Right: Unknown American, *[Susanna Posing in front of a Tree]*, 1964–1969

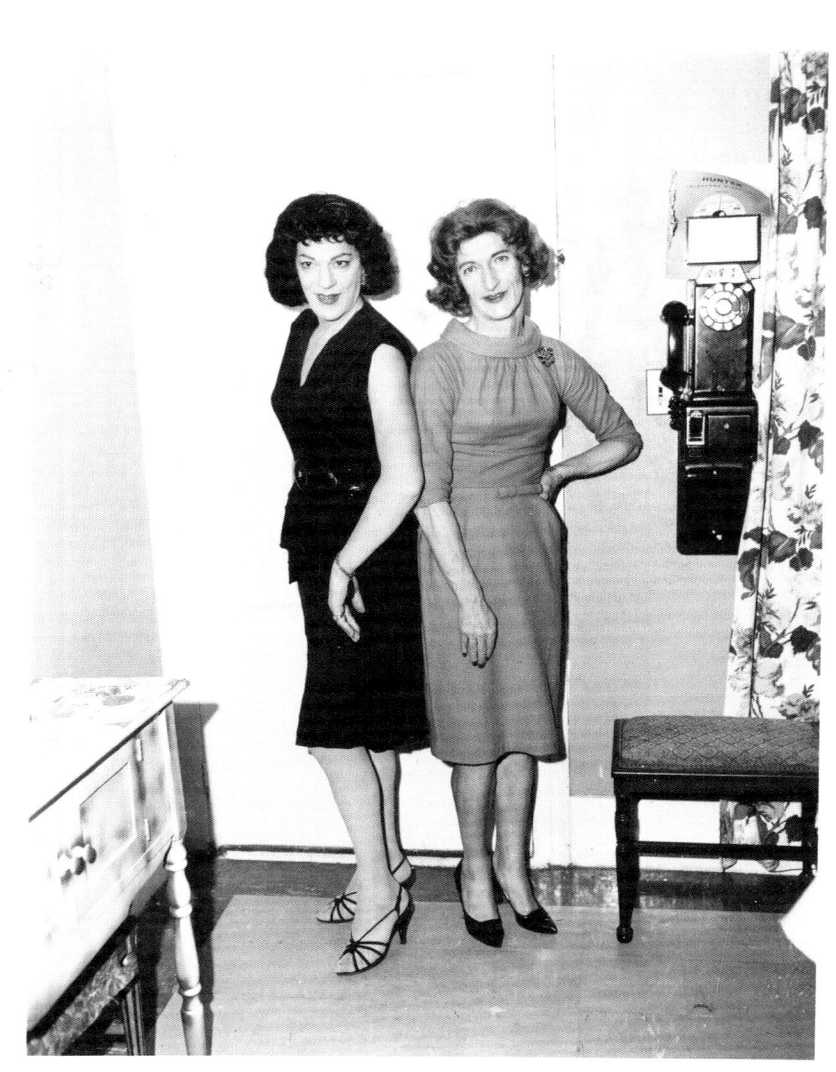

66   Unknown American, [*Susanna and Friend by the Telephone*], 1955-1963

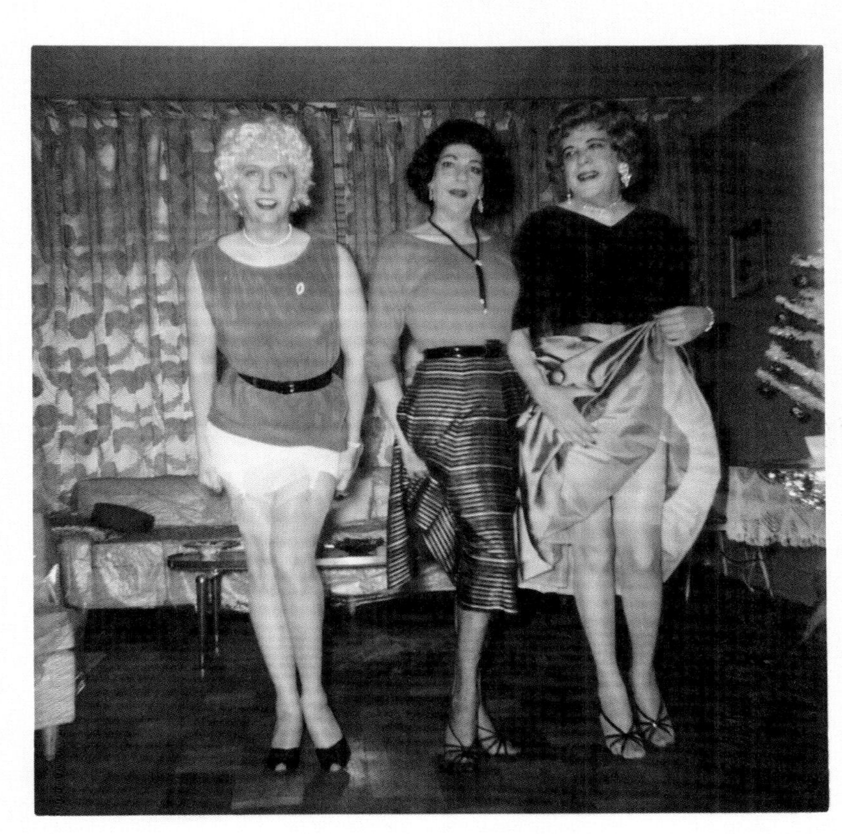

Unknown American, *[Susanna and Two Friends Showing Some Leg]*, 1960s

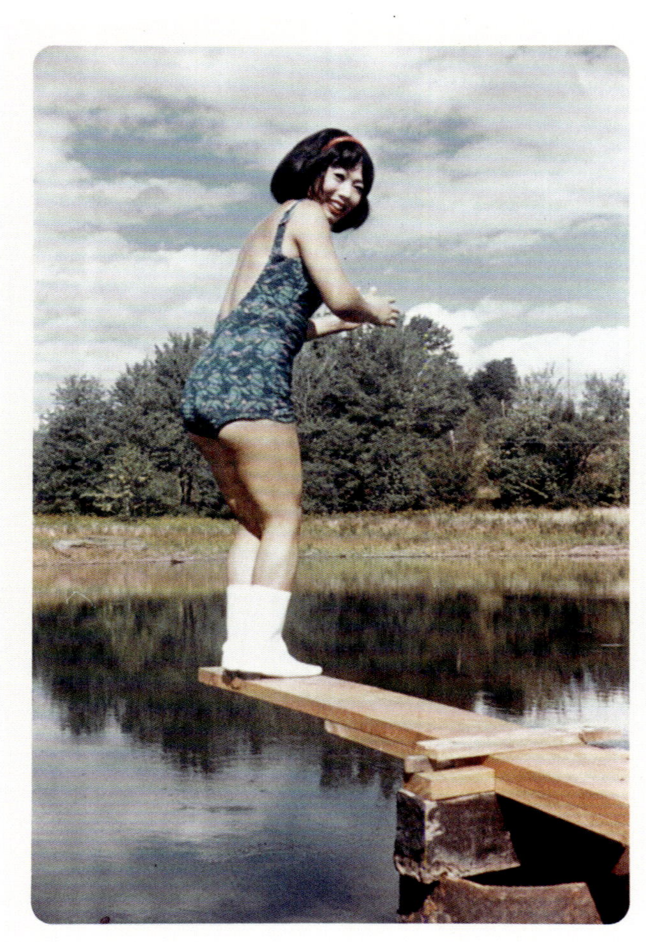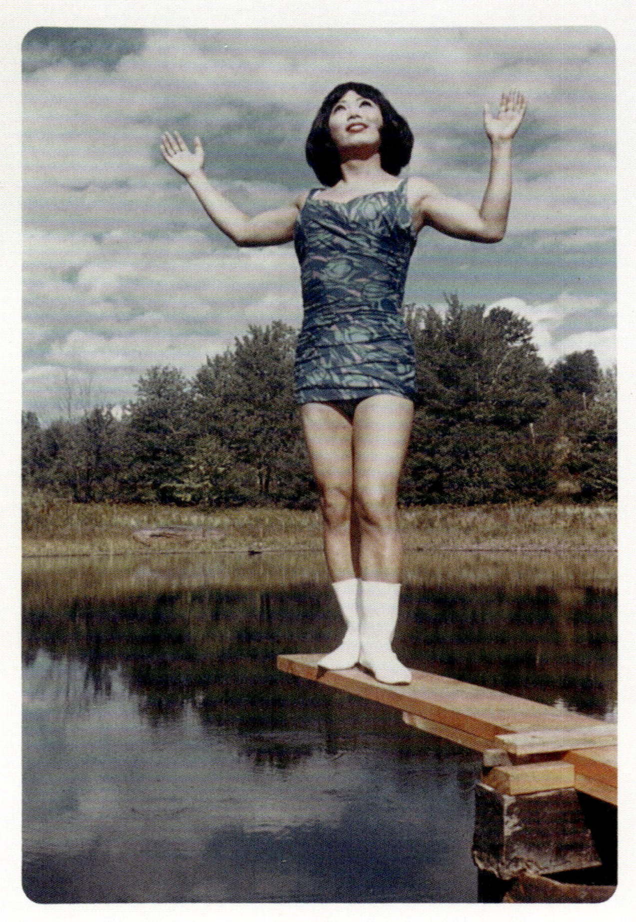

68   Left: Unknown American, *[Lily Diving]*, 1966. Right: Unknown American, *[Lily on the Diving Board]*, 1966

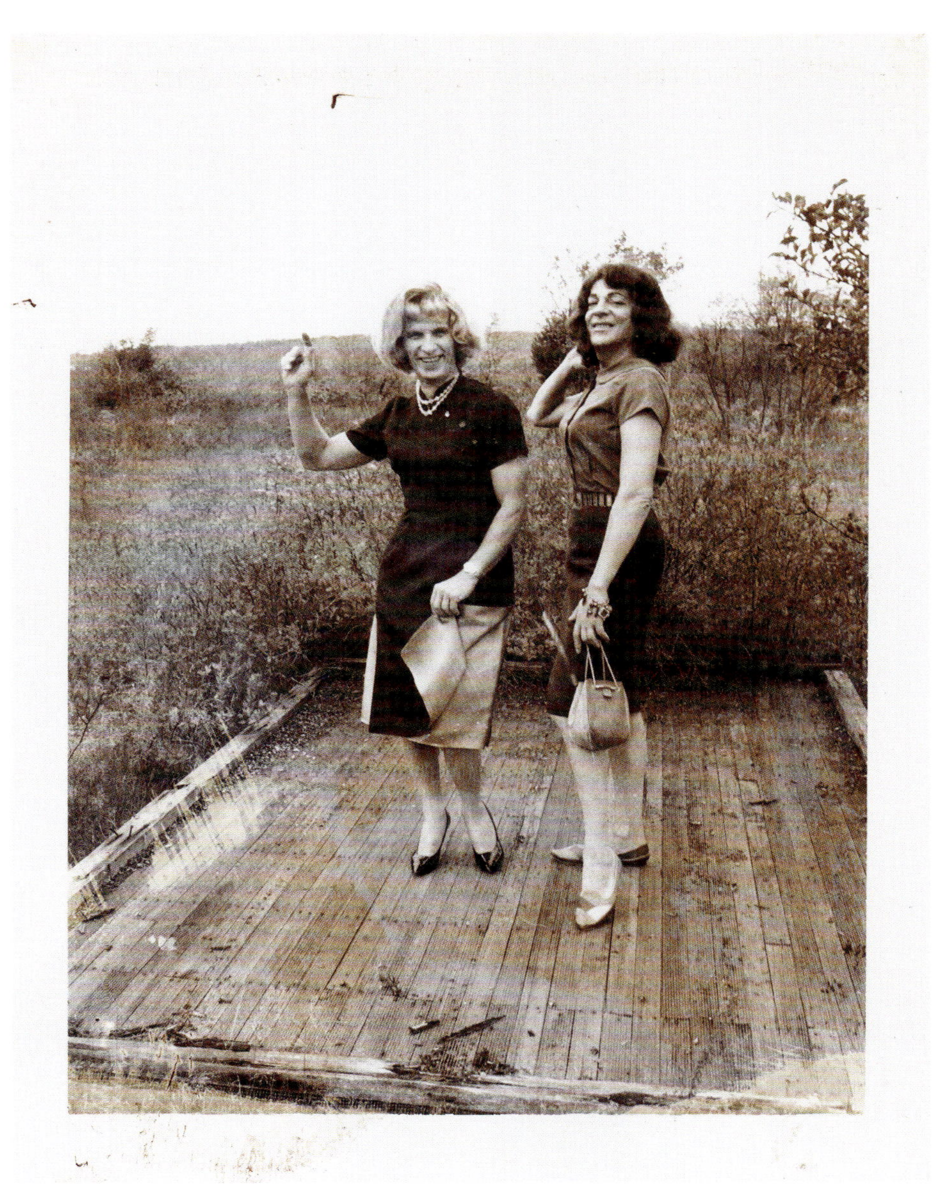

DANNY LYON

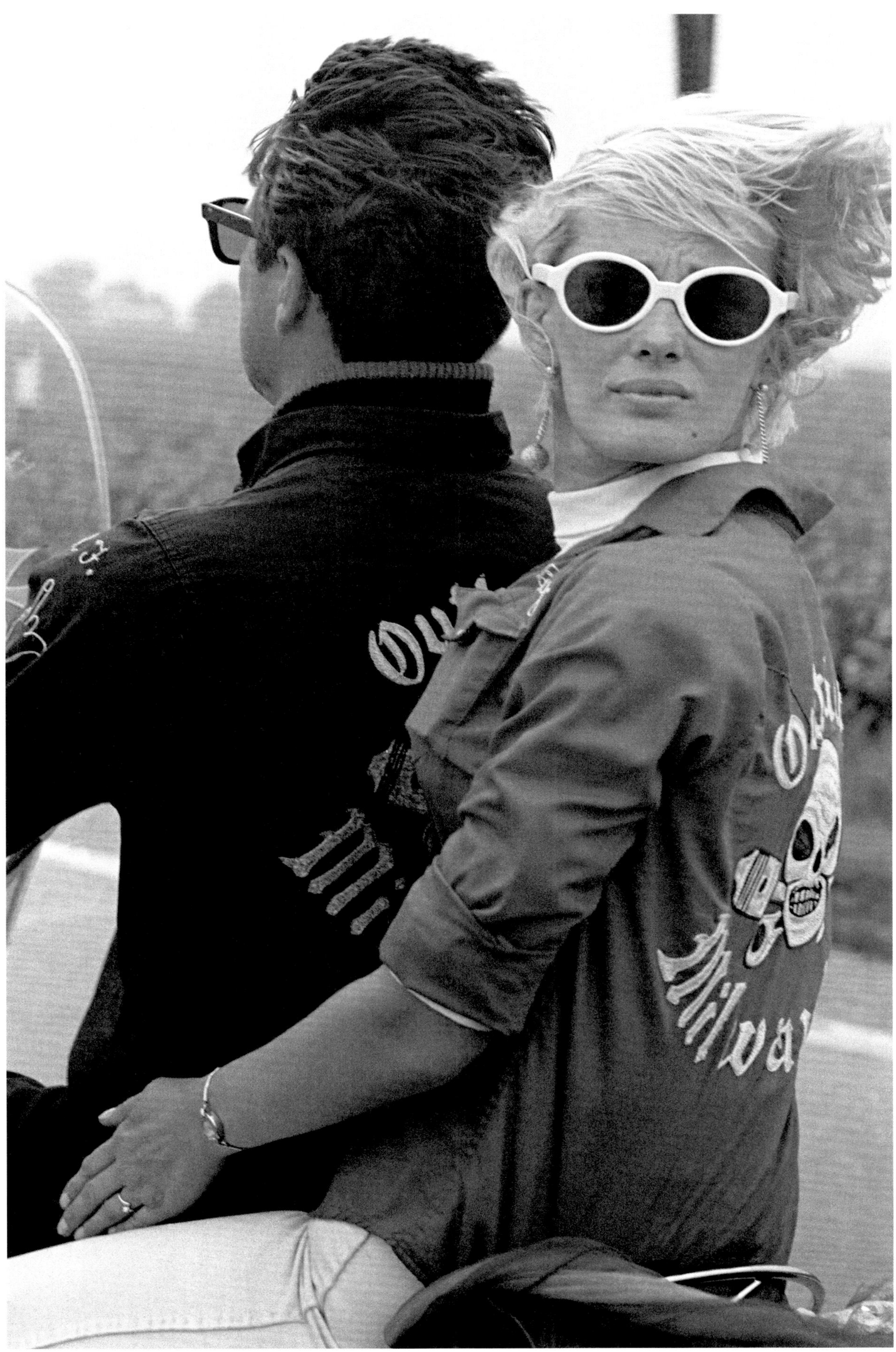

In *Crossing the Ohio River, Louisville, 1966* – one of Danny Lyon's (b. 1942, USA) most iconic and celebrated photographs – the viewer is literally thrust into the picture, as well as into the heart of the twentieth century, at full throttle. In the image, both a rusting nineteenth-century railway bridge and the languid American river it spans read clearly in the distance, yet the road, in the foreground below, is pure blur, rushing through the frame from left to right with the speed, force and all-consuming power of a riptide. Tearing across its surface is a man dressed in black astride a stripped-back Harley-Davidson, his greased pompadour rendered wild by wind and acceleration. He momentarily glances backwards over his right shoulder, yet is propelled ever forwards, his unworn helmet sitting on the handlebars and seemingly leaning into the unknown of the oncoming open road. Embroidered onto the back of his shirt a grinning skull, flanked by two crossed pistons, grits its teeth and smiles menacingly at all that has past; above it, in blackletter script, the name of an infamous motorcycle club – the Outlaws.

In the mid-1960s, after studying history at the University of Chicago and spending several years documenting the turbulent struggle and stoic determination of the civil rights movement as a staff photographer for the Student Nonviolent Coordinating Committee, Danny Lyon bought a 1956 Triumph made of spare parts, joined a notorious biker club, and began to explore the cultures and communities that centred around motorcycles. It may seem like a strange turn for Lyon to have shifted both his attention and lens away from the likes of Martin Luther King Jr, Stokely Carmichael and the historic marches, sit-ins, clashes and funerals occurring throughout the American South, and instead focus upon groups of adrenaline junkies and rebellious misfits, some of whom would stop by the side of the road to have a picnic with, as he described it, 'a nine-foot original Nazi flag marking the spot'.[1] Yet, in a time when police, politicians and even National Guardsmen were openly intimidating, incarcerating, beating and bludgeoning thousands of peaceful protesters on a regular basis – as witnessed and captured by Lyon himself during the preceding years – those who aspired to live outside the law (the 'Outlaws') offered a difficult yet fascinating alternative response to the status quo. Attempting to escape the strictures of a flawed society through antisocial nihilism

and speed-induced abandon – rather than fighting to change it via righteous activism and non-violent protest – these 'bikeriders' were nevertheless in many ways pursuing a common American dream, albeit via very different means: essentially, one of freedom. As Lyon explained recently, at its heart, his work has always been 'about the existential struggle to be free. That is what unites everything I have done.'[2]

Drawing from cowboy legends, pirate mythology, pulp fiction and Hollywood tales such as *The Wild One* (1953) and *The Wild Angels* (1966), the motorcycle-obsessed subjects of Lyon's book *The Bikeriders*, first published in 1968, are imbued with fantasy as much as reality and represent a creative fiction as much as an objective fact. They pose and posture – for neighbouring bikers and neighbourhood kids, for the camera and for one another; they rest their elbows upon their motorcycles with conspicuous casualness, and self-consciously slouch like a moody Marlon Brando. Similarly, Lyon's photographs themselves indulge in an unapologetic and often romanticised subjectivity, and draw their strength from the photographer's deeply embedded and proudly earned position within this community, rather than from the distanced perspective of the traditional photojournalist. In a sense, Lyon assumes the role of an insider among outsiders, and in doing so grants the viewer newfound insider status as well. 'The material in this book was collected between 1963 and 1967 in an attempt to record and glorify the life of the American bikerider,'[3] Lyon writes in the introduction to its most recent edition. 'It is a personal record, dealing mostly with bikeriders whom I know and care for. If anything has guided this work beyond the facts … it is what I have come to believe is the spirit of the bikeriders; the spirit of the hand that twists open the throttle on the crackling engines of big bikes and rides them on racetracks or through traffic or, on occasion, into oblivion.'[4] Lyon's eye insists that as we fly freely down the open highway alongside our comrades, or drink beer in crowded parking lots or the lush Midwestern fields among them, we carefully relish rather than critically reflect upon the experience.

Because of its intimately immersive and unapologetically subjective approach, Lyon's photographic work has often been aligned with the New Journalism movement of the 1960s, alongside the non-fiction writings of notables

such as Truman Capote, Norman Mailer, Joan Didion, and 'gonzo-journalist' Hunter S. Thompson, who published his own accounts of living with and riding alongside bikers – *Hell's Angels: The Strange and Terrible Saga of the Outlaw Motorcycle Gangs* – just a year before the release of Lyon's. (In fact, in 1966 Thompson sent a strongly worded letter to Lyon encouraging him to leave the Outlaws, writing, 'I think you should get the hell out of that club unless it's absolutely necessary for photo action. I've seen the Angels work and they scare the hell out of me.'[5]) Yet Lyon cites the seminal book *Let Us Now Praise Famous Men*, published in 1941 with text by James Agee and photographs by Walker Evans, as the primary source of inspiration for his work. More specifically, and perhaps surprisingly, it was the voice of Agee rather than the eye of Evans that served as a catalyst for Lyon's own vision. 'To tell the truth,' he stated in a recent interview, 'Agee's writing had a more profound effect on me at the time than Evans's photographs.'[6]

In the preface to *Let Us Now Praise Famous Men*, Agee clearly states both his and Evans's proto-New Journalism position from the outset as one that 'tr[ies] to deal with [our subjects] not as journalists, sociologists, politicians, entertainers, humanitarians, priests, or artists, but seriously'.[7] He continues, 'It is an effort in human actuality, in which the reader is no less centrally involved than the authors and those of whom they tell … more essentially, this is an independent inquiry into certain normal predicaments of human divinity.'[8] Similarly, Lyon's own independent, insider approach – which as he himself admits is dedicated to not just the recording but also the glorification of his subjects – involves the viewer as much as the photographer, and in a sense delves deep into the everyday humanity of his bikeriders while also elevating them to a similarly divine status, perhaps not so much in line with Judaeo-Christian tradition but rather that of classical Graeco-Roman mythology. As Lyon once explained it, 'They were heroes to me, all of these people.'[9] And through his photographs we are thrown upon the back of their heavy metal chariots, forever riding among these half-men, half-gods as they roam the Elysian plains of America's open roads – fearless, determined and wild – on an endless quest for freedom and a spirited odyssey of abandon, adventure and whatever comes their way.

Aaron Schuman

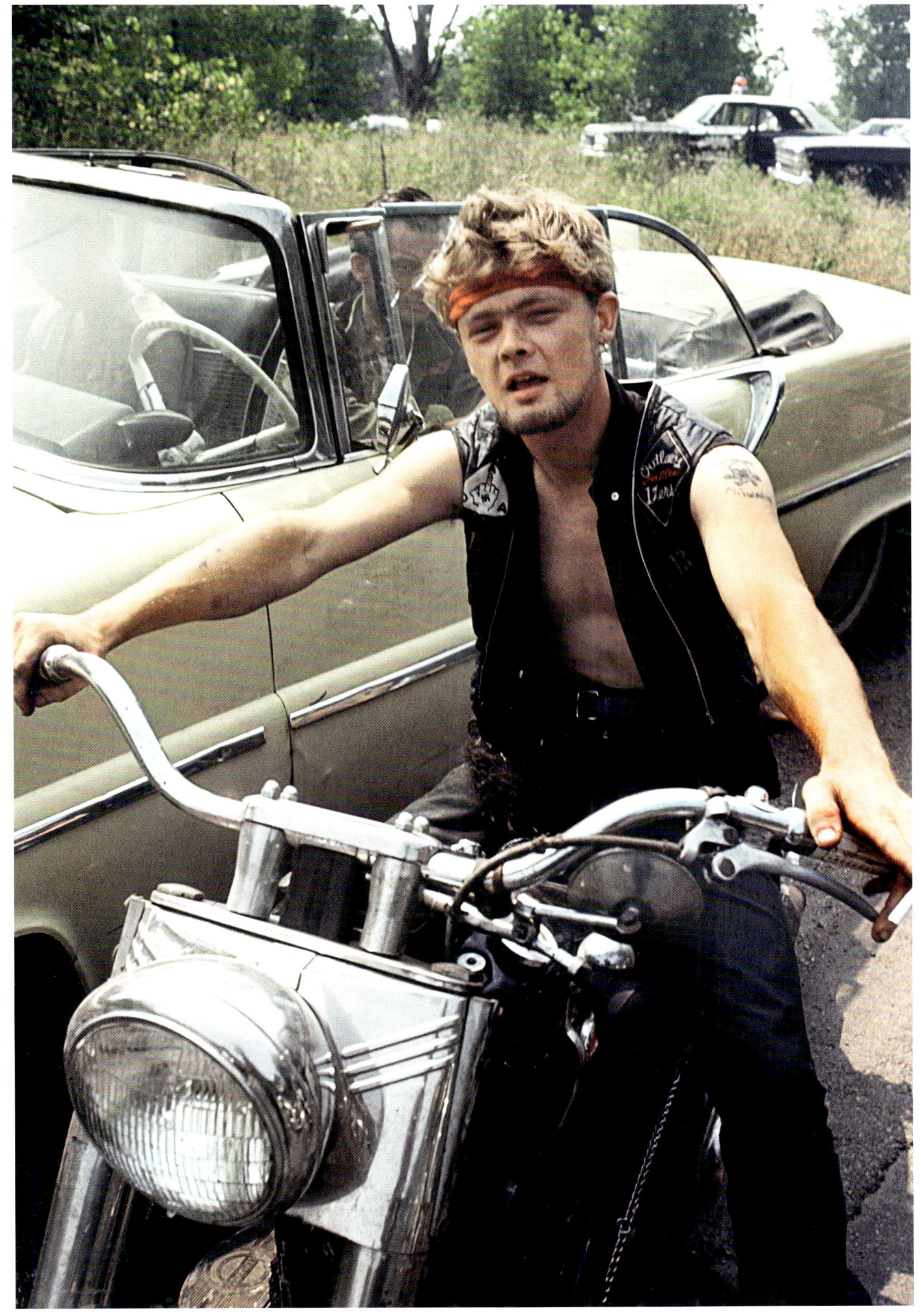

From 'The Bikeriders', *Indiana Dunes*, 1966

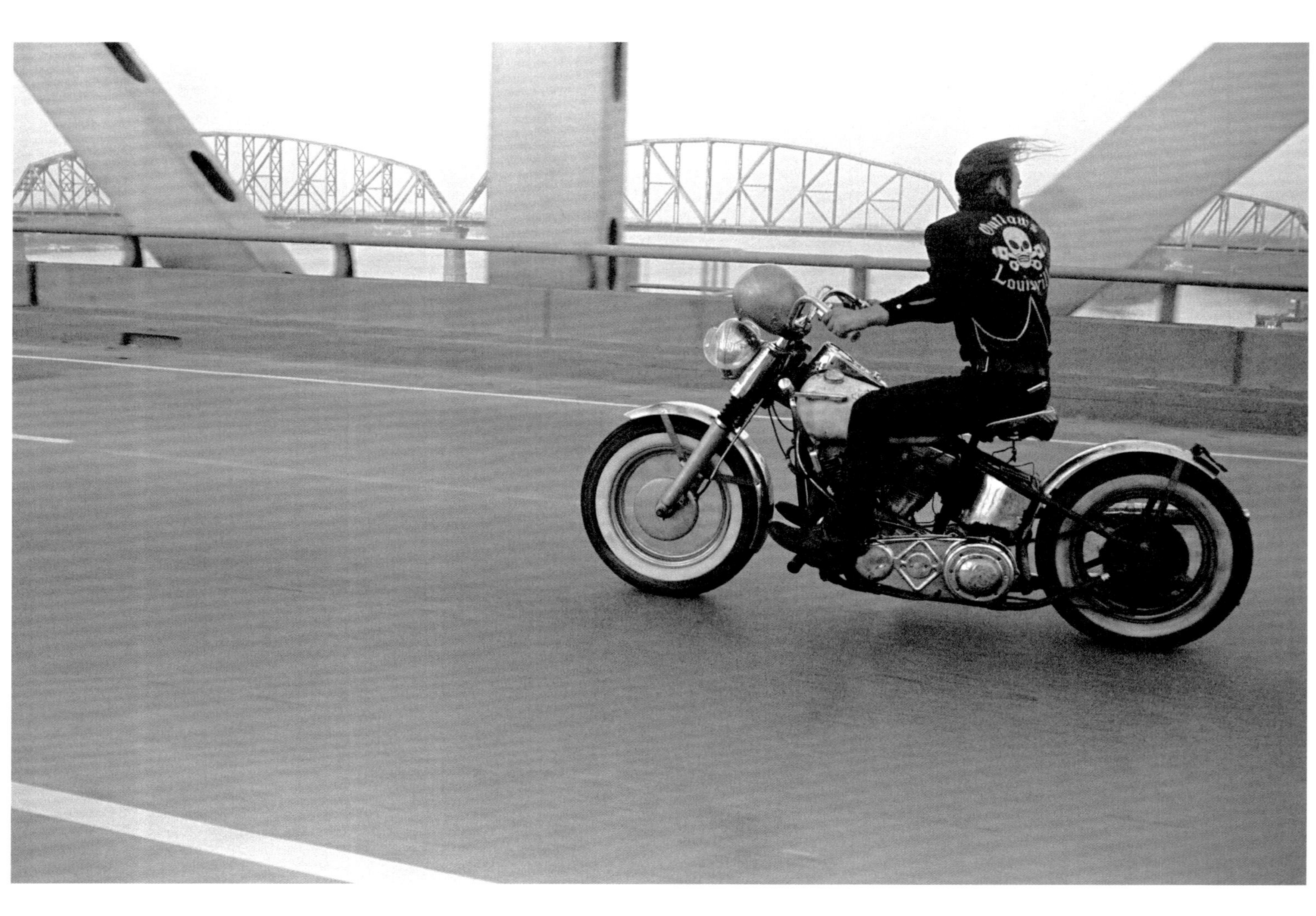

74   From 'The Bikeriders', *Crossing the Ohio River, Louisville, 1966*

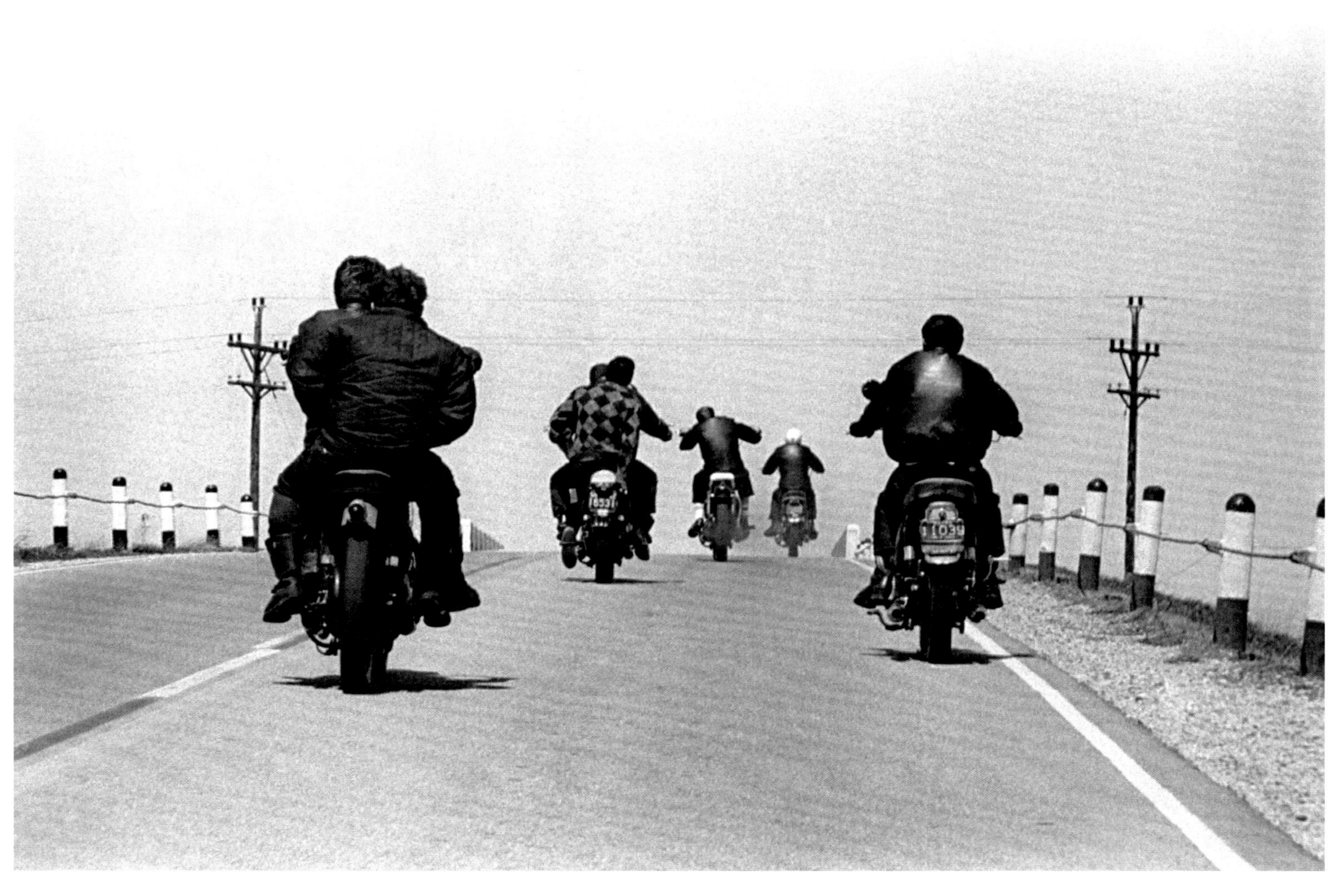

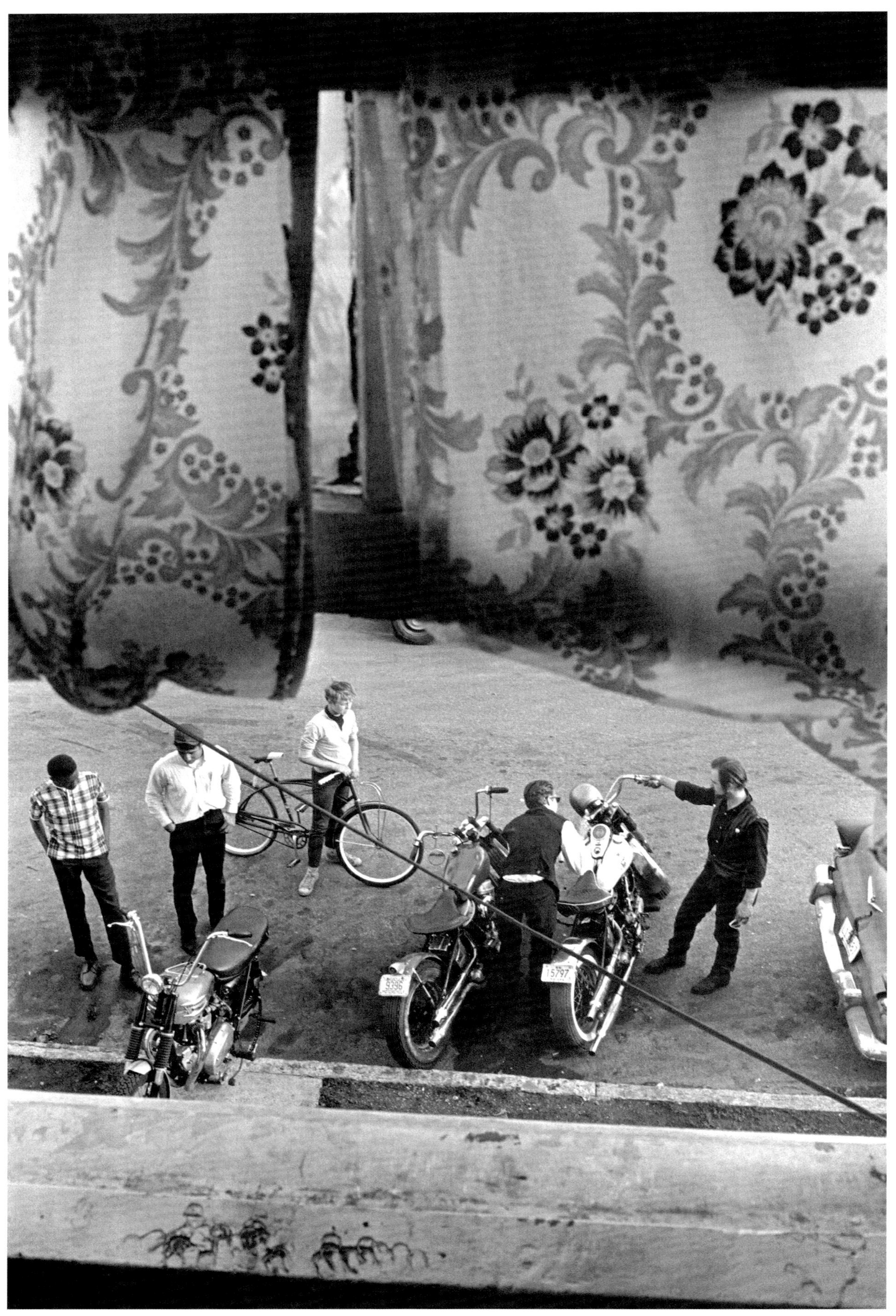

76   From 'The Bikeriders', *From Lindsey's Room, Louisville*, 1966

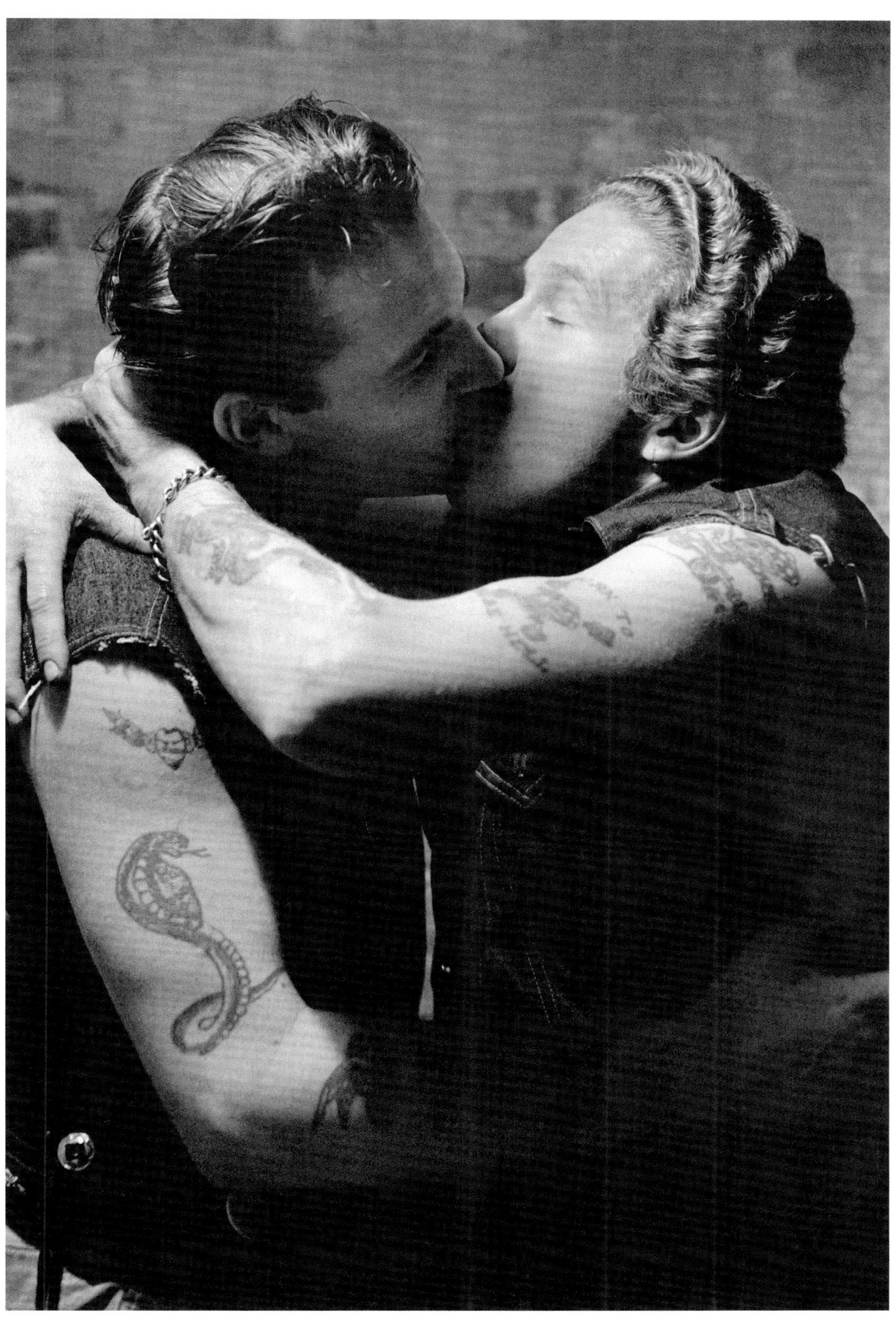

From 'The Bikeriders', *Corky and Funny Sonny, 1965*

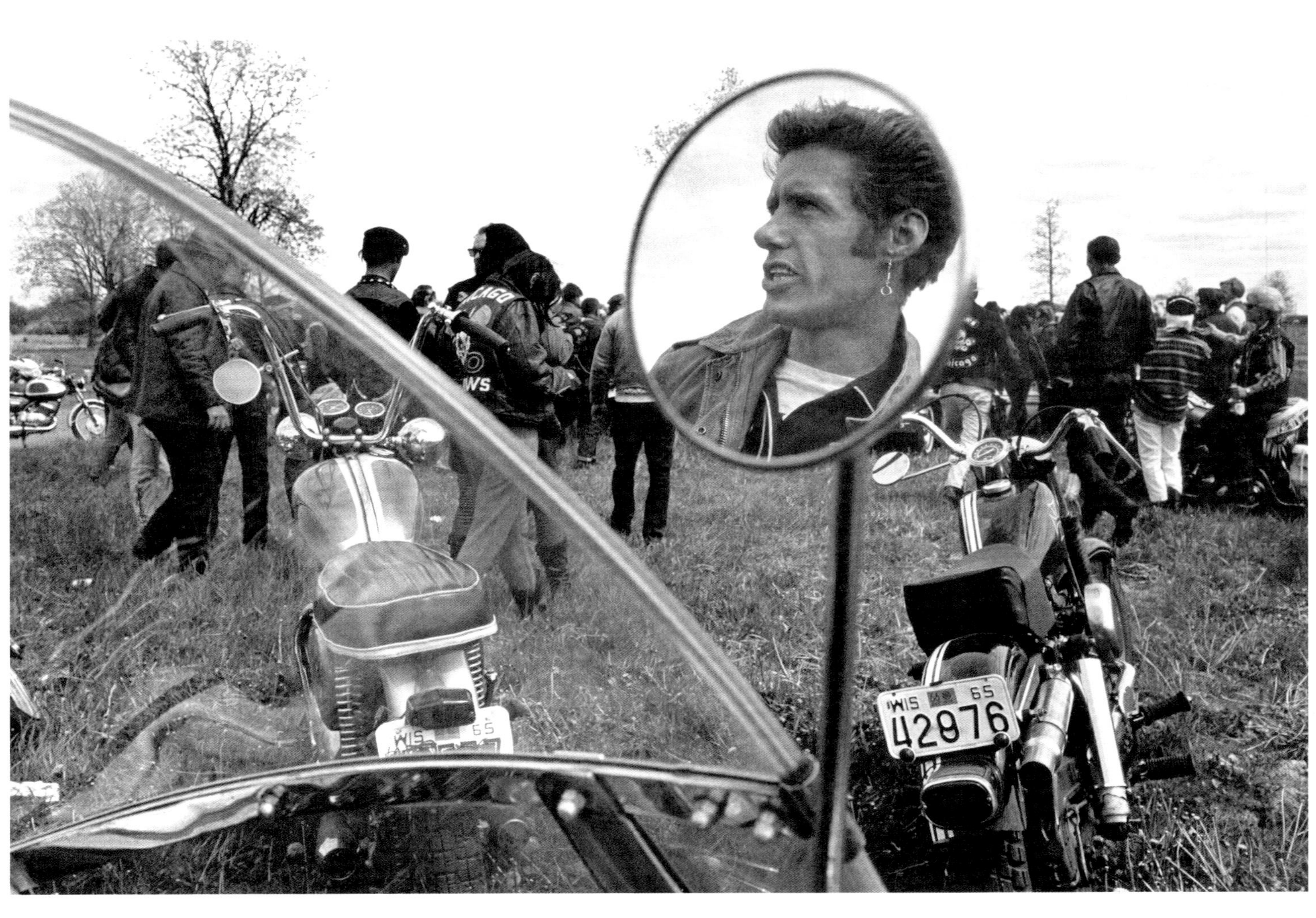

78   From 'The Bikeriders', *Cal, Elkhorn, Wisconsin, 1966*

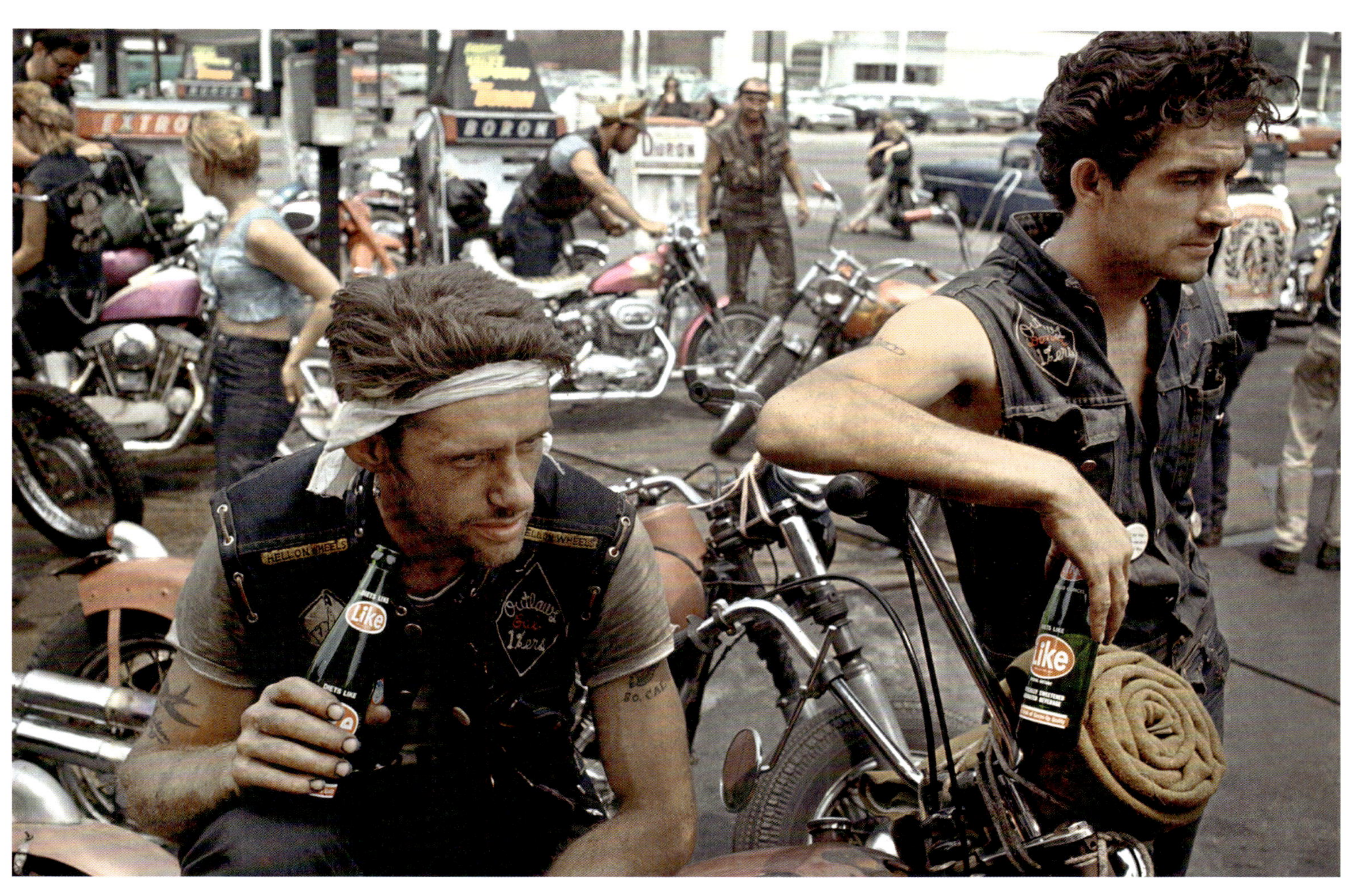

From 'The Bikeriders', *Cal on the Springfield Run, Illinois*, 1966

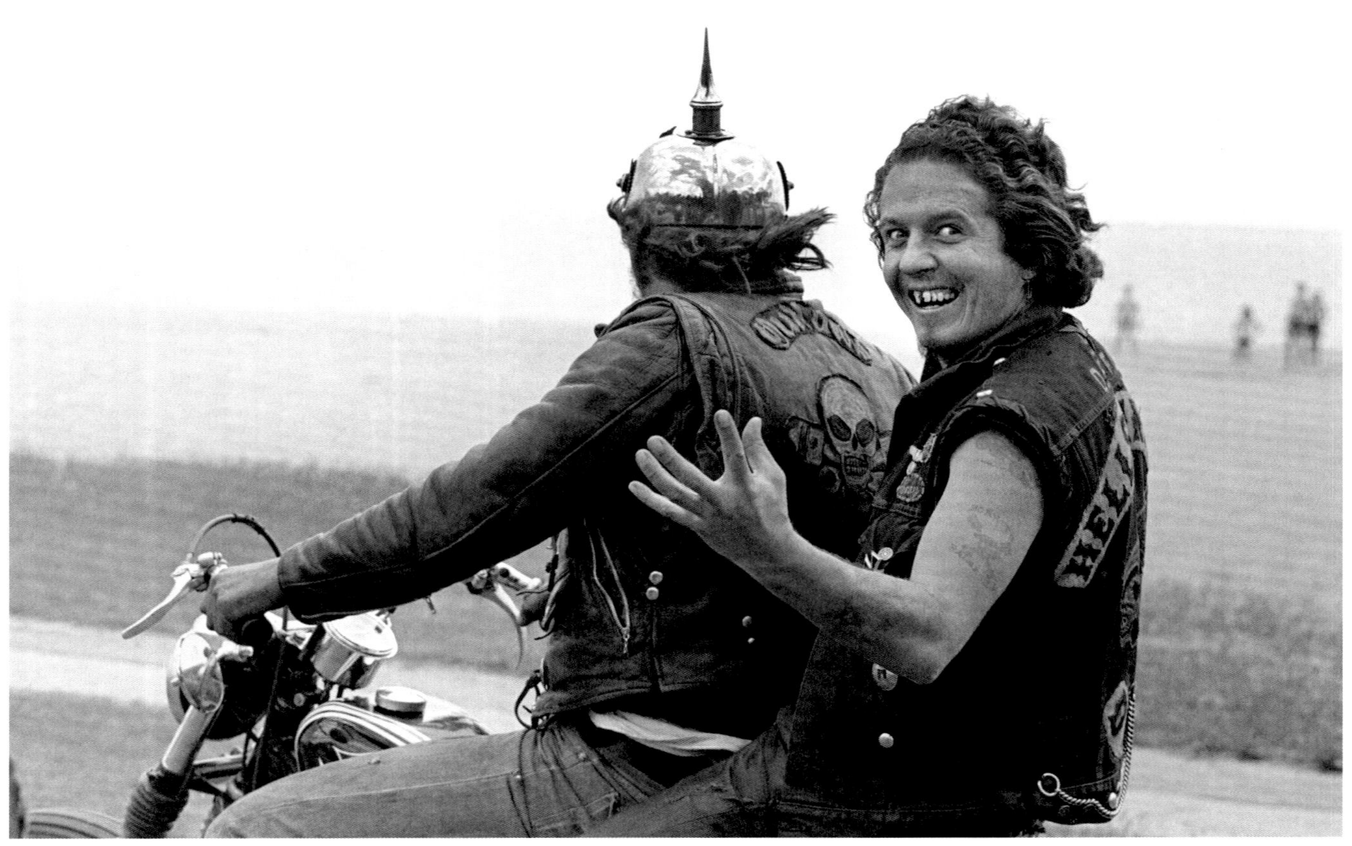

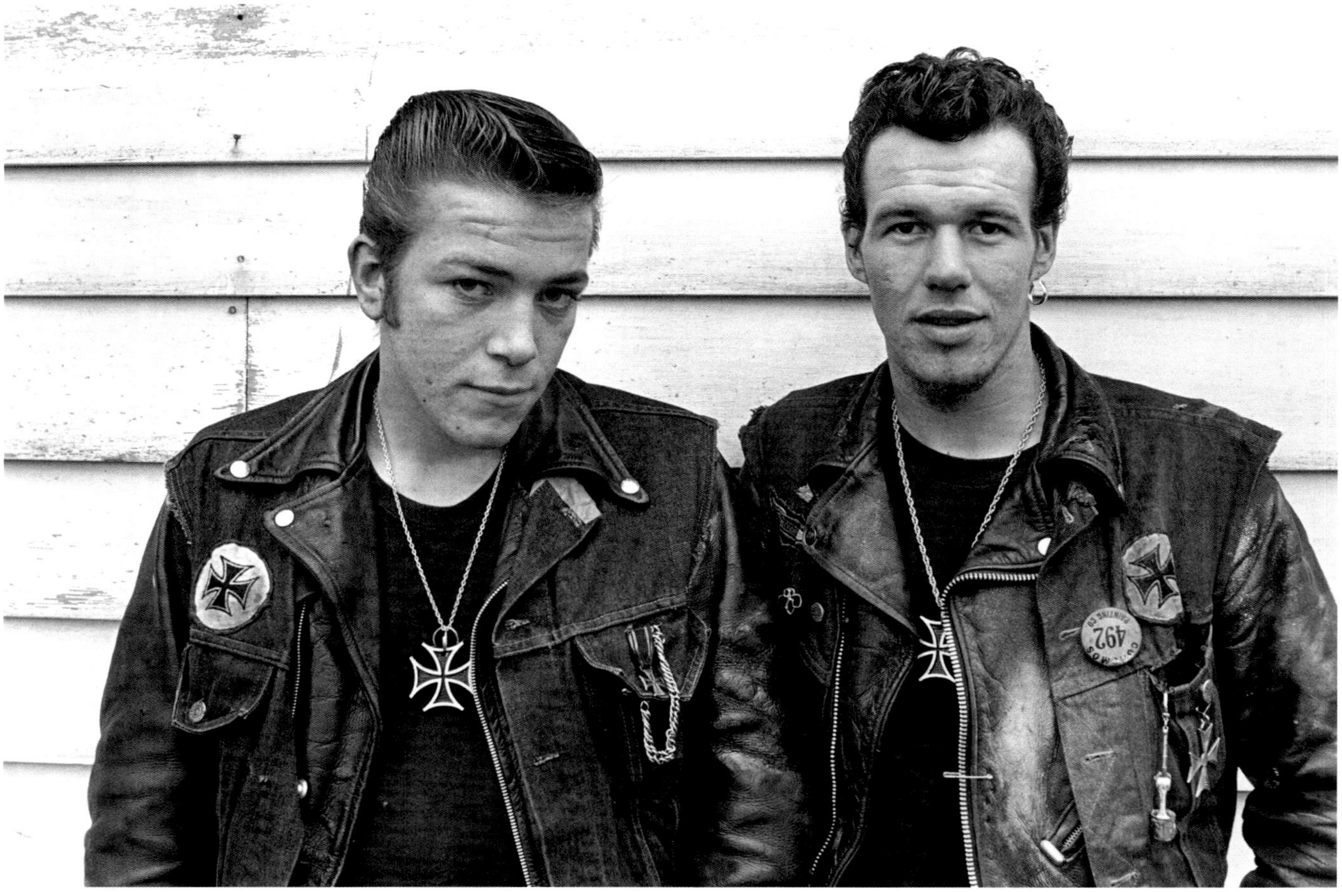

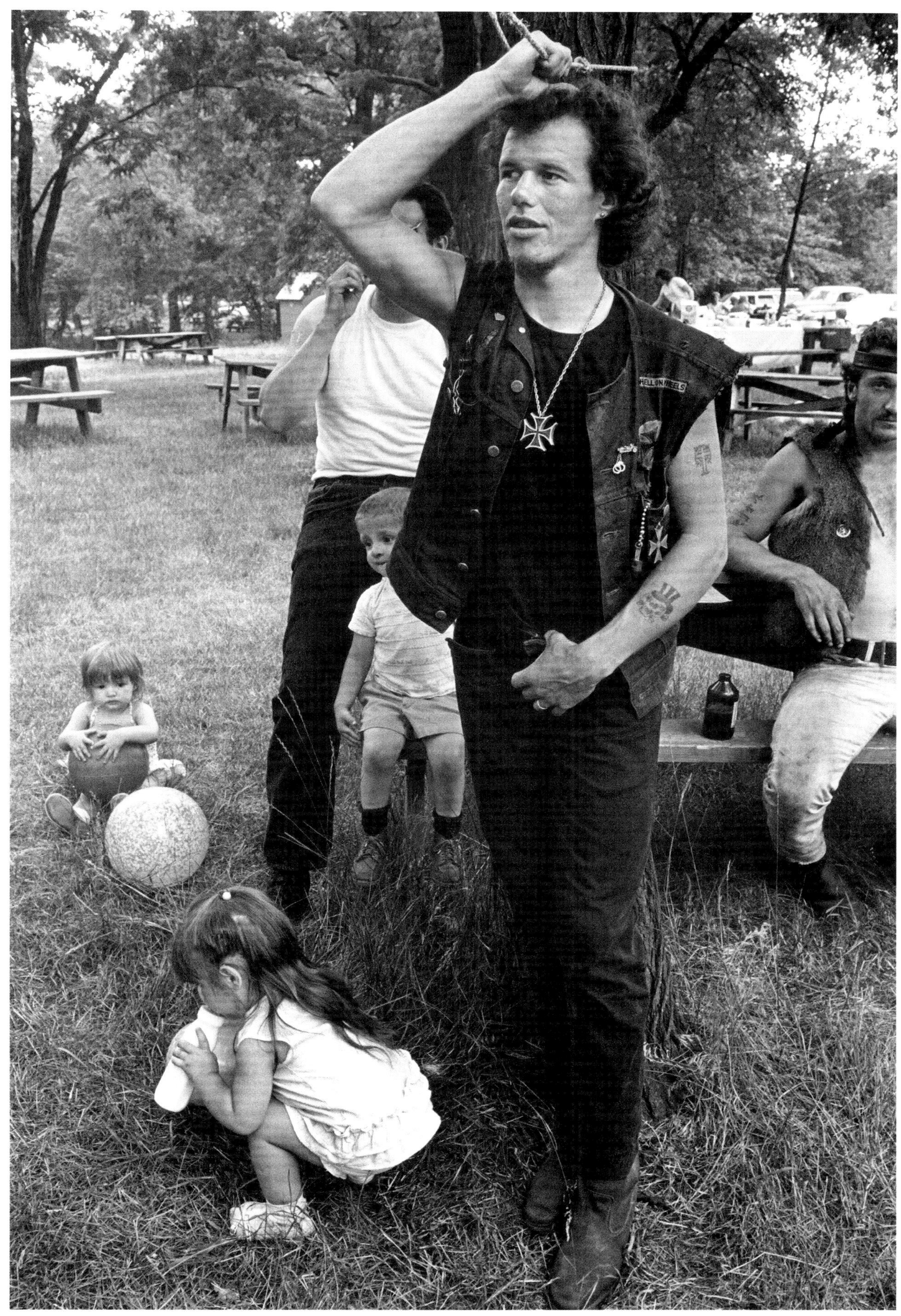

LARRY

CLARK

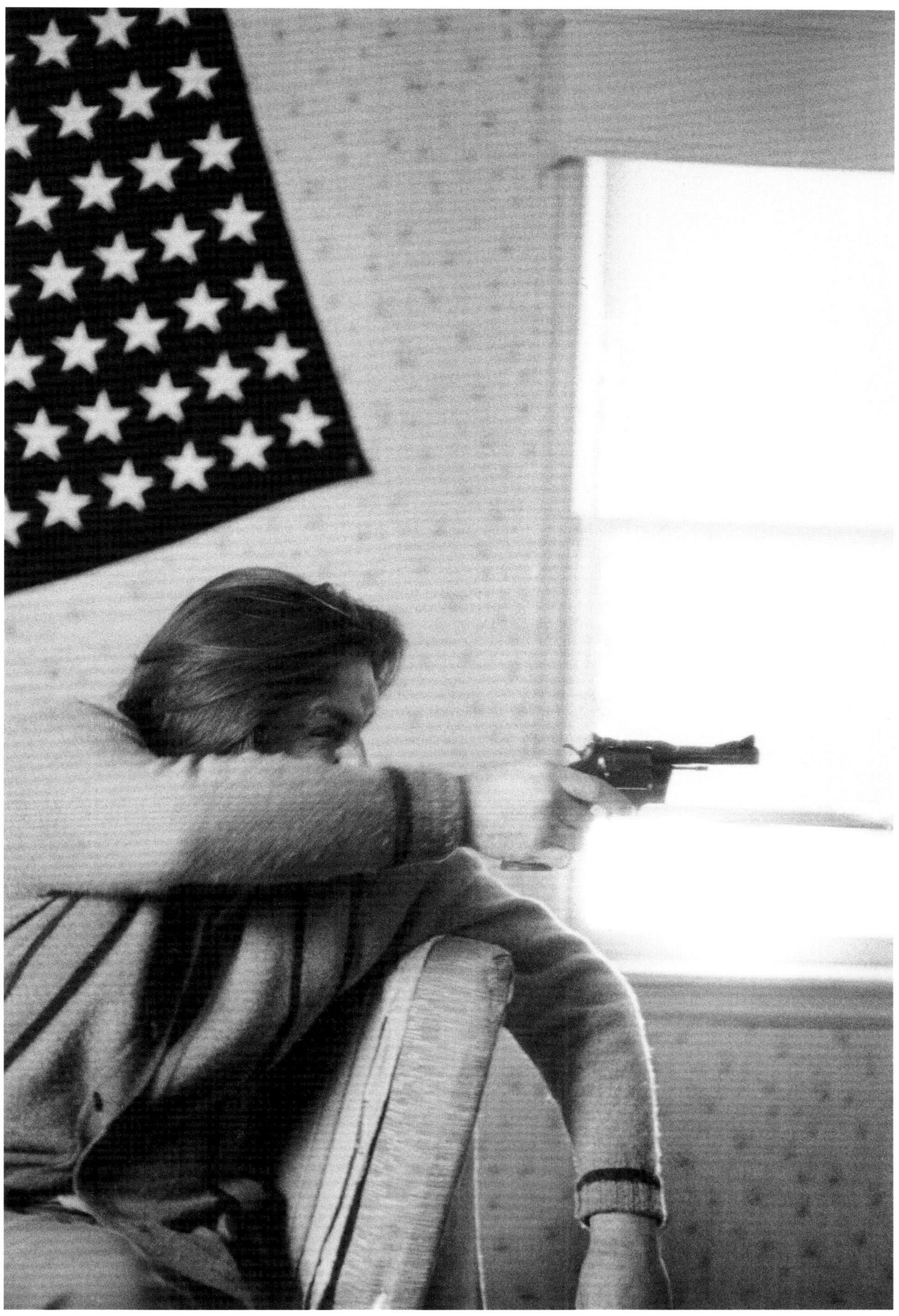

In 2010, during a conversation between the artist Larry Clark (b. 1943, USA) and his close friend and fellow photographer – and ultimately the first champion and publisher of his 1971 book *Tulsa* – Ralph Gibson, Clark remarked, 'I was lucky to be 12 years old when rock 'n' roll really busted out. I saw Elvis in Tulsa at the fairground on his first tour of the United States … It was just amazing. He came out and did a half an hour without stopping. It was really dirty.'[1]

Of course, this particular recollection helps to situate Clark precisely within a very specific historical, geographical and cultural landscape: a baby-boomer, growing up in 'America's Most Beautiful City' (as described by *Reader's Digest* in 1957) at the dawn of a seismic generational revolution. But it also subtly offers remarkable insight into how Clark, as an artist, would eventually reckon with, rebel against and redefine the upbeat mythology and clean-cut aesthetic of the mid-twentieth-century American Dream – by busting out, being relentless and getting 'dirty' himself. 'I'm like a child of the Eisenhower era,' he explained to the photographer Ryan McGinley during a conversation at the Whitney Museum of American Art in 2003, 'everything was hidden, everything was secret, there were all these things that weren't talked about. Drugs … Alcoholism … Child abuse … Nothing was talked about. I mean, it was a perfect America. There were no problems. But I saw all this stuff going on … One of the reasons I started making art was, I said, why can't you show everything, you know?'[2]

A topless woman straddles a bare-chested man on a bed, amid a tangle of sheets; she offers her right arm, clenching her fist into his chest as he carefully inserts a needle into her vein; blood is beginning to rush into the attached syringe as he prepares to push its plunger down with both thumbs (p. 92). A man in a collegiate-style cardigan twists around on an upholstered chair, his longish, clean mane of hair swept back; an outdated American naval flag, covered in stars, is crookedly pinned to the floral wallpaper above him. His eyes squint, straining to focus, as he swings his right hand up and points a Colt. 38 revolver sideways, blinding midday sunlight pouring in from the window behind (p. 83). A boyish character with a coiffed blonde pompadour sits on a bed behind two friends,

the right leg of his trousers rolled up; he injects a shot of amphetamine into his calf; moments later his face contorts ghoulishly with painful ecstasy, as the rush hits him hard. Two nude young men – one flaccid, the other semi-erect – flank a naked teenage girl in a poster-strewn bedroom; they assist her as she bites down on a piece of cloth and slides a needle into the crux of her right arm, focused and determined. A Christ-like figure lies moaning and bleeding on a bed, a gaping gunshot wound piercing his upper thigh; a young woman weeps next to him, a purse-sized pistol resting crookedly on a nearby chair. A small baby, only several months old, lies peacefully in a tiny open coffin surrounded by ribbons and flowers; a grandfatherly figure with tidy hair and a dark funereal suit leans over her, placing another bouquet by her side.

Throughout *Tulsa*, it is clear that the subject matter alone of Larry Clark's photographs is often both brutal and shocking. Shot from 1962 to 1971, during several trips that Clark took back to his hometown throughout his twenties – between stints as an art student in New York, a soldier in Vietnam, and a drug-addled transient roaming from town to town (and from girlfriend to girlfriend) around the United States – *Tulsa* aims to unflinchingly 'show everything' of Clark's childhood friends and their associates, many of whom grew up to become misfits, addicts, criminals, deadbeats, and dead bodies long before their time. Despite being set mostly within a seemingly banal 1960s domestic suburban context, content-wise these images are entirely antithetical to notions of 'a perfect America', and confront the viewer directly with harsh scenes of lives normally hidden from the mainstream or consigned to the unmentionable margins of society.

Yet it is not simply the stark content or revealing nature of Clark's images that makes them particularly unique or remarkable. From John Thomson's mid-nineteenth-century photographs of Chinese opium dens to Jacob Riis's turn-of-the-century documentation of 'stale beer dives' and flophouses in New York's Lower East Side; from Brassaï's explorations of underground nightclubs and brothels in *Paris by Night* (1931) to Weegee's coverage of murder and criminality in his *Naked City* (1945), depictions of addiction, sex, violence and vice have been long been prevalent and prominent

within the history of photography. As has been remarked on ever since its publication, what most notably sets Clark's *Tulsa* apart from previous photographic works is the position that he takes as the photographer of these scenes – not as an objective observer, fly-on-the-wall documentarian or voyeuristic outsider, but rather as a deeply embedded insider and participant whose eye is unflinchingly and unapologetically autobiographical.

As the critic and curator Andy Grundberg wrote in 1984 (citing both *Tulsa* and Clark's follow-up of 1983, *Teenage Lust*, as prime examples of photography at its most avant-garde), 'the tendency of documentary photography has always been to define its subject matter as whatever is foreign to the photographer … One direction contemporary documentary practice might take, then, is towards recording the "I" instead of the "Other", centering itself on what the photographer's life is rather than on what it is not, and acknowledging the crucial presence of the photographer on the scene.'[3] As both Clark's typewritten preface to *Tulsa*[4] and one particular photograph reveal, Clark's presence, participation and the personal nature of these photographs quite literally sit at the heart of this work. In *Untitled* (1971; p. 93) – presumably taken by one of his friends, but nevertheless notably entitled a 'selfportrait' – Clark himself sits on a chair, front and centre; he is shirtless, holding a cloth loosely in his left hand and nodding off into a drug-fuelled haze, while his friends spray aerosols into rags, huff them, and flash Vulcan salutes in the background ('Live long and prosper', so they say). Here, the 'I' and the 'eye' become one, and the traditional delineations and relationships between photographer, subject and viewer become muddled and confused, in a sense aggressively challenging what documentary photography itself is, and simultaneously pulling us in, revealing unexplored perspectives and suggesting entirely new possibilities – both profoundly powerful and deeply personal – for photography itself.

But it is also vital to recognise that Clark's aesthetic approach – despite its rather blunt, casual and occasionally accidental appearance at first glance – was also carefully considered, crafted and controlled. 'When the book came out in 1971,' he once explained, 'I actually had someone who didn't know I had done the book

say to me, "There's this amazing book out of
the best photographs that I've ever seen, but
the guy's a lousy photographer."'[5] Yet, as Clark
implied earlier, from the outset his ambitions
were more those of a progressive artist rather
than of a conventional documentarian, and the
unconventional look of his images was the result
of deliberate photographic decisions.

The book is presented chronologically in quasi-
filmic manner (hinted at by film strips, made
in 1968, which are printed at the centre of the
book), and the earliest photographs – dating
from 1963 – are shot at close-range using a
50mm lens, giving the pictures a straightness
and natural intimacy that feels genuinely
uncontrived. In seemingly bare surroundings
his subjects ponder, pose and preen like James
Dean, true rebels without a cause; they smoke
and hunt and shoot up and drive, all the while
with Clark (and subsequently us) close and
almost too comfortable by their side. The
resulting photographs are in a sense very
familial and infused with a true, brotherly love.

Then, as the book's sequence progresses into
1971, Clark, although remaining physically
close, visually pulls back by switching to a
35mm lens. Fights break out, black eyes and
bullet wounds appear, drug use becomes more
rampant, sex less intimate, and death itself
begins to loom large, all the while the wide-
angle lens simultaneously distancing and
enveloping us within the vortex of the scene as
it rapidly spirals downwards into darkness and
despair. Furthermore, as Clark explained in
1977, even his choices regarding photographic
exposure while both shooting and printing *Tulsa*
were aimed quite literally towards helping us
see deep within the darkness, with light itself
becoming brutal and blinding: 'I do a lot of
burning and dodging when making a print …
There's not a straight print in the *Tulsa* book.
When I'm photographing I always try to shoot
against the light. The film can't handle this and
everything gets burned up, since I'm exposing
for the shadows.'[6]

Ultimately, Clark's *Tulsa* represents a
remarkable turning point in documentary
photography during the latter half of the
twentieth century, whereby the pursuit
of photographing in the shadows – at the
margins of society – began to demand that
photographers themselves no longer be

marginalised but instead become central
to their own work, that they refrain from
adopting a traditionally polite distance or a
conventionally acknowledged aesthetic and
instead translate their own experiences via
their own means, both in terms of approach and
style. In both their intimacy and immediacy,
as well as in their content and form, Clark's
photographs not only reveal what was otherwise
hidden but resonate deeply with the unique
voice and personal experiences of Clark himself,
all the while quietly echoing with the final,
melancholic verse of the opening number on
that fateful night at the Tulsa fairground, way
back in 1956: 'Although it's always crowded,
/ You still can find some room, / For broken-
hearted lovers / To cry there in the gloom; / And
be so – where they'll be so lonely, baby / Well,
they're so lonely / They'll be so lonely, they
could die.'[7]

Aaron Schuman

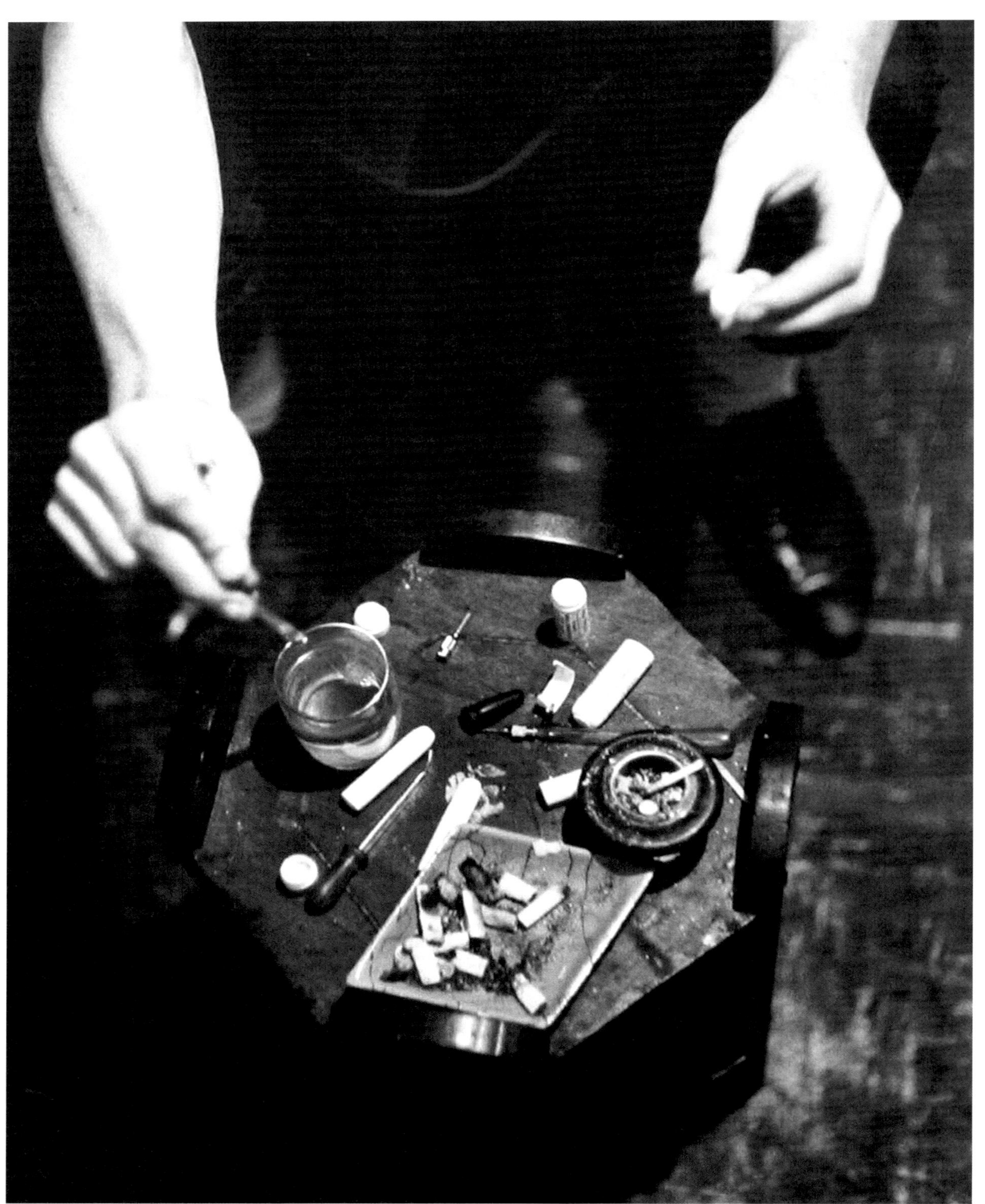

86   From 'Tulsa', *Untitled*, 1963

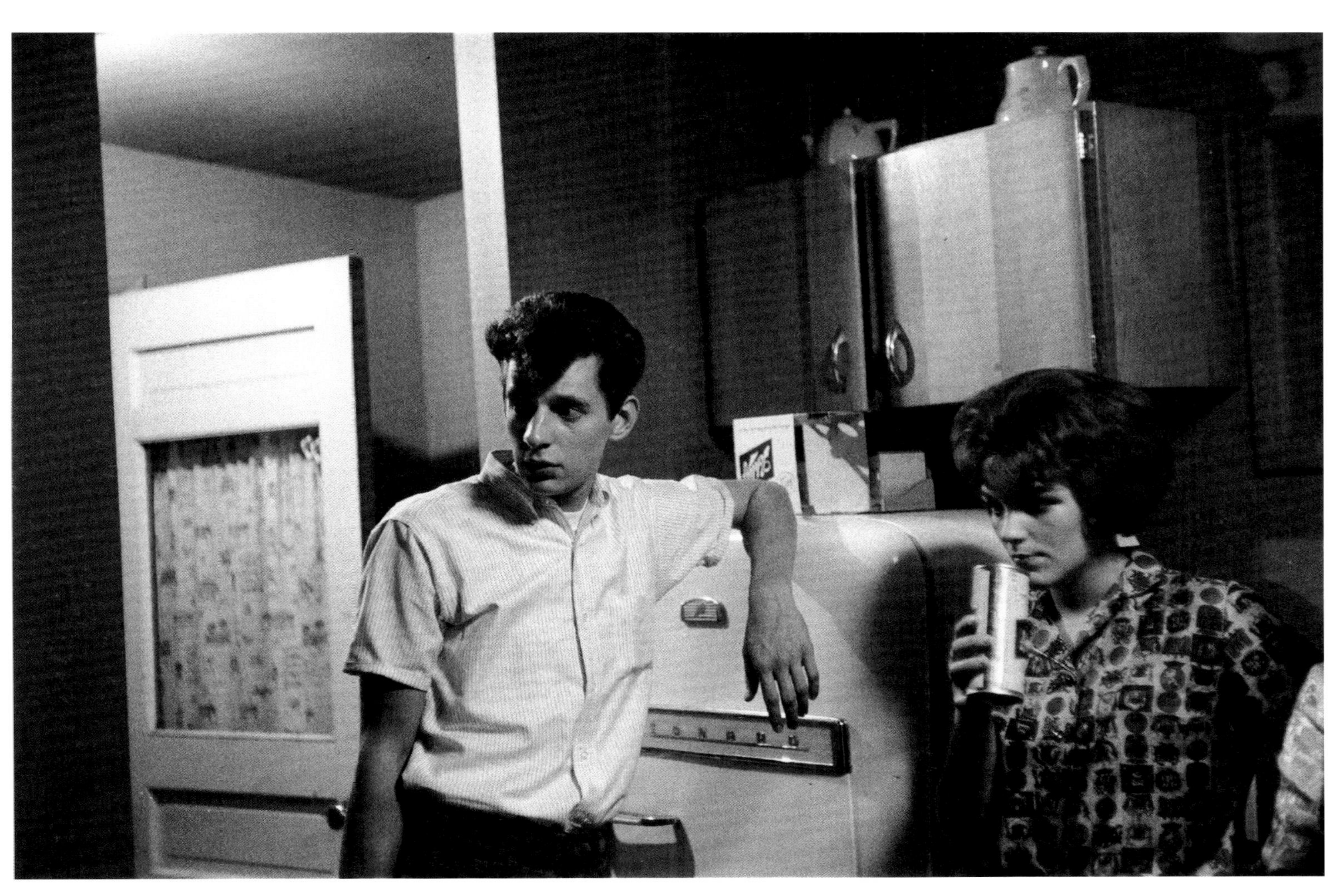

From 'Tulsa', *Untitled*, 1962

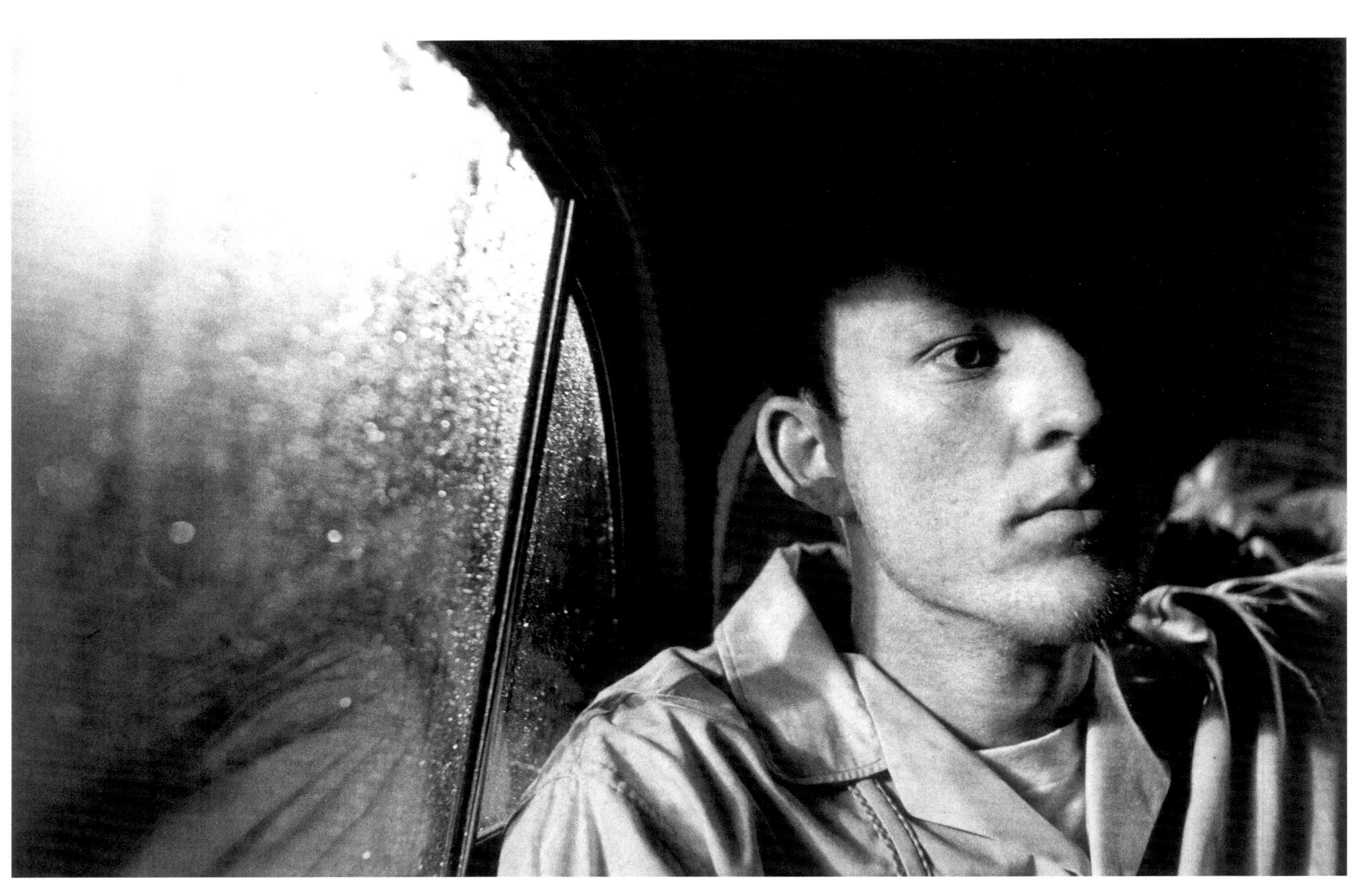

88   From 'Tulsa', *Untitled*, 1963

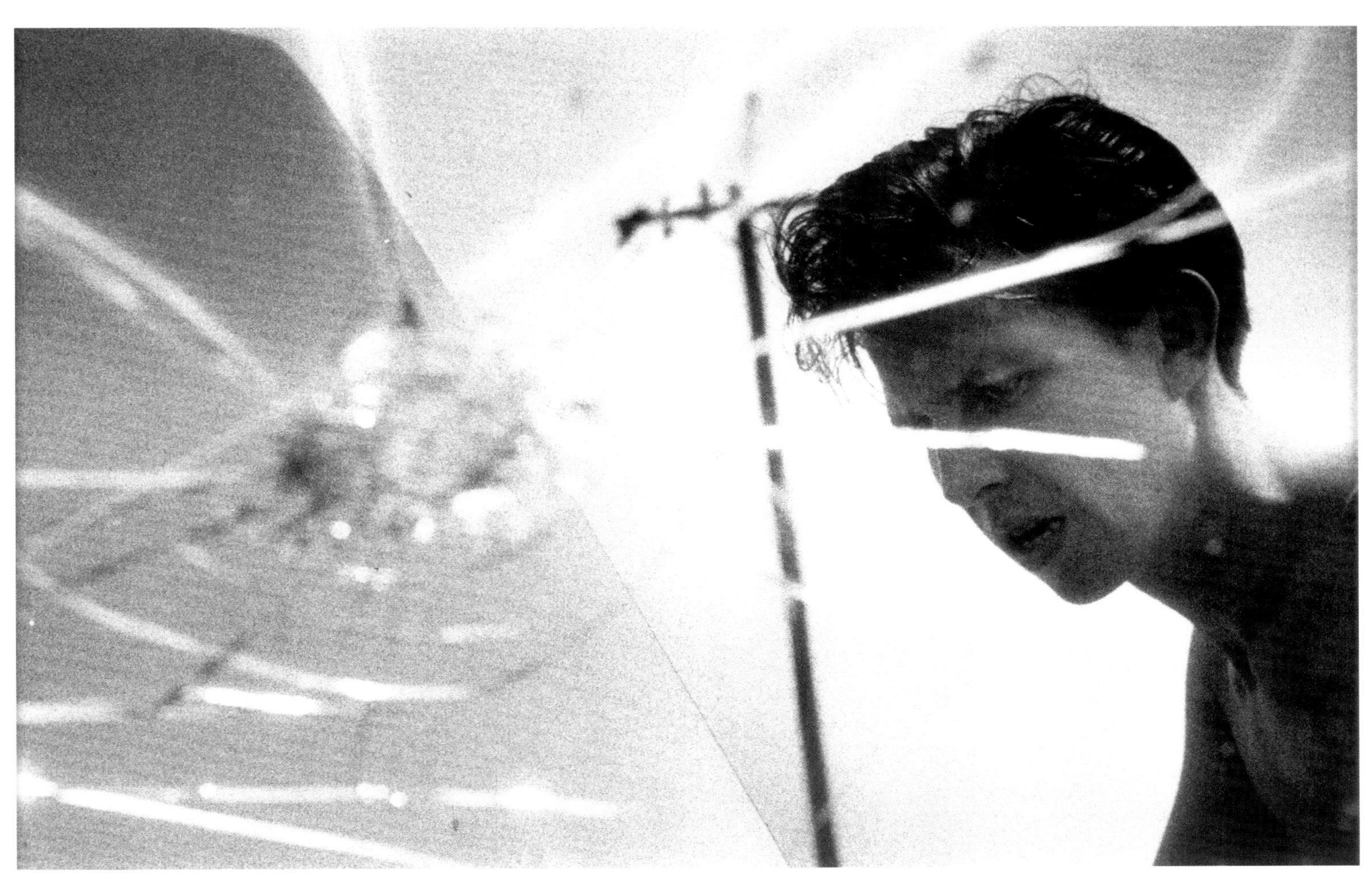

From 'Tulsa', *Untitled*, 1963   89

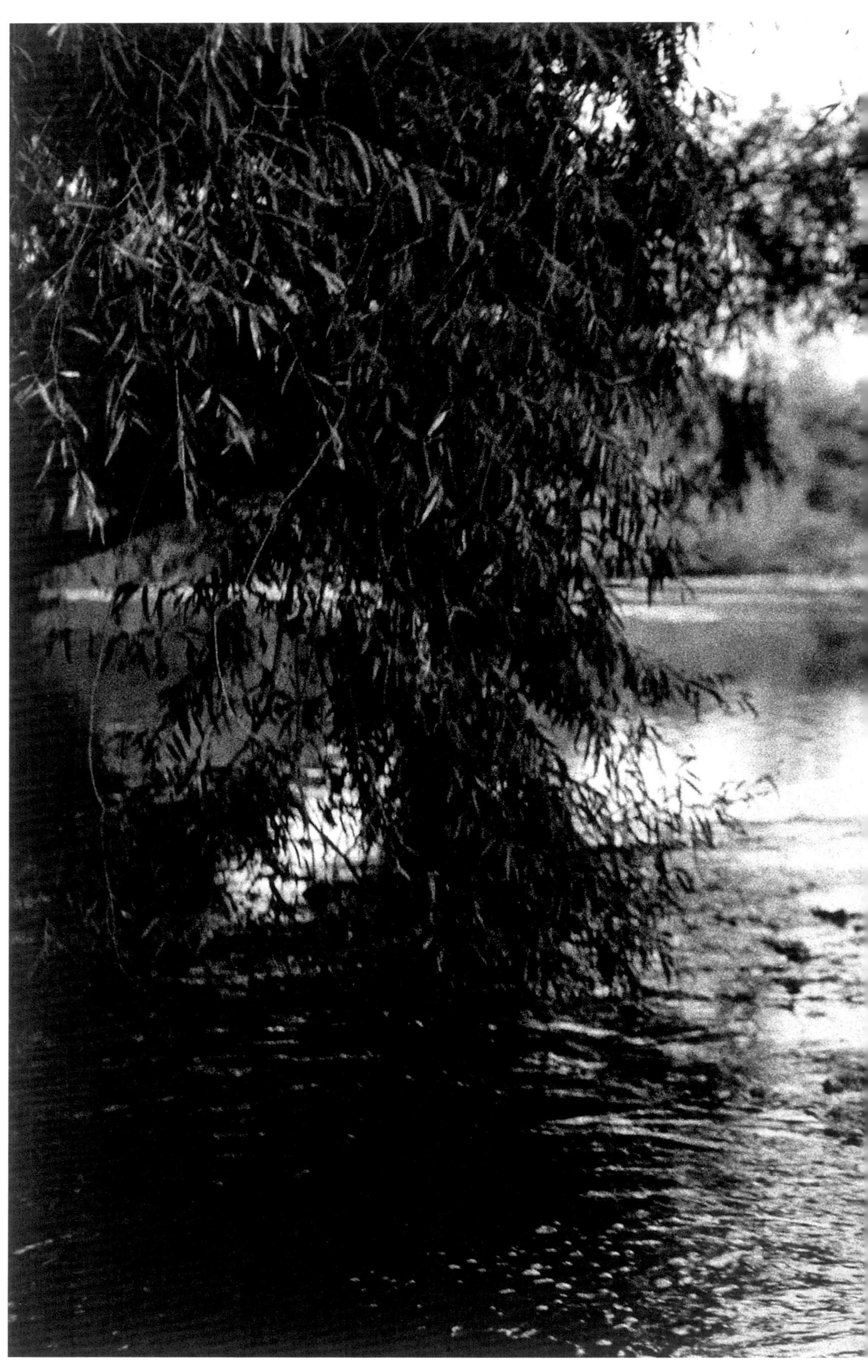

90   From 'Tulsa', *Untitled*, 1963

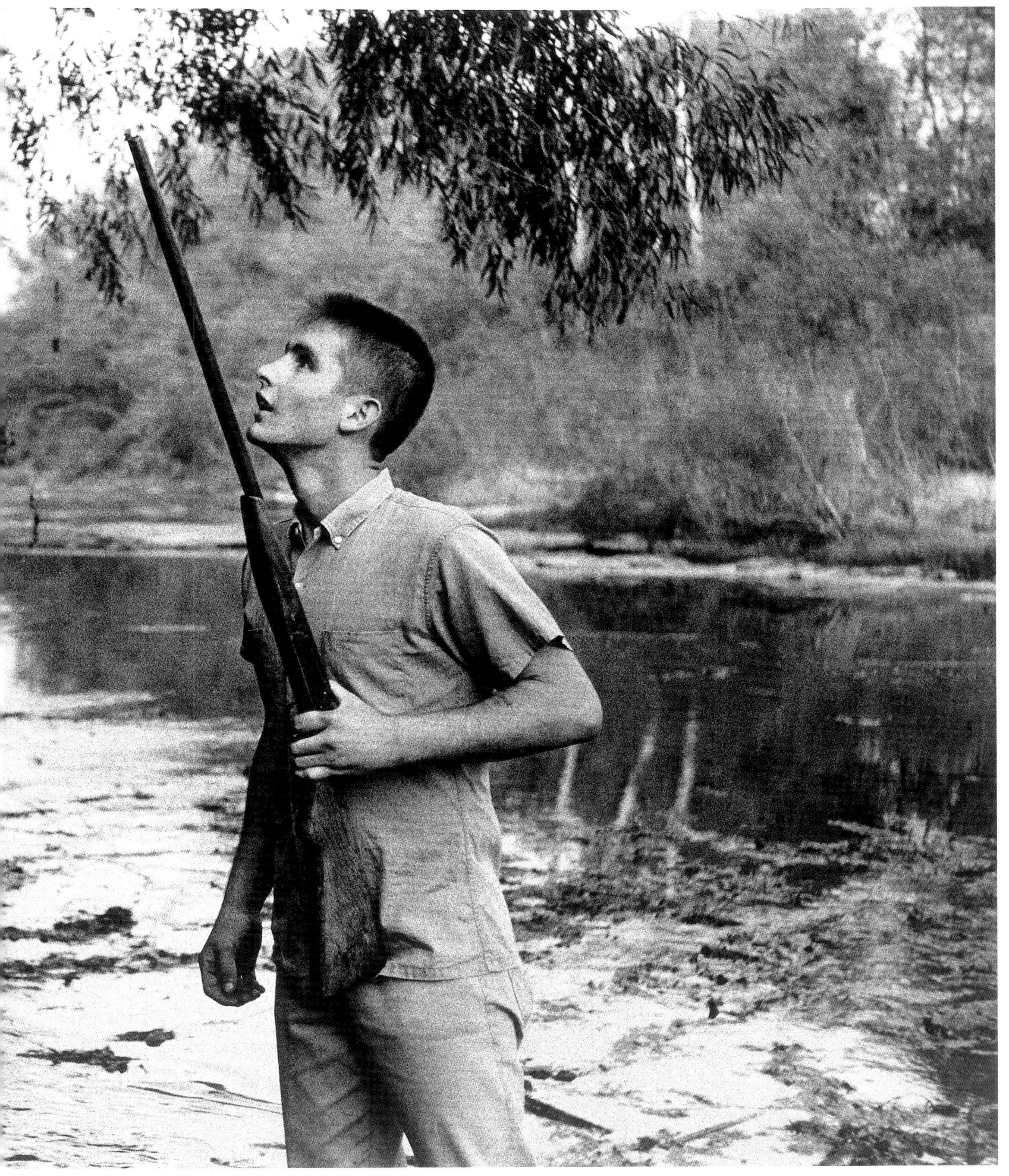

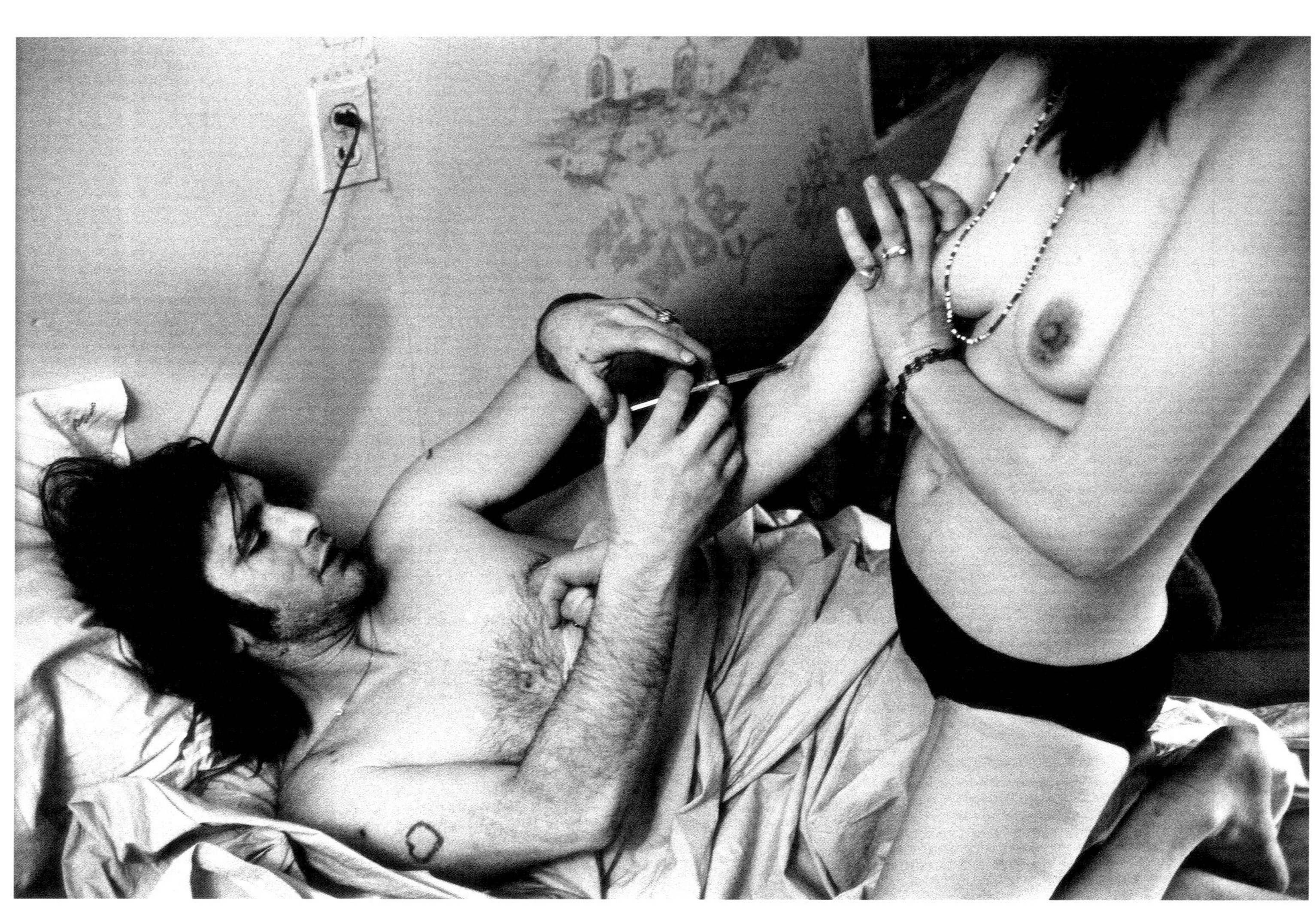

92 From 'Tulsa', *Untitled*, 1971

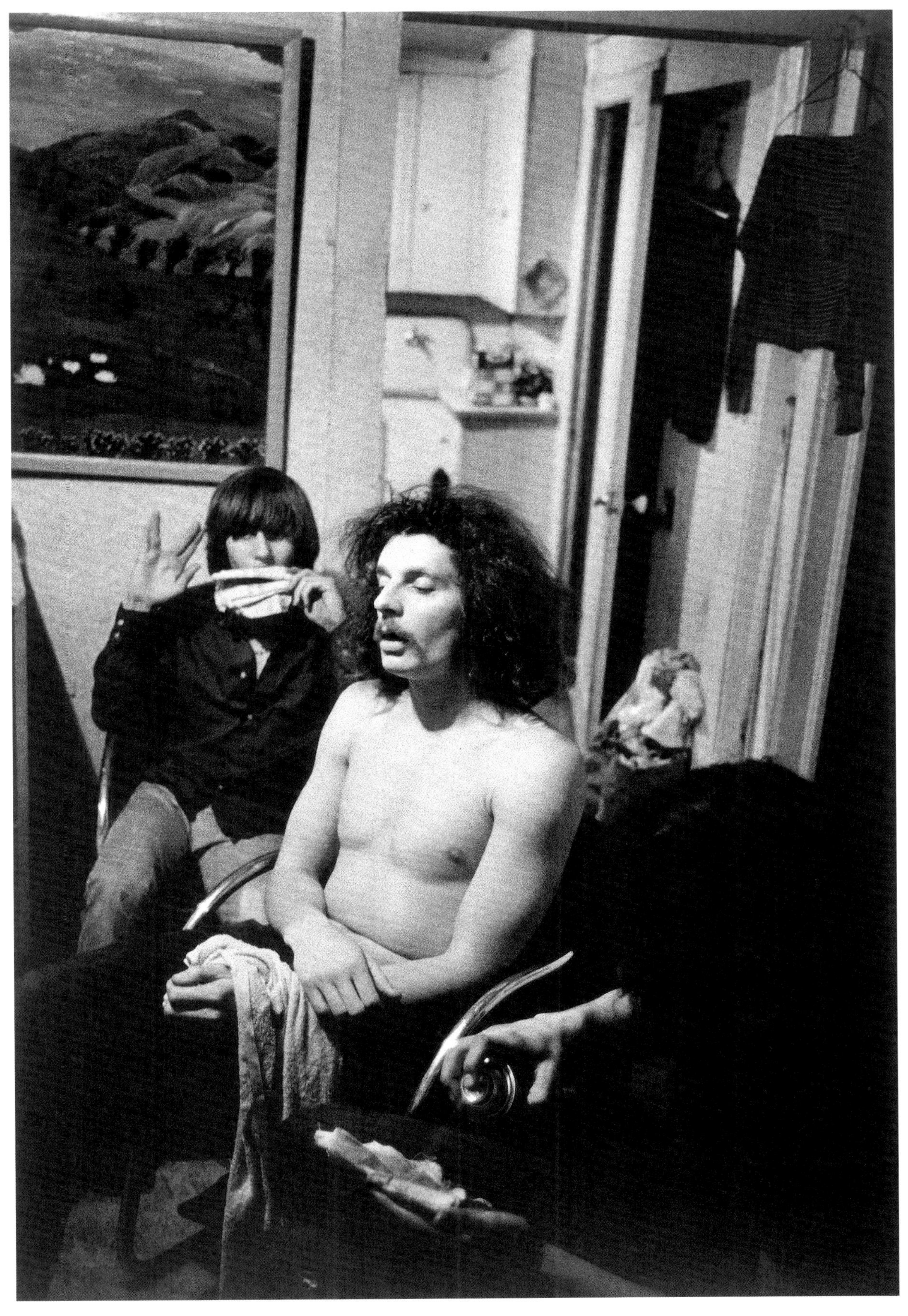

From 'Tulsa', *Untitled*, 1971

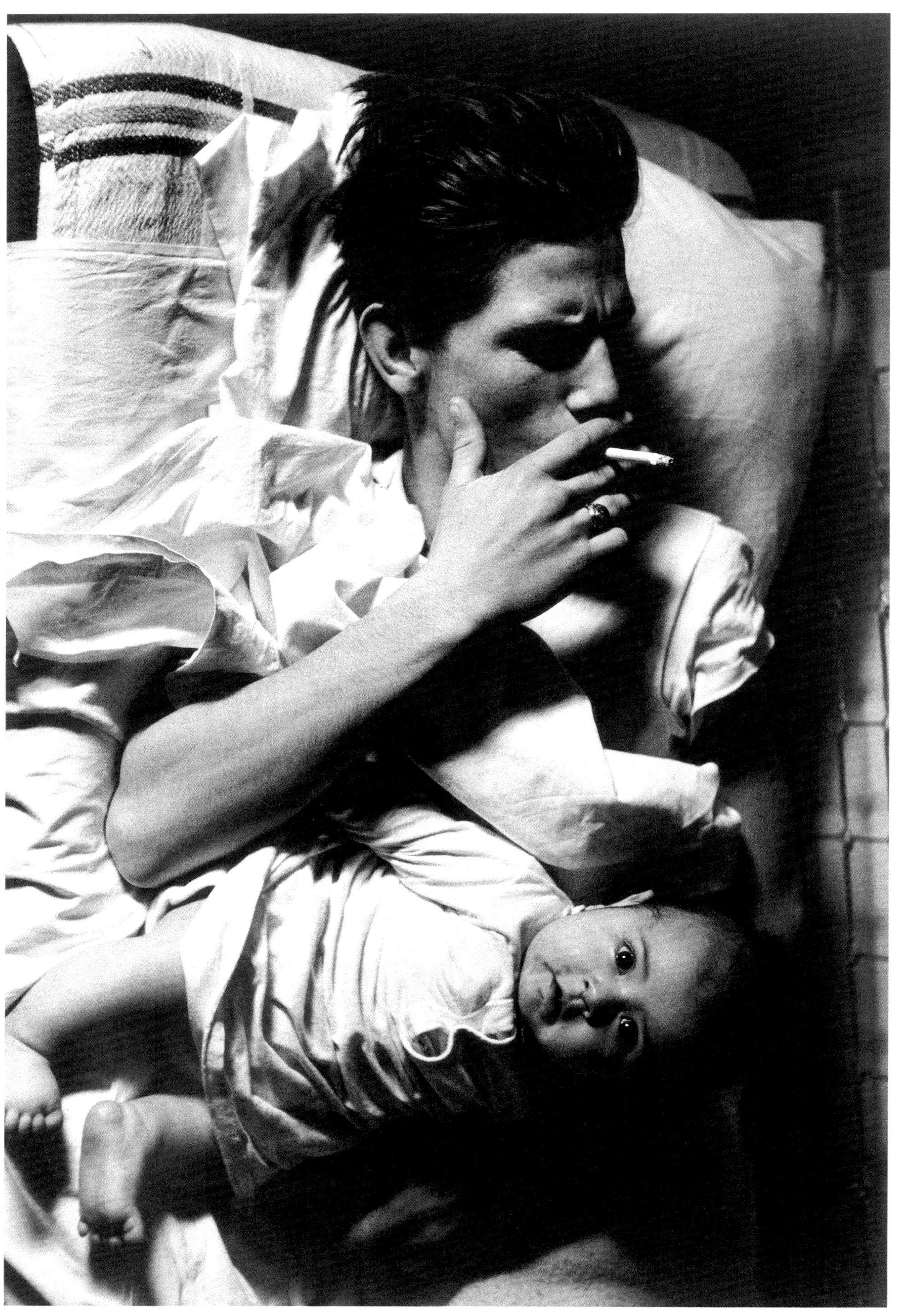

94   From 'Tulsa', *Untitled*, 1963

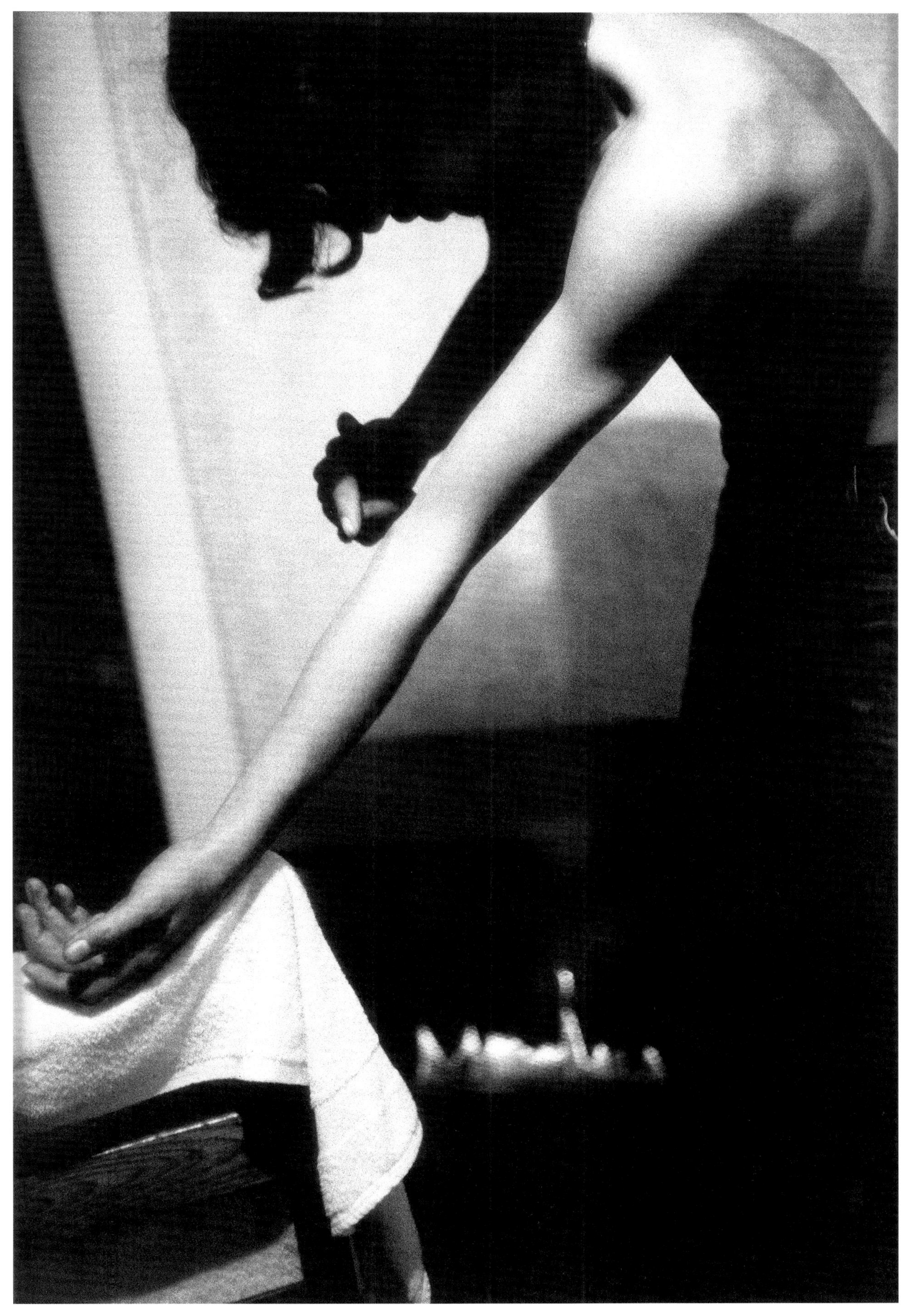

SEIJI

KURATA

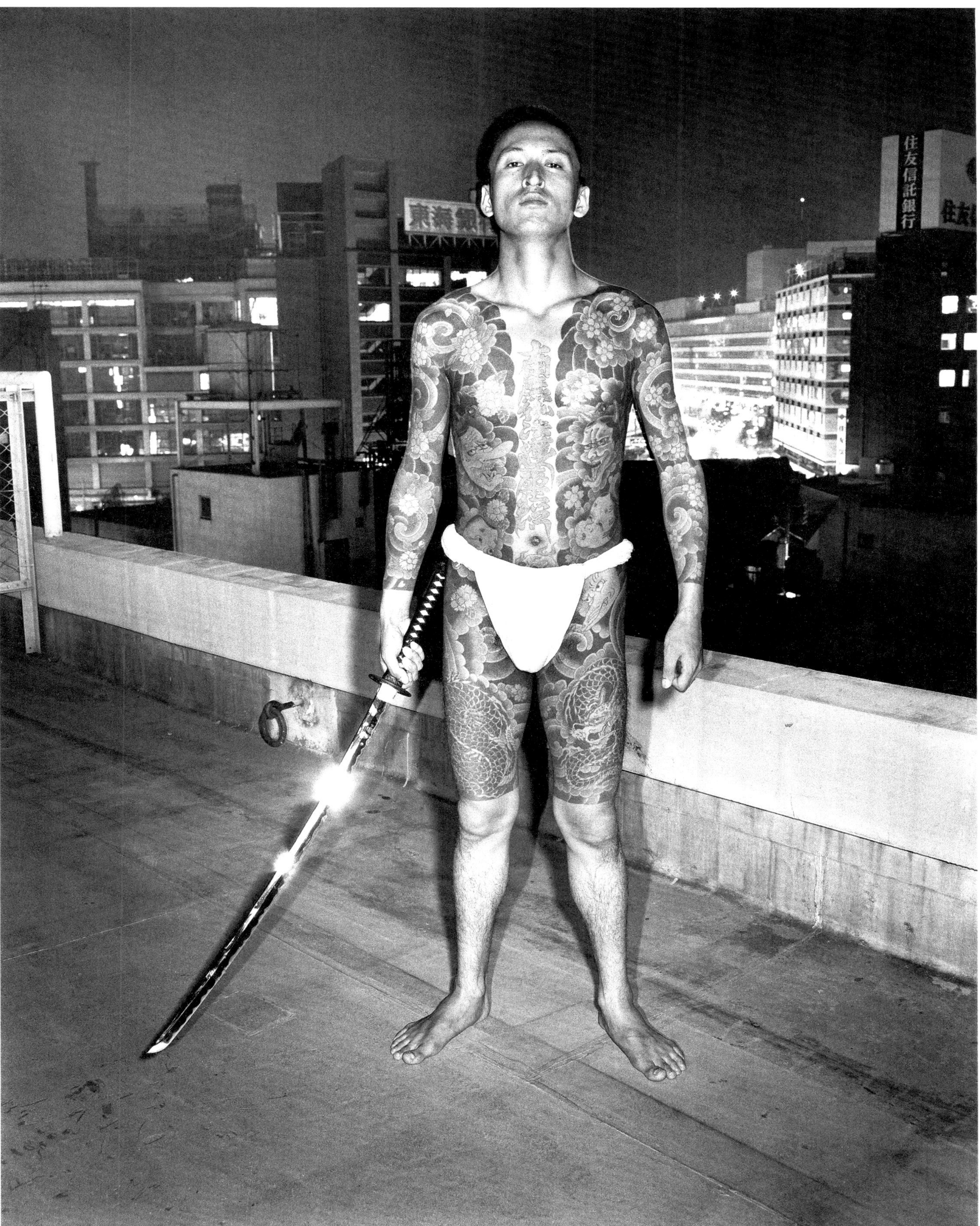

The front cover of Seiji Kurata's (b. 1945, Japan) *Flash Up* shows a photograph of a yakuza gangster on a Tokyo rooftop at night, standing proudly with his elaborate body tattoo and katana sword. Lit by the flare of Kurata's powerful electronic flash, he is sentry to the book's cherished content, the willingness with which he offers himself up to the camera both resolute and menacing (p. 97). *Flash Up* promises close-combat photography, a revelation of the darkest corners of the city's underbelly. And as the flash bounces back off the katana's extended blade it more than hints at the photographer's complicity.

In 1975, Kurata began photographing at night in Ikebukuro, a working-class district in the northwest of Tokyo, recording the denizens of its clubs and gambling dens as well as the frequent disturbances of its violent street life. The photographer wielded his medium-format camera 'with respect', as he termed it, firing his strobe light in an act of exchange with those he photographed (he later hinted at the intricate, sometimes physically threatening negotiations his work entailed).[1] *Flash Up*, like so much Japanese photography of this period, is intensely voyeuristic. But it is a voyeurism that constructs a world self-contained and shrouded – even in light. It is entirely free from either the political longing or the condescension of, say, its British equivalent. After two decades of social upheaval in Japan, the yakuza on guard on *Flash Up*'s front cover seeks also to preserve something.

Kurata understood that subculture requires to be narrated, and *Flash Up* follows a clear-cut path through Ikebukuro and Shinjuku nightlife. It begins with the joy and welcome of the streets, an arena of subversive performance and ordinary pleasures. Passers-by, children, hostesses and their clients: all seem accustomed to the burst of Kurata's strobe. The book soon takes a darker turn as police round up gang members and attempt to clean up after violent street battles. Like Weegee before him, Kurata seems always to be there with his camera, whether in the midst of an arrest, recording a kicking on the street or capturing the bloody carnage of a motorbike accident. But unlike Weegee, Kurata has little sympathy for the authorities or, indeed, a contract with a picture agency. His allegiance lies, quite clearly, with the people of the streets, the *bōsōzoku* (motorcycle gangs), the prostitutes and, always, the yakuza.

Flash Up, then, is both abject and fond, violent and amoral. Through its aesthetic of reciprocal, 'random' exposure, Kurata shows us how the street corners hang together: the ties of friendship, duty and trade that bind the transvestites and hostesses to the clubs and gangsters, as well as to the paramilitary ultranationalist organisations that wielded influence to the very apex of Japanese society. In the 1970s this was a relatively open culture: the Tokyo yakuza had local offices, while the ultranationalists paraded in public (including, as *Flash Up* reveals, against trade unions) and supported activities in local communities (p. 105).[2] Sexual commerce attracted none of the prudishness or regulation that it did in the West, and the yakuza funded a popular film industry to promote their culture of violence, ritual and obligation (Kurata's book is shaped, I suspect, by that genre's 1970s realist turn). In this context, *Flash Up* is less reportage than the evocation of a way of life, less a subcultural shock than a knowing affirmation.

The book is also an evocation of the photographer's way of life, and *Flash Up* was Kurata's bid to join the heavyweights of Japanese photography. Since the mid-1970s he had been informally schooled by many of its leading figures, taking part in the various loose-knit organisations that offered training, publishing and exhibiting opportunities. These groupings were a legacy of the 1960s – collective, disputatious, deliriously hedonistic – and *Flash Up* was in part their product. But while deferring to his illustrious elders, Kurata also produces an aesthetic that is knowingly different: less morally pointed than Shōmei Tōmatsu; more pragmatic about desire than Nobuyoshi Araki; less obsessive and subfusc than Daidō Moriyama. 'I miss those times,' wrote Kurata a decade later, 'everything seemed so easy to understand.'[3] In a sense, *Flash Up* is the last great statement of 1960s photography in Japan, a book whose fate was also that of illuminating what had become of its counterculture.

The proud yakuza on the cover of *Flash Up* reappears with other gang members towards the middle of the book as they wrap their loincloths and pose in cramped apartments and public baths to exhibit their torsos for the camera (p. 109). These images reveal what *Flash Up* is really about: a sense of belonging, one in this instance embodied by the painful

ritual of the full-body tattoo, loyalty and subjection (supposedly of ancient origin) written on the flesh. But here we approach the central ambiguity of the book, for the gangster tattoos might also embody the pain of existence, a cry for identity at the very moment when the force of yakuza ritual was beginning to subside. By the late 1970s, the Tokyo gangs were becoming deterritorialised, under pressure from the police and from the loss of their street operations to new forms of financial corruption. Kurata, I think, recognised their anguish – he later wrote of a simultaneous atrophy in the regime of the image – and it explains, too, the rumours of his own masochist attachment to the subjects of the book ('If I hurt,' maybe he thought, 'then I am truly of them'). The tattooed yakuza personify belonging under the threat of dissolution, a submission to archaic ritual *and* a flesh-bound resistance to the displacements of the present. *Flash Up*'s profane illumination, then, is also the cut of the Real.[4]

Flash Up ends with a long sequence of photographs devoted to the clubs and gambling dens of Ikebukuro, an affectionate and matter-of-fact delineation of its complex libidinal economy. These were the seedier establishments of Tokyo's fluid *mizu shōbai*, or nightlife (literally the 'water trade'), famous for the warmth and experience of its women. Kurata focuses overwhelmingly and generously on the actors in this drama: the hostesses, the clients, the transvestites, the tourists and the ever-present yakuza, now conspicuous in their Al Capone suits. Tokyo nightlife was an elaborate play, one scripted almost entirely around the willingness of women (or those who looked like women) to service men.[5] Kurata narrates this corporeal comedy without elaboration. His exultant scenes – cut from the flux of the night – express something of the sanctuary and cheer promoted by the clubs. It is a striking feature of *Flash Up* that it contains so few images of television screens: throughout the book the single pulse of Kurata's strobe is fired in opposition to TV culture's more pervasive mediation. As he later wrote about the place he loved and lived to photograph, 'Eroticism has always been at its heart but, like fast food, it has broadened as technology interacts with people, things, and money.'[6] *Flash Up* fights to capture this more palpable eroticism, or at least to sustain its passing. Like the yakuza on the cover, preservation is Kurata's hope and, in a way, his transgression.

Duncan Forbes

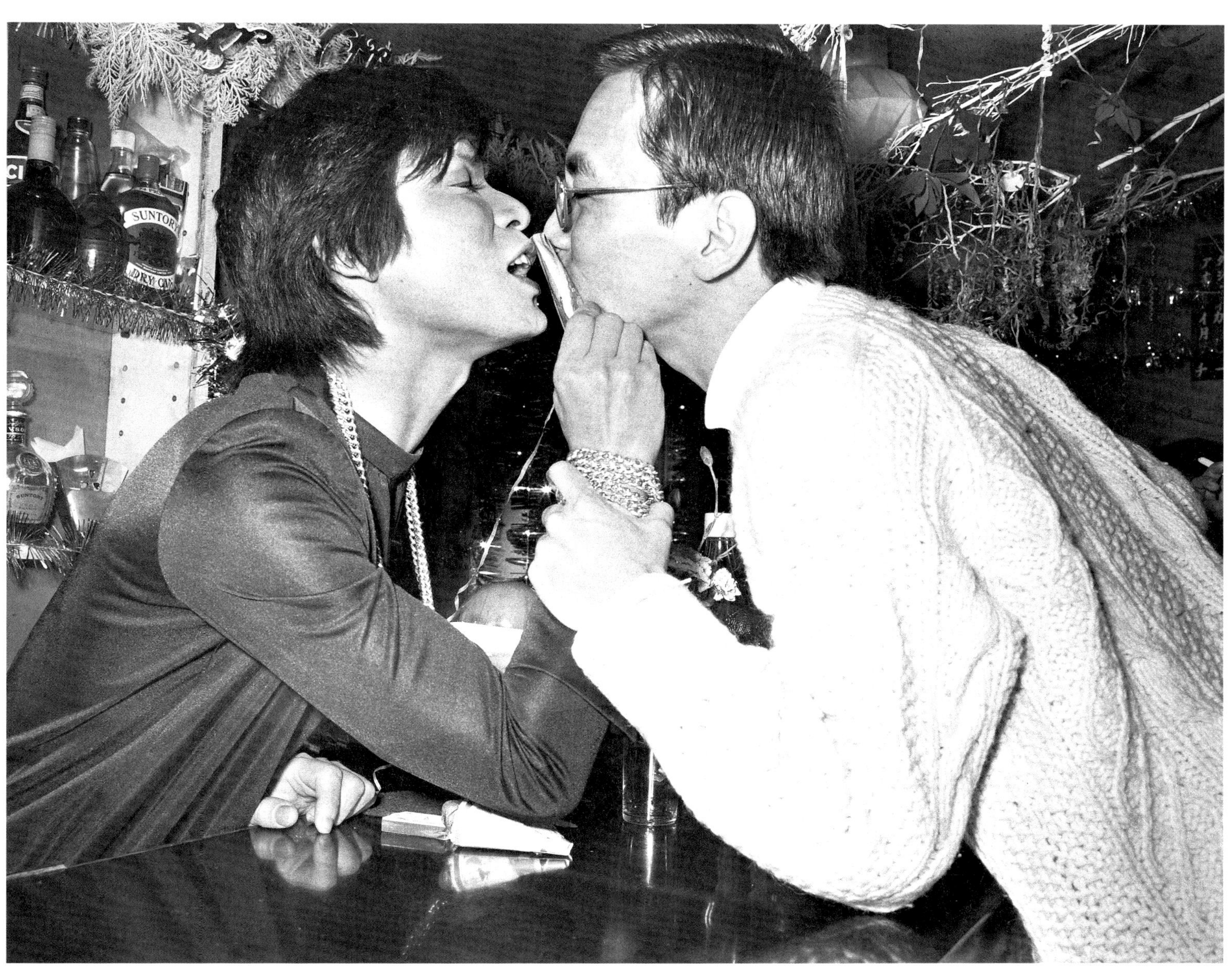

Gay Bar at Christmas Time, Ebisu Street, Ikebukuro, Tokyo, 1977

  After the Night Shift, Ikebukuro 2-chōme, Tokyo, 1978

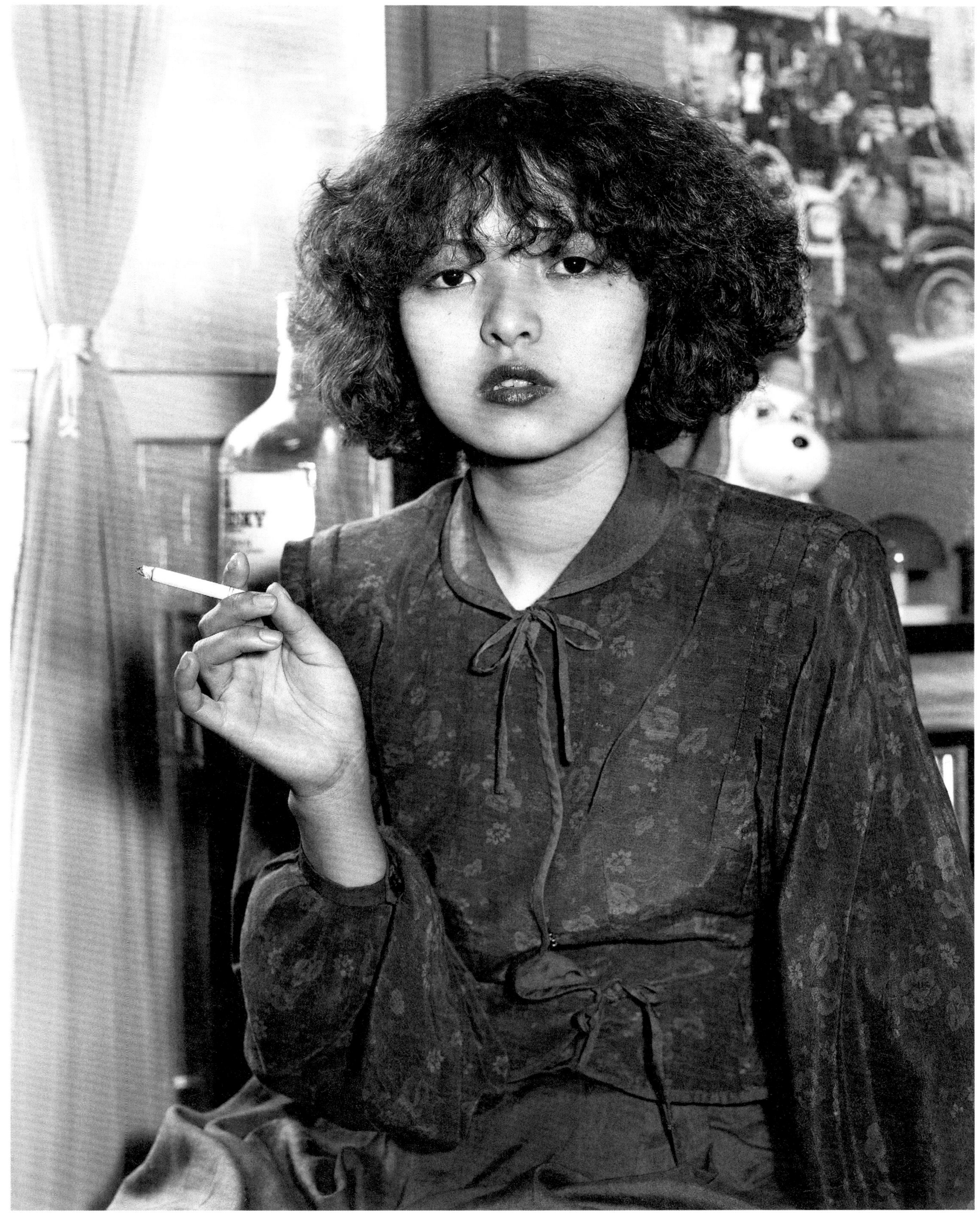

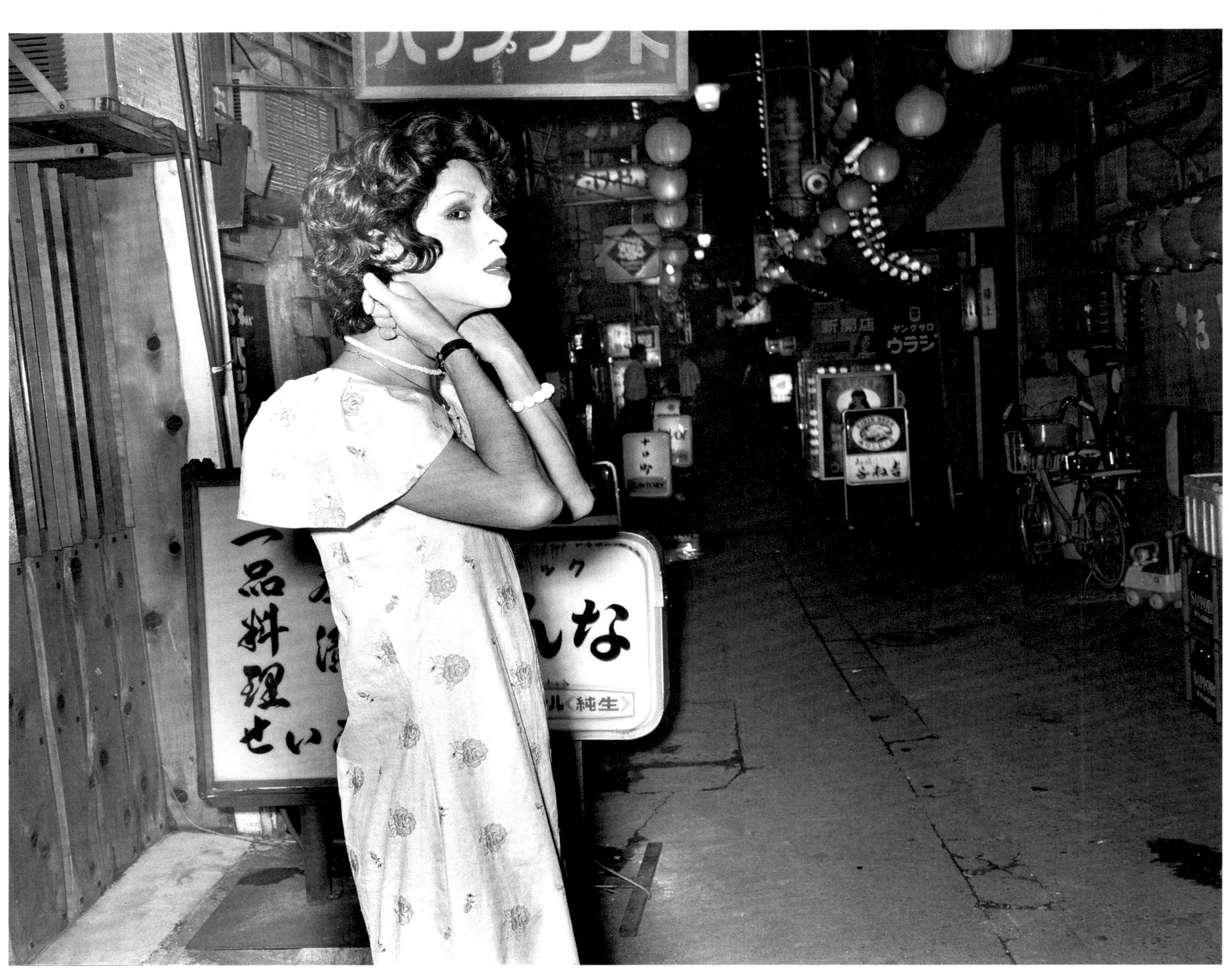

102 *Even Though There's No Sign of Any Customers ..., near Hikarimachi Ohashi, Ikebukuro, Tokyo, 1975*

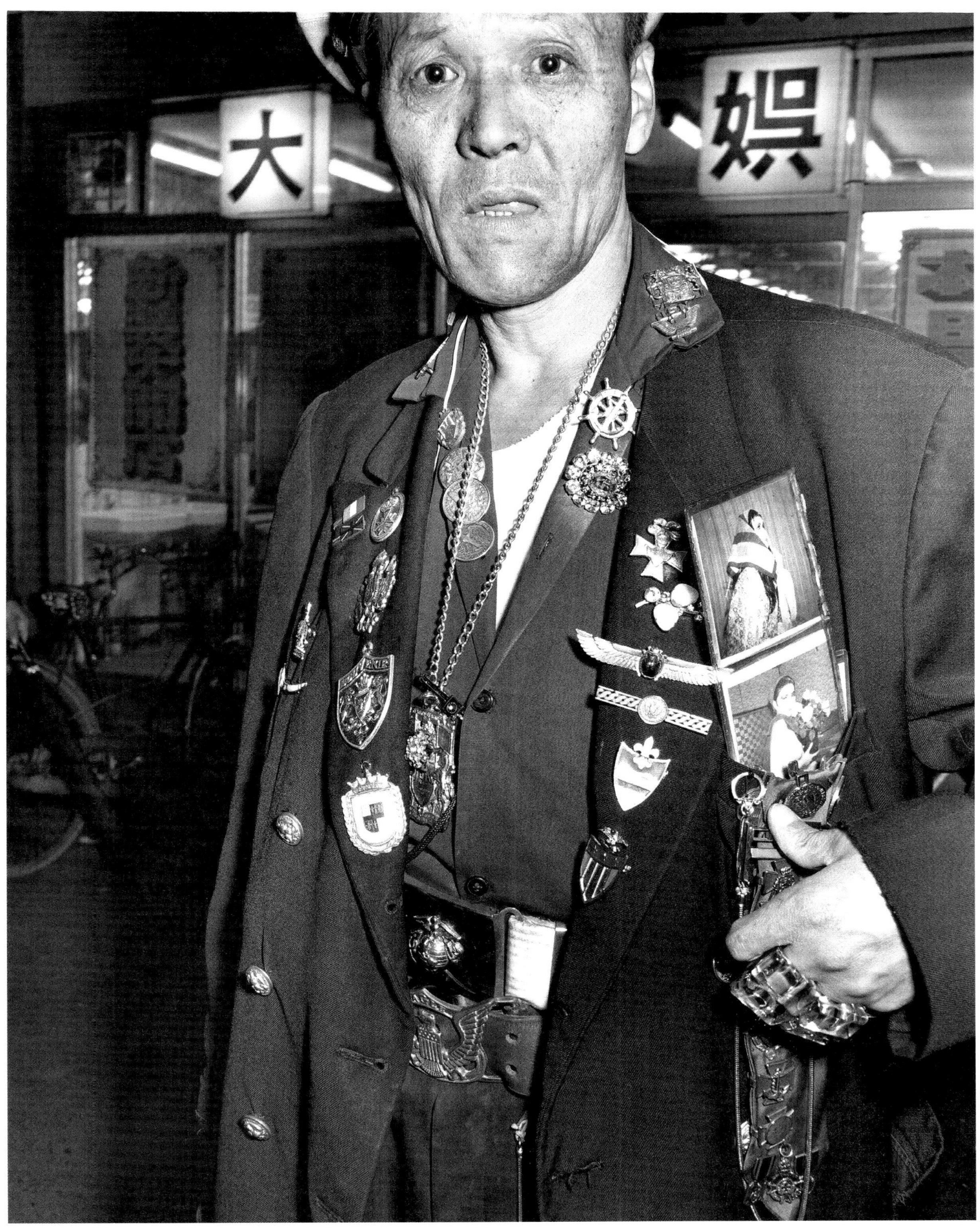

Unbalanced Man in Front of Pachinko Hall, Romance Street, Ikebukuro, Tokyo, 1975

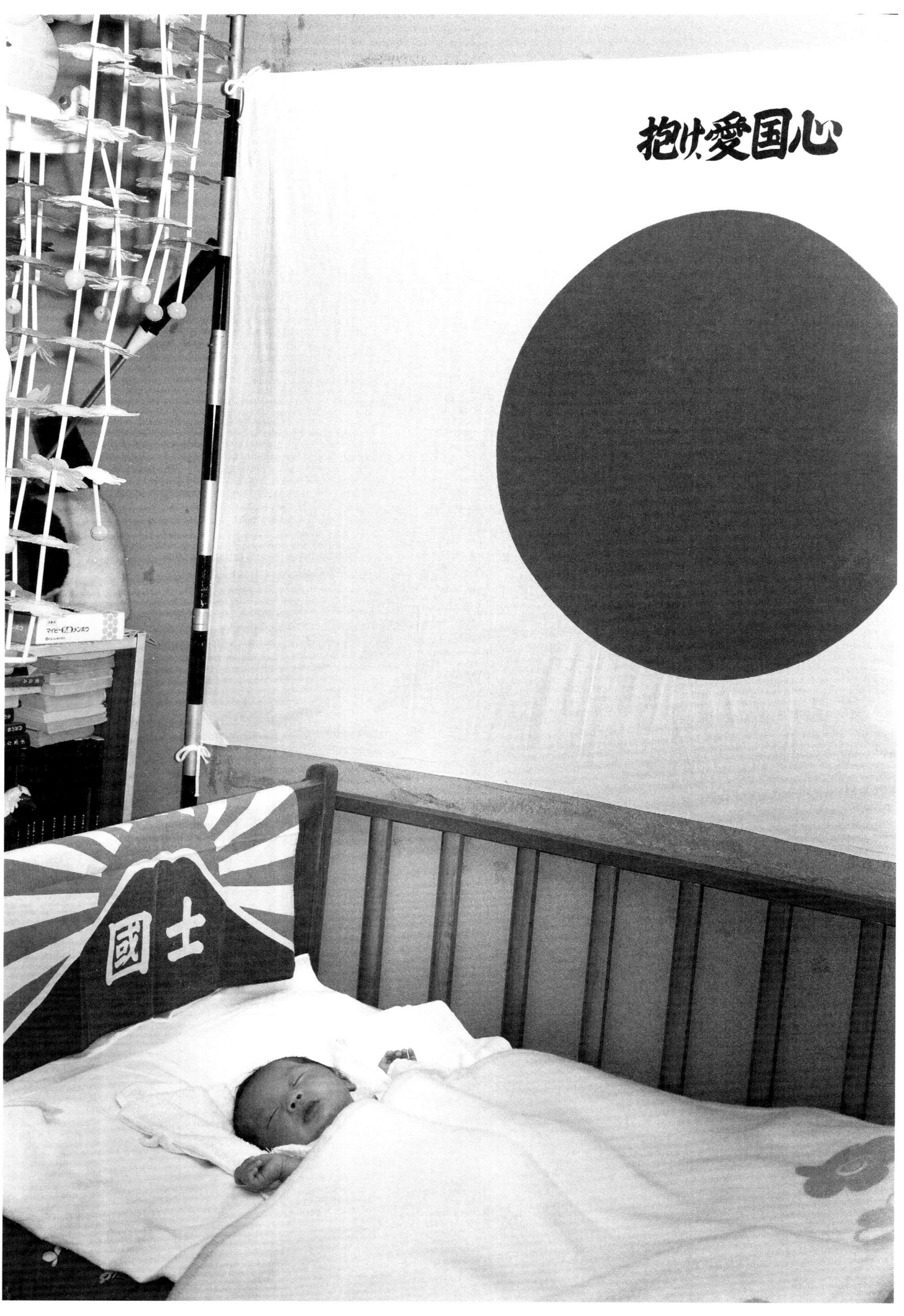

104 *Right-wing Baby*, Kami Ikebukuro, Tokyo, 1979

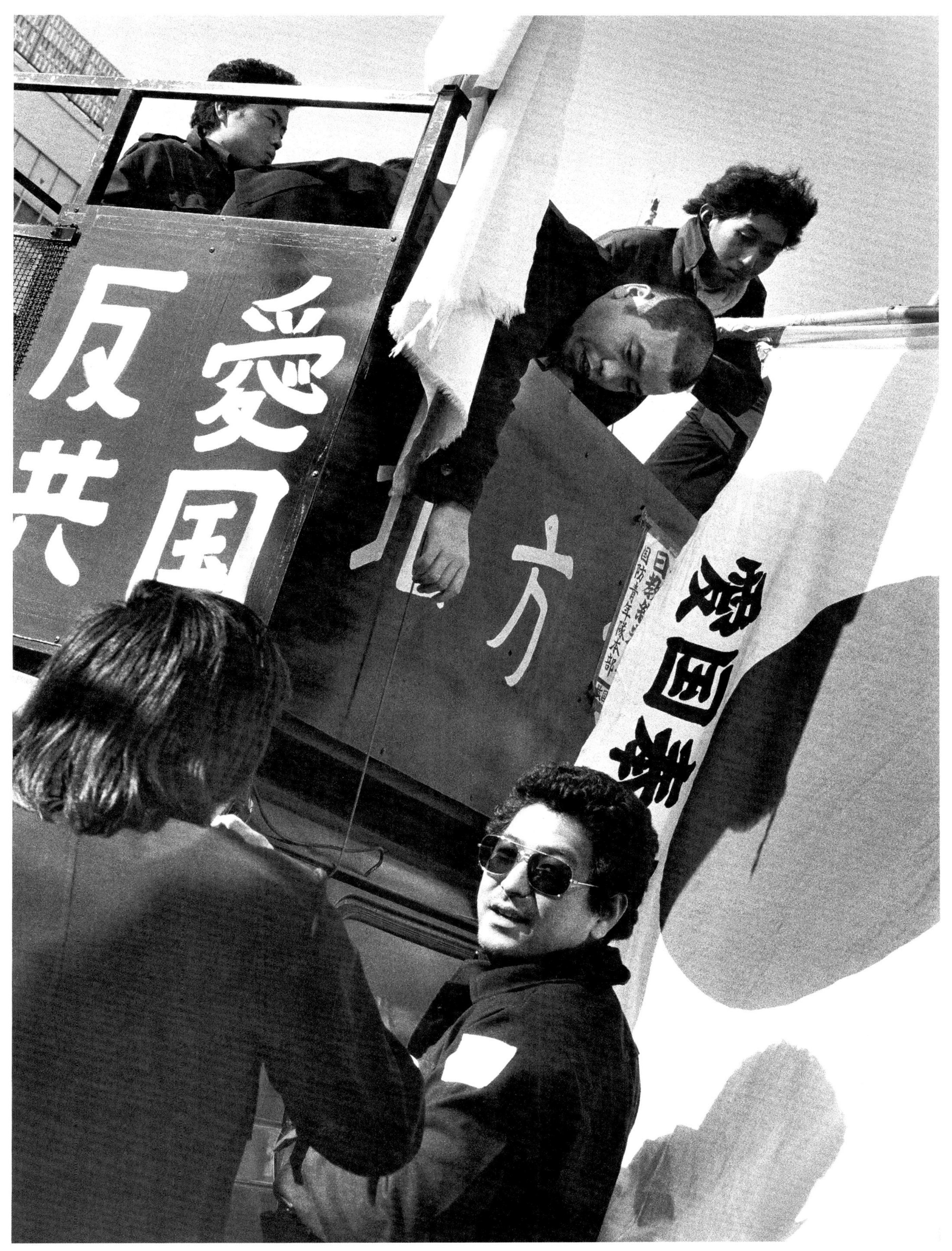

Young Right-wingers Gather at the Meeting of the Anti-Japan Teachers' Union, Ibaraki, Mito City, 1979

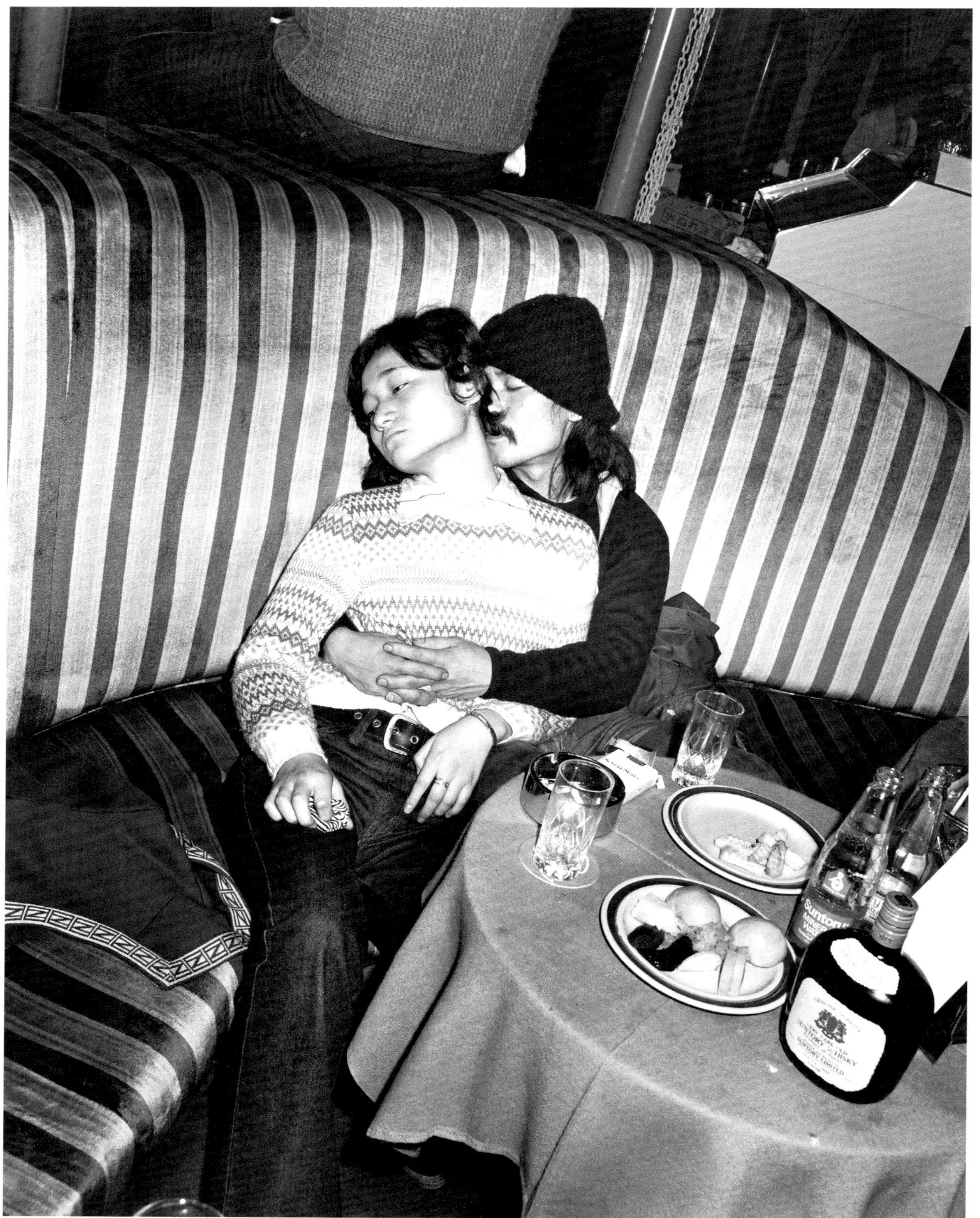

106 *Teens at the Disco, Ikebukuro, Tokyo, 1978*

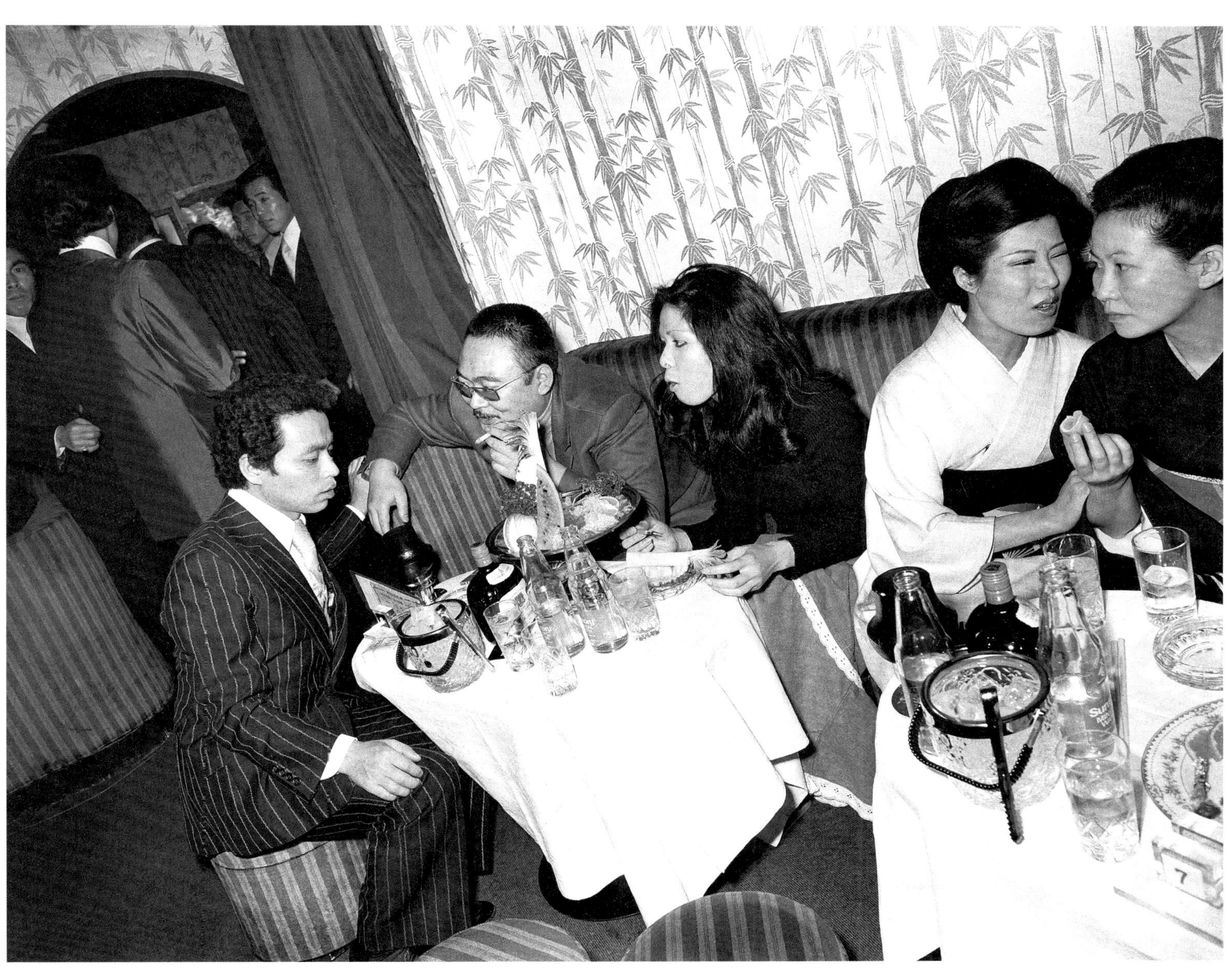

Christmas Party, Host Club, Bungeiza Street, Ikebukuro, Tokyo, 1975

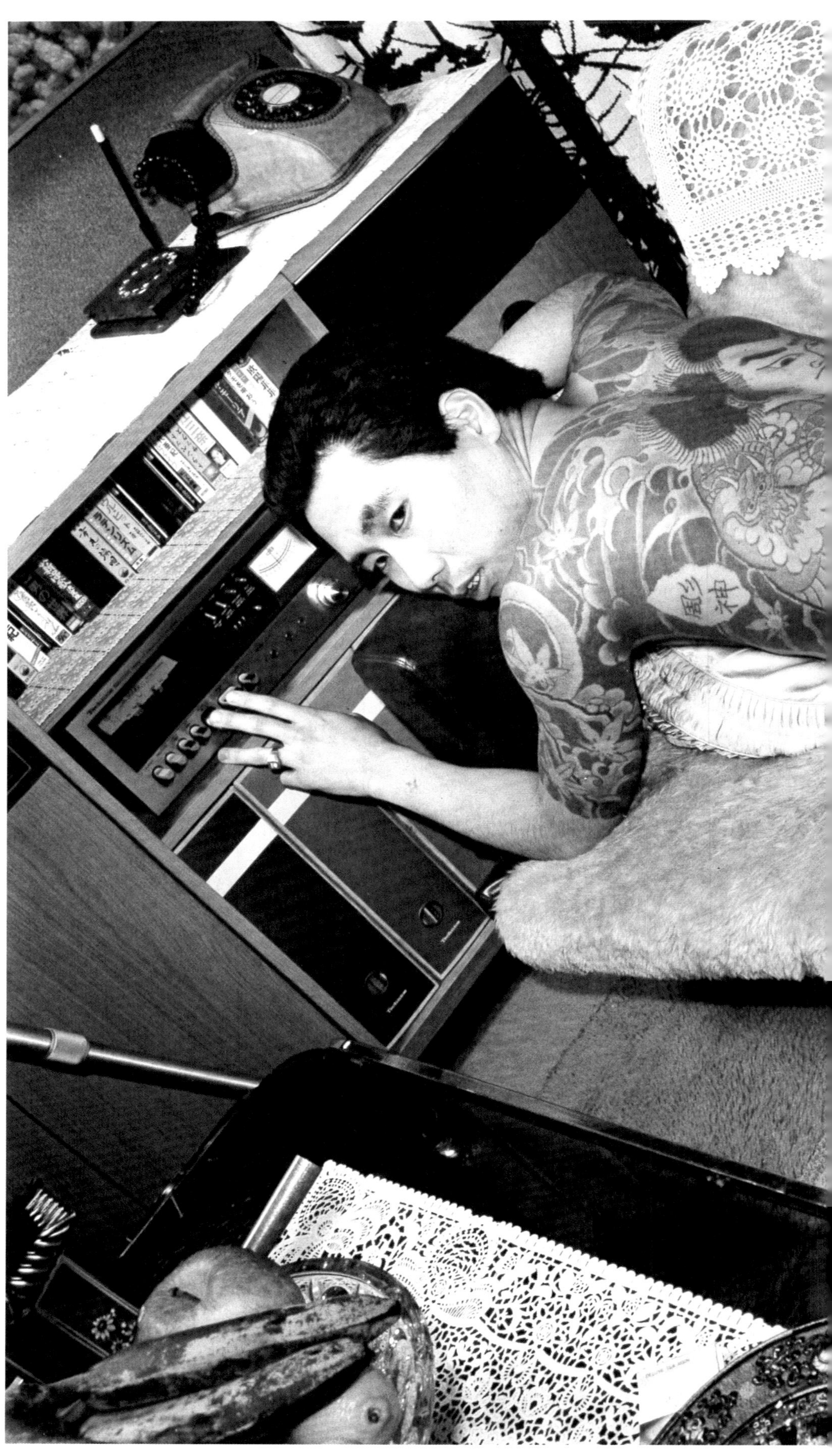

108 *Big Brother and the Siamese Cat*, Chihaya-chō, Toshima-ku, Tokyo, 1978

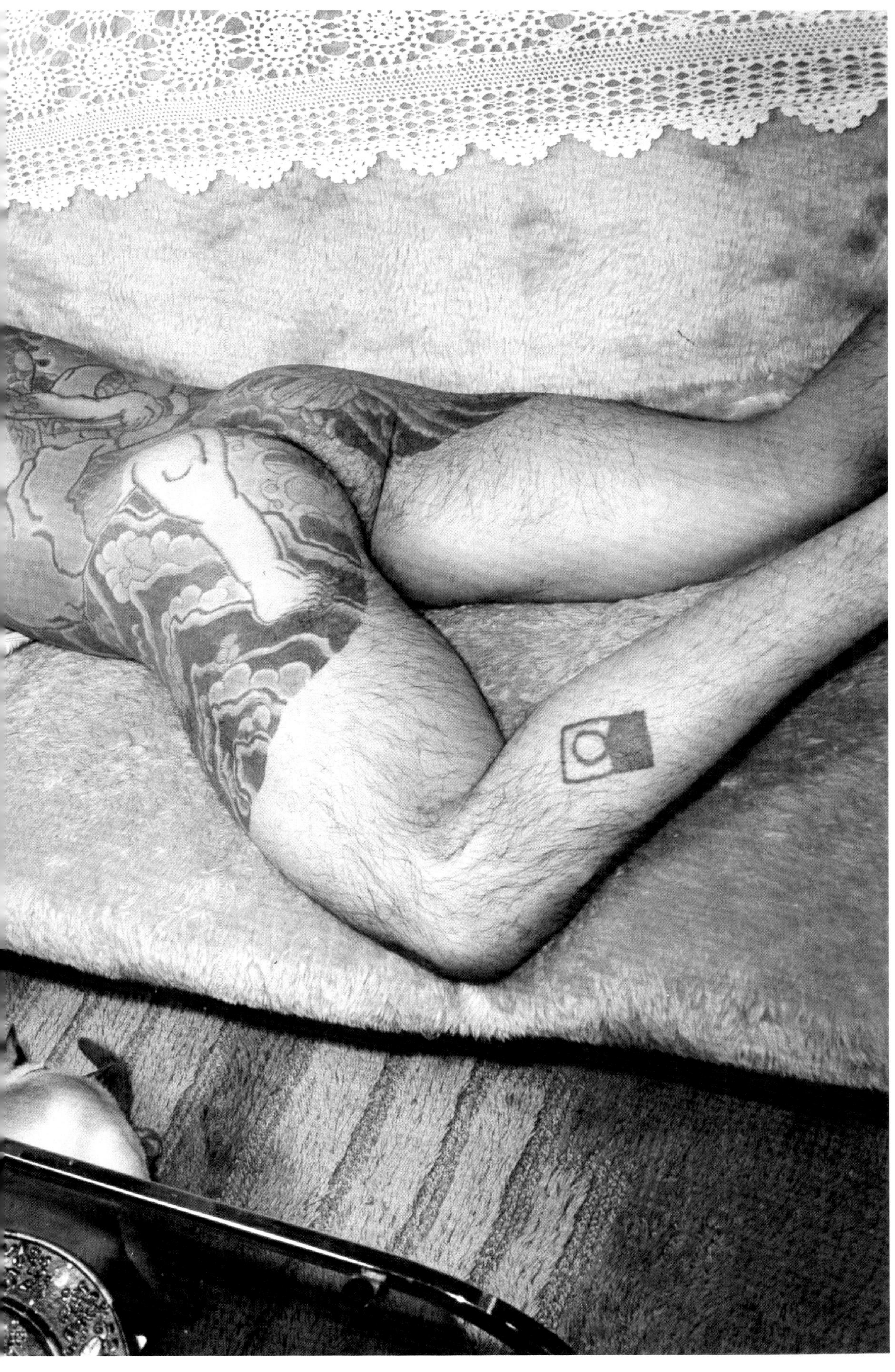

IGOR

PALMIN

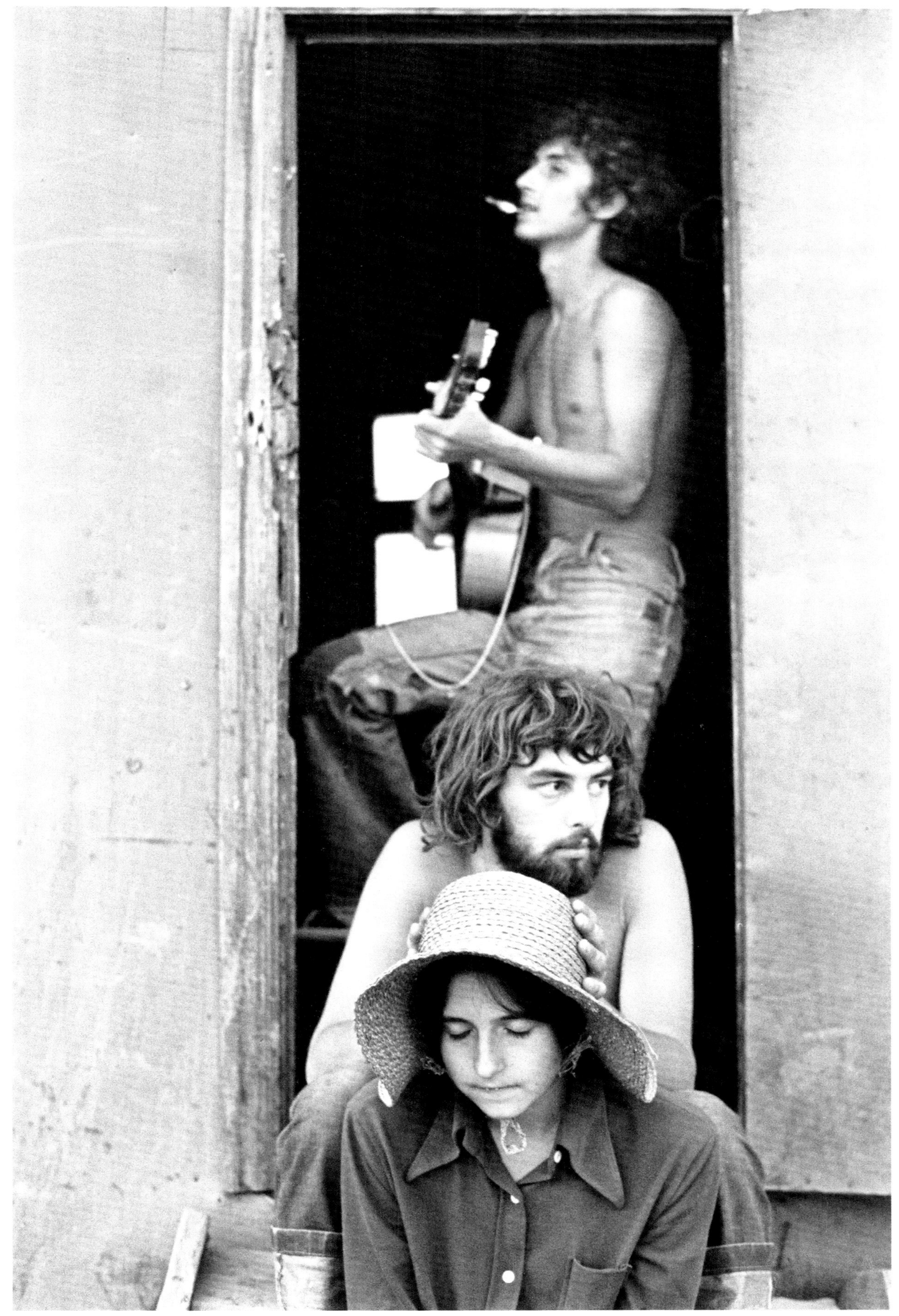

Igor Palmin's (b. 1933, Russia) photographs have a dreamy, otherworldly quality to them.[1] They seem to exist in a timeless and nameless place, characterised by barren earth and high skies devoid of chronological or geographical markers. Yet the knowledgeable eye places the pictures in a specific time and mood. The photos of forlorn countercultural youths populating an apocalyptic post-industrial landscape were easily decipherable to those late Soviet citizens who, like Palmin and his hippie subjects, spent their lives beneath the Soviet mainstream and at its margins. For them, the photos portrayed both the specific setting of an archaeological summer expedition – familiar territory to many Soviet bohemians – and a wider mood of aimlessness, alienation, irony and detachment – emotions that had become integral, even essential, to existence under late socialism. The photographic series *The Enchanted Wanderer* and *The Disquiet*, shot at the site of an archaeological expedition in southern Russia on the same day, capture the dilapidated environments the socialist economy created, yet also hint at its ruthless power, embodied in the oversized machines and brutally man-made landscapes. The human inhabitants of this landscape seem to be coincidental in their presence – a far cry from the conquerors of nature who had traditionally populated Soviet photographs of industrial progress.

At a first glance, the hippieish flower children are at odds with the desolate environment they inhabit. Their youth contrasts with the lifelessness of their surroundings; their wavy skirts, loose shirts and wind-blown long hair defy the straight, geometric lines of their environment. And yet they somehow also belong in this world of ramshackle trailers, vast and empty concrete storage halls, boats stranded without water and unfinished buildings that would never be completed. Like their surroundings, the hippie youngsters in Palmin's pictures seem to exist without purpose or motivation. They too seem to live in a world that is full of allusions to progress, yet is lost in its own timelessness. Their bell-bottoms, their hairbands, their trendy shoes, their notebooks and guitars, and their drawings on the wall of their trailer, sporting English slogans, a peace sign and opium poppies, link them to the big global counterculture of the 1960s and '70s, which they know is somewhere out there. Yet, like the landscape, they are caught in the 'here and now' of the photograph, ruptured from past and present. They too embody the contradictions of late Sovietness, where industrial failure provided the background for countercultural self-fashioning and where freaky youngsters have taken the place of socialist workers in animating the scene. Rather than building socialism like those who dug the pits, constructed the concrete bunkers and manoeuvred the cranes, they laze about in harmony with the wind, sand and dust. They wander the remnants of socialist production, yet they appropriate them for their purposes. They do not work with them. They use them as background to their individuality. And that was also very characteristic of late Soviet life.

Organised by Soviet universities and institutes, archaeological and scientific expeditions became one of the Soviet intelligentsia's favourite vehicles for escaping, at least temporarily, the gaze and control of the authorities. Around the campfire, many miles from Moscow, one could almost pretend that one lived in a state that did not dictate how to make art, write history or dress properly. Many otherwise gainfully employed intellectuals volunteered to spend their summers doing odd jobs in remote regions, helping to find the traces of a mystical comet or discover Russia's Scythian past. The official expedition was a recognised phenomenon of unofficial culture. In 1977, Moscow archaeologists assembled an expedition to Arzgir in the Stavropol Krai to explore Bronze Age burial mounds. Igor Palmin was hired as the expedition's photographer. His hippie subjects were recruited as unskilled labourers to help with the manual tasks of excavating. Here the organisers tapped into a reservoir of countercultural acquaintances, who wanted to get away from the stress of the big cities with their hostile policemen, zealous Komsomol patrols and disapproving parents and teachers. Or they simply needed an entry in their work ledger, since it was illegal in the Soviet Union to be idle for more than two months. On expeditions one was generally among *svoi* – people like oneself, even if age, occupation and style varied widely.

Palmin felt immediately drawn to the young people housed in the trailer on the edge of the compound. He felt a complicity with and connectedness to their silent rebelliousness. Palmin, while a whole generation older than the youngsters, was fascinated by their restlessness and studied difference and indifference. He too had been an instinctive and uncompromising enemy of the Soviet order from his early teenage years. His school years in Voronezh had been overshadowed by the arrests of several dozen of his schoolmates, who were involved in an anti-Stalinist youth organisation. While this so-called 'Communist Party of Youth' was led by earnest communist youngsters who wanted to construct a better version of socialism, Palmin professes that his creed was always a blanket rejection of the socialist world order. He considered himself an entirely un-Soviet person. In this he foreshadowed the attitude of his young hippie friends, whose declared aim was the avoidance of and non-engagement with anything Soviet. Sure, one had to live in and with the socialist structures, since one had to go to school, work, receive an apartment, get married and divorced within the Soviet bureaucracy. Yet by the 1970s there were many spaces in which official culture could be blended out or where it existed only as the butt of ironic jokes, hence neutralising its pervasive effect. The Soviet hippie world was one made up of alternative symbols and rites, interspersed with cruel persiflage of the stale slogans of the ageing socialist project. It followed Western ideals (here personified by the young 'Bob Dylan' and his guitar (p. 111)) and was at the same time very Soviet – not least because it was so adept in taking such excellent advantage of the possibilities late socialism offered: cheap living, guaranteed work and a well-developed cultural underground.

The Soviet underground of the 1970s was by no means entirely underground and was indeed quite visible, at least to most urban dwellers. The hippie community was one, but not the sole, shaper of this loose network of artists, musicians, writers, dissidents, yogis, bohemians, collectors, illegal traders, religious believers and many other shades of non-conformists who carved out an ever more encompassing slice of life from Soviet normality. The first signs of hippie life in the unlikely environment of the Soviet Union can be recorded around 1967–8, when some youngsters in the larger towns and in the western borderlands let their hair grow (to very modest length, at this stage), donned hairbands, painted flowers on their jeans and adopted slogans of peace, love and rock 'n' roll. When

Palmin photographed Moscow representatives of the species in 1977 in the Russian steppe, the capital's hippies had already survived several waves of repression, lived through ideological and cultural transformations and split into a variety of different but related groups.

His 'Enchanted Wanderer' – a title taken from the nineteenth-century novel by Nikolai Leskov, in wide circulation among the underground – was the young Moscow hippie Sergei Bol'shakov, who went by the names of Ryzhii (Ginger) and Liutik (Buttercup). Sergei was typical of much of the Soviet capital's hippie community as he came from a privileged background with parents working in high-ranking positions in the party and state *nomenklatura*. Like his friends, he embraced the idea of hippiedom as a meaningful alternative to a Soviet life, which he perceived as consisting of nothing but lies and hypocrisy. By 1977 Sergei had decisively broken with the possibilities that his promising origins could have afforded him in the Soviet system. He had dropped out of the highly competitive and prestigious Moscow Engineering Physics Institute (MIFI), which trained scientists for top-secret work in the military and nuclear sectors. He had also feigned insanity to escape the Soviet army, received a diagnosis of schizophrenia and spent time in a psychiatric hospital, whose perfidious system he understood only too well since his mother was a leading psychologist. Indeed, Sergei's and Palmin's paths had crossed once before, thanks to Sergei's friend Ofelia, who was closely linked with the Moscow network of non-conformist artists that also formed Palmin's intellectual and social circle. After bulldozers crushed an improvised open-air exhibition of this group at Belyaevo in full view of the Western press, the Moscow city council reluctantly granted two sanctioned exhibitions to the non-conformists on the grounds of the VDNKh, the All-Union fairground established during the Stalinist period. In the second of these exhibitions, Ofelia's artistic group, tellingly called Hair (*Volosy*), was invited to participate. Palmin photographed the unfolding drama that took place during the opening and in the following weeks, when endless queues of eager visitors snaked around the exhibition grounds. The KGB had confiscated some of the artistic works on the day of the opening, including a hippie flag tailored by Ofelia and her friends which

bore the – to communist ears, dangerous – slogan 'Country without Borders'. The artists, led by Palmin's friend Oscar Rabin, who mounted a dustbin and spoke to the assembled crowd of participants, journalists and guests, refused to open the exhibition until the items were returned. The flag never came back, but Ofelia tailored another one overnight, this becoming one of the most noted pieces of the exhibition, as indeed were its makers. During the heady two weeks of the exhibition, the members of Hair were present in their hippie finery. Palmin captured them lounging in the sun on the steps of the high-Stalinist House of Culture. The picture is all subversion: the solemn neoclassical columns of the House of Culture are defiled by the nonchalant hippies, whose demonstrative ignoring of the authorities is underlined by the presence of two hapless Soviet policemen observing them from afar. Palmin's future 'enchanted wanderer' sits deep in conversation in the picture.

Unbeknown to both Palmin and Bol'shakov, this picture was to be the first step in a creative partnership depicting young, rebellious youths in Soviet environments. The narrative of the pictures from the exhibition and that present in pictures taken two years later in Arzgir are essentially the same: young people searching for life and meaning in the rubble of a gigantic social experiment whose rigidity turned them into outcasts. Ironically, these bored, countercultural youngsters (and a few stray dogs) give life to the otherwise stale and bleak landscapes of late socialism. Palmin's original idea was to photograph the whole band of exotic counterculturals who had joined the expedition, yet only a few were willing to pose for the photos, and finally only Sergei remained, traversing the surreal landscape as the 'enchanted wanderer'. Before that, Palmin had captured a still of life in their small, dusty trailer: a table strewn with smoking paraphernalia; a girl named Olga cooking on the single hotplate; a young man named Igor looking into the distance, smoking and reading (p. 117); the wall decorated with hand-drawn pictures and posters; a picture of the *Mona Lisa*; jackets on pegs on the wall (p. 116). These pictures are full of allusions to labour, yet there are no toilers. Instead the energy of these youngsters clearly went into a very different endeavour. One photo that Palmin did not include in his selection of *The Disquiet* was a close-up of

a drawing pinned to the wall that showed a small figure with glasses attacking a giant poppy with a saw. For those in the know, this picture referred to the Soviet hippie practice of extracting the seeds of poppy flowers in order to boil them into *mak*, a kind of raw opiate, or to brew *kuknar*, a narcotic tea. Not being able to follow the Western craze for LSD (this was only available in Soviet military laboratories and with only a few exceptions did not make it into hippie hands), Soviet hippies developed a variety of domestic drug cocktails made from ingredients available to them. Poppies grew everywhere: from the front yards of small village houses near Moscow to the fields of western Ukraine, Central Asia and the Russian south. It did not take the archaeological field-hands long to find the nearest poppy supply.

Drugs enlarged the world for Soviet hippies. For many like Ofelia, Sergei, Igor and Olga it was part of the hippie way of life, which Ofelia had termed a 'system of life', since it was not only a decision of style but a fundamental reckoning with the prevailing morality and official world view. Drugs made hippies travel (both physically and spiritually) in a country that had too many borders. Drugs confirmed their non-conformity and otherness. Yet drugs also destroyed the languid coexistence between hippies and Soviet society that prevails in Palmin's pictures. The hippies in the expedition got into trouble for their poppy business and were almost sent home. Olga died of a drug overdose in the 1990s, as did the hippie legend Ofelia. Igor emigrated to the USA. Sergei remained cynical about Soviet life and became even more cynical about post-Soviet life. It took more than thirty years before Palmin, thanks to modern social media, would hear from his subjects again. Yet once upon a time they had shared a brief period of their lives in the dusty steppe of southern Russia, in a habitat that was so stagnant that time seemed to stand still, yet so full of hidden dynamics that Palmin labelled both picture series he shot there with titles implying movement. The hippies struck him as seekers and searchers who had not yet found what they were looking for. The Soviet Union stood still. But at its margins there was movement, heralding the seismic changes that were soon to come.

Juliane Fürst

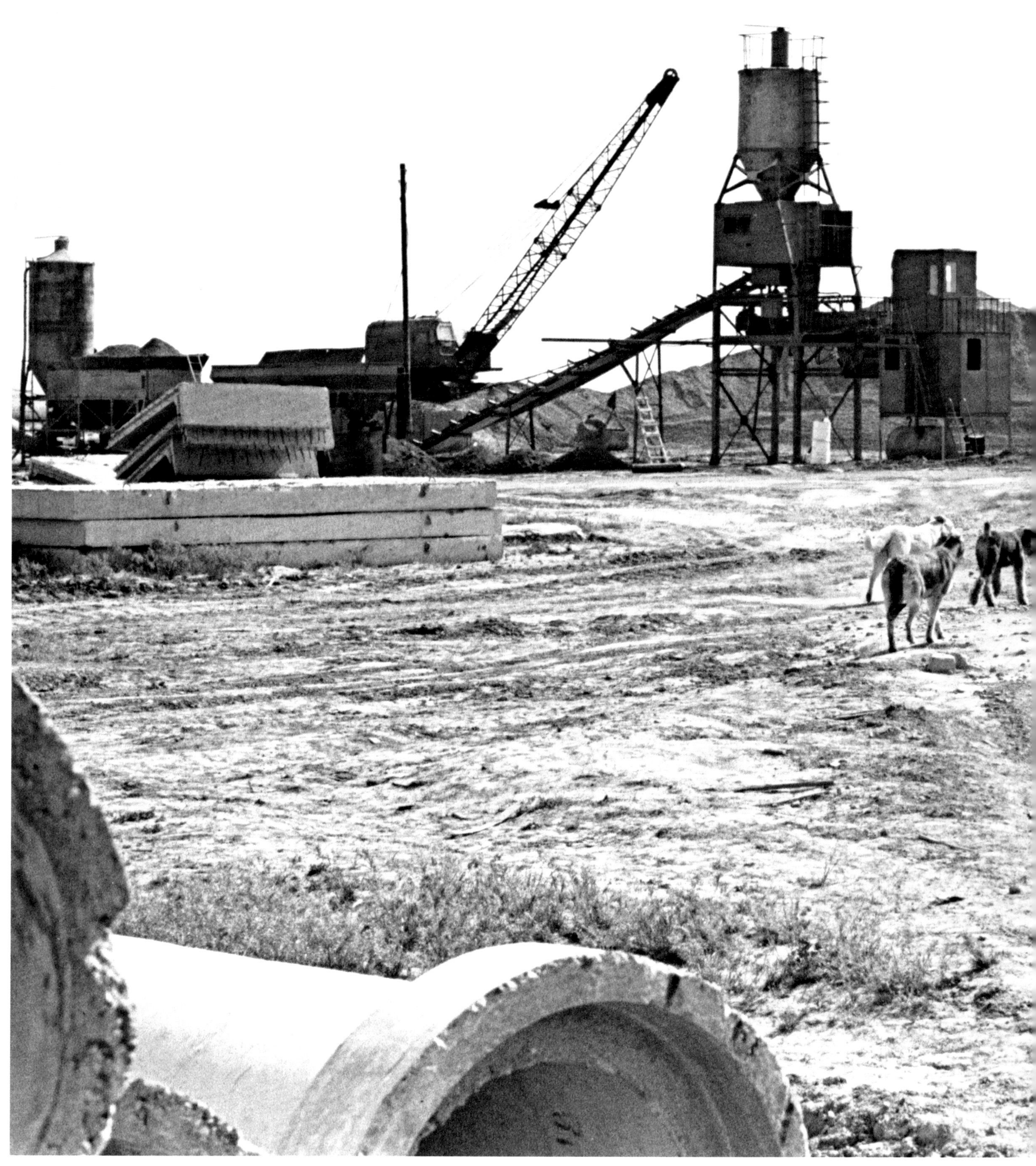

114 From 'The Disquiet', *Untitled*, Arzgir, Stavropol Krai, USSR, 1977

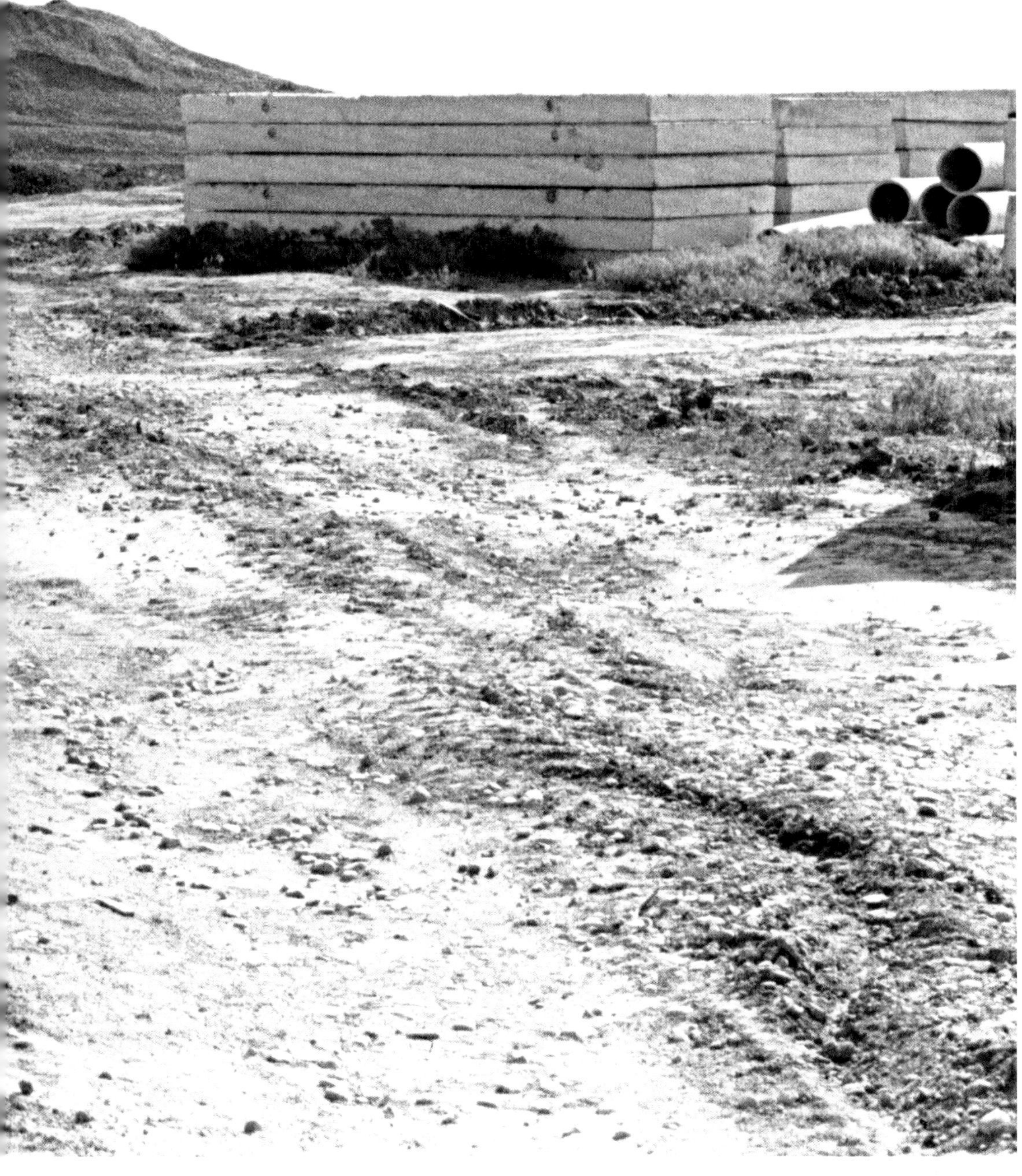

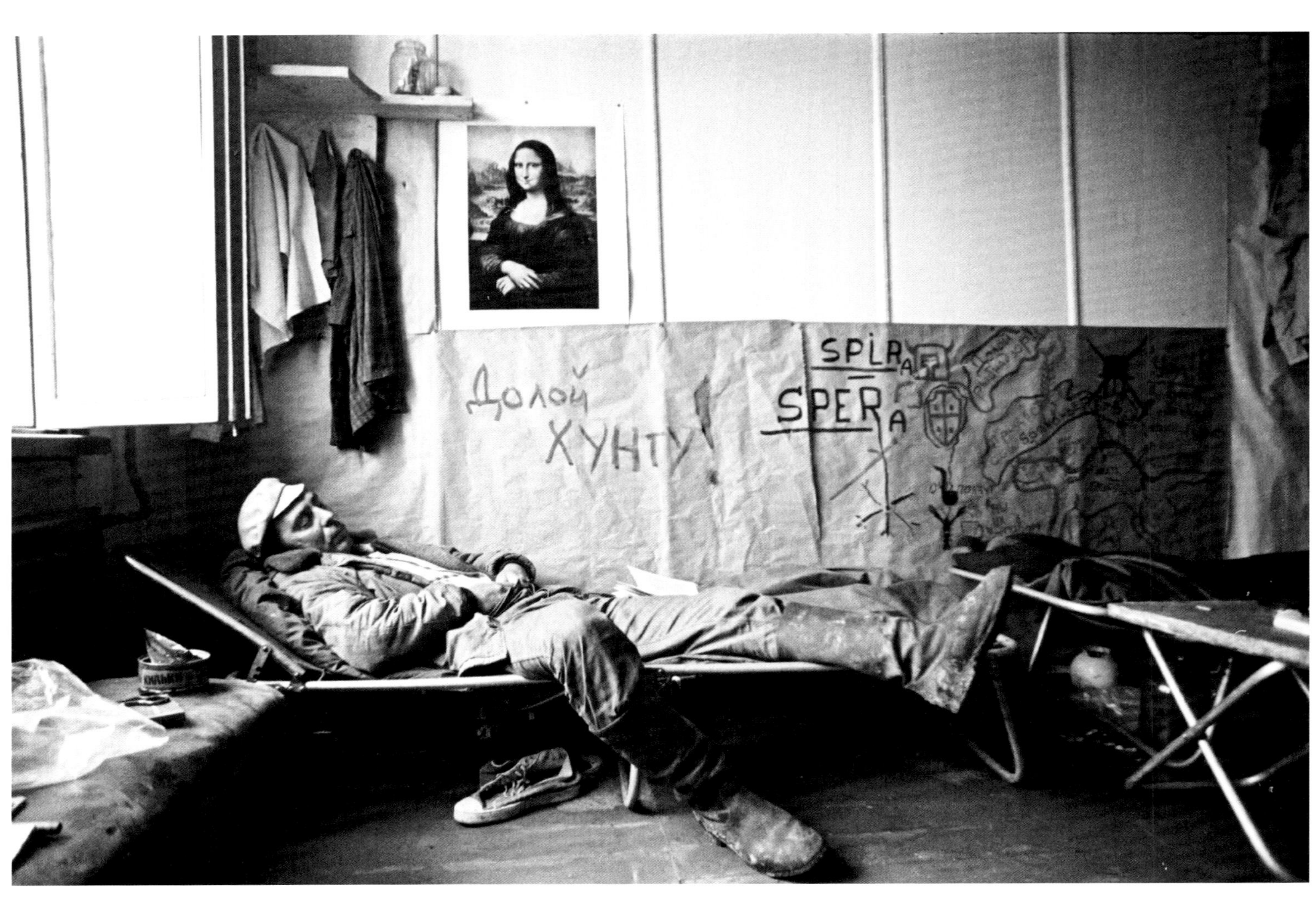

116 This page and opposite: from 'The Disquiet', *Untitled*, Arzgir, Stavropol Krai, USSR, 1977

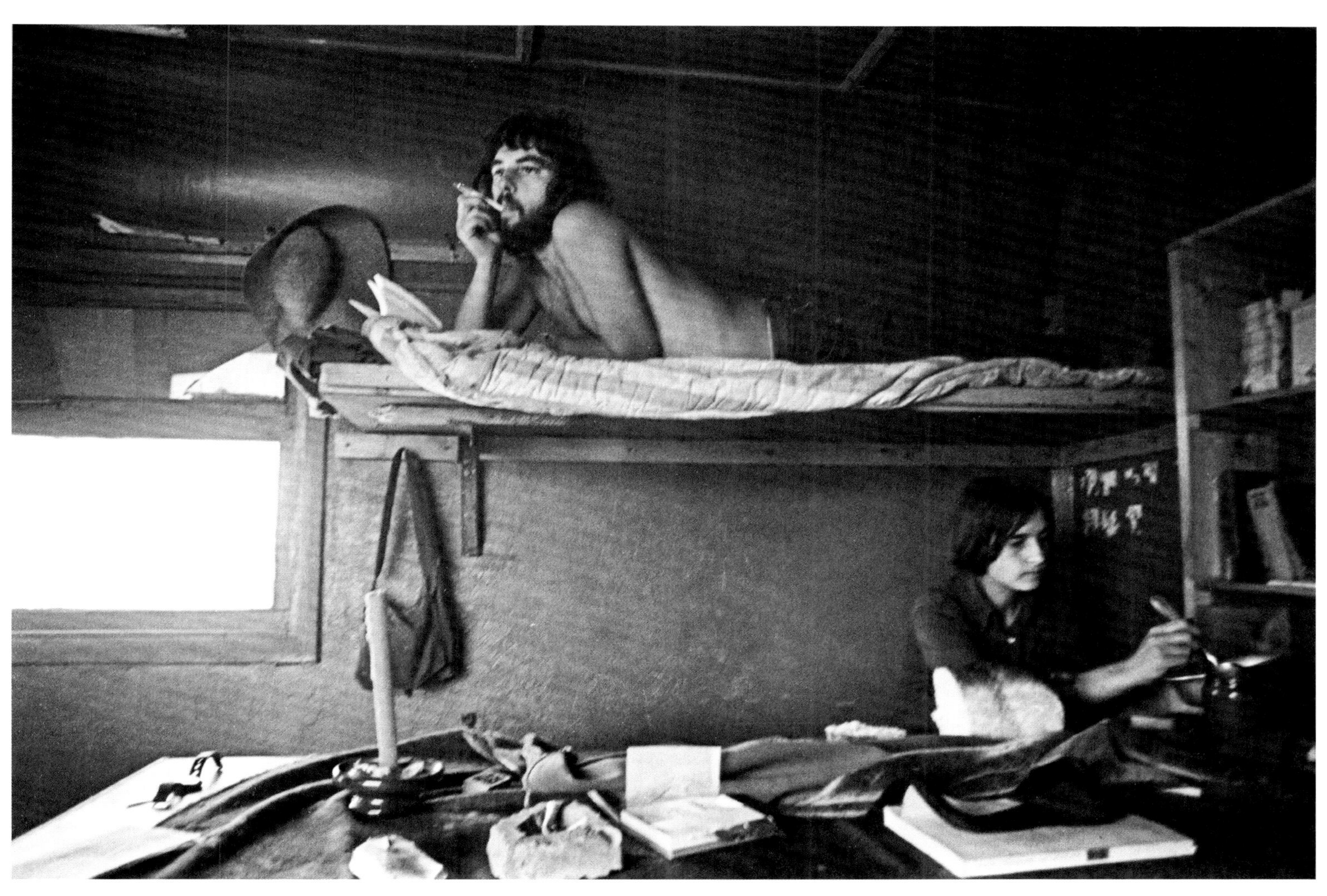

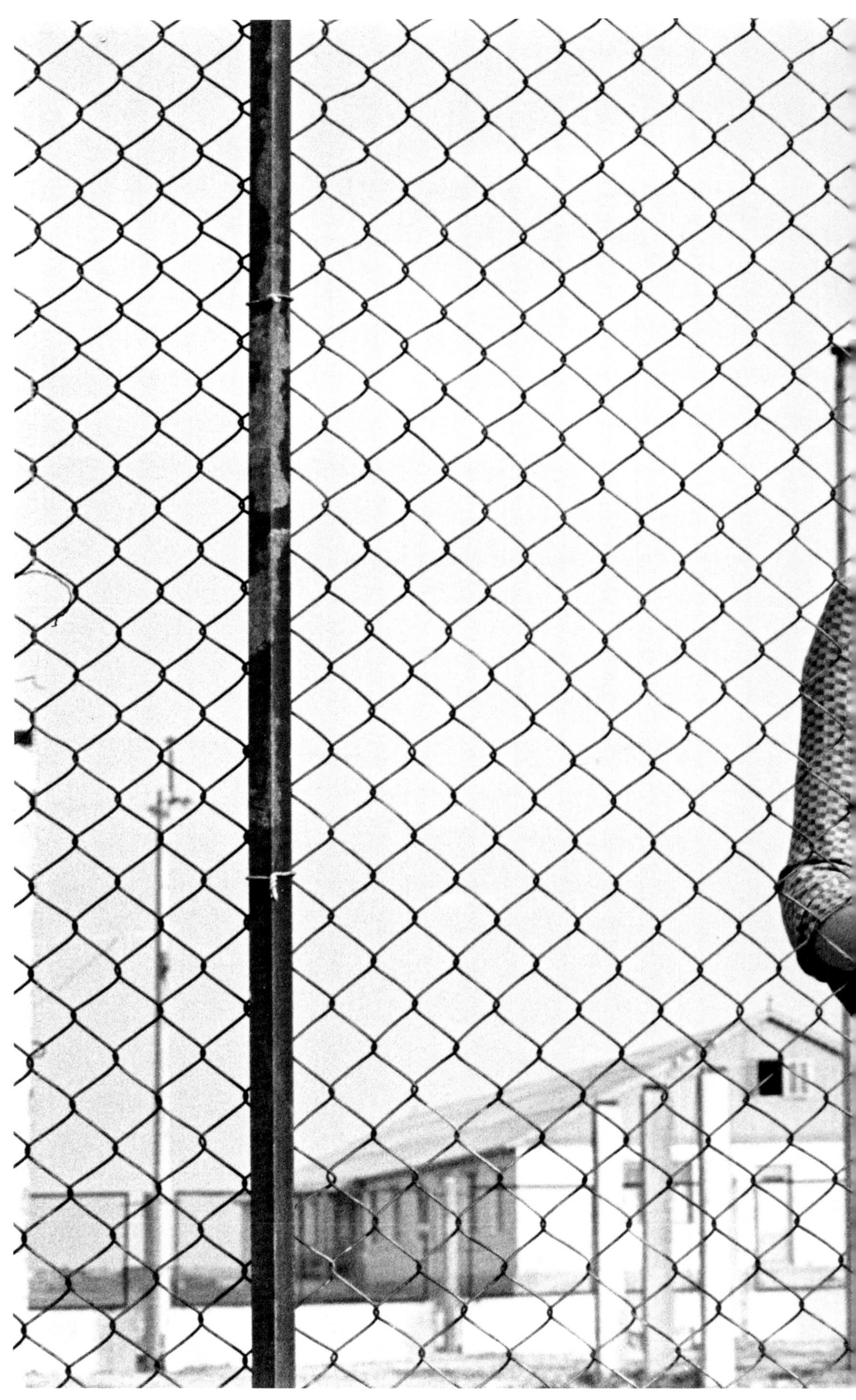

118 From 'The Enchanted Wanderer', *Untitled XVI*, Arzgir, Stavropol Krai, USSR, 1977

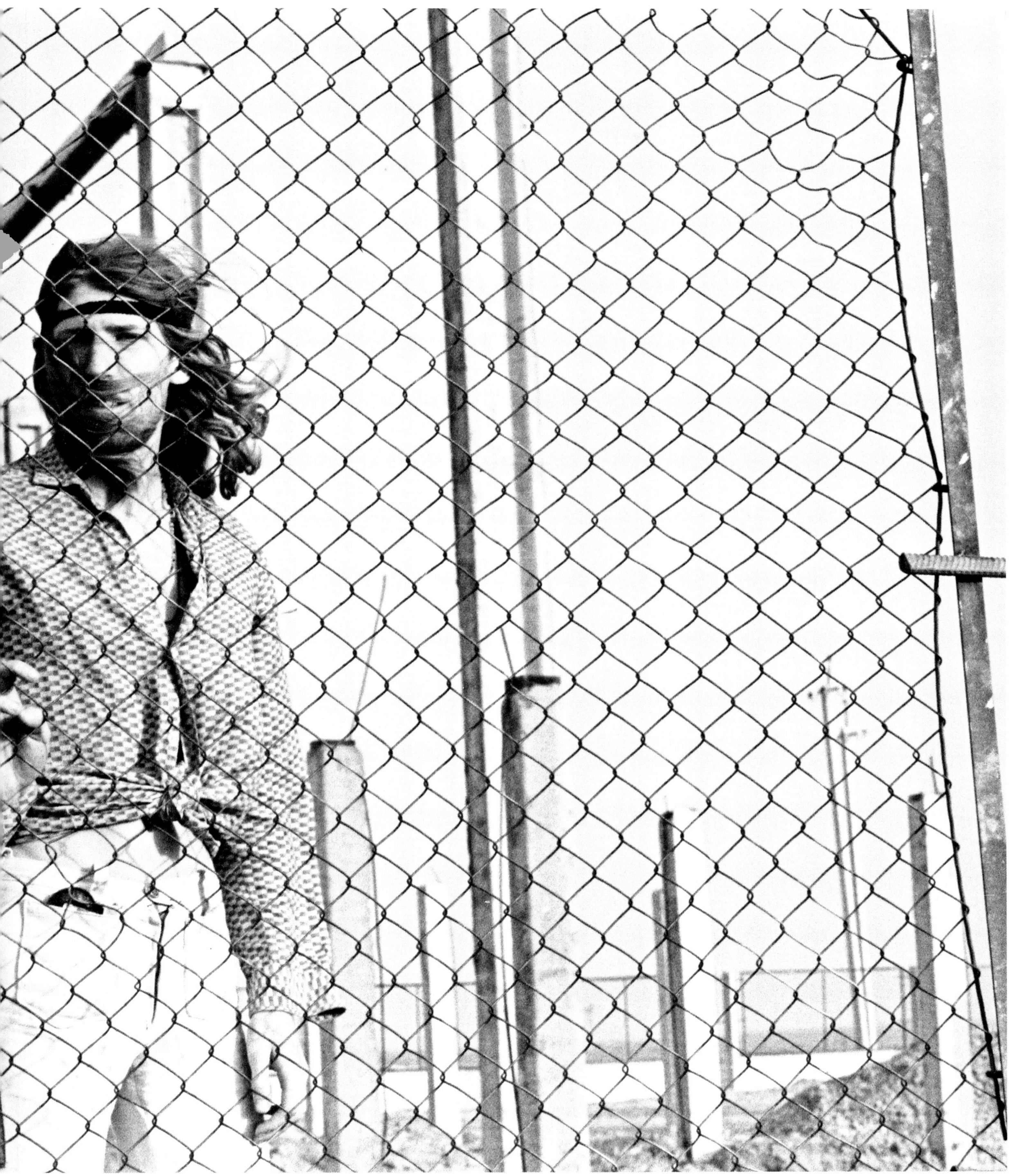

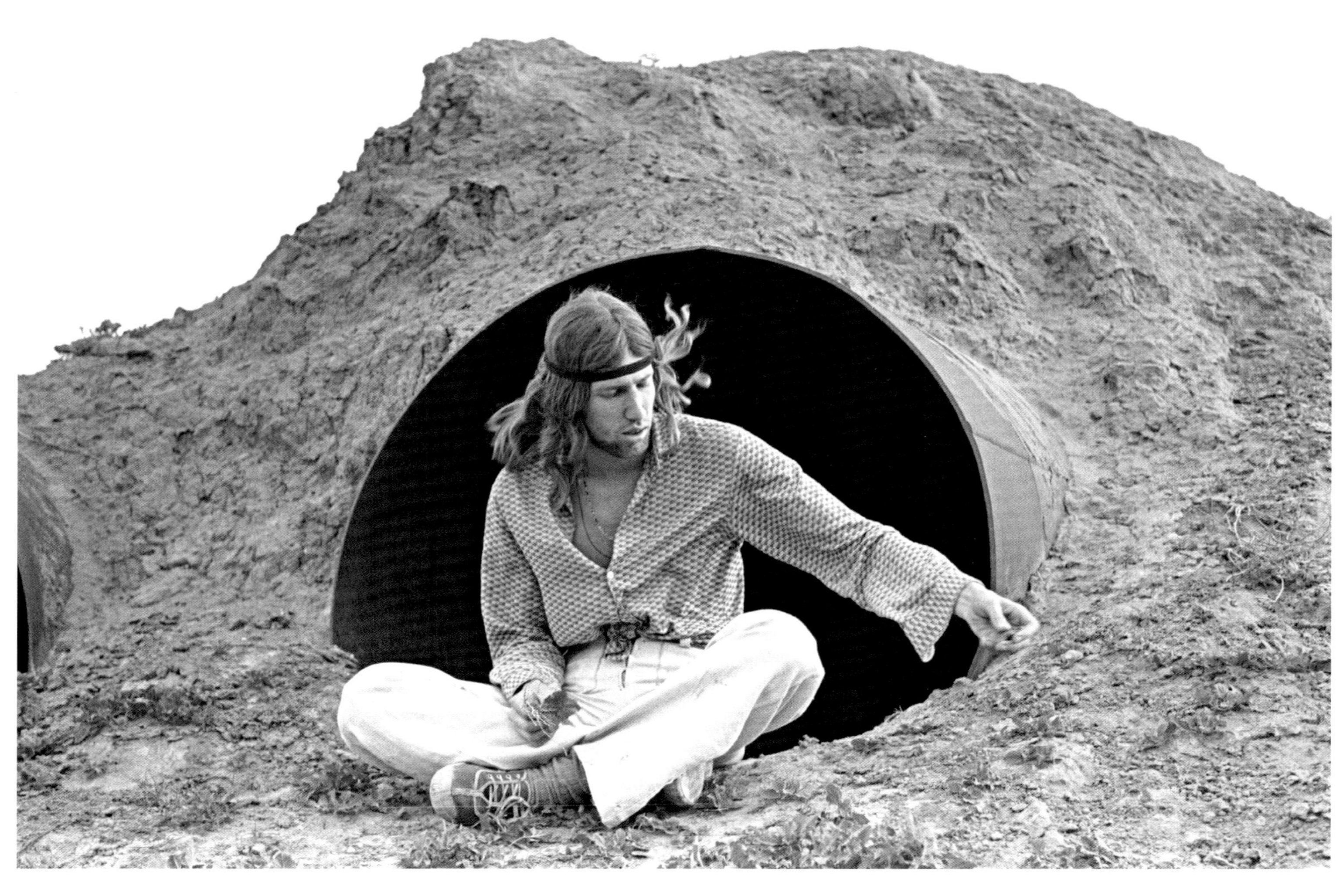

120 From 'The Enchanted Wanderer', *Untitled XVII*, Arzgir, Stavropol Krai, USSR, 1977

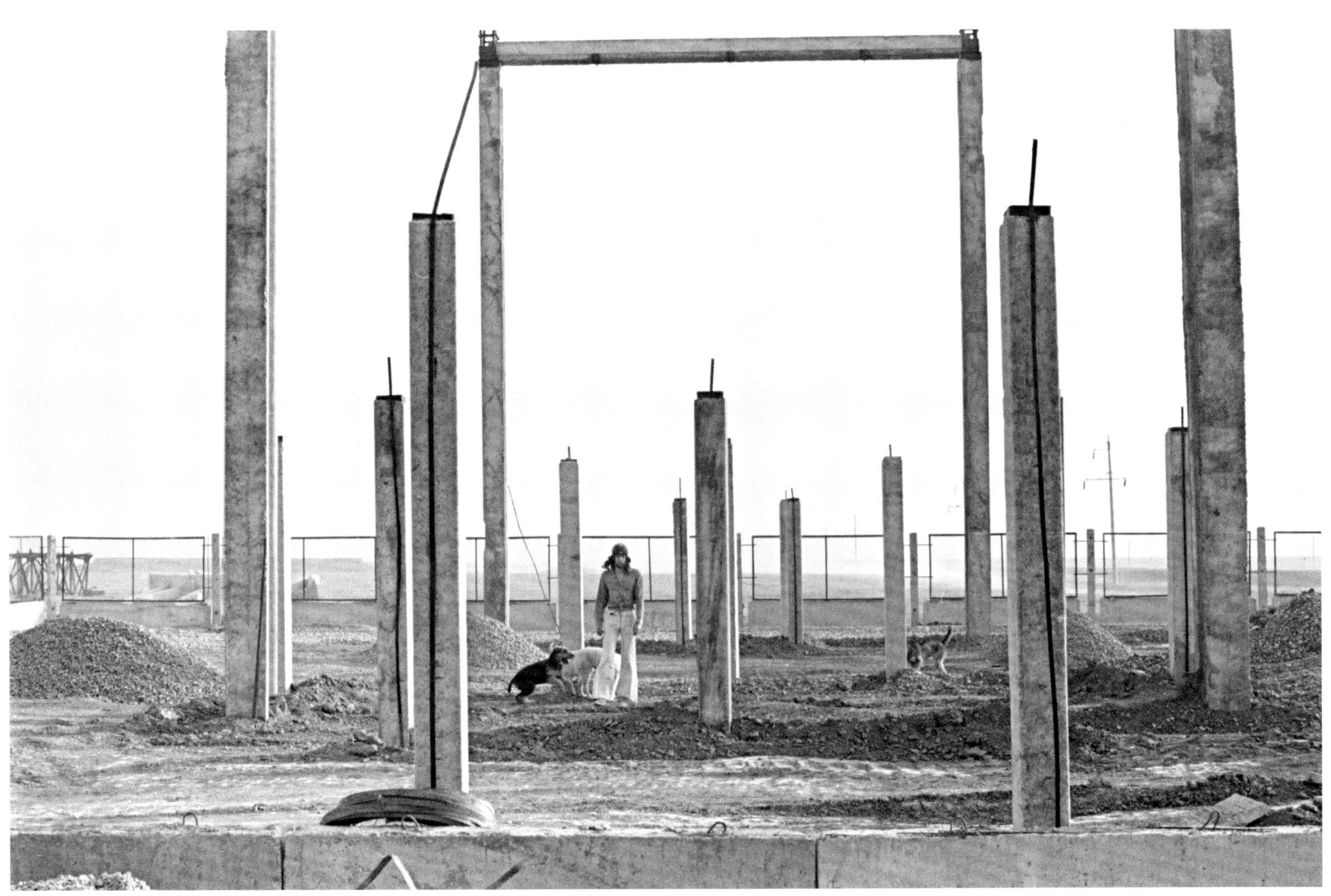

From 'The Enchanted Wanderer', *Untitled XIV*, Arzgir, Stavropol Krai, USSR, 1977

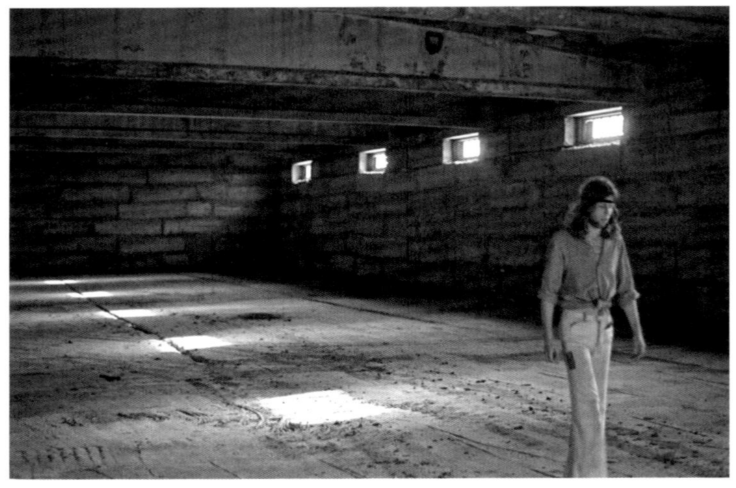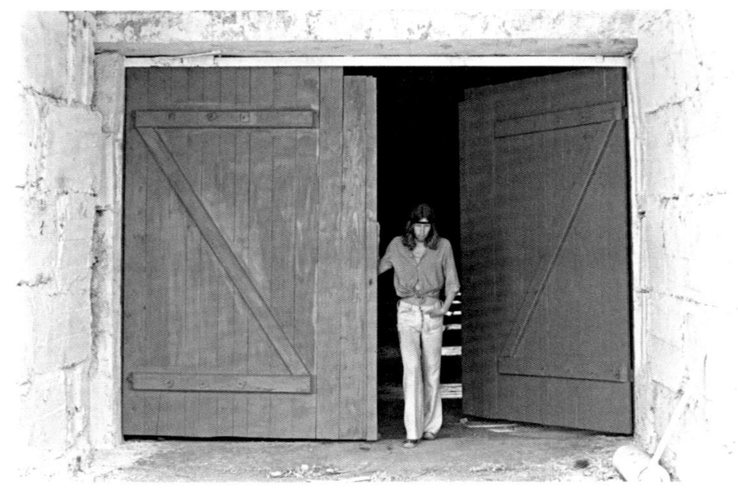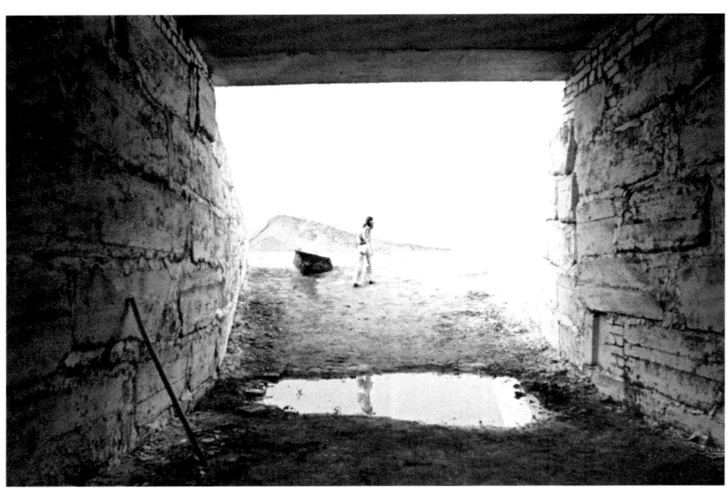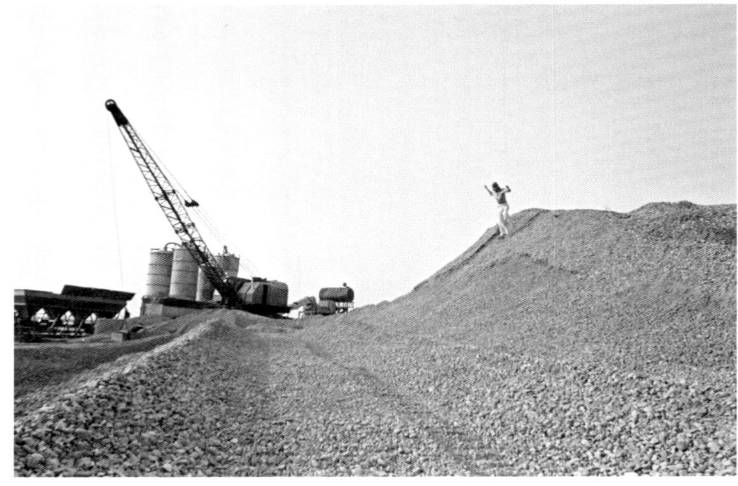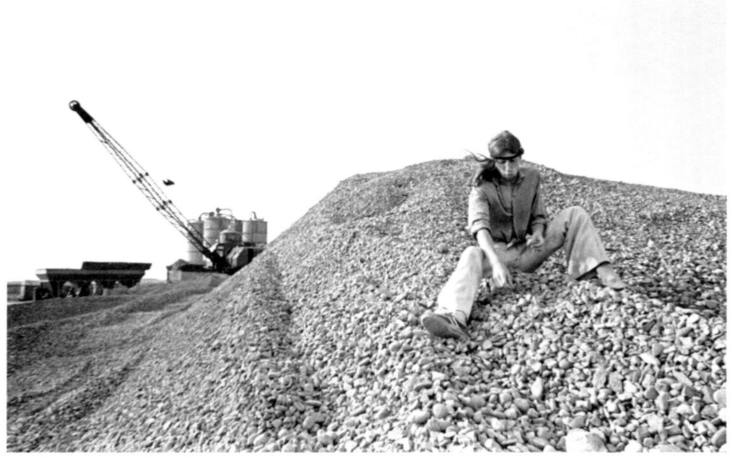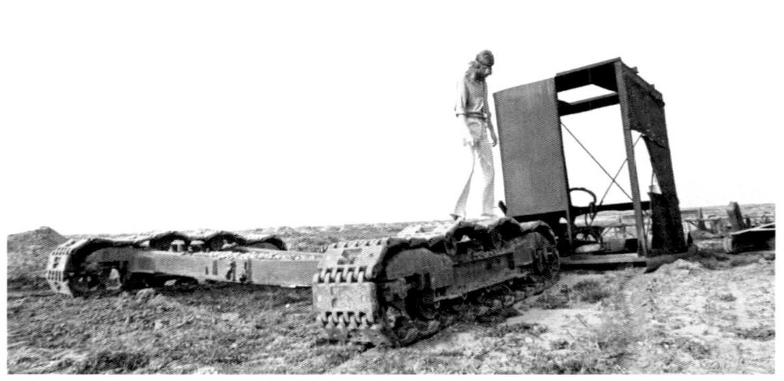

122 From top, left to right: from 'The Enchanted Wanderer', *Untitled II; III; IV; VI; VII; IX*, Arzgir, Stavropol Krai, USSR, 1977

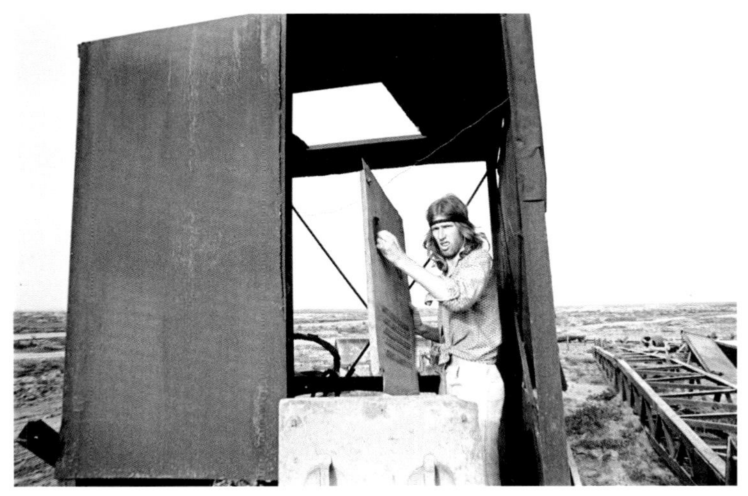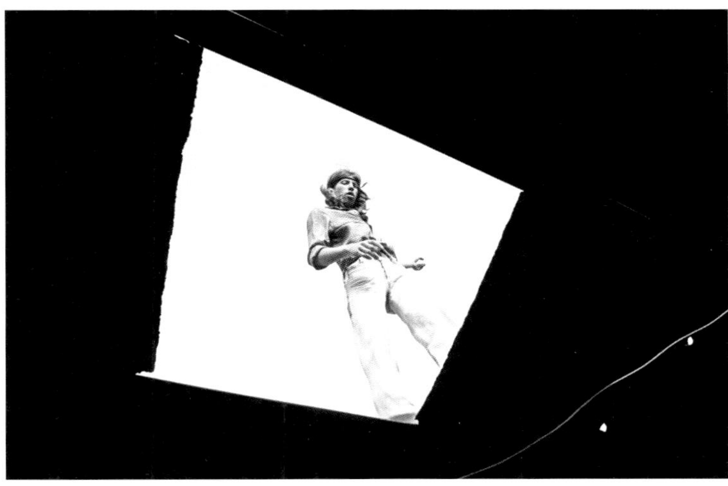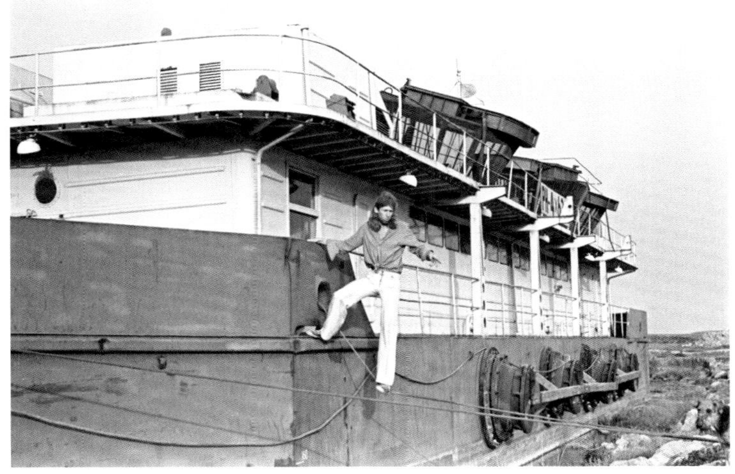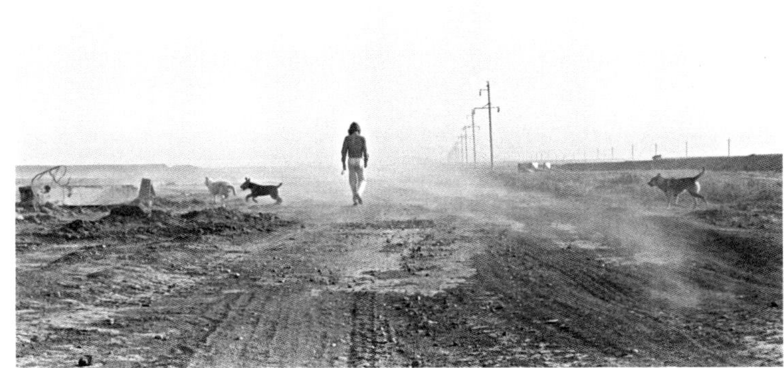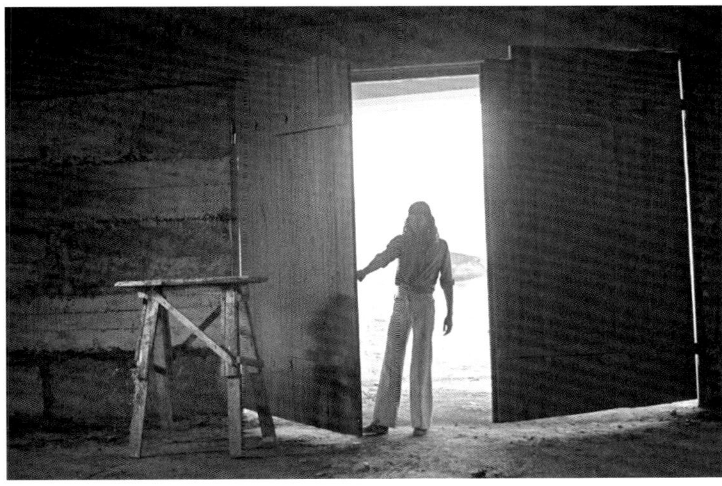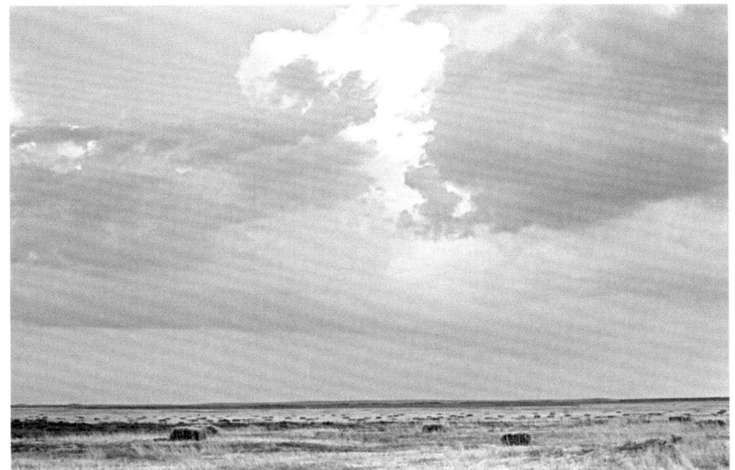

From top, left to right: from 'The Enchanted Wanderer', *Untitled X*; *XI*; *XIII*; *XIX*; *XXI*; *XXIV*, Arzgir, Stavropol Krai, USSR, 1977

WALTER

PFEIFFER

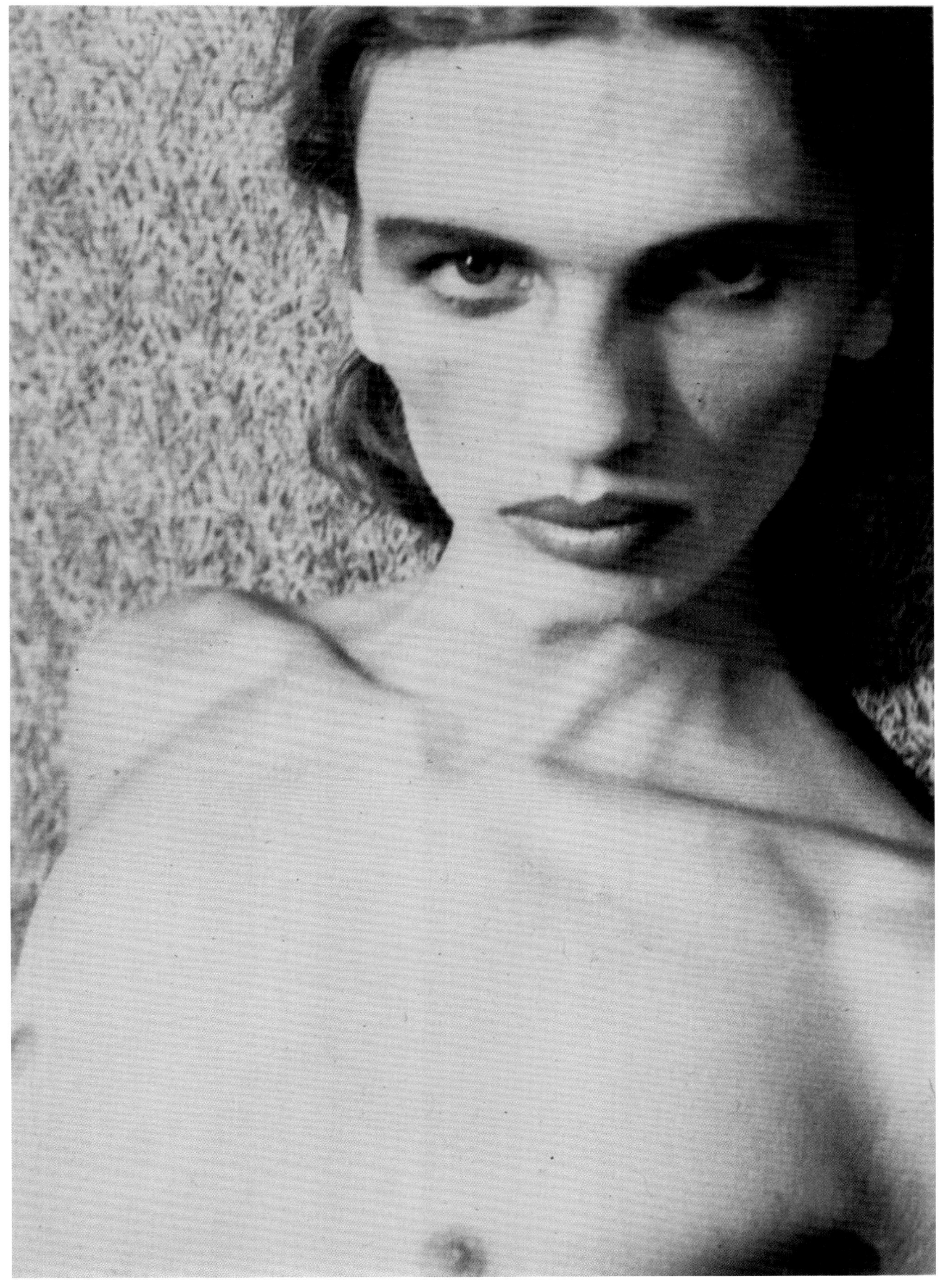

Walter Pfeiffer's (b. 1946, Switzerland) style readily connects with the preoccupations of contemporary image-makers such as Jack Pierson, Collier Schorr, Wolfgang Tillmans and Ryan McGinley; yet he emerged in the 1970s with an earlier generation of photographers that included Larry Clark, Duane Michals and Peter Hujar, all of whom explored the instability of gender and sexuality in relation to the male body. What is distinct about Pfeiffer is how his career has navigated a generational shift in working with and presenting queer subjects, from a practice operating on the periphery to its newfound centrality in the commercial image economy, exemplified by its accommodation by fashion.

Writing in the introduction to Peter Hujar's book *Portraits in Life and Death* (1976), Susan Sontag identified two impulses in photography: one that 'converts the world itself into a department store' and another that 'converts the whole world into a cemetery'.[1] The theory evoked how photographs aestheticise and commodify subjects as much as they ossify them, by marking the beauty of their moment in front of the camera as time passes.

Pfeiffer's work first garnered attention in 1974 as part of the group exhibition *Transformer: Aspects of Travesty* at the Kunstmuseum Lucerne in Switzerland, curated by Jean-Christophe Ammann, who would become Pfeiffer's long-time editor. The title references Lou Reed's album of 1972, and *Transformer* was the first museum exhibition to explore transvestism and non-normative sexualities, in representation drawn from art, fashion and music. (The exhibition was restaged by the Richard Saltoun Gallery, London, in 2013.)

Pfeiffer exhibited a set of photographs of Carlo Joh, taken over a number of months in 1973. They charted, across black-and-white images printed on cheap documentation photo paper, a young man in differing states of gendered appearance, oscillating between naked, made-up and in drag (pp. 125, 127). Pfeiffer recalls that the sequence 'started with Carlo Joh in his blossom and beauty, and every time … he came – we photographed maybe once a month – he got thinner, and you see this in the pictures'.[2] The compulsion to document was shared by the subject, as Carlo Joh brought lamps and a camera to every session and did his own

make-up. Pfeiffer in return made the framing for each photo and directed the sittings in his apartment. Carlo Joh died prematurely soon after the photo sessions ended, and before Pfeiffer first worked with Ammann on selecting the photographs for display.

The work has an intense beauty, depicting a person at their moment of becoming, before it is taken from them. As portraits, they show the strength and vulnerability of the young man in the visual register of his glamour, and his decline. Pfeiffer was compelled to document Carlo Joh: 'I had to photograph him as my muse. If you want something deeply, it has to be; you have to make it. If not, you are not strong enough.' Like Sontag's theory, Pfeiffer's photographs of Carlo Joh are able to raise the department store and the cemetery – rather like Hujar's *Candy Darling on Her Deathbed*, taken in the same year (a portrait of the Warhol superstar in declining health, now regarded as a significant image of trans identity). What makes it particularly apt in Pfeiffer's case is that he actually worked as a department store window dresser before he became a photographer.

Pfeiffer's training in the commercial gaze taught him how to construct visual seduction, and it translated readily into a self-taught mode of photography that placed value on the look of things. Pfeiffer still prepares for each shoot he works on by arranging large-scale mood boards in his studio, technicolour cornucopias of cascading bolts of cloth, wrapping paper, photographs, posters and plastic props: a queer material culture of sorts, as if he still has the shop window in mind.

Pfeiffer now produces editorial fashion for titles including *Vogue Paris*, *i-D*, *Self Service* and *Dazed*, and in turn for fashion advertisers such as APC, MSGM, Pringle of Scotland, Hermès and Helmut Lang. One of the reasons for Pfeiffer's late-blooming success in fashion is his ability to direct an attitude about bodies without having to rely on clothes, which suits the homogeneous nature of much contemporary fashion.

As a young man with aspirations to be an artist, Pfeiffer knew about the closed, elite world of fashion – in the 1970s he travelled to Milan to buy his shoes, and he read fashion magazines, loving the otherworldly photographs of Guy Bourdin – but he 'didn't know that I would ever

get into this world … now, everyone wants to be there'. It is telling that the world of fashion, so distant to Pfeiffer as a young man, would not only come to embrace him as one of their own but would also co-opt his territory of image-making produced on the periphery as its own.

When shooting his first photobook, the now cult, out-of-print *Walter Pfeiffer, 1970–1980* (the cover of which features a Ken doll with his hand in his shorts) (pp. 128–35), Pfeiffer was told by his editor, Ammann, that he must publish the full extent of what he had captured, as the future might not be so permissive. It would be easy to argue, as the twenty-first century heralds a newfound visibility for queer visual culture, celebrated not just in museums and galleries but also within aspirational commercial imagery, that Ammann got this wrong. And yet, just like the subject matter that this aspect of photography tends to coalesce around – what Pfeiffer calls his 'beauties' – this visibility might yet be merely provisional, particularly as we enter today's new political landscape. Asked what propels him to photograph beauty, Pfeiffer replied: 'Because you do not know how fast she is fading.'

Alistair O'Neill

Adapted from an earlier version published as 'Elements of Style' in *Aperture*, 228 (Fall 2017)

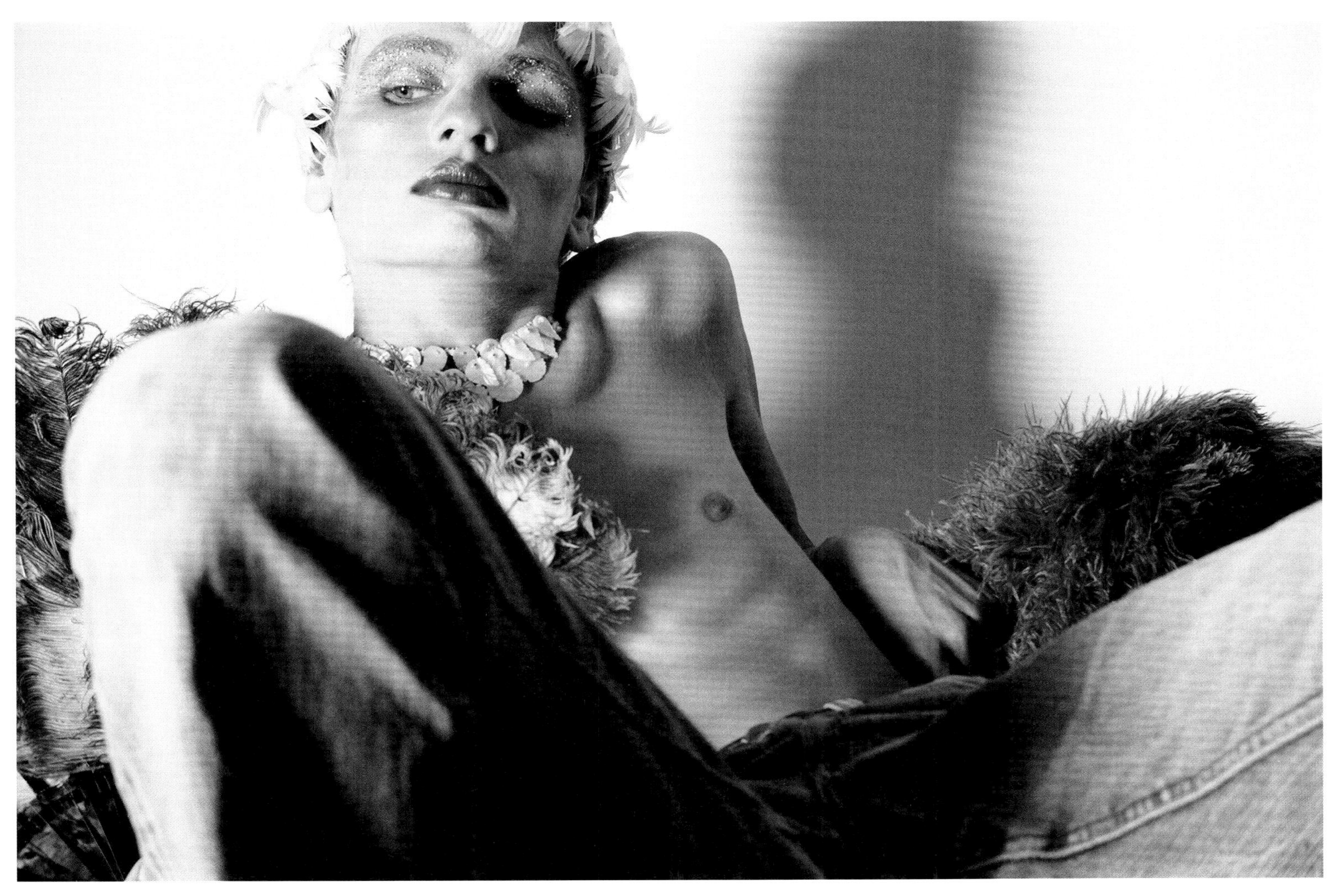

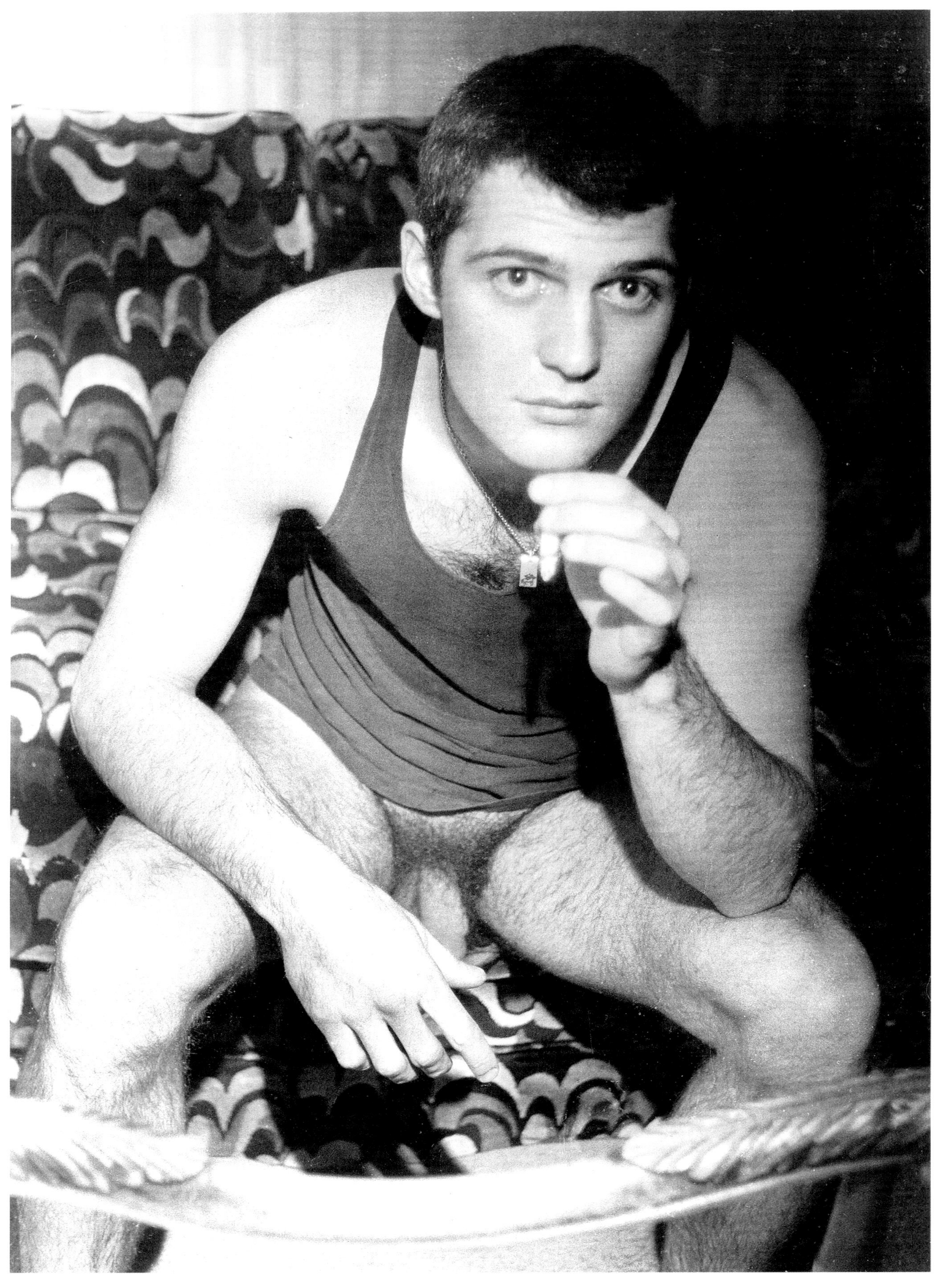

128 This page and opposite: from 'Walter Pfeiffer, 1970-1980'

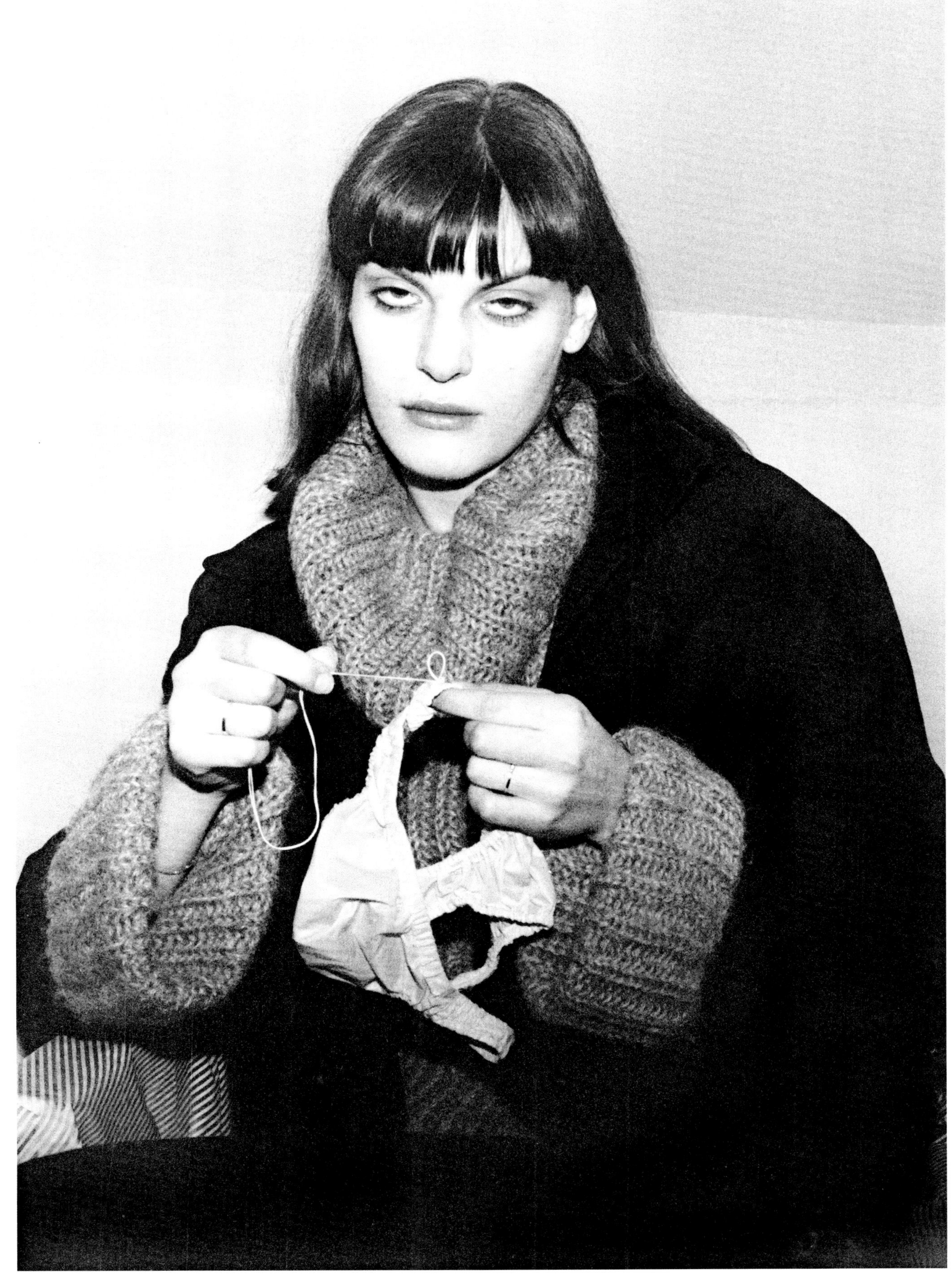

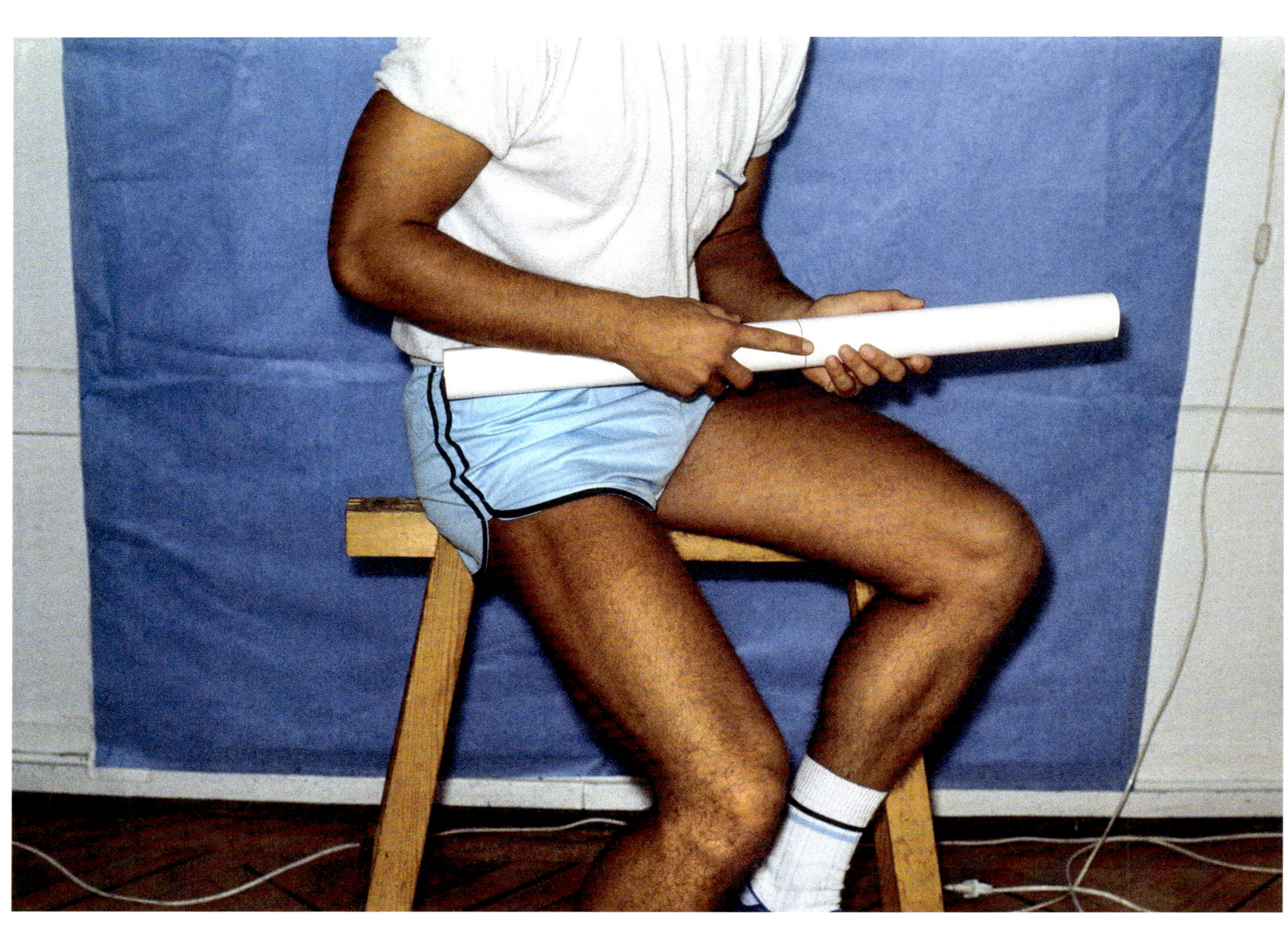

130 This page and opposite: from 'Walter Pfeiffer, 1970-1980'

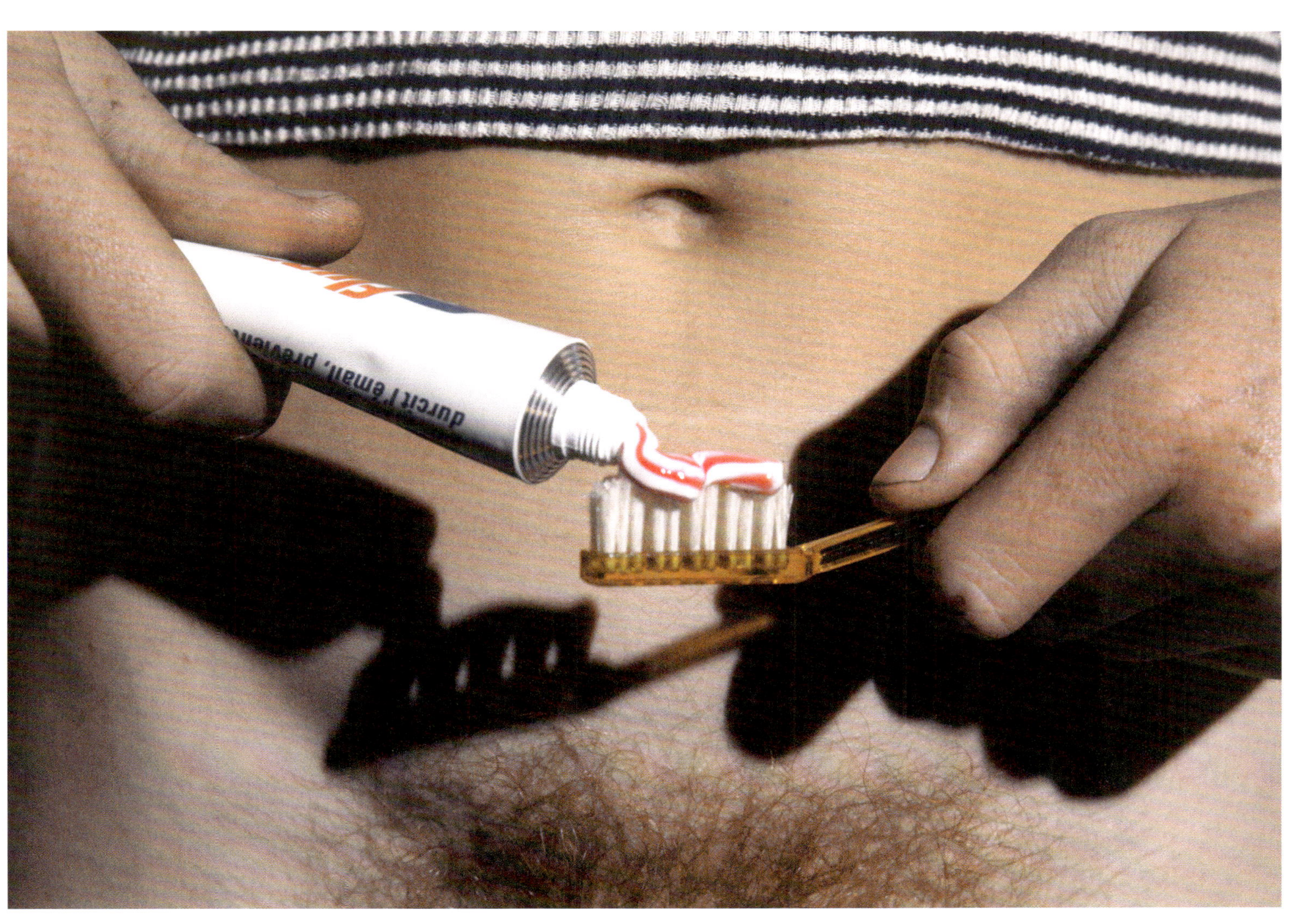

durcit l'émail, prévient

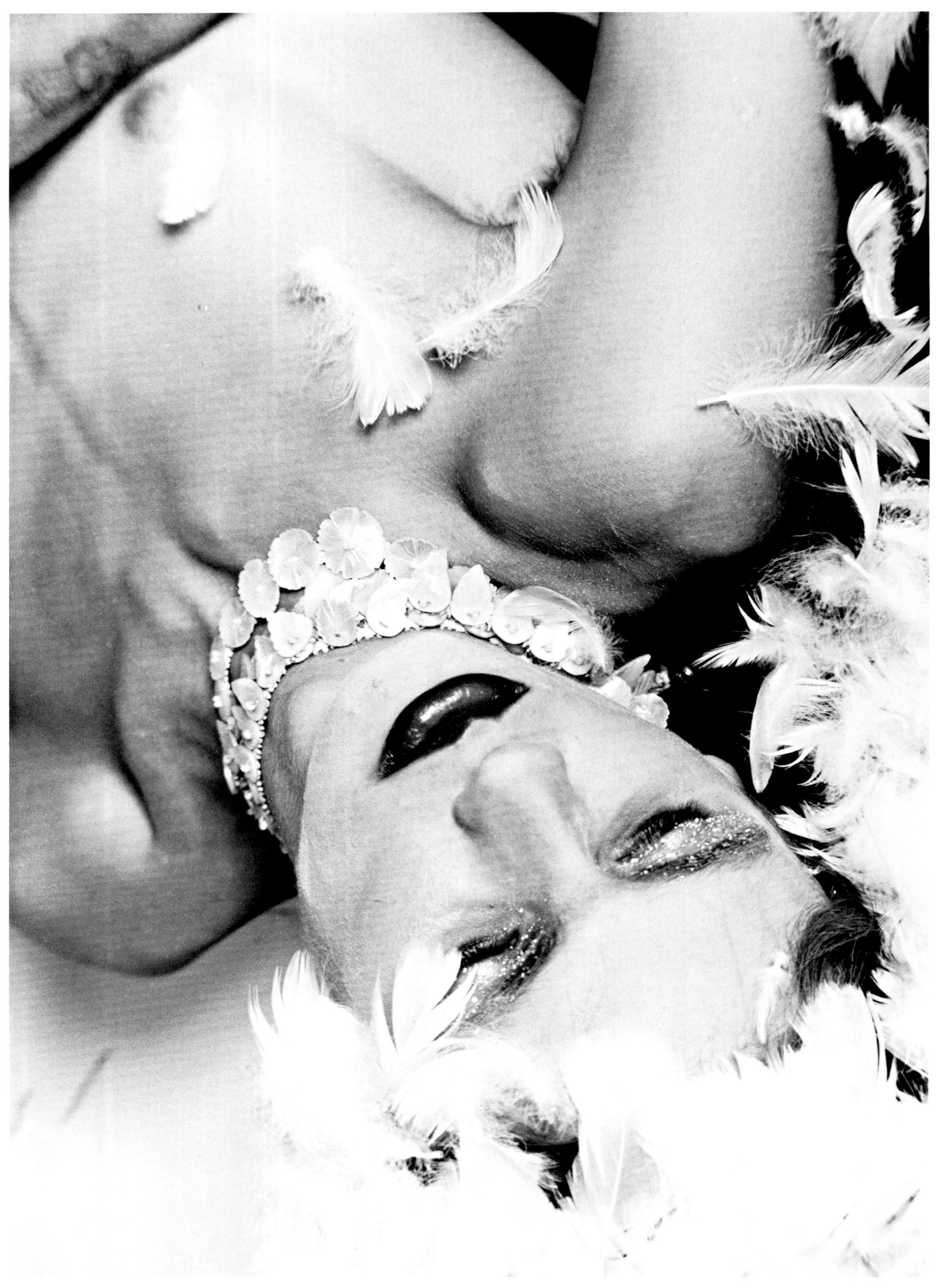

132 This page and opposite: From 'Walter Pfeiffer, 1970-1980'

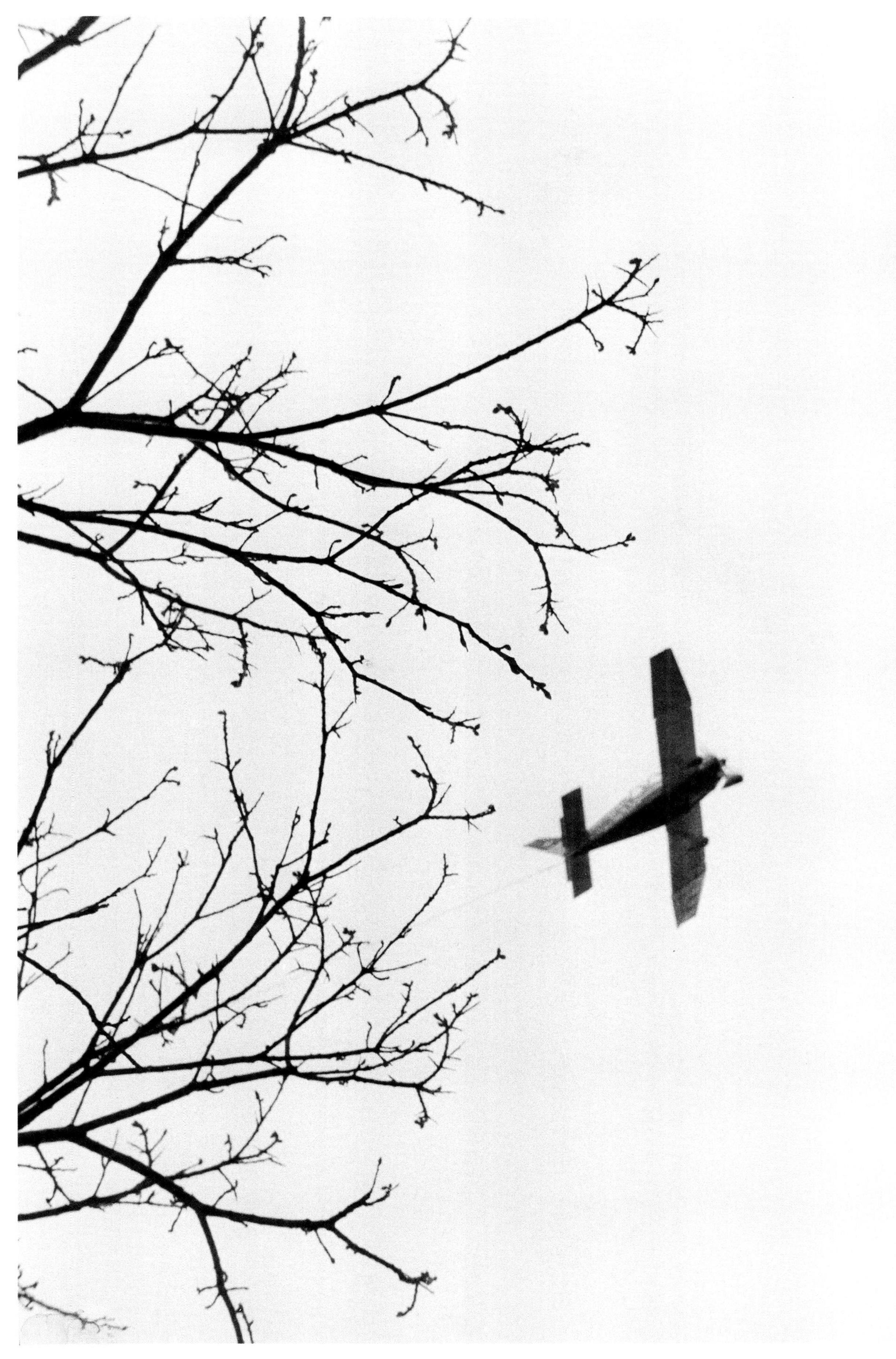

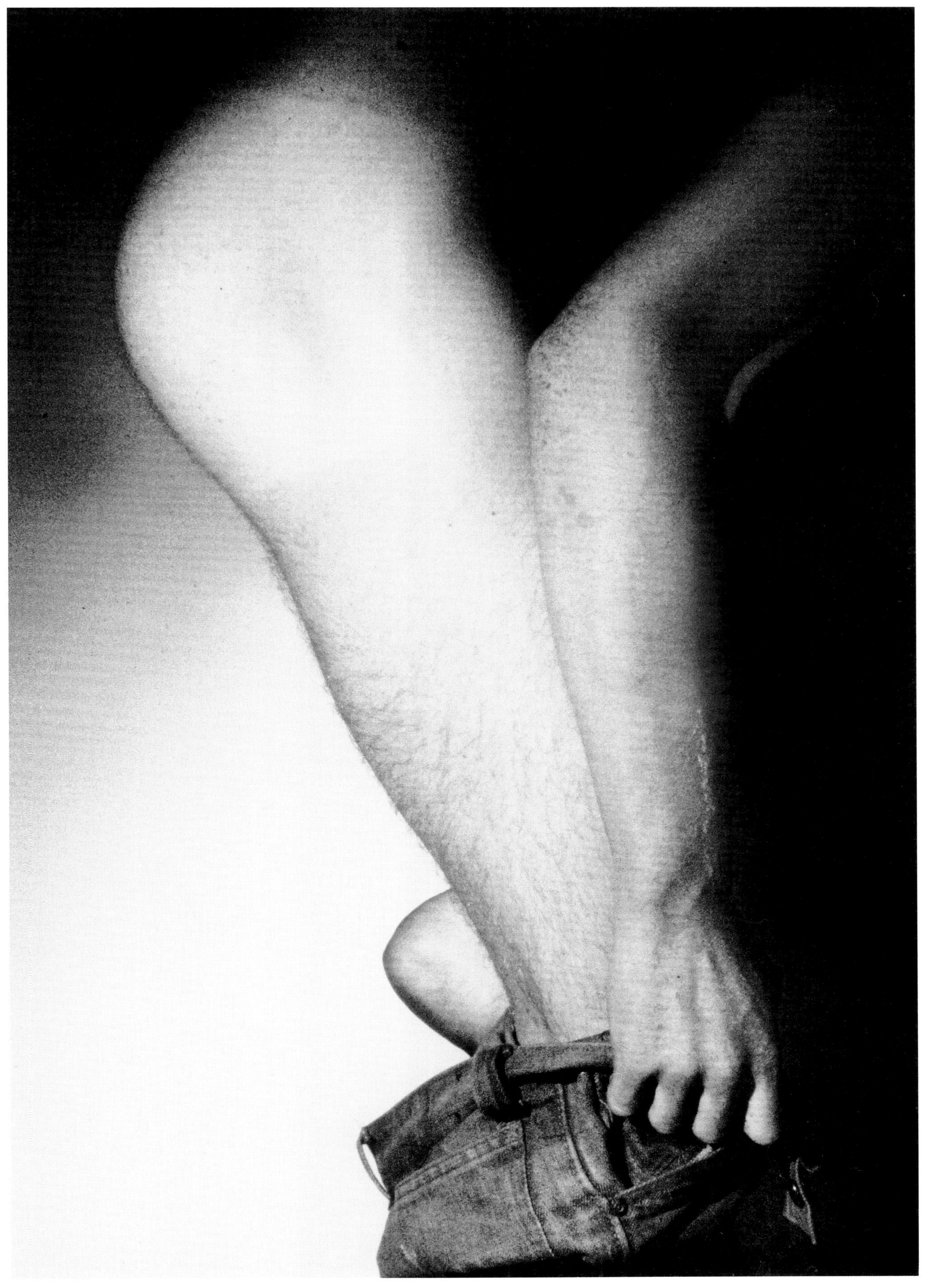

CHRIS

STEELE-PERKINS

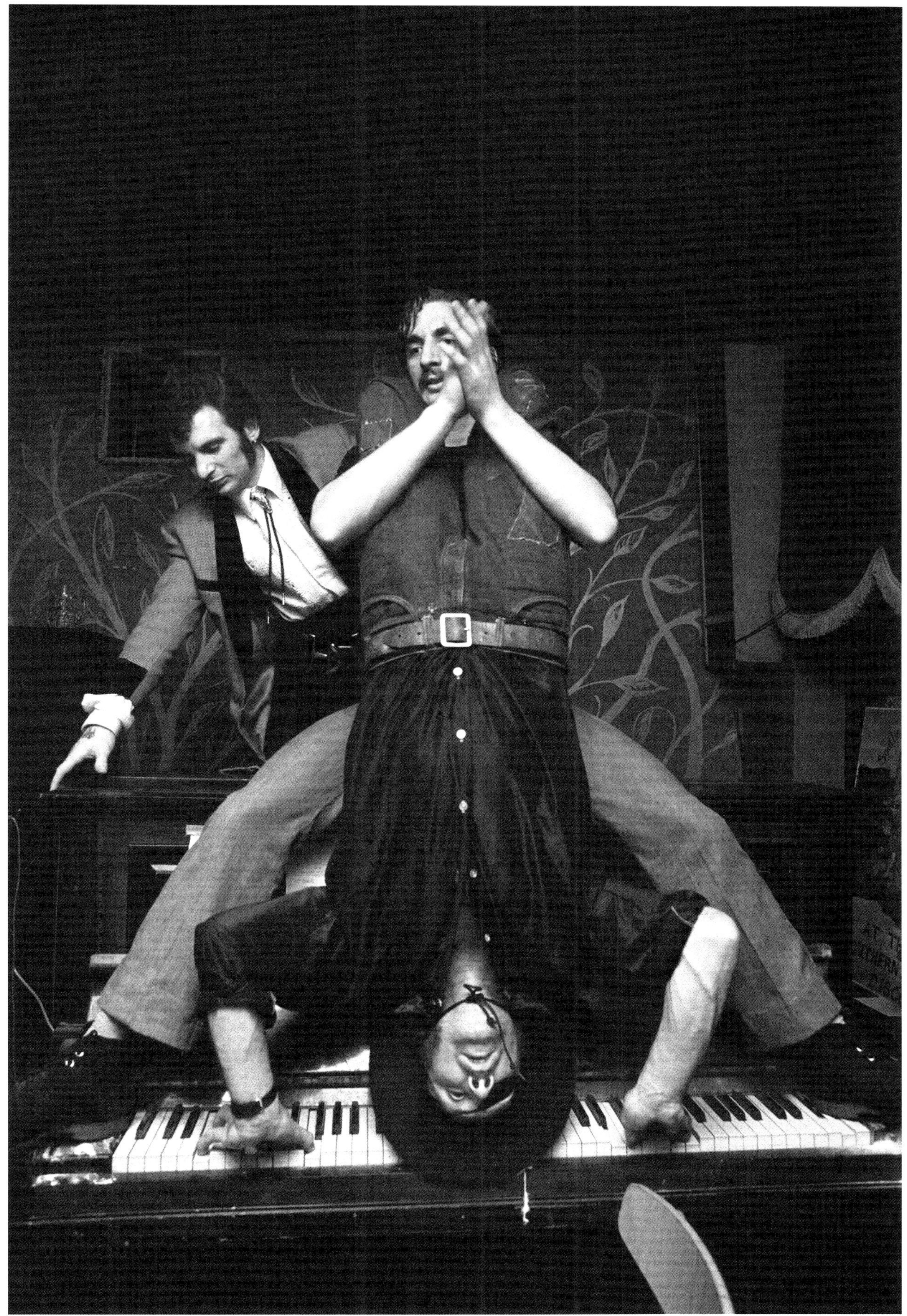

In one of the key images from *The Teds* by Chris Steele-Perkins (b. 1949, Myanmar) we are presented with the sight of a tattoo on a man's densely freckled back. Its cack-handed lettering reads: 'Don't follow me I'm lost to' – only for the sentence to be punctuated by an image of an archetypal Teddy boy, readily identifiable by the Brylcreemed quiff. While the photograph brings to bear just one facet of a style that denoted this complex and first youth subculture of the modern age, the act of conspicuous display that it documents seems a fitting symbolic record of the broader life and style memorialised by Steele-Perkins's camera.

If photography is 'the process of rendering observation self-conscious', as the influential and late, great John Berger noted in *Understanding a Photograph*,[1] then Chris Steele-Perkins has made comprehensible a message about the people, places and events that nurtured the scene, which he recorded with an impeccable, unerring sense of the zeitgeist. What began as a small commission from the now long-defunct *New Society* magazine to document, with the journalist Richard Smith, the second- and third-wave revival of the Teddy boys during the 1970s, grew and matured into a reverberating study of this youth movement over many years. It was first published as a monograph in 1979 by Travelling Light/Exit, then rereleased in 2002 by Dewi Lewis before a revised edition was again issued by that same publisher in 2016. It is now considered a masterpiece of British social documentary photography.

Against the backdrop of post-war gloom in the 1950s, the Teddy boys emerged in front of the eyes of Steele-Perkins, who, then still an impressionable child, looked on with wonder and excitement at the fashion, music culture and swagger. Conversely, his father would rail against these groups of youths, for they represented rebellion – a border of resistance against the constraints and expectations of their parents – and burned clothes that Steele-Perkins, inspired by such trends, had bought, even threatening to turn him over to them if he didn't behave himself. Suffice to say the concept of the 'teenager' was born, and so too was this indefatigable working-class youth culture, partly adopting and adapting the sartorial signatures of Edwardian dandies (and shortening the name to 'Teds'). First among its

features were the three-quarter-length drape jackets, in dark shades and often made of velvet and cut with trim collars and pocket flaps. They were accompanied by high-waisted drainpipe trousers, often revealing the socks, accessorised with a skinny tie held together with a medallion – cross-bones, skulls, eagles, dollar signs and other American iconography – and the outfit completed with either winklepickers or crêpe-soled shoes usually made from suede, known as brothel creepers or beetle crushers, as the footwear of choice.

'The gear: it's smart; it's great stuff; it's much smarter than flared gear. The hair: it's tidy; it's not long and straggly. You walk down the street and you get all the old people – the original people who was there in the fifties – looking at you and saying, "Ah, look there's Teddy Boys". You get great screws from people. You get people looking at you as if you were really brilliant like, as if you were really great,' a Ted who spoke to Richard Smith is quoted as saying in the book.[2]

With their eclectic lineage and rock 'n' roll antics, the Teddy boys were keen to be photographed, since appearances were everything and the capture served only to enrich their self-perception of their image. Bricklayers or butcher boys suddenly became transmogrified through dress into a 'somebody', to be feared or exalted. Such spectacle, such to-be-looked-at-ness, offered a vision both actual and artificial, something that can only be considered an excess, producing a 'propensity to peacock', as Steele-Perkins puts it.[3] The challenge, then, was to balance genuinely candid moments with more staged scenes in which the Teddy boys overtly posed for the photographer.

Steele-Perkins was present at dance halls, houses, pubs and seaside promenades, bearing witness to both public displays of tomfoolery and behind-the-scenes episodes, affording him a position of photographic spokesman, whether as insider or outsider. Rules and codes, behaviour and interaction are seen through a continuum of lived events, sequences of life on the fringes; ageing Teds, young Teds, drunk Teds, dancing Teds, smoking Teds, sneering Teds, snogging Teds, tongue-tied Teds, rockabilly Teds, jiving Teds, fighting Teds, knife-wielding Teds, urinating Teds. Over the course of taking these photographs,

Steele-Perkins identified some of the riotous behaviour and proud eccentricity at the heart of these tribes, largely underpinned by overt male sexuality. Diehard members bred animosity towards spin-offs or other youth cults, and a reputation of violence developed that led them to be blamed for many of society's ills. Chronicles of lives going as fast as possible, in which Steele-Perkins immerses himself, forms the bulk of the work, yet care is also given to photographing his subjects from the front, singularly, and then in pairs or threes, with no picturesque effects; instead the images, and even the gestures he captures, seem frozen. There is a strong atmosphere of confrontation, of a literal face-to-face encounter – emphasised by the lack of background detail or any *mise en scène* – that focuses intently on the photographed subjects themselves. Moving between the two approaches, Steele-Perkins always seems to find the right distance.

In fact, Steele-Perkins's sustained attention to this strain of existence – one that performed its identity so readily for the camera – actually moves beyond the illusion of protection and belonging that style gives, to provide anthropological insight and speak volumes about the society from which this multifaceted subculture emerged. As such, what *The Teds* offers – in part through the further contextualisation given by Smith's accompanying text vignettes – is a subjective perspective, insofar as the body of work both mythologises this lifestyle and at times peels back the layers of its construction, with respect, without judging.

It also serves as a salute to the fact that the Teddy boys remain the most influential movement throughout the history of youth culture – paving the way for the mods, rockers, punks, New Romantics, Northern Soulers, ravers and beyond – one that Steele-Perkins has confronted in terms of its identity and status within the larger culture of Englishness, grounding the work in a reality that is fast-living, maligned, nostalgic and superseded.

Tim Clark

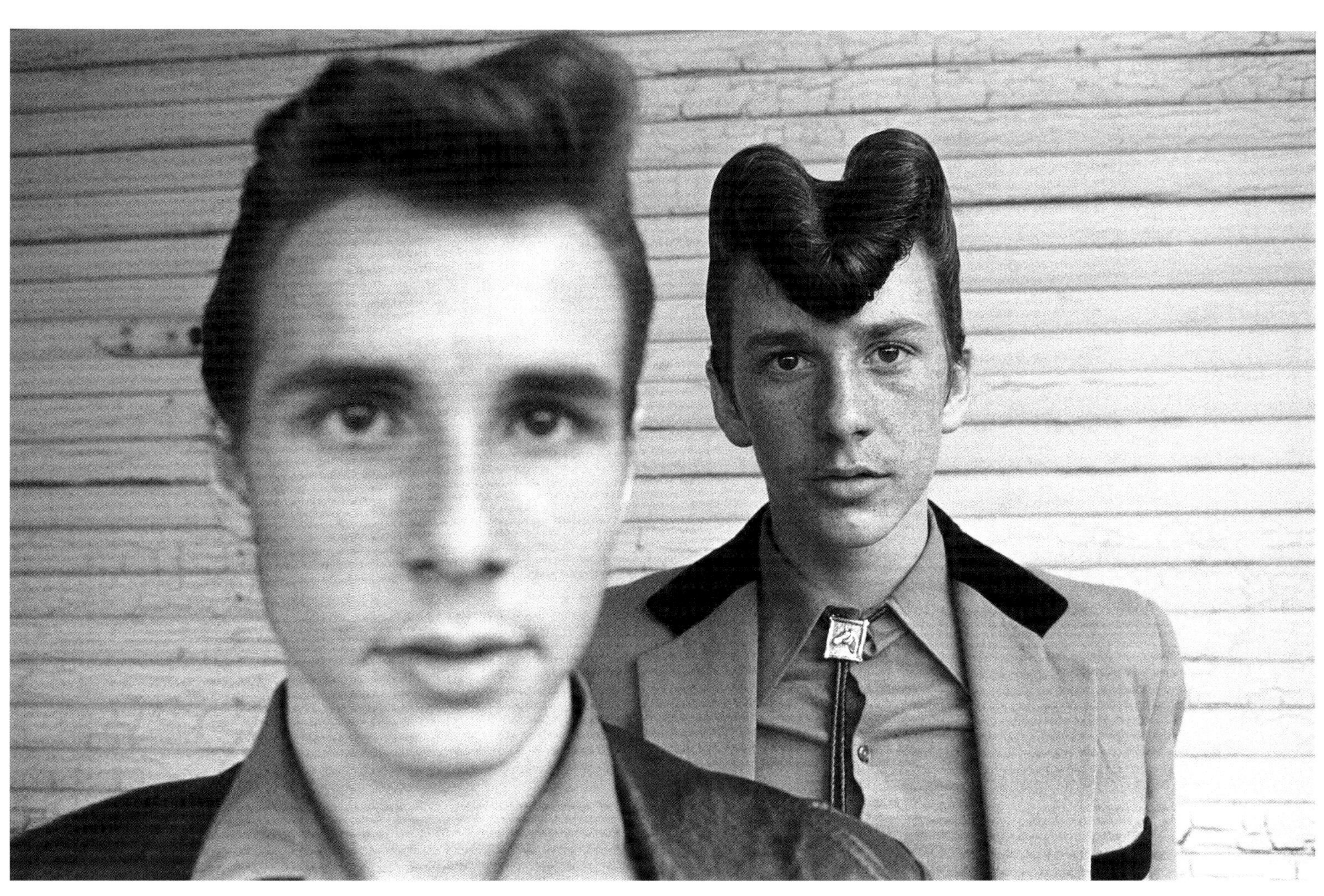

From 'The Teds', *Two Teds at Southend*, 1976   139

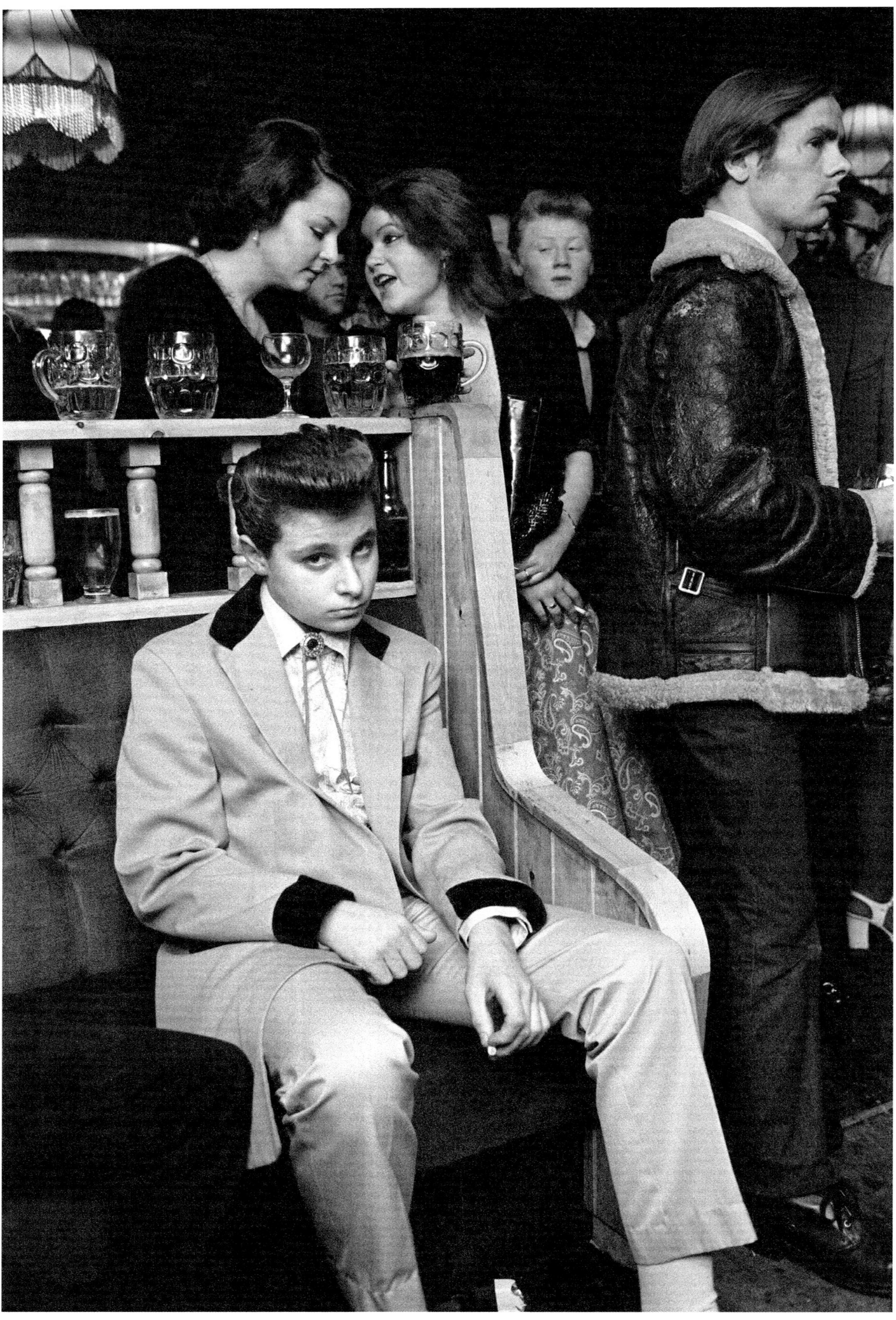

140 From 'The Teds', *The Adam and Eve*, Hackney, London, 1976

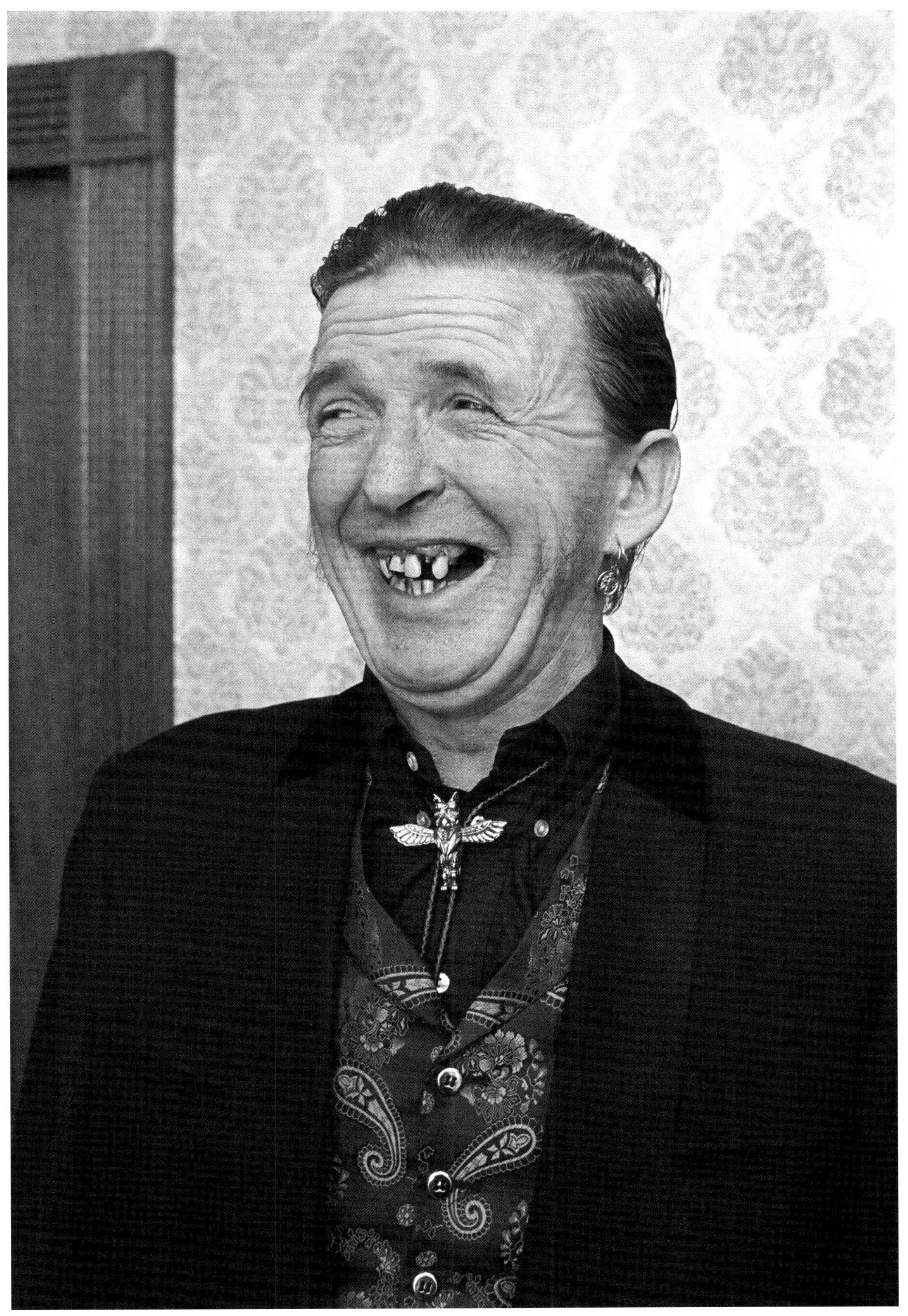

From 'The Teds', *Stcn the Man*, 1976

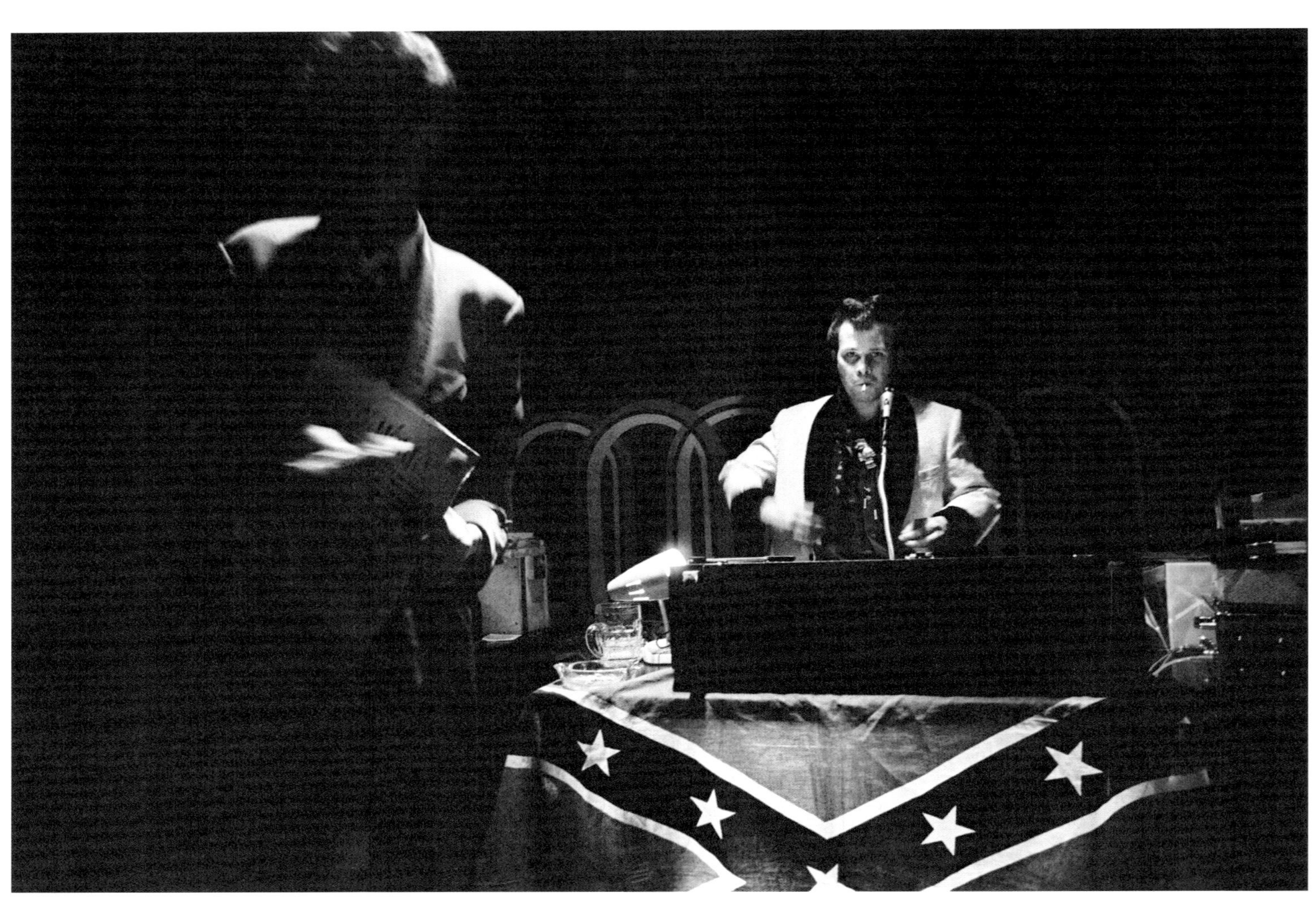

142 From 'The Teds', *Fifties Flash*, 1976

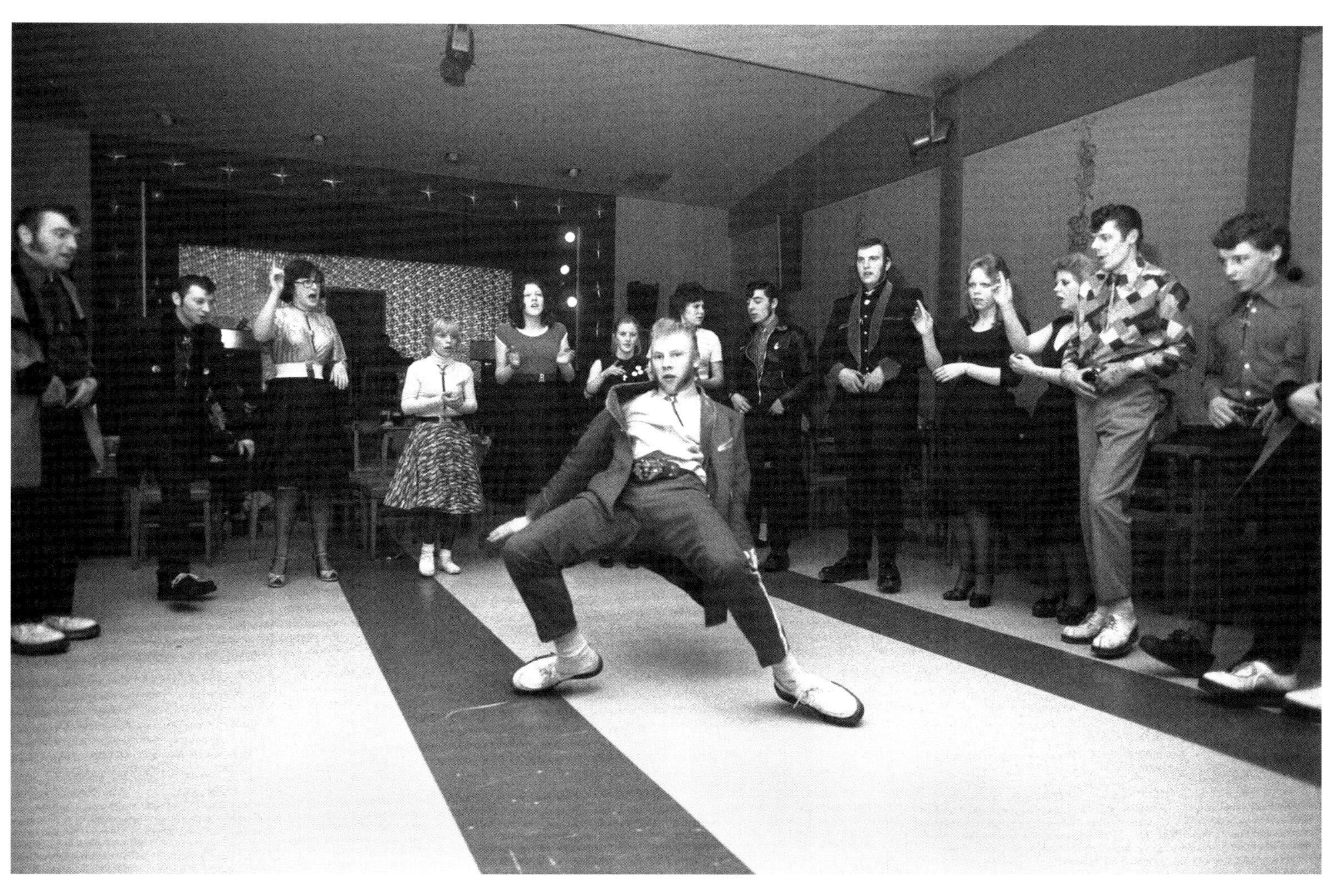

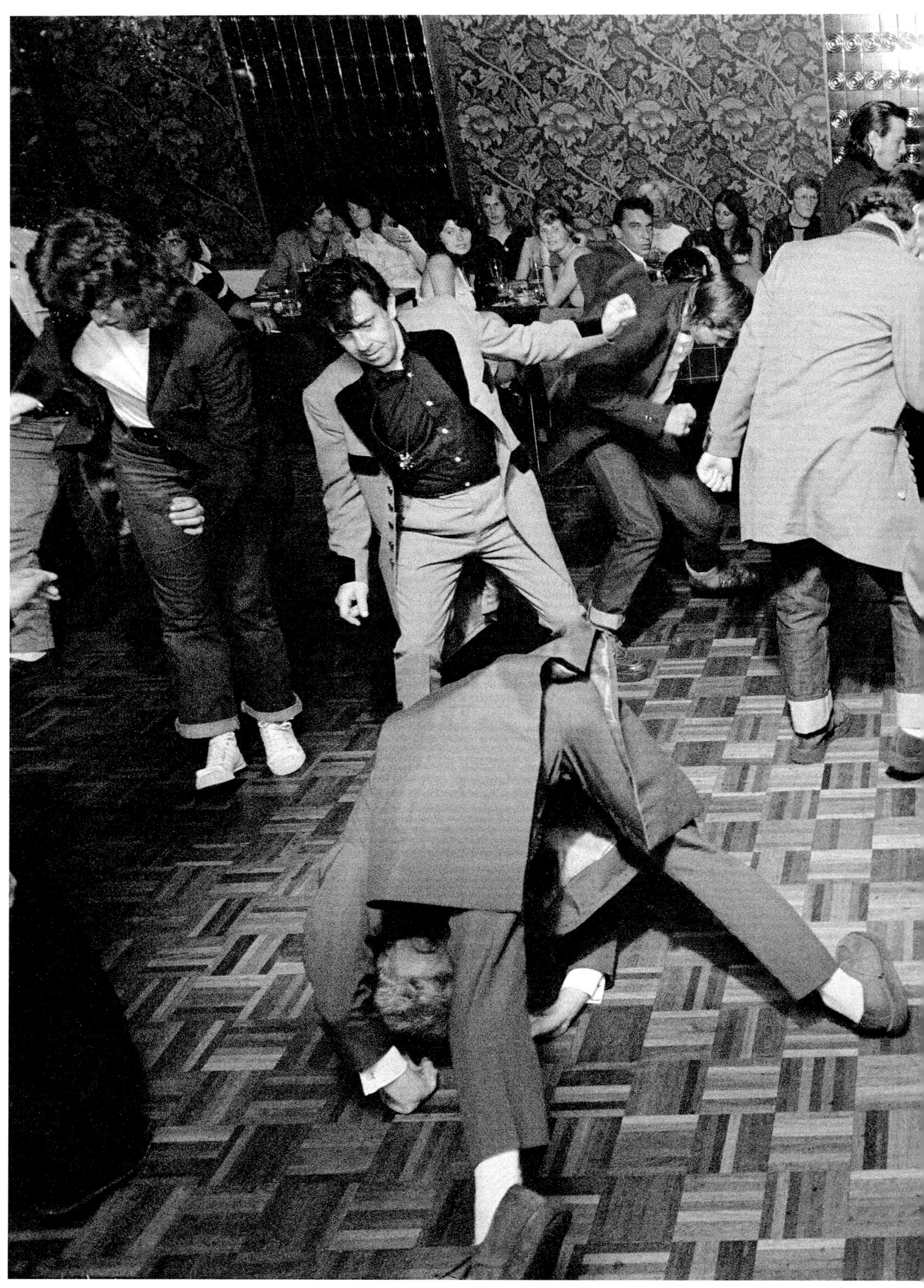

144 From 'The Teds', Bradford, 1976

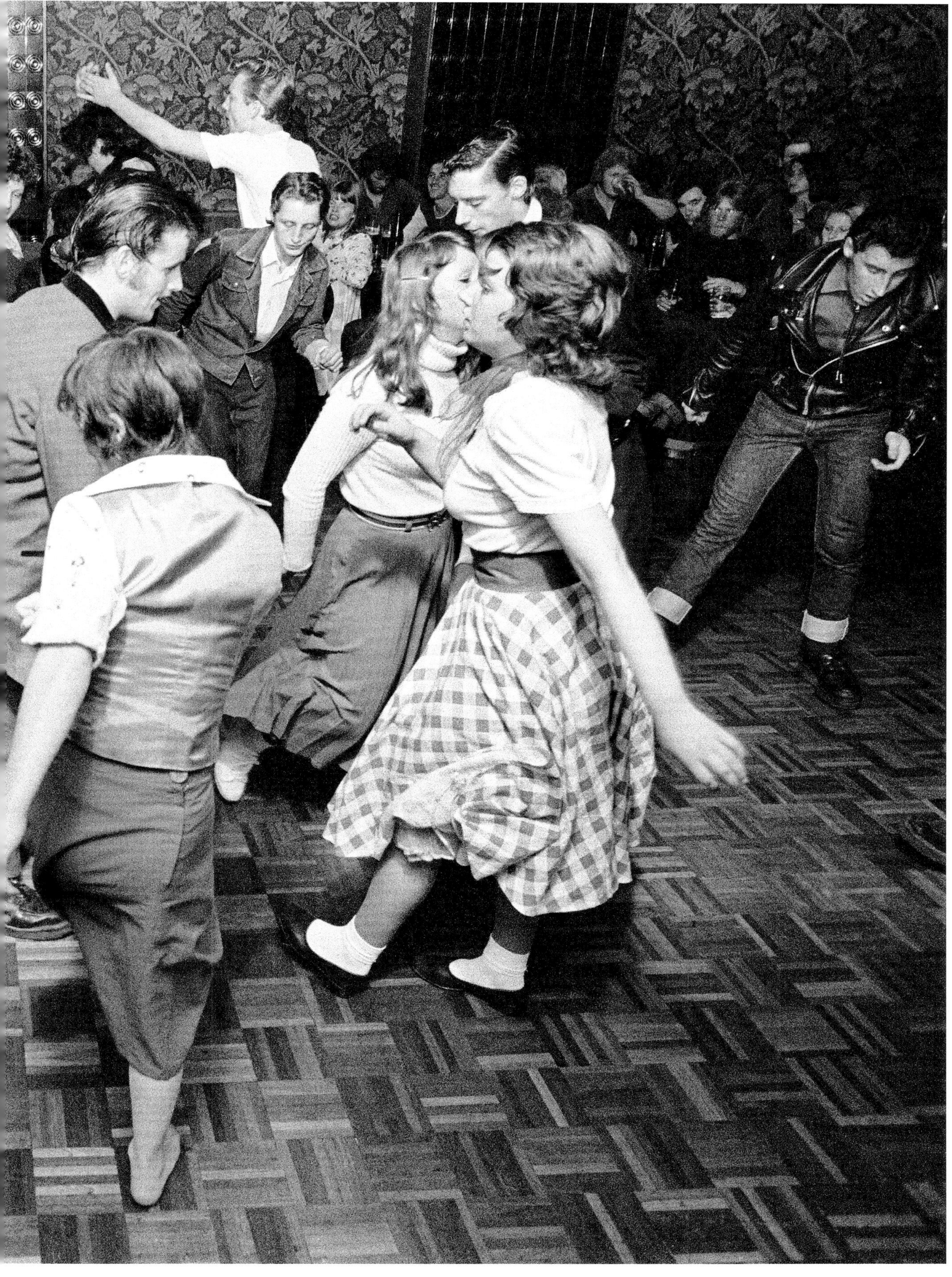

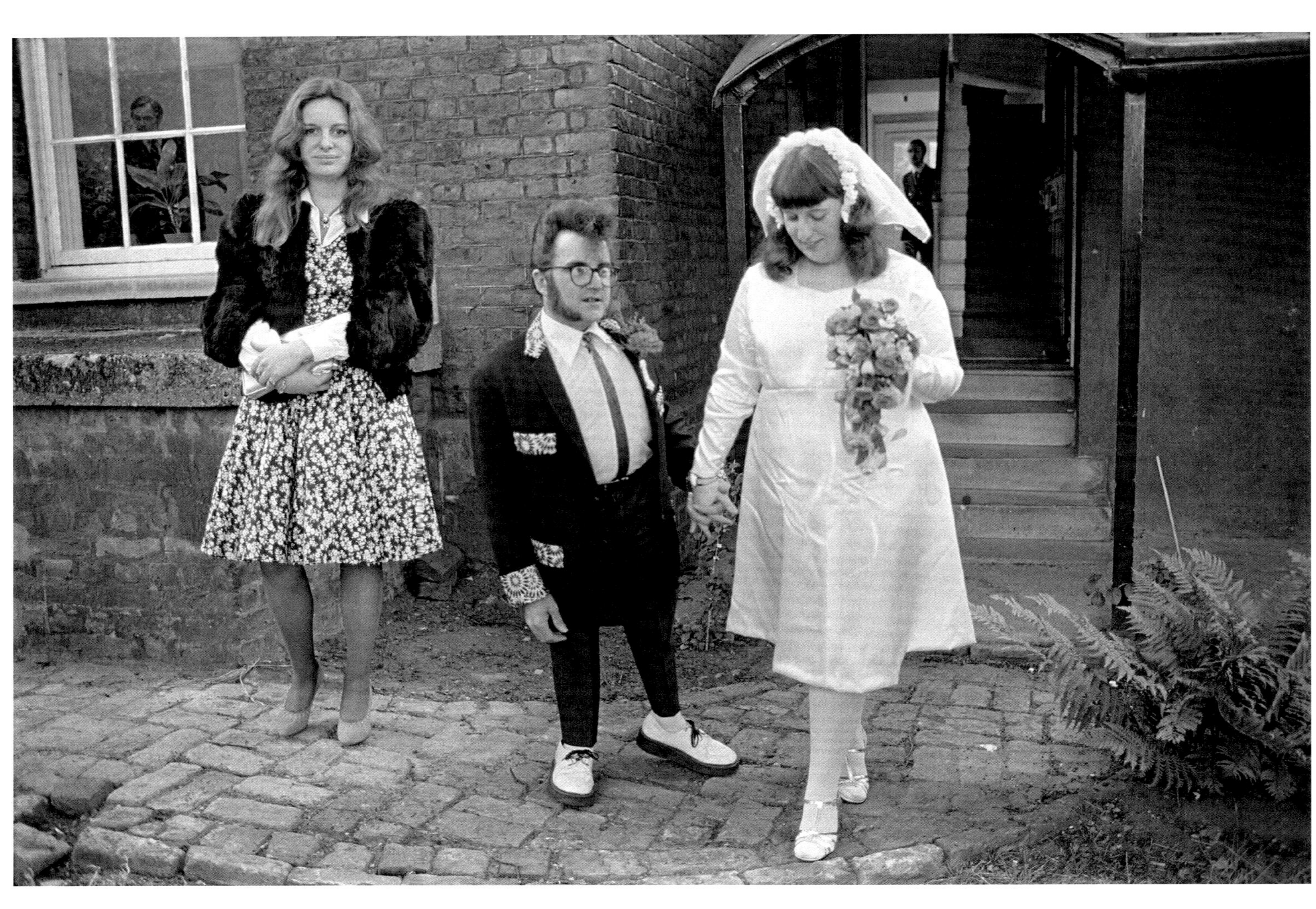

146 From 'The Teds', *Tongue Tied Danny's Wedding*, 1976

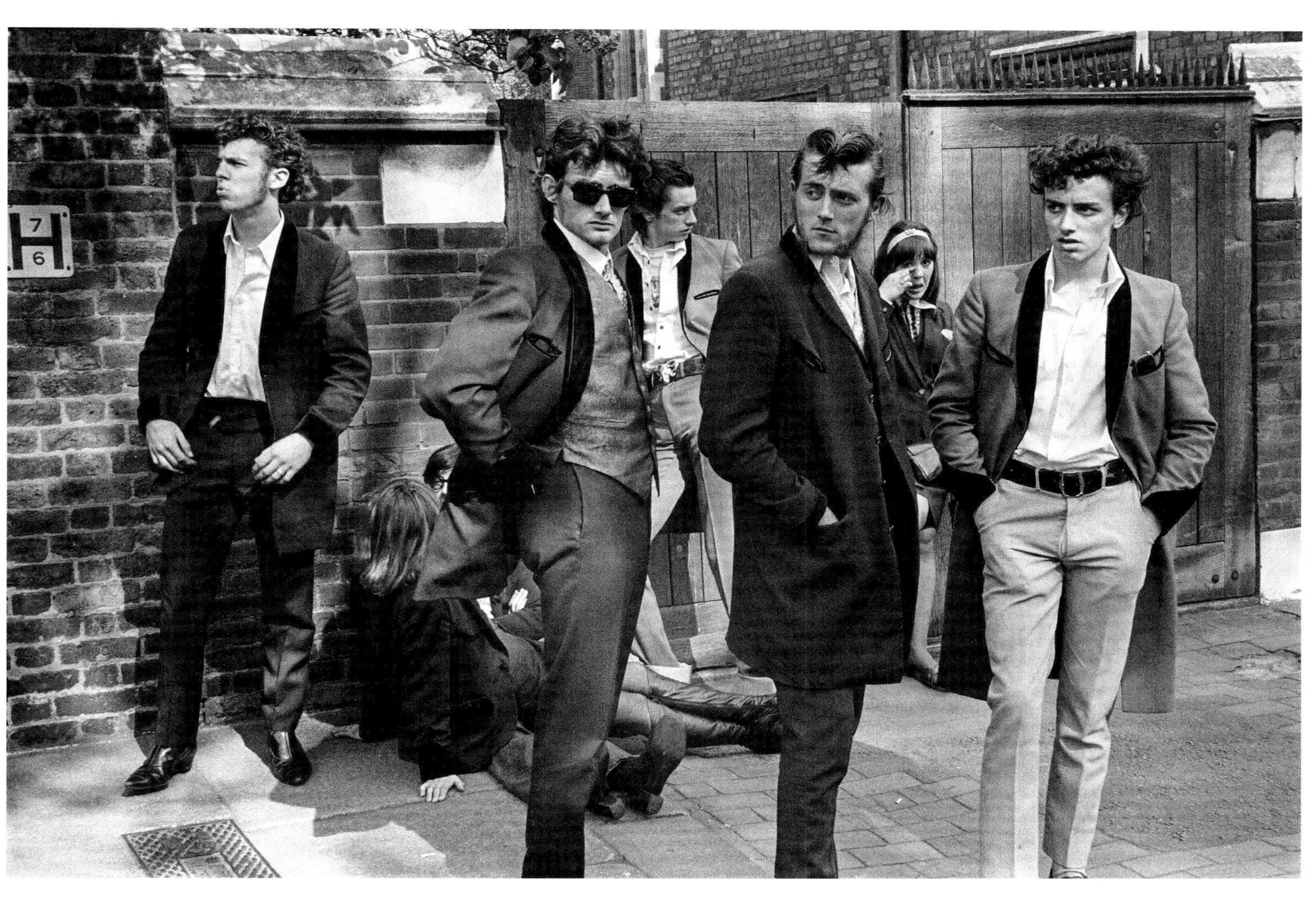

From 'The Teds', London, 1976

PHILIPPE

CHANCEL

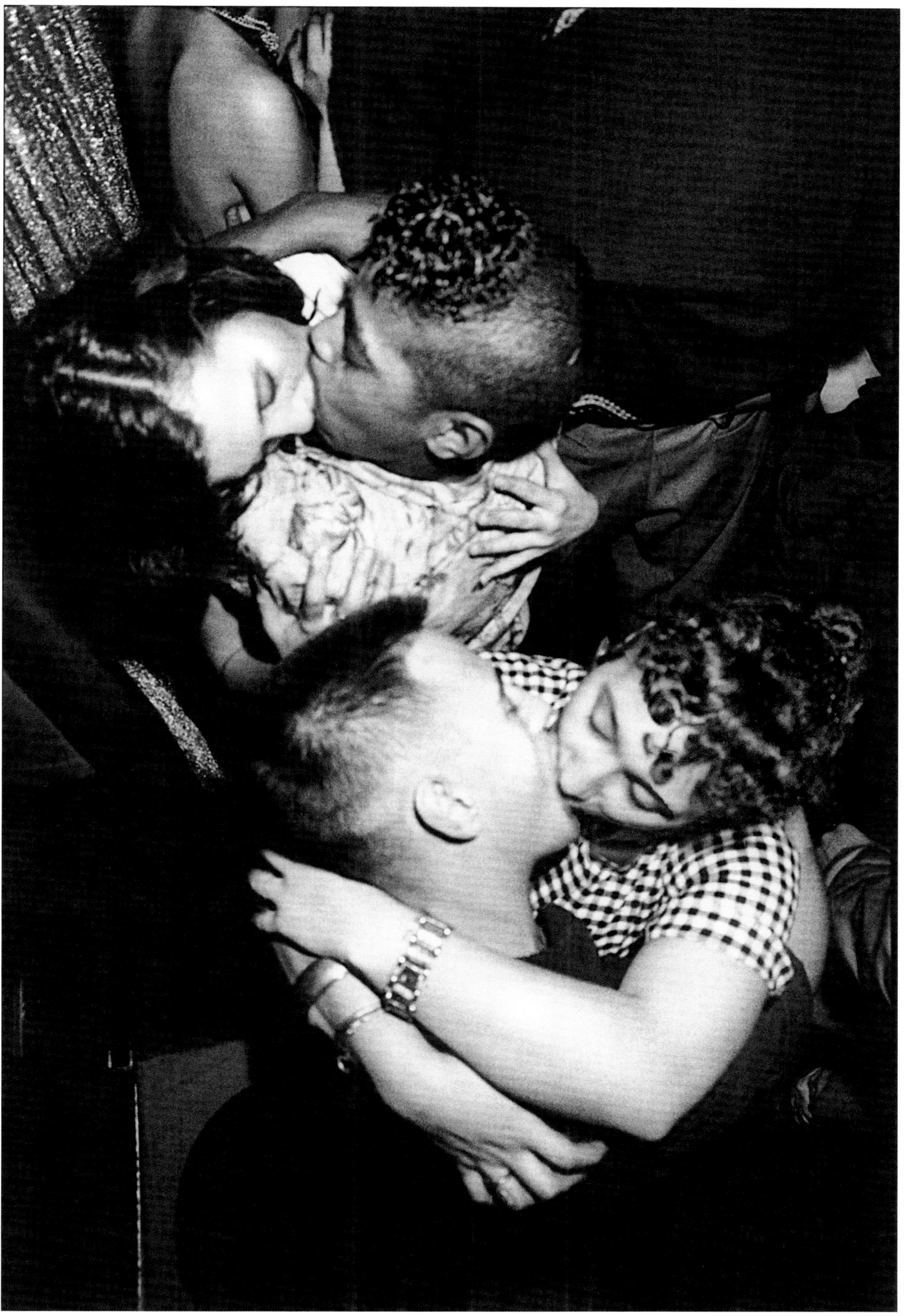

At first glance, Phillipe Chancel's (b. 1959, France) images of young urban revellers look curiously out of time, more redolent of Memphis, Tennessee, in the 1950s than Paris in the 1980s. The clothes, hairstyles and tattoos all speak of another youth cultural era: the post-war decade in which American and European teenagers emerged for the first time as a social and cultural phenomenon with their own tastes, attitudes and style.

In America, rockabilly music, a hybrid of white rural country and western and black rhythm and blues, was the first defining outburst of the certain kind of unfettered, inchoate youthful energy that would characterise all the 'rebel' music to follow, from the primitive thrust of countless 1960s garage bands to the amphetamine momentum of punk in the late 1970s. In his book *Country: The Twisted Roots of Rock 'n' Roll* (1977) the American author Nick Tosches writes: 'What made rockabilly such a drastically new music was its spirit, a thing that bordered on mania.'[1]

That spirit, preserved on original vinyl records from the time, has lived on in the devotion of several ensuing generations of youthful devotees, self-styled rockabilly rebels whose boredom with, and disaffection from, the mainstream has been channelled into a kind of retro-rebellion built on an obsessive attention to image and style. In the early 1980s, following the seismic subcultural rupture that was punk, French youth, like their counterparts in Britain, began rifling the subcultural past for inspiration. A new wave of rockabilly fans sprang up around groups like Stray Cats and The Meteors. Their followers were younger and more style-conscious than the more slavishly retro Teddy boys, whose appearance – drape coats, tight jeans, brothel creeper shoes – seemed so old-fashioned in the 1980s as to be anachronistic. (The British photographer Chris Steele-Perkins captured one of the last manifestations of Teddy boy culture in his photo-book *The Teds*, published in 1979 (pp. 136–47)).

In early 1980s Paris it was this vibrant, but essentially nostalgic, youth cultural milieu that drew the attention of several French photographers, including Gil Rigoulet, Gilles Elie Cohen and Philippe Chancel. 'Like them, I am 20 years old,' Chancel later wrote of his discovery of two Parisian gangs, the Vikings and the Panthers, 'The spirit of the time is one of the tribes, the style.'[2]

Unlike many gangs in Paris at the time whose members espoused ultra-right-wing views and racist attitudes, these gangs were made up of members from multiracial backgrounds (the Vikings) or predominantly first- and second-generation West Indians (the Panthers). They were outsiders not only in defiance of the mainstream, but within a predominantly reactionary subculture. Indeed, the main reason for the Panthers' existence was to combat the many ultra-right street gangs that had formed in Paris during the late 1970s. Named in homage to the 1960s American revolutionary organisation the Black Panthers, they were in the vanguard of what would later become a wider network of left-wing gangs nicknamed 'Antifa' and *chasseurs de skins* (skinhead hunters). Their style was borrowed from the US military – vintage Air Force flight jackets and caps – and many of them were skilled in martial arts.

The Vikings were a less consciously political gang made up of young kids from various ethnic backgrounds – 'black, blanc, beur' ('black, white, Arab', *beur* meaning French of North African origin), as Chancel would later put it, referring to the popular French phrase used in the 1900s to describe the country's multi-ethnic culture.[3] As if in acknowledgement of their difference, they had named themselves after the American group The Del-Vikings, who were the first rock 'n' roll vocal group of the 1950s to include both black and white musicians. Revealingly, the Vikings referred to themselves as 'cats' (as in the 1950s American jazz slang term 'cool cat') and were in thrall to an idealised version of 1950s American youth culture: extravagant retro outfits, vintage cars, dance crazes from the early days of rock 'n' roll – as immortalised in George Lucas's classic retro coming-of-age film *American Graffiti* (1973).

In Chancel's photographs, it is the style, the music and the youthful energy of this subcultural moment that predominates. The girls are dressed up in faux furs, headscarves, flared dresses, their piled-up hair held in place with bright plastic hairpins. The boys wear Hawaiian shirts, baggy pleated trousers and trainers (sneakers), their hair sculpted into quiffs. Though the Vikings and the Panthers socialised together, drinking and partying at the same clubs, the latter look older, more street-smart, less eager to please Chancel's camera.

Amid the wild partying there are more ominous images: a lad brandishing a wooden club; a shotgun in the boot of a car (p. 153); baseball bats being hidden in kit bags. Like all street gangs, the Vikings and the Panthers had marked out their own turf, which spread out from Parc de la Villette, then a wasteland at the northeastern edge of the city awaiting redevelopment, to the Gare de l'Est in north-central Paris. The Vikings alone had around one hundred members in the early 1980s, and alongside the more combative Panthers they engaged in regular violent battles with other gangs in music venues and on the crowded alleyways of the sprawling flea market at Clignancourt. Their main rivals were the Teds and the Rebels, both of whom shared the same style and musical taste as the Vikings and the Panthers, but who sported Confederate flag patches on their jackets as an emblem of allegiance to the racist politics of the old American South.

All of these incidents took place against the turbulent political backdrop of early 1980s France, when the left-wing government was grappling with rising unemployment, which in turn fuelled the initial rise of a new kind of ultra-nationalism. In the French municipal elections of 1982, two centre-right parties formed alliances with the ultra-right Front National in a number of towns. In Paris, the Front National leader, Jean-Marie Le Pen, was elected to the local council in the 20th arrondissement with 11 per cent of the vote.

At a time when the immigrant population of France was becoming increasingly scapegoated as the cause of the country's social ills, the existence of the Vikings and Panthers could be viewed as a kind of street-level response to the hardening of attitudes in the French body politic and on the streets of the capital. At some point, though, their alliance of difference was fractured by the increasingly violent nature of their everyday existence. A bout of street fighting between the two gangs erupted in the streets of Montmartre in 1983, for reasons that remain unclear. 'I don't know why, [but] the gangs got into a violent fight, one evening, in

the Montmartre neighbourhood,' mused Gilles
Elie Cohen, another photographer who had also
immersed himself in the gangs' world at this
time. (In 2000 he made the documentary film
Rock contre la montre, about his time among the
gangs.) 'There were fewer and fewer meetings.
People would fall silent as I arrived. The scenes
of violence became more frequent. About 20
years later … many had died [a] violent death.'[4]

Chancel's fly-on-the-wall images of the Vikings
and the Panthers capture these disaffected
Paris youths at a brief moment when that
violence had yet to escalate into a kind of
inexorable self-destruction. In truth, though,
violence had always defined them as much as,
if not more than, the music they listened to and
the clothes they wore. In the end, it undid many
of them. These photographs evince a different
energy: the wild, rebellious exuberance of youth
expressed though the sartorial signifiers of
another time. Here, the original rebel yell that
defined 1950s rockabilly echoes across decades
and continents to express the same, essentially
adolescent, discontents, but in a radically
different socio-cultural context. In the process
of being appropriated by angry young Parisians
from various ethnic backgrounds, it shed its
white, southern American roots and was born
again as a complex expression of belonging
– to the gang, the tribe, the style – and not-
belonging: to the mainstream, the country,
the national(ist) identity. Its spirit somehow
endures, evading the deathly trappings of
nostalgia, its spirit still a thing that borders
on mania.

Sean O'Hagan

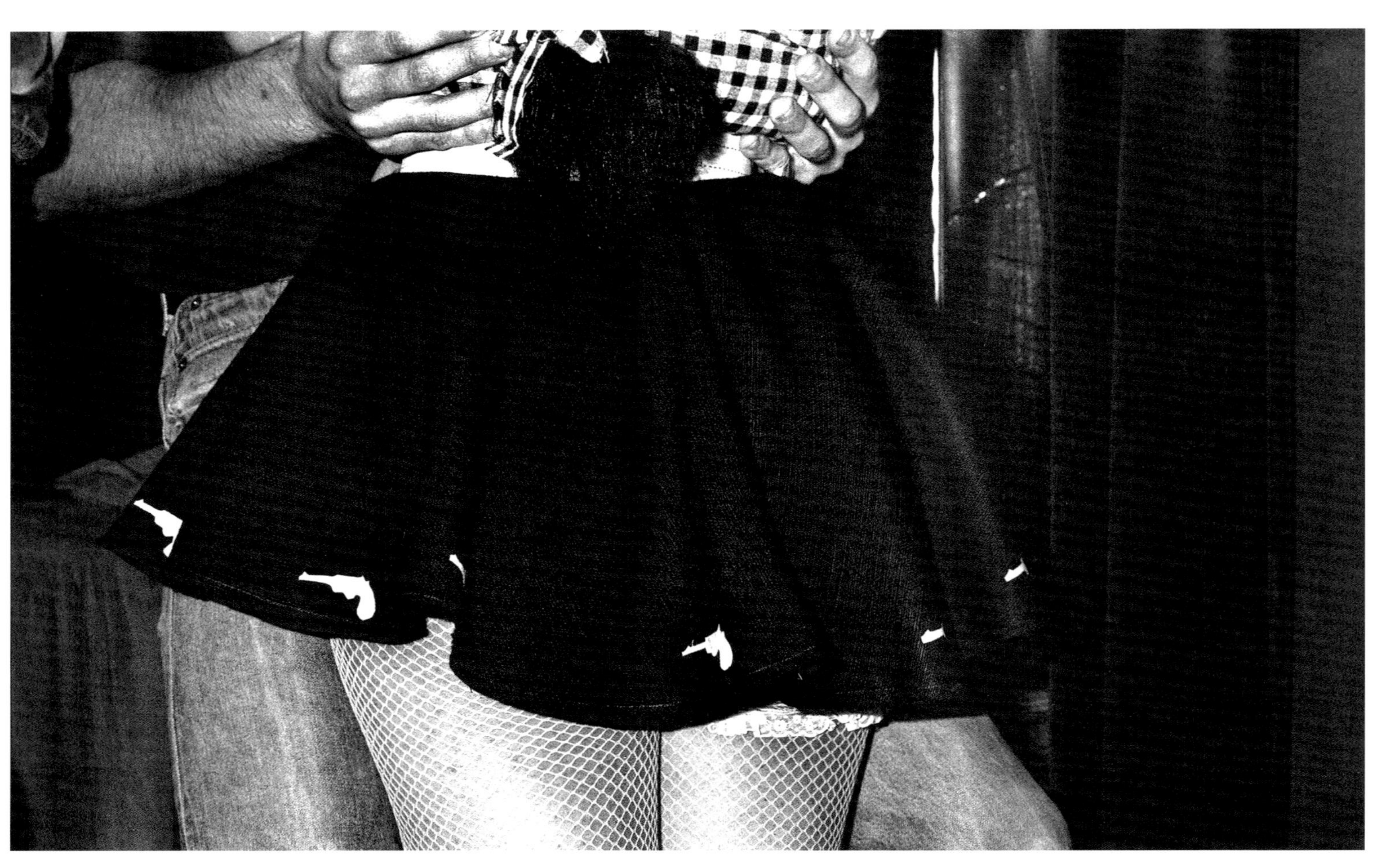

  This page and opposite: from 'Rebel's Paris 1982'

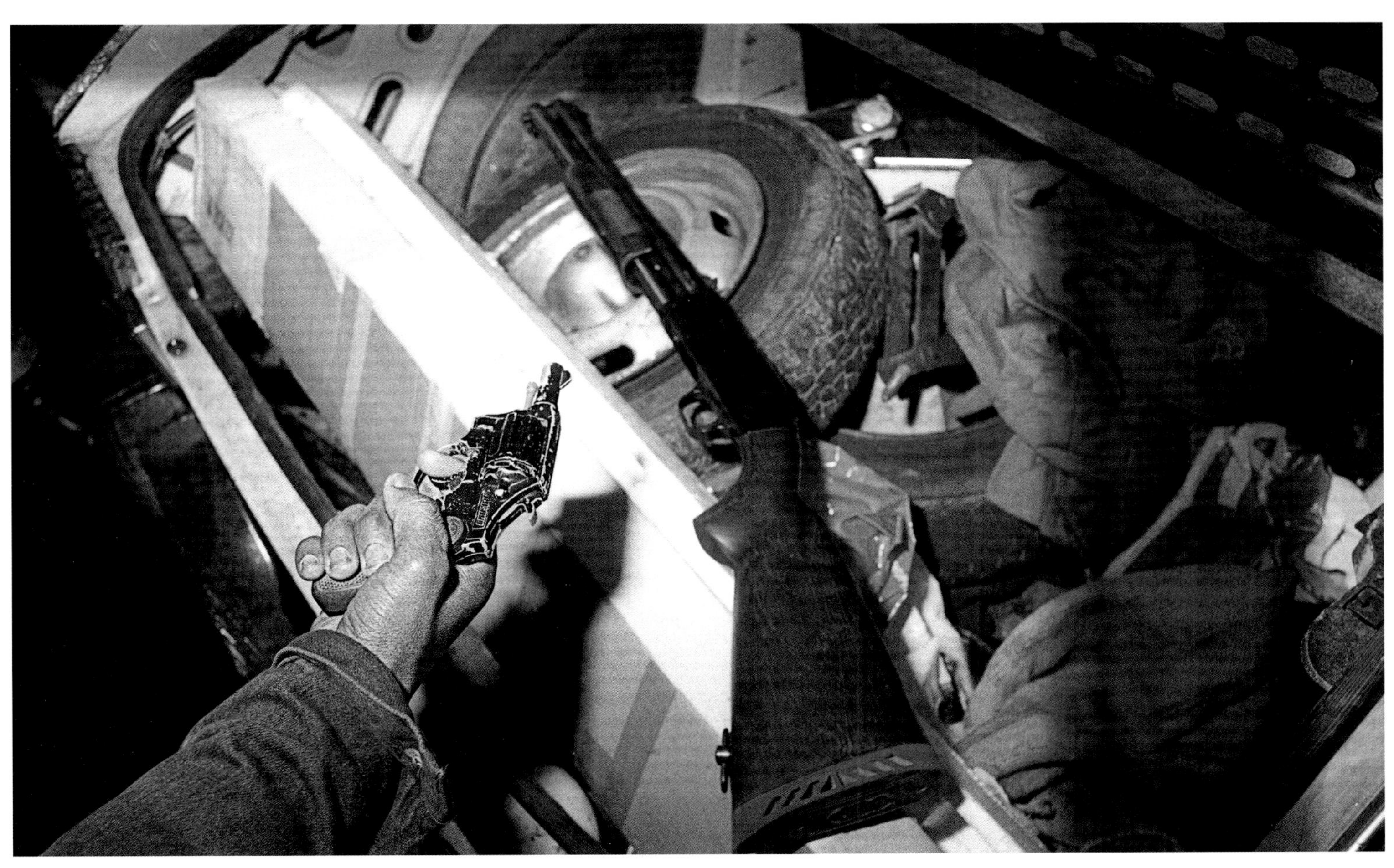

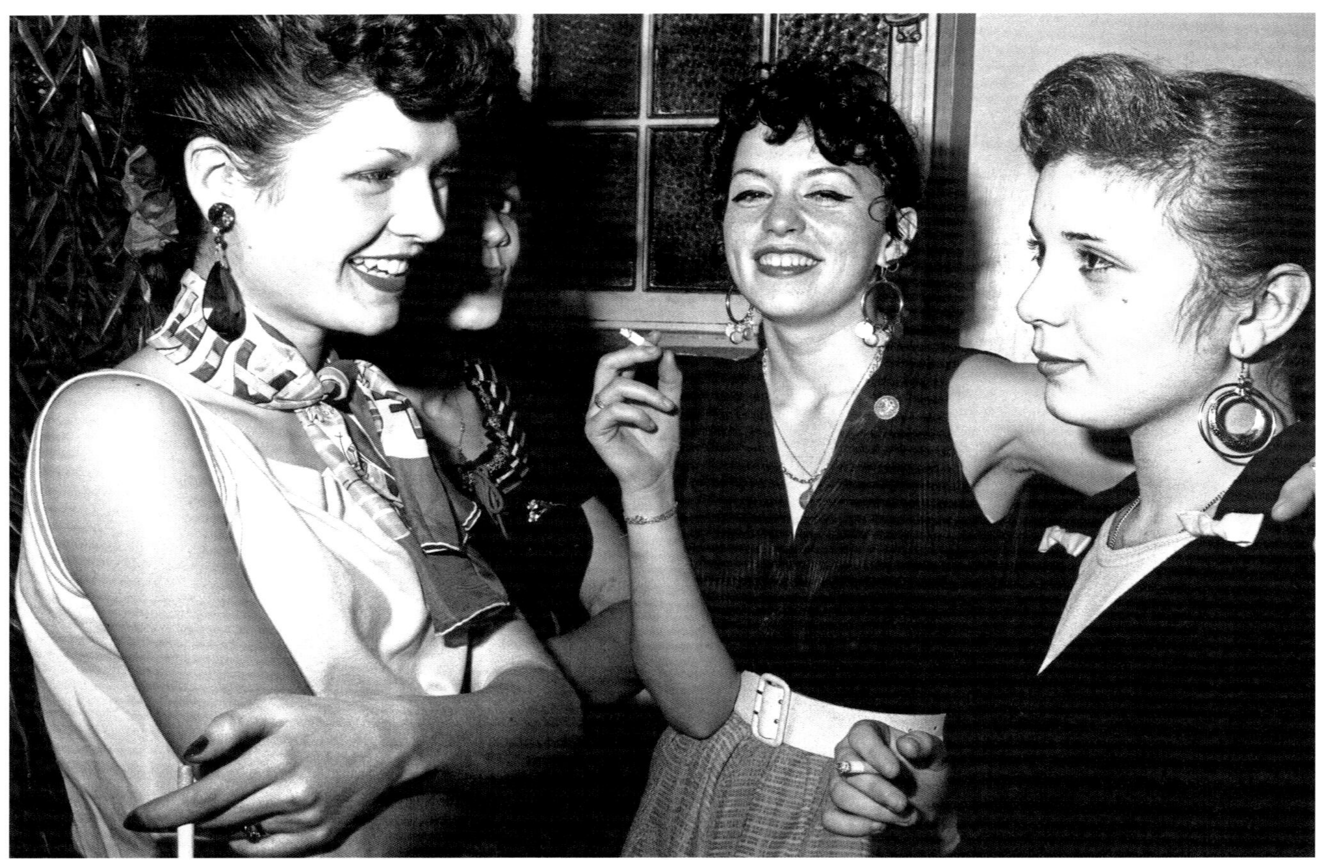

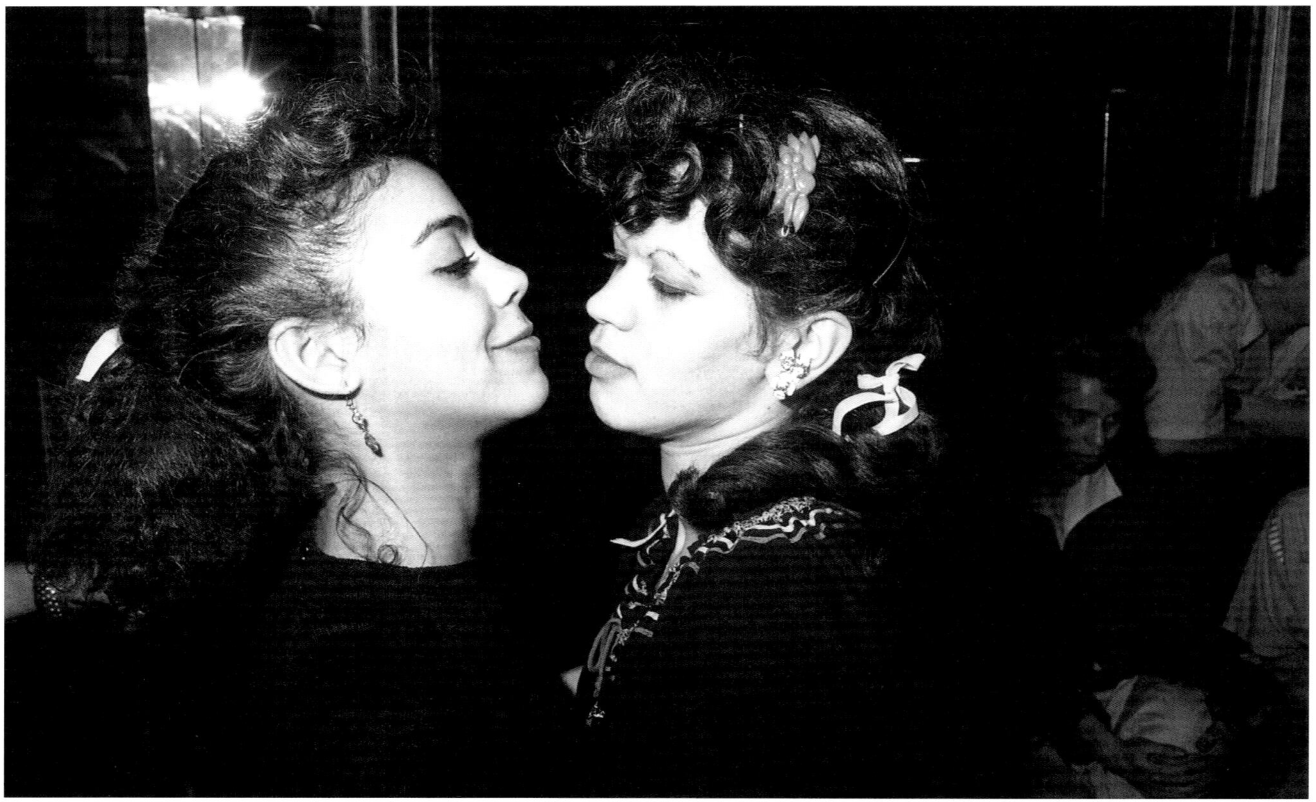

154 This page and opposite: from 'Rebel's Paris 1982'

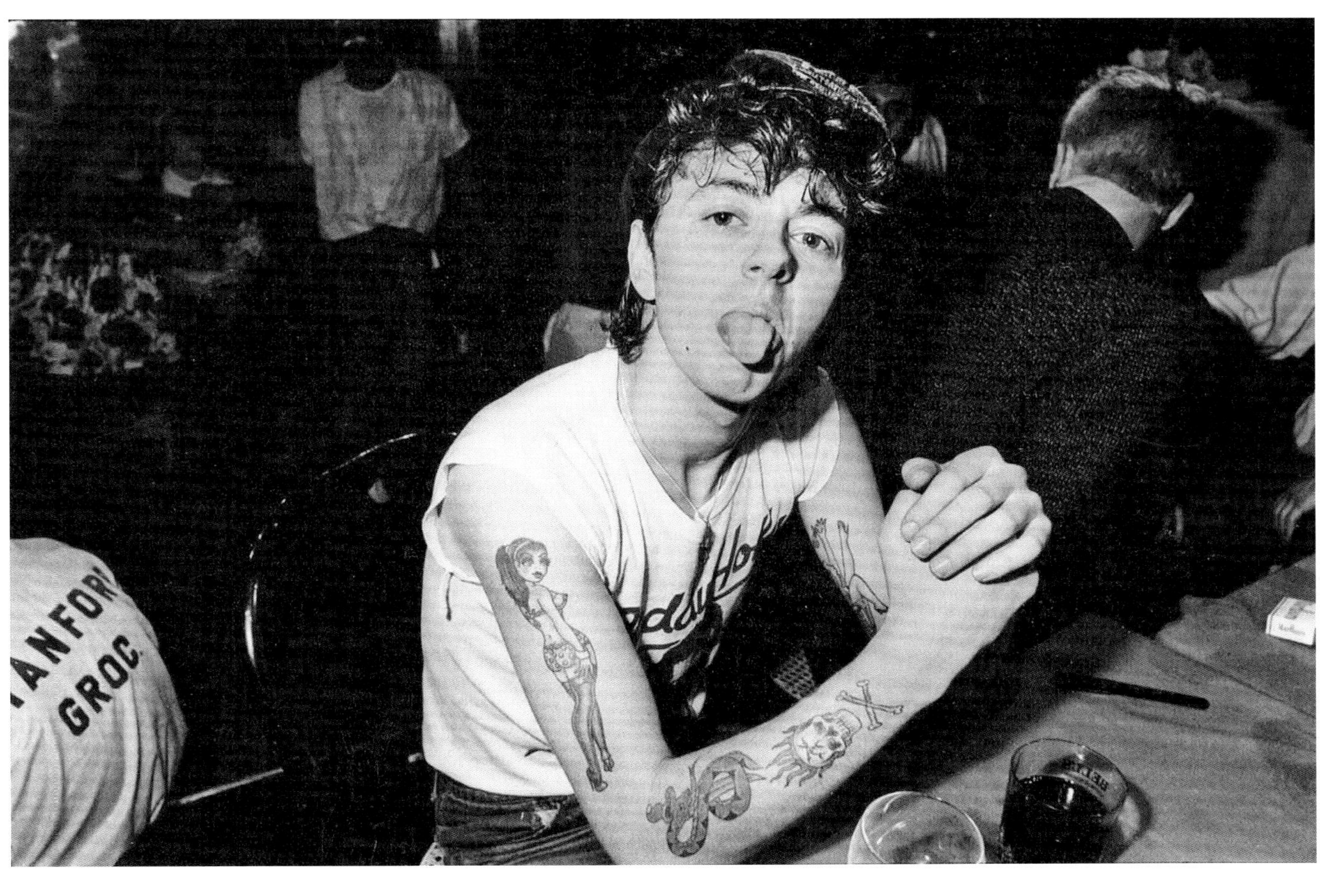

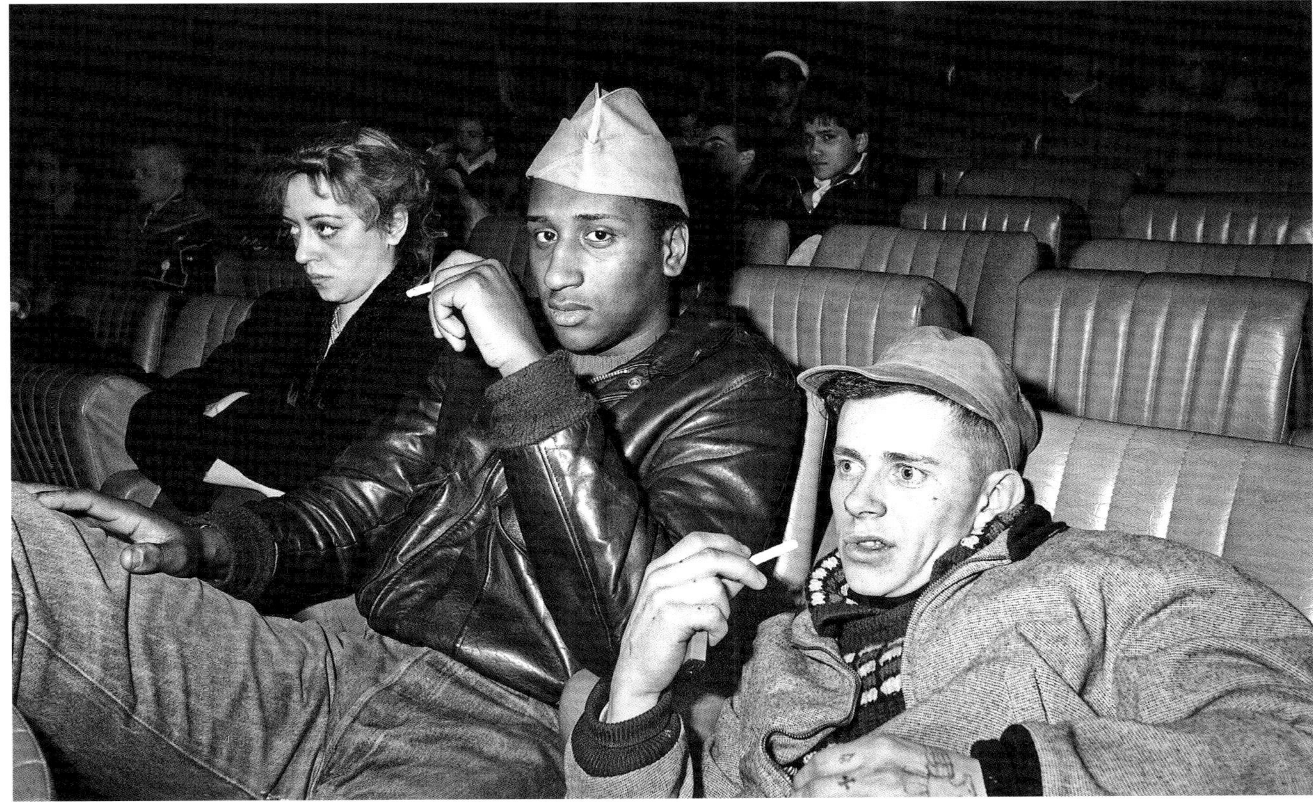

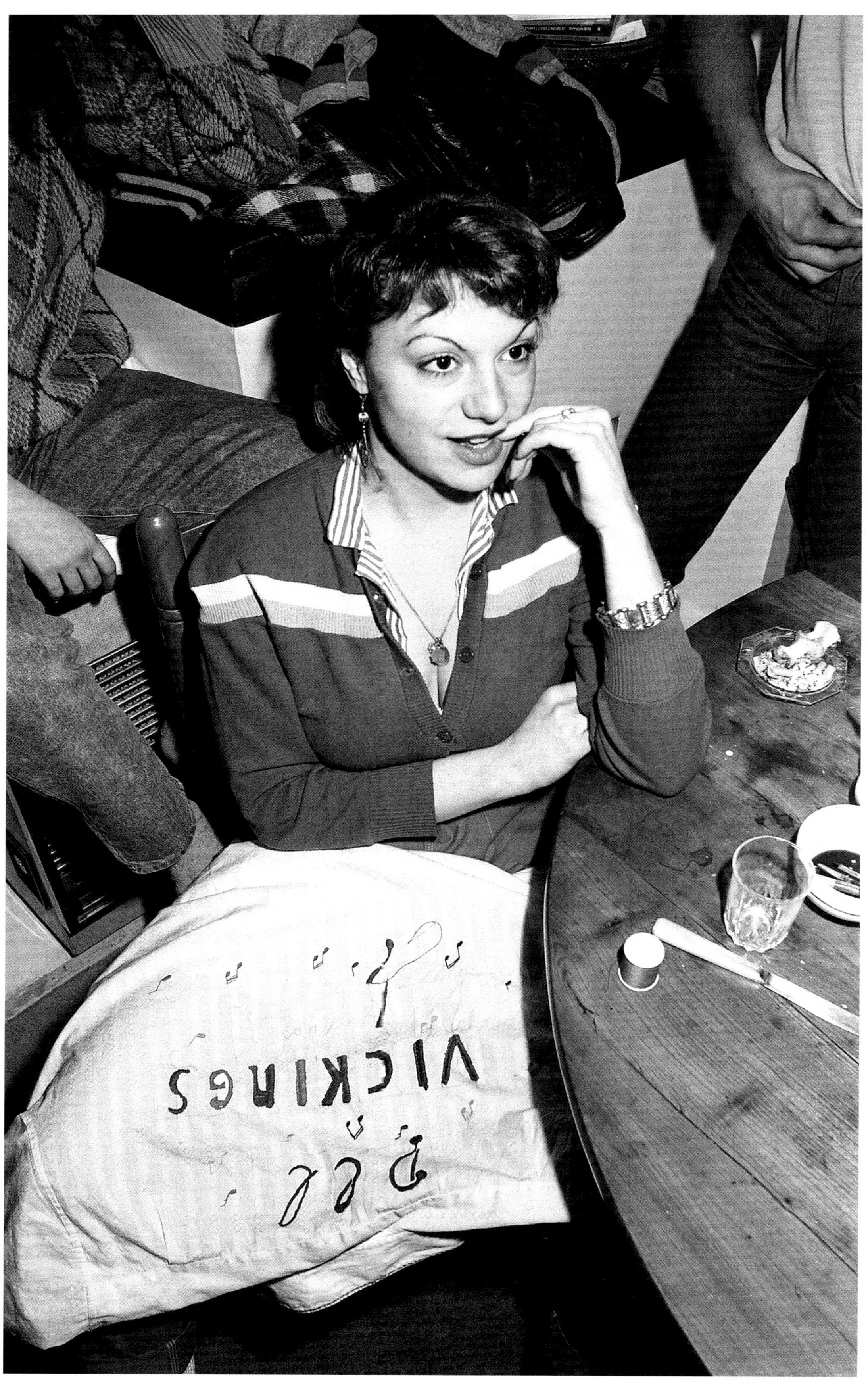

156 This page and opposite: from 'Rebel s Paris 1982'

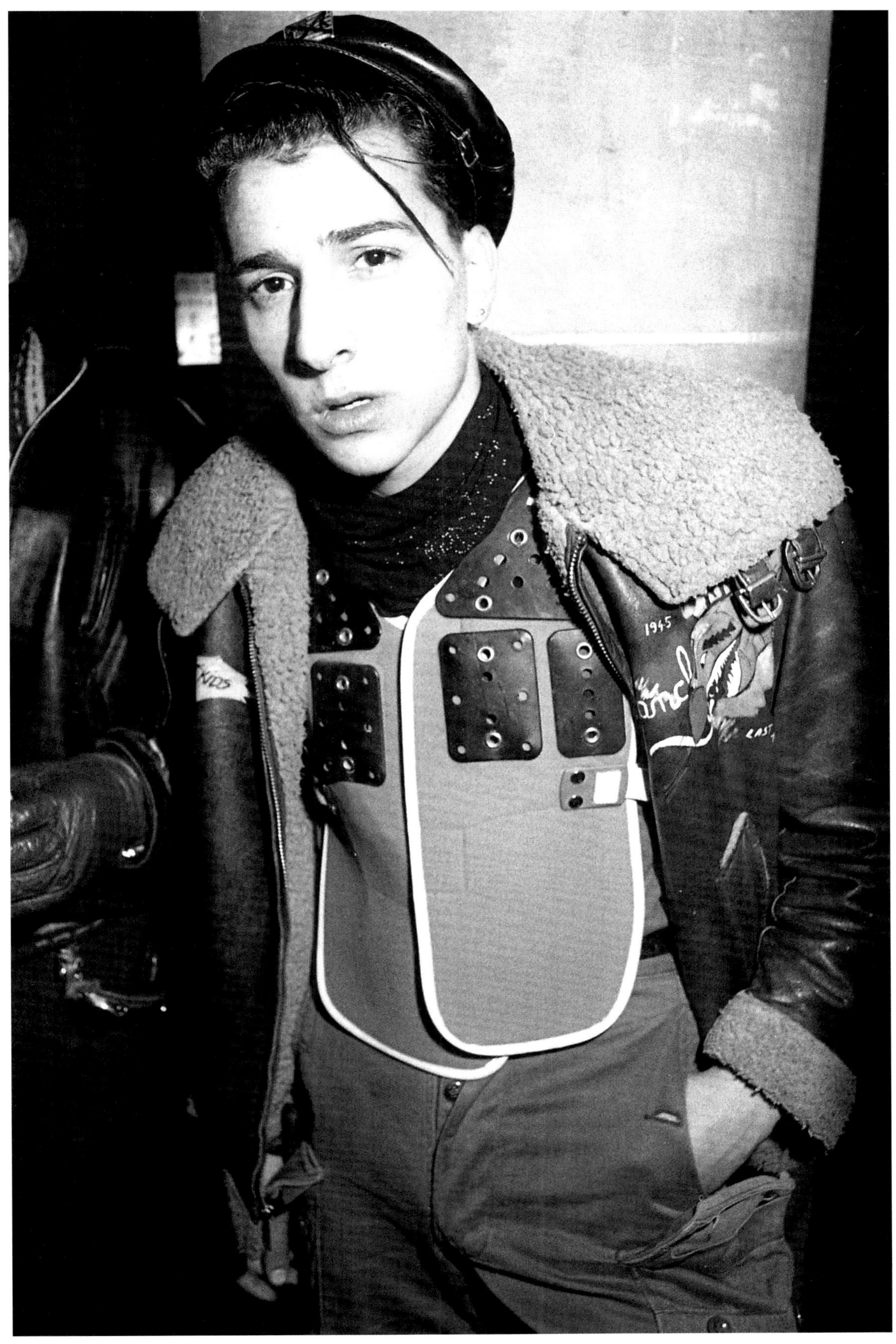

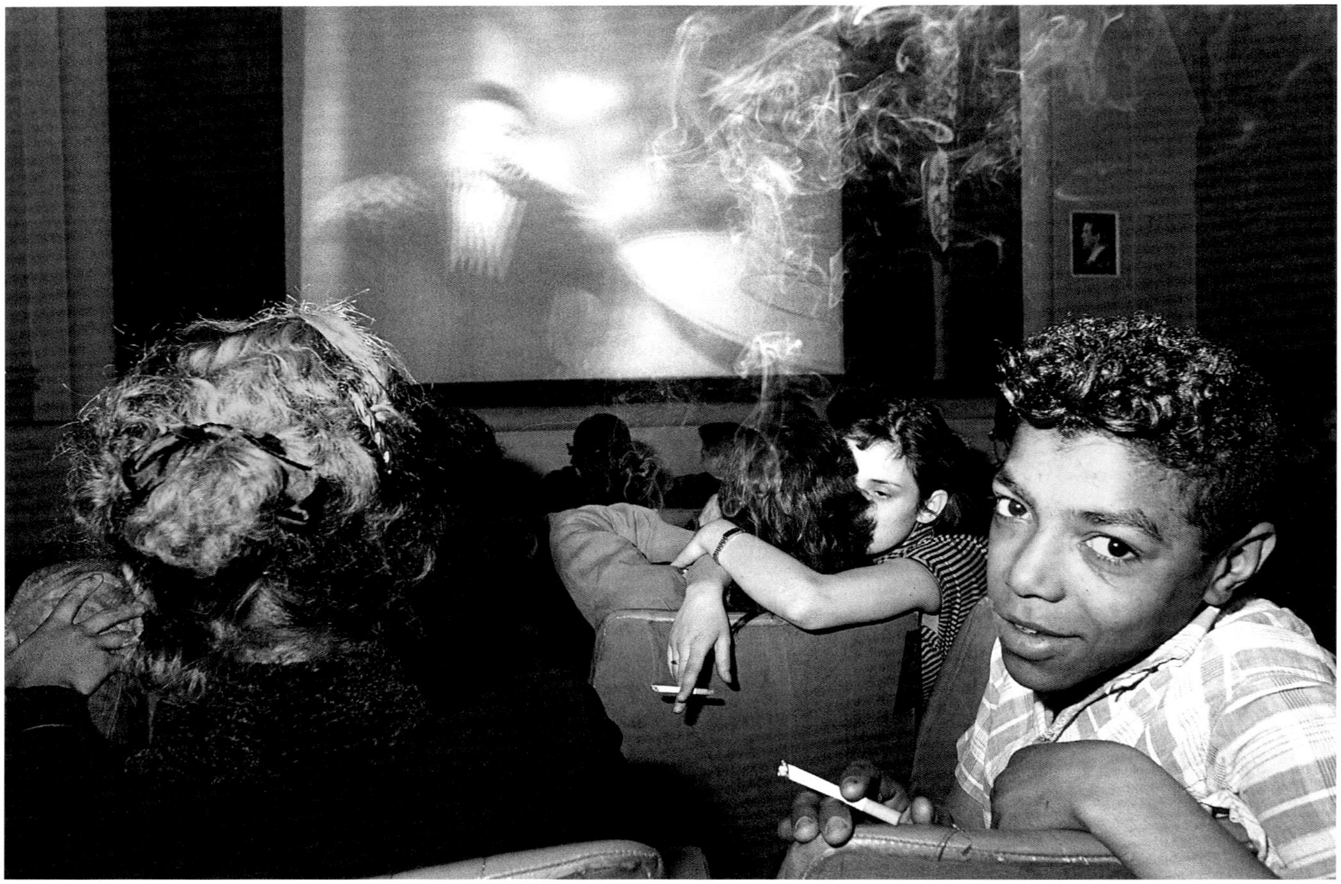

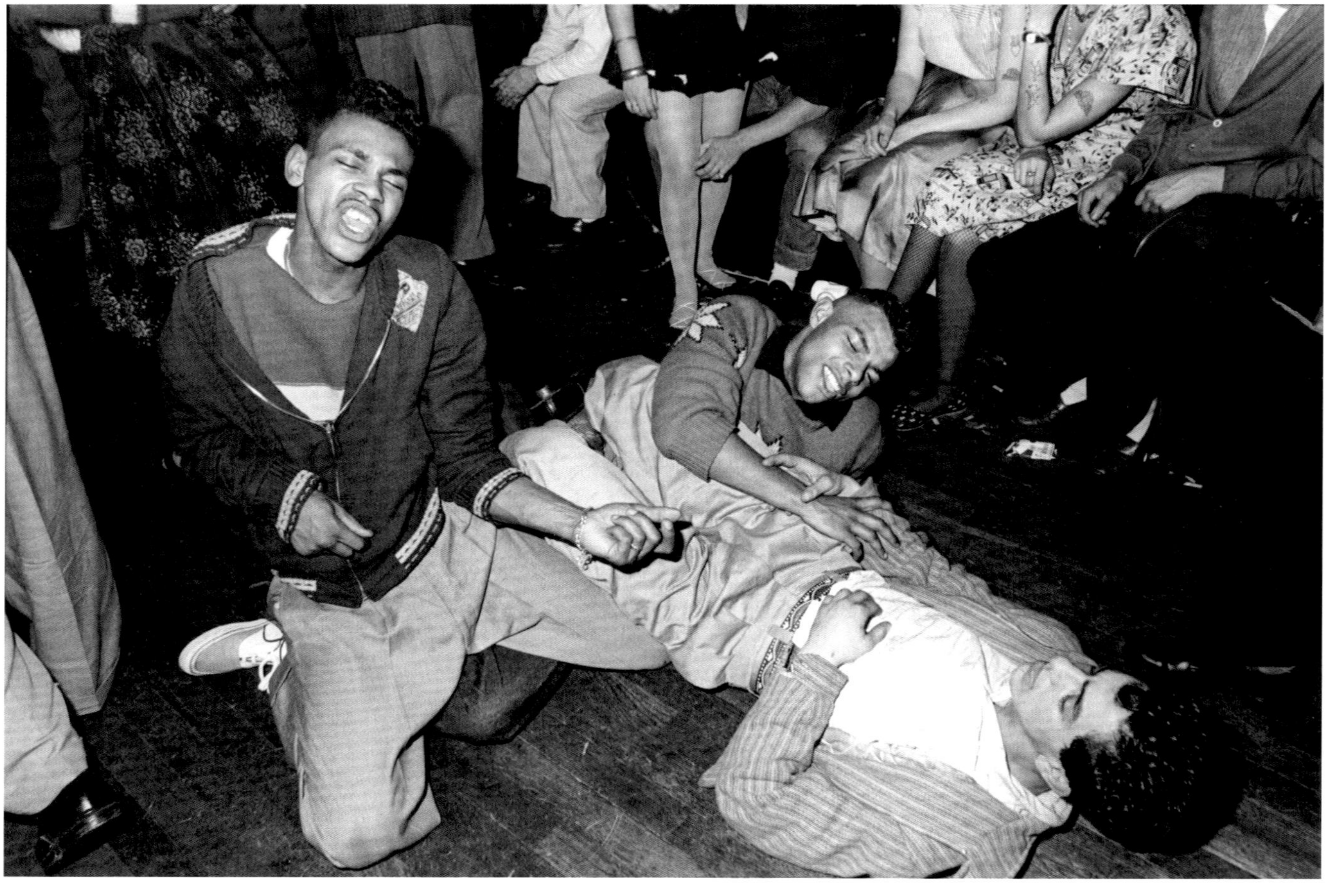

158 This page and opposite: from 'Rebel's Paris 1982'

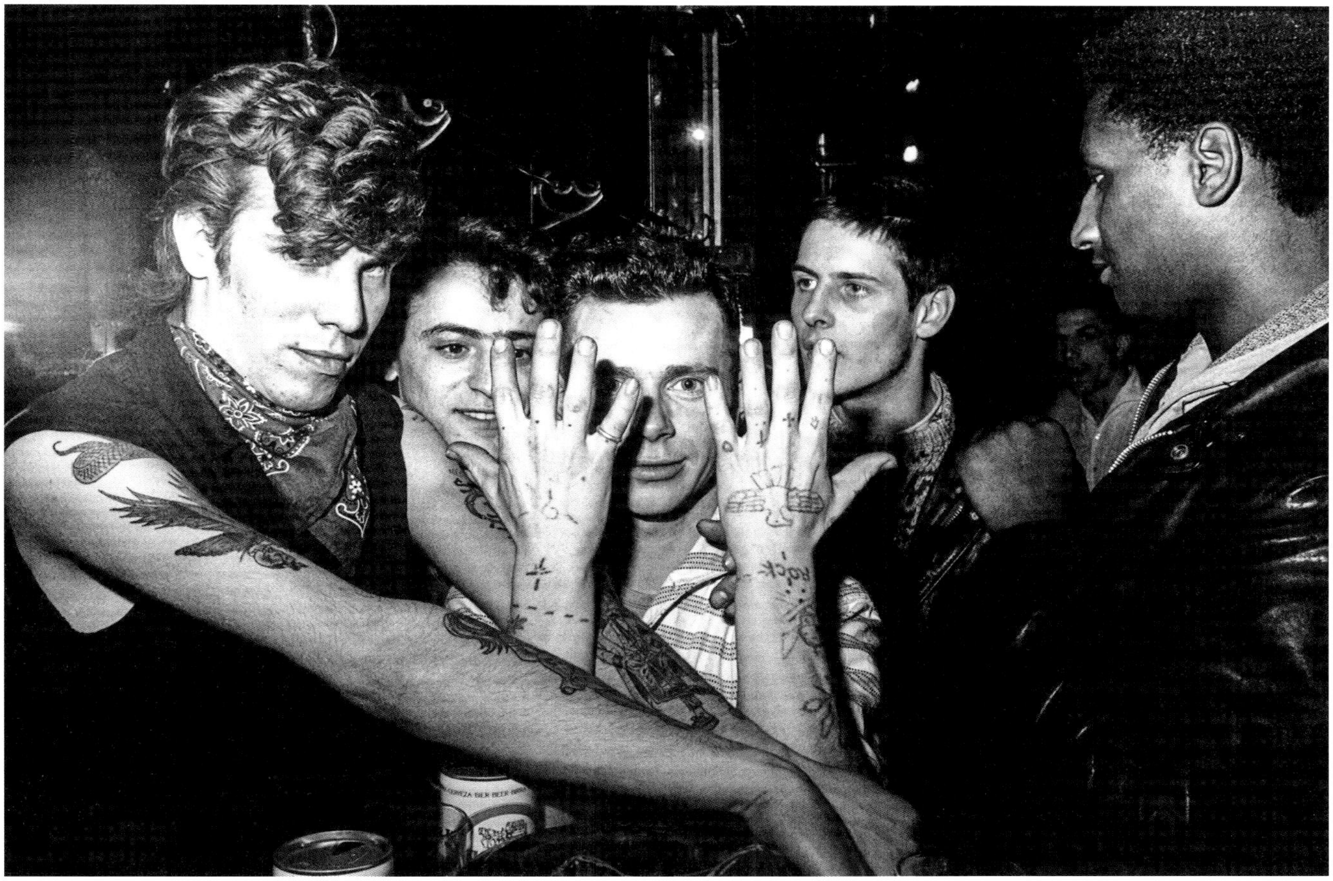

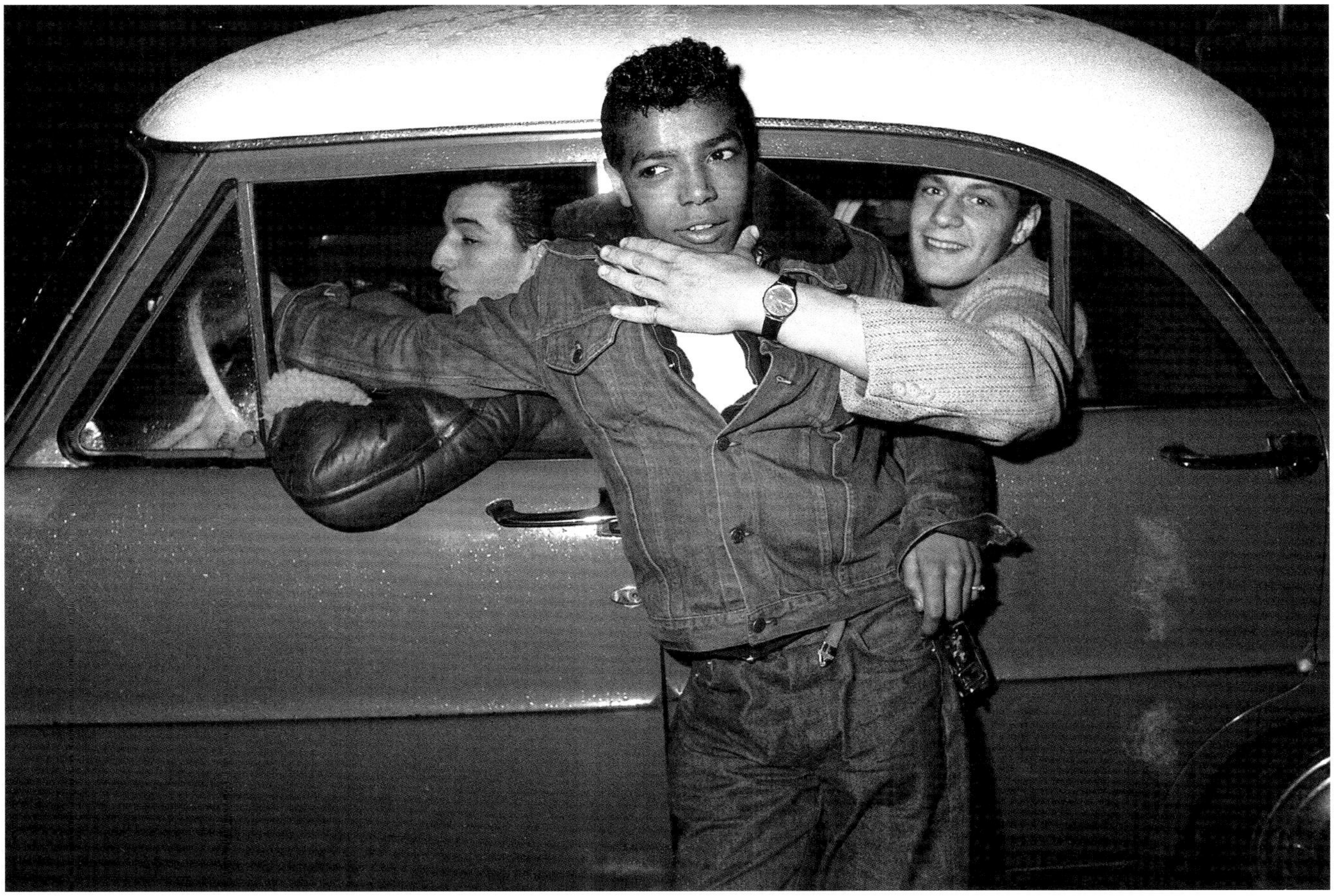

PAZ ERRÁZURIZ

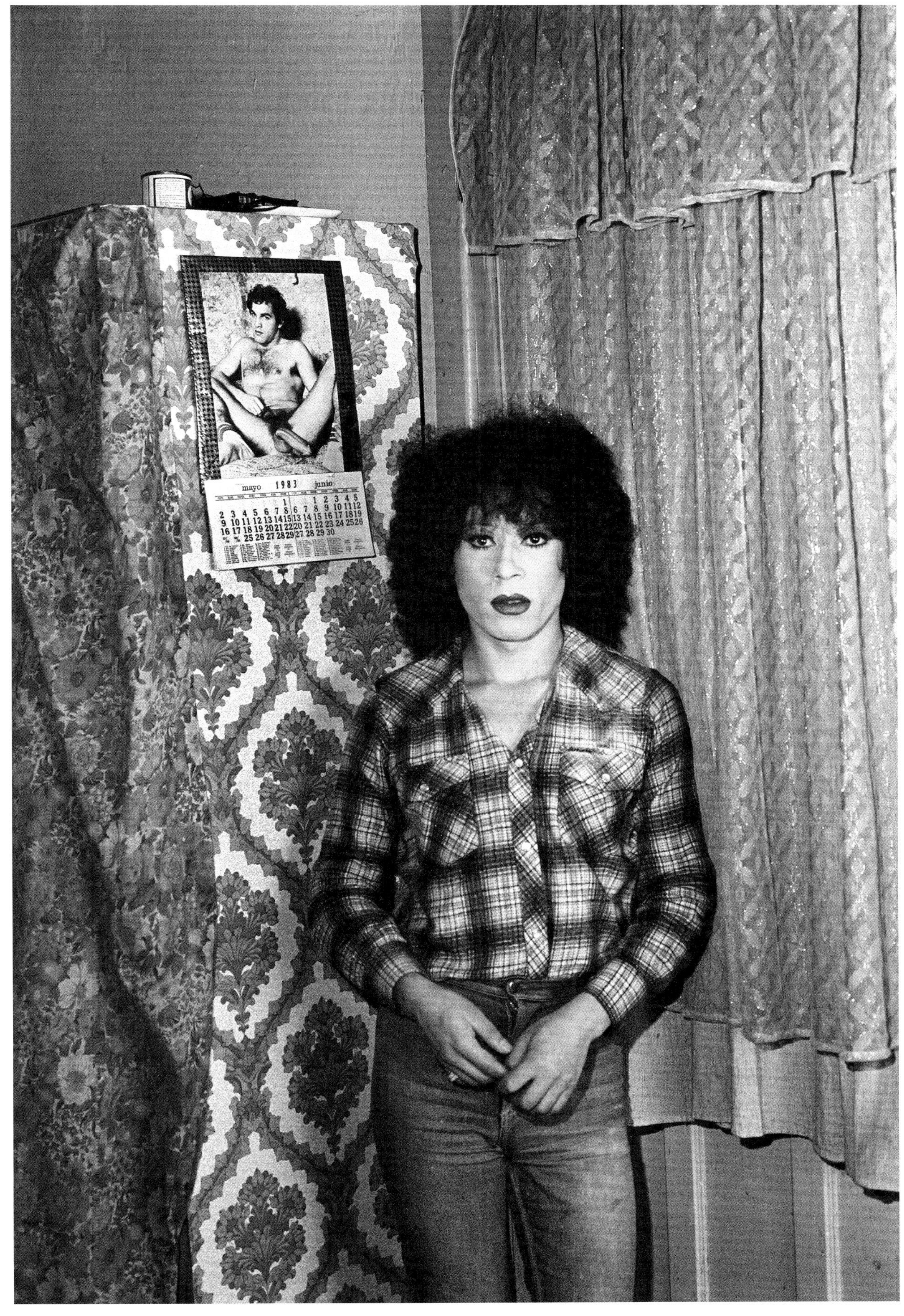

mayo 1983 junio

A former schoolteacher, Paz Errázuriz (b. 1944, Chile) had only recently begun taking pictures when the right-wing army chief Augusto Pinochet seized power in Chile in September 1973, following a bloody military coup in which Salvador Allende, the country's socialist president, was ousted.

The new regime hinged on terror. Censorship, curfews, enforced segregation and political persecution were the norm. Throughout, the then 28-year-old Errázuriz photographed fervently, often in secret and at great personal risk. Within two months of Pinochet's accession, for instance, nearly 20,000 men and women considered opponents to the new order had been rounded up and confined inside Santiago's national stadium, where they were beaten and tortured. Many were never seen again. Indeed, official figures released in 2011 suggest that more than 40,000 Chileans were imprisoned, tortured or slaughtered during Pinochet's seventeen-year rule. Entire families and communities were seized, without a shred of evidence against them.

The consequences were particularly severe for anyone promoting a narrative opposing that sanctioned by the junta. Protest and freedom of expression were quashed ruthlessly by Pinochet's secret police, who singled out journalists and photographers for intimidation and arrest. Certainly, taking pictures on the street was considered an open act of rebellion. It fell under the 'contempt for authority' provisions of the Code of Military Justice, which criminalised 'insults' to public order. And if you were a woman, so much the worse, because in choosing to work outside the realm of the home you were contradicting the traditionally submissive domestic role propagated by Pinochet and his ideologues.

Errázuriz, though, shrugged off such constraints and set about making work, building her own darkroom and teaching herself first the rudiments, then the finer points of the craft, flouting curfews and regulations as she went. 'For me, it was a form of activism,' she explained in a 2003 interview.[1] 'Photography let me participate in my own way in the resistance waged by those of us who remained in Chile. It was our means of showing that we were there and fighting back.' From the beginning, Errázuriz was – shrewdly perhaps – drawn

to documenting what was happening on the perimeter rather than centre stage. She sought out particularly those Chileans who had been in some way disenfranchised or targeted cruelly by the regime. For instance, one of her earliest series depicts the large numbers of people who had been made homeless by the new order and who now slept on the streets.

In 1981 she co-founded an organisation for photographers who, like herself, were operating under the radar and in opposition to the military regime. Partly it was safety in numbers – they would go out into the streets in groups as a means of protecting themselves, and made sure of their legal rights. But the AFI (Asociación de Fotógrafos Independientes) had another, unforeseen effect. Suddenly, members began discussing what it meant to be a photographer – and more importantly, a Chilean photographer. The dialogue kick-started a process which Errázuriz later described as 'like discovering ourselves … I think it gave me a deeper and more extensive knowledge of my country … It gave me a pretext for digging into my obsessions and needs.'[2]

The sequence of photographs titled *La manzana de Adan*, or 'Adam's Apple', began the following year when Errázuriz, who had already made some pictures of female prostitutes, befriended a clan of male cross-dressers, some of whom also worked as prostitutes, who were living and working in clandestine brothels across the cities of Santiago and nearby Talca, about 300 kilometres south. Created in collaboration with the journalist Claudia Donoso, who interviewed the men, this near decade-long undertaking portrayed what life had become like for a community forced by the regime to live furtive, insecure lives, in constant fear of the authorities.

The relationship between Errázuriz and the group began with two transvestite brothers named Pilar and Evelyn and their mother, Mercedes, an illiterate, widowed woman whom they supported with their earnings. So as not to make the men – who were understandably traumatised by what had happened to them – feel under further scrutiny, Errázuriz and Donaso went as far as to live in the brothel with them for stretches of time. 'I wanted to portray their lives, in their way,' Errázuriz later explained. 'I guess my point of view has been an

anthropological one. I do not comment on their lives, I wanted to be more of an accomplice, than a foreigner or an outsider.'[3]

Having suffered in secrecy and silence for so long, the men came to welcome the acknowledgement that camera and pen now offered them, unfurling crocus-like in the morning sun to speak willingly of the beatings, verbal harassment, torture and killing that had marked their lives since Pinochet had come to power. 'We were … in Valparaíso [a town on the coast to the north of Santiago] when the coup occurred,' remembered Pilar. 'They took all of us to a ship moored in the port. They took us there blindfolded, in a van. For six days I was left there, piled up with the others, in the hold. The first thing the soldiers did was cut our hair; they pulled it by the roots and afterwards they pissed on us. They kept hitting us. They hung Tamara and Tila with a rope and made them spin turning them round and round. They threatened to throw us overboard. They were some thirty of us homosexuals on board. We were released one by one.

'They killed several of us during the coup. They killed Mariliz who was really pretty, just like Liz Taylor. This happened over Christmas. Her body was found in the Mapocho river, full of bayonet holes. At the Legal Medical Institute we were told: "These are not knife wounds. They were made with bayonets."'[4]

In the photographs, the contrast between what has happened to the men in the past and the day-to-day life that has had to continue is marked. Behind the eyeshadow and foundation, however exquisitely applied, and in among the net curtains, plug-in heaters and floral wallpaper standing in for their latest temporary home, the tension is unmistakeable. It sears from their eyes into yours.

Evelyn committed suicide; Leyla was killed by the police. Most others in the group fell victim to AIDS. It was so early in the epidemic, Errázuriz later recalled, that they died without knowing what it was that ravaged them. She remains in touch with the group's sole survivor.

The photographs remained secret for many years – it would have been too dangerous for all concerned to exhibit them. Errázuriz and Donoso waited until Pinochet stepped down

from the presidency, in 1990, to publish their
book. Since then, Errázuriz, now 74 and
internationally revered – she represented Chile
at the Venice Biennale in 2015 – has returned
over and again to the lives of those who find
themselves on life's margins. She has turned her
lens on nomad minorities and circus performers,
as well as the elderly and those confined to
psychiatric wards – groups who seem to lack a
voice everywhere, dictatorship or no. In gifting
them a voice, it seems, she has found a strident
one of her own.

Lucy Davies

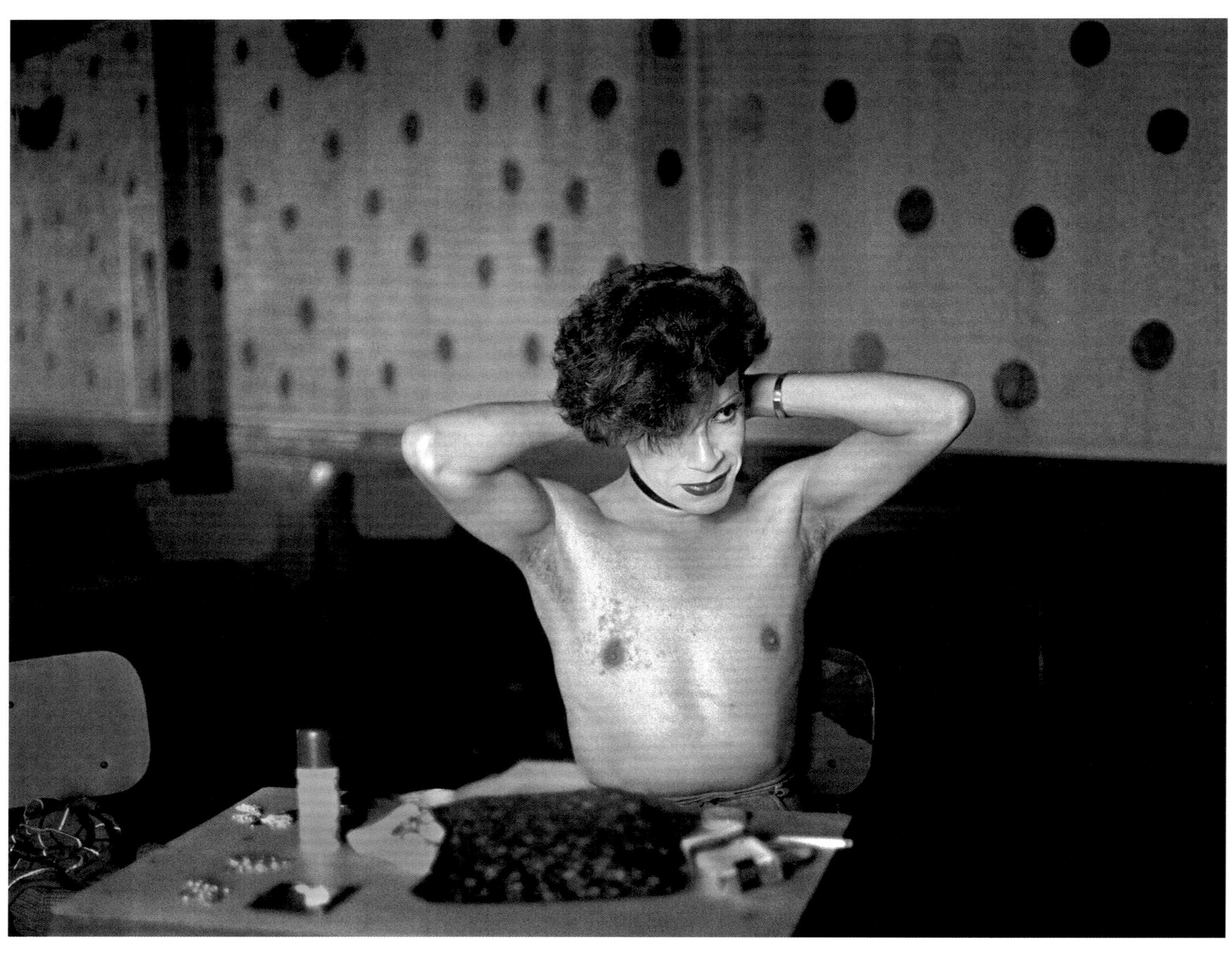

164 From 'La manzana de Adán' (Adam's Apple), *Evelyn, Santiago*, 1983

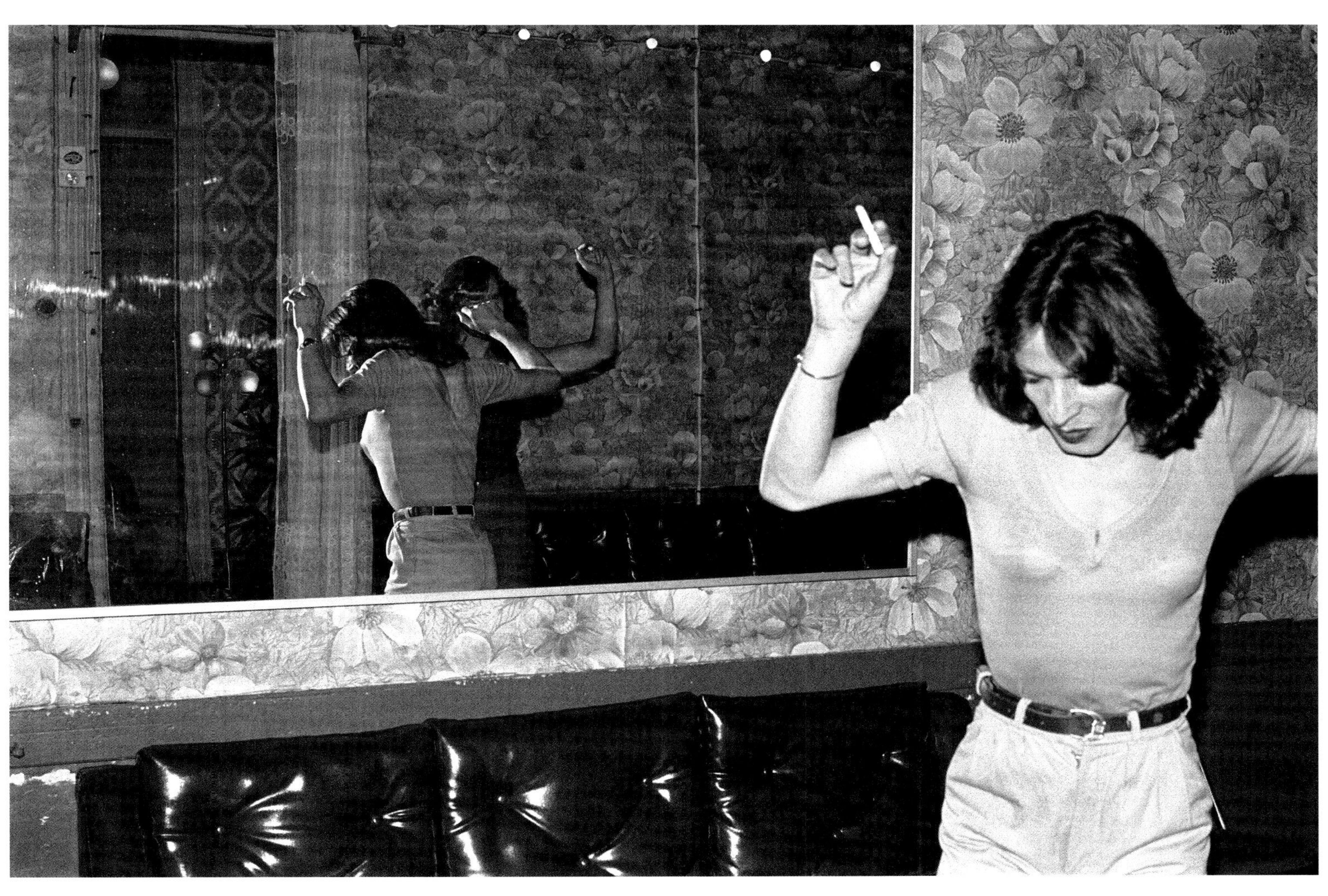

From 'La manzana de Adán' (Adam's Apple), *La Palmera, Santiago*, 1983

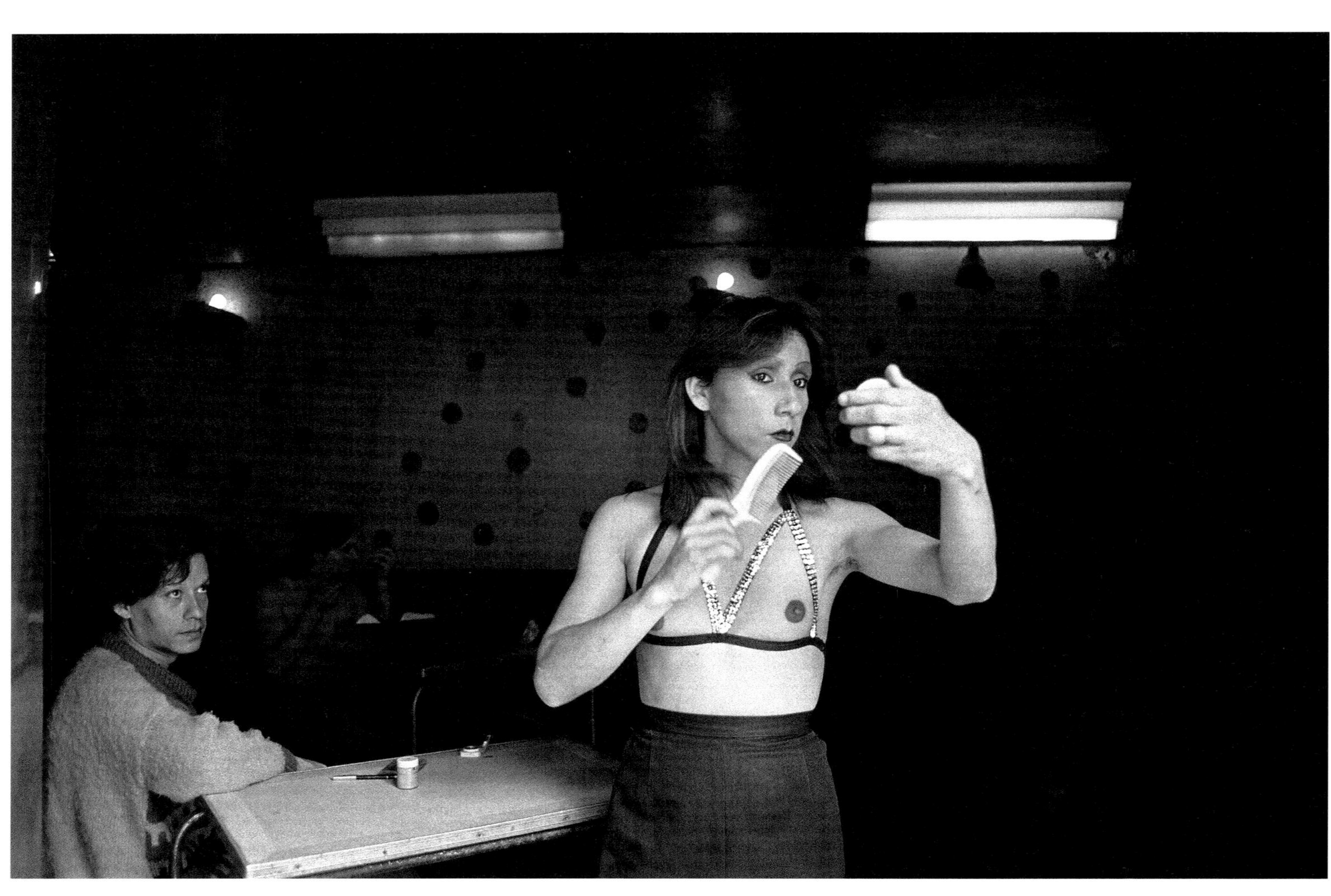

166 From 'La manzana de Adán' (Adam's Apple), *Macarena, Santiago,* 1983

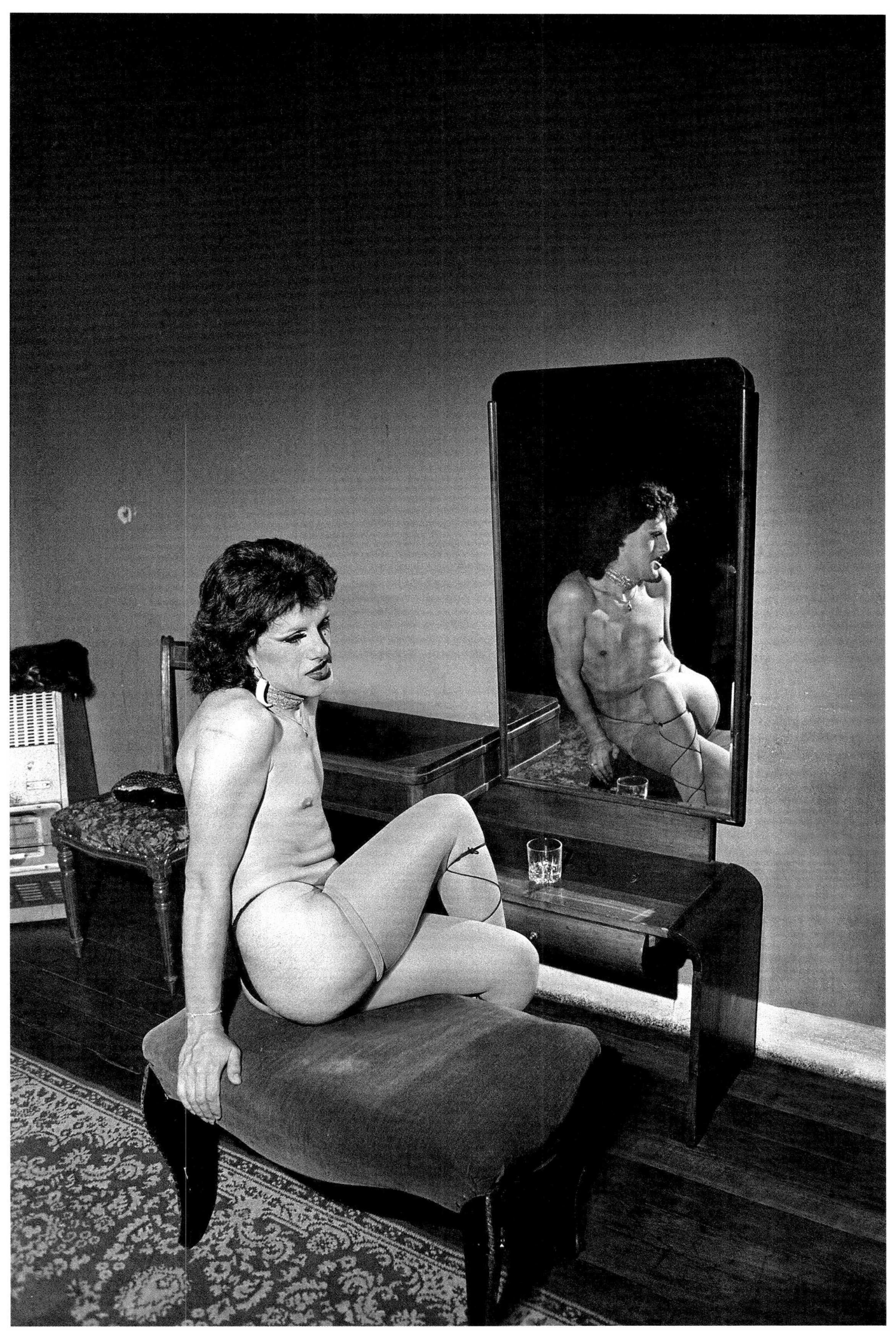

From 'La manzana de Adán' (Adam's Apple), *Pilar, Santiago*, 1983

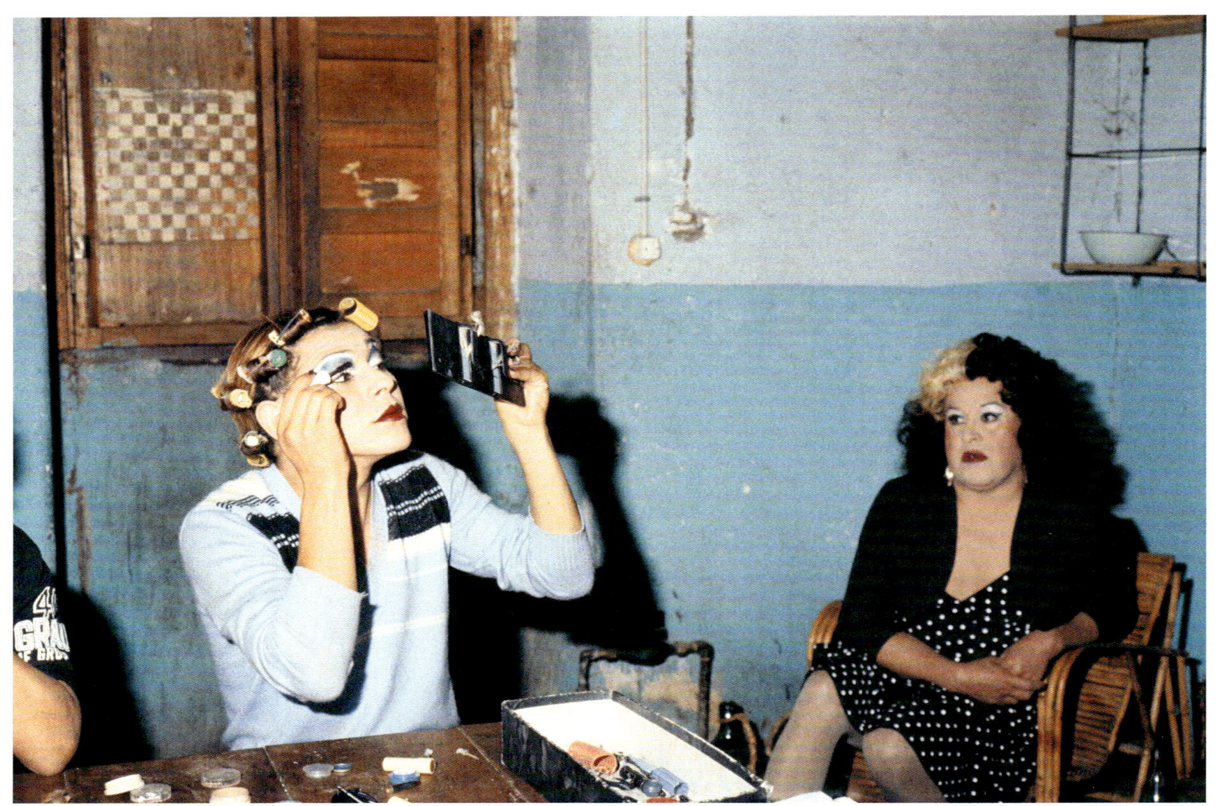

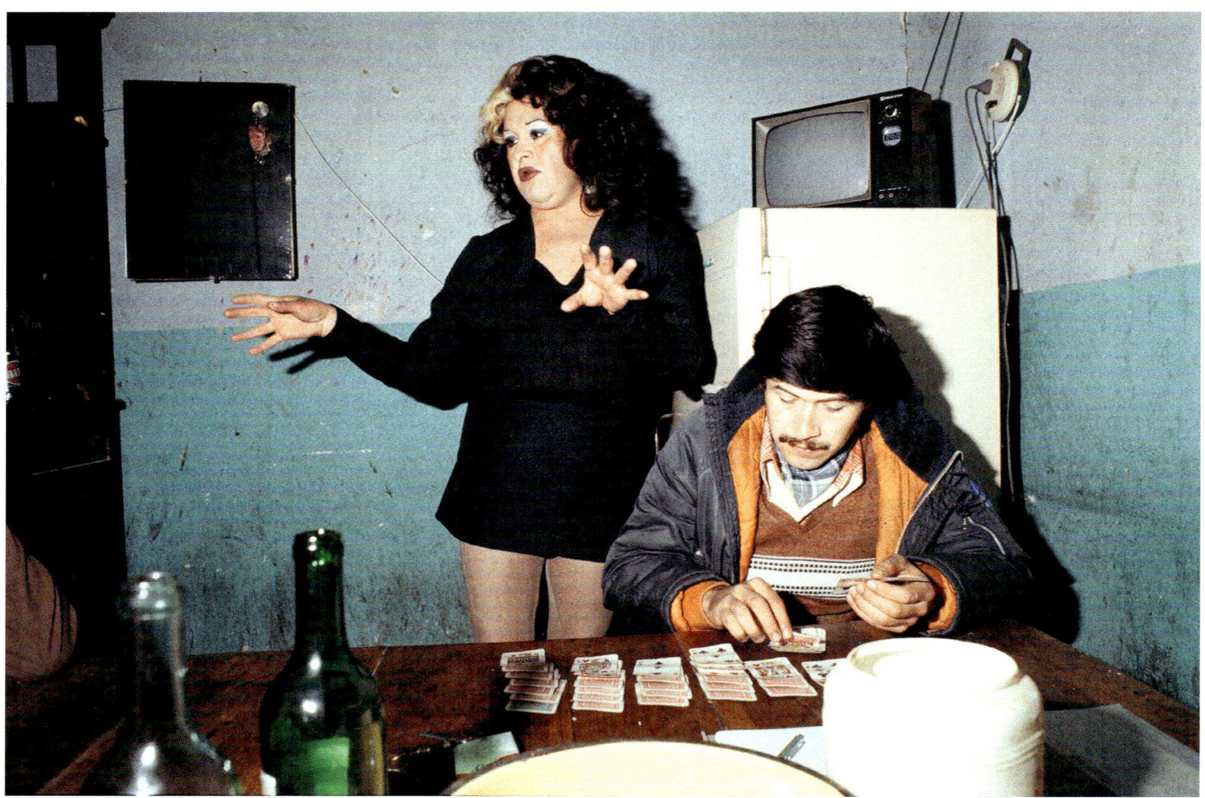

Top: from 'La manzana de Adán' (Adam's Apple), *La Jaula, Talca,* 1983
168 Above: from 'La manzana de Adán' (Adam's Apple), *Susuki, La Jaula, Talca,* 1983

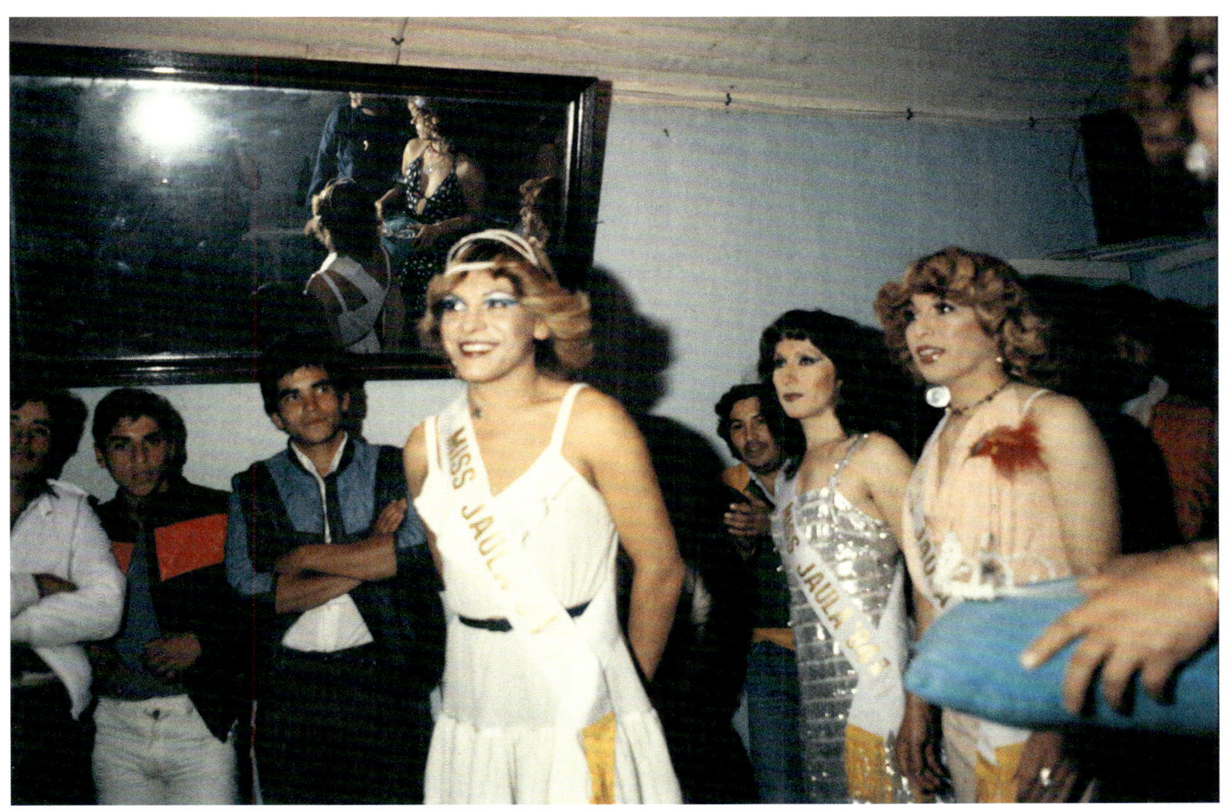

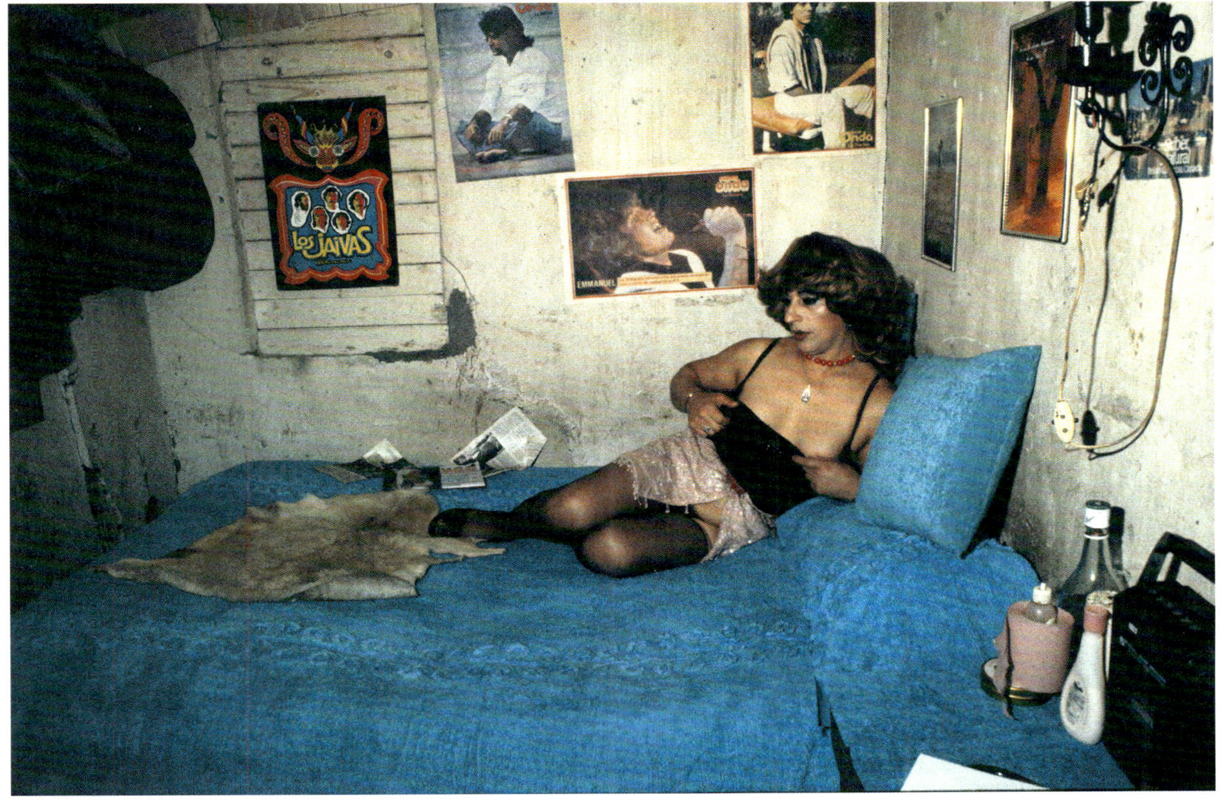

Top: from 'La manzana de Adán' (Adam's Apple), *La Jaula, Talca, 1983*
Above: from 'La manzana de Adán' (Adam's Apple), *Nirka, La Jaula, Talca, 1983*

170 From 'La manzana de Adán' (Adam's Apple), *Evelyn, Santiago*, 1983

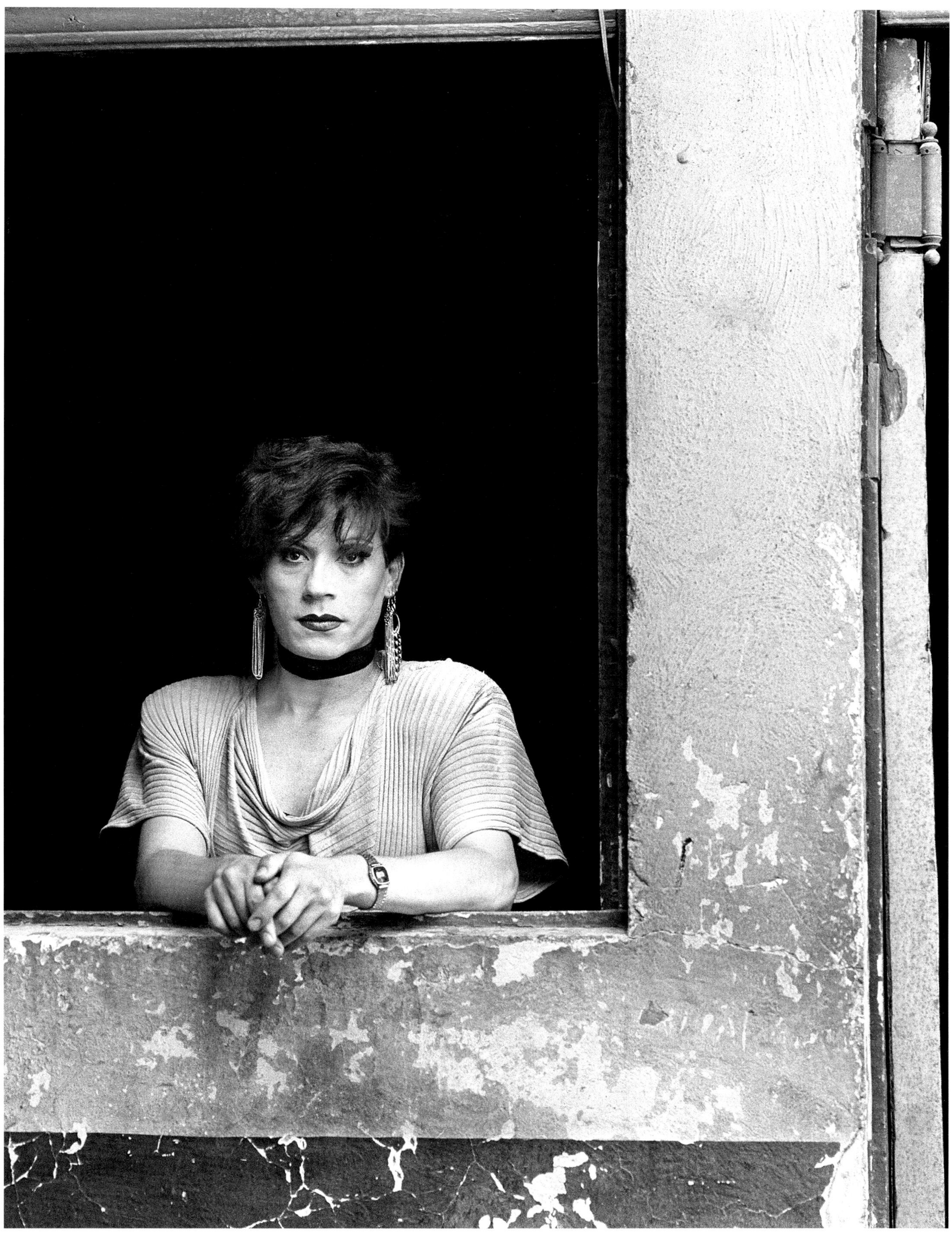

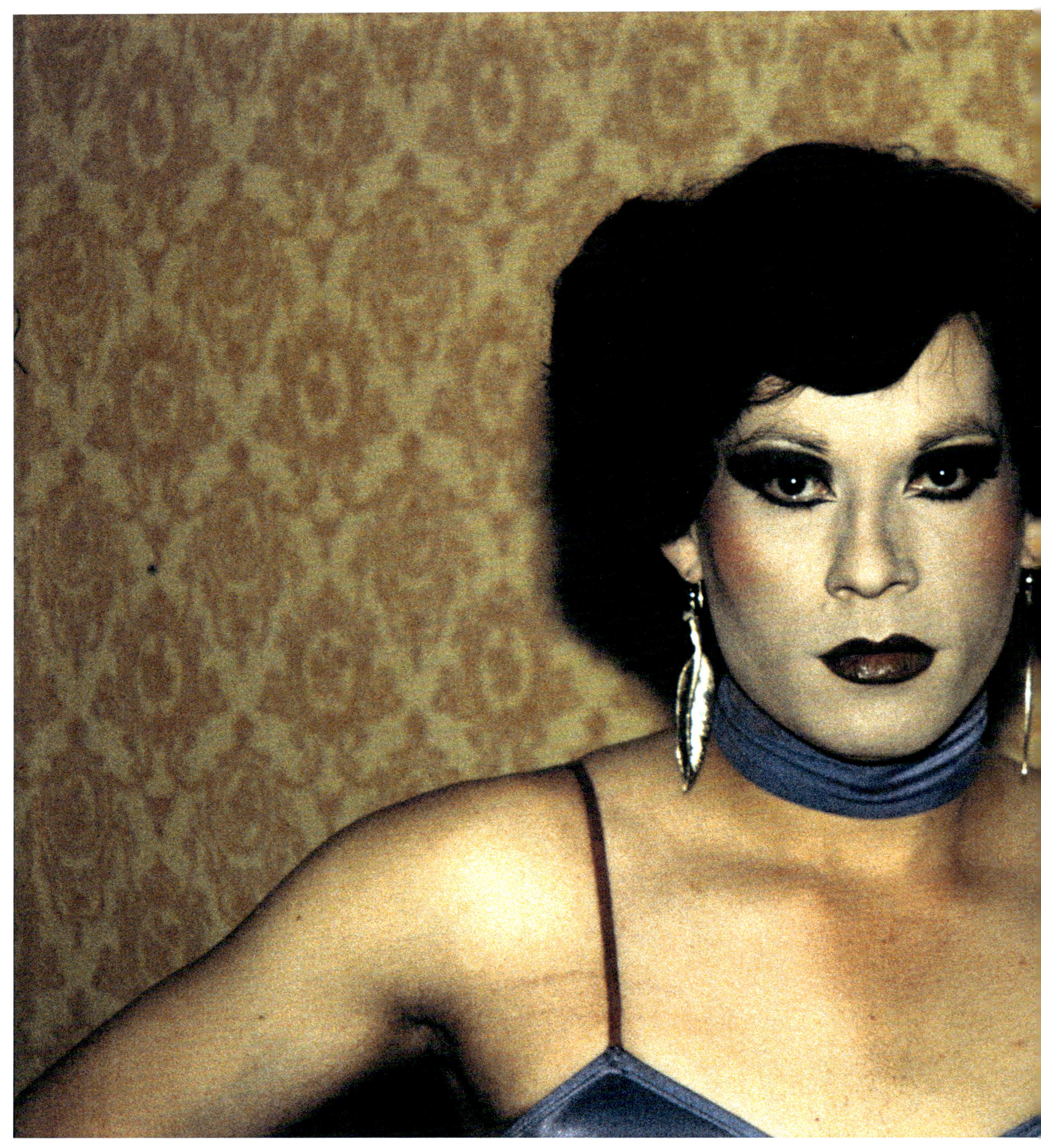

172 From 'La manzana de Adán' (Adam's Apple), *Evelyn, Santiago, 1983*

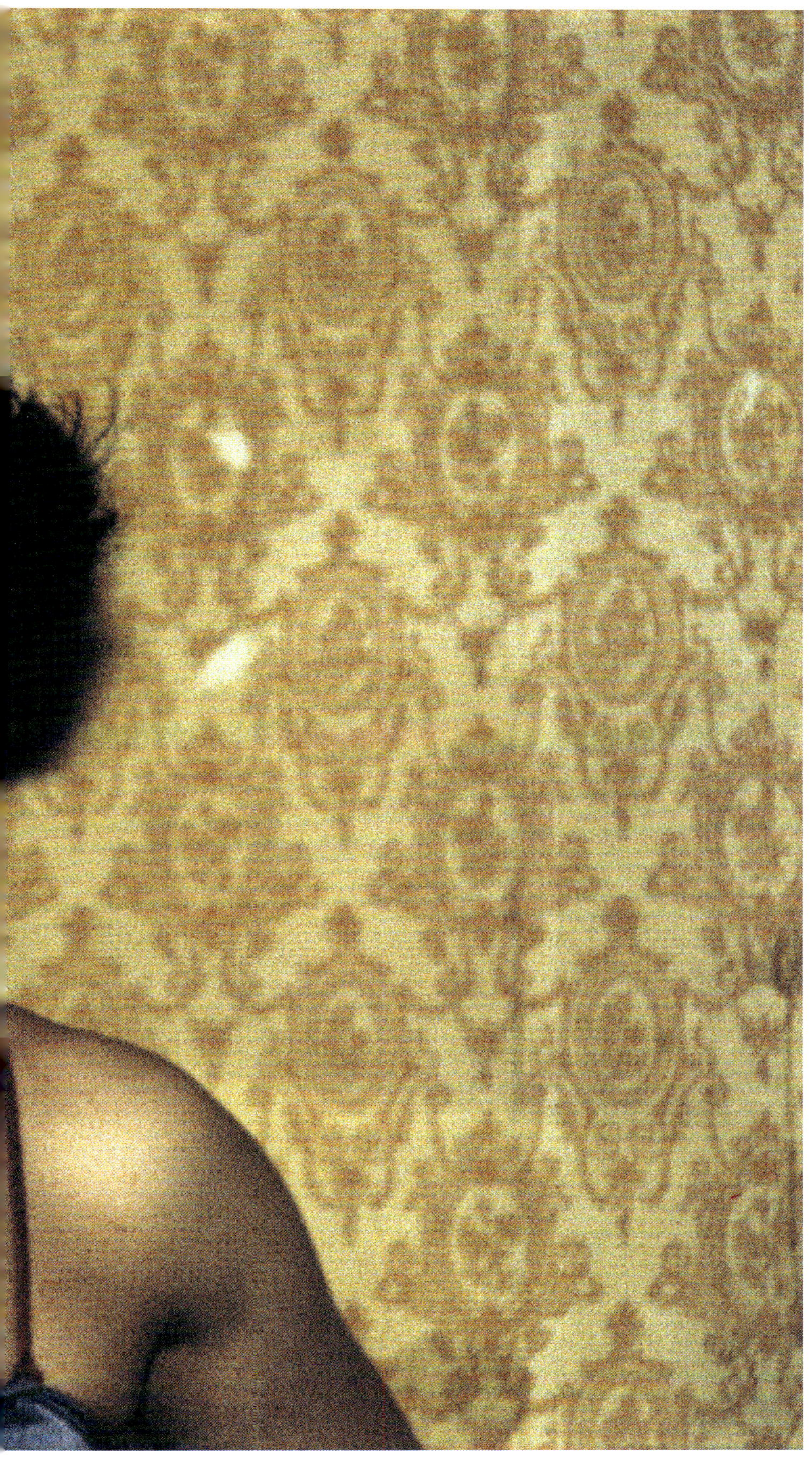

MARY ELLEN

MARK

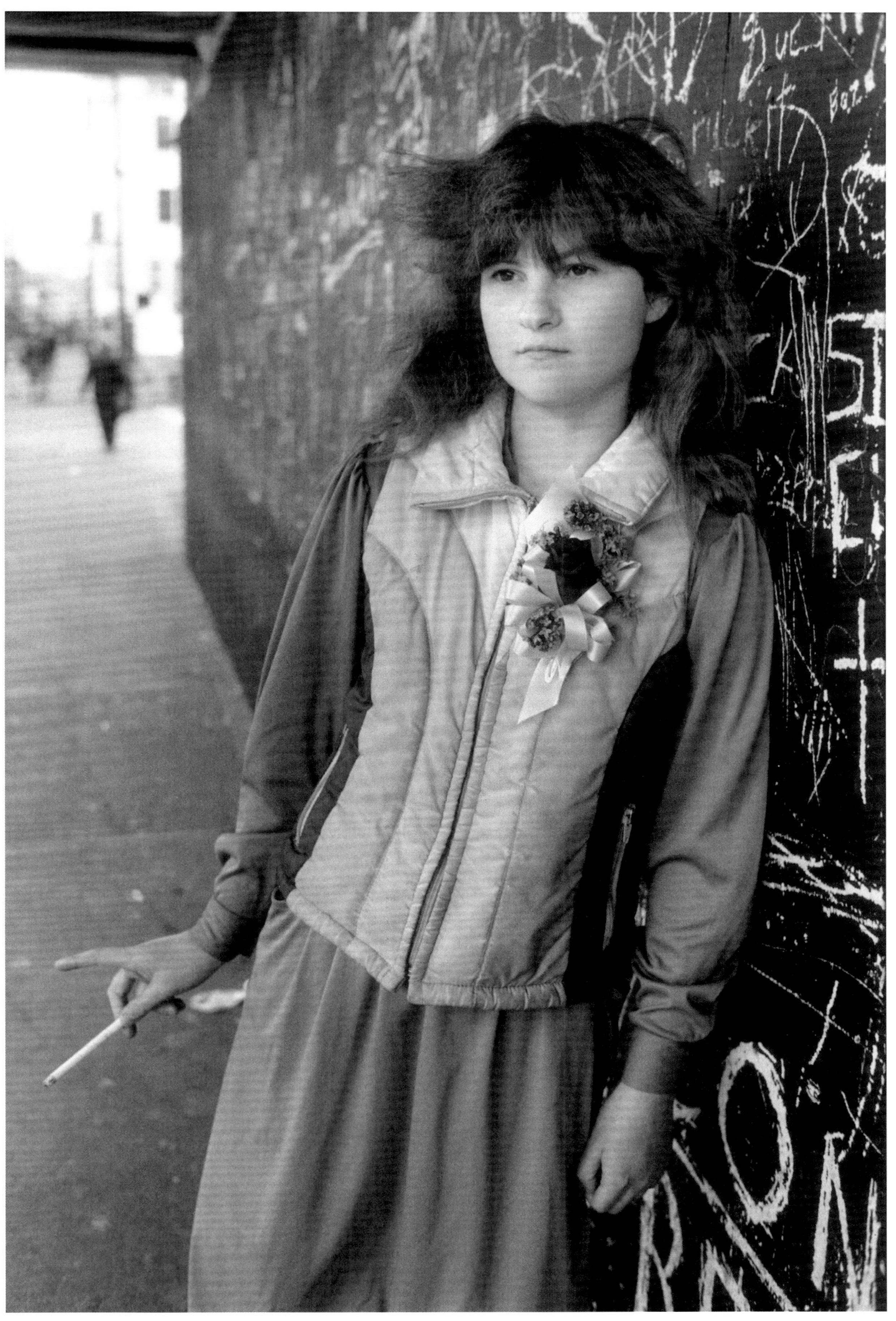

'You're still very beautiful,' says Mary Ellen Mark (b. 1940, USA; d. 2015) to Erin Charles, 22 years after she first met her between First and Second on Pike Street, Seattle, in 1983. It's because Mark has that gift of sight, seeing real beauty in whoever she photographs, that we will never forget 'Tiny', a former street kid who by the street's own laws really should be dead by now.

Against the odds, Tiny has outlived Mark herself, who died in 2015, and her image will survive us all. Her thirteen-year-old face, framed by a black veiled hat, will haunt those of us who look. *it could have been me*. All dressed up in a black cocktail dress for a Halloween party (p. 179), Tiny might be a model in a fashion shoot today. Insouciant, she blows a gum bubble, looking straight down the lens of the camera. She could probably look anyone in the eye, even the old men who desired and paid for her prepubescent body. Especially them.

Sixteen, Tiny's T-shirt says, but she isn't (p. 178). In another image, this child-woman is seated, her face tilted upwards as if in supplication; her mouth, with its pronounced cupid's bow, distinctively downturned. A through-the-looking-glass smile. *it could have been me*. In a fairground, dwarfed by rides that toss bodies this way and that for pleasure, Tiny clutches a toy horse – perhaps a prize-win – with both arms, as though she might prevent it from cantering towards freedom (p. 180). Tiny holds on. We see her again, clasping a small black dog, its lead snaking around her arms. Standing in the middle of a road, they lean into one another, as though they know they won't make it alone. Any minute now a truck might hurtle from the horizon. Flatten them. Every photograph seems on the edge of disaster. This particular disaster will be averted though; it won't happen today, because the photographer has their backs. Maybe photography really can save lives.

Mark is by her own description a 'humanist' photographer, but she isn't in the business of redemption. She neither glamorised Tiny's life nor disguised its frequent tragedies. The daughter of an alcoholic mother and an unknown father, Tiny made the street her home, taking her kittens with her the day she left. She spent time in juvenile detention, became viciously addicted to crack, gave birth

to three children whose biological fathers she never knew, though they paid her for the trick. She had to be *Streetwise* – the title of Mark's long-term project, and of Mark's husband Martin Bell's documentary – taking the choices available to her, finding ways to numb the pain and earn money. Mark listened to her hopes for a different life; dreams of a horse farm, diamonds, a baby. The last wish came true, ten times over.

Mark and Bell, without children of their own, once offered to adopt Tiny, but she wouldn't accept the condition – to enrol in school. Photography was a means to get close and stay close, and that cemented a relationship between a New York artist and a Seattle street kid that would never have existed otherwise. It has also provided Tiny with a family album, and an alternative method of making money. Each time a picture of Tiny was published, Mark would send a little cash, even in the days when she wouldn't approve of the use to which it would be put. Her ethics of seeing extended beyond photographic practice and turned contemporary criticism on its head. Susan Sontag, writing about Arbus, and other practices she found deficient, famously described the camera as a kind of passport 'that annihilates moral boundaries and social inhibitions, freeing the photographer from any responsibility to the people photographed'.[1] Mark carried the kind of responsibility towards Tiny that is a corollary of love.

At stake for Sontag was the inside/outside debate, central to documentary photography and brilliantly rendered in a 1994 essay by Abigail Solomon-Godeau that examines the perceived contradiction at the heart of photographing other people: that authenticity can only be gleaned from 'inside', while an objective approach is only possible from the outside.[2] Mark escaped such binaries too. In a very obvious sense, Mark was 'outside' the world of Tiny, and Rat, Lulu and Dewayne (these last two died young and now have plaques on Pike Street), but she was intuitively inside. Using her camera, she *saw* their world; she understood its hierarchies, its currencies and its laws. By taking such an interest in these lives so starved of attention and affection, Mary Ellen Mark made magic with flat surfaces. She sent us through the looking glass to the lives that most have not had to endure. While

much photographic criticism focuses on the superficiality of the medium, we can clearly see how the photographer herself is implicated – from the Latin *implicare*, meaning to fold in or enfold – within the image. *it could have been me*. Mark perfectly understood the role of her intimate, voyeuristic exteriority: 'One thing's for sure: In this kind of social documentary photography I do, you're never a fly on the wall like you are when you photograph a disaster or war and the event is more important than your presence.'[3]

Mark's commitment to the vulnerability of the female body, its subservient position in patriarchal society, was lifelong. A woman of the 1970s, the feminist movement would have been proud to call her one of its own. She often worked with women, was most curious about them – from female patients in Ward 81, a maximum security psychiatric institution in Salem, Oregon, where she lived for a month, to the women who sold sex to survive on the infamous Falkland Road, Bombay (Mumbai), India. So iconic was one of her images – of a transvestite sex worker in Falkland Road, 1978 – that in 2017 a young photographer appropriated it and inserted it into his own photograph, because he had been unable to capture the essence of that experience. It is interesting to note that Mark actively wanted to make 'iconic' images, a concept that postmodernism made unfashionable, though such images, by their very nature, have prevailed.

Sontag wrote that 'photographs objectify: they turn an event or a person into something that can be possessed.'[4] Something contradictory is happening here. We are witness to how Mark was in fact possessed by Tiny: by her eyes, by her mouth, by her way of being in the world. By her beauty.

Where is Tiny now? Blink and you'll miss her, as the saying goes. She's thirteen years old, you'll find her just a few streets away, turning her next trick. Cities hide the stories they don't want us to see behind advertising hoardings of clean, affluent people having the time of their lives. Mary Ellen Mark asked that we look closer. *it could have been you*.

Max Houghton

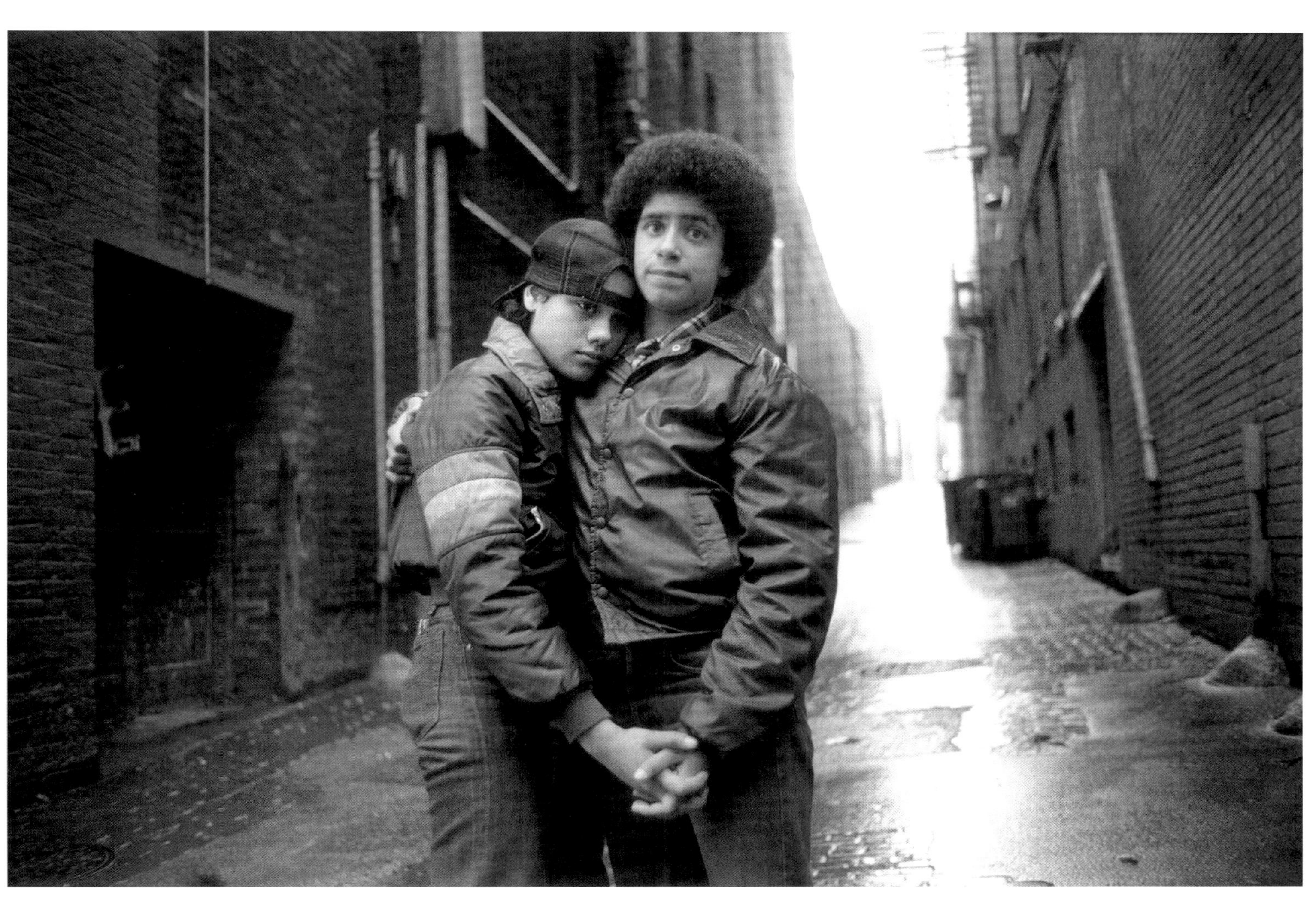

From 'Streetwise', Seattle, Washington, 1983

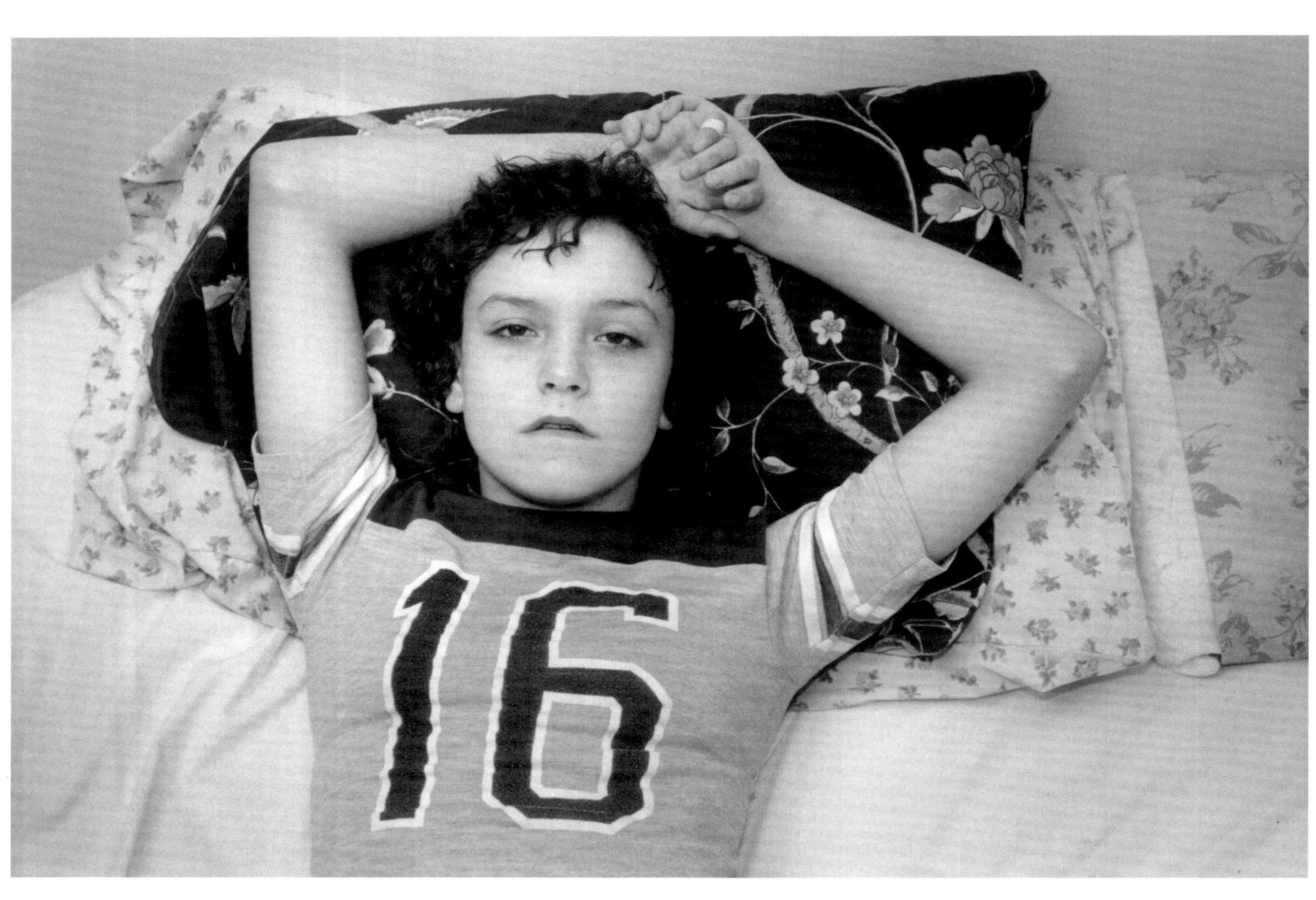

178 From 'Streetwise', *Tiny, Seattle, Washington, 1983*

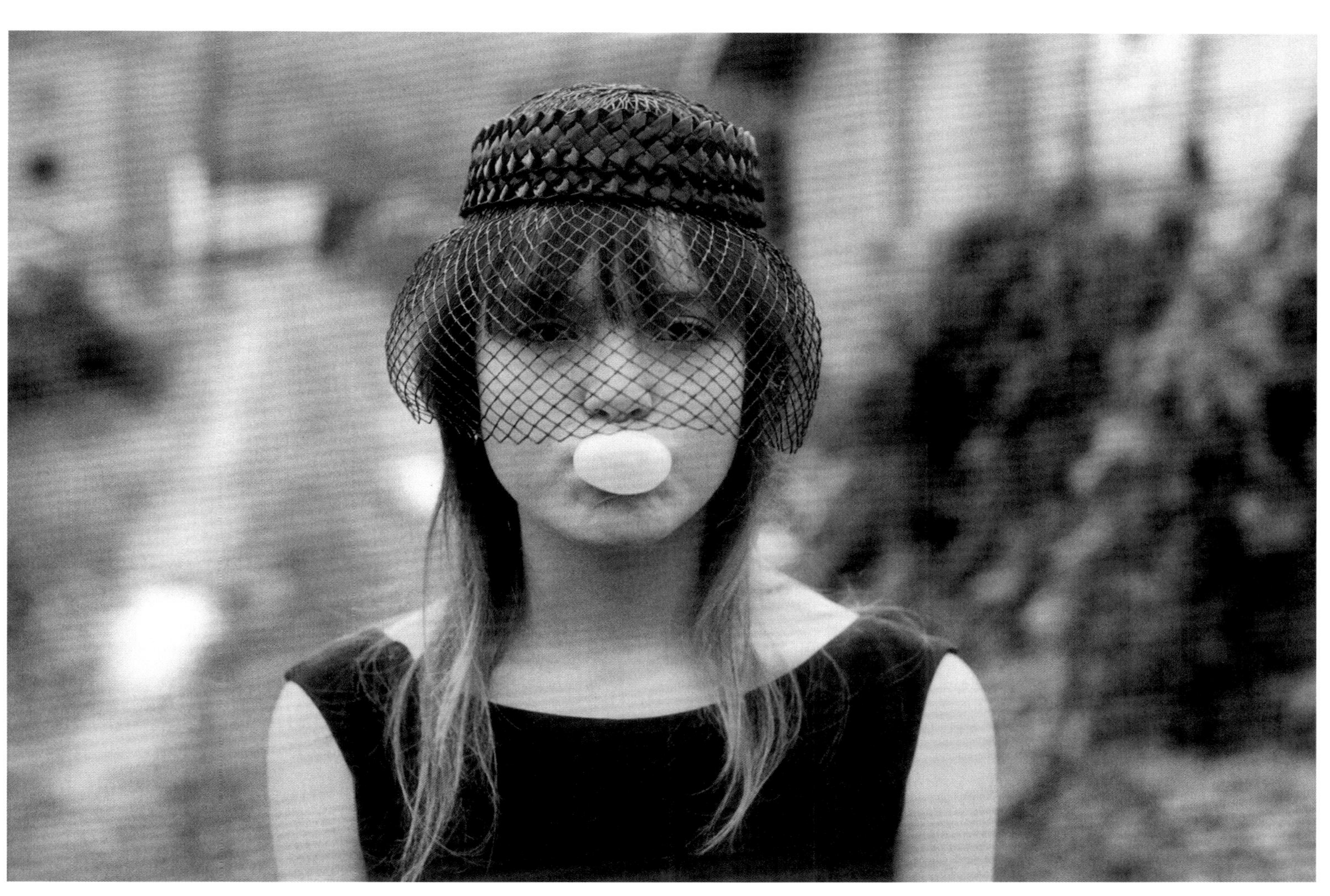

From 'Streetwise', *Tiny Blowing a Bubble (During 'Streetwise')*, Seattle, Washington, 1983

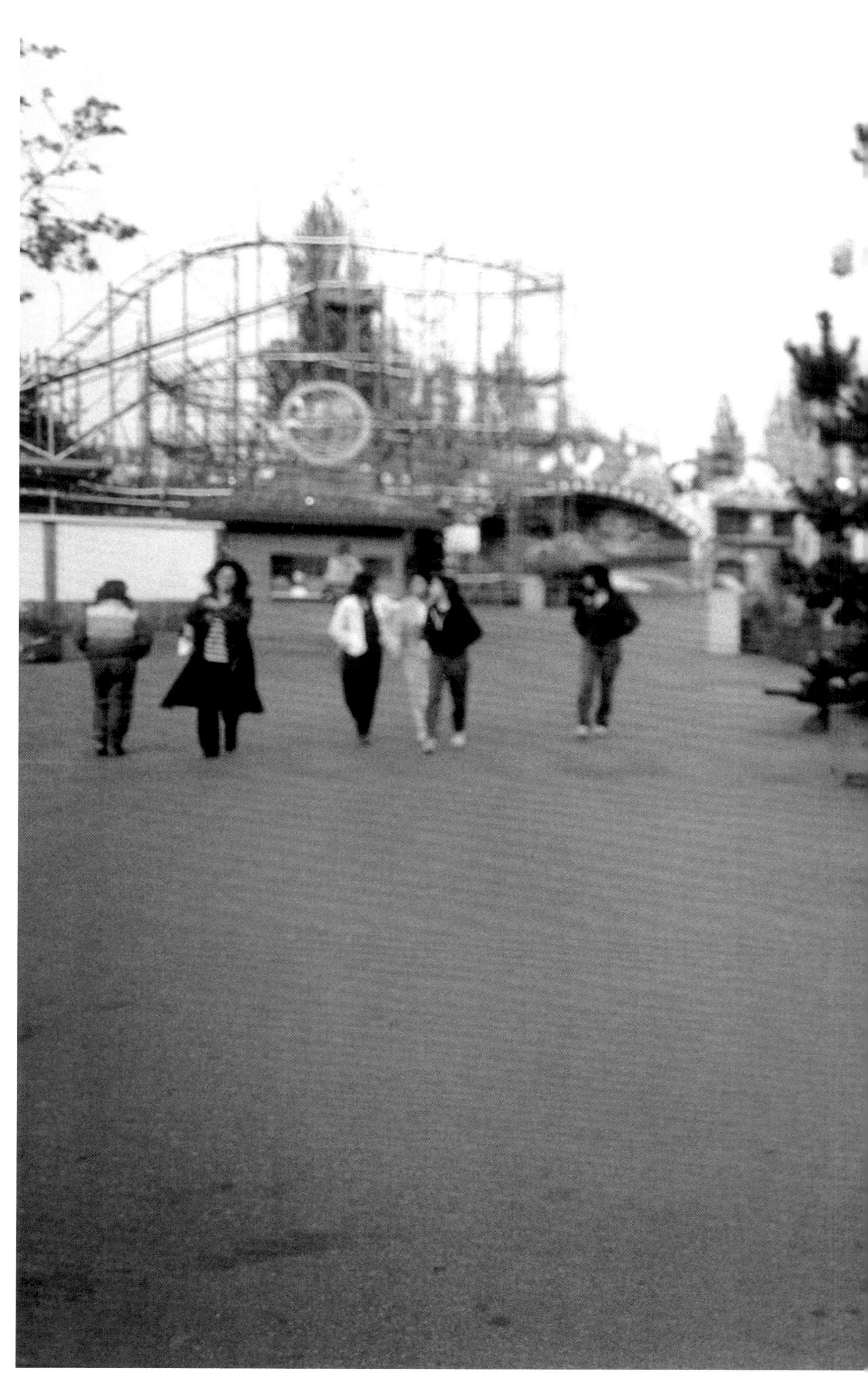

180 From 'Streetwise', *Tiny*, Seattle, Washington, 1983

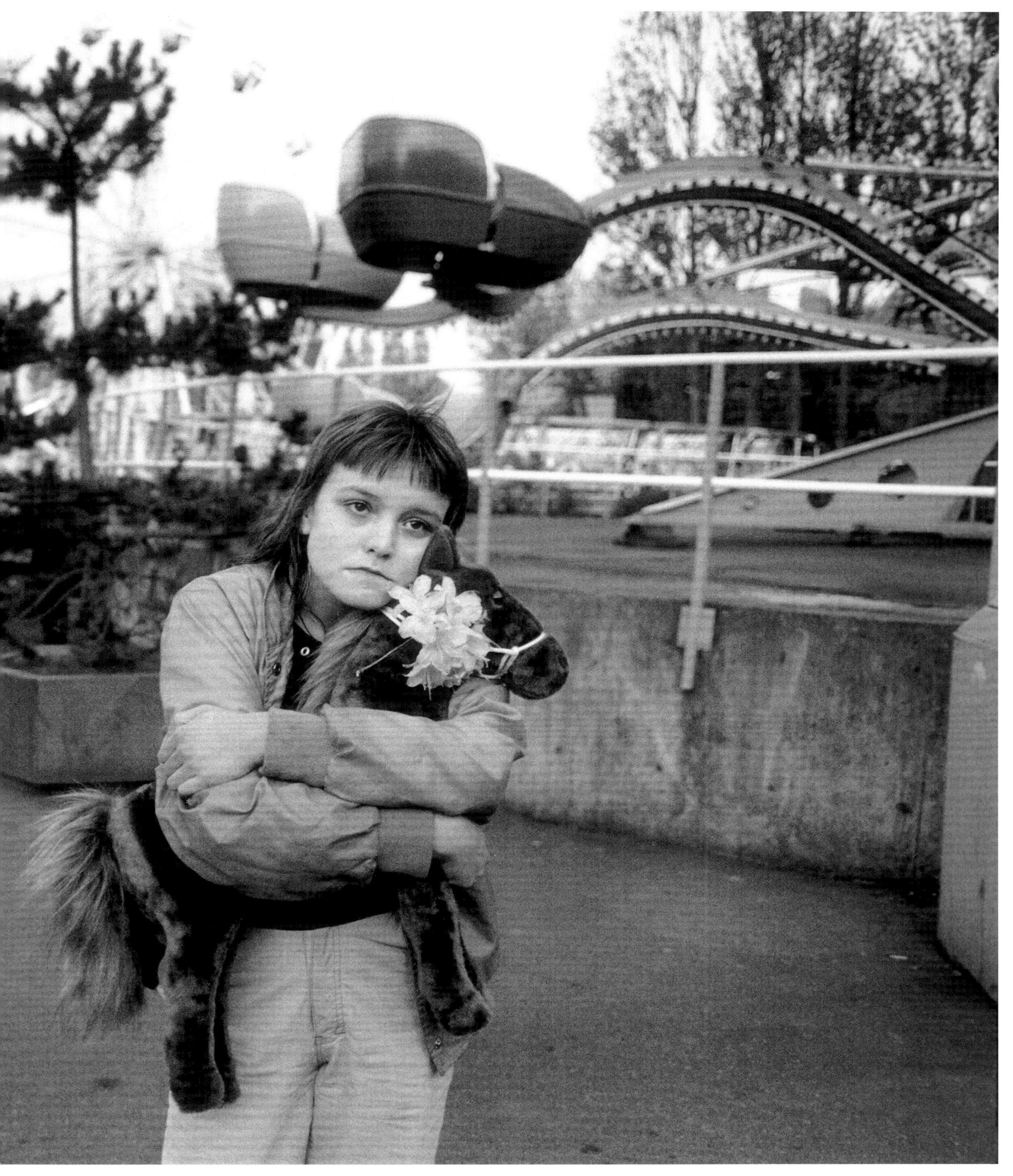

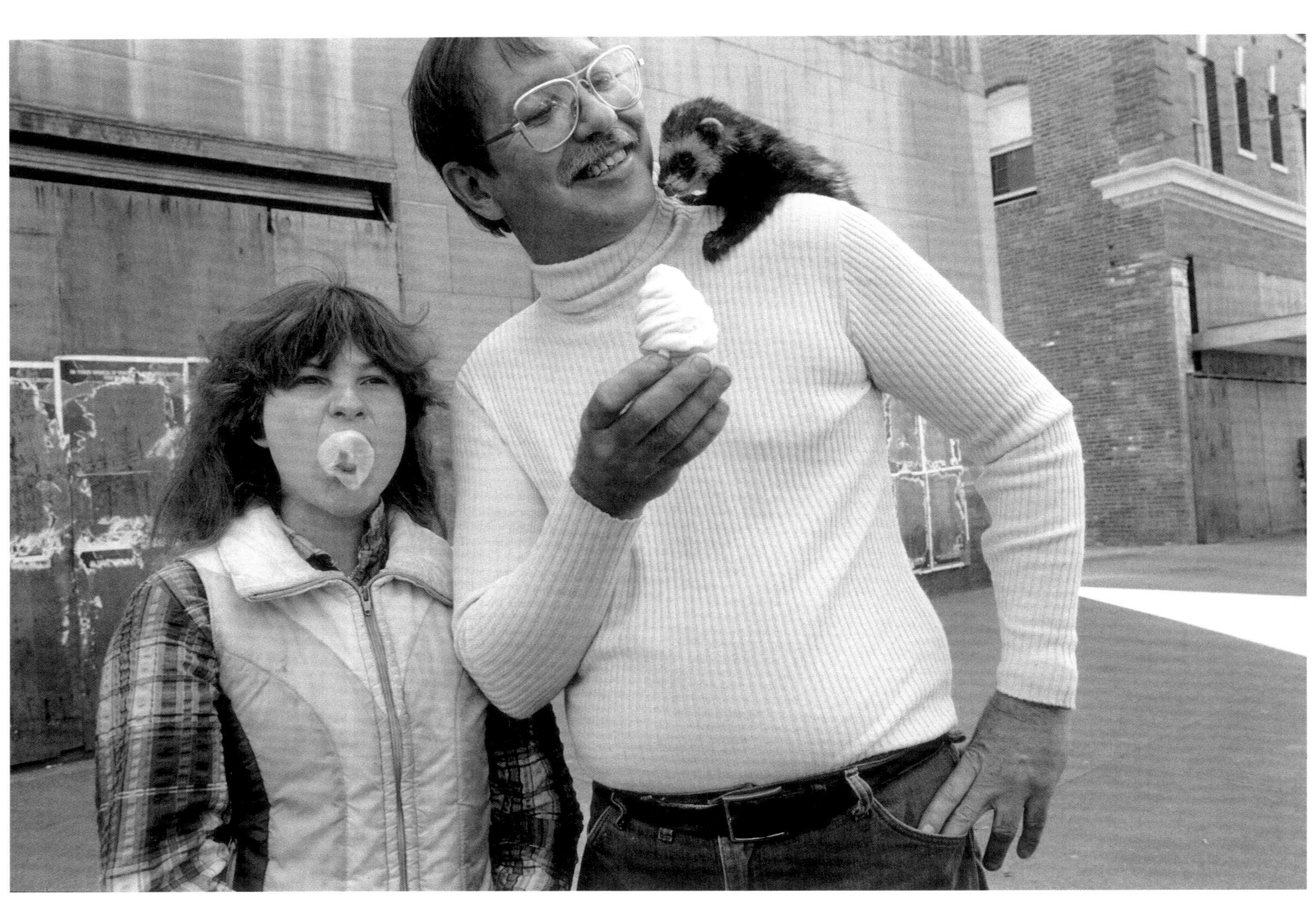

182 From 'Streetwise', *Laurie and the Ferret Man on Pike Street*, Seattle, Washington, 1983

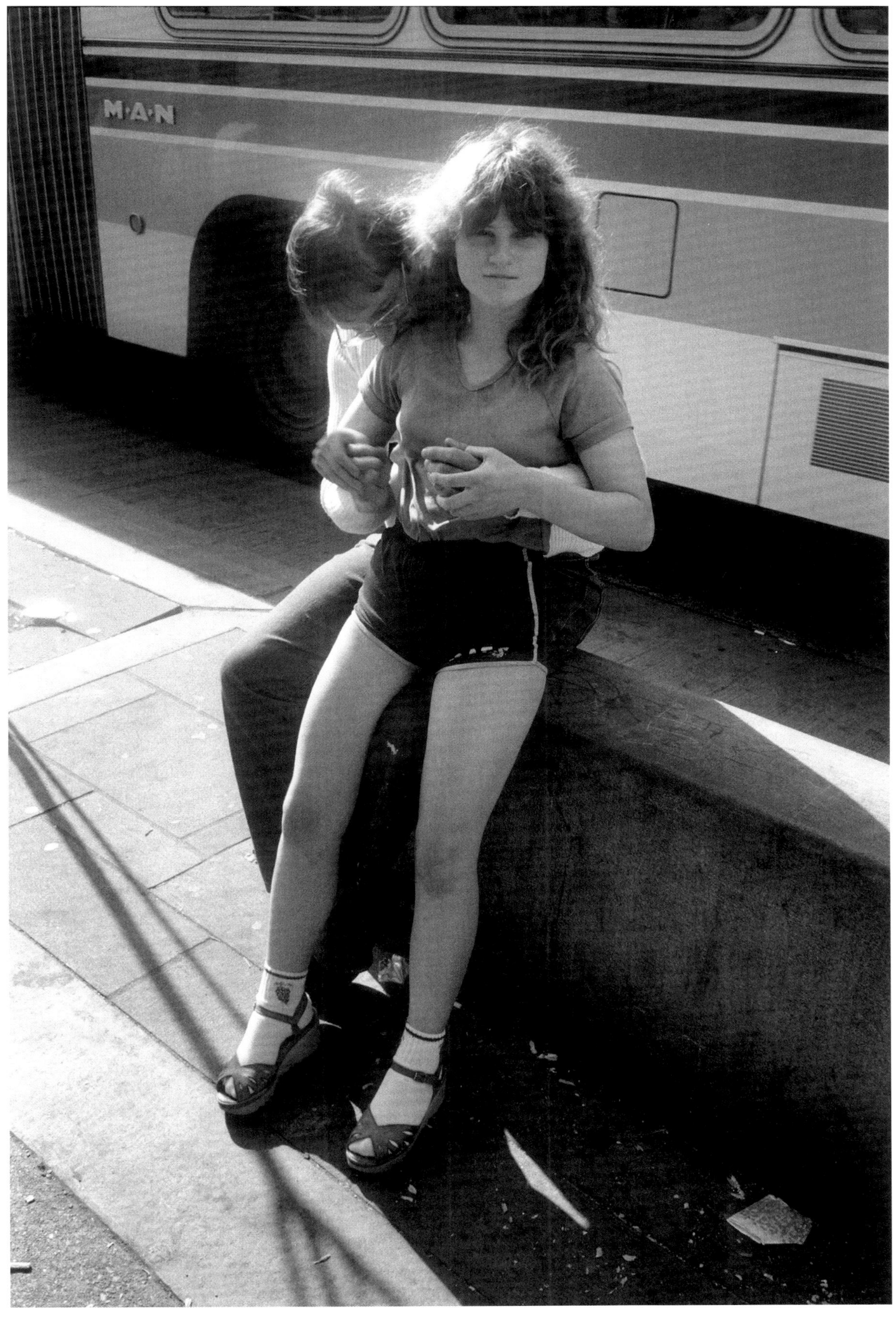

From 'Streetwise', *Pike Street*, Seattle, Washington, 1983

JIM

GOLDBERG

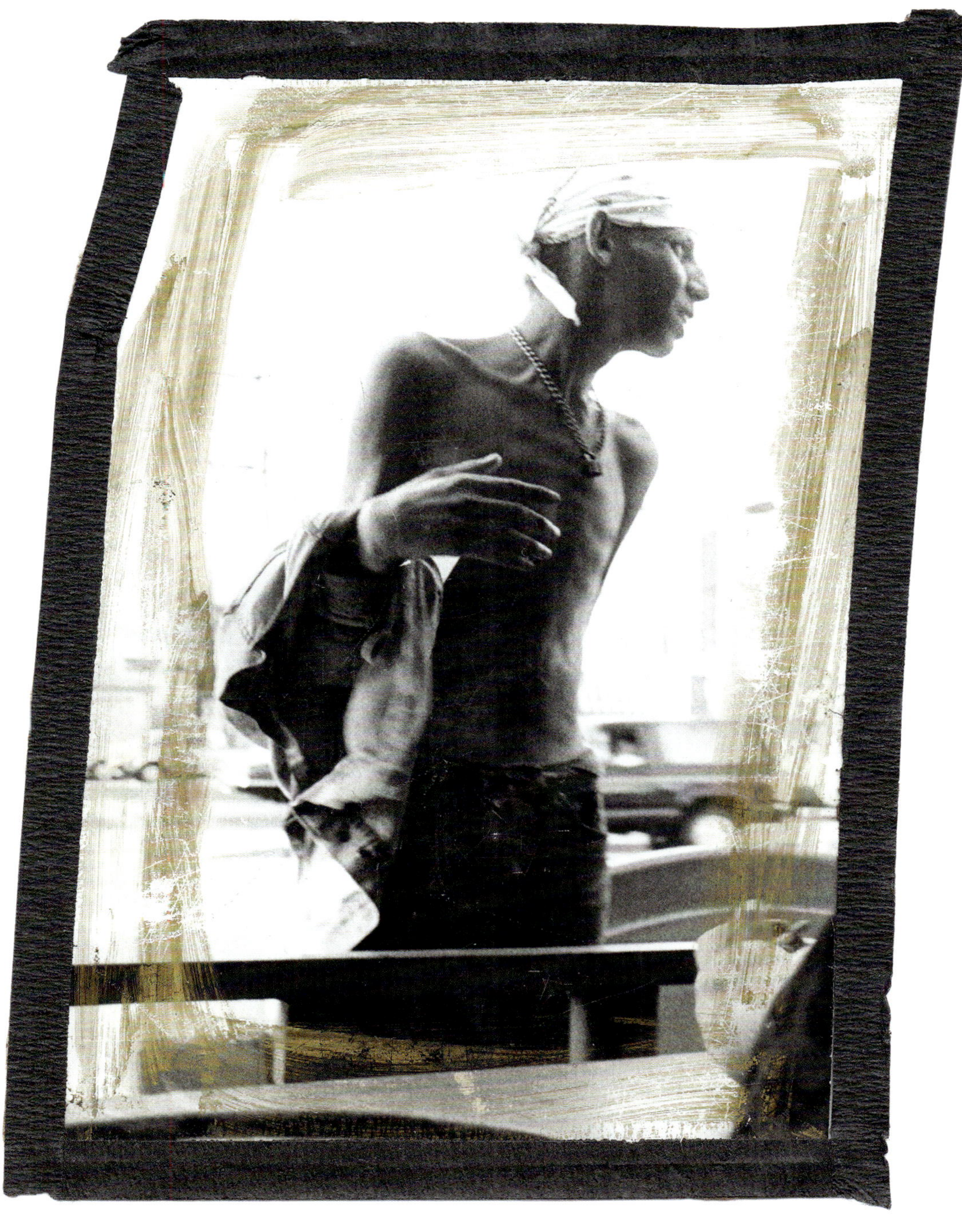

born a wicked child
raised by wolves

a screamin kamakazi
i never will crash

First published in book form in 1995, Jim Goldberg's (b. 1953, USA) *Raised by Wolves* weaves several individual stories into a larger story of teenage homelessness on the streets of Los Angeles and San Francisco. Comprising photographs, film stills, collages, interviews, handwritten testimonies and snatches of biography, it creates a wilfully fractured narrative in which shifts in time and place echo the uncertain, chaotic thrust of the itinerant lives it traces.

Having jettisoned the received 'truths' of photojournalism for a more multi-layered, impressionistic approach, Goldberg also subverts the established documentary approach by using blur, graininess and often radically cropped images to evoke the energy of lives lived on the run, not just from the authorities but the adult world. Goldberg's authorial voice frames the interviews used throughout – a still, calm centre in a work driven by the often unreliable testimonies of the protagonists, not least that of 'Tweeky' Dave, a central character whose autobiographical anecdotes veer from the truthful to the self-mythologising according to his mood.

Out of these fragments and confabulations, though, a greater truth emerges: a sense not just of what it takes to survive on these unforgiving streets but of how doggedly determined and creatively inventive an artist must be in order to evoke the everyday uncertainty that attends the lives of children who are living on the run: from authority, the adult world and themselves.

Goldberg spent six years (1987–93), off and on, with his adolescent subjects. In that time he observed their daily grind of hustling, having sex, scoring and taking drugs, being busted by the cops, interacting – or not – with their social workers, hanging out on the street and in squats, and killing time in diners and fast-food joints, forever on the move through the same neighbourhoods in search of a trick or a high.

Like much of Goldberg's work, *Raised by Wolves* is the product of an immersive approach that depended on him developing a close relationship with his subjects. There is no detached observation here, rather a kind of collaboration. As with his other series, *Rich and Poor* (1985) and *Open See* (2009), Goldberg involved his subjects in the creation of the finished work. For *Raised by Wolves* he uses their handwritten testimonies and journal entries alongside transcripts of interviews he conducted with the homeless kids, their parents, siblings, social workers and the police.

The narrative is punctuated by official documents – an enforcement notice from a landlord with the words 'FUCK U ASSHOLE' scrawled on it – and more personal ephemera: a letter of apology to a long-lost parent, and even a 'to do' list that, unconsciously or otherwise, mocks the often mundane practicality of the straight world: 'things 2 do tomorrow / get high! / see echo / see jim / see misha / eat maybe / maybe sleep?'

The list was written by Tweeky Dave, a veteran street survivor who alongside Echo (real name Beth), a relative newcomer to the itinerant life, is the central character of Goldberg's narrative. The first voice we encounter, though, belongs to Goldberg himself, the all-seeing but invisible narrator. In the living room of a suburban New York house he interviews Echo's mother, a social worker, while they watch home movies of a once intact and functioning family. We learn almost immediately that the young homeless woman we will encounter first fled the family home aged thirteen, to escape her sexually abusive stepfather, Ray, a police officer. All that follows is framed by that revelation.

As is immediately apparent, as a photo-book *Raised by Wolves* is almost novelistic in its style and structure, but it is the images that give the narrative its visceral power and sense of immediacy. On the page, the lives of these damaged children unfold with a kind of inexorable self-destructive energy that is by turns compelling and unsettling. What emerges, too, from the deft juxtaposition of images and words, is the sense that these kids are clandestine, almost ghostly presences on the Californian city streets, semi-invisible to the adult world save for the roving gaze of sexual predators and police officers.

In its entirety, though, *Raised by Wolves* is not just a photo-book or an exhibition, but a multimedia project that also exists in the films and audio recordings that Goldberg also made during his time among the adolescent homeless. In one dismally illuminating sequence, Tweeky Dave and Echo sit side by side in a fast-food joint, thinking aloud in abstract fits and starts as they chew on burgers and fries. She is striking and withdrawn; he is fawning and insistent, a stick-thin, wolfish presence. The ambience is redolent of various American indie films that deal in chemical and sexual transgression, from Gus Van Sant's *Drugstore Cowboy* (1989) to Larry Clark's *Kids* (1995), but there is an enervation here that is well-nigh impossible to recreate on celluloid: the weary stoicism of the drug-dependent street survivor.

Though Goldberg grounds the book in the interwoven experiences of Tweeky Dave and Echo, there are close to a hundred 'characters' in the cast, many of them just fleeting presences. Goldberg, too, becomes a character in his own multimedia novel, befriending the pair and helping them out when things inevitably become desperate. His role is a complex one: witness, narrator, editor and shaper of the narrative, but also friend, confidant and perhaps even enabler. Throughout, though, he encourages them to engage to whatever degree they want – or can – in the story he is constructing around them. It is inevitably a compromised collaboration – Goldberg maintains creative control of their narrative – but he is upfront throughout about his motives and machinations.

Raised by Wolves is also an elegy, and one punctuated by what turn out to be often bleakly ironic memorial artefacts: a skateboard with a sticker that reads, 'Next Stop: The Twilight Zone'; a T-shirt emblazoned with the words 'Cheap Trick'; Tweeky Dave's denim jacket covered in felt-tip scrawls – 'Hollywood Dope Fiends 4 ever', 'Fuck the system up the ass'. When Tweeky Dave dies of liver disease, the last person he calls is the photographer who befriended him. Goldberg inherits his jacket – and his ashes. No one else claims them; no one else wants them. He would have disappeared without trace but for his appearance in this work. It is his only memorial and in itself an artefact that assures his place in posterity. There is redemption here, too. Beth falls pregnant, has a healthy baby called Amber and returns to her family home, where she has another daughter, Julie. Her itinerant life, like her street name, becomes an echo.

Who, then, are the wolves of the book's title? Are they the parents who did not, or could not, protect their children? Or the adults who prey on their vulnerability? Or the older children who school them in how to survive on the streets? The question echoes through the narrative, unanswered. In one photograph, a youth in a leather jacket stands on a hillside with both middle fingers raised defiantly at the city below. The wolves are out there, everywhere, hiding, like these children, in plain sight.

Sean O'Hagan

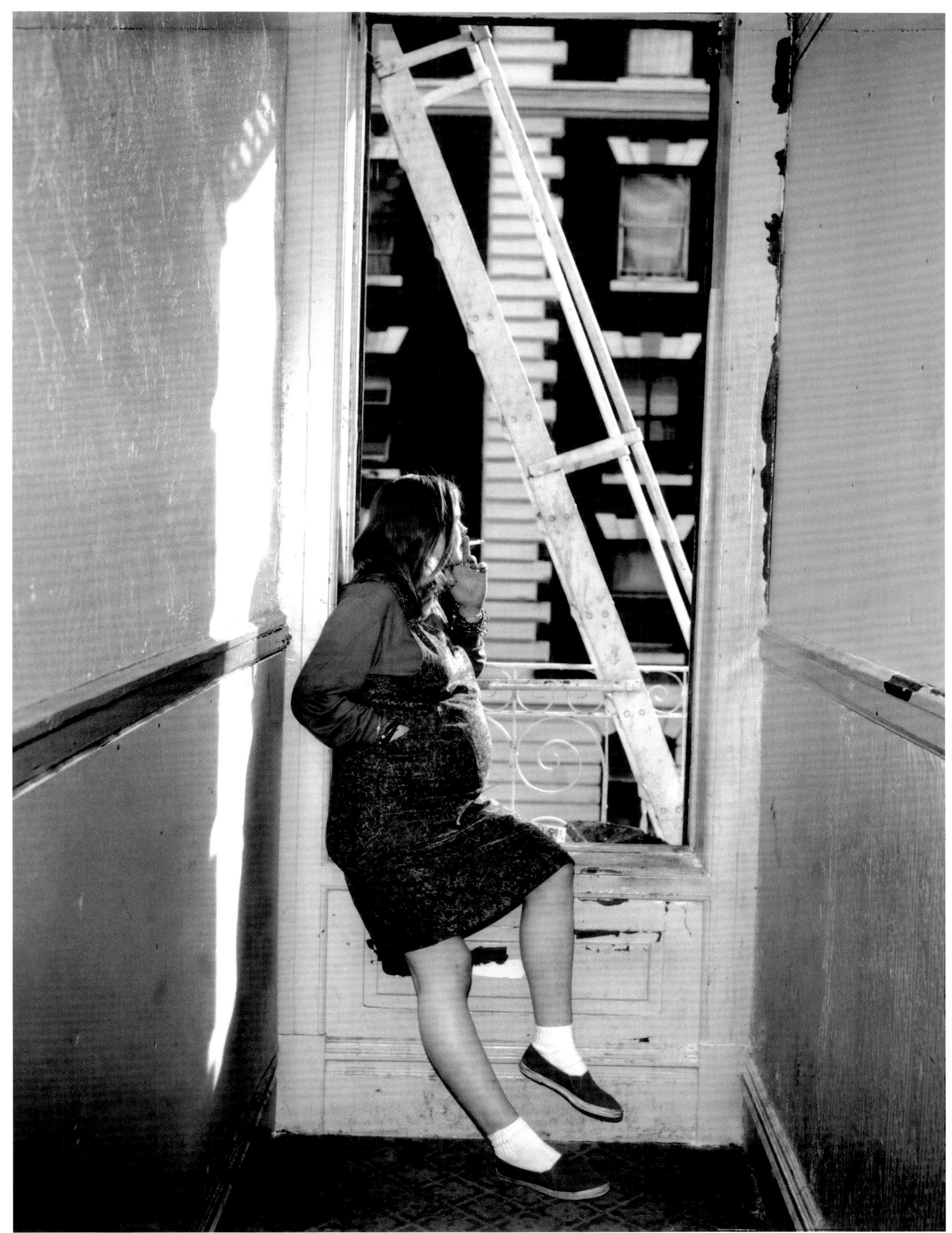

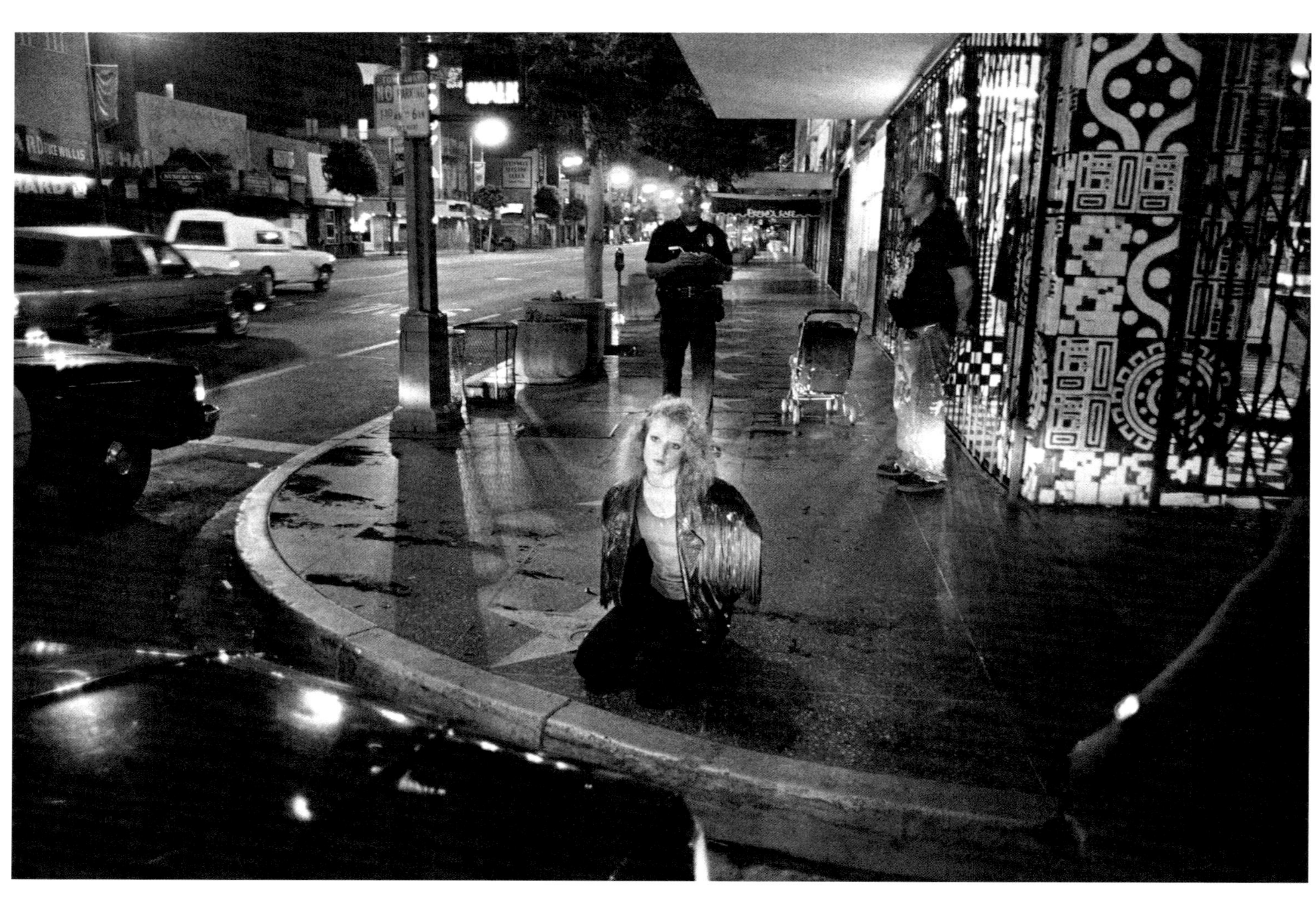

188 From 'Raised by Wolves', *Hollywood Boulevard, 3 a.m.*, Hollywood, California, 1988

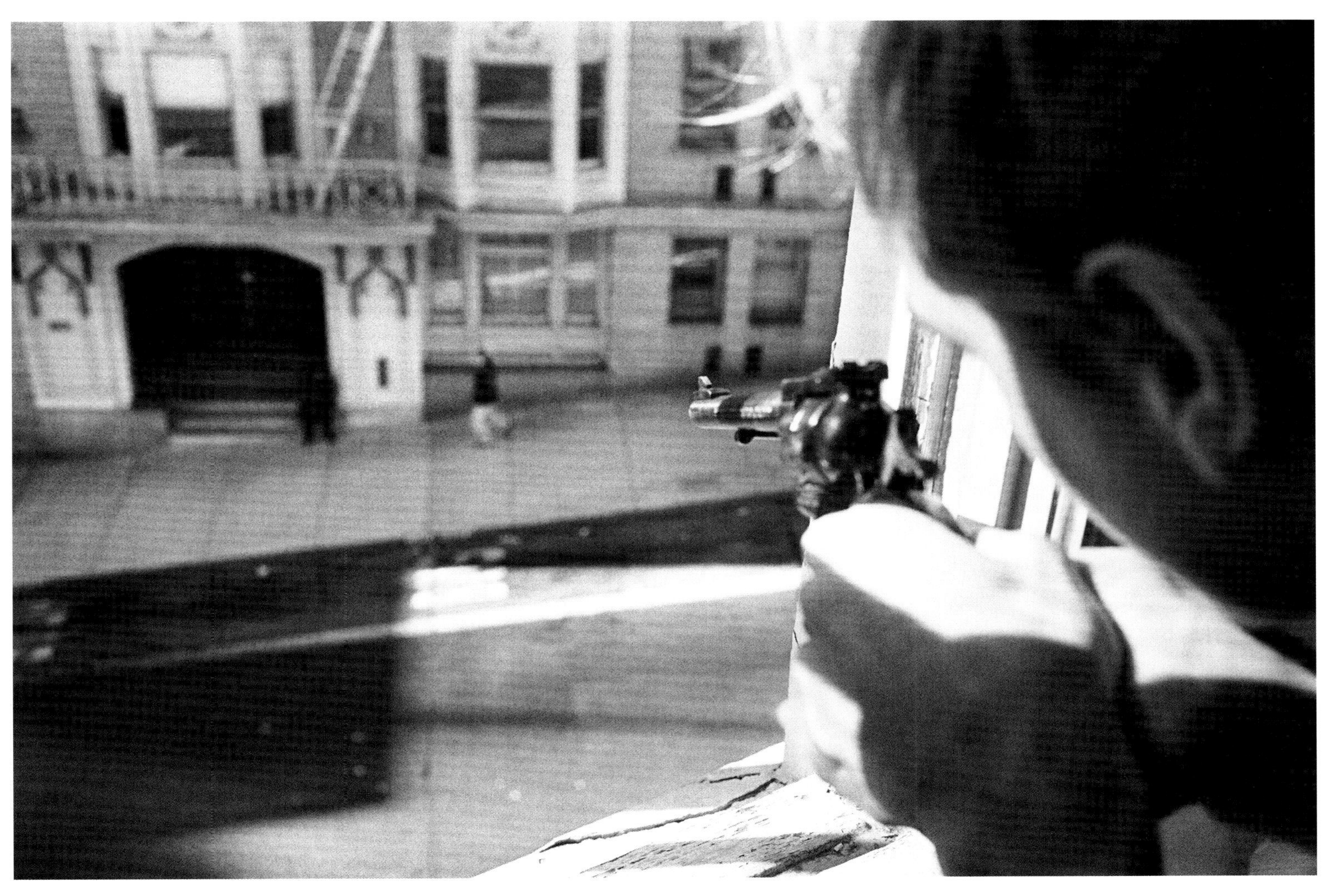

From 'Raised by Wolves', *Tank, Room 17, Riviera Hotel*, San Francisco, California, 1987

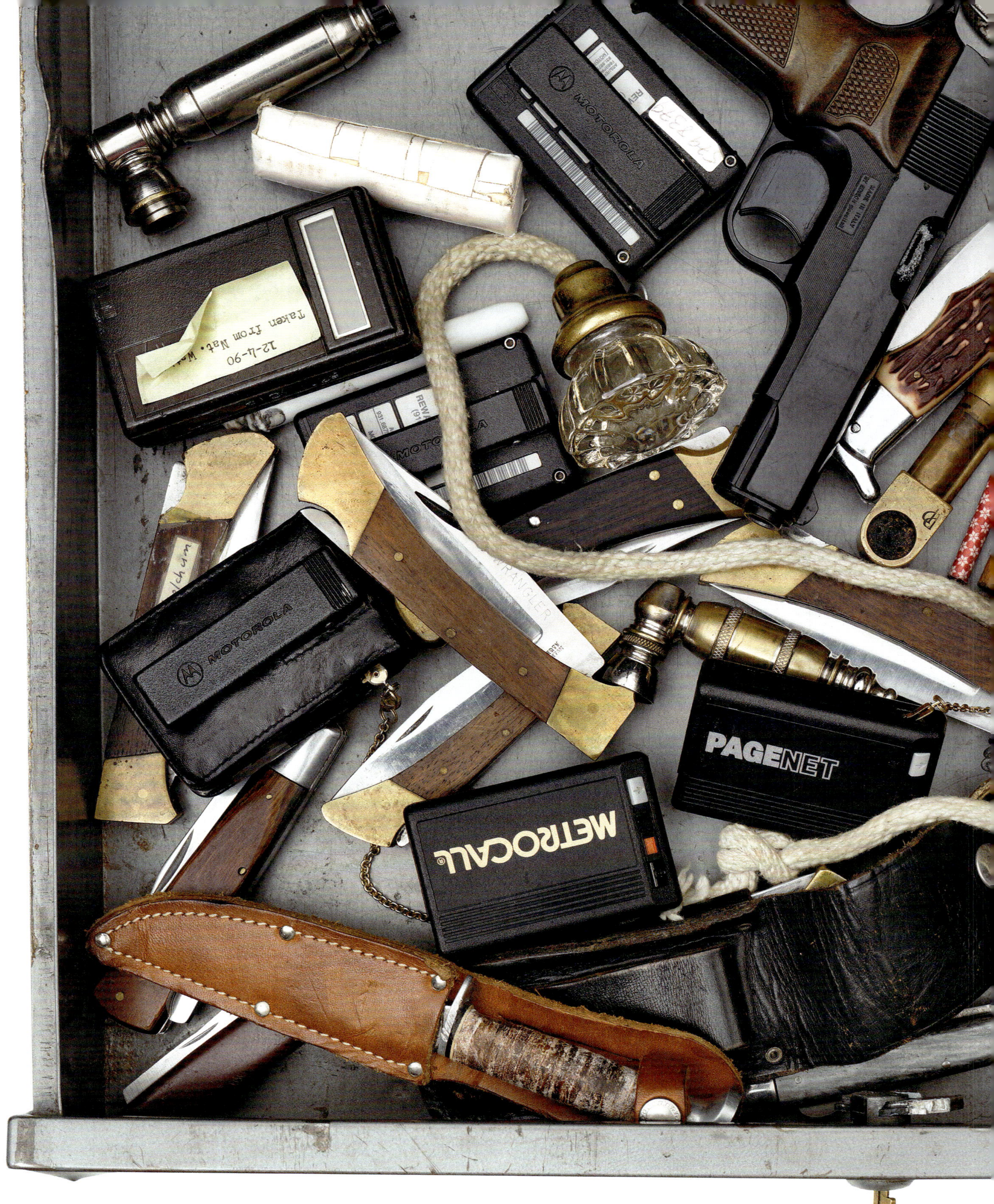

190 From 'Raised by Wolves', *Confiscated Objects*, San Francisco, 1992–1993

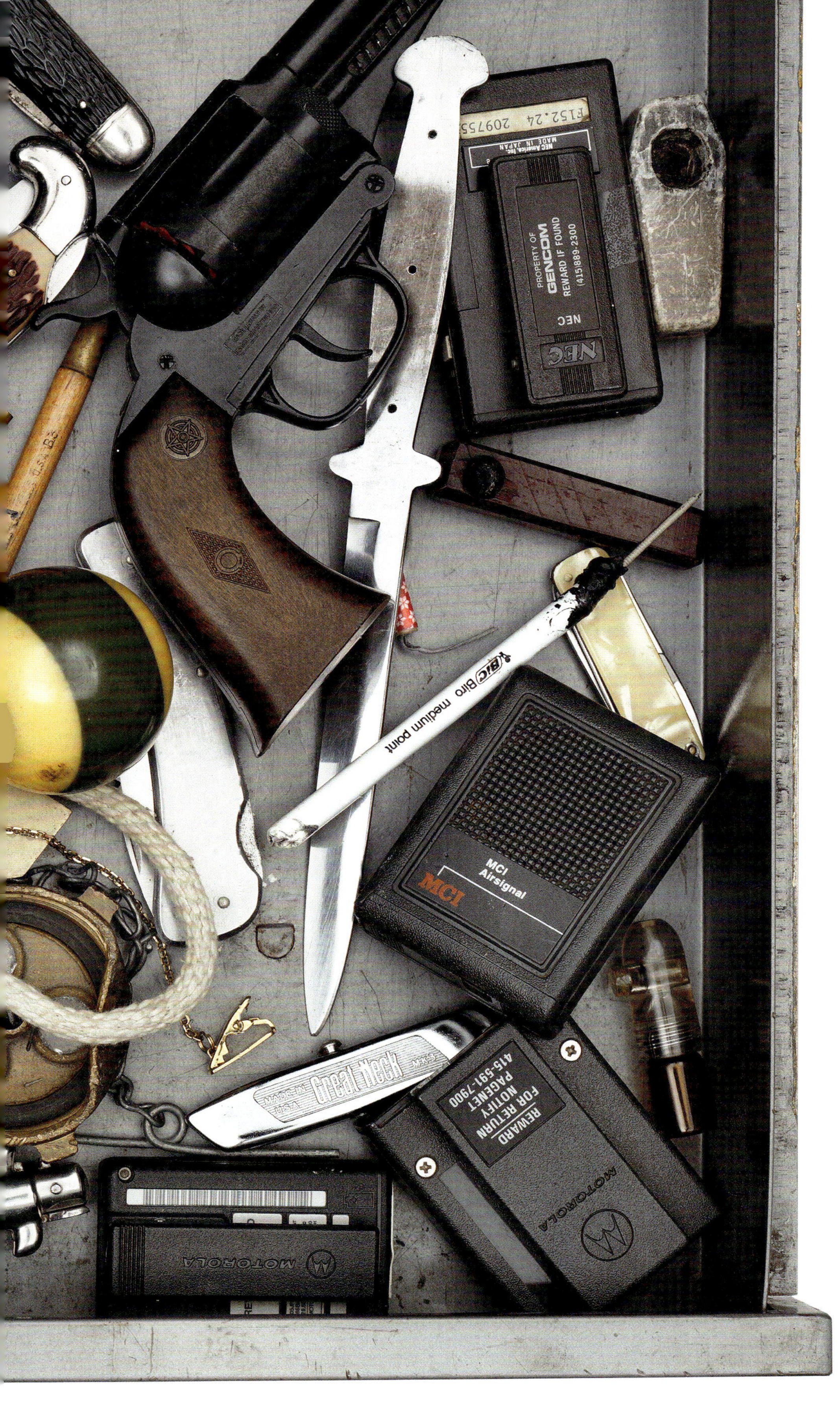

F152.24 209755
NEC America Inc.
MADE IN JAPAN
PROPERTY OF
GENCOM
REWARD IF FOUND
(415)889-2300
NEC
NEC
BIC Biro medium point
MCI
Airsignal
MCI
Great Neck
MOTOROLA
REWARD
FOR RETURN
NOTIFY
PAGENET
415-591-7900
MOTOROLA

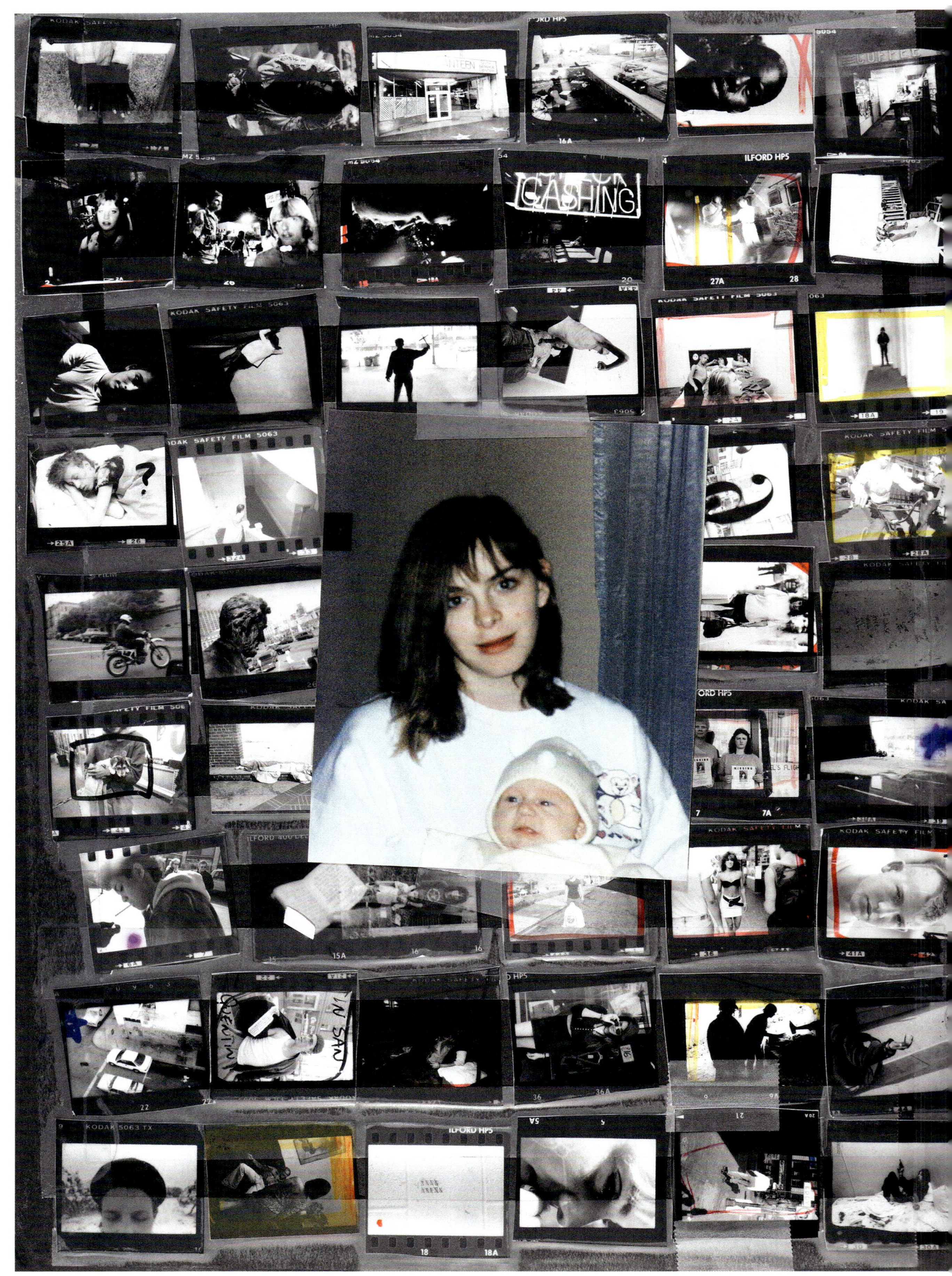

192 From 'Raised by Wolves', *101 Pictures*, San Francisco, 1982-1986

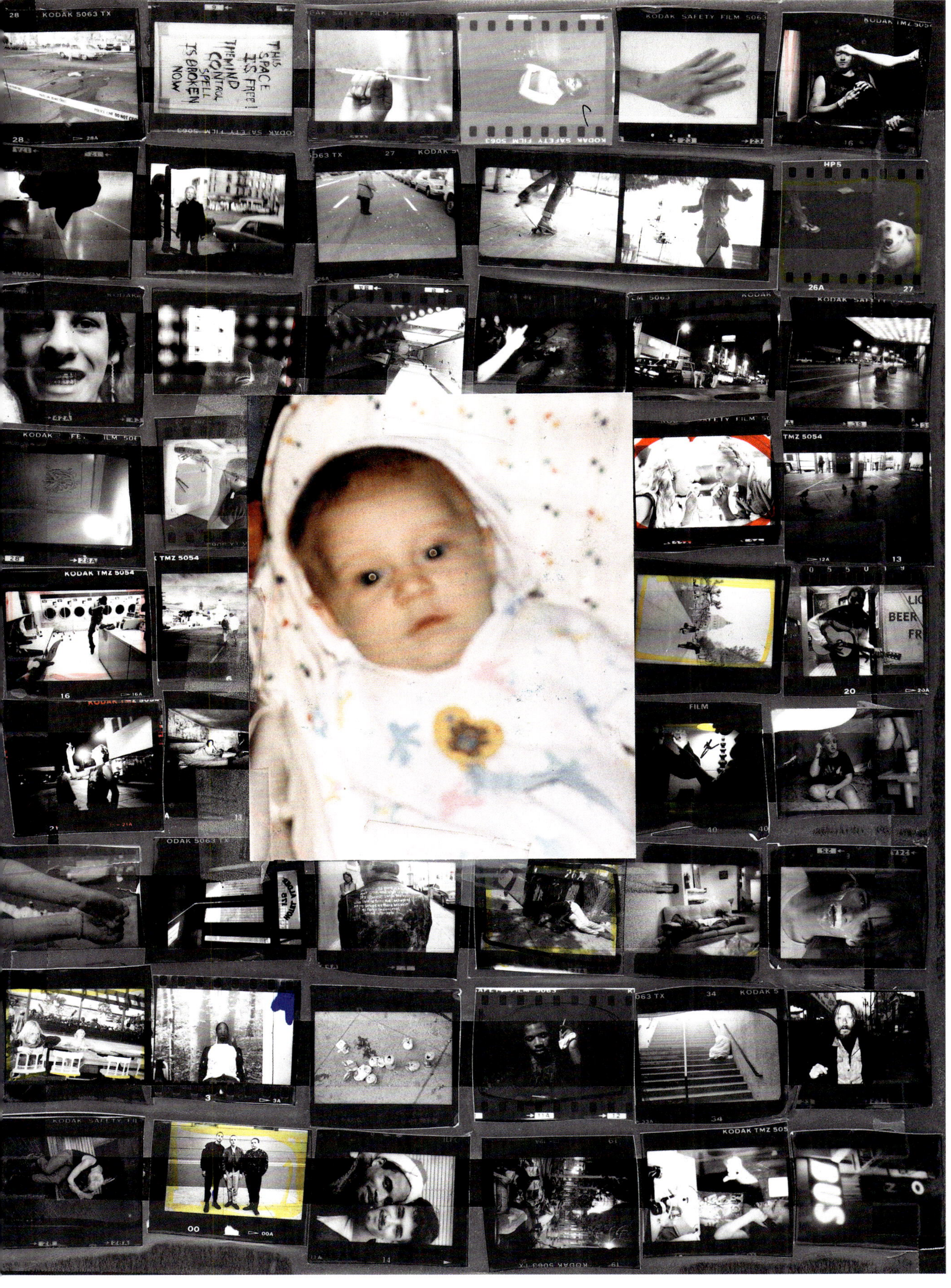

THIS SPACE IS FREE!
THE MIND CONTROL SPELL IS BROKEN NOW

BORIS

MIKHAILOV

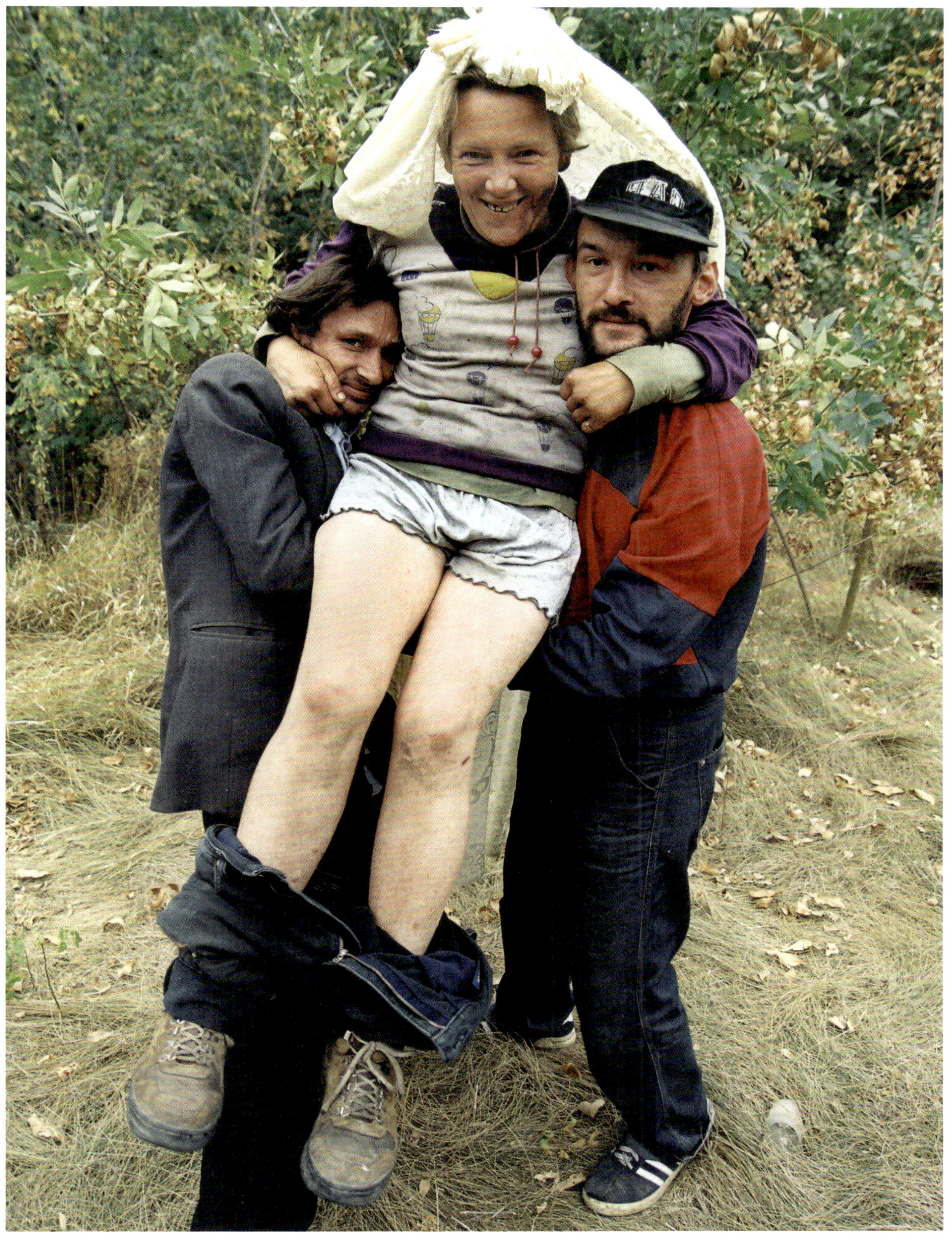

A few years after the breakup of the of the Soviet Union, Boris Mikhailov (b. 1938, Ukraine) returned to his hometown, Kharkiv, in the Ukraine. The wild desolation that he was faced with, due to the crisis triggered by the country's lack of energy reserves and the ensuing relentless inflation, was the starting point for his most desperate and wide-reaching visual poem: *Case History*. Made up of more than four hundred photographs shot between 1997 and 1998, it is the painful yet cathartic expression of a total political failure: first of Communist ideology, then of the democratic reforms ushered in by Mikhail Gorbachev under the appellatives 'Perestroika' and 'Glasnost', and lastly of Western-style capitalism. The only characters in this series are the so-called *bomzhes*: homeless people who lost everything in the sudden shift towards a market economy, like in a nuclear wind: houses, clothes and the very teeth from mouths that have nothing left to chew. It is the end of history (in keeping with the theory of Francis Fukuyama: here any simulacrum of progress indefinitely falls by the wayside), told by Mikhailov with his own unique blend of affliction, amusement, liveliness and hunger.

The Wedding originates here. It is the impossible child of a clearly sterile parent. A sort of spin-off revolving exclusively around a single, grotesque vicissitude. The protagonists are a couple of *bomzhes*, chanced upon like all the others in the ferocious outskirts of the city, who were called upon to stage a fake wedding. It is the apotheosis of a process of control and *mise en scène* that underpins this phase of Mikhailov's production. While previously the Ukrainian photographer asked his subjects to pose for him, miming situations of everyday life arranged on the basis of the clichés of religious representation (*Case History* offers a vast selection of atrocious series of pieties, falls, flagellations, crucifixions and depositions), here his requests go even further. We shift from the corruption of the biblical story, with wide-eyed figures against dismal settings (reminiscent of Pasolini's *Gospel According to St Matthew*), to a sort of post-apocalyptic soap opera. The table-turning is radical. Television actors chosen exclusively for their good looks are replaced by two absolute wastrels, bereft even of clean clothes, decency, good taste and – most of all – sex-appeal. As Boris Groys writes, 'the contrast between the outward appearance of

these old, infirm and disfigured bodies on the one hand, and their owners' endeavours to enact erotically suggestive love scenes with these very same bodies on the other, seems insufferably indecent.'[1]

Mikhailov plays out the entire series on the tension between erotic drive and its denial. Every image contains a more or less explicit sexual invitation that does not induce the slightest arousal on our part, denying any organic stimulus shot after shot. And yet on the other hand, sexual desire seems to be the only emotion left to the two newlyweds, forever busily kissing and touching one another or rubbing against each other, like corrupt and unproductive epigones of *Juno* and Alfred Jarry's *Supermale*. On the other hand, dignity has been violently subtracted from both – as Mikhailov goes to great lengths to highlight, instead of attempting any pointless yet moralistic undertaking of soul-searching and recomposition. There are no profound gazes or severe expressions in his portraits, but just the brutal degeneration of surfaces: wounds, pustules, deformations, outgrowths and vulgar gestures, reiterated and displayed like trophies. The outcome is a sense of deep-seated embarrassment that envelops onlookers in the place of the subjects themselves. We are embarrassed for them, like before the hapless (yet knowing) participants in a reality show on trash television, lowering our gaze from their faces even before they detach their eyes from the camera lens.

The two protagonists of *The Wedding* are rotting away, their bodies visibly decomposing while they are still alive. As anti-heroes, this is the clearest symptom of their anti-immortality: they are clearly younger than they appear to be, but a pernicious mix of fatigue, poverty and illness has swept away all traces of their true age. We are unable to understand exactly how old they are, for they inhabit a different space-time. Instead of a photographic document, this work by Mikhailov looks more like a sci-fi legend. The atmosphere is very similar to that imagined by Cormac McCarthy in *The Road*: in an indefinite future, after an equally unclear catastrophe, nothing remains of humanity but a primitive state of life, entirely bereft of any technological or energy resources, with no other animals around and caught in a constantly tense and hostile climate. Unlike what happens in

the novel, however, Mikhailov's characters still seem able to have a good time. They are in fits of laughter, clowning around, enjoying themselves. Gripped by outbursts of unstoppable biological motility, they engage in entirely irrational or completely hedonistic behaviour. They even have a whale of a time while reciting the farce cooked up by the photographer, who opts to do away with any photojournalistic ambiguity in favour of staging a cringe-worthy theatre of the absurd. They are the worst actors one might possibly imagine to interpret a love story. Yet in their total and obscene readiness to satisfy the demands of the photographer in exchange for a handful of roubles, they make the perfect couple to be featured in a work of sublime pornography, in the etymological sense of the representation (*graphé*) of prostitution (*porneía*).

Francesco Zanot

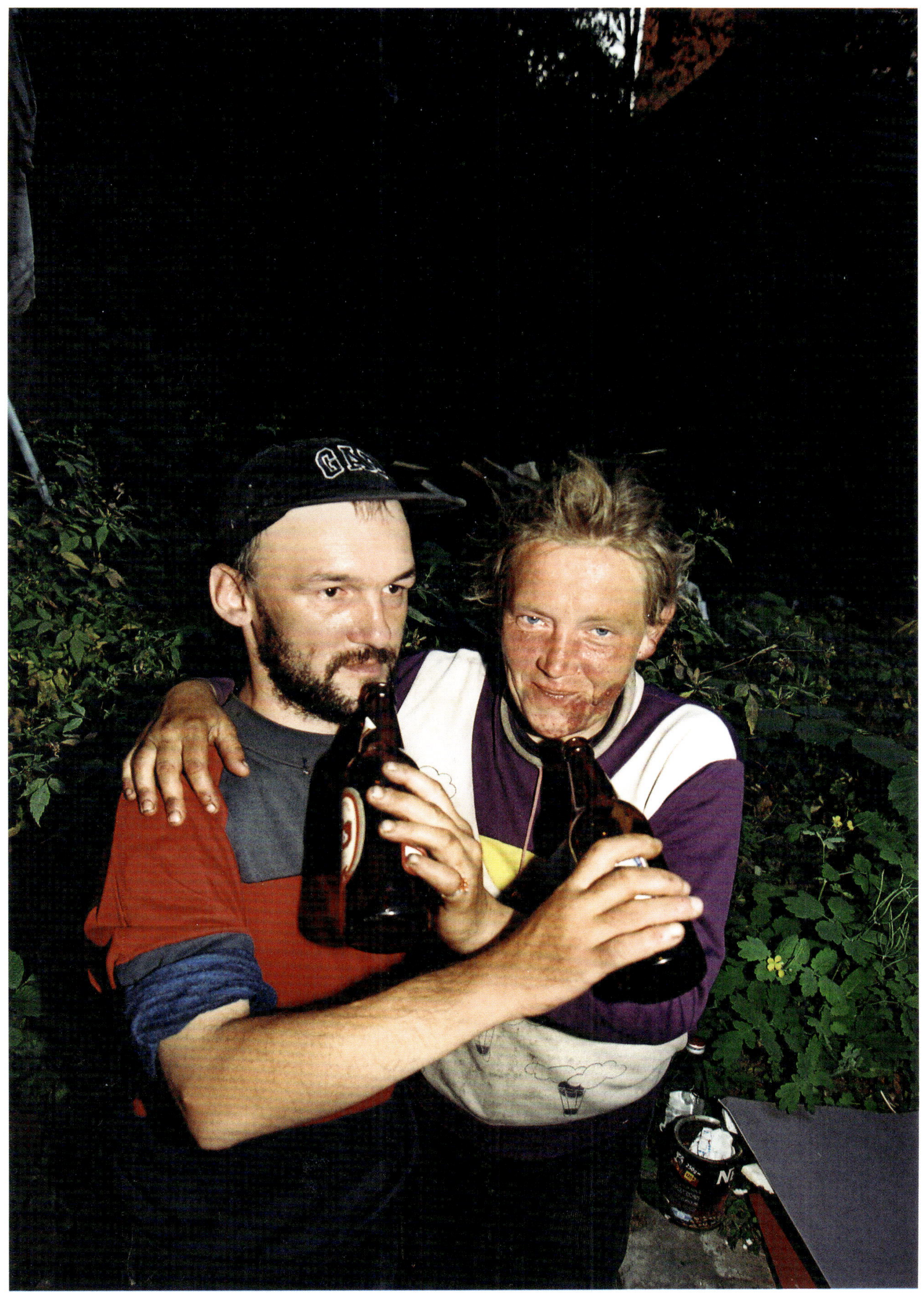

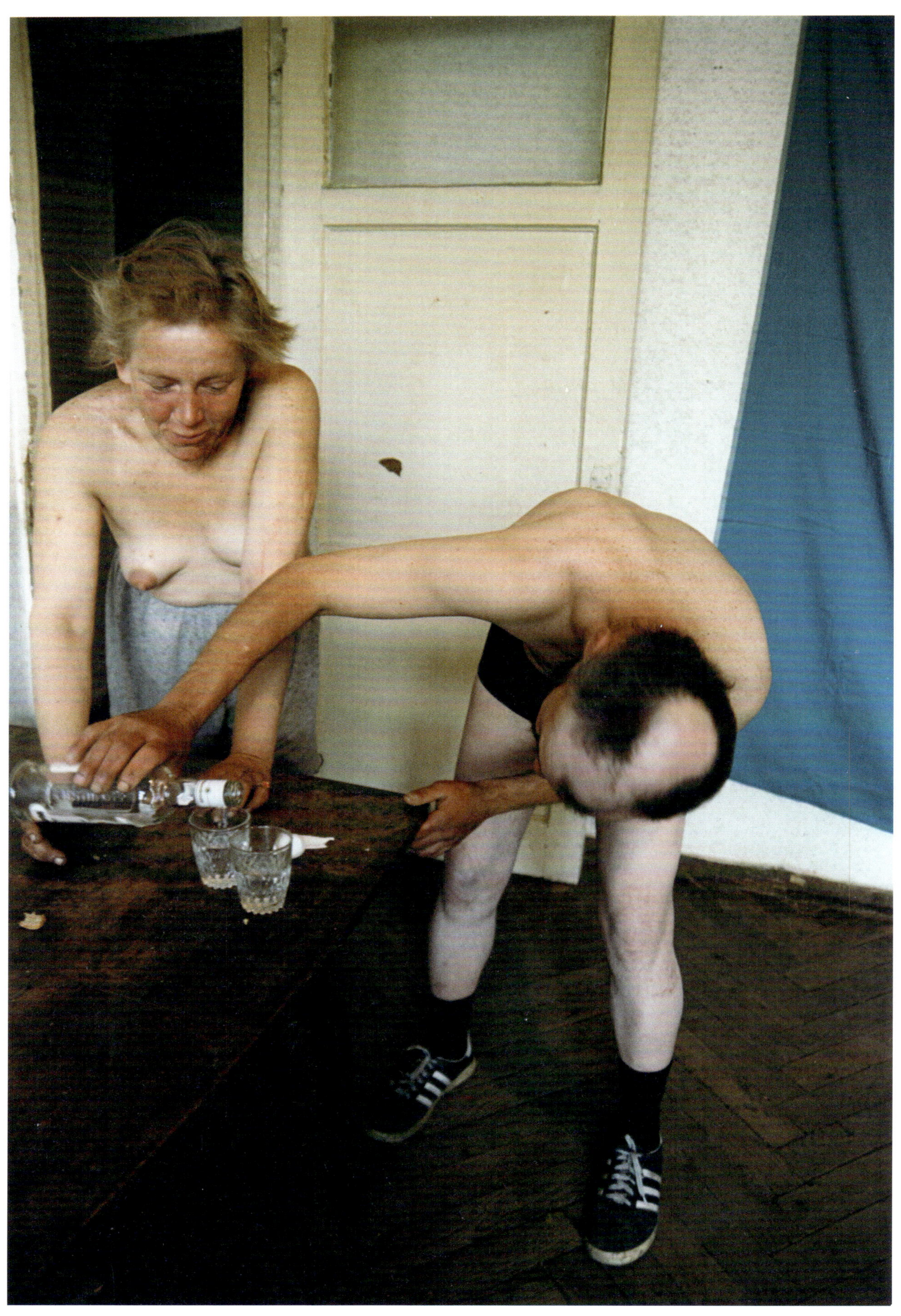

198 This page and opposite: from 'The Wedding', 2005-2006

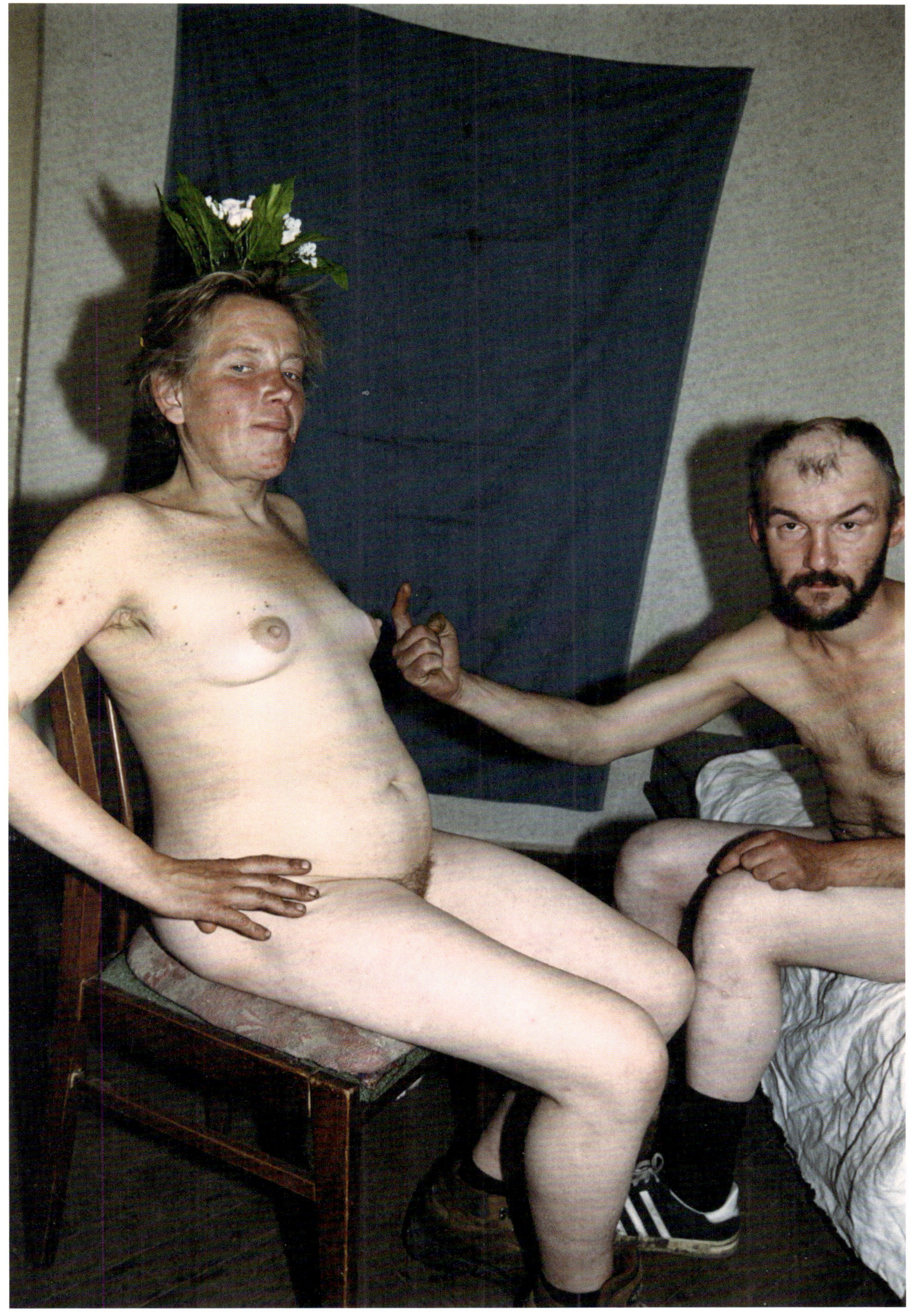

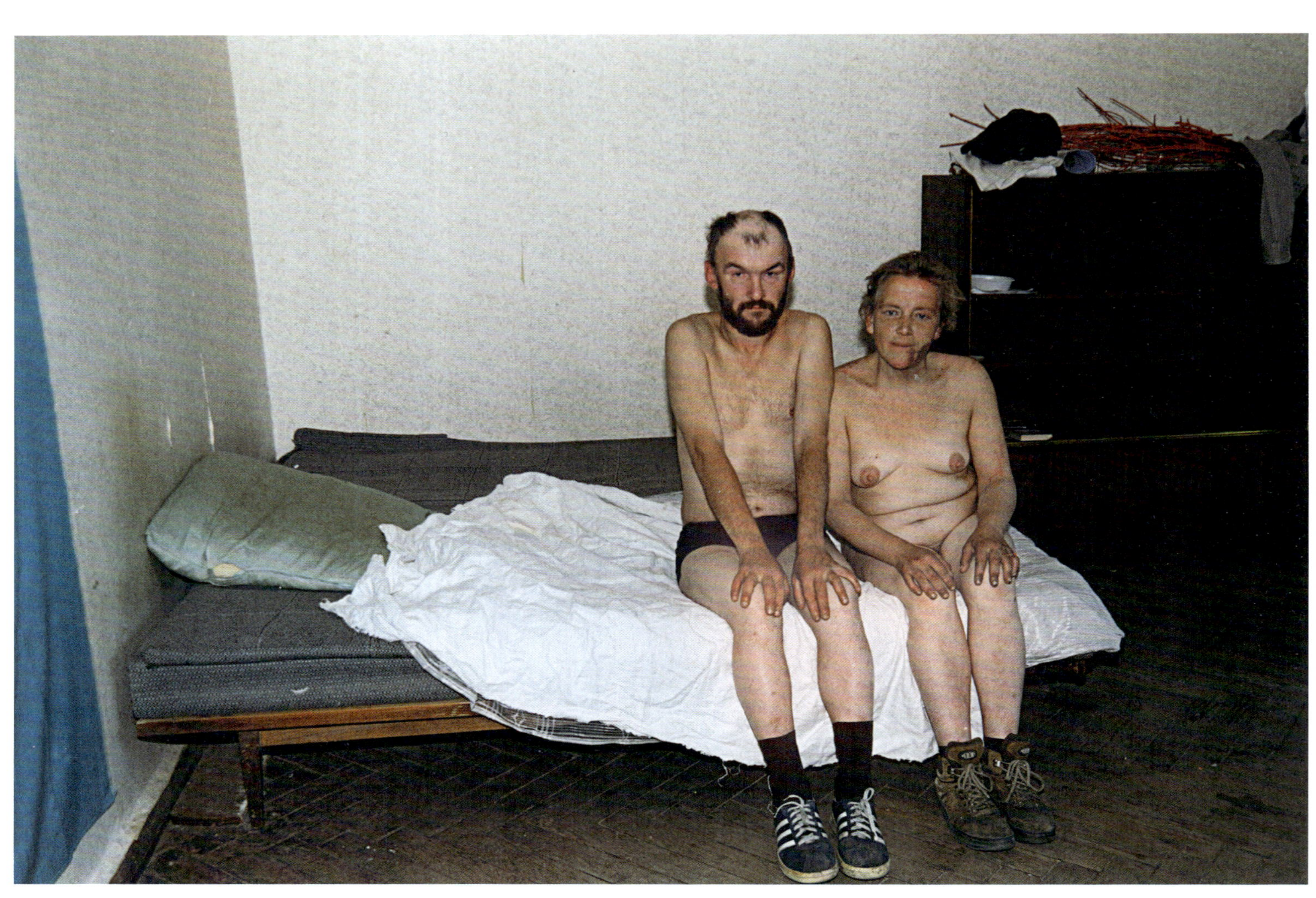

200 This page and opposite: from 'The Wedding', 2005-2006

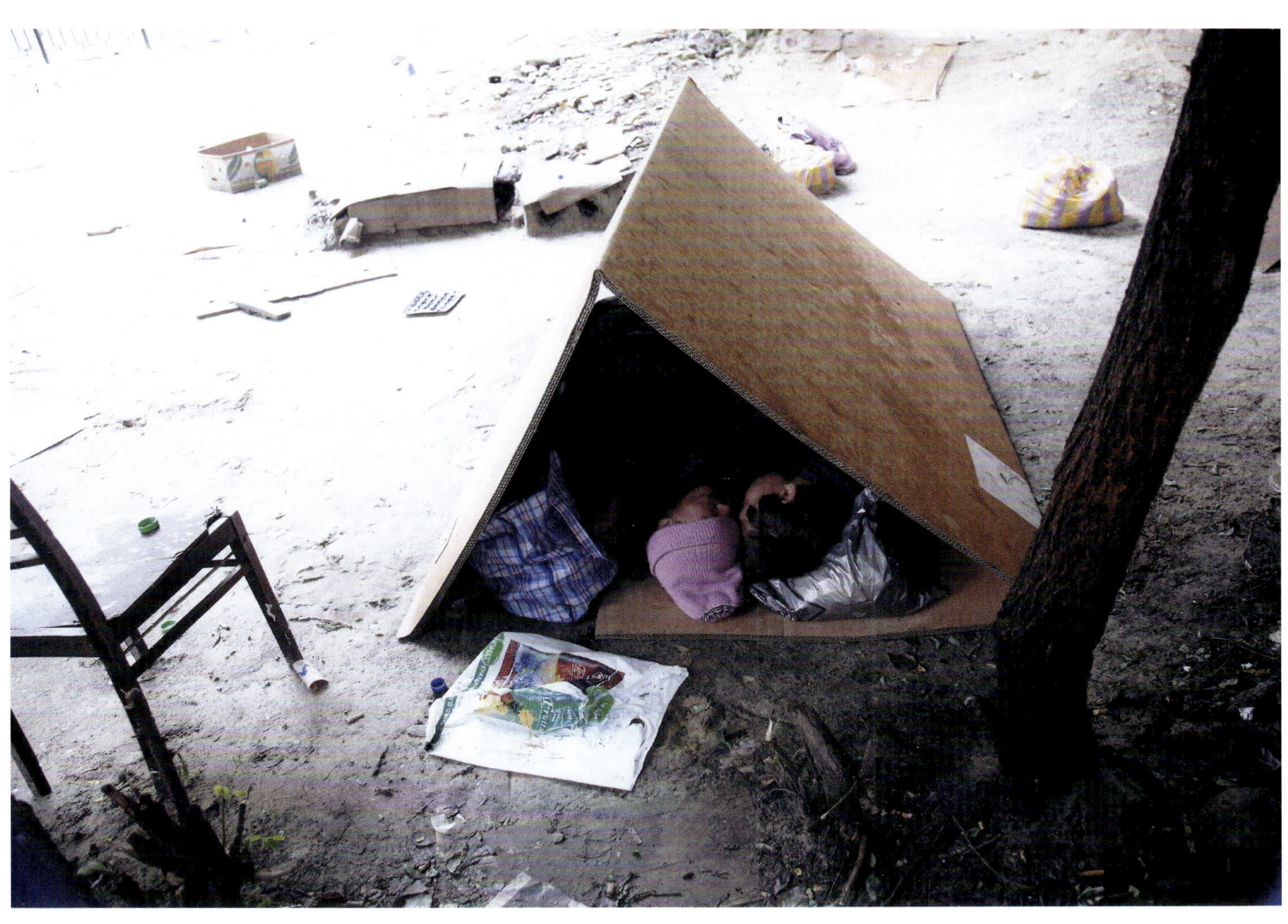

DAYANITA SINGH

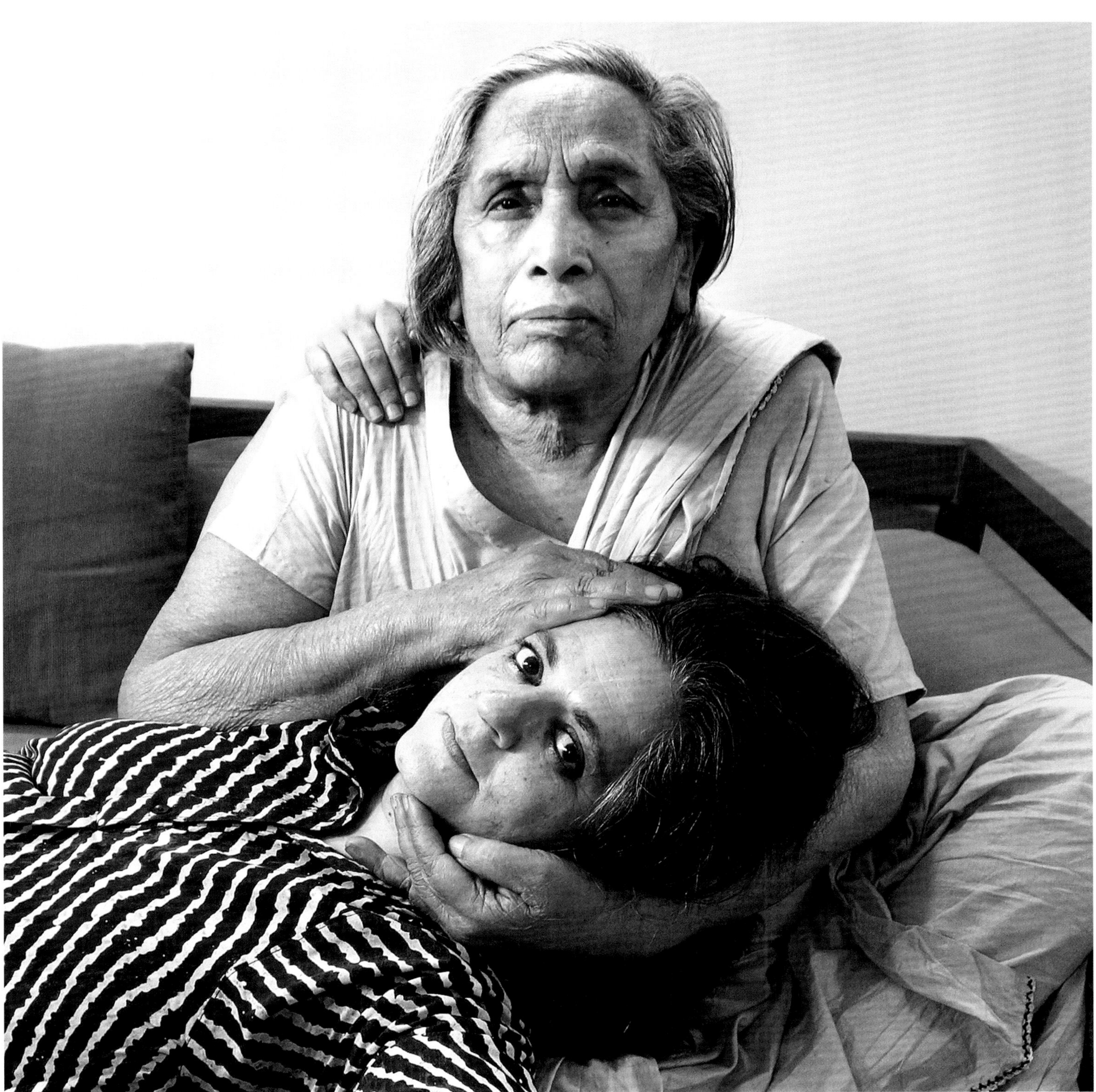

Over the last three decades, Dayanita Singh (b. 1961, India) has become one of the most singular practitioners working at the rich intersection of art and documentary photography. She studied at New York's prestigious International Center of Photography, eventually returning to India. In 1989, she was commissioned by *The Times* (London) to photograph the eunuchs of New Delhi. At that time there were around one million eunuchs in India, mostly castrated boys. Each neighbourhood of a city is assigned a group of eunuchs, who, invested by the community with magical powers, bless the area in exchange for money. Well aware that the world's media saw India as either exotic or calamitous (or both), Singh was seeking out a place for herself in the male-dominated world of photojournalism. But she was also looking for something much more meaningful, beyond the clichés. At a household of eunuchs deep in the city, Singh was introduced to Mona Ahmed, a beautiful and charismatic person. Mona is a female name; Ahmed is male. Ahmed's early years were spent as a boy. After castration, she lived as a woman, Mona, and underwent the first of three genital reassignment operations. But it was too painful to continue. Slowly, Mona Ahmed came to identify as a third sex, in a world that recognises only two.

The first meeting between Dayanita Singh and Mona Ahmed went well. Several rolls of film were shot as the two started to get to know each other. But Mona was wary of the media, and had friends and relatives in England who still knew her as male. She changed her mind about the day's photography. Singh returned the film to Mona, telling her editor it had been damaged during processing. It was a gesture of the trust and equality that has since become the hallmark of all Singh's photographic interactions. Mona recognised Singh's sincerity, and a rich friendship began to develop. Meanwhile, Singh was beginning to work on what would become a major study of her own friends and relatives, as domestic patterns shifted from extended networks to nuclear families.

Mona adopted a baby daughter, Ayesha. Soon Singh was close enough to Mona that she would be invited to photograph Ayesha's grand, three-day-long birthday parties, to which eunuchs came from all over India, and even from Pakistan and Bangladesh. Over time, however, Ayesha began to socialise more with others in the household. Despite her enormous love for Ayesha, Mona struggled with parenthood and took to drinking, and an already precarious life quickly began to unravel. Becoming an outcast among outcasts, preferring to live in a graveyard of ancestors, Mona grew isolated. Ayesha was taken away. But Mona's bond with Singh continued to grow; the psychological balance shifted as Mona went from being something of a symbolic guardian for the young photographer to a more fragile, dependent, lonely and troubled soul. Their friendship grew deeper still, transcending all labels of gender, class or nationality; just two individuals with a profound bond in a difficult world. That bond lasted until Mona Ahmed died in the summer of 2017. Singh remains in contact with Ayesha.

In 2001, more than a decade into their relationship, Dayanita Singh's photographs of Mona Ahmed became public. *Myself Mona Ahmed*, a ground-breaking book, was made with the pioneering publishing house Scalo. Stylistically, the photographs appear to belong to the classical mode of 35mm, black-and-white, humanist observation. But in the book they are set in counterpoint with the text, which comprises profoundly honest and frank emails sent by Mona, via Singh, to Walter Keller, one of the founders of Scalo. Mona's words also supply the captions for the images. So while Singh's name is on the cover, below that of Mona Ahmed, it is clear that Singh is as much a facilitator as an author here, stepping back from the images in order to allow the subject to tell her own story, in all its complexity.

The book's hybrid weave of word and image, fact and fiction, diary and declaration belongs to the important lineage of necessary experiments that has always been present within photography. And yet, like the marginal subjects that demand untried means of expression, such books are often marginalised themselves. Today, Dayanita Singh is renowned for the originality of her many photographic publications, which always find new forms for what needs to be articulated. For Singh, this commitment really began with *Myself Mona Ahmed*, a book now celebrated both as a study of a friendship with a bravely unique person, and a beacon of what is possible with images and words.

For over 25 years, Singh remained restless, never quite reconciling herself to a final arrangement for the work made with Mona Ahmed. While the book could have emerged only from the depths of that particular bond, it is often interpreted as a study of 'a eunuch' or even 'an Indian eunuch', when what has really mattered is both more universal and more personal than this. Eventually, in 2013, Singh decided to film Mona, while keeping a relation to the fixed view of the photographic image. She explained: 'For some time now, I had been playing with the Mona work, trying to find another form for the work, something that could be a true portrait of Mona. I always felt that … I had never been able to do justice to her uniqueness. Finally, I found the form with the moving still image, which is a still portrait of Mona, listening to her favourite song. At first, she appears like someone who has just woken up, then she gets the song and finally she becomes the song.' Shot as a single take, the camera never leaves Mona's face as it moves through a lifetime of emotions. Singh's profound attachment to Mona is palpable, and is underscored by the title of the film: *Mona and Myself*.

David Campany

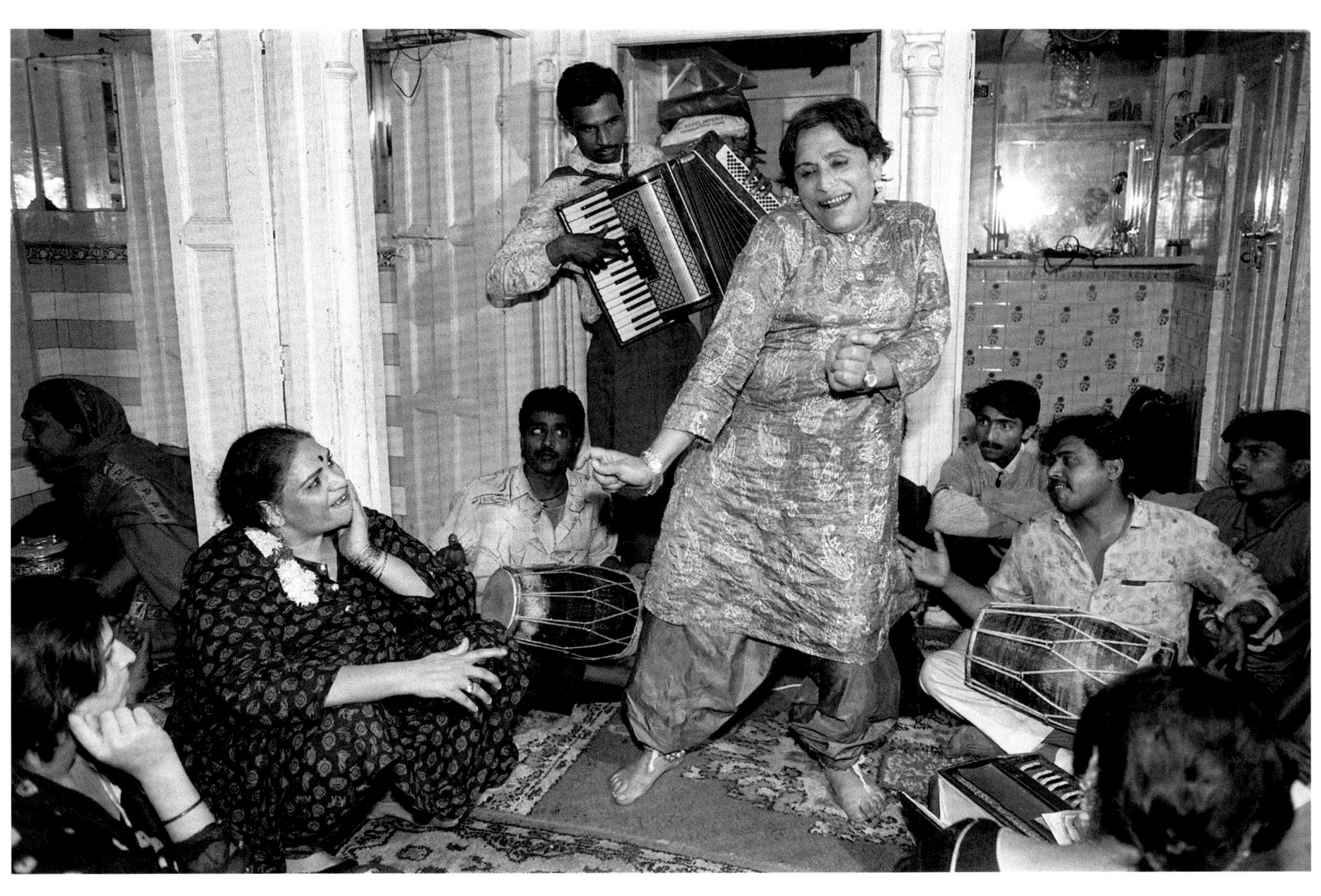

I get this strong urge to dance from within, Ayesha's second birthday, 1991   205

206 *To bless the newborn child, I am dancing in front of the house*, 1994

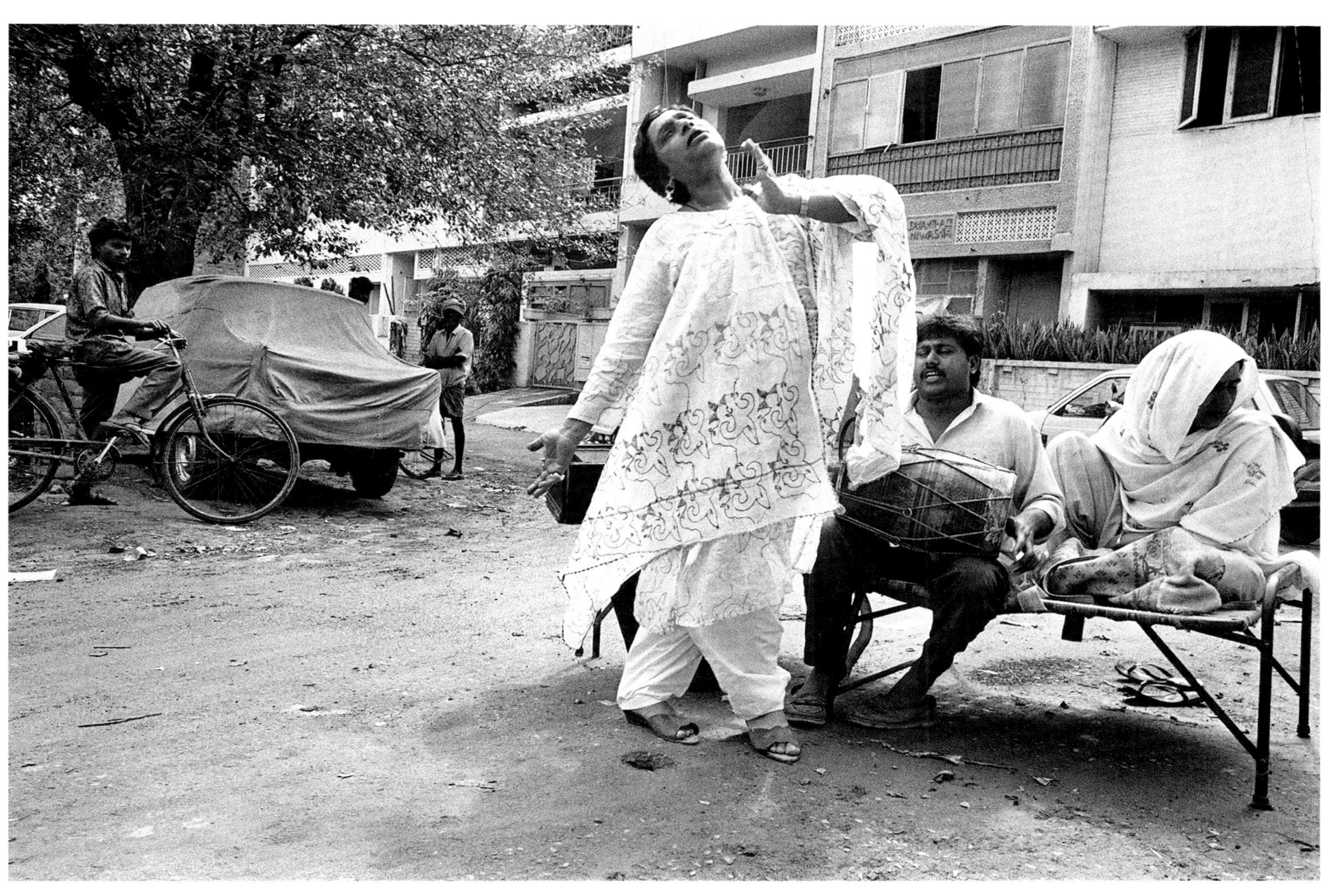

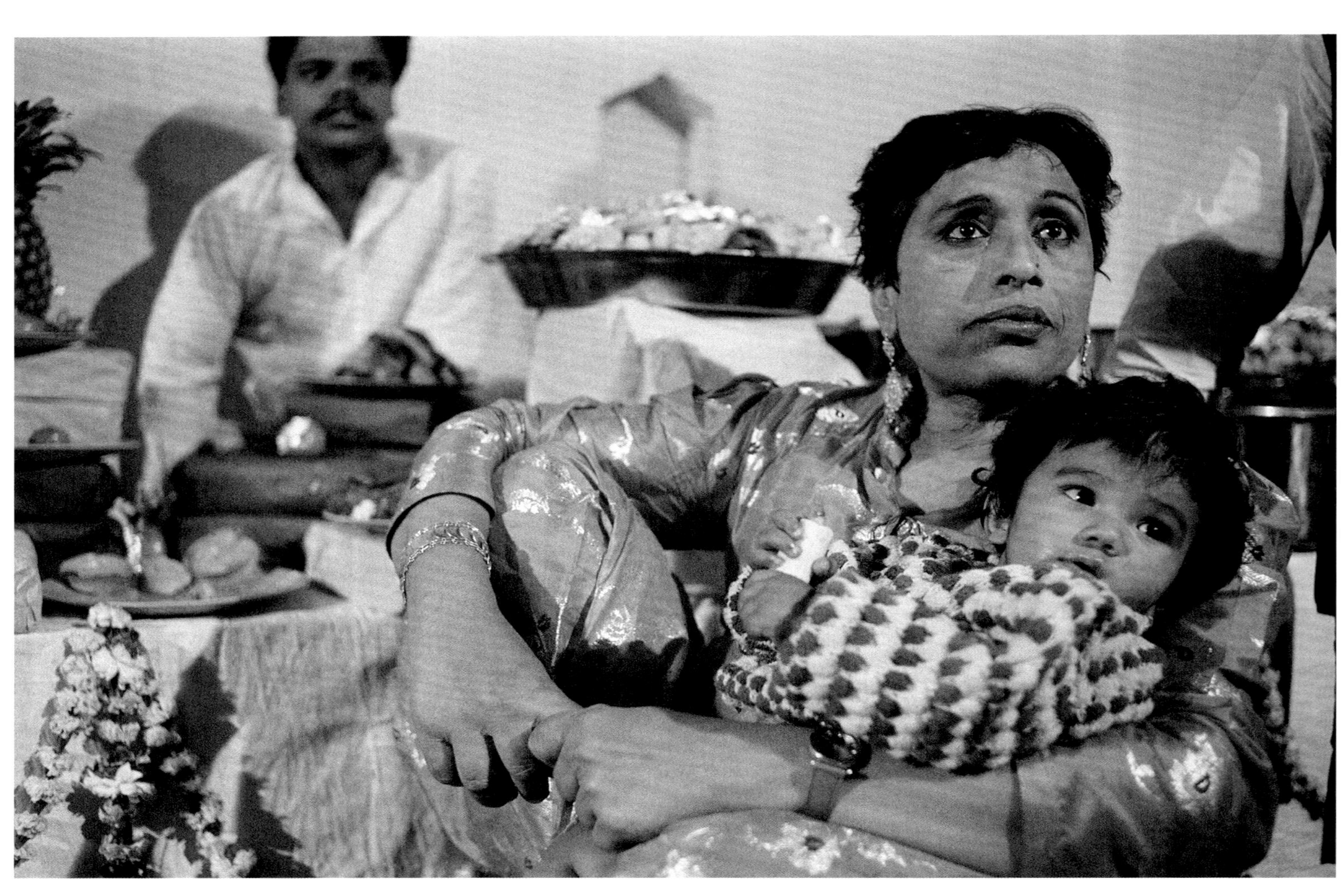

Ayesha fulfilled my dream of becoming a mother, so I celebrated her first birthday for 3 days and 3 nights and invited over 2,000 eunuchs from India, Pakistan and Bangladesh, 1990

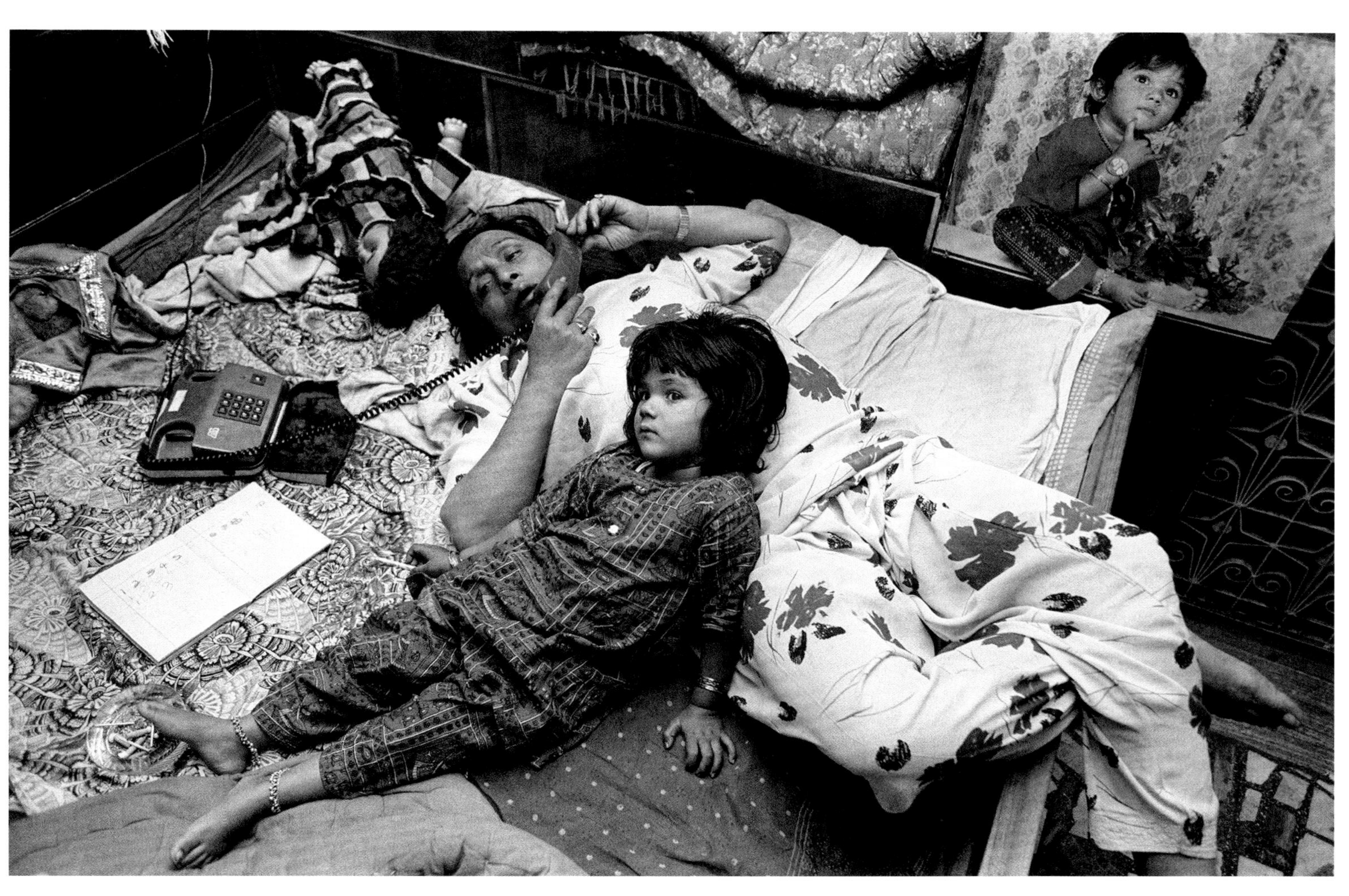

We lie around like a normal mother and daughter, 1992

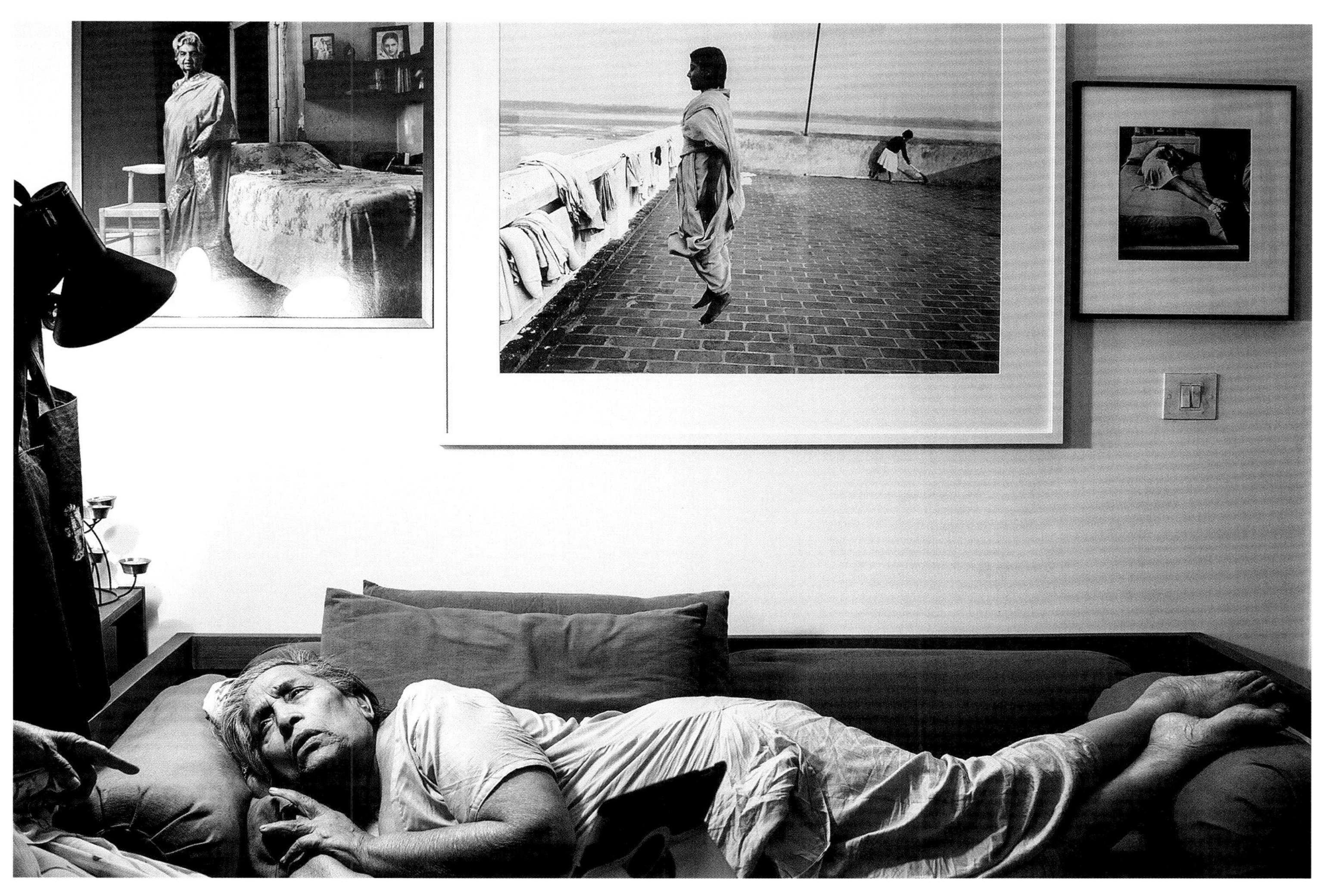

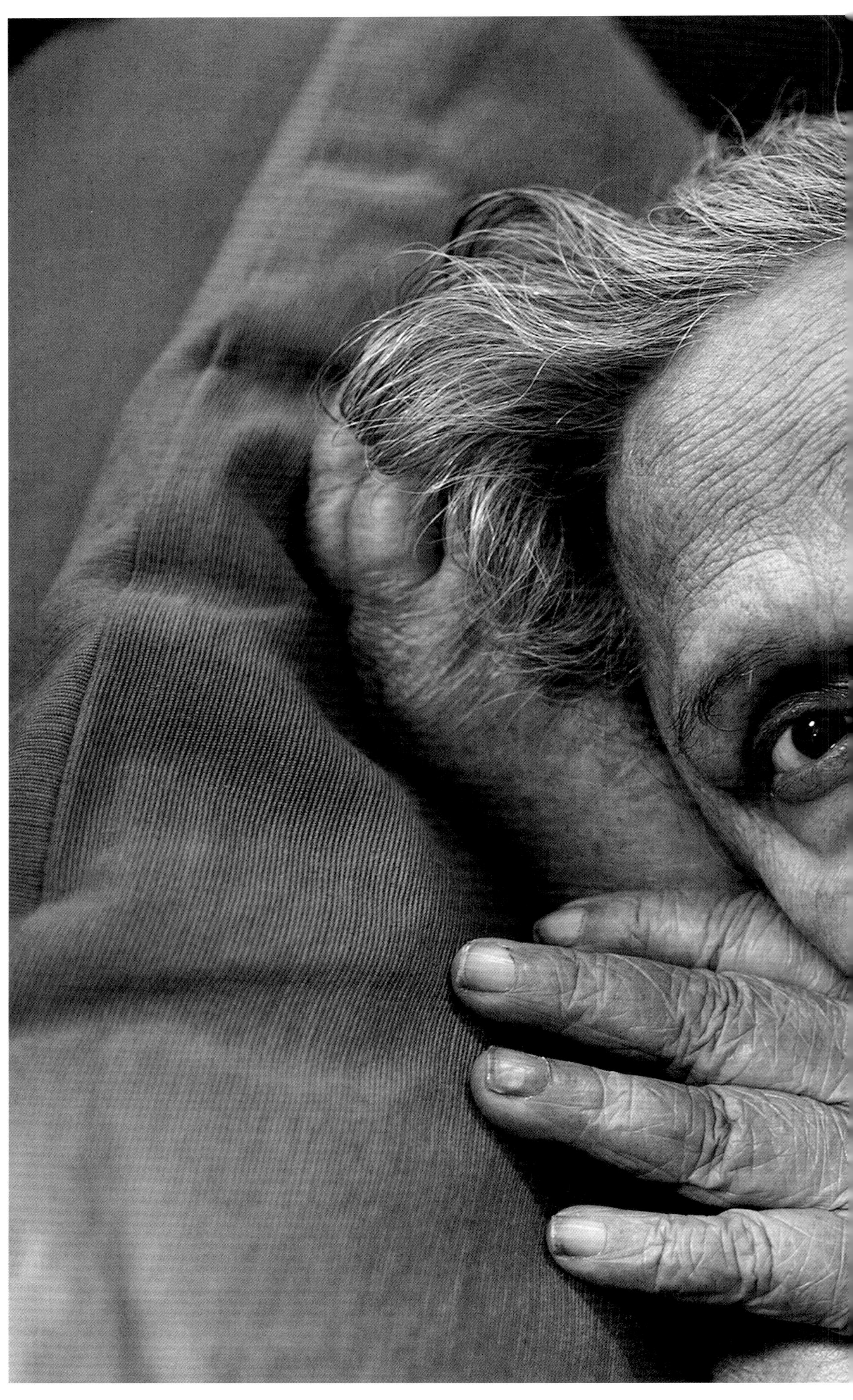

212 Film still from *Mona and Myself*, 2013

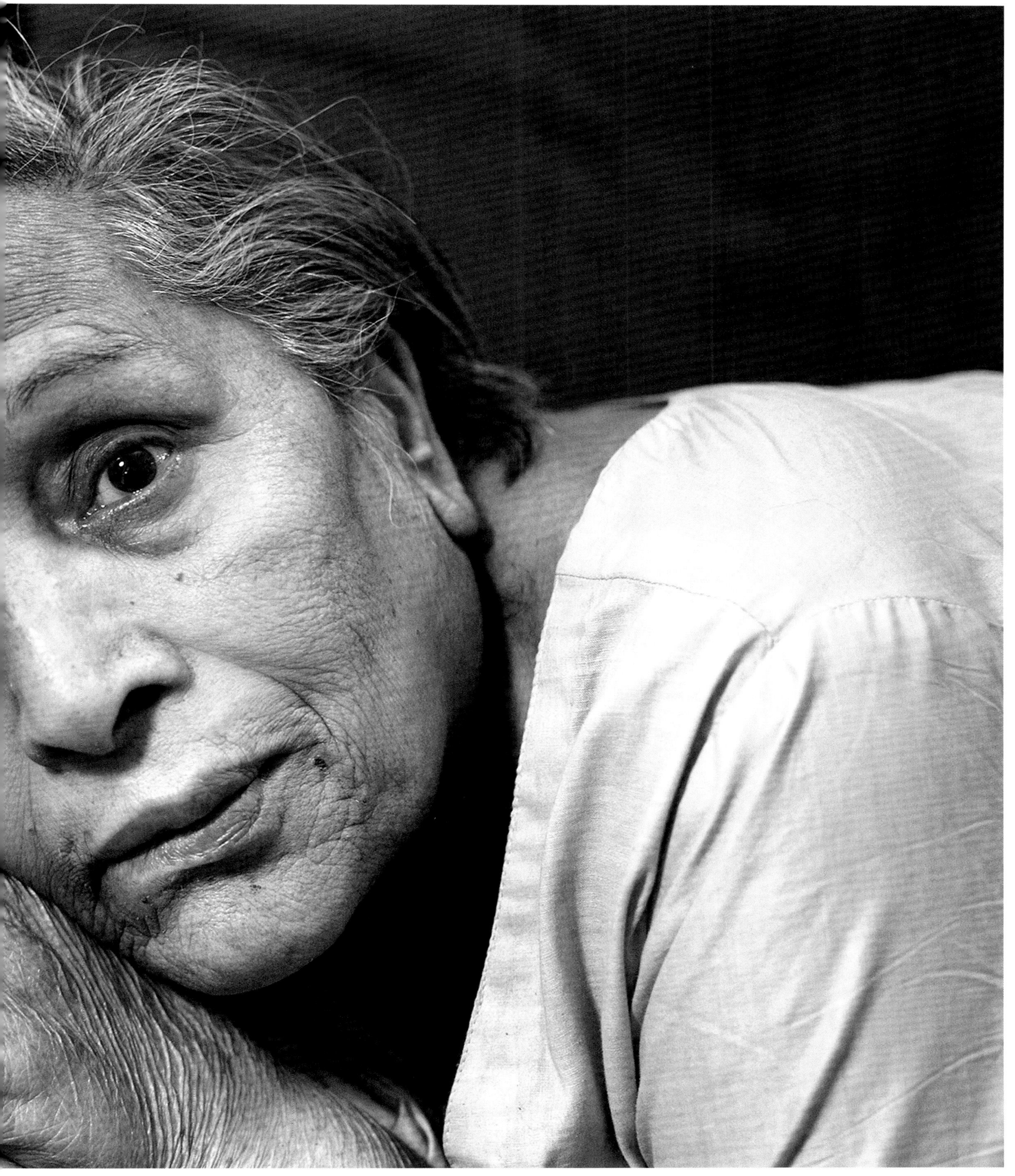

ALEC

SOTH

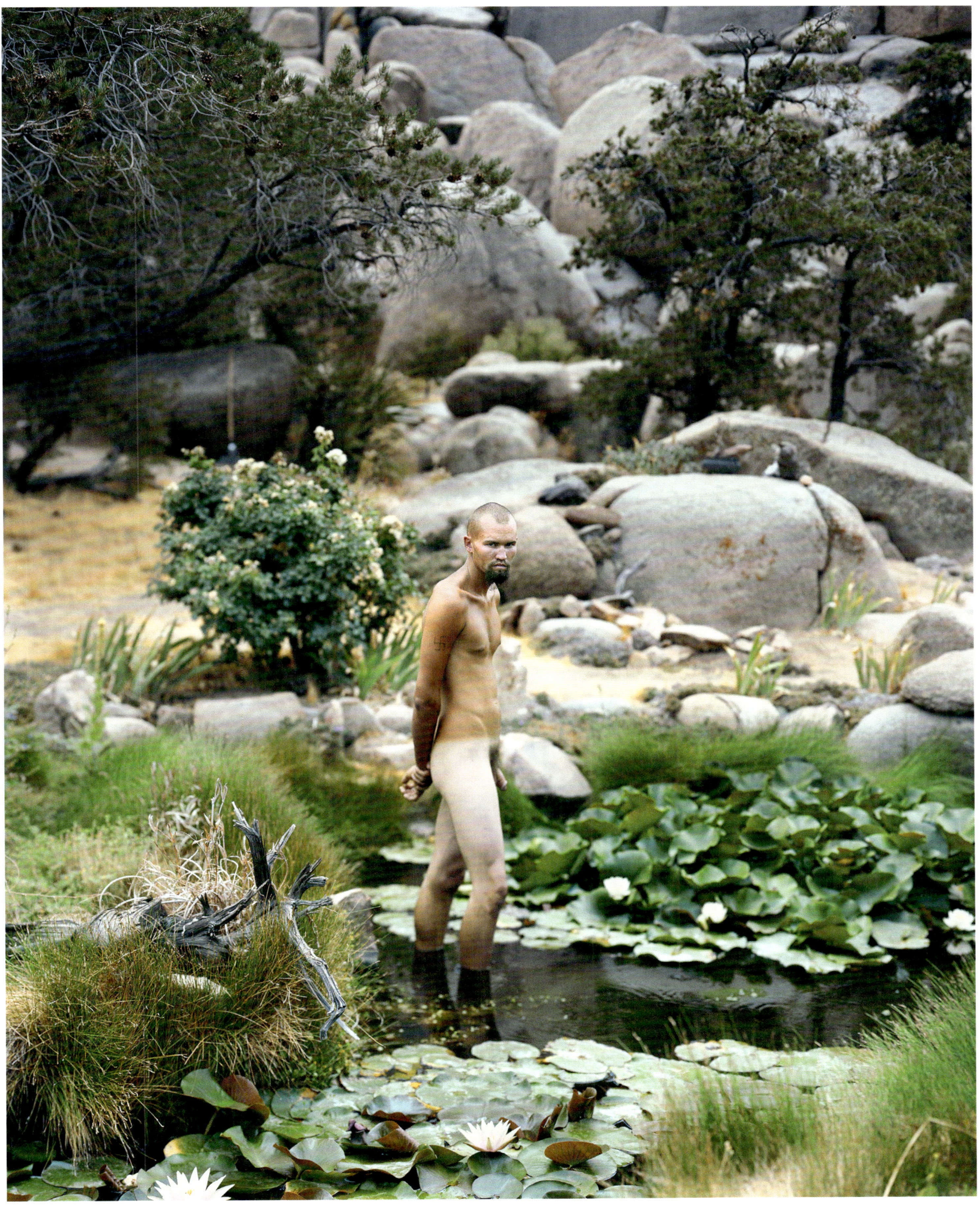

Broken Manual is a particular hybrid of a work of art and a practical survival guide. It all started with a genuine impulse that grasped Alec Soth (b. 1969, USA) around 2007, in the wake of the two works with which he had risen to international fame, gaining a place of great respect within the contemporary photography system: *Sleeping by the Mississippi* (2004) and *Niagara* (2006). It was at this point that he felt the desire to run away. To leave everything behind and get far away from it all. To abandon all kinds of prefabricated norms and hide himself away. This is why, for a certain period of time, he suspended his photographic work and drove around rural America in search of a cave to buy. It had to be somewhere he could seek refuge any time he felt the need. And then the subprime mortgage catastrophe exploded. Lehman Brothers filed for bankruptcy. The Dow Jones index collapsed, burning thousands of billions of dollars in a few short days. This was the start of the great crisis. Soth was thus forced to give up on his project; yet he did find a way to sublimate it into his work. First of all he built a little model of a cavern with a tree and a treehouse nestled amid the branches. What had been only in his imagination was finally given a concrete form. Then he began to work on the idea of *Broken Manual*, through which Soth not only stages but also experiences his own evasion from the impositions of conventions and society.

First and foremost, *Broken Manual* represents an escape from the rules and compartmentalisation of photography. Within it we may in fact find highly different images, both colour and black and white: still-life images of isolated objects against perfectly uniform backdrops; sweeping rural landscapes; dwellings portrayed down to the tiniest detail; portraits of apparently unsuspecting subjects. In contrast with any monolithic approach, Soth puts together an openly anti-typological work. He rejects all distinctions between genres in order to give life to a magmatic language, an all-out photographic Esperanto arising from a democratic melting pot. The result is doubly disorienting. First of all, it is not clear what the photographer found there in front of him and what instead he manipulated and staged. Accustomed as we are to the certainties generated by photography, *Broken Manual* provokes an experience of confusion and disturbance. What's more, we lack the hallmarks by which we would determine and

recognise Soth's style, deployed here in such an unstable way as to remain unidentifiable. *Broken Manual* works like a game of hide and seek, within which the photographer takes shelter in order to get away from any attempt at intromission, just like the subjects do that are featured in this work: hermits who have moved away from their own communities in order to construct an intimate and personal universe in which to live in complete isolation.

All the portraits of *Broken Manual* are of hermits dispersed in the woods and forests (the role of which is paramount: there may be no hermit without nature). The objects captured by Soth belong to them, just like the more or less comfortable dwellings that house them. The landscapes are those that open up before them every day. There are those who live surrounded by scale-model aeroplanes while wearing a pilot's overalls, those who spend the whole night awake in a sort of inversion of the normal biological cycle, those who keep a bunker full of dried foodstuffs and technical equipment ready to face any sort of emergency. While constituting the search for an entirely private space and language, *Broken Manual* is also a form of nearness in regard to these bearded individuals, in corners as far flung as possible from civilisation. Ultimately, they are the ones who provide the models for Alec Soth's solipsistic undertaking. His photographs are a study of their faces, their bodies, their things, their spaces, their thoughts and their utopias, but at the same time they pay tribute to a string of disappointments. None of these people give the idea of being solid and happy; on the contrary, they appear to be at the height of their fragility, engulfed in their own shadows and fears. For this reason, each of Soth's images corresponds to a caress, while *Broken Manual* stands out as the chronicle of a series of failures. It does not work as a breviary; it is cryptic and largely incomprehensible, and leads in the direction of a foregone defeat, to which he seems not to lend too much importance, just as we all pretend to be unaware of our own 'biological failure', charging towards our destination at great speed, 'in inverse ratio to the square of the distance from death', as Tolstoy writes.

What matters is the process, *Broken Manual* thus suggests. And it is this very logic that guides Soth in the creation of his imagery. As occurs in Land art (Soth carried out

experiments similar to the performances of Richard Long at the start of his career), the work corresponds to the experience had by the artist in space. For him it is fundamental in this case to have set foot in a number of places endowed with a special meaning: the wood near Lincoln, Montana, in which the Unabomber built his hut; the monastery in Kentucky which Thomas Merton withdrew to; the hotel room in Butte, Montana, from which a famous picture was shot by Robert Frank, hermit *sui generis* who moved to Nova Scotia to escape the chaos of New York. The heart of Soth's work lies along this path. It is a matter of presence and participation. The photographic image represents only a trace. A souvenir. It does not need to be beautiful, composed, correct: it just needs to be there. In *Broken Manual* we see a number of grainy portraits of the faces of hermits. These are details of photographs shot from very far away and then enlarged to the point of blurring all details. The faces of those men are transformed into death shrouds. Unrecognisable, they could belong to anyone, to the photographer or to the viewers of his images. All of a sudden, as if placed in front of a mirror, we see ourselves. We are 'the others'.

Francesco Zanot

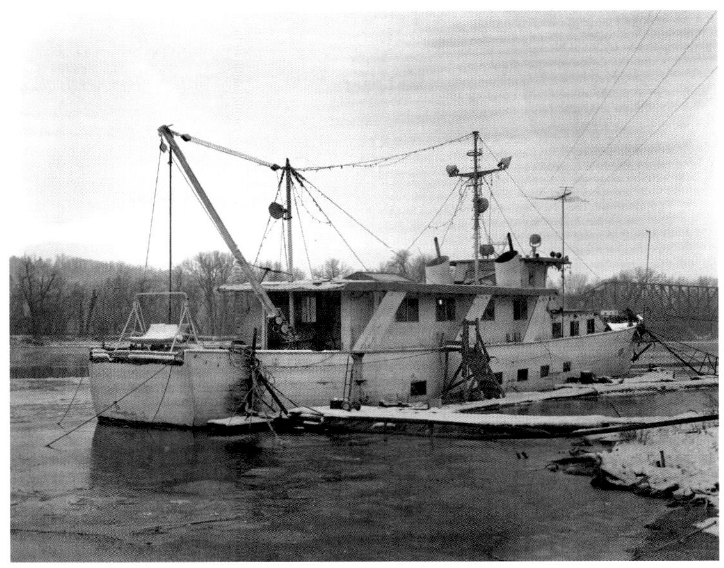 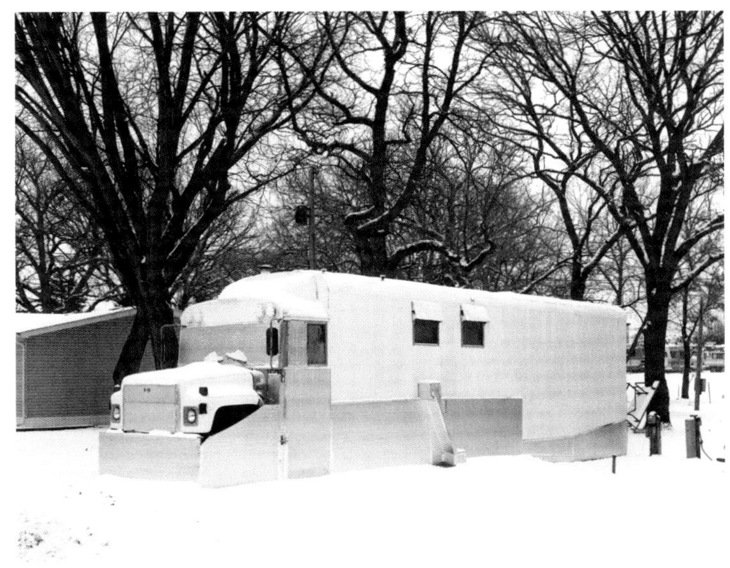

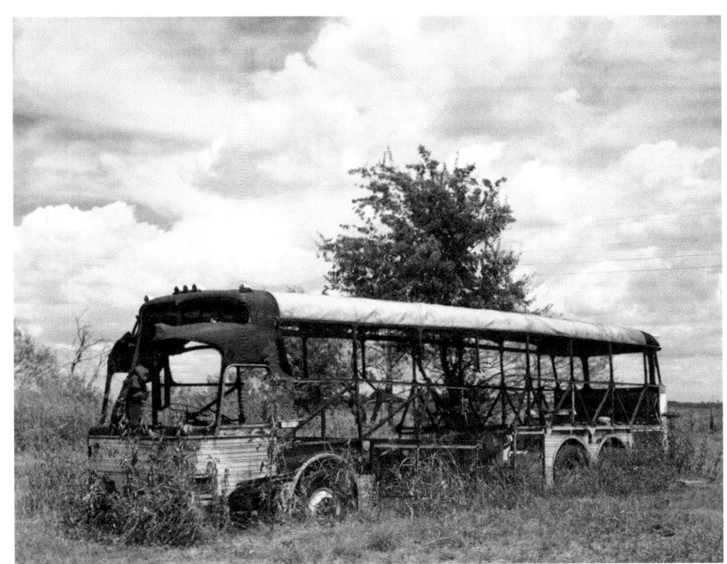 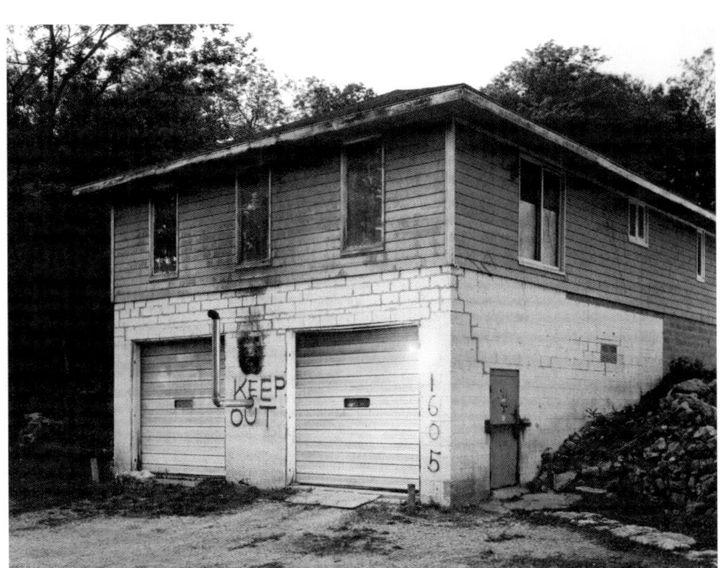

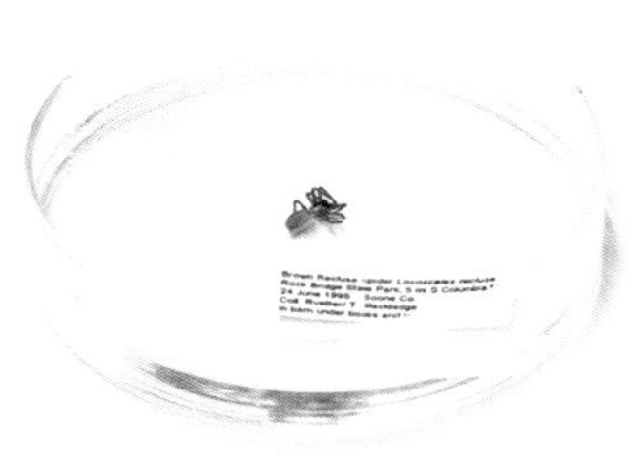 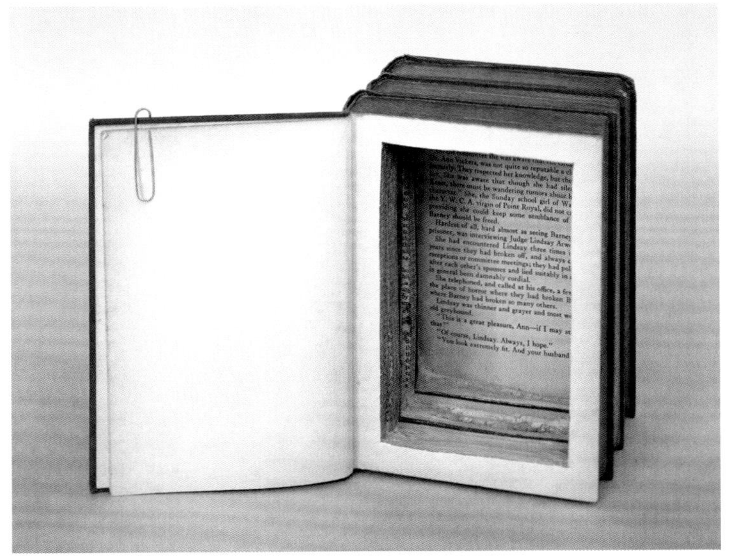

From top, left to right: from 'Broken Manual', *USA*, 1995; *1999_13ZI009*, 1999; *Branch Davidson Bus*, 2007; *Dogpatch, MO*, 2007; *2008_08zI0157*, 2008; *2008_08zI0063*, 2008

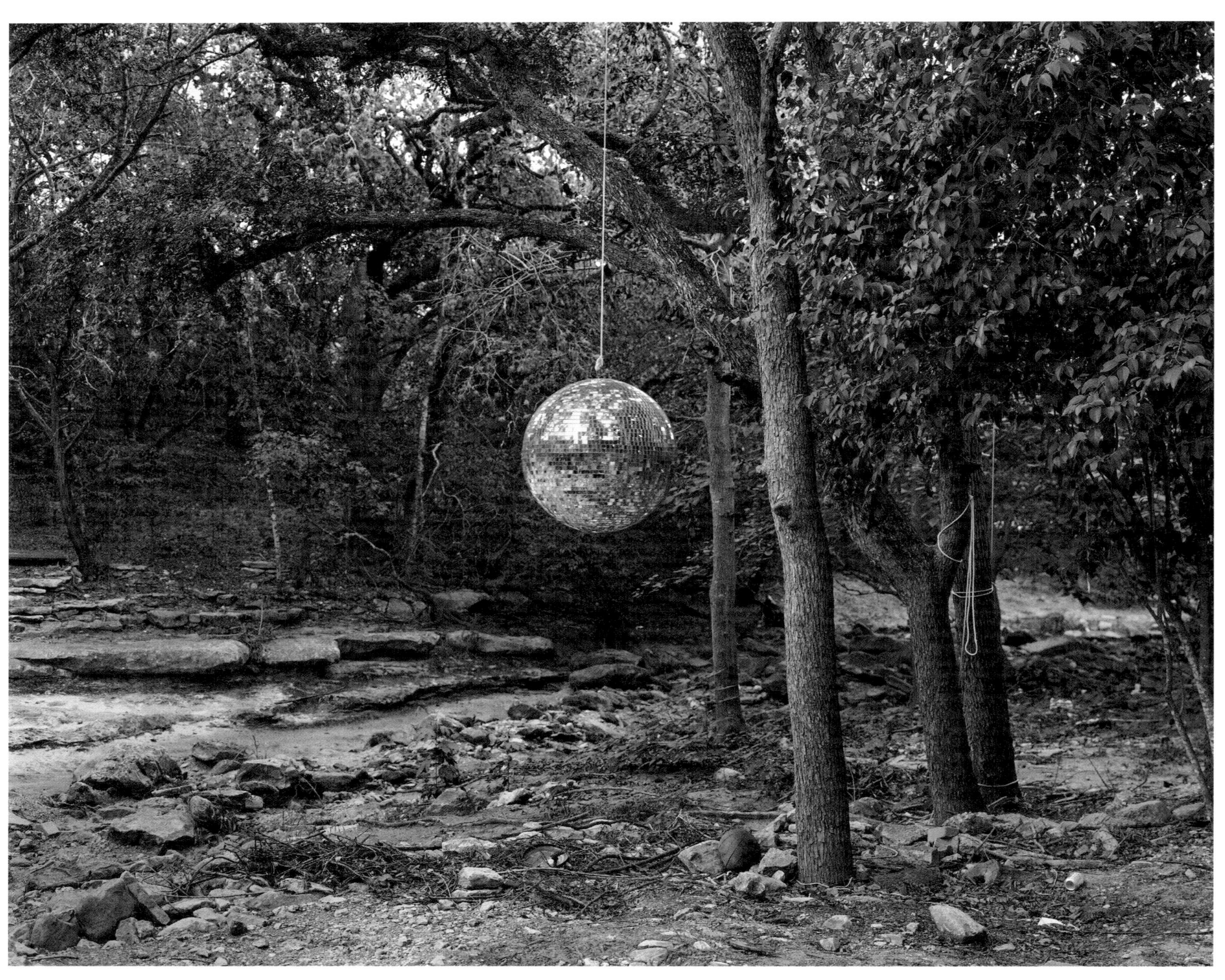

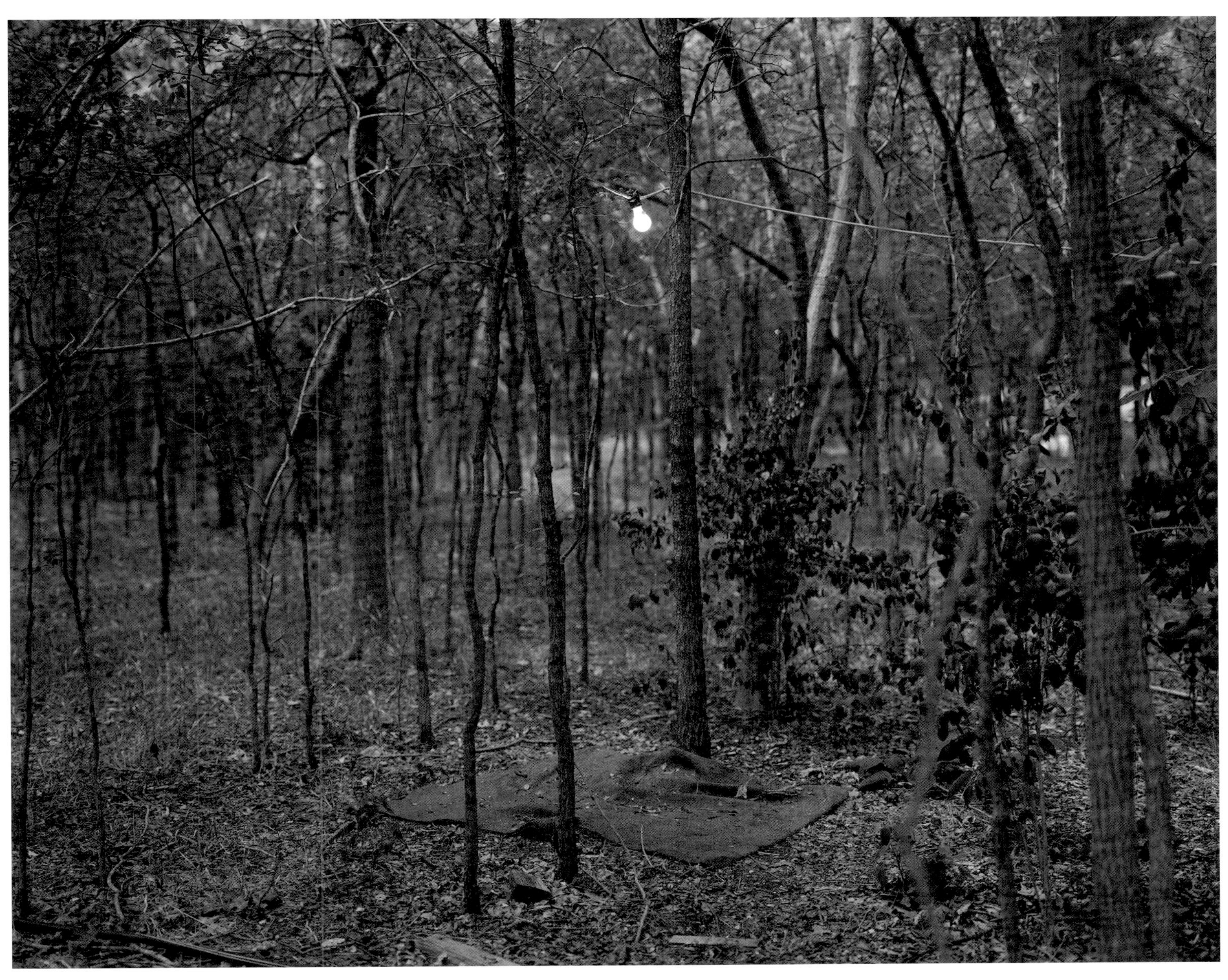

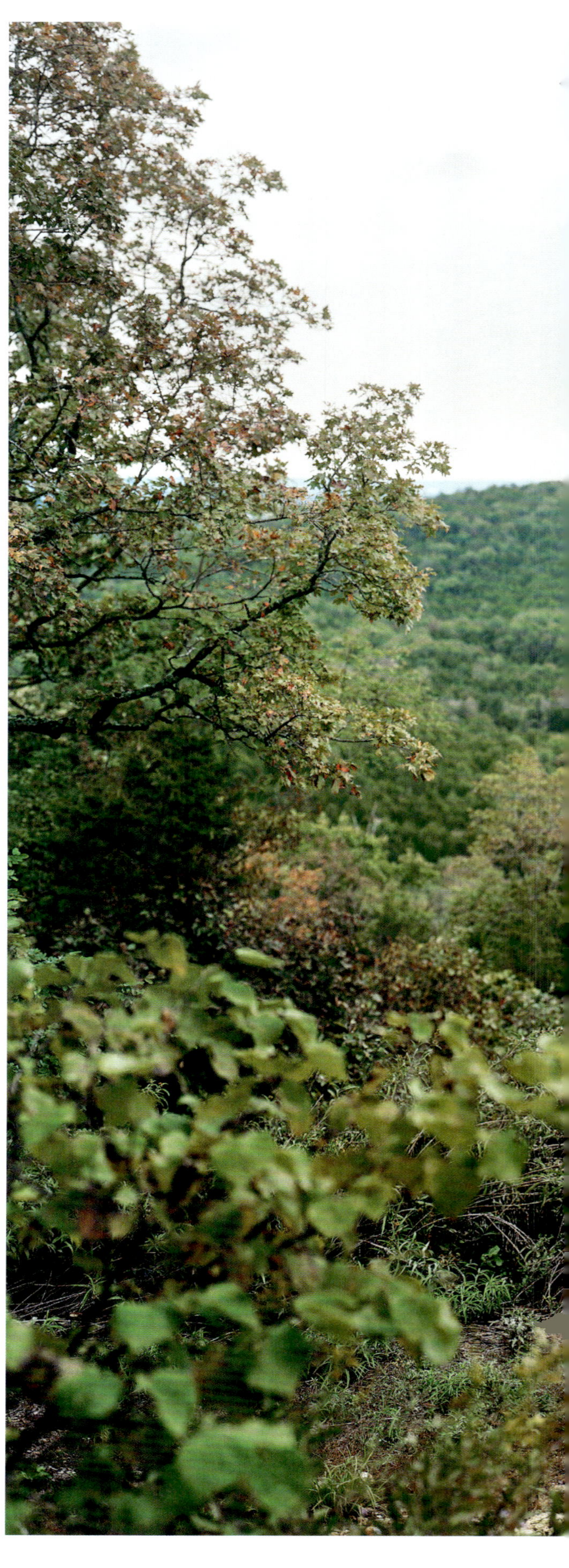

220 From 'Broken Manual', *The Arkansas Cajun's Backup Bunker*, 2007

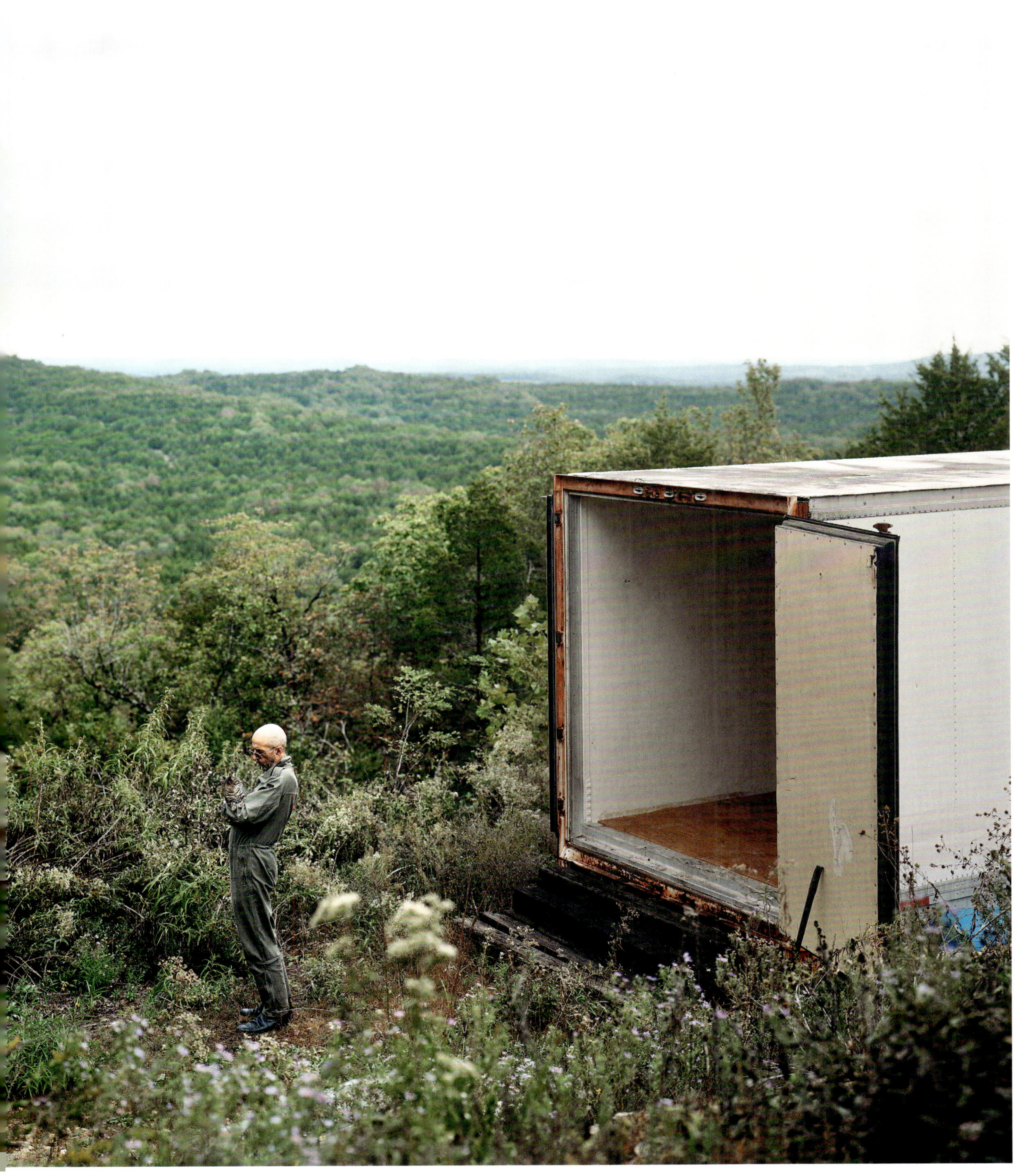

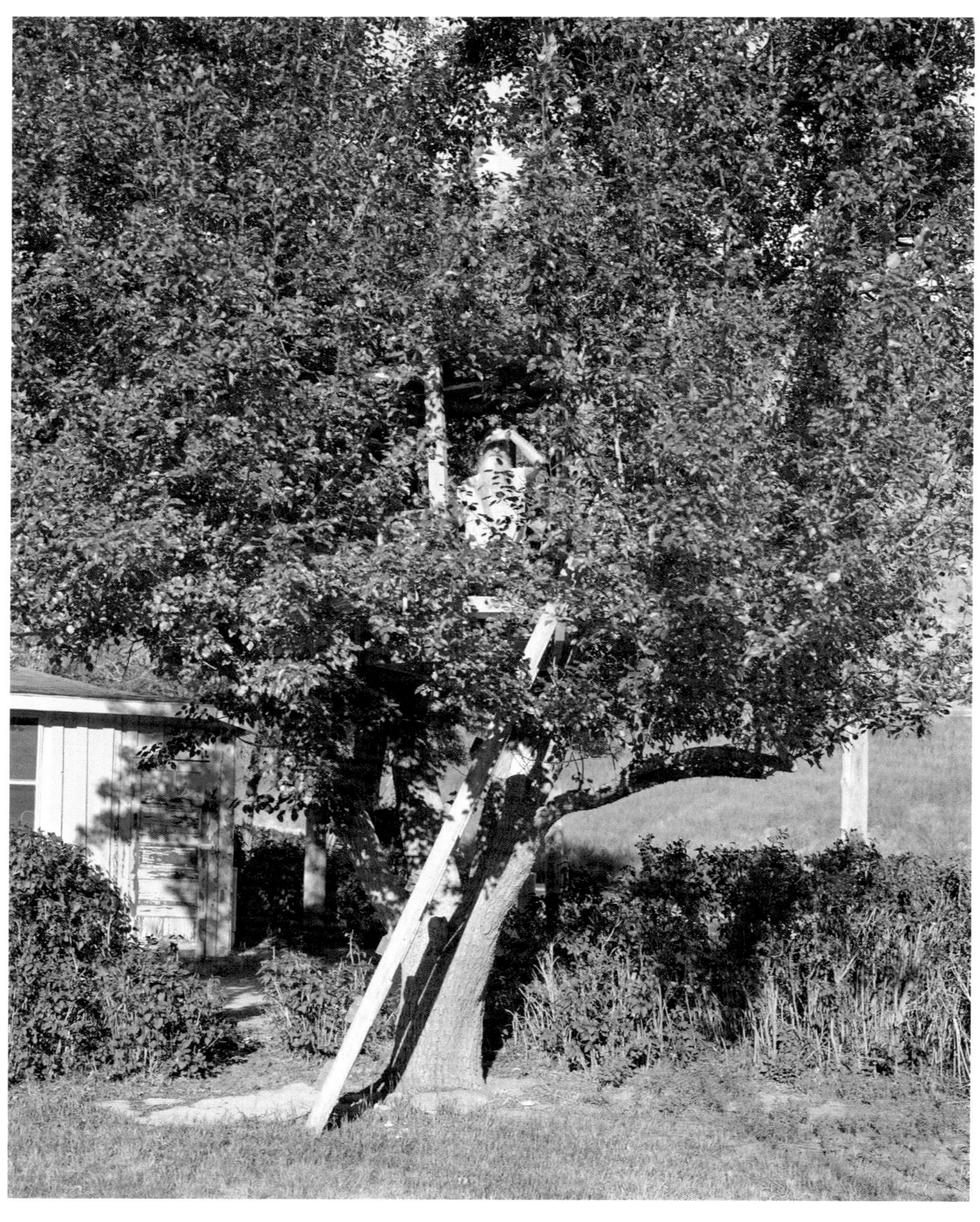

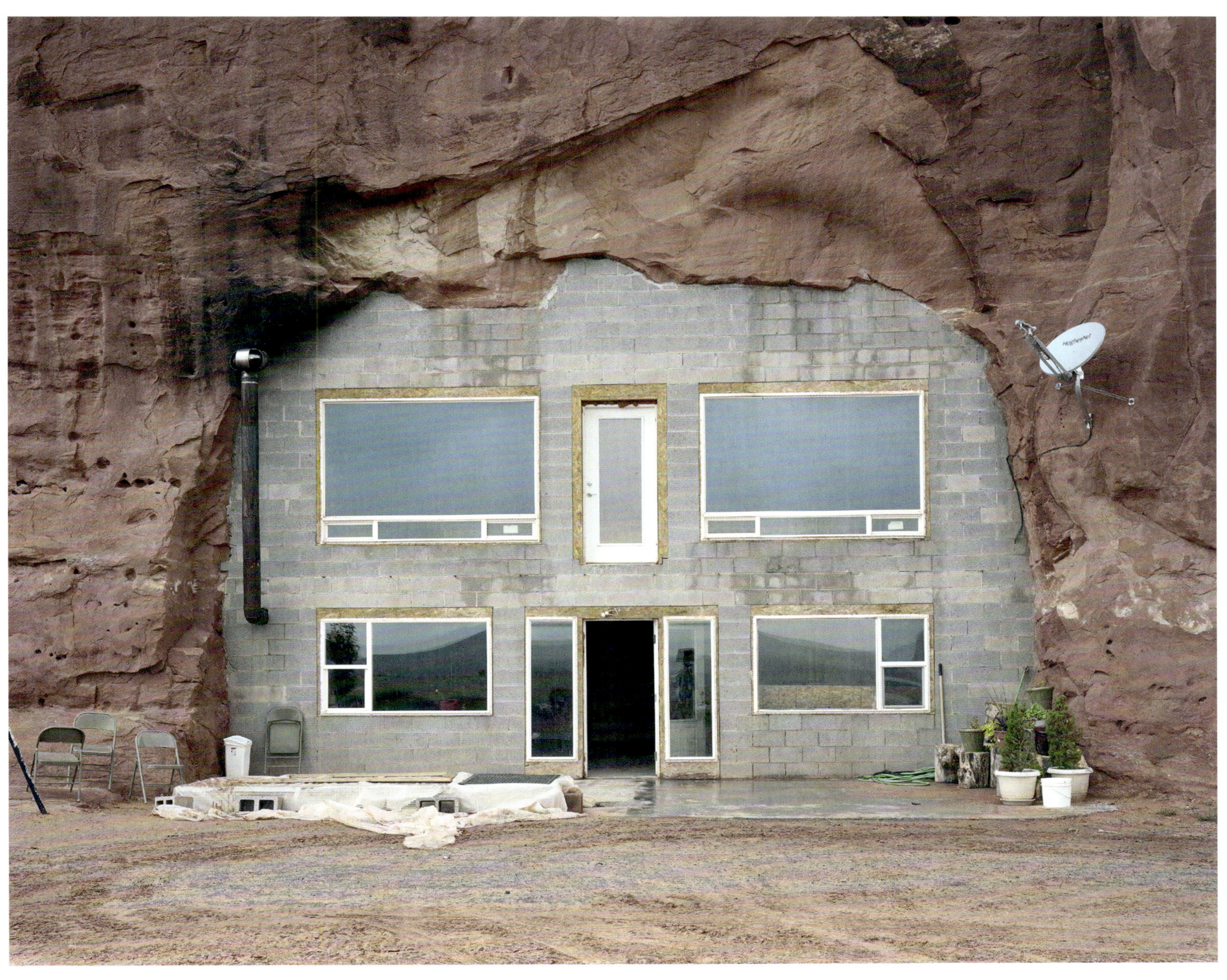

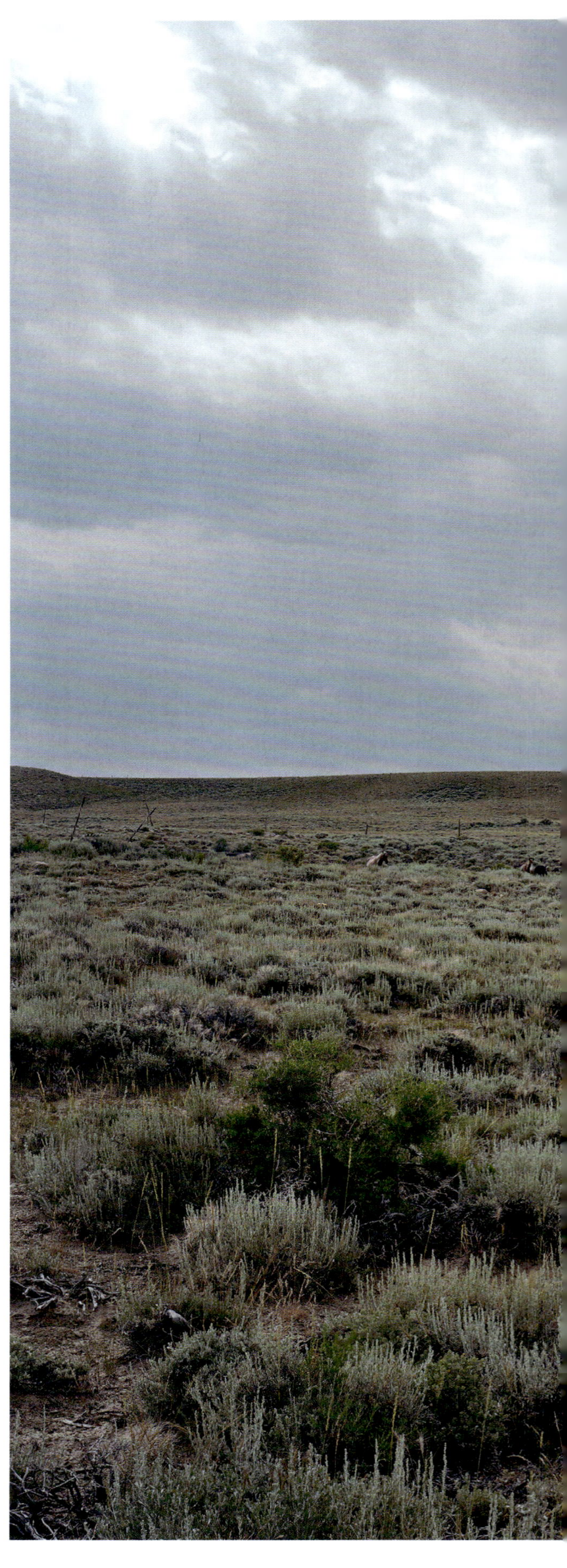

224 From 'Broken Manual', 2008_08zI0047, 2008

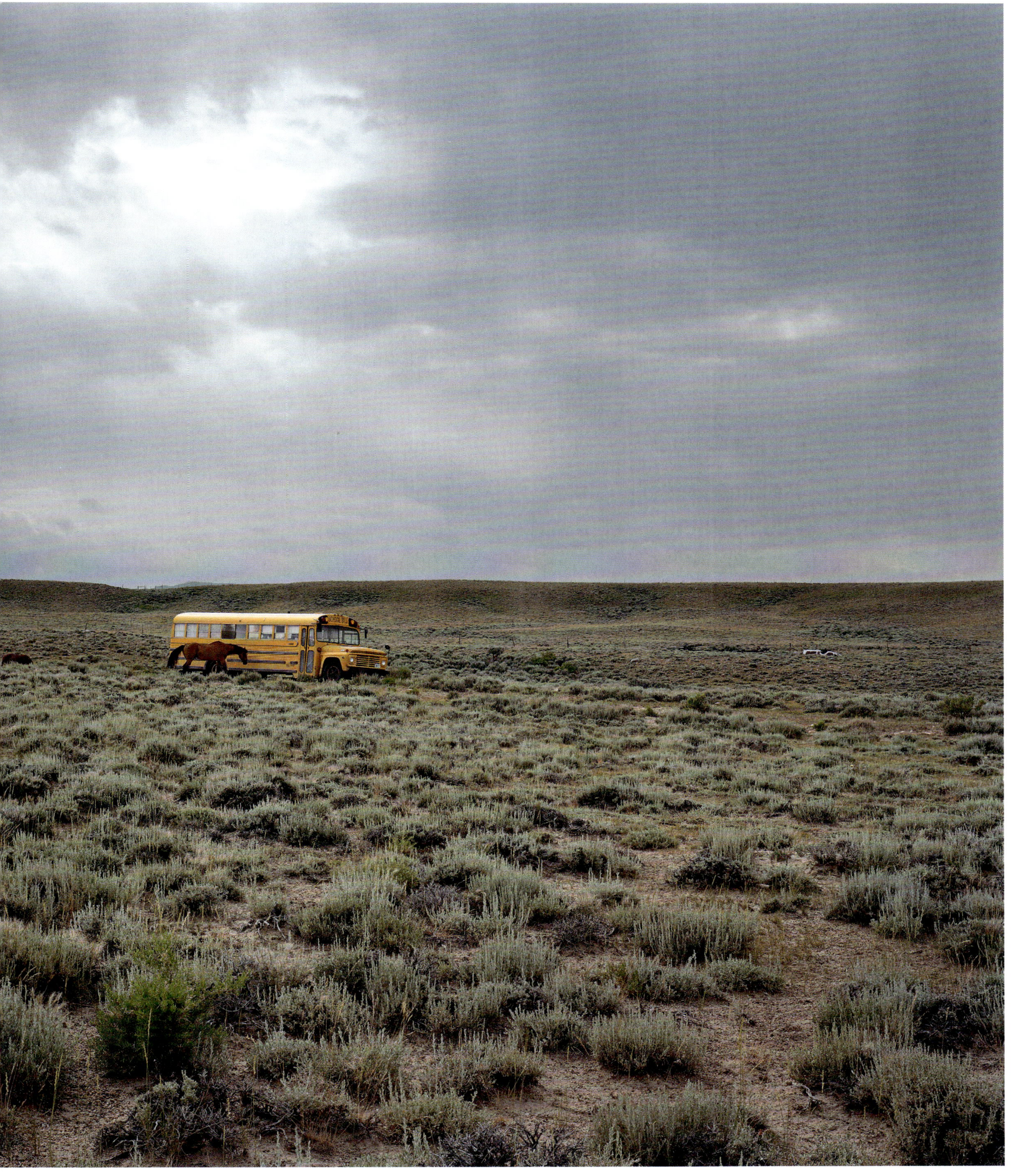

PIETER

HUGO

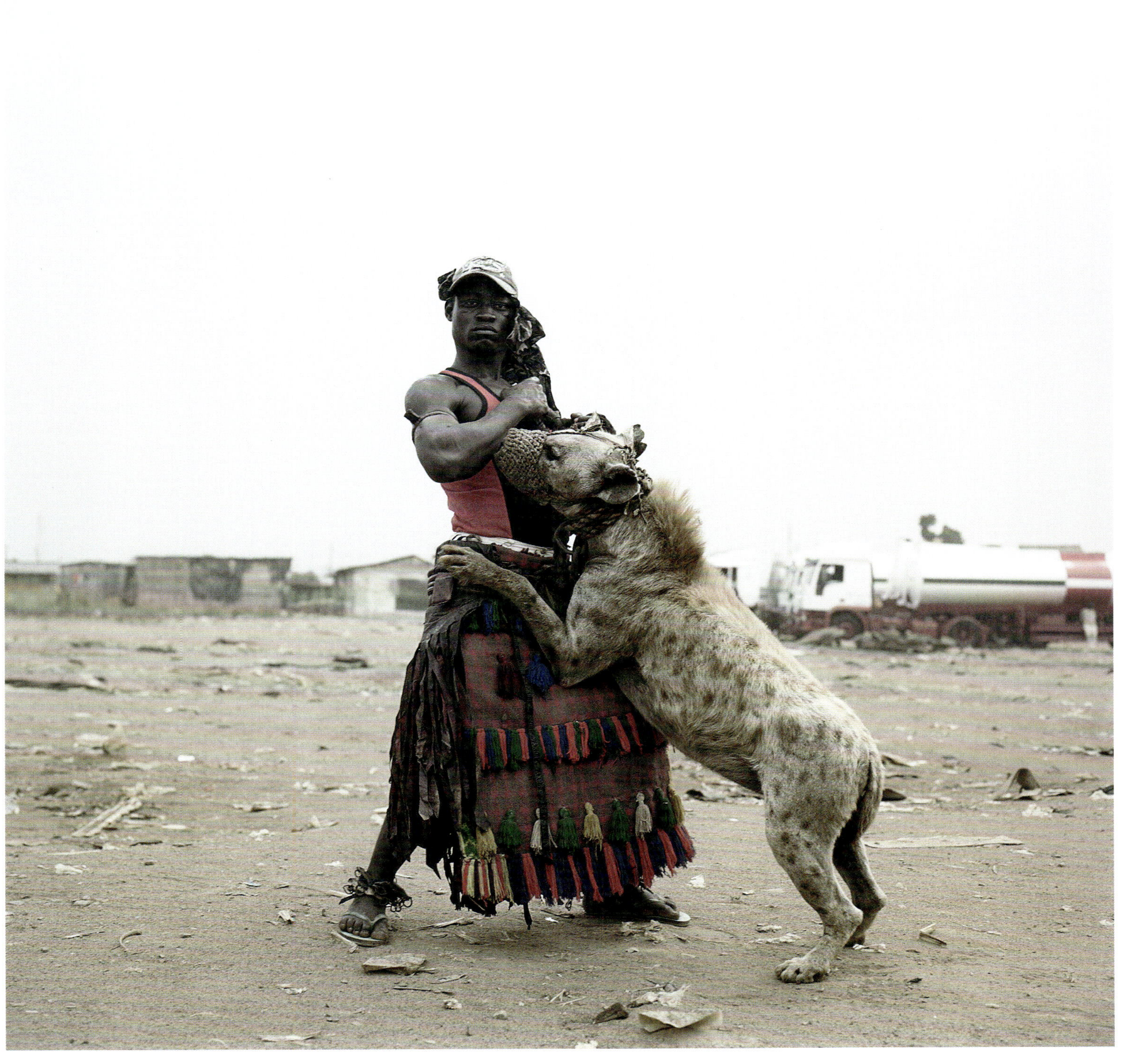

The outsider has long been a presence in photography, drawing the gaze of practitioners as diverse as Christer Strömholm, Diane Arbus and Boris Mikhailov. The South African photographer Pieter Hugo (b. 1976, South Africa) has also chosen to document the lives of those who exist on the periphery of society, in his native country and across the continent. The result has been an often complex engagement with race and representation through a practice that merges portraiture, documentary and immersive observation.

In his series *The Hyena and Other Men*, Hugo's subject is a group of urban nomads whose outsider status prompts a mixture of fear, awe, repulsion and curiosity in those who encounter them on the streets of Nigeria's largest city, Lagos. The Gadawan Kura (hyena handlers) are portrayed by the state and the populist media as criminals who use their captive beasts – muzzled and chained hyenas – to threaten and extort their supposed victims. Hugo's series is, among other things, a riposte to that demonisation. He describes them as 'itinerant minstrels' who survive by selling traditional medicines and staging street performances featuring the beasts that they travel with and live alongside: four monkeys, a python and three hyenas.

It is the hyenas that arrest our gaze, drawing us in even as we recoil from their feral presence and abject existence. The hyena is perhaps the most mythologised and misunderstood outsider of the animal world, and the Gadawan Kura have, by association, absorbed – and exploited – their almost occult aura. 'Many people in Nigeria still believe hyenas are witches,' Hugo told me in 2008, 'or that they are humans who have been reincarnated as wild beasts to cause mischief and havoc in the night. There's also the fact that the African hyena just looks kind of otherworldly.'[1]

Constantly harassed by the authorities, the Gadawan Kura survive on the fringes of Nigerian society by continually keeping on the move. Hugo travelled to Nigeria in 2005 intent on finding them. It proved difficult. Locals were cagey when asked for information about them, particularly by a towering white man with a South African accent. He arrived in Benin on a tip-off to find that the Gadawan Kura had been and gone. Driving around Abuja at dusk,

frustrated by another long and unproductive day on their trail, he suddenly caught sight of them for the first time.

'We found them living on the periphery of the city in a shantytown – a group of men, a little girl, three hyenas, four monkeys and a few rock pythons,' he wrote in his introduction to the book *The Hyena and Other Men* (2007), 'performers who used animals to entertain crowds and sell traditional medicines. The animal handlers were all related to each other and were practising a tradition passed down from generation to generation.'[2]

Over two weeks, Hugo photographed the troupe as they performed on the streets to often feverishly excited crowds, but he was dissatisfied with the results. A full two years later he returned to Nigeria, spending more time with them and becoming friendly with some of the handlers. The hyenas, though, were a different matter. Weighing up to 90 kg (200 lb), their uncanny appearance – those huge, muscular necks, fearsome jaws, patches of raised fur and almost scrawny legs – seems designed to strike fear into humans and other animals. Even when bound, muzzled and chained, they evince an aura of simmering malevolence and brute violence. 'I was always wary of the animals,' Hugo told me, 'Up close, a hyena is an almost overpowering presence. It is a wild animal however much it has been subdued. I never felt comfortable being close to them, and their effect on local people was so powerful that you could easily start to believe some of the mythology.'[3]

The hyenas, spectacularly ill-suited by temperament to captivity or domestication, were subject to harsh treatment from their handlers. 'There were a lot of big sticks,' elaborates Hugo. 'When I asked people about the cruel treatment of the animals in Nigeria, they just looked at me as if I was mad. It simply isn't an issue there.'[4]

The complex dynamic of the human–hyena relationship is embedded in Hugo's carefully composed portraits, which eschew the edgy drama of the street performances for a more formal stillness. Isolated on deserted suburban streets, beneath concrete flyovers or on the edges of shanty towns, the men and their captive beasts exude an even more unsettling presence. These in-between spaces reflect the

marginal existence of the Gadawan Kura, while also emphasising the feral otherness of their animals. Everything here seems makeshift, sun-bleached and drained of colour, from the shacks and cracked concrete walls in the background to the clothes worn by the Gadawan Kura – T-shirts and hand-woven, often ragged, skirts.

In one artfully composed group photograph, two monkeys sit upright among the men while a young girl perches on the back of a hyena. In its formal composition and sense of enforced attentiveness, the photograph borrows many of the tropes of an extended family portrait – which, in a way, it is. The presence of the monkeys, though sitting upright and posing like the humans around them, stirs something unsettling deep within us. Likewise the young girl who has grown used to interacting with a hyena as if it were a pet dog or small pony. These images raise so many questions about the complex psychology of this itinerant collective, about our relationship with animals and about the ways in which photography and performance are intertwined (Hugo paid the Gadawan Kura for their time and they, in their turn, enjoyed performing for his camera).

For all that, it is the bigger picture that most interests Pieter Hugo: how these itinerant outsiders operate within it and illuminate it. '[The Gadawan Kura] exist and survive in a place that is neither here nor there. They are transgressive but what they do is either allowed or overlooked by the state. Their way of life is almost medieval, and they survive like this in the most oil-rich country in Africa. Sure, the hyenas and the baboons are dramatic but it's all the big questions that hover over the images that I'm interested in.'[5]

Sean O'Hagan

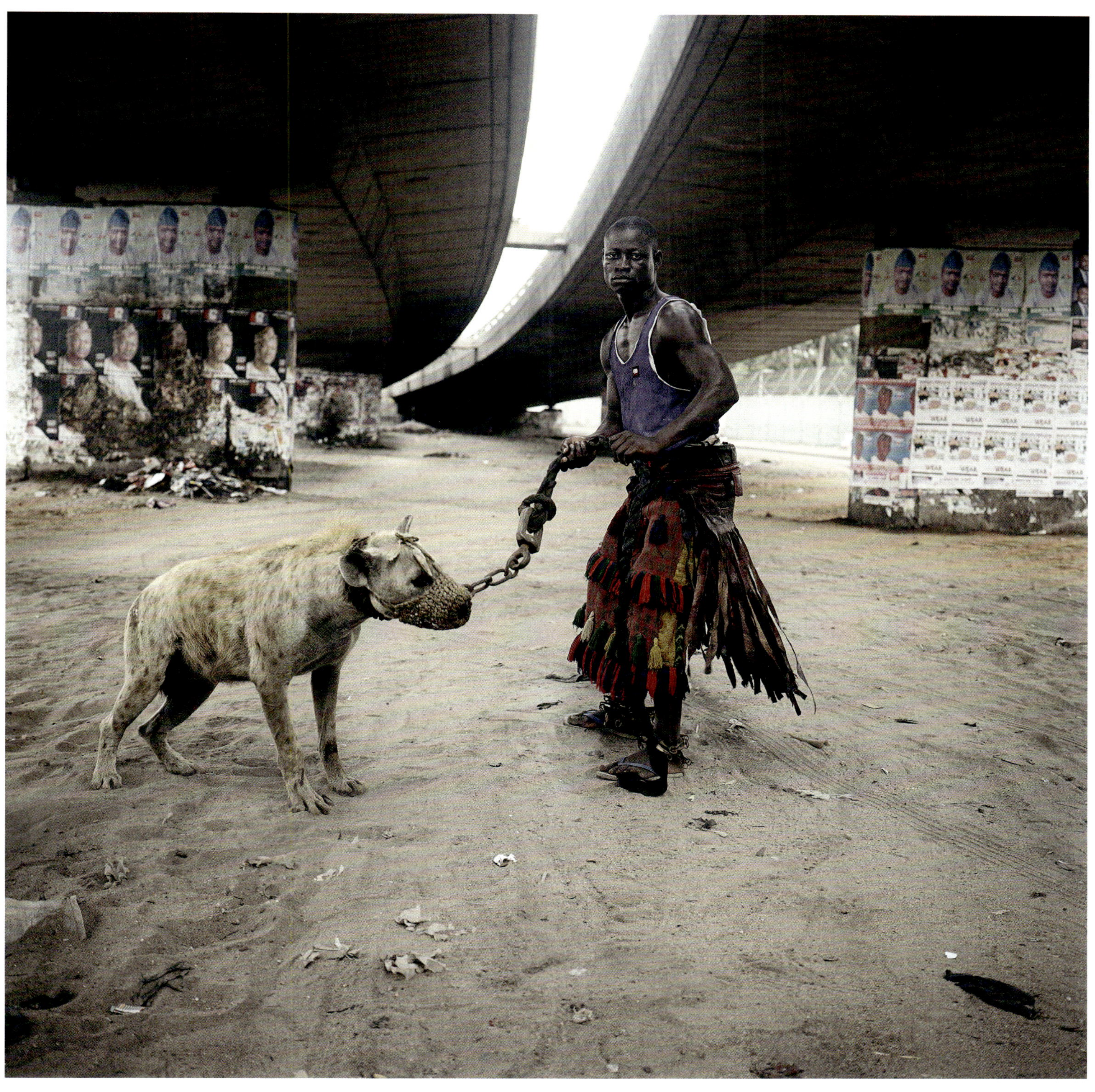

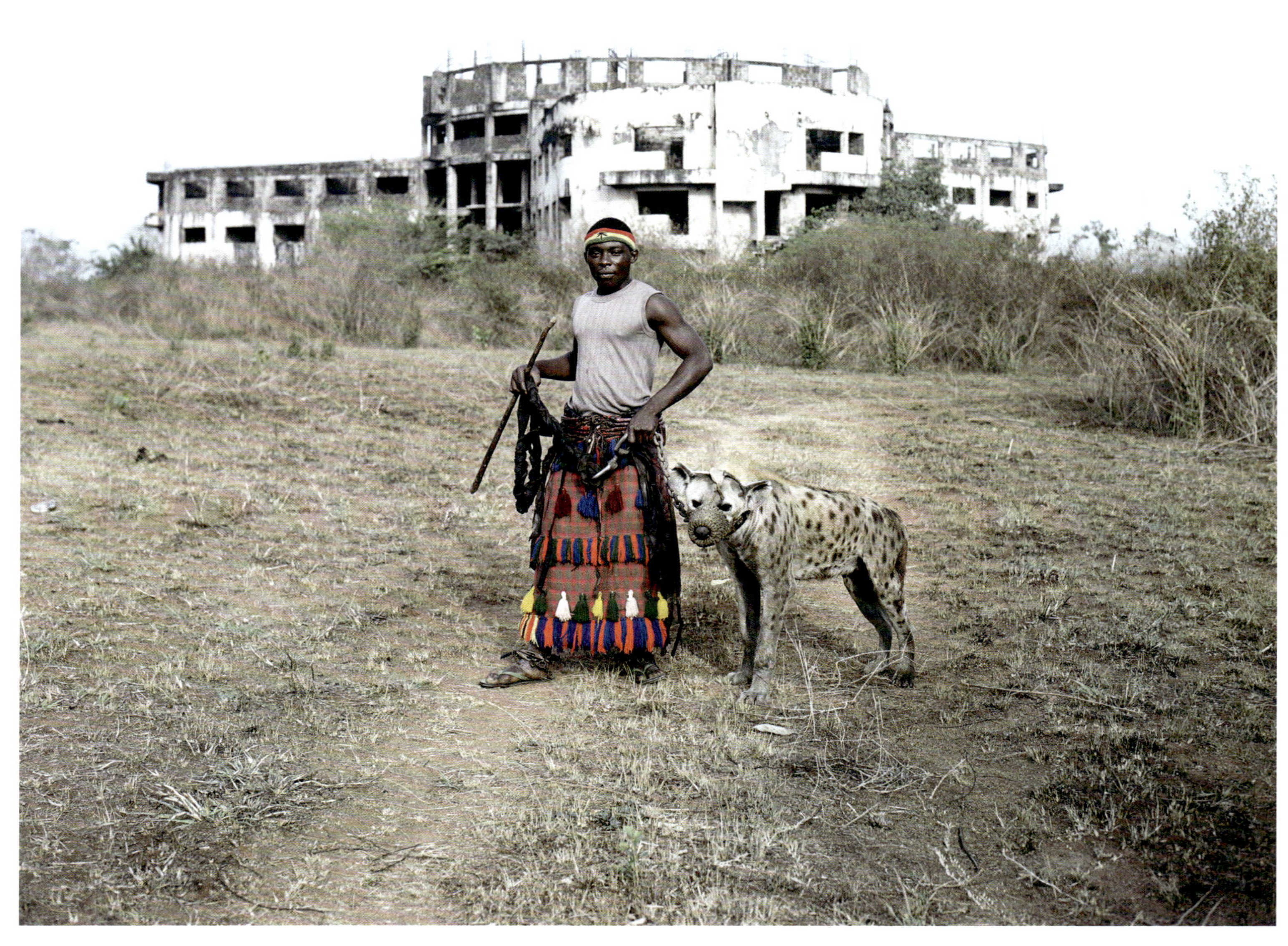

230 From 'The Hyena and Other Men', *Mohammed Rabiu with Jamis*, Ibusa, Nigeria, 2007

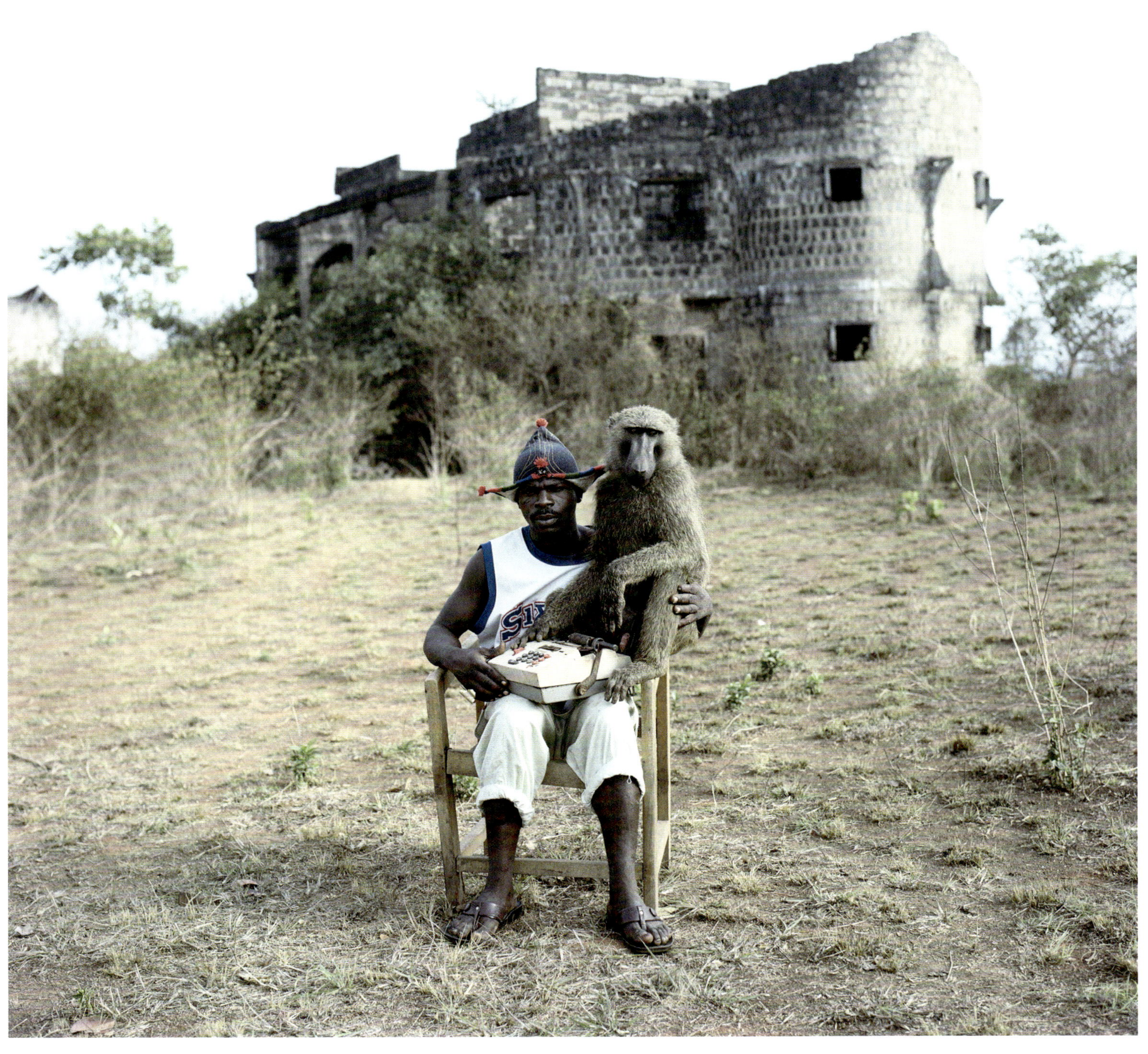

From 'The Hyena and Other Men', *Abdullahi Ahmadu with Emeka, Ibusa, Nigeria, 2007*   231

KATY

GRANNAN

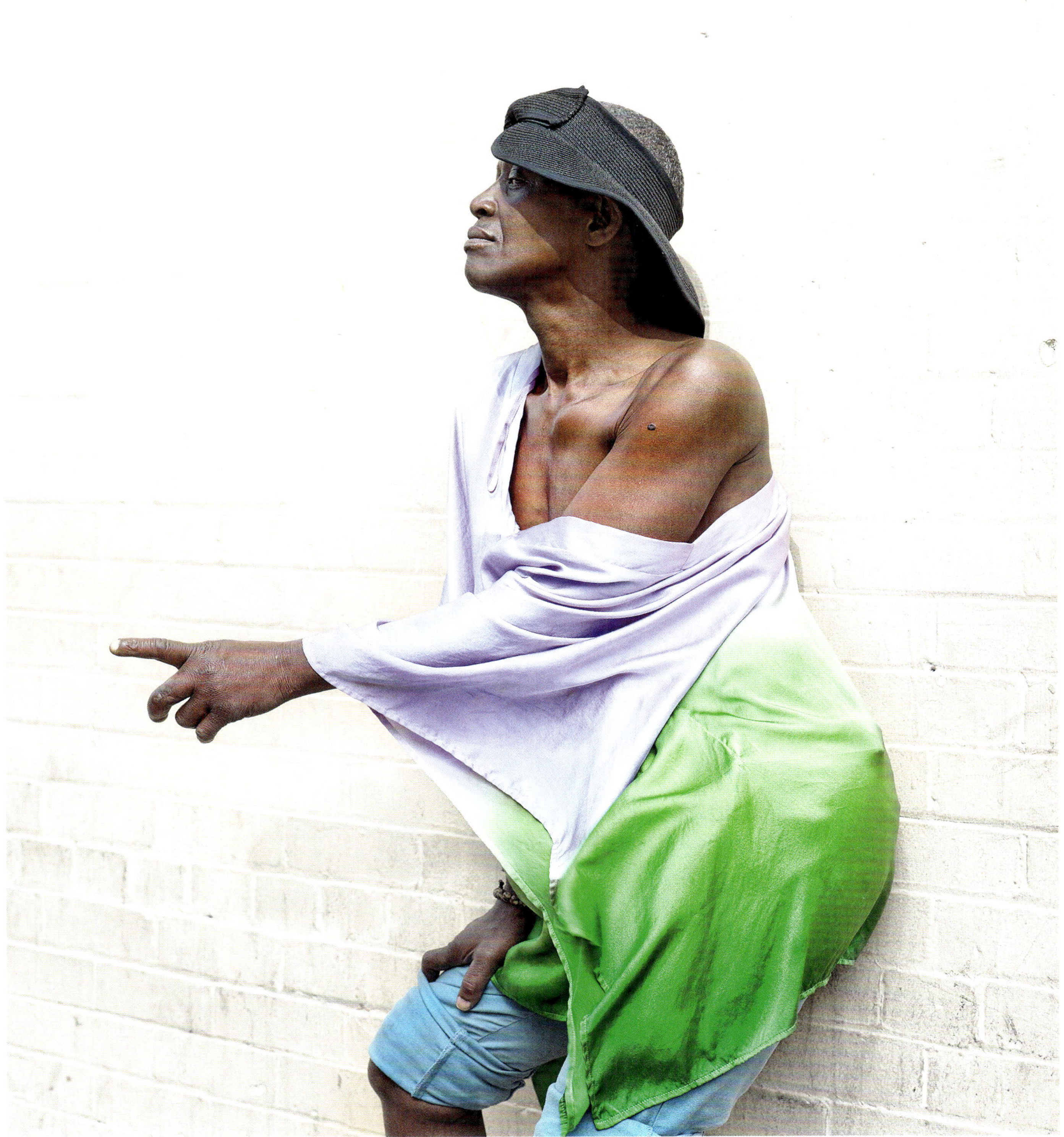

Diane Di Prima, 'Revolutionary Letter #1'[1]

How do we take on the complex task of reconciling ourselves to the human body? How do we confront the myriad ways in which it is traversed by our own complex – often frustrated – aspirations, or the ways that it is limited by the strictures of the world, and fixed by the penetrating gaze of others? Katy Grannan's (b. 1969, USA) work both provokes and addresses these questions. For twenty years, her portraits have pivoted around the dynamic and fraught relationships between our sense of self and the plasticity, the fragility, the recalcitrant and transformative capacities of the human body within the confines of culture, economy and social space.

In her debut monograph *Model American* (2005), her measured use of light heightens the disjuncture between self-image and self-possession, and grounds that tension in the difference between an internal and external conception of the body.[2] Her portraits are careful, if not tender, redolent with a beauty that foreswears any attempt at flattery. Throughout the series, the photograph's relation to the body is governed by the difficulty of remaining centred within an essentially contested space.

Grannan's subsequent series *The Westerns* (2007) models the body as the locus not so much for self-discovery as reinvention. Where earlier portraits are more tempered in tone, if not in content, the newer pictures develop a sharper psychological edge, proposing the body as a place of making.[3] Freedom in these portraits is grounded in non-conforming gender expression and in her subjects' mercurial relationships to their bodies, rendered often as if in improvised revelry. Such revelry is heightened by the new presence of western light in the pictures, following Grannan's move from New England to California, and in her three subsequent series exhibited in this group show that western light has both a catalytic and coruscating effect on her portraits' textured sense of life.

The portraits in *Boulevard* (2011) were made in front of the numerous white walls that line the streets of San Francisco and Los Angeles. The portraits cumulatively craft a stark sense of the liminal existence of city dwellers arrayed along the radiant streets of Californian cities shaped by the westward arc of the American Dream.[4] Figures are thickened in density by the pulsing white walls that frame them, and each momentary gesture registers like a sharp-edged retinal trace against the envelope of brightness that surrounds it. These are portraits shaped by a kind of grace inassimilable to reigning Western ideals, because their subjects bare their ageing, their tremulousness or their disaffection with a brazenness equal to the 'ruthless and indiscriminate' light that moulds them into such sharp relief.[5]

In the wake of *Boulevard*, Grannan began to trace the north–south sweep of Route 99 through California's Central Valley, loosely following the trail of Dorothea Lange and retracing her Depression-era steps. Grannan's travels there resulted in two photographic series, *The Ninety Nine* and *The Nine* (2014), as well as a feature film of the same name.[6] In such towns, for those ill-trained or unfit for the information economy, the resilience of the human body marks the outer limit of economic opportunity. Given this, the body's inscription into Grannan's luminous and sparse photographic frames directs our gaze towards its vitality, its visible histories, its beauty, and often towards its pain.

Many of these portraits are suffused with an emotional intensity that may prompt in us (quite reasonably) a desire for the cessation of what often resembles trauma. But if the cause of this is not circumstantial but systemic – if the source of the pain is not the picture, but the continuum of life that it intimates – then a tempering of the image would only displace the problem, rather than sketch its possible cause. Where there is pain, it is rendered in the portraits as immanent and inescapable, which suggests not only that it is endemic to the work of living at the margin, but moreover that it *cannot* be decisive if it is in fact intrinsic to daily life.

Grannan's transition from film to digital capture freed her in this newer work to photograph at microscopic fractions of a second, lending some portraits an instantaneity that registers the quiver in a stray strand of hair, while bonding that immediacy to a narrowed frame that sculpts its subjects into statuesque form. This cultivates a tension between solidity and speed, or between the fleeting and the transcendent. Moreover, the latitude of digital capture preserves the extraordinary severity of this western light, which often acts as a radiant assault on the fragility of the figures in the portraits. It is this immediacy, and its capacity to lend *presentness* to the frame, that has the effect of transposing the intensity of each picture onto a sense of regular and extensive time, rather than into a register of exceptional revelation.

The tensions that emerge within and between Grannan's portraits are then contextualised and altered by the black-and-white street scenes and landscapes in *The Nine*. These pictures counteract the strict compression of the portraits, radically expanding our sense of the place from which they have emerged. The landscapes and scenes in *The Nine* underscore the complexity of familial relationships, the scarcity of urgently needed resources, the habitual nature of addiction, the open-ended desertion of exurban obsolescence, and the resilience of those intimate bonds that socio-economic pressures seem designed to rupture. These pictures skirt the edges of a landscape in which strip malls, workshops and scattered chain motels constitute the interior of a town whose periphery has been shaped by the needs of mass transit and by relentless mechanisation.

If we can recognise in Bakersfield or in Modesto the existence of towns whose principal economic function is to resupply lives led elsewhere, then we can recognise the relative powerlessness of these individuals when set against the pitiless dearth of real political will.

The title *The Ninety Nine* reminds us that we are
each of us an integer within the systematic logic
of capitalism, and that the odds of our success
(or survival) decrease drastically in proportion
to our distance from the number one.

Grannan's pictures frame singular men, women
and children seeking subsistence, or perhaps
mobility (an essential American freedom),
in a landscape denuded of opportunity and
the images confront us with a starkness and
severity that we may either reject or struggle
to absorb. If for William Carlos Williams
there were 'no ideas but in things', it seems
that in Grannan's photographs there are no
disembodied truths.[7] The body is the matter in
which we live, and our resistance to its frailties
is of a piece with our increasing distance from
one another.

Stanley Wolukau-Wanambwa

Adapted from an earlier version
published in 2015 on the website *The
Great Leap Sideways*, formerly available
at www.thegreatleapsideways.com

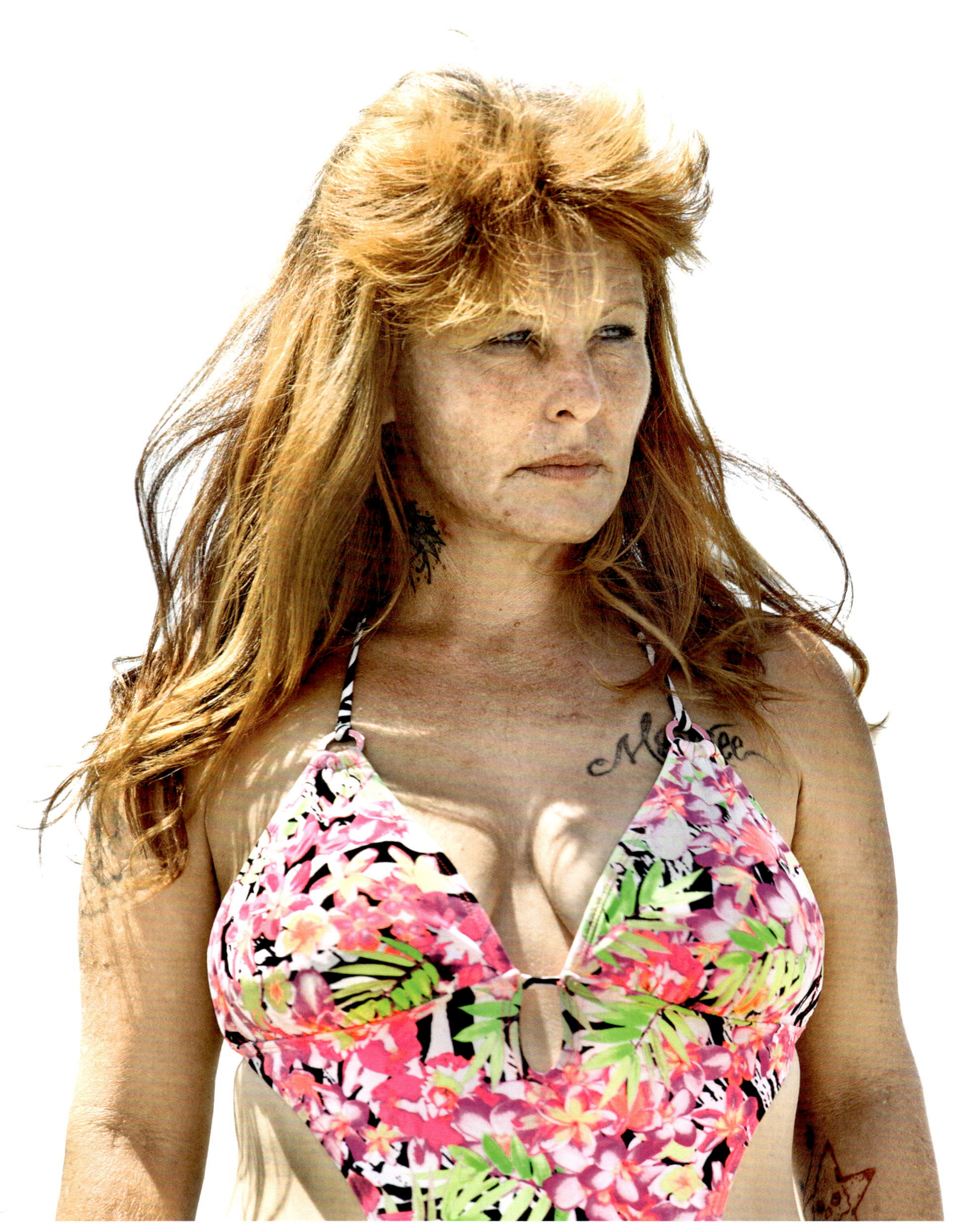

236 From 'The Ninety Nine', *Anonymous*, Modesto, CA, 2013

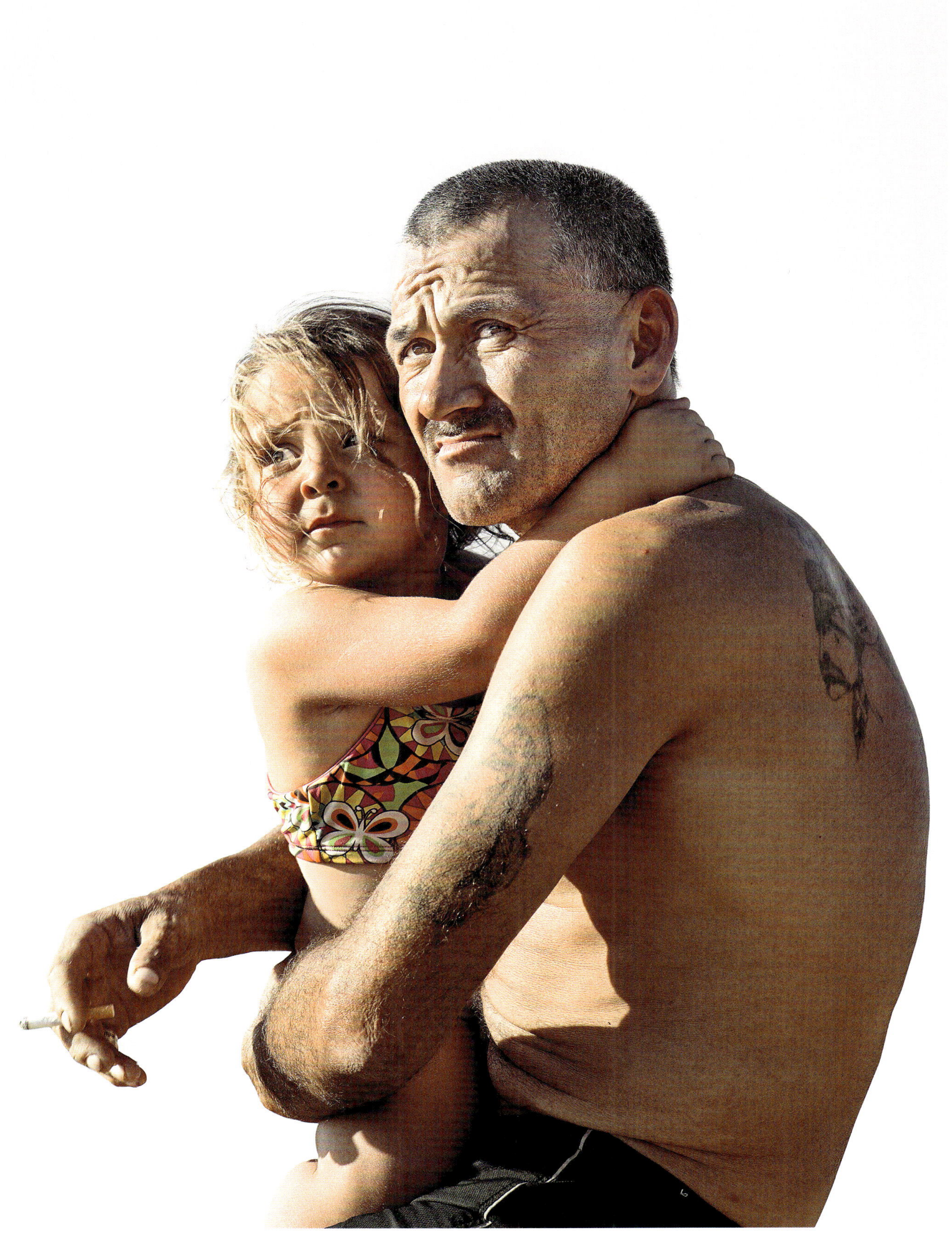

From 'The Ninety Nine', *Anonymous*, Bakersfield, CA, 2011

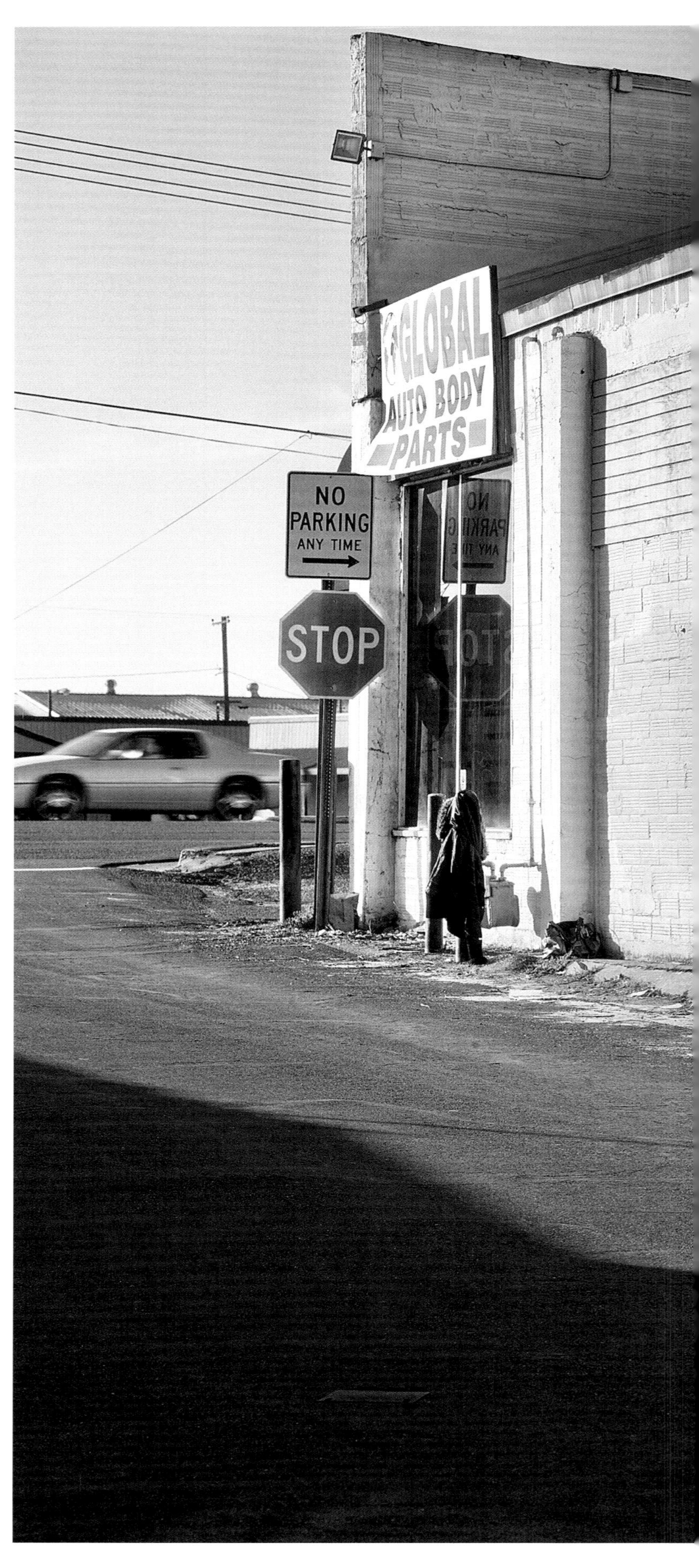

238 From 'The Nine', *Inessa Waits Near South 9th Street*, Modesto, CA, 2012

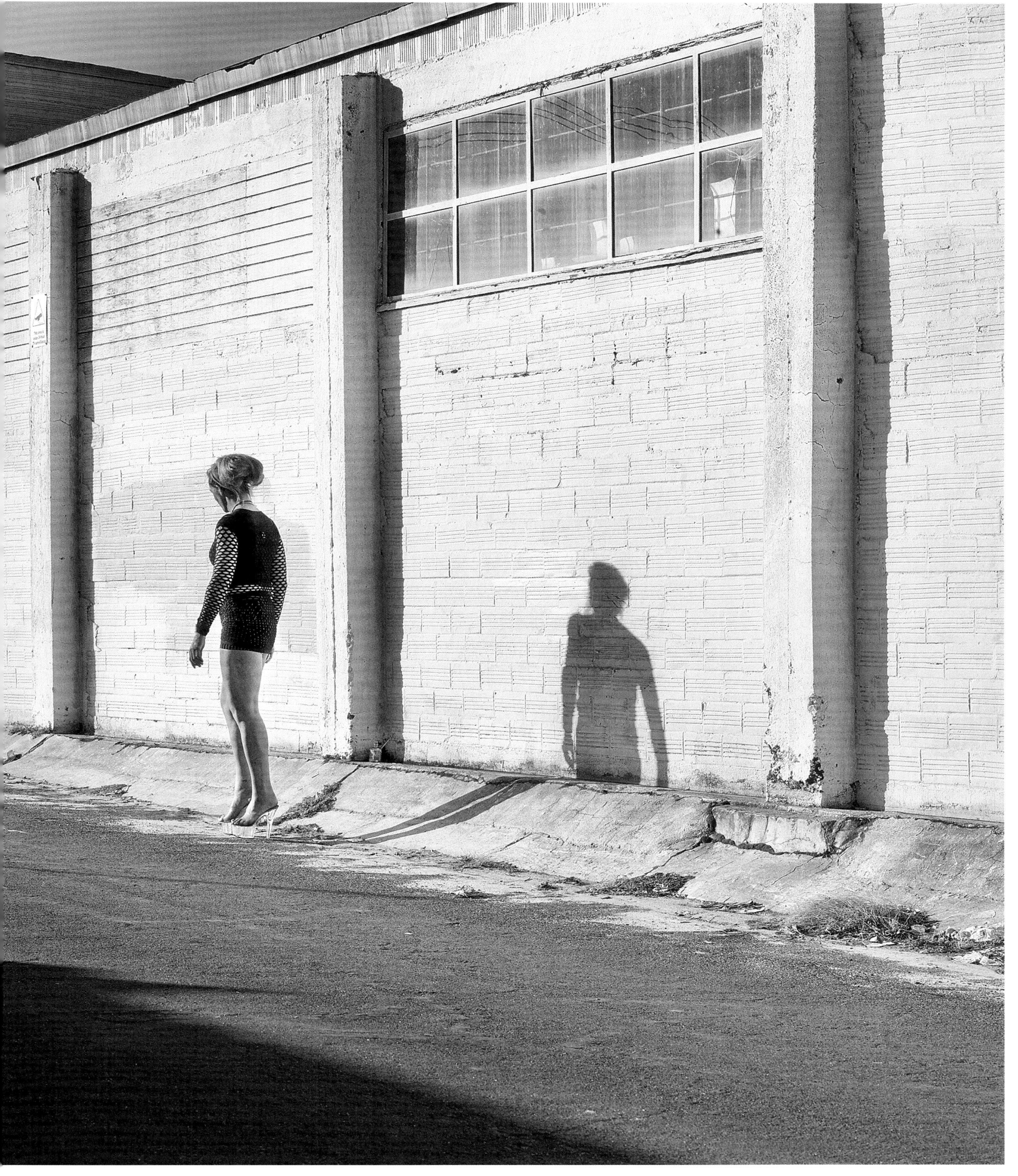

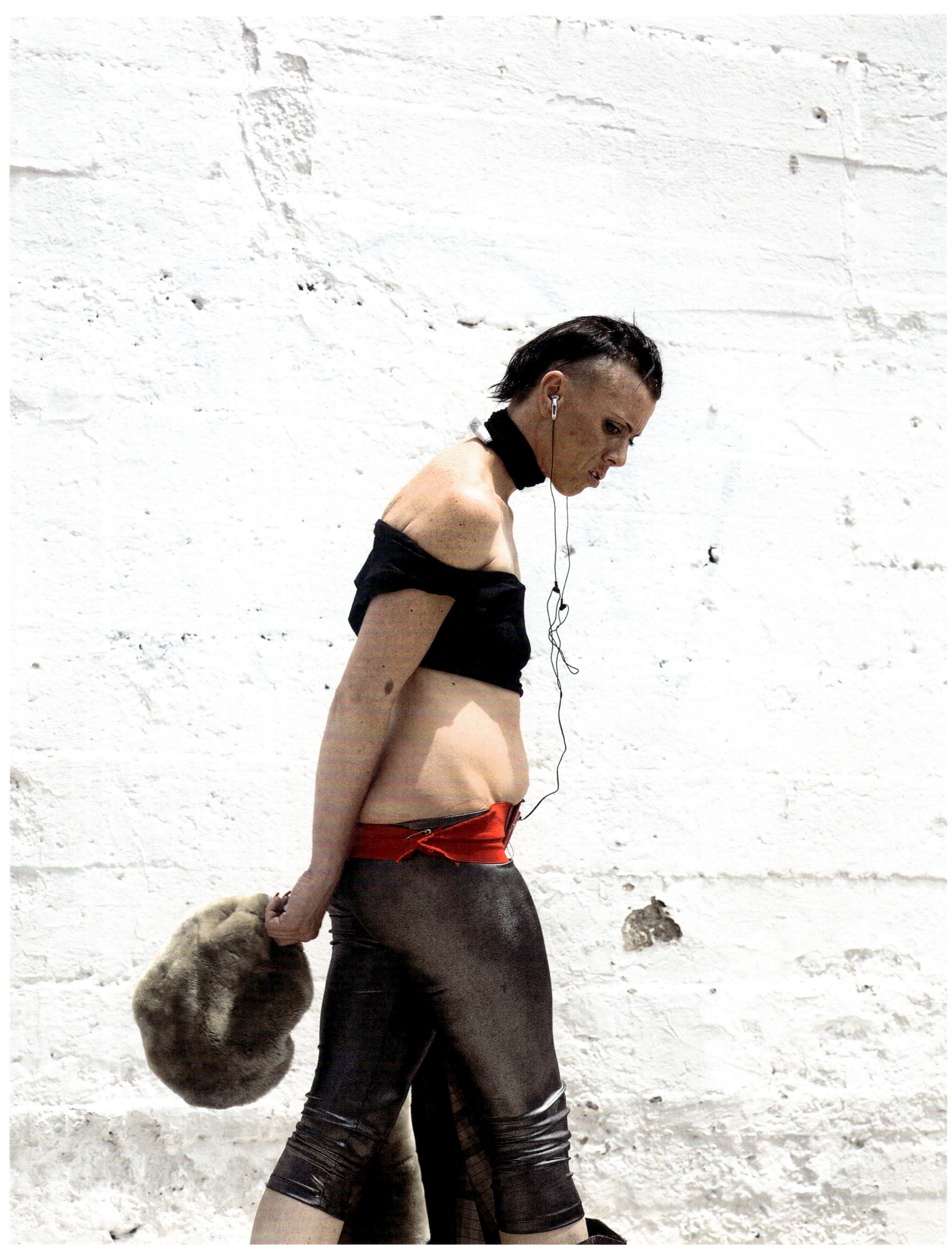

240 From 'Boulevard', *Anonymous*, San Francisco, 2010

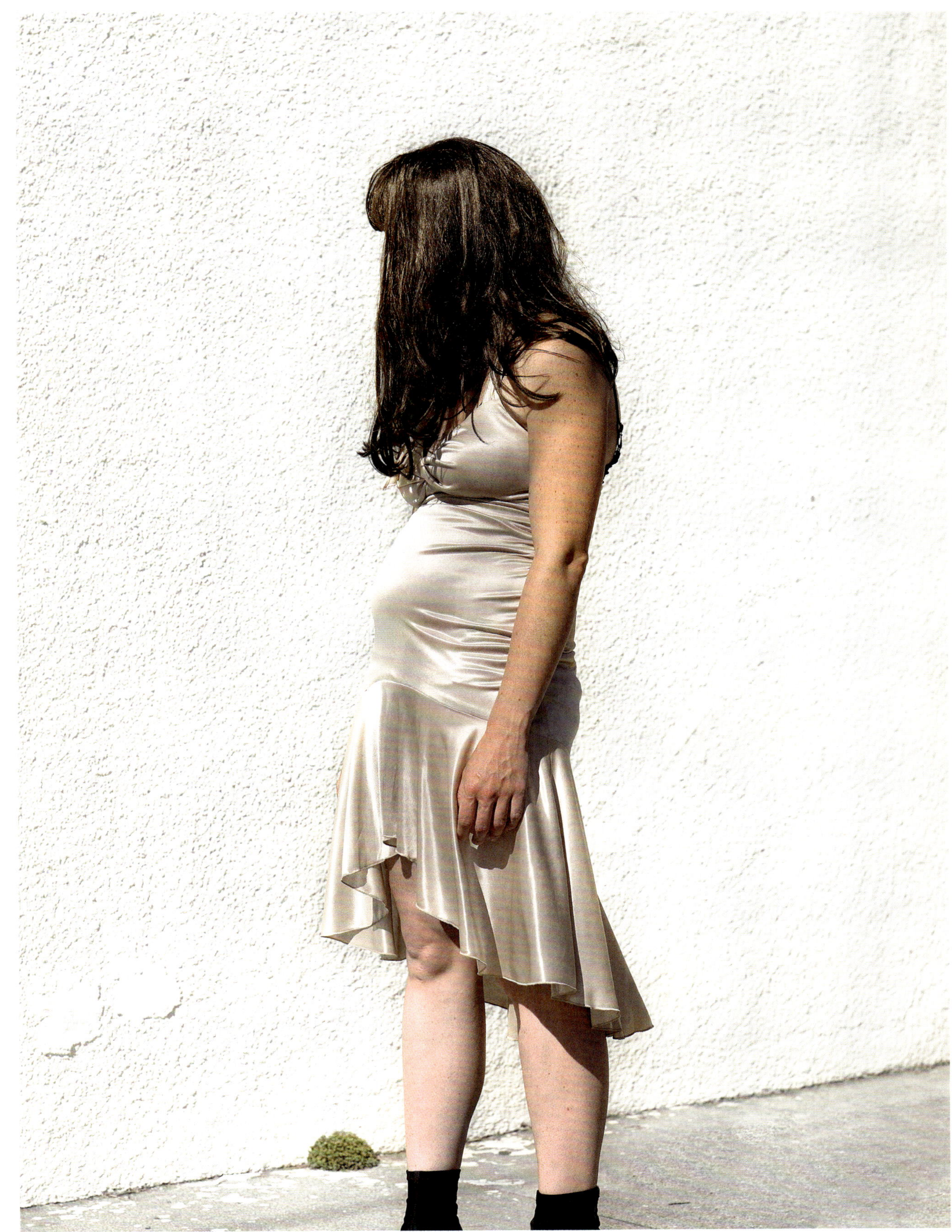

From 'Boulevard', *Anonymous*, Los Angeles, 2008

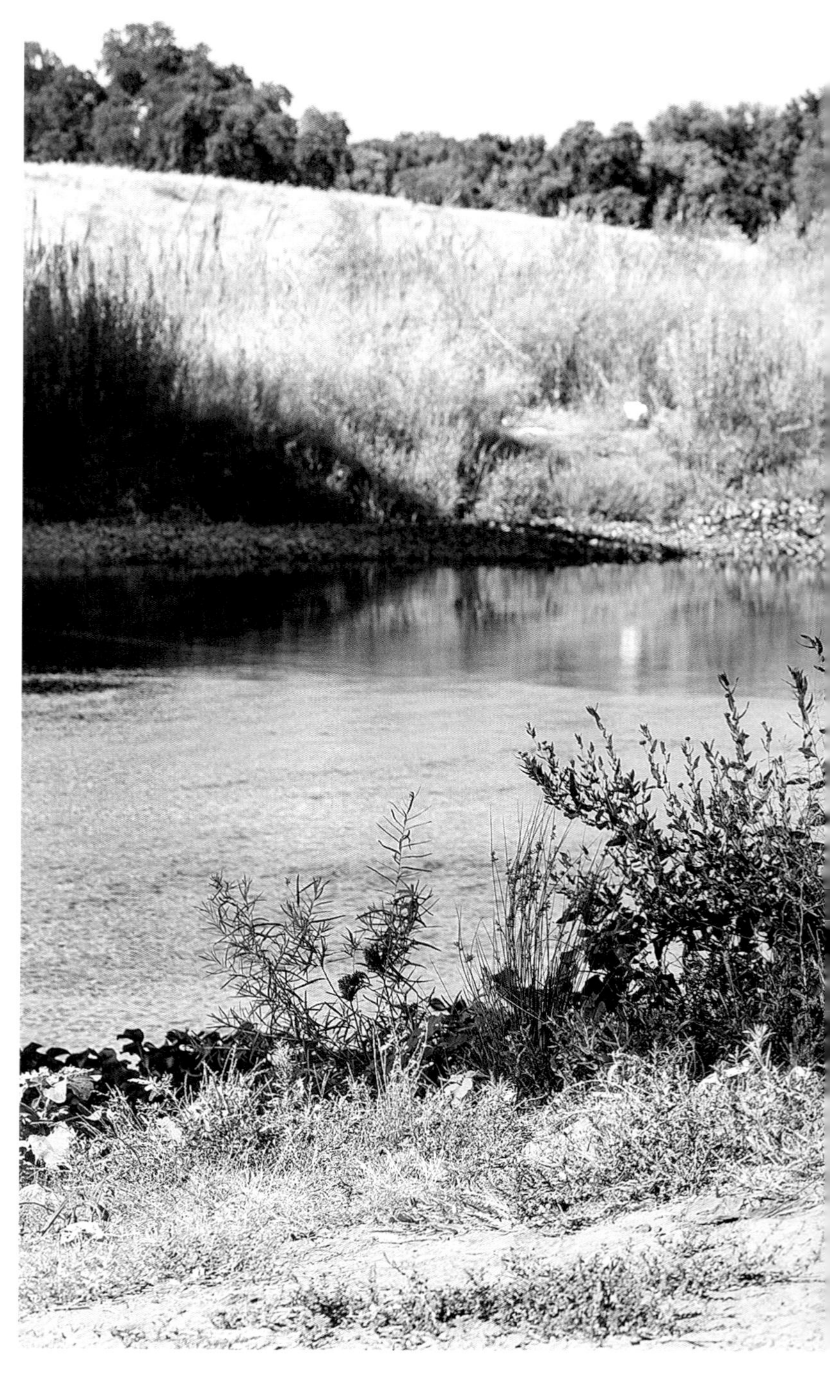

242 From 'The Nine', *April and Robert on Mattress Under 9th Street Bridge, Modesto, CA, 2013*

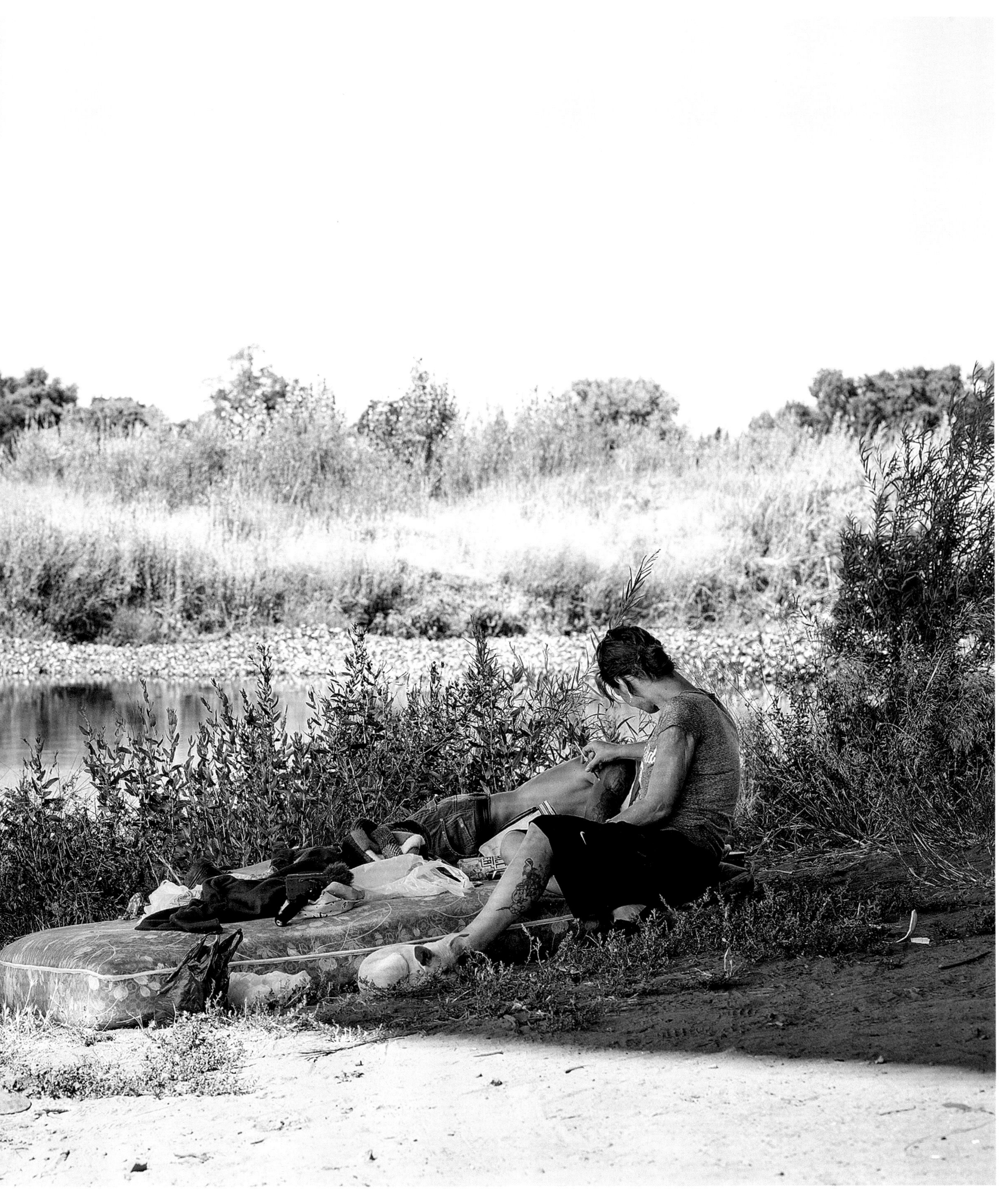

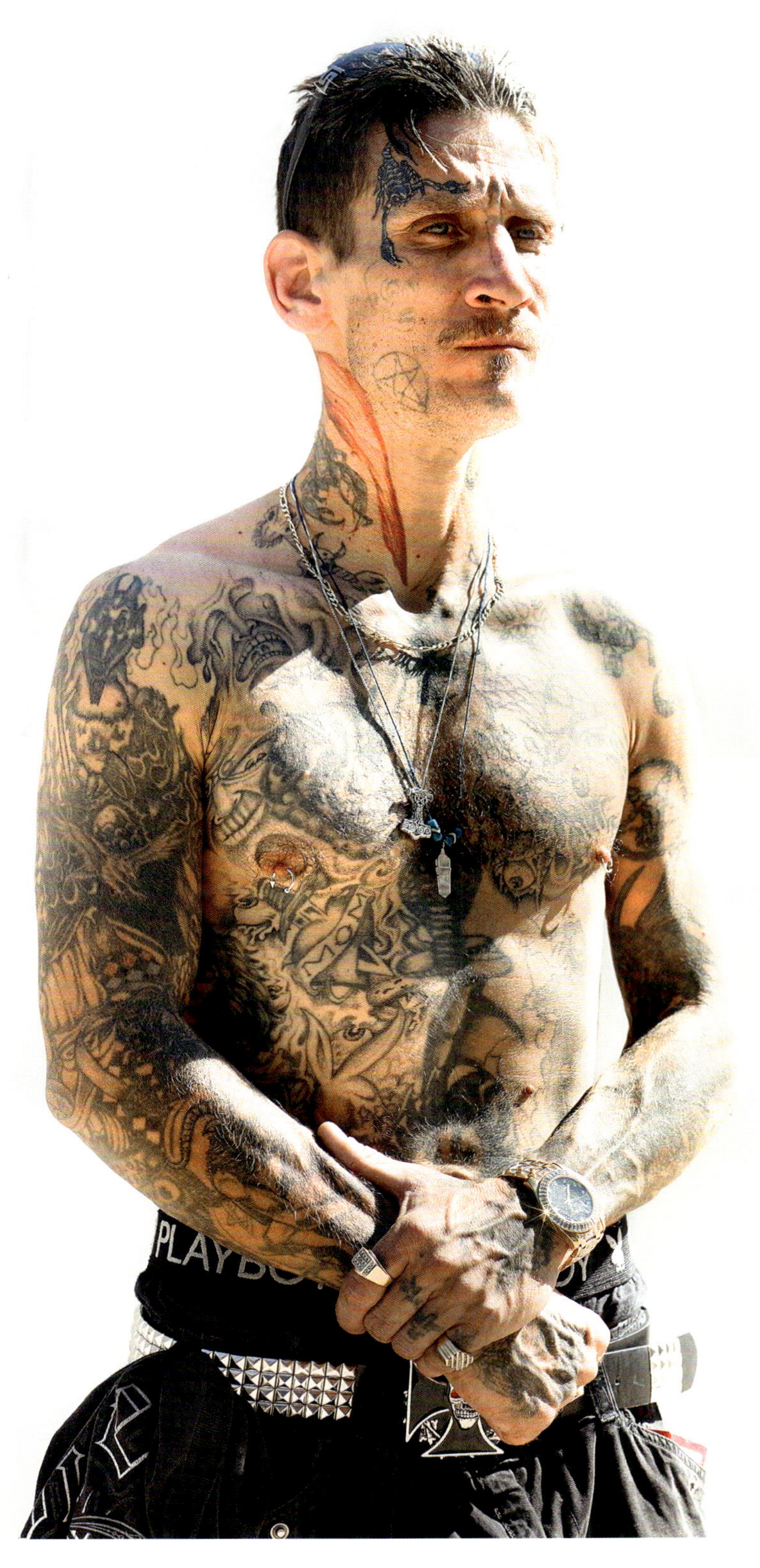

TERESA

MARGOLLES

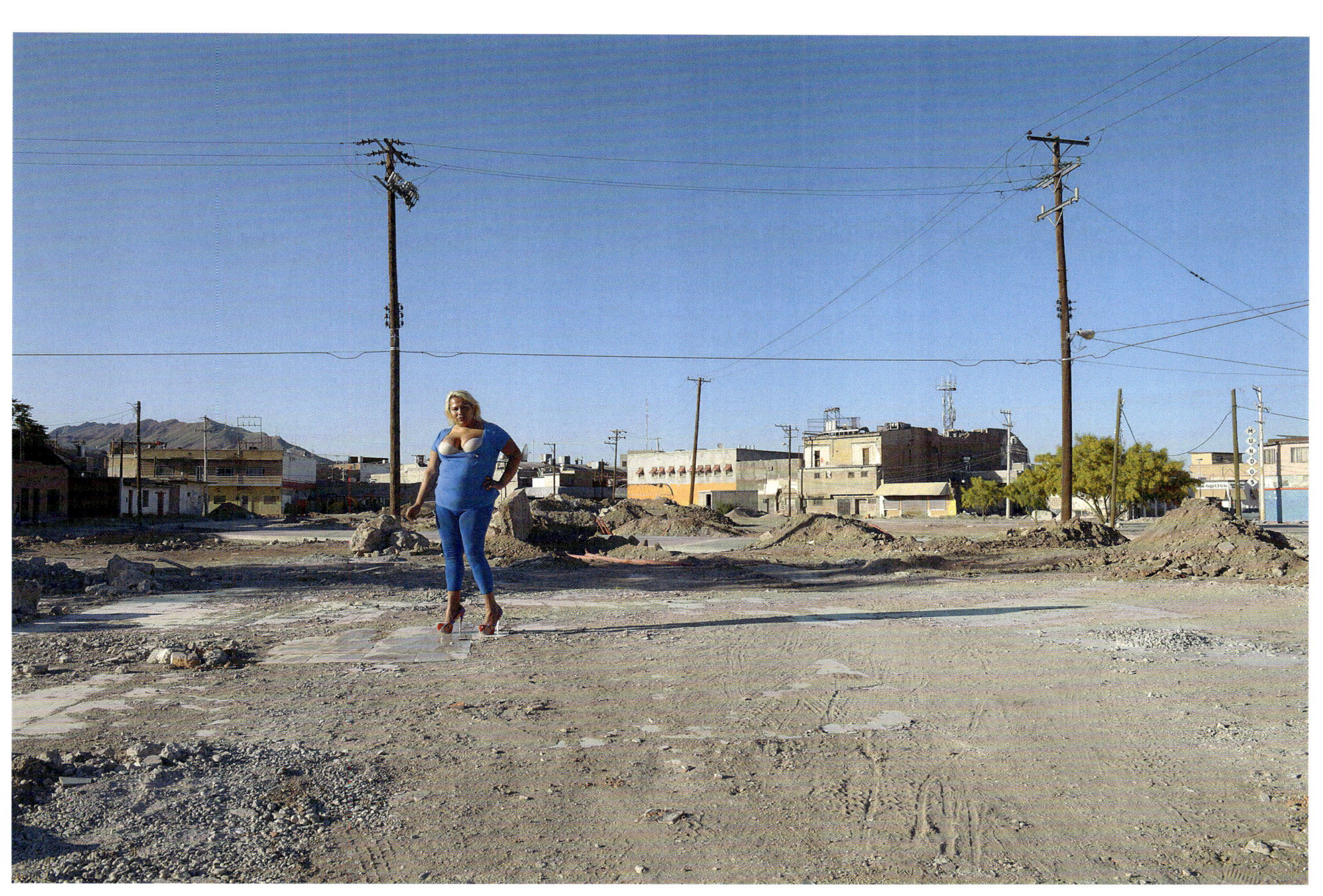

Teresa Margolles's (b. 1963, Mexico) *Pista de baile* (Dance Floor),[1] a series of works documenting the physical transformation of the nightclub scene of Ciudad Juárez, Mexico, appears at first to be part of a new visual vocabulary for the artist. The large, framed photographic portraits of transgender sex workers posing on the remnants of dance floors in various demolished sites awaiting reconstruction have an unexpected clinical distance. For an artist who usually incorporates a very focused physicality in her work the medium of the series is surprising, even if the content is not.

Margolles first gained critical attention in the mid-1990s as a founder member of the Mexico City-based art collective SEMEFO.[2] In their early collaborative work *Carousel Lavatio Corporis* of 1994, exhibited at the Museo Carrillo Gil,[3] embalmed parts of real horses were displayed encased in a strange carousel-like metal cage. The work shocked visitors with its use of dead animals, its odours of decay and by appearing to cross the line between art and reality in its stark evocation of cruelty and suffering in the context of the funfair.

The contrast of pain, violence and play as political metaphor deployed in this work was to become a key element in Margolles's later artistic vocabulary; this attribute and her work's politically revealing and interventionist approach have led to widespread recognition of her art outside Mexico. As an artist she has worked unflinchingly to reveal and mourn the injustices confronting both herself and her audiences.

Margolles's work has frequently explored the relationship of artwork to audience by blurring the definition between spectatorship and complicity. Her solo show *Muerte sin fin* at the Museum für Moderne Kunst in Frankfurt, held in 2004,[4] which used the transmutability of materials to break from the traditional confines of the art object, established Margolles as a major player on the international art scene. The exhibition was framed by two related works, *En el aire* (In the Air, 2003) and *Aire* (Air, 2003). In these pieces, water previously used to wash the bodies of the dead in the morgue of Mexico City was transformed into bubbles (in the former case) and into steam

(in the latter) to create a humid atmosphere in the room. Despite the sanitisation of the water, the idea of its derivation was enough to create interwoven, emotionally charged responses: fear, disgust, sadness, anger. The gallery audience was contaminated by the work with or without their permission.

The materials that Margolles uses in her art (blood, body parts, contaminated water) break taboos of realism and representation and impose a sense of complicity on the part of the audiences of her installations. In a work such as *What Else Could We Talk About?*, created for the Mexican Pavilion at the Venice Biennale in 2009,[5] the reuse of bodily fluids contaminated with the 'real' processes of the afterlife repelled and frightened many. Margolles took the decaying Venice palazzo and intricately entwined her processes of working into the fabric of the location. Cloths soaked in blood collected at the sites of distant violence hung from the walls, blending with the faded opulence of the silk coverings as silent and powerful reminders of worlds outside the boundaries of the art fair. On the ground floor of the otherwise empty and dark space hung an enormous mural of mud. Dug from the sites of the discovery of murder victims, the mud clung to the cloth; never allowed to dry, it was sprayed from behind with water, dripping the contaminated liquid slowly into the gulley below. With every passing day of the biennial the liquid impregnated the floors of the palazzo with the remains of this distant violence, as each day the cleaner's mops coated this complex and literally multilayered work with yet more layers of meaning.

Through these key creative interventions, Margolles forced her audiences to recognise those aspects of the politics of violence traditionally hidden within the international art world, and to confront the violence of the drug wars destroying the lives of the Mexican families with whom she worked to create the concept that informed the work.

In terms of content there are two obvious precedents in Margolles's work for the *Pista de baile* series. In 2000 she exhibited the embalmed, pierced tongue of a dead drug addict. This work, *Lengua* (Tongue),[6] a combination of Catholic imagery and political revelation,

explored the fact that 'despite popular wisdom, death is not egalitarian. Social taxonomies are re-inscribed not only in the causes of death but also in the fate of our remains.'[7] The embalmed tongue, bought from the family of the victim, was part of an overall work that gained its meaning from the very process of its making and exhibiting. The fact that the family were willing to agree to the creation of the work in exchange for the cost of the dead man's burial adds to the implicit social critique within the work, and its exhibition in Los Angeles was a poignant reminder of the impossibility of the victim to escape the circumstances of his own poverty. *Lengua* was there to speak for the silent, to impact in death as it could not in life – a fragment of the everyday reality of death on the streets of any big city forcing its way into the 'safe' space of the gallery.

Subsequently, Margolles explored the so-called *maquiladora* murders that have taken place since the passing of the North American Free Trade Agreement (NAFTA) in 1994, which precipitated the murder of many young women in Ciudad Juárez.[8] Many of the hundreds of women who have been killed had worked in the factories of companies that switched production south of the US–Mexico border to benefit from lower costs. As with *Lengua*, the victims are the poor and the unrepresented, and the sheer enormity of the tragedy is difficult for an artist to engage with. Margolles's response, the installation *Lote Bravo, Lomas de Poleo, Anapra y Cerro de Cristo Negro* (2005), showed a video/sound piece of a seemingly endless car journey around the sites of the murders, with the sounds of the desert night. The scale and loneliness of the video is reinforced by an accompanying sculptural installation of handmade bricks. Though the bricks echo the minimalist aesthetic of Carl Andre, the sand used to make them is imparted with a more focused political meaning by having been collected at points within Cuidad Juárez where the bodies of victims had been found.

In both these earlier projects Margolles worked collaboratively with members of the populations that her work was addressing so as to gain greater insight into the subjective realities of these victims of crime and social inequality. The materials and visual vocabulary used might differ, but the need to direct audiences towards her particularly eloquent vision of the forgotten in society remains a constant. In *Pista de baile* Margolles has returned to the scene of a different type of crime, showing the marginalised world of the transgender sex workers whose existence is under constant threat and whose environment has been destroyed, in order to question the links between money and power. The murder of one of her subjects, Karla, during the process of developing this project gives the work both urgency and pathos. In these works, artist and audience again become complicit, for as passive observers of injustice they too become guilty. It is only through embracing empathy and an engagement with political change that these works can be truly understood.

Oriana Baddeley

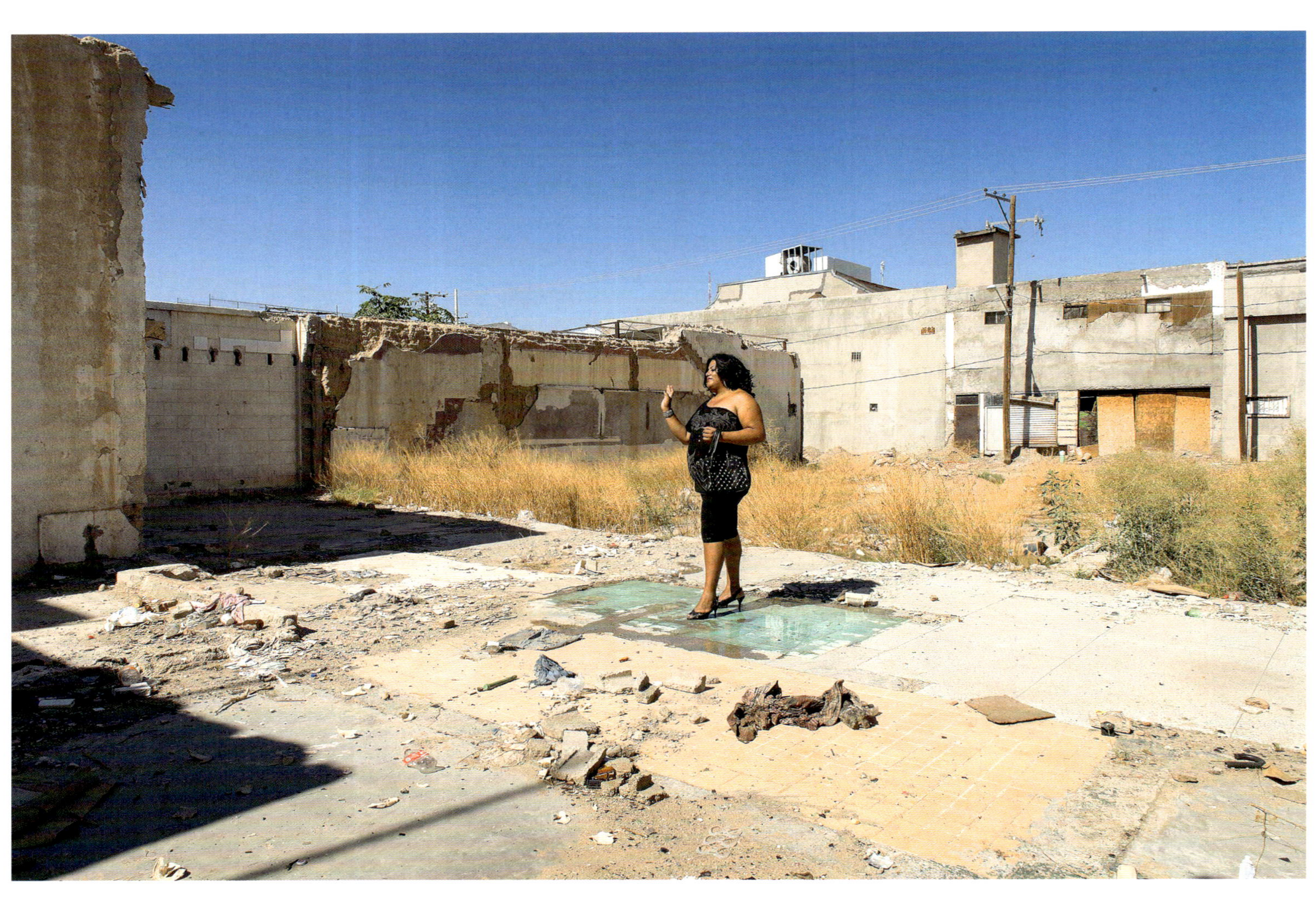

Pista de baile de la discoteca 'Eduardo's' (Dance Floor at Eduardo's), 2016
250 Transgender sex worker standing on the dance floor of a demolished club in Ciudad Juárez, Mexico

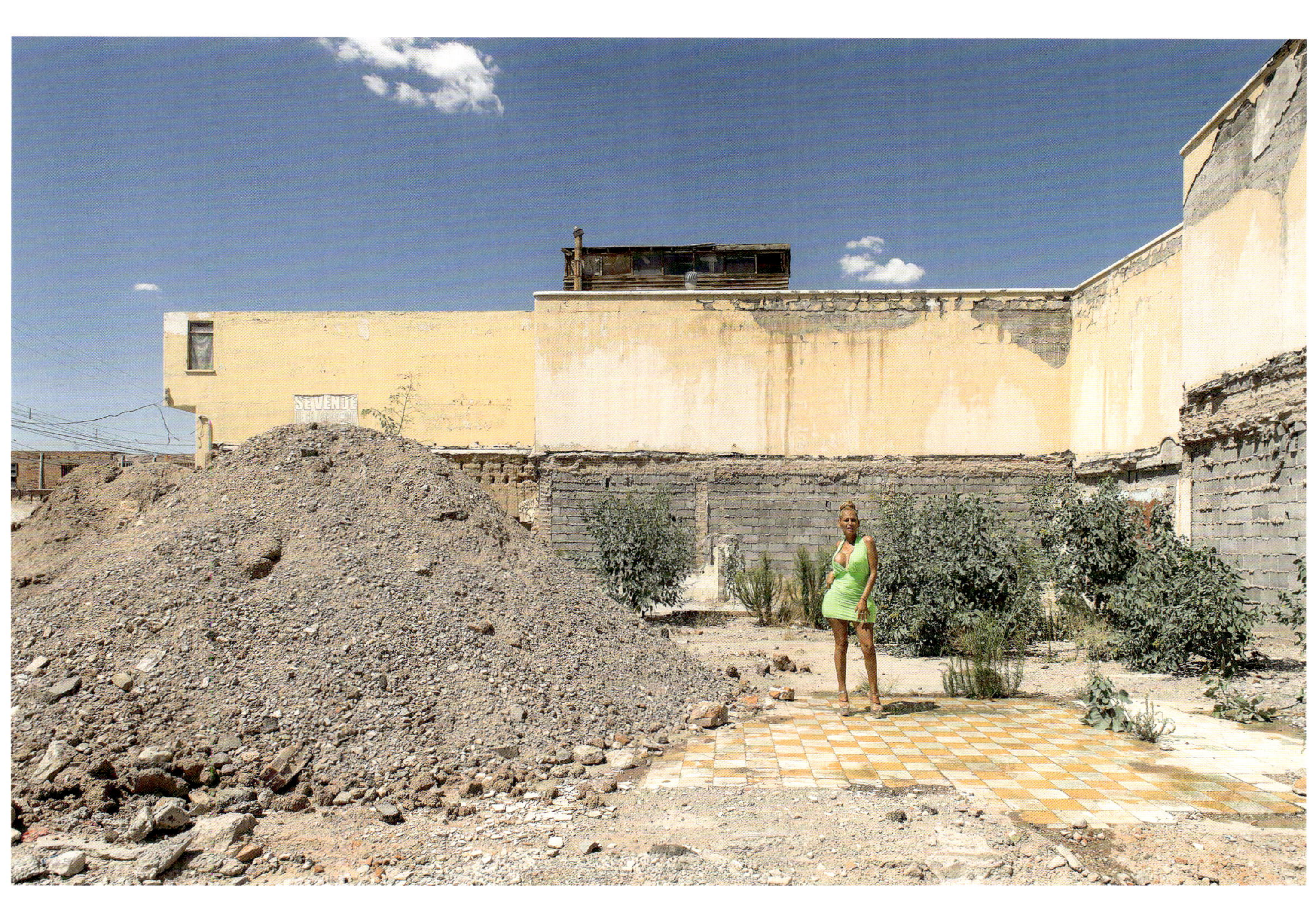

Pista de baile del club 'Arthur's' (Dance Floor at Arthur's), 2016
Transgender sex worker standing on the dance floor of a demolished club in Ciudad Juárez, Mexico

This page and following: Teresa Margolles, *Revisión del archivo de Don Luis Alvarado, años 60, 70 y 80, en los clubs alrededor de la calle Mariscal, Ciudad Juárez, Mexico* (Revisiting Luis Alvarado's Archive: The Nightclubs around Mariscal Street, Ciudad Juárez, Mexico, 1960s–1980s), 2016

In 2011 Teresa Margolles met Luis Alvarado (b. 1929, Mexico), a street photographer who documented the nightlife around Mariscal Street in Ciudad Juárez between 1960 and 1990. While researching and digitising Alvarado's archive, Margolles discovered what she describes as 'important documents of a fragment of the history of Juárez', capturing this borderland city dominated by brothels, gambling dens and inexpensive alcohol. Carefully selected and arranged by Margolles in the slideshow *Revision del archivo de Don Luis Alvarado*, Alvarado's images portray a certain lawlessness and foreshadow the socio-economic changes generated by Mexico's economic experiments under the Border Industrialisation Program (1965) and the North American Free Trade Agreement (1994).

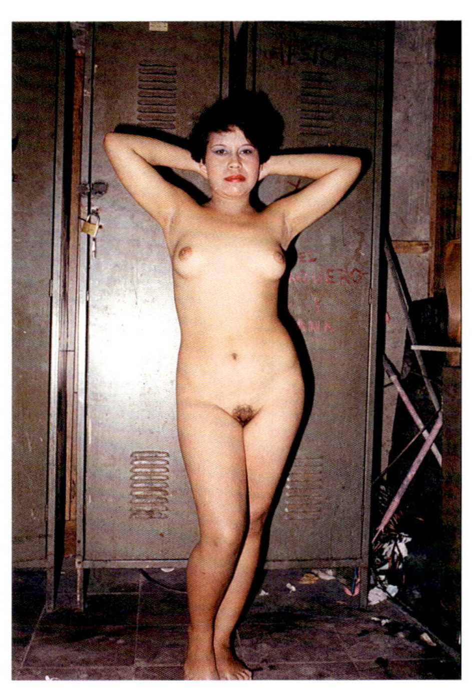
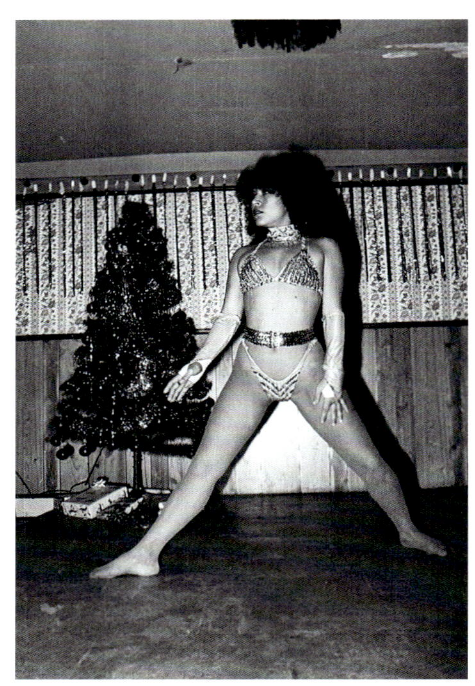
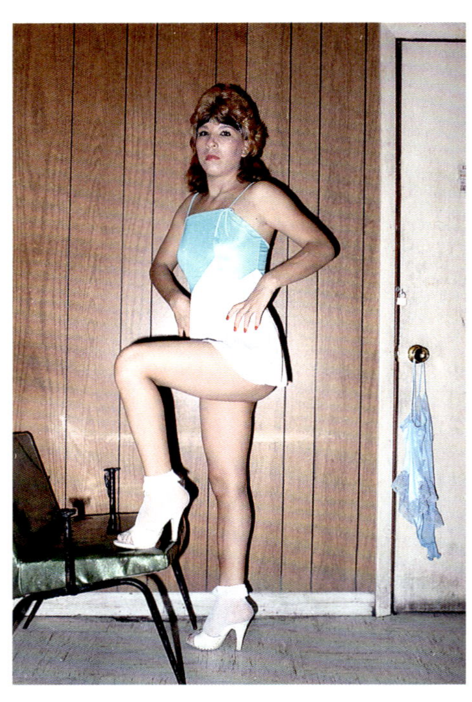
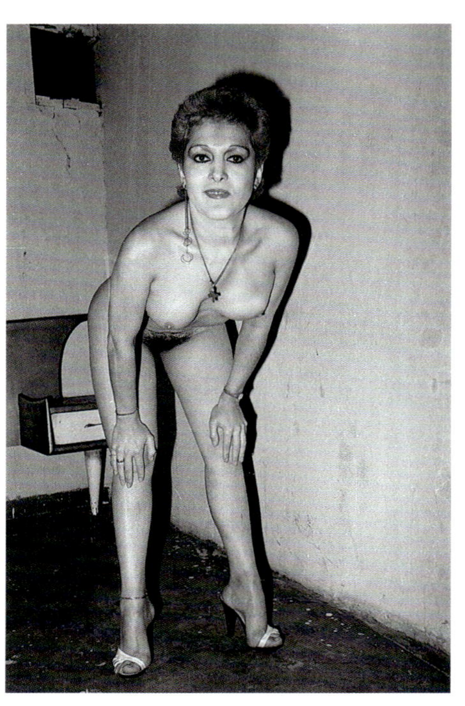
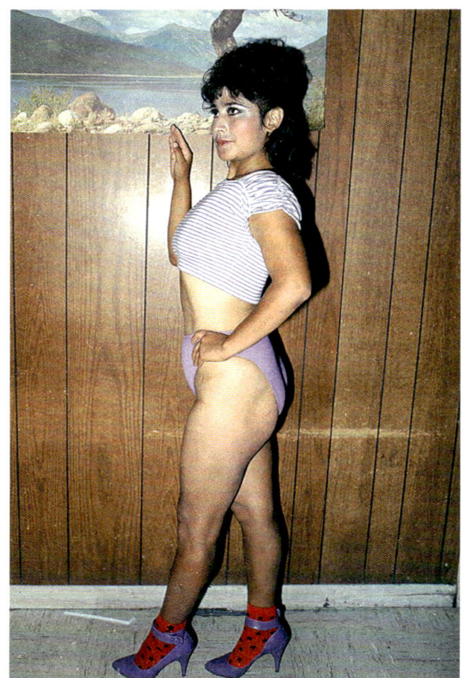
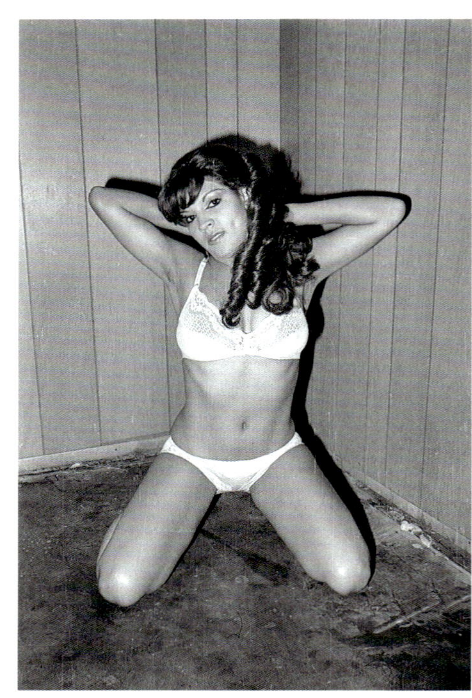

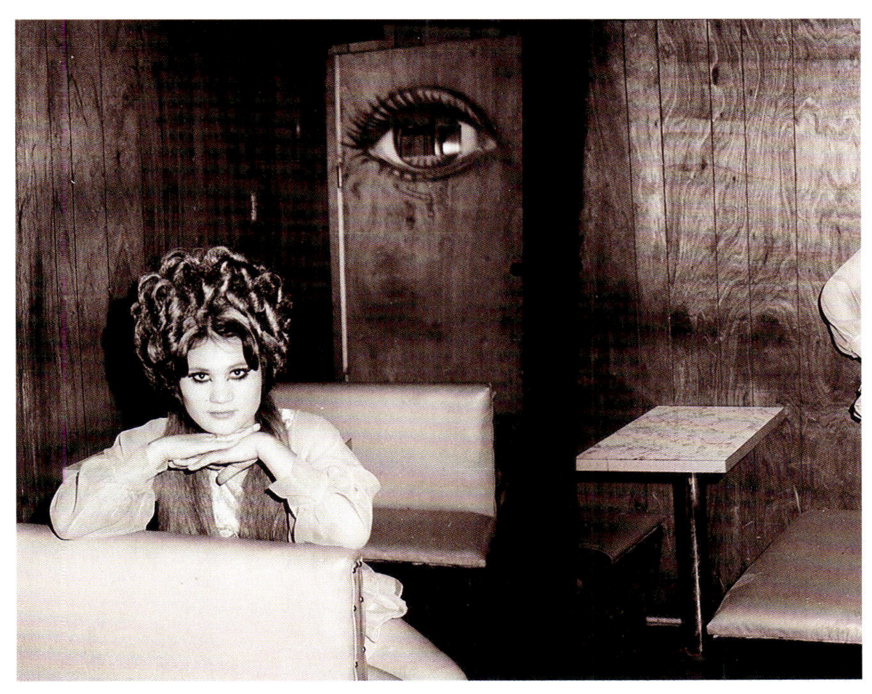

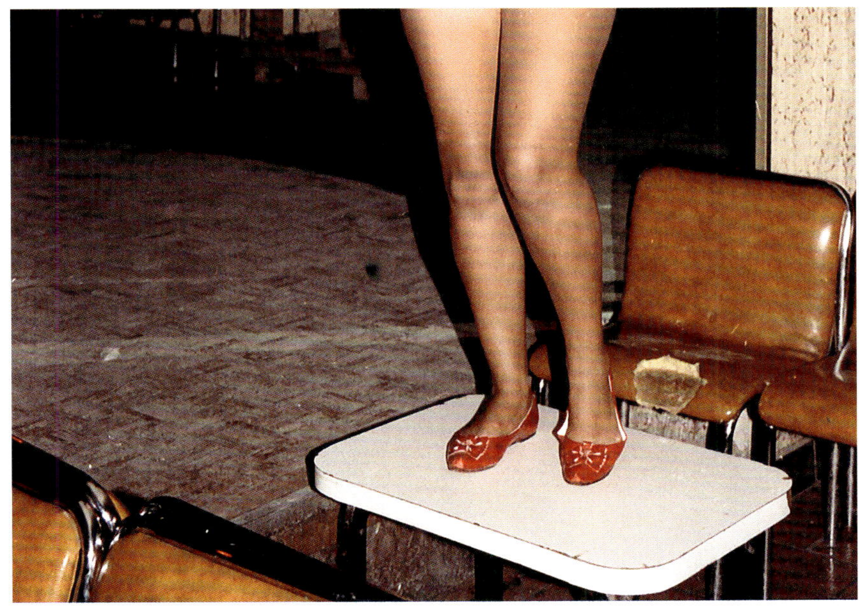

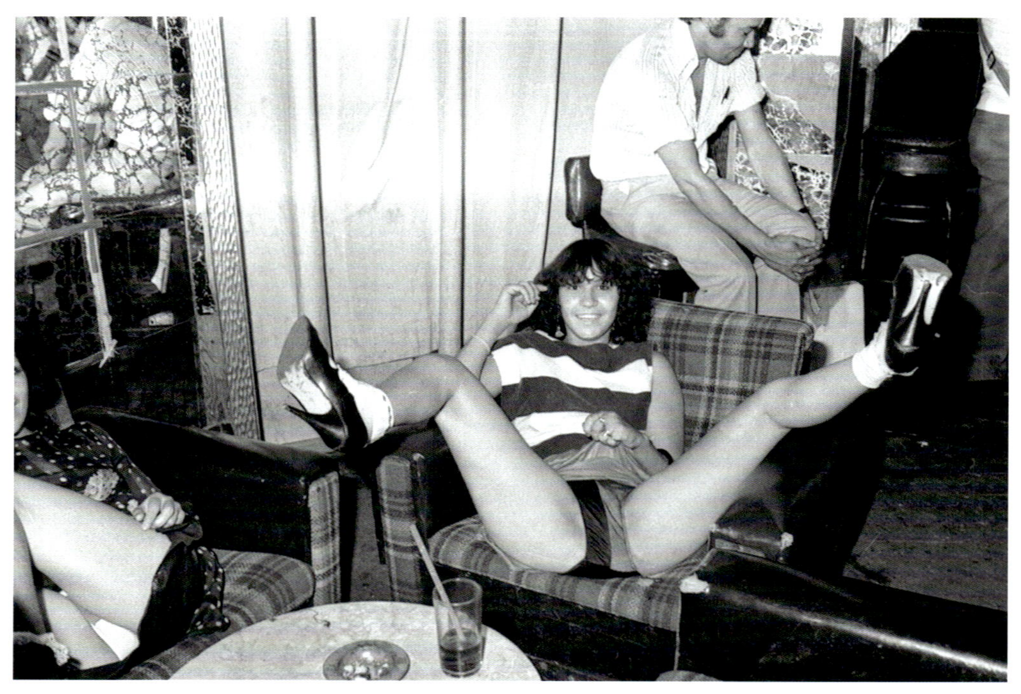

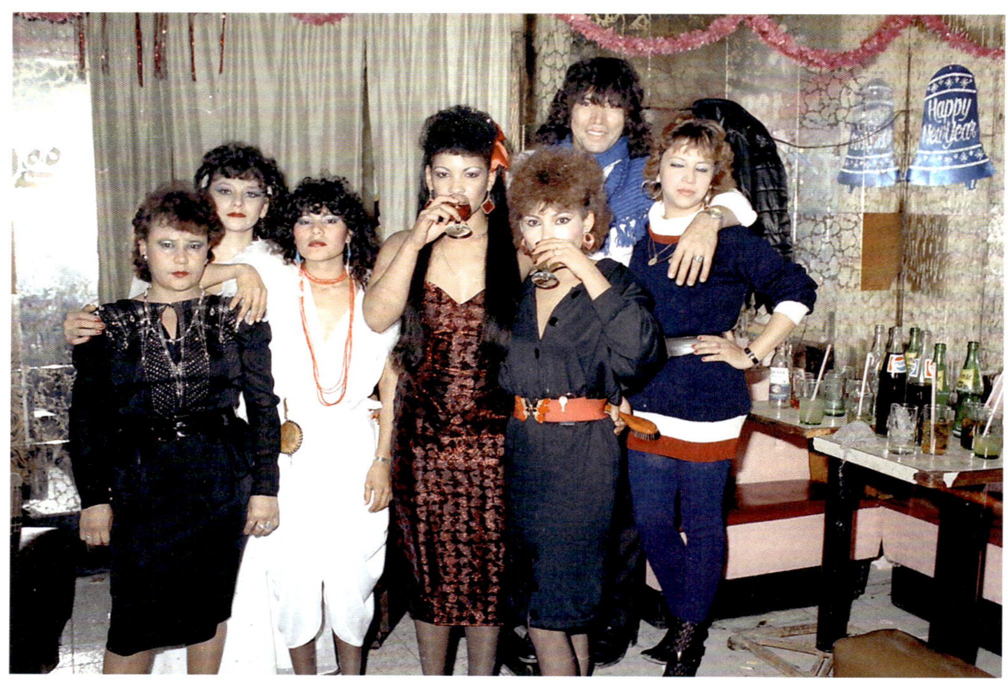

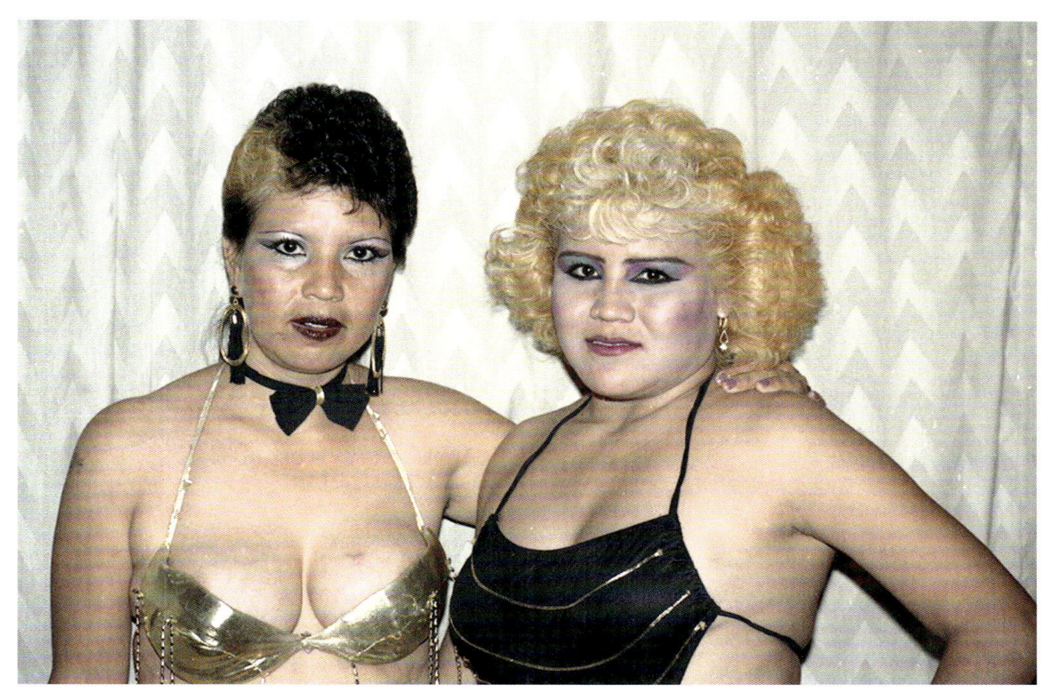

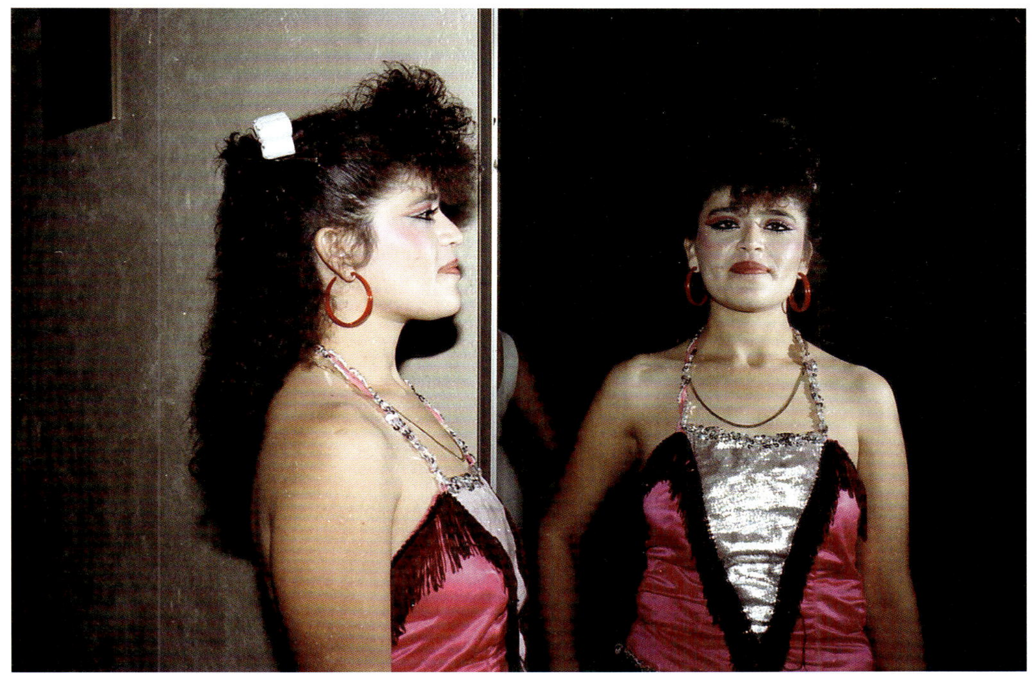

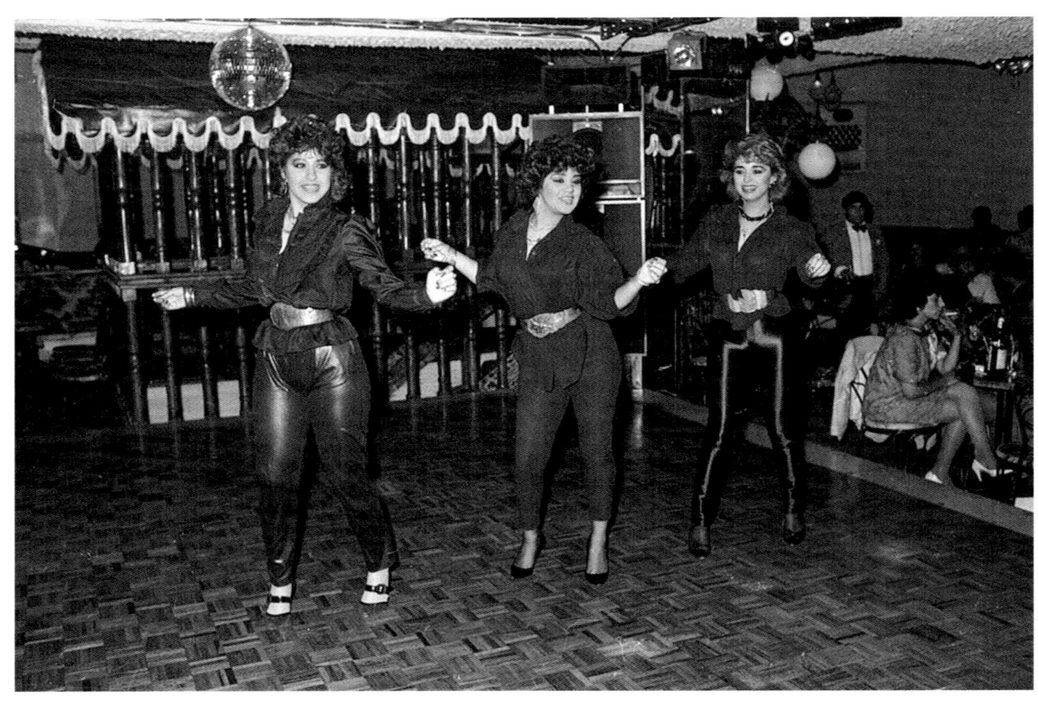

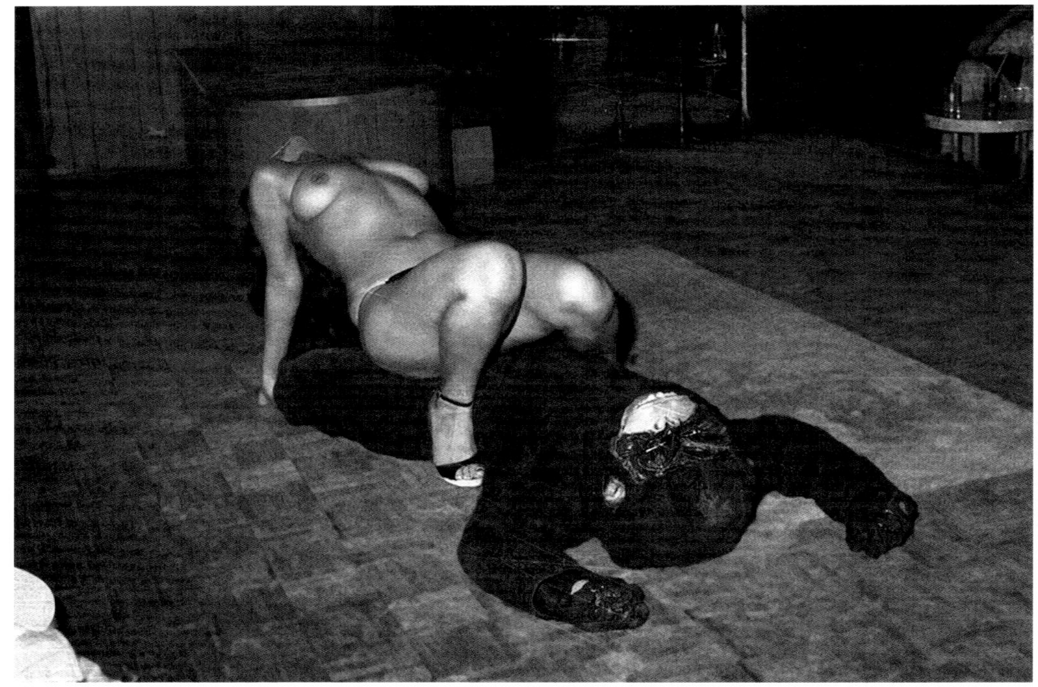

ARCHIVAL MATERIAL

Between 1960 and 1980 the American transgender activist
Virginia Prince (b. 1912, USA; d. 2009) ran and edited
the bi-monthly periodical *Transvestia*, with a total
of 100 issues published. Its stated aim was to 'provide
expression for those interested in the subjects of unusual
dress and fashion … to provide information to those
who, through ignorance, condemn that which they don't
understand … [and] to provide education for those who see
evil when none exists'. A story-driven magazine, it was
published by and for the burgeoning transgender community
that was beginning to reveal itself in 1950s America.

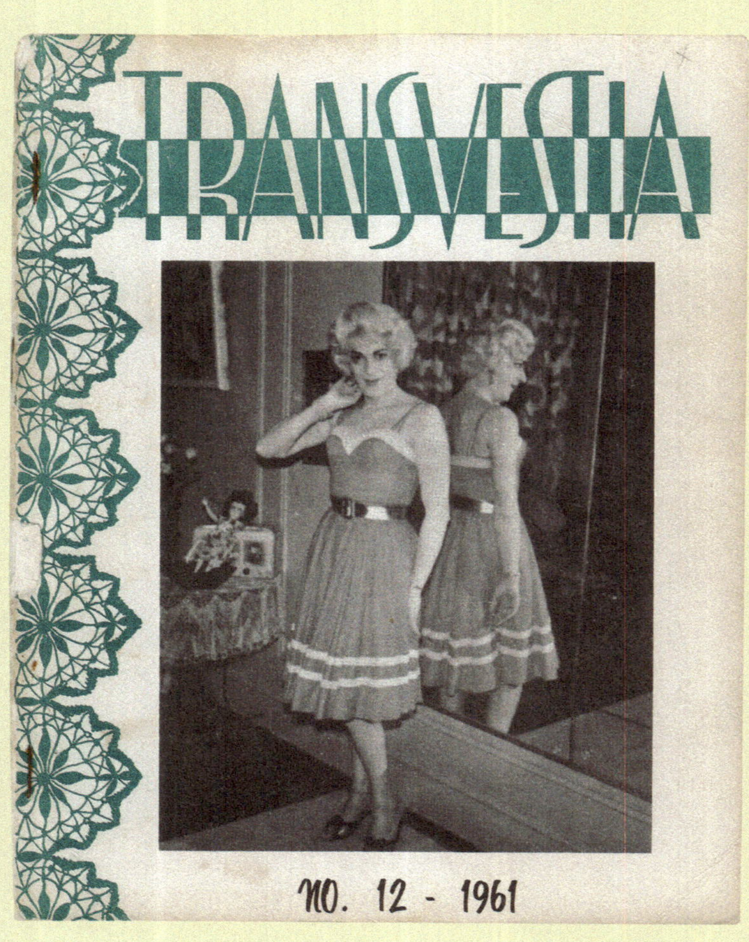

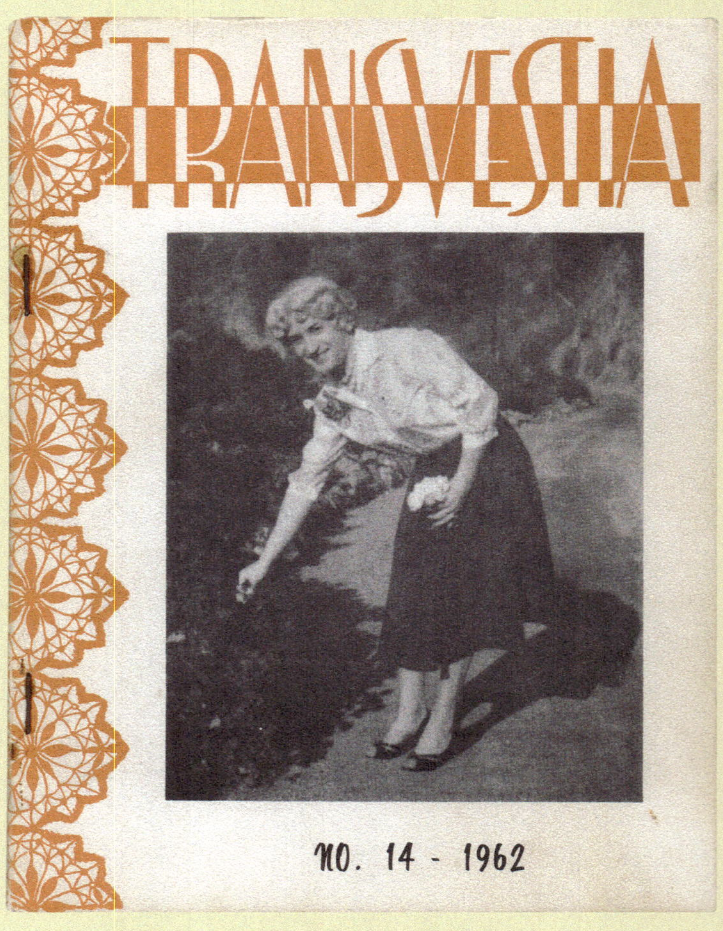

260 *Transvestia* (covers), edited by Virginia Prince, December 1961–1967

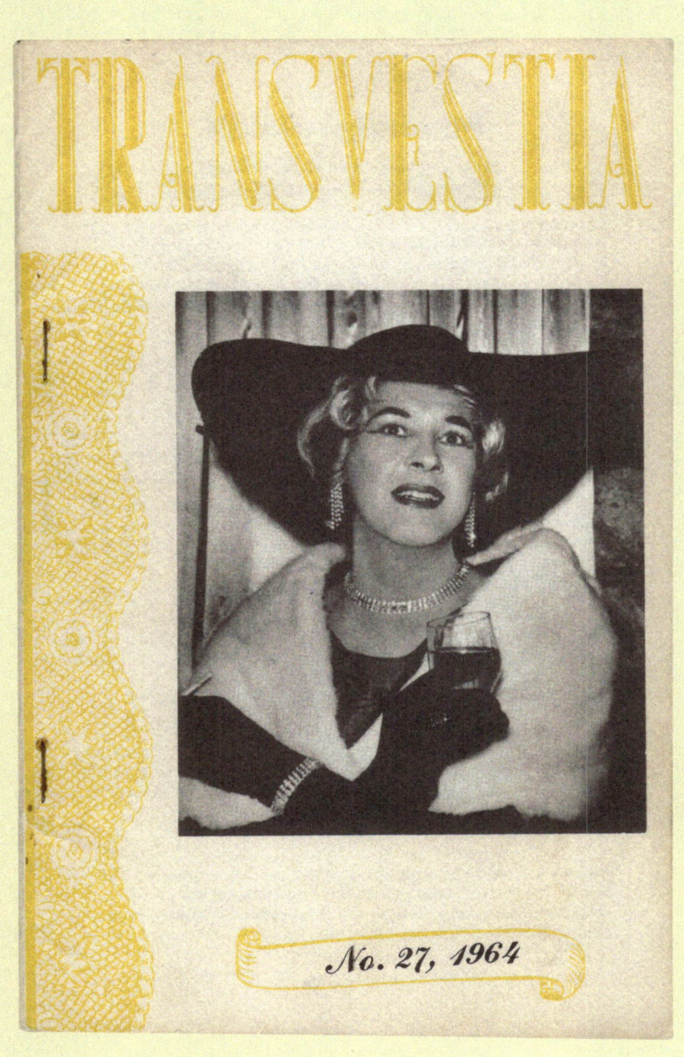

TRANSVESTIA

No. 27, 1964

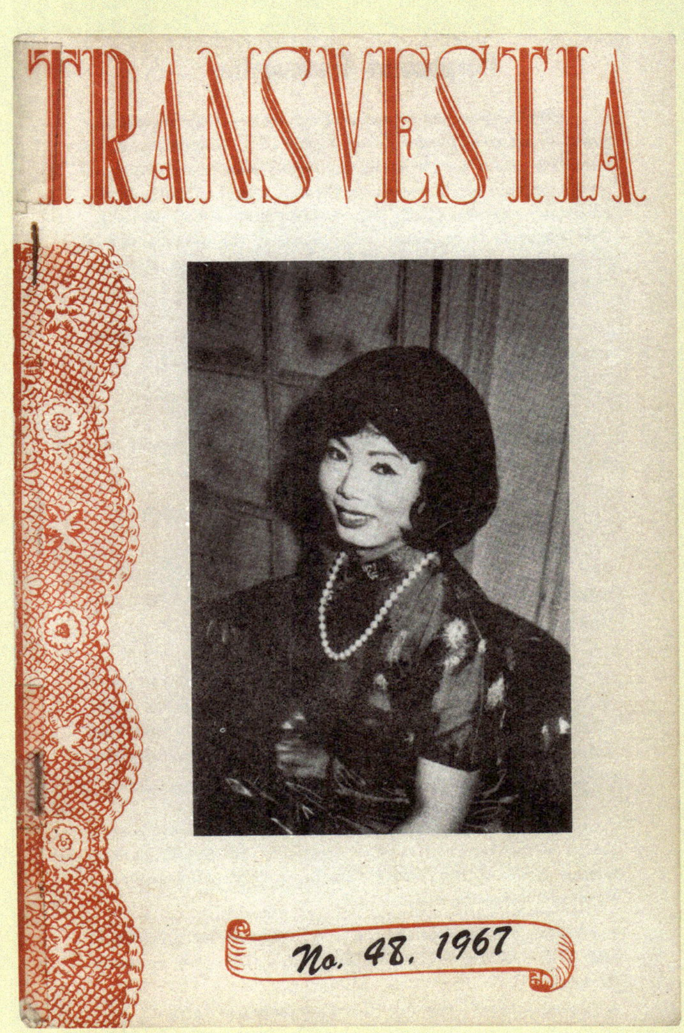

TRANSVESTIA

No. 48, 1967

"SUSANNA SAYS..."

Hi:

A quick note from Virginia drops like an alarm-clock bell at 5 AM when one's sleep is at it's deepest. Just a reminder that the column is due. Another summer came and went and with it a multiplication of experiences and dreams come true. New friends came to add their baggage of TV wealth to our common space capsule. Meet Shanghai Lili, the perfect Chinese doll, barely 5' 4" or thereabouts, the envy of her taller sisters. Our first meeting at Susanna's NY apartment entailed 3 solid hours of Polaroid color shots, the first time that Lili could have her picture taken by somebody else. Up to then it was all self-portraits. Then came Lili's first visit to our country place. I assumed she would arrive at my apartment Friday evening carrying the usual mountain of suitcases that almost every TV carries for one week-end of dressing up. To my surprise, a cab pulled up in front of our house, and this cute Chinese girl emerges carrying just a small suitcase and her hand-bag. She explains with a smile: it was easier to dress at home and come already dressed for the week-end. And there were other friends that I had heard about but never met until now.. there's Rita from the Bronx...a wonderful person and lots of fun to be with...and Ellen, a charming gal... the kind of person you like on first sight...Musn't forget Sally and Julie from Texas. Sally and Lorelei spent a week-end at Casa Susanna this Summer (their-honey-moon)....Lorelei (a gorgeous creature) got her baptism of fire spending an entire week-end surrounded by TV's...her only complaint is that Sally just was won't learn to take care of her clothes (as a girl should)... Sally just smiles at Lorelei and states that Sally feels like a lady of leisure and besides, Lorelei does such a beautiful job of ironing that Sally would feel ashamed even to try her hand at the iron. Shortly after that week-end I had the opportunity to visit Texas (on business) but naturally managed to squeeze a marvellous TV evening at Sally's with the added joy of meeting Julie who drops a long stretch just for the occasion. The TV yakketty-yak went on (as you can well imagine) until the wee hours of the morning. That evening made the whole long trip to Texas really worth while.

There was an old dilapidated barn at Casa Susanna. It is now becoming (after being fully renovated) a potential entertainment hall. Incredible though it sounds for a TV hideaway, the first item of entertainment to make it's appearance at the barn was (excuse the expression) a pool table. Not a very lady-like vehicle for fun...but we must admit we've had many a pleasant afternoon shooting pool on high heels. Right Sally? We've also proven this summer that to take TV pictures it isn't always necessary to stand in front of the camera making believe we are some sort of Rita Hayworth or Elizabeth Taylor...we decided to register on film the healthy expression of fun and joy that pervades a TV gathering, and one afternoon five TV's gathered on the lawn in front of the country house to take funny pix...One of them shows 3 TV's dumping a fourth one into a garbage can...another portrays a jealousy scene in which one TV is stabbed with a pitchfork by her sister TV while the others look on with horror...or again there's a volley ball game in progress...plus shots candid camera style...unposed and unexpected...these show the TV as she really looks to others. An extremely profitable exercise to spot one's weak points...I promise to send some of these most unconventional shots as soon as a certain TV friend of mine sends me the copies she promised...I'm sure Virginia would not object to printing them as part of TV fun.

We've also discovered a little place some 5 miles away from the resort (bar-pizza combination) owned by

a Hungarian lady and her husband. They are wonderful
people and enjoy having a group of TV's coming into
their place for pizza. We've been there three times
altogether (all dressed of course) and it has been a
fabulous experience for those TV's who had never, but
never, been out in public. Right, Elaine? The reaction
from the rest of the people at the place? Zero. I'm
sure a good many of the bar customers read us as soon
as we walked in, but the beauty of the whole scene
was that it didn't make one whiff of difference either
to them or to us. All they could see is that we were
having a wonderful time. In a funny sort of way it is
nice to be read so that you can show the on-lookers that
we are having a ball in a discreet, non-scandalous,
lady-like way. Quite different from the popular image
of the screaming drag queen. It is indeed a pleasure
to see TV's "loosening up". It is a form of magic to
observe how the nervousness and tension slowly fade
away as the relization makes itself felt: I am in a
restaurant, I am sitting at this table..the waiter is
serving me and he treats me as a human being, better
still, as a girl...No guilt, no shame, no fear.......
psychiatrists: take note! The beauty of the entire experience is that the lady who owns the place knows that
we are TRANSVESTITES and she goes out of her way to make
us feel at home. She and her husband, and later the
bartender, come to our table and sit with us..the juke
box is playing some Greek music and our hostess invites
us to try that type of folk dancing...and we get up and
hold hands, and form a circle and we dance...a couple
of the customers at the bar are curious and approach
our circle...five minutes later they, too, are part of
the dance group....As when the clock strikes 3 AM..we
depart....the place is closing....and we wish we could
have stayed there for hours and hours...but there's
always another time, another week-end...Did we make a
good impression? We feel we did, otherwise our hostess
would not have reiterated her warm invitation for us to
return. She and her husband even walked with us to our
car. The important thing here was that we behaved in
accordance with the image we should always keep in mind
when dressed in front of other people.

At this point I'd like to repeat something I've

been insisting upon for a long, long time the right
movements, the right walk, and at least a teeny-weeny
attempt to soften that booming chest reverberation,
just enough not to be too noticeable if you should ever
be in public. And this means a little effort, a little
rehearsing, a little checking up on movements in front
of a mirror or in front of a friend who can criticize
and suggest improvement. For those TV's who insist in
puffing away holding the cigarette as they always do
in their male lives let me bring up a statement made
to me by a TV wife: Lorelei. She told me that then she
was in college and she began to smoke, she spent plenty
of time in front of the mirror rehearsing the MOST FE-
MININE WAY to handle that cigarette...how to make the
hand motions as pretty as possible...in a way, the cigarette is today what the fan used to be a century ago
(or still is in some social circles in Spain for instance)....a tool to enhance attractiveness....move-
ments that must be harmonious with the mood and the
personality and the moment......Now I ask: if a fabu-
lously attractive GG (such as Lorelei) took the trouble
to improvw her movements in front of a mirror, how much,
much more vital it is for a TV to check and re-check.
And I don't mean that this applies only to those who
venture out in public. No indeed. Even in the company
of a wife, or a relative, or another TV.....there's
nothing nicer than to present as smooth an image as
possible. In some areas there's nothing we can do
about....height, skeletal frame, feet, hands, muscles,
etc....but in those areas where something can be done,
there's just no excuse if we don't at least make an
effort. One of the nicest compliments a TV can get from
a non-TV is not that she looks beautiful or pretty (the
friend is probably lying) but that she looks <u>real</u>.

Jody has come up with a dream: she wants to ice-
skate this Winter. We have a lake at the resort..it
will probably freeze....and Jody is already picturing
a group of TV's skating in full regalia (those tiny
short skirts are simply adorable) sliding over the white
surface of the pond. I admit I'd love to try on an outfit like that, but I'm afraid I would spend most of the
time just sitting on the ice. Frankly I prefer the
summer....Joan and Susanna are the only girls who have

enjoyed swimming in that lake "a la femme". What to
do about the wig? Just go behind some bushes, take off
the wig and put on your bathing cap. Leave the wig inside your beach bag. Swimming does NOT mess up your
make up as long as you do not attempt to dry your face
with a towel....just let the sun do the drying...then
add a bit of face powder and you are all set. It is
also convenient to have for such ocassions an extra
set of falsies and an extra set of hip pads...when you
come out of the water you won't be able to wear them
until next day. Daphne from Canada was a bit more practical...she just let her brother do the swimming. One
word of warning: a girl's bathing suit leaves a tell-
tale marking on your chest and shoulders. As you tan,
the skin under the straps stays white. It's quite a
tattoo for at least a couple of months. (Solution to
this is to cover yourself beforehand with a good sun
screen like "Sea & Ski" or "Tartan". I did this in
Hawaii with no marks at all.   Virginia)

    Susanna's dancing lessons are progressing. So far
the teacher has been working mostly on posture and re-
laxation...he has promised me that my neck will be at
least half an inch longer and THINNER as a result of
the exercises I'm doing. Back of the neck and between
the shoulder blades he has found a vicious area of tension...which must be dissolved....The hip joints and
the shoulder joints were equally stiff and locked....
they must be loosened. He attributes part of this tension to my transvestism. He points out that the simple
fact that when one is compelled to hide an important
part of one's personality the result has to be tension.
A couple of amusing incidents have taken place during
these lessons. When my brother arrives at the studio,
he only lets me wear a full skirted dress, long opera
hose and dancing pumps. No wig, no makeup, since he has
to dash to work right after the dance lessons. It is a
huge studio which I have all to myself. One morning
the teacher had me lying on the floor, flat on my back
while he was kneeling astride of my legs bending over
me and working with his hands straightening my spine.
Suddenly a side door opened and a telephone repairman
walked in on his way to the roof....you should have
seen his face when he took in the scene on the floor.

With a whispered "excuse me", he took off. Another
morning, the teacher very seriously tells me he must
warn me of an unforeseen result his lessons might
bring about: it seems that he has a friend who is a
psychiatrist and has mentioned to him the fact that he
has a TV student. The psychiatrist feels that as we
work to bring out the feminine we are also relaxing
and developing the male personality....and he thinks
that it could well happen that Susanna would end by
disappearing entirely as her brother became stronger.
In other words as you learn to dance in dresses you
might just be killing the girl-within! I assured my
teacher that I wasn't one bit worried over his friend's
theory because ever since I've been taking these lessons
both Susanna and her brother feel physically better..
true..but as usual it is Susanna who wants to do the
dancing. HE is not interested. At any rate I must meet
that psychiatrist. We ought to have a very nice and
illuminating chat. But even with this threat of extinc-
tion Susanna feels marvellous....it is one of the most
worthy investments I've ever made in my life...Of course
it takes a teacher who is not only good but fully aware
of the TV's mental and physical problems.

    Cynthia warmly recommends the new pressed face
powder "corn silk"....it looks terrific on her face,
but again not everybody has a face like Cynthia's. And
this brings me to the closing note for this issue: the
gathering at Sheila's in early October. As usual it was
fun...and as usual we devoured the goodies that only
Clarissa knows how to fix. Joan and Susanna celebrated
one more birthday trying to convince themselves that
they are both one year younger...Joan looks younger but
she is cheating - Betsy from Rhode Island and Pamela
from England (this is Pamela #2, also a Limey) were
ecstatically happy. It had been a long time of absten-
tion for both of them....Pamela even gathered enough
courage to leave Sheila's house without changing back..
and Wilma's brother (who was kindly doing the driving)
treated Pamela to an extra 40 miles of travelling by
sneakingly taking the wrong road back to New York.

    Wilma asks me to warn TV's against buying the new
small size Polaroid. She says they do a very poor job.
    And thus ends another chapter in TVland.

We'll be back with more gossip and rambling in the
next issue of TRANSVESTIA.

Love,
SUSANNA

REMINDER

Sometimes readers get so used to TRANSVESTIA that
they forget that Chevalier has many other things to
offer also. While speaking of TRANSVESTIA, may I re-
mind you that anything is new until you have read it.
There is nothing dated about this subject of ours. So
back issues of the magazine are just as good reading
as the current issue and they are cheaper too. Person-
ally I would like to clear out the back issues to make
space and to realize some badly needed capital, so
don't forget - 6 issues for $20. ($3.33 each)

Then there is the FEMMEMIRROR, a monthly news-
letter made up of your own comments, ideas, etc. Support
it with contributions and it can become a very interesting and chatty addition to your library. For those
interested in clippings and what goes on elsewhere
there is the CLIPSHEET. This too is made up from readers contributions, so please help us out here.

In addition we have printed a number of separate
stories ranging from the short little TV TALES thru
a collection of short stories like SCARCITY OF NURSES,
to full length stories like FATED FOR FEMININITY,
MALE ACTRESS, CARNIVAL and TALES FROM A PINK MIRROR.

Don't forget either that Chevalier offers special
merchandise to you too, the REALISTIC FALSIES, PHANTOM
FANNY, and PRETTY PANTIES. I can also supply WIGS at
less than going rates.

Please get details from the price list on the last
page and please use the snip out order form too. It
will help in filling and tracing orders. Send for any
of these items to:

CHEVALIER PUBLICATIONS BOX 36091 LOS ANGELES 36, CALIF.

74

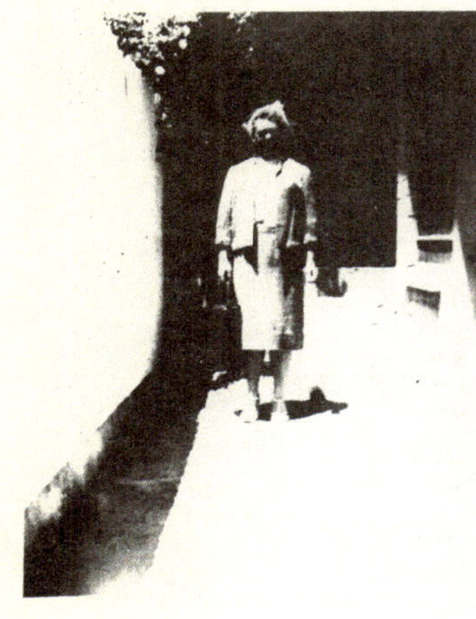

PATRICIA

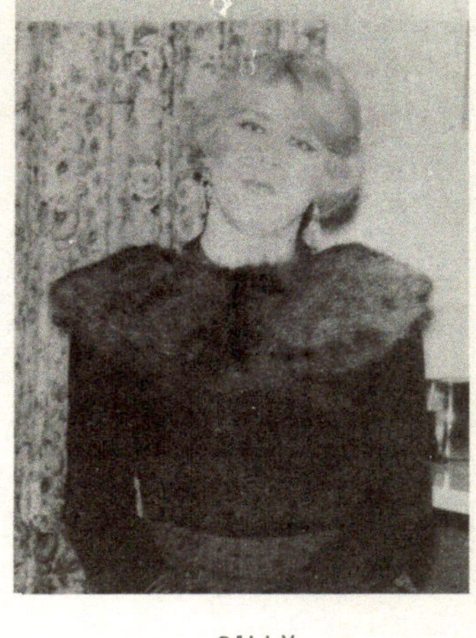

SALLY

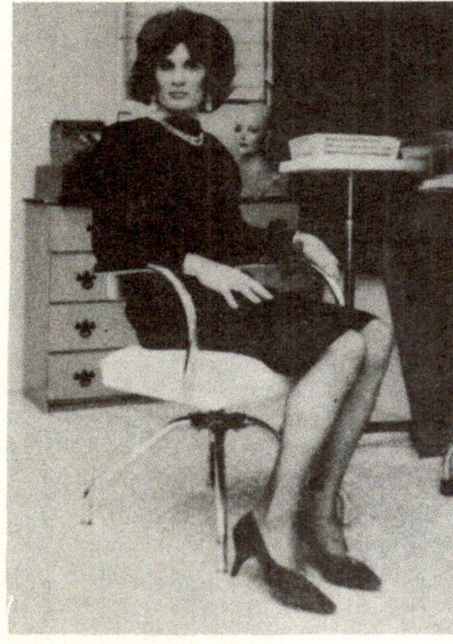

DEE DOROTHY 52-L-1 FPE

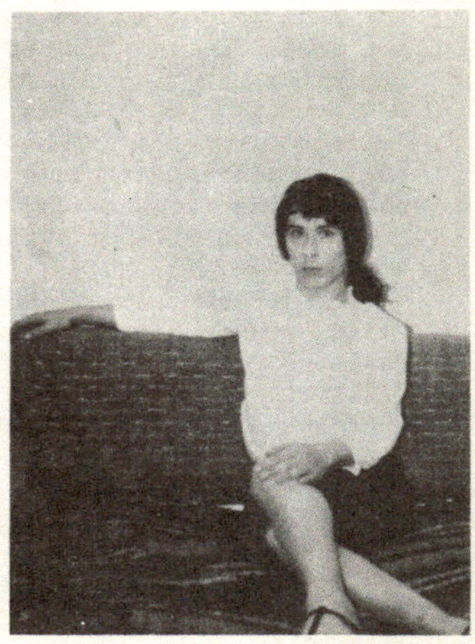

BRENDA - COLO.

75

In June 1960 *Esquire* published an intimate and insightful report about a gang of
teenagers from Brooklyn, New York. As an early insider account of youth subcultures
in the US, the photo-essay by Bruce Davidson, accompanied by a text by the writer
Norman Mailer (b. 1923, USA; d. 2007), offered a romanticised view of American
youthful rebellion.

BROOKLYN MINORITY REPORT

Photographed by Bruce Davidson

"SHE THOUGHT THE RUSSIANS WAS COMING"

An inside view of the aspirations of embattled youth

by **NORMAN MAILER**

THESE photographs (overleaf) by Bruce Davidson are very good, but I am not the one who has need to advertise them for they caught me up directly, so directly that I took an assignment from Esquire to write a short commentary to appear alongside of them.

I never did get to meet some of the citizens in these pictures. Bruce took the photographs many months ago, and the gang has dispersed a bit since then. I am as sorry as the reader that I will not, for example, be able to tell you anything about the girl who is fixing her hair. Let it go. That was summer and this is a thin little report on life in winter with an editorial at its end for those who insist on a reading diet which is fortified by a message.

I first went down to Brooklyn to see the gang on a bone-cold February afternoon this year. They were waiting for Davidson and me in a candy store about a half mile from their turf, a parlor they had begun to use lately because their own was too small. The new place had a juke box, and three booths to the rear, and when we entered five or six girls and a dozen boys were milling around in the back.

For the first minute, a bit of tension: nothing all-out hostile, more an air of stony curiosity, studied on their part, studied on mine. One cannot get around it—there are situations which belong more to the movies than to life, and all of us were obeying an archetypal scene in a gangster movie or a Western—a stranger had come to visit.

This mood shifted quickly enough. Bruce had already told the Royal Dealers, which is the fictitious name we might as well use, that Esquire Magazine had bought his pictures. (For a year he had been friendly with these kids and the sight of him with the Leica up to his face had come to seem as natural as lighting a cigarette.) Now a few of them had been let in on the new information that a writer was here today to write them up, and this explanation for my presence passed around quickly. They were picked up by it. Conversation began to go, and before fifteen minutes we had found a common ground; we were passing back and forth our prescriptions for odd kicks.

Had I ever heard of ground aspirin being mixed with tobacco and rolled in a cigarette?

No; that one I hadn't heard of.

"That's the most, man—I was out of my skull for two hours."

"You creep, you're a fag," said one of the kids to the kid who had been out of his skull.

"No, man, that aspirin is a boss kick."

Laughter. General derision. It seems somebody had offered marijuana to the kid with the aspirin and he had punked out.

So the stories went. Whitey had taken fifteen saccharine tablets once. "Man, that's a drag. I was throwing up all afternoon," said Whitey.

We discussed dried leaves, and nutmeg, and Sterno; one of them had even heard of a way to find some juice in lighter fluid.

Then talk shifted to the Dealer's account of a rumble they had been in last summer, a big rumble which made the newspapers. Ten of them had been brought to court for beating up a kid in the park, and they were now on probation. Since none of them were going to school any more, they were using up a good part of the money they made at work to pay off their various lawyers. One of the kids was talking now about his case. Not a member of the Royal Dealers, he had gotten into trouble for something else.

"What's your lawyer charging you?" Whitey asked. Although he was the smallest of the Juniors, a thin, brooding kid of sixteen with clean, proud features, he seemed the natural leader.

"Two and a half," said the other.

"Two and a half bucks?"

A sneer. "Two and a half cents."

"What'll you get?"

"I don't know."

"A year, you bastard. You deserve a year."

I never found out what the act had been. Conversation turned back to the rumble. The Dealers had been cutting through the park last summer when they saw a Puerto Rican gang which had eyes for them. One of the Seniors was with them, Terry, a big kid about twenty who had done some boxing in the Army and had natural military ability. He collected the Dealers in a nest of bushes at the peak of a small hill, and sent four of the Juniors down to serve as decoys on the paved path in the draw below, a run of thirty or forty yards down the hill. It had seemed close enough, but when the Puerto Rican gang attacked, they struck so suddenly that the decoys were dropped hard. One of them got a baseball bat on the side of his skull, and bled badly. He was unconscious by the time Terry led the charge. But the Dealers' cavalry took the day. The Juniors, beefed by Terry the Senior, beat up on the Puerto Ricans. After forty seconds the other gang was in flight. Terry picked up the decoy with the bleeding head, and carried him under his arm all the way out of the park. Whitey, who has heart in a rumble, was the last to leave—he gave a final clout to the casualty he had been fighting, and said, "This is from the Dealers."

Back to their turf by separate ways, they had all collected in the candy store. I could hear how their voices must have sounded, because in combat, after a fire-fight, we would all be a little hysterical, and would all be laughing and sing- *(Continued on page 137)*

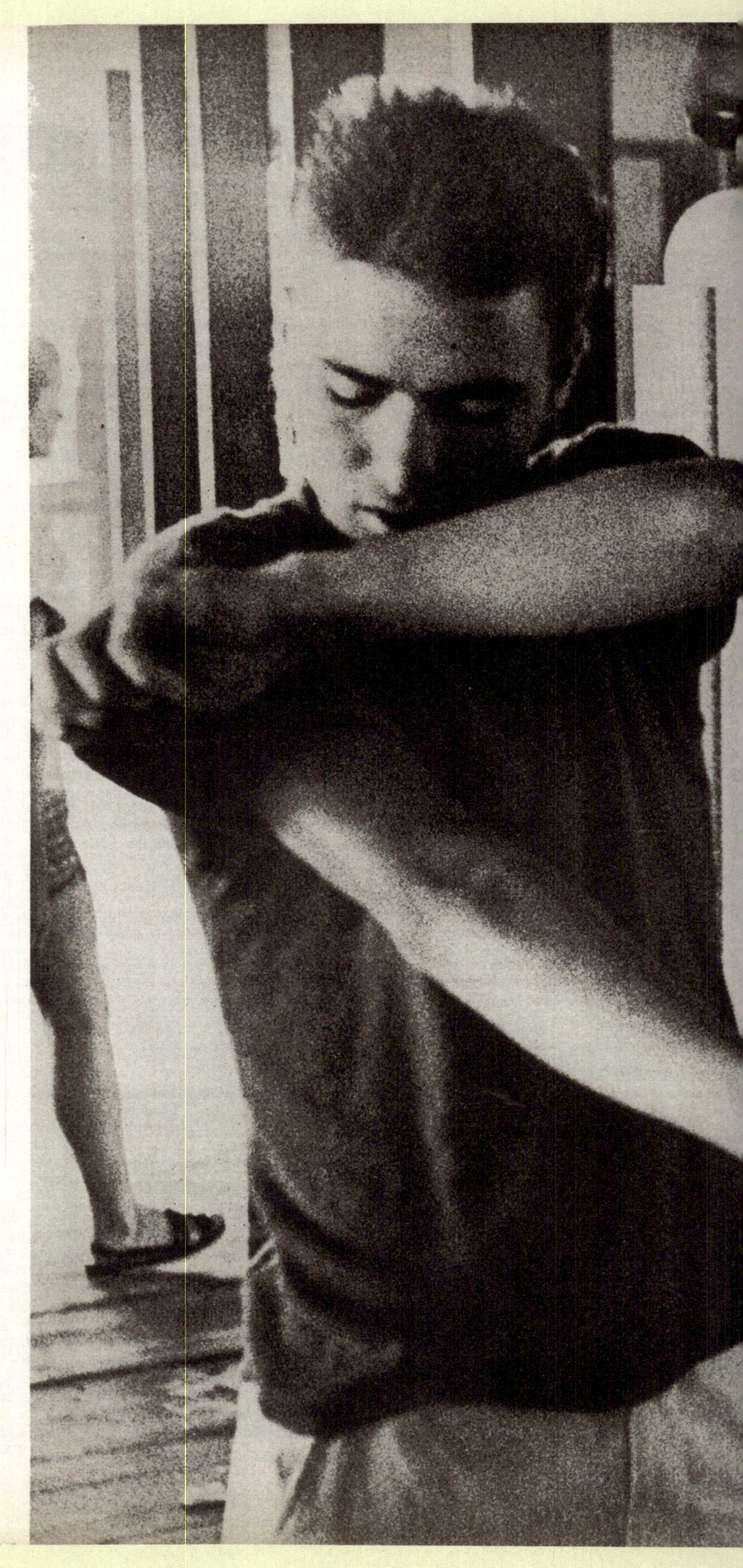

*Preoccupation of teen-agers with self and
appearance is caught in scene at Coney
Island. At Ocean Time Bar, there are no
mirrors in the rest rooms, so the mirror
of a cigarette machine is used instead*

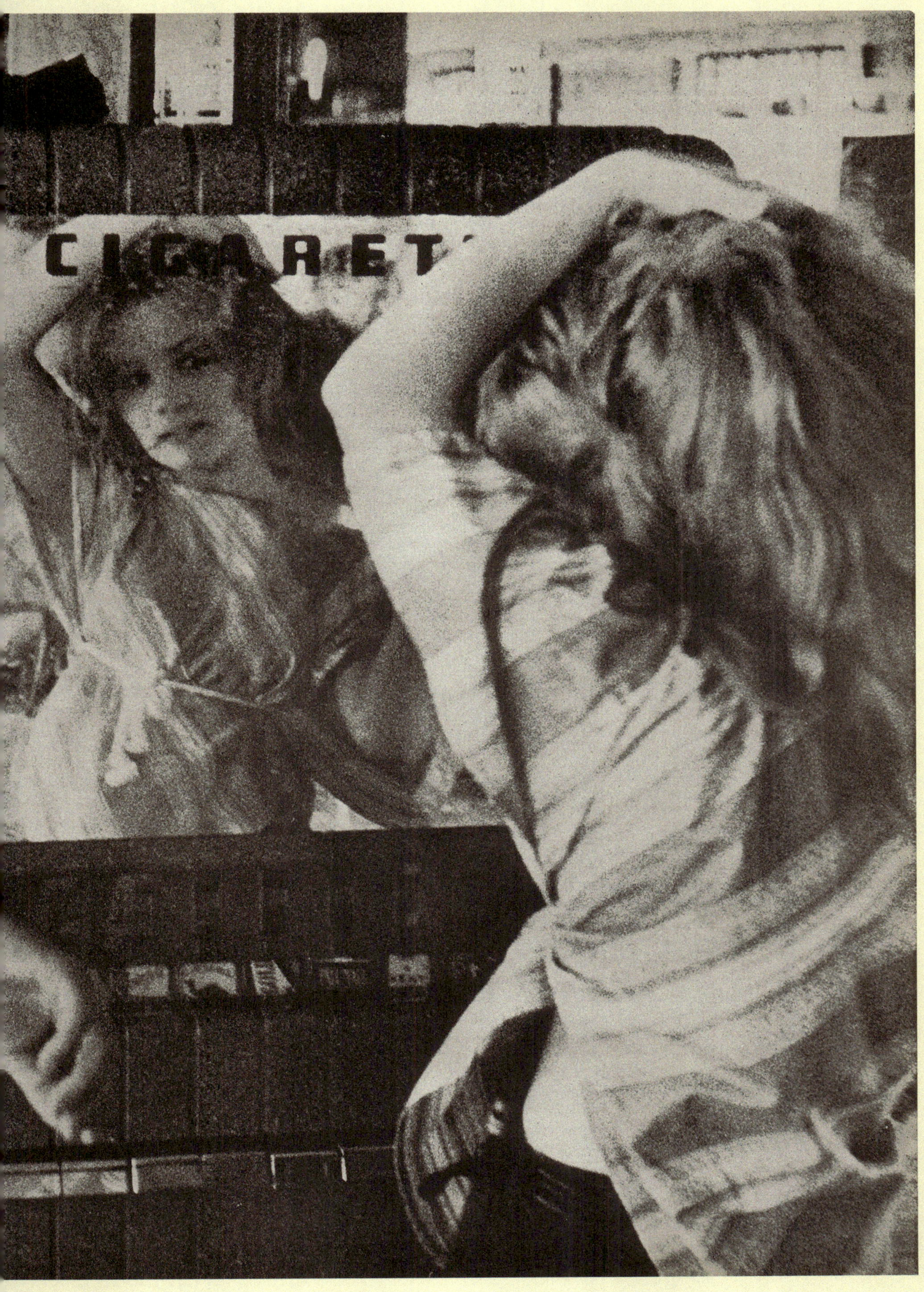
CIGARET

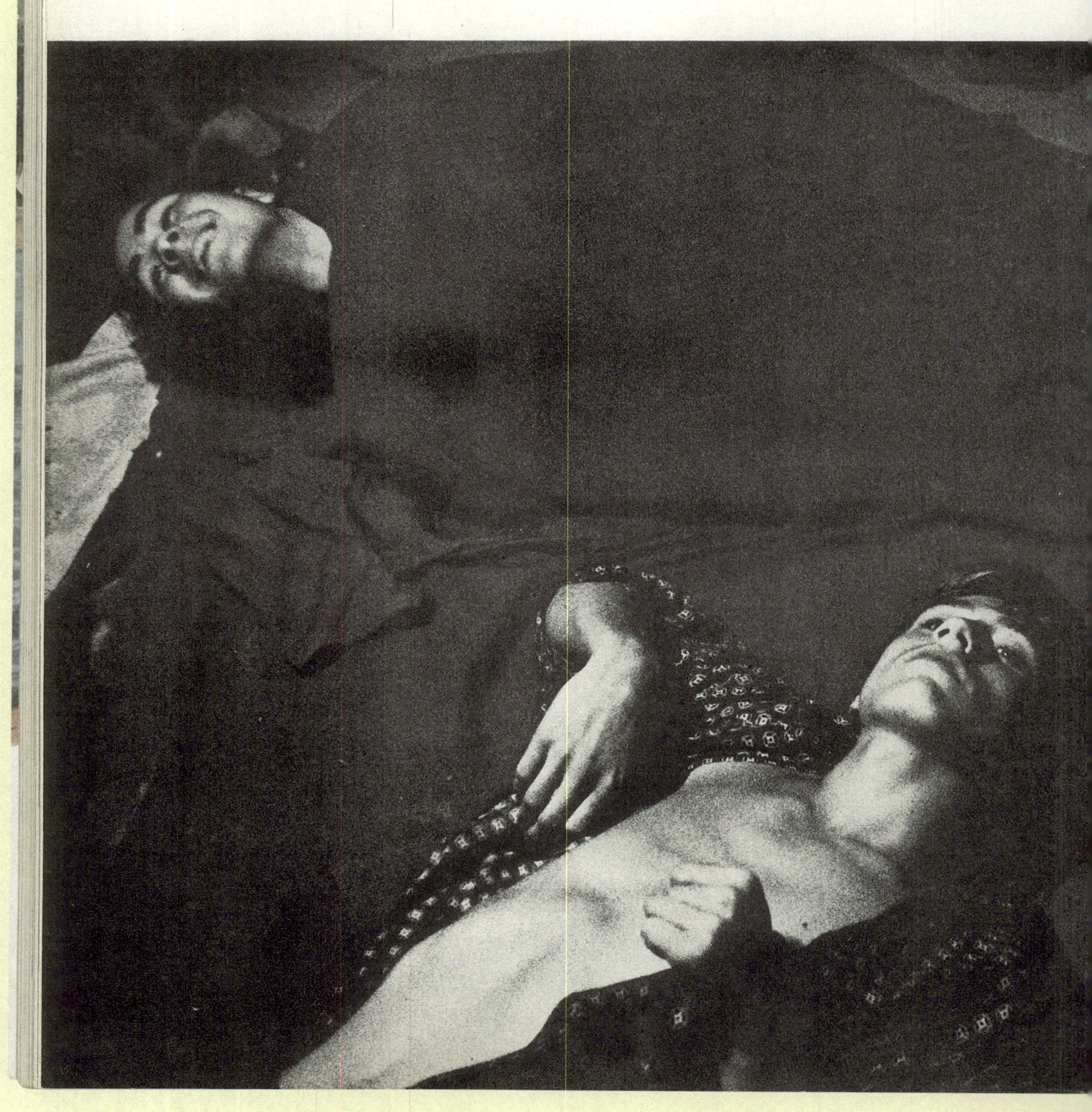

After a Fourth of July celebration at Coney Island, the boys
(left) *spread their coats in the sand and spend the night under
the boardwalk, listening and talking through the night until the
morning birds make hungry sounds. On a hot summer night*
(below) *at a crowded basement party, a steel support pipe
cools and hides a pair of young lovers. A back-seat window*
(see the double-page picture overleaf) *closes off the summer
street, giving a young couple some precious moments alone*

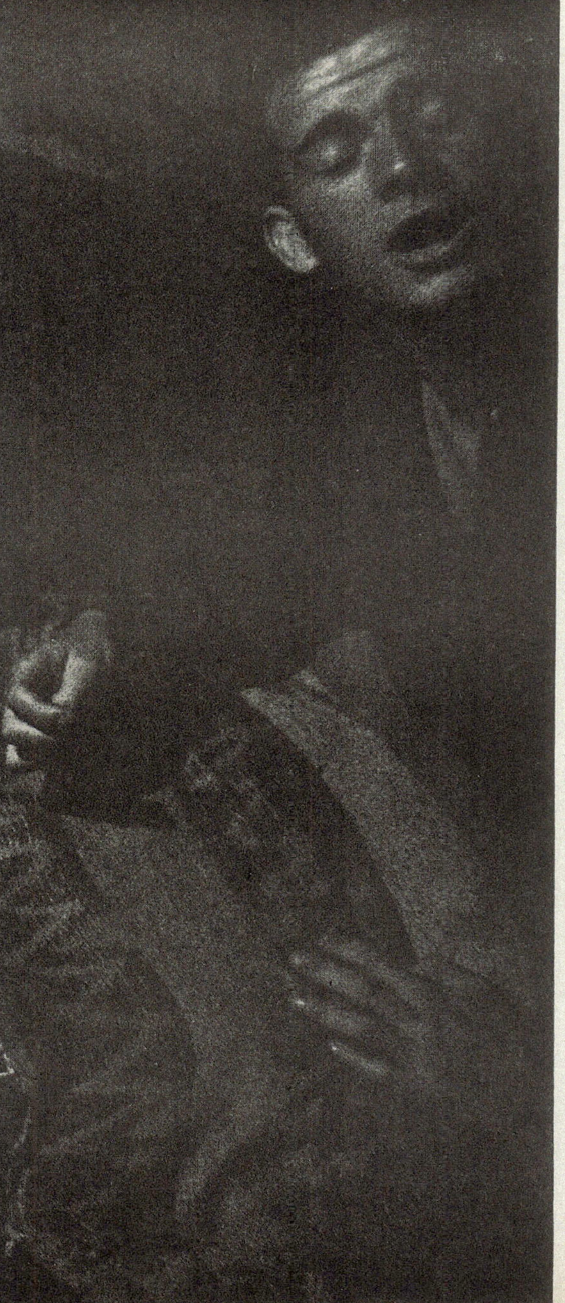

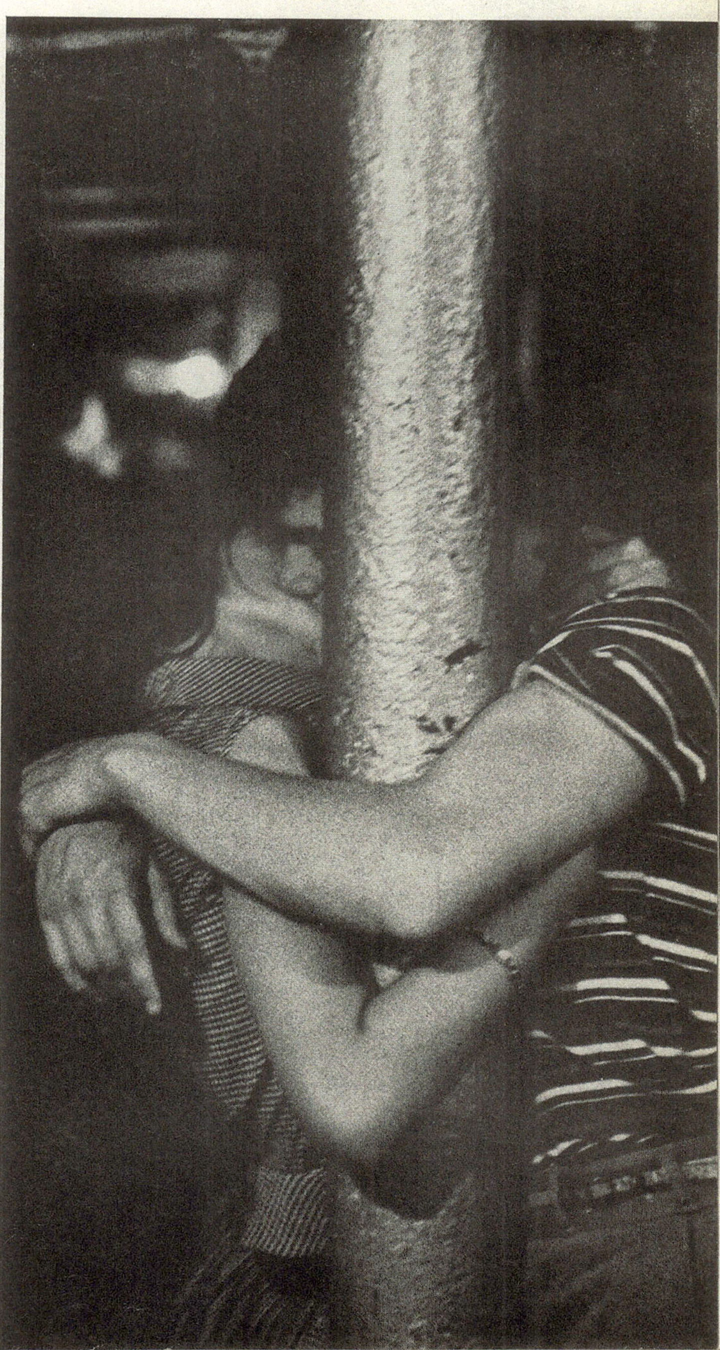

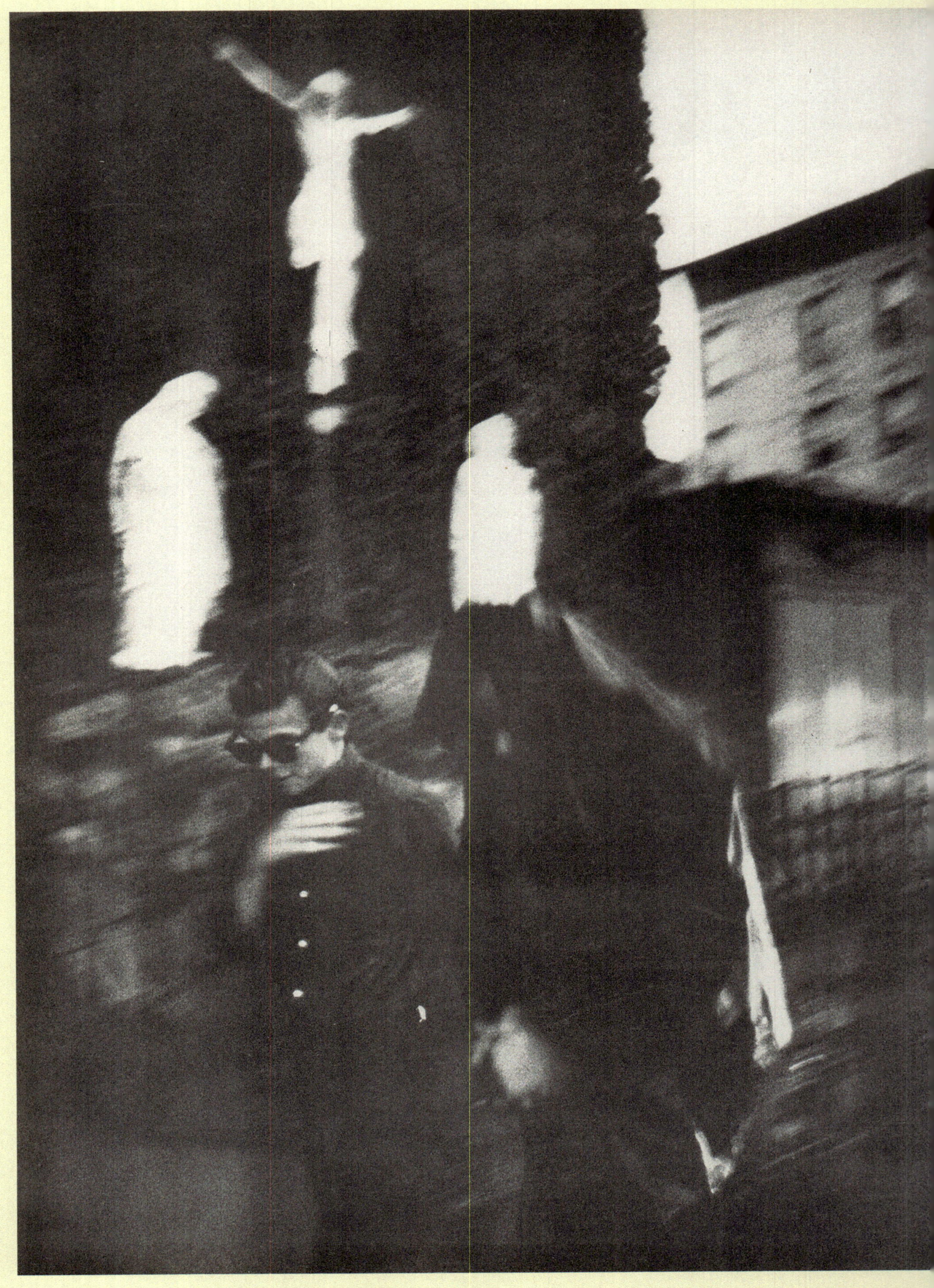

ing out at once about what had happened to us and how, and where we had been. Those were some of the few good moments in the war. So the Dealers had been staking out their claims in the candy store for star roles in the gang legend of the battle. They were home from the war, and full of charge. They would have new cartel with the chicks.

But the police have the Greek sense of Nemesis. The siren of a squad car sounded outside the door of the candy store. "This is from the Dealers," Whitey had made the mistake of saying, and the kid who had been left by the gang which lost gave the message to the cops when they arrived on the scene at the park.

It was a dull, hot, newsless day in summer, so it made the newspapers. All too inaccurately according to the Dealers. Ten vicious juvenile delinquents beat up a cripple, went the jazz. "Hell, man, it wasn't like that at all," one of them said, "it was a fair rumble." We'll never know. Once a newspaper touches a story, the facts are lost forever, even to the protagonists.

Now it was February, a quiet scene. Since that rumble, the Dealers have been cooling it. Of necessity. But talk of the rumble had stirred them up. Not long afterward, we went out of the candy store into the iron-grey cold, and took the subway down to Coney Island. A couple of Dealers were going to get tattoos.

We had just missed a train and it was empty on the subway platform. The kids began to put on a production for me. Ricky, a short, heavy Italian kid went out to the very end of the station, and urinated on the tracks. There were jokes about hitting the third rail, and when they got to the point of saying what Ricky would lose, and how little he would lose, he turned to the others, about five of them, and pulled out a Japanese knife, one of those small, sharp, steak knives which are inserted into a wooden scabbard and cost about a dollar, and he waved it at us, and ran up the platform stairs about ten steps. "You guys think I'm not tough. Come up here and I'll kill you. I'll kill the first one. I'm Al Capone—you watch out for me." And a good imitation it was, of Rod Steiger as Al Capone.

I had a water pistol in my pocket, a small model of a short-barreled forty-five which I had taken on impulse earlier in the day from Bruce Davidson who had been about to drop it in a trash barrel. I flipped it up the subway stairs to Ricky, shouting, "Quick, man, here's a gun." In the air, it looked real and Ricky had a natural look of dismay, not knowing whether to catch or to drop it, and if it were loaded would it go off? Or was it a gag? That much went over his face, and then he dropped it, and the gun made a tinny, clanking little sound, the inimitable sound of a toy, and the other Dealers roared in mockery. But Ricky had talent and for a young actor he can use a prop with the best. The gun went into his right hand, the knife into his left, and the brown scabbard for the steak knife went into his mouth like a cigar. "All right," he said, lining us up with the gun, waving it like a movie murderer, "this is the St. Valentine's Day massacre. You're all dead. In one minute you're all gonna get it. Bop. Bop. Bop. Bop—" mowing us down. Johnny, one of the best fighters in the Dealers, about eighteen, good-looking, a little taller than the rest, rushed him, and they scuffled on the stairs, Ricky at a disadvantage because he had to put down the knife. Just then a train came in. It was going in the wrong direction, but it was the right kind of diversion. Ricky broke loose from

Johnny, ran down the stairs back to the platform, and approached the open door of the train. A ten-year-old kid was sitting across the aisle, and Ricky waved the gun at him through the open door. The kid took it well, half-scared, half-grinning, and then the door closed, and Ricky began to walk along the platform, rapping on windows in order to study the expression of the people who turned around to see a gun about three feet from their mouth. If street robbery were a trade, this could serve as apprenticeship, for one might learn quickly which types will freeze and which will not when an adolescent is pointing a gun at them. Ricky had time for four or five close, quick studies before the train picked up too much speed. Then one of the other Dealers pushed him from behind and scared him royally because he was only two feet from the side of the moving train, and the distance was halved before he recovered. Then Whitey, Johnny, and the first Dealer took hold of Ricky and made a play of pushing him into the train, but Ricky broke loose—six inches from contact with the moving side wall of the subway car—and started to shoot again at all of us. "Bop, bop, bop. Bee-owww—" offering us ricochets as well. Johnny went over and whispered something to him. As Ricky bent over to listen, Johnny backhanded him in the belly, and then ducked back as Ricky tried to slug him on the arm.

Our train came in. We had a car almost to ourselves, and all the way to Coney Island they asked me questions about combat. How many grenades had I carried ? How many would they let you carry? Had I ever killed anybody? Did I carry a gun now? And vague talk of pot. Johnny had a dream. He would collect two pounds of pot, and then he would go away for a couple of years and travel around the country—there were a lot of things he wanted to do once he got on the road. It turned out he was the reader in the Dealers. He was reading *The Beat Generation And The Angry Young Men* now, and he liked Kerouac. He had been trying to read my piece, *The White Negro* in that anthology, but it was too hard. "It's deep. Like I know, man, you got to think," he told me with a grin.

That day, Davidson and I stayed with them at the tattoo parlor while Whitey and another bought new tattoos. Medical science has come to the tattoo parlor, and the inner sanctum was in surgical white with sterilizers and antiseptic procedure. But love of the tattoo is a subject in itself, and I don't know that I am the one to write about it. Leave it that the kids covet and worry every choice of a tattoo the way a bride picks each piece of furniture for her bedroom. The fear of making a mistake is heavy, because a coiled serpent on the arm demands that you develop the strength of a serpent or else you're phony, and a Betty Boop on the calf—well, you might end up marrying Betty Boop.

A couple of nights later in a bar Ricky said, "I'm going to put a naked dame on my arm."

"What'll your wife say when you get married?"

He didn't hesitate a minute. "I'll put her name under it."

But then some of the Dealers have a gone wit when they're drunk. I met Terry that night, a big one, twenty as I mentioned, with a black leather jacket, good features, blank face, and a string of bon mots. The longer we drank, the faster they came. "You know who I'd like to make," he told me; "one of those jazz singers. I'd like to make her right on the floor while she's singing. I'd like to drill her." Talking of the past and past happiness he said,

"She had a set of knockers on her would choke a mule—she was boss, man." But the best I remember was the tale of his evening with a society girl: "When I came up to her door in my hopped-up '50 Mercury, va va, hoo hoo, hmmm, she thought the Russians was coming." Much later that night, at three in the morning, we took a race through the park in my no-longer-hopped-up '53 Studebaker, Bruce Davidson, Terry, Johnny and myself, and Terry led me to the historic ground where the Dealers had their apocalyptic rumble and he went over the terrain with me, the two of us, reconsidering the problem like old Civil War generals warm with nostalgia. It was a good night.

Altogether I saw the Dealers three times. The last trip I took my wife, and a friend and his girl, to one of their dances, but the evening never came off right, because the air of decorum was heavy. I had been promised in advance that a fight would start that night, but it never did. The dance was given by another club in a veteran's hall, and the Dealers were only one of four or five gangs present so everybody was on best behavior, and the evening ended early—a couple of kids pulled out the rubber plugs in the tanks on the water closets in the men's room. That flooded the floor, and in disgust the bartenders closed the dance down early. We took Terry, Johnny and Whitey back to the Village to hear some jazz, but they were off their turf and subdued that night.

I⟨T⟩ occurs to me, as I read over what I have written, that this piece is anti-climactic. I wonder if that is not right. Because I sometimes think the drama of the rumbler, the would-be rumbler, and the adolescent along for the ride is not too far away from the sweat of any artist, any salesman, any adventurer, any operator. Their imagination is too vivid, and so they spend the days and nights of their adolescent years waiting for the apocalyptic test which almost never comes off. It is common in any editorial about juvenile delinquents to speak of wasted lives and growing blight, but what junk these editorials are, for there is not one root to juvenile delinquency, but two. For all the talk of broken homes, submarginal housing, overcrowding in the schools and cultural starvation, the other root is more alive, and one kills it at one's peril. It is the root for which our tongues once found the older words of courage, loyalty, honor and the urge for adventure. It may be that when one gets to know them well, some of the Dealers are bad pieces of work, but I would gamble that most of them are rather good pieces of work, bright, sensitive to what is true and what is not true in what you say to them, loyal if they like you, and in congress together they are as alive as a pack of monkeys. They suffer from only one disease, the national disease—it is boredom. If their conversation runs the predictable river-bed of sex, gang war, drugs, weapons, movies and crazy drunks, well, at least they live out a part of their conversational obsession, which is more than one can say for the quiet, inhibited, middle-aged desperadoes of the corporation and the suburb. If we are to speak of shadows which haunt America today, the great shadow is that there is a place for everybody in our country who is willing to live the way others want him to, and talk the way others want him to, with our big, new, thick, leaden vocabulary of political, psychological, and sociological verbiage. Yes, there is a place for everybody now in the American scene except for those who want to find the limits of their growth by a life which is ready to welcome a little danger as part of the Divine cocktail. ‡‡

WALTER PFEIFFER, SCRAPBOOKS, 1969-1985

Walter Pfeiffer began collecting and collating visual curiosities in
1971 when he was working as a stylist in a department store in Zurich.
Juxtaposing personal photographs of his friends with found objects such
as postcards, film posters and newspaper clippings, Pfeiffer created
several scrapbooks offering a peek into his queer world.

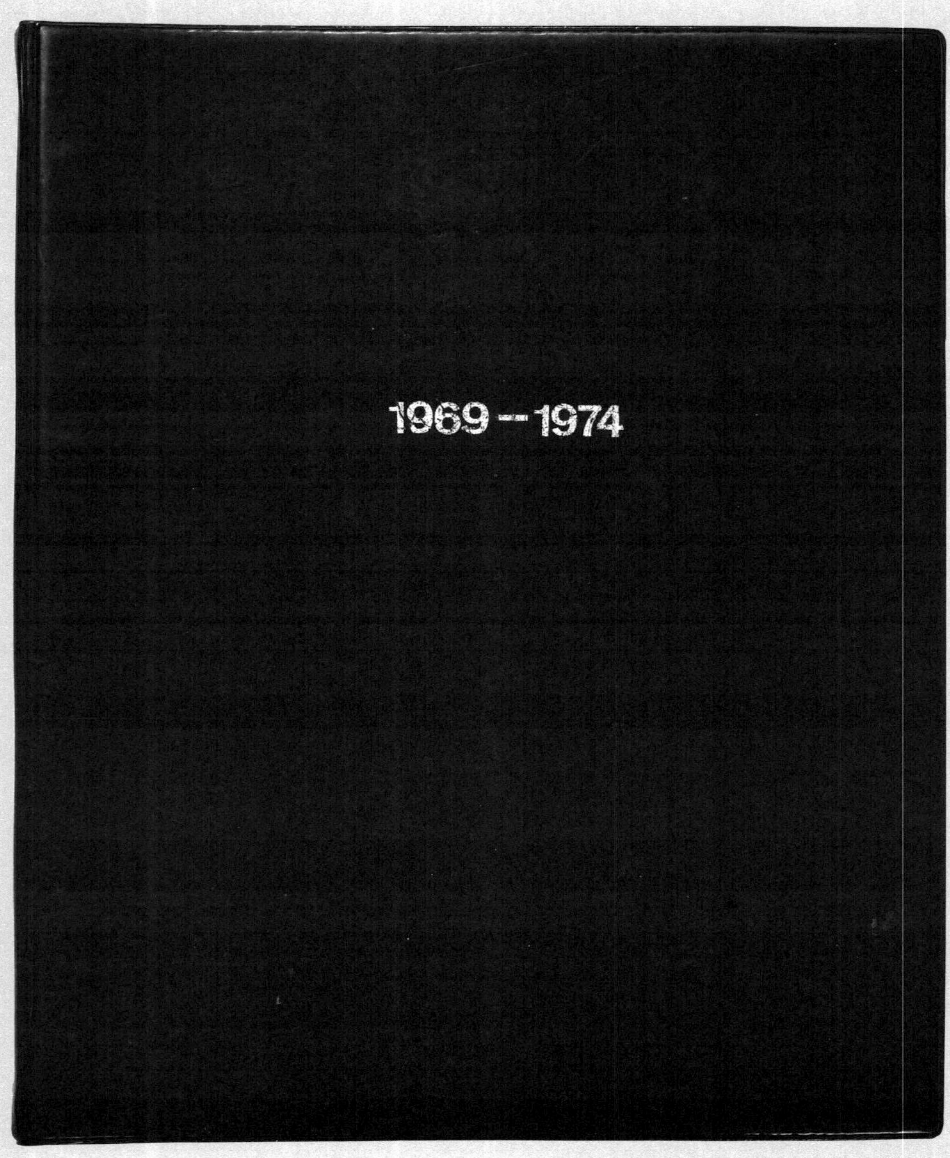

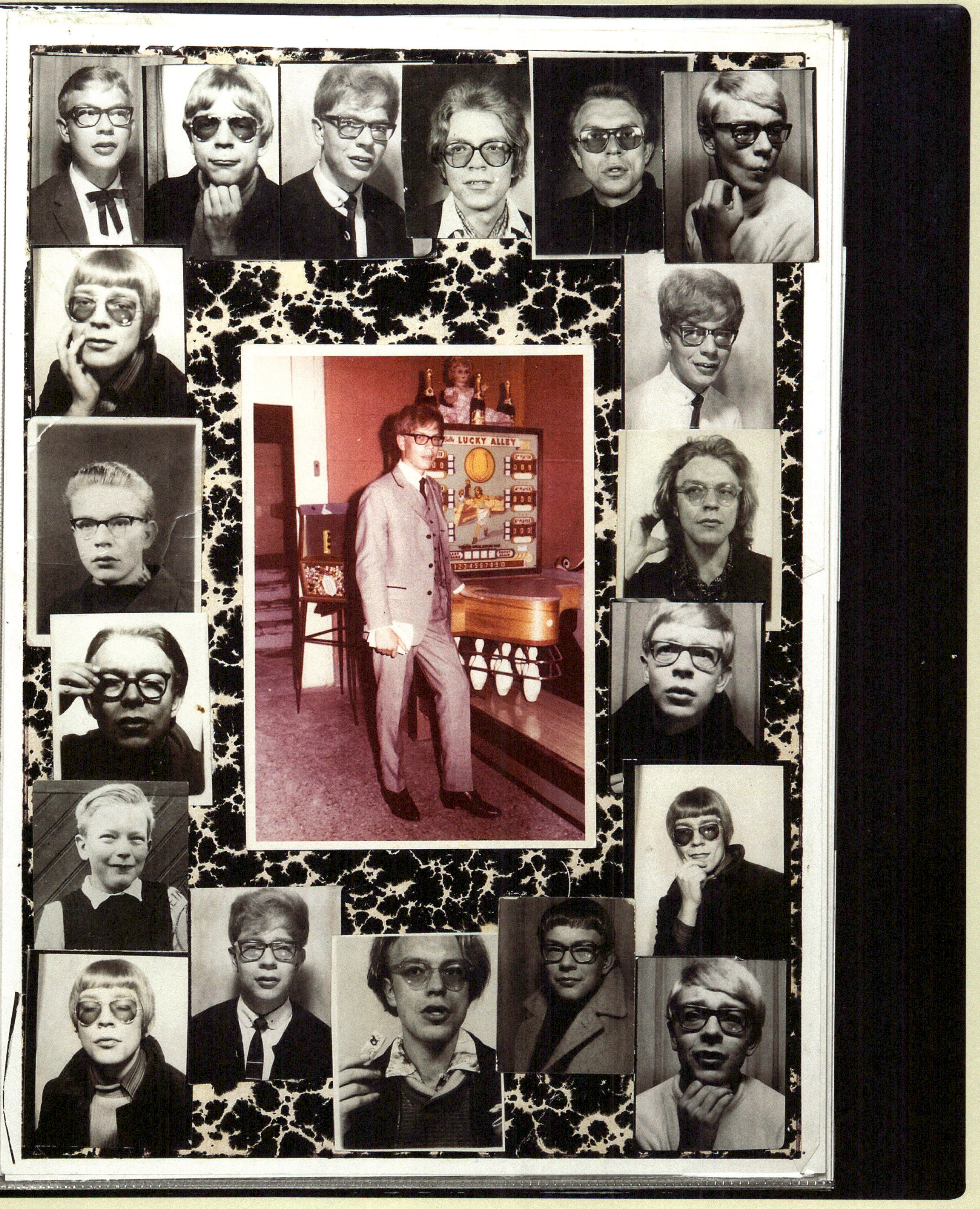
LUCKY ALLEY

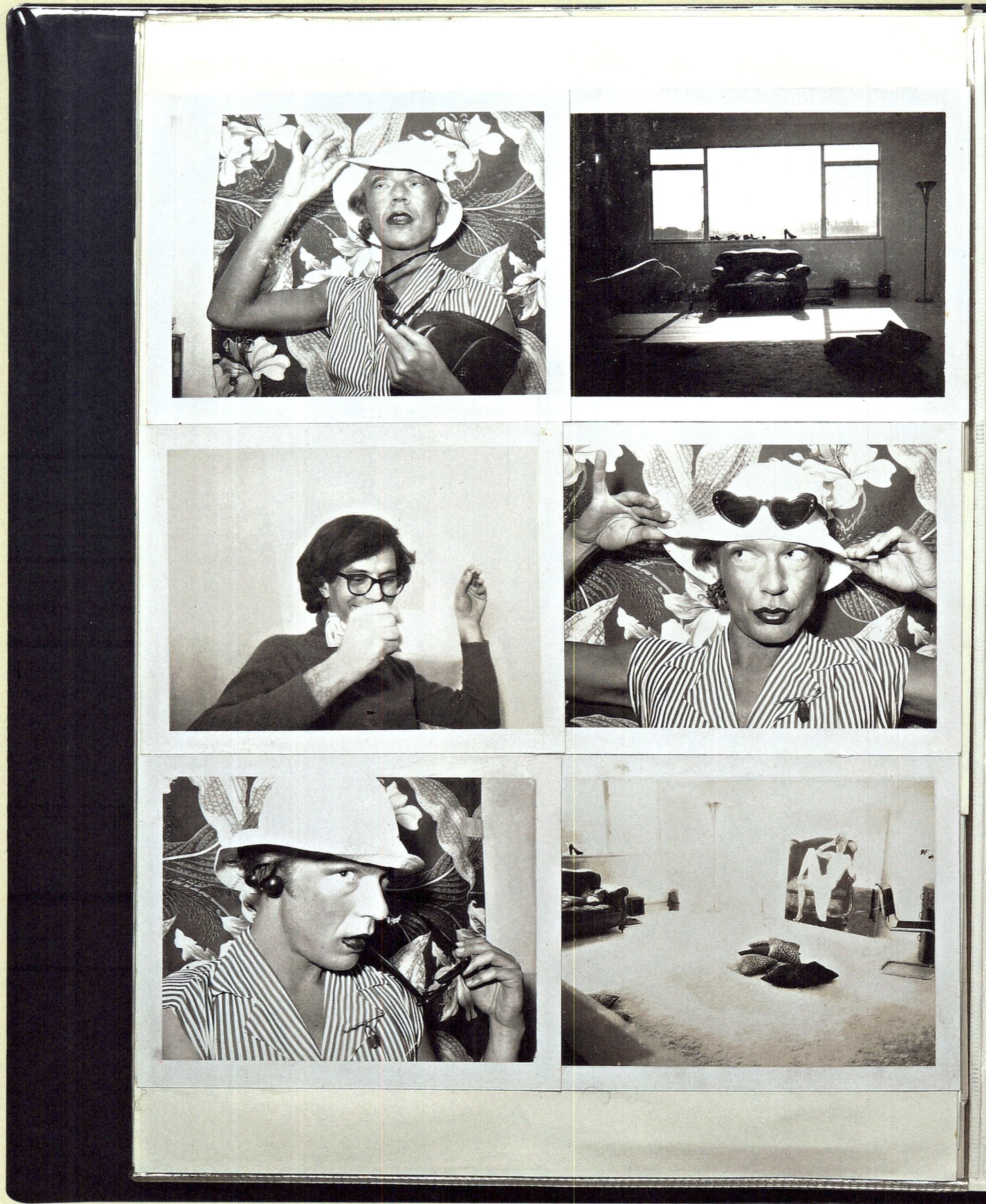

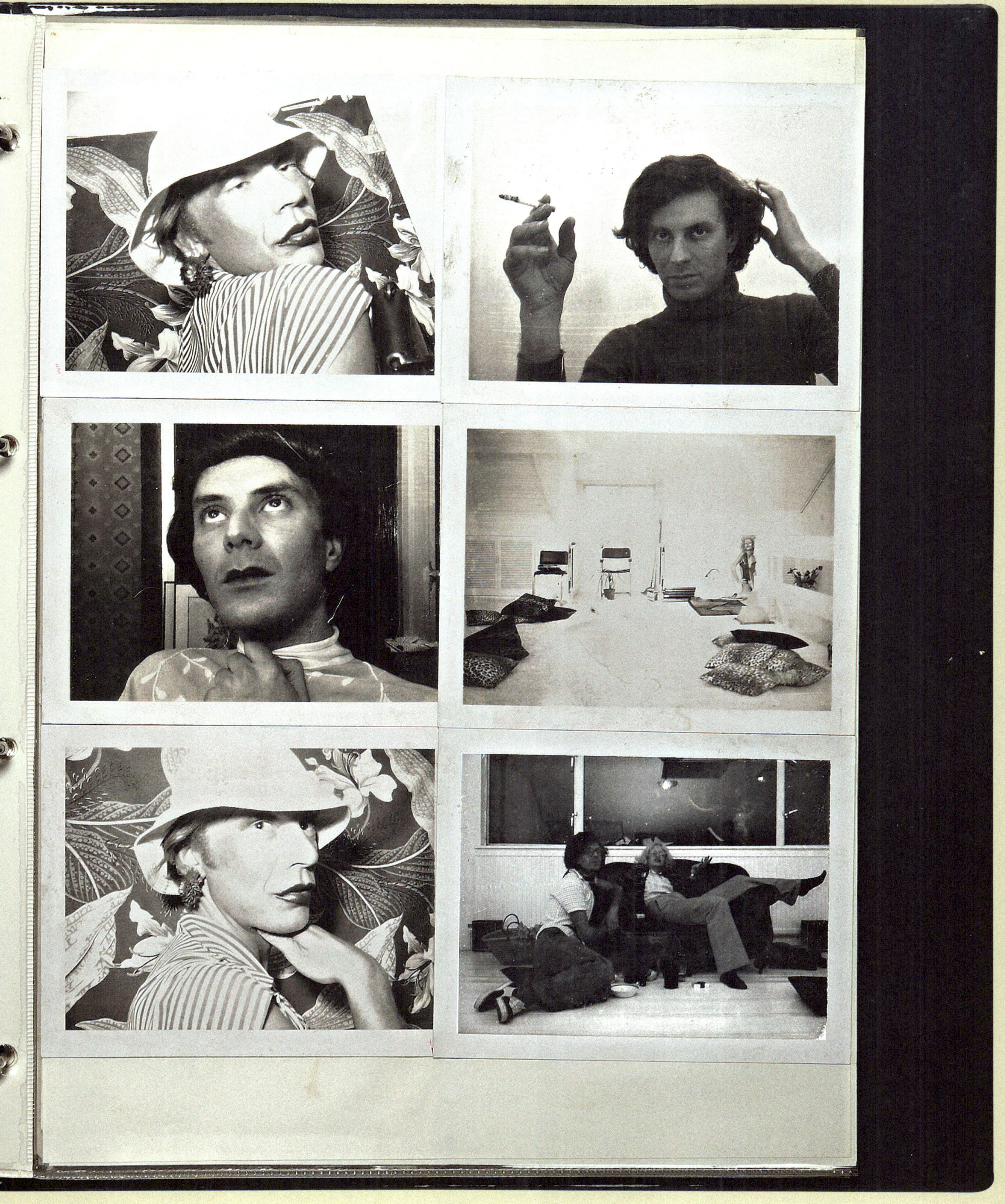

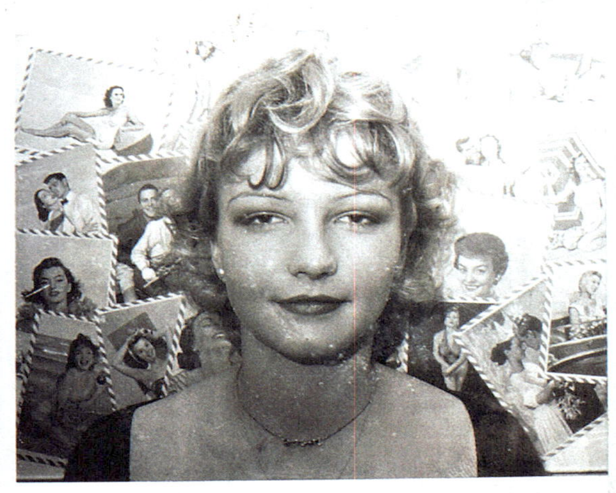
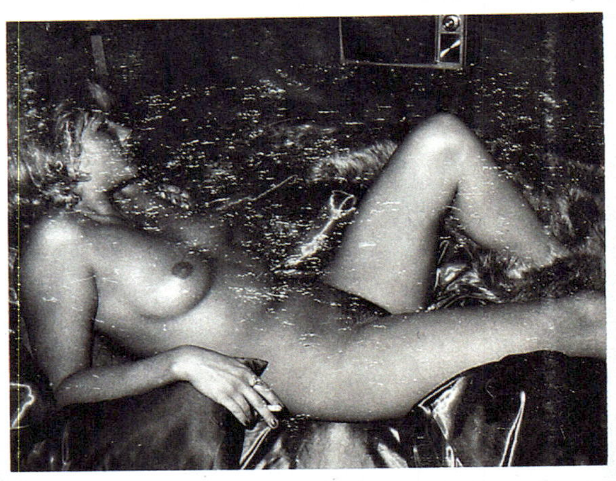
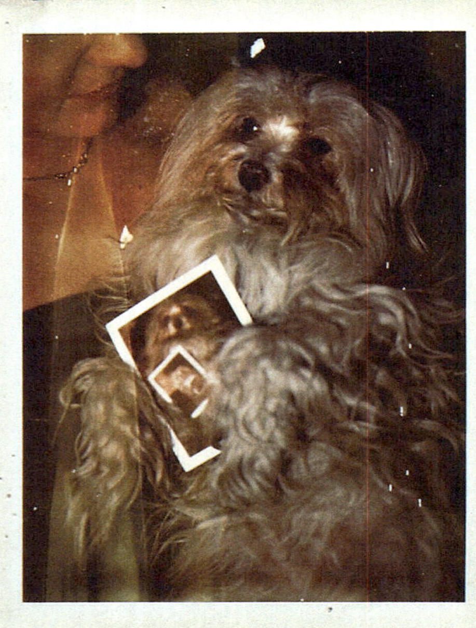
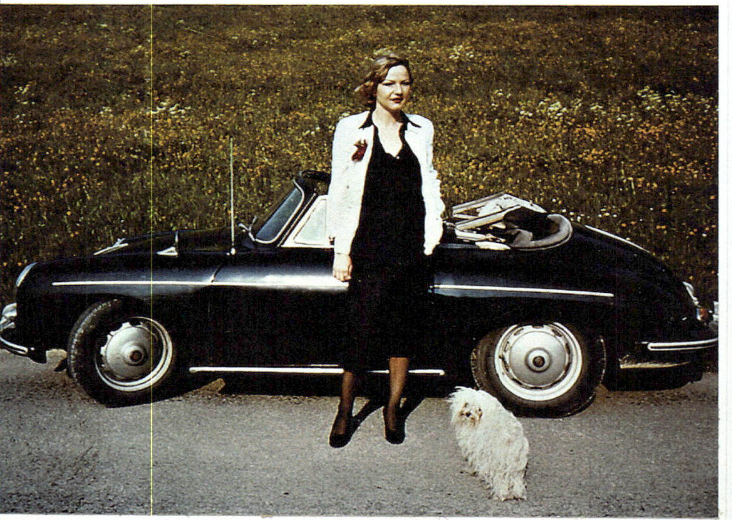
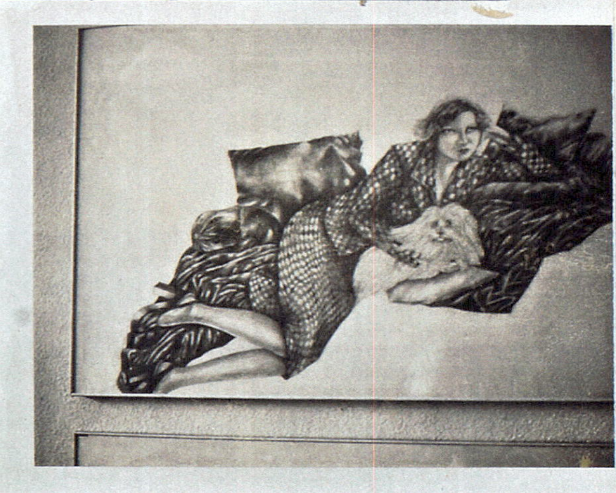
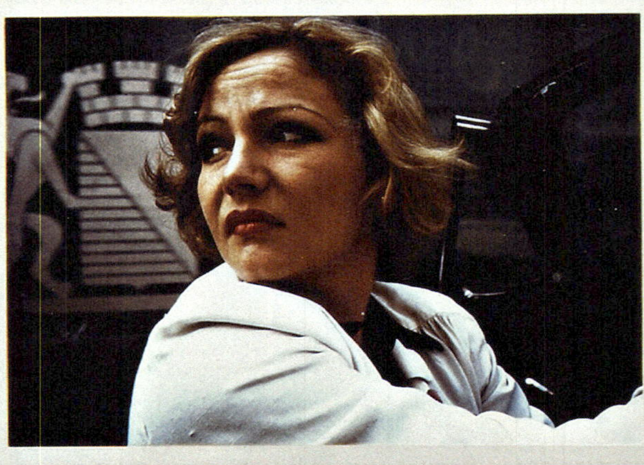

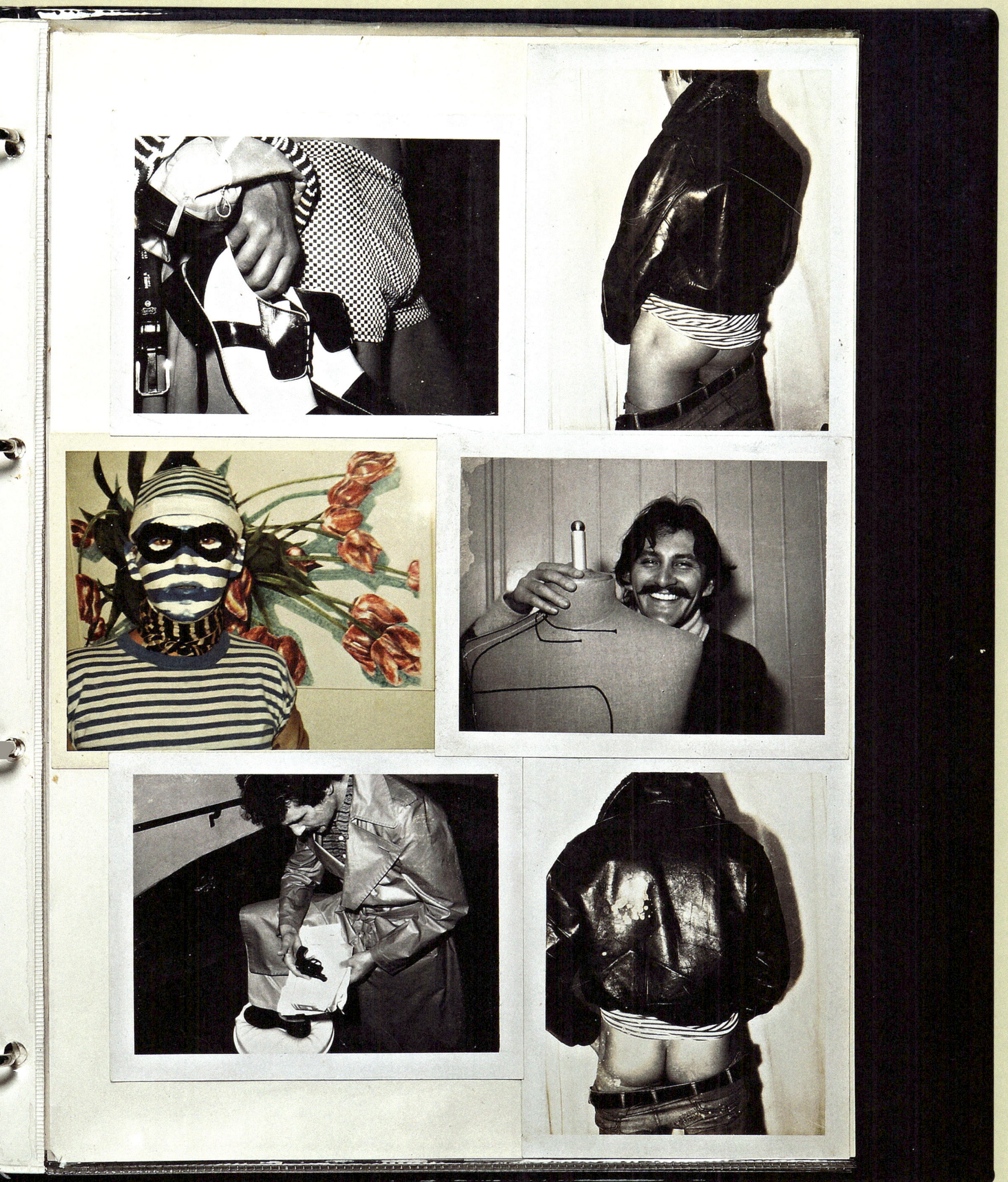

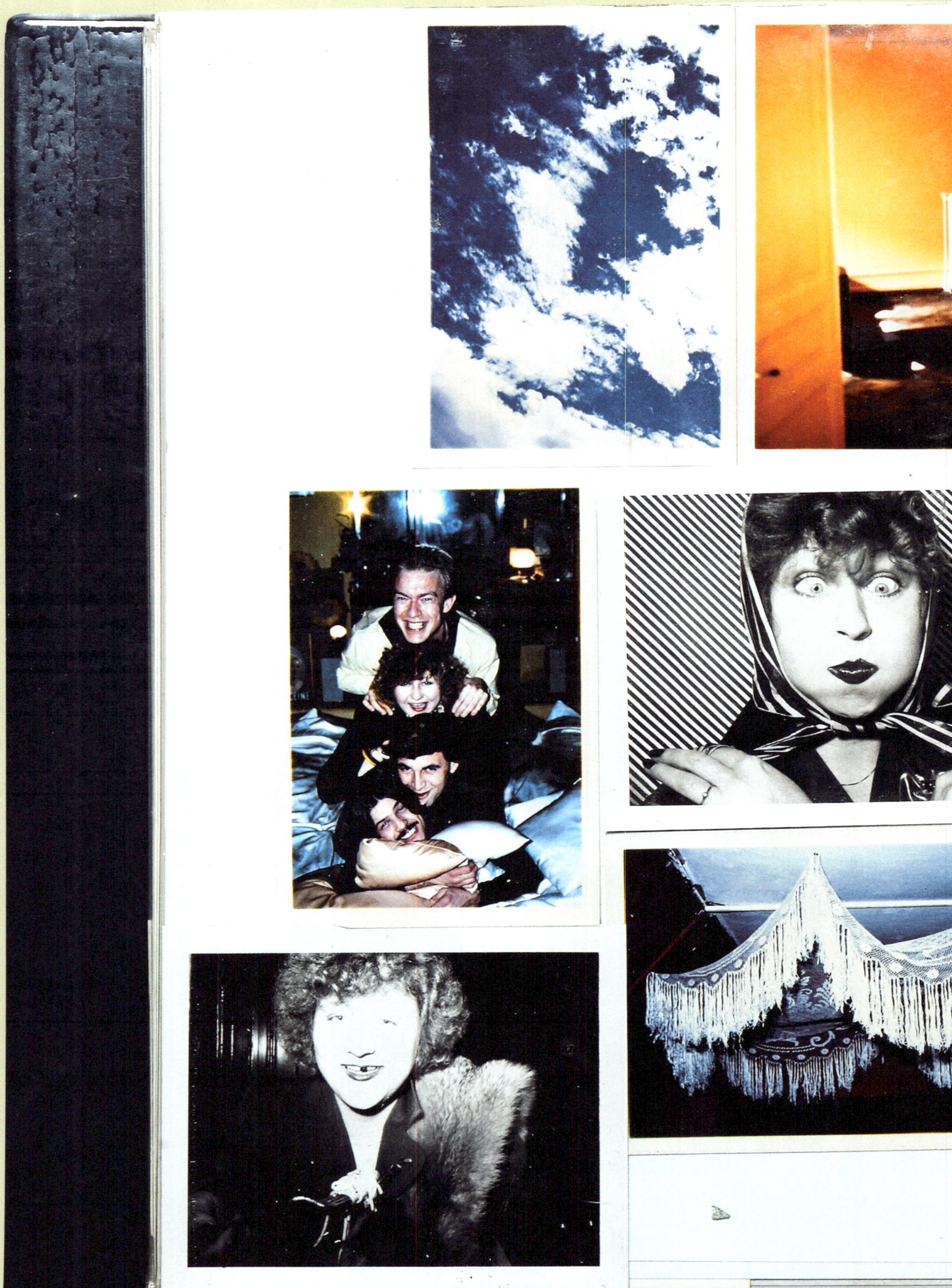

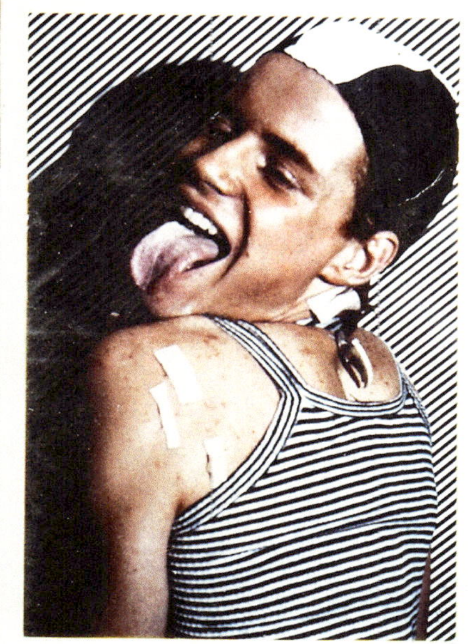
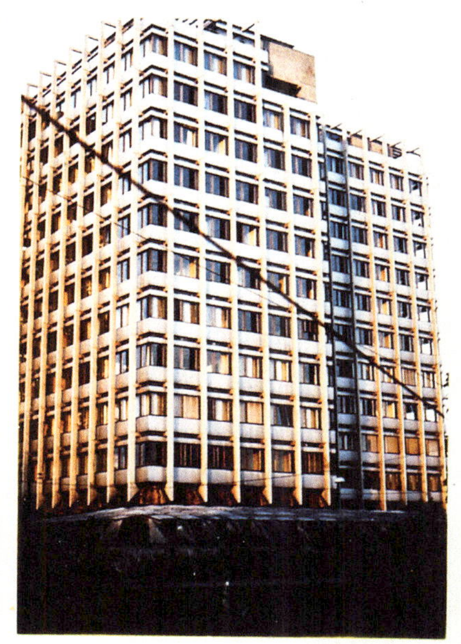
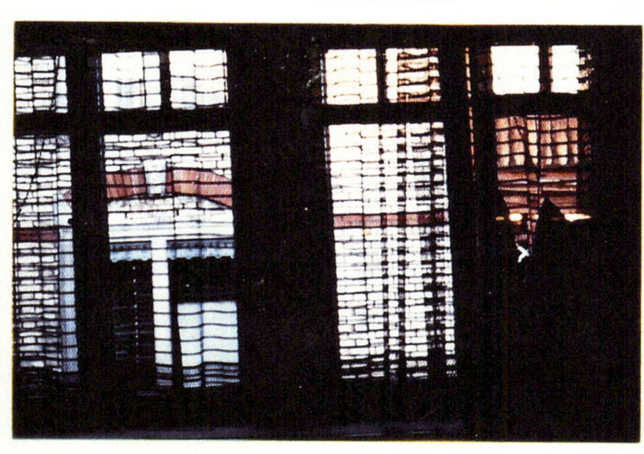
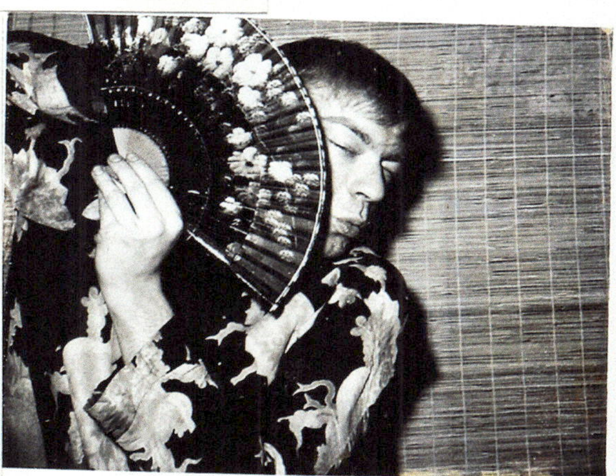
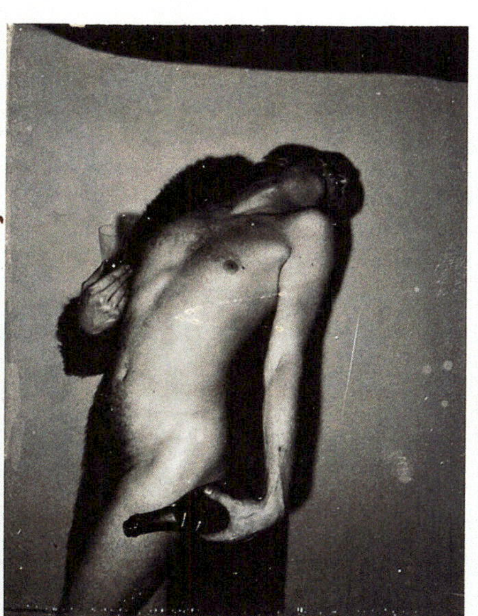
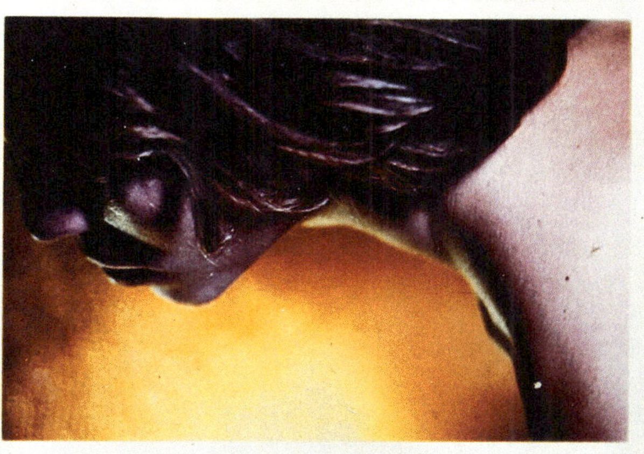

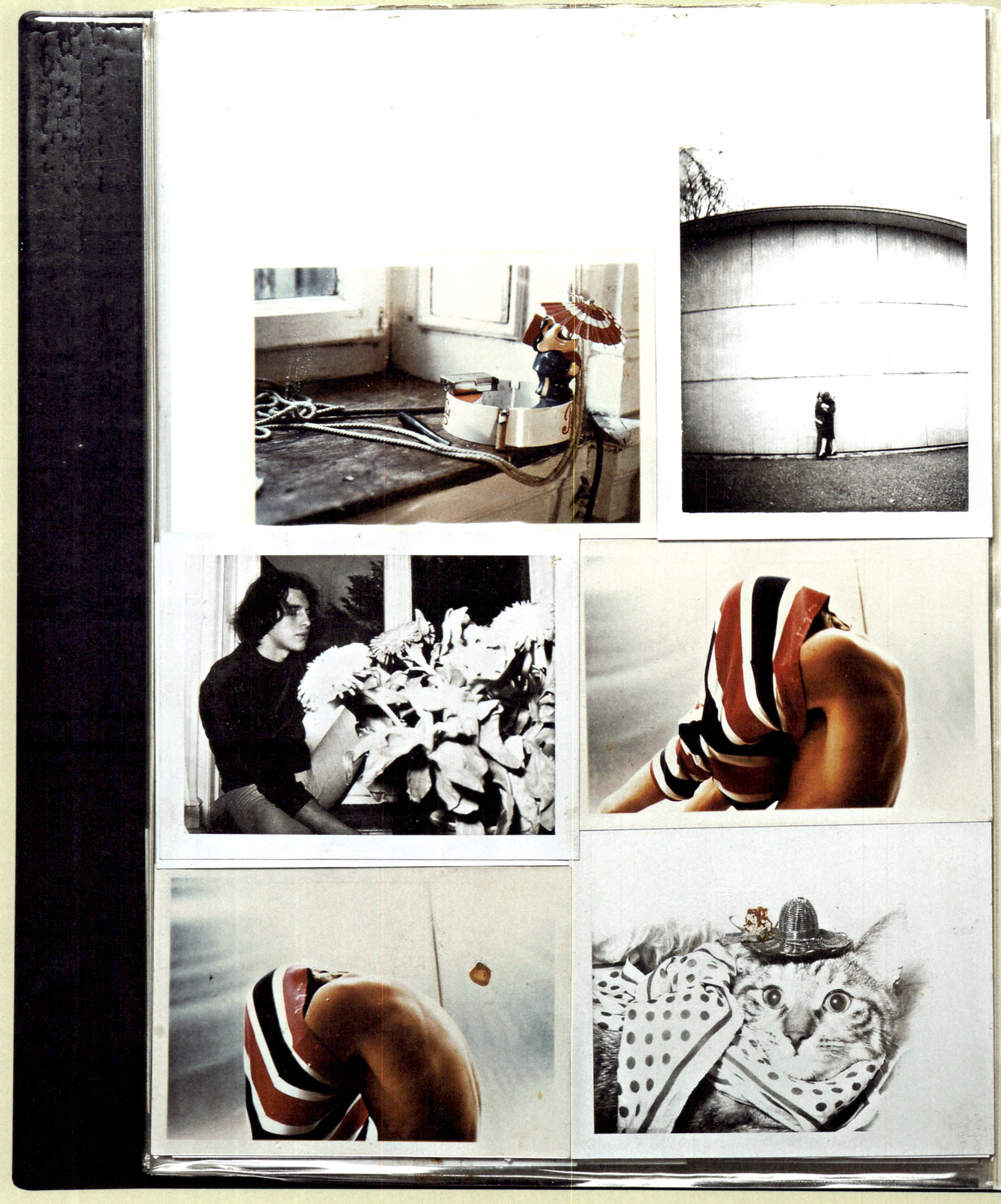

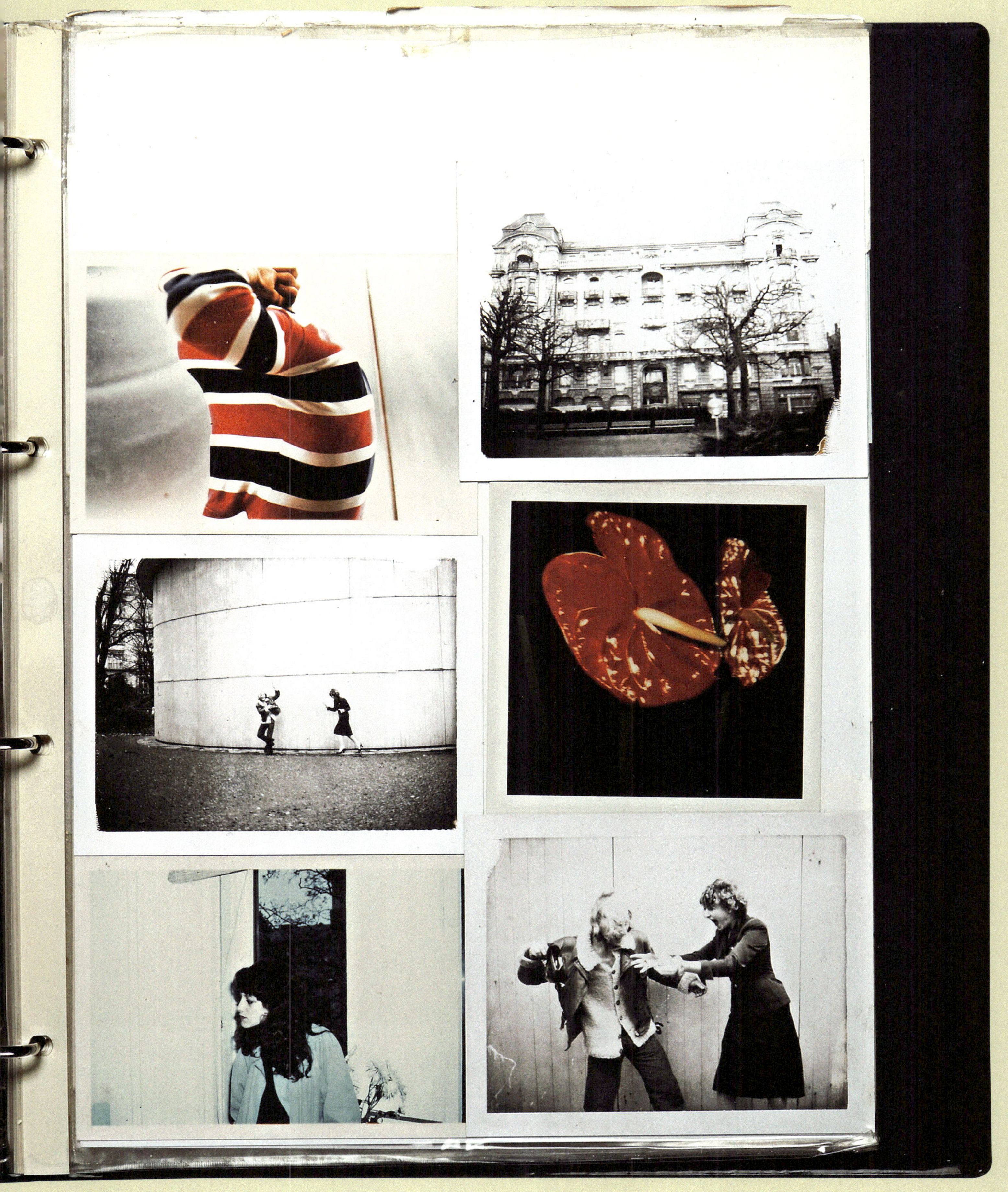

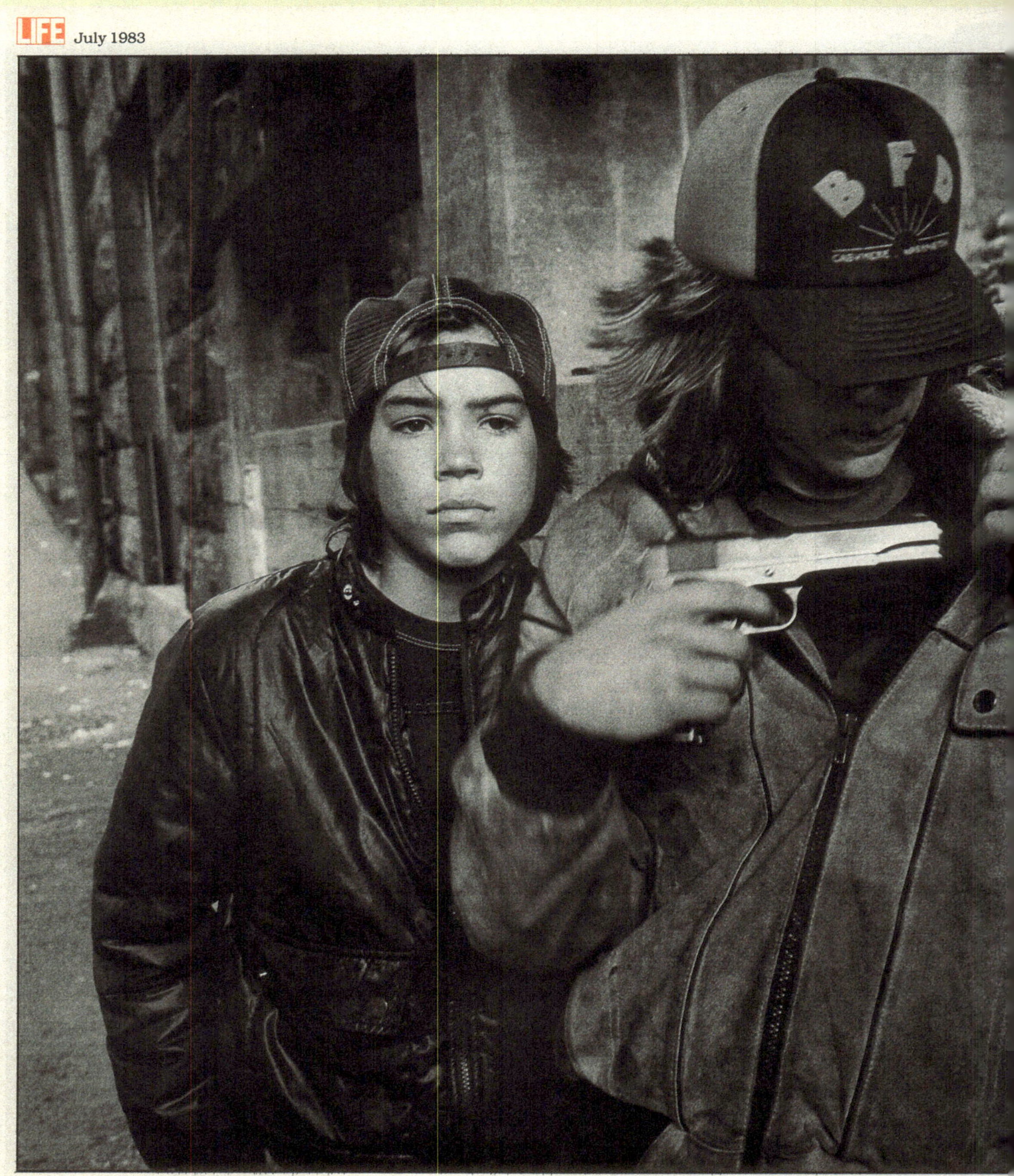
LIFE July 1983
Streets of the L
34

Mary Ellen Mark first photographed Tiny and her runaway peers for *Life* magazine in 1983. Together with the author Cheryl McCall (b. 1950, USA; d. 2005), Mark travelled to Seattle and immersed herself in the street lives of homeless and abandoned teenagers around Pike Street Market. After the assignment Mark maintained close contact with her subjects and initiated the documentary *Streetwise* (1984), directed by her husband, Martin Bell.

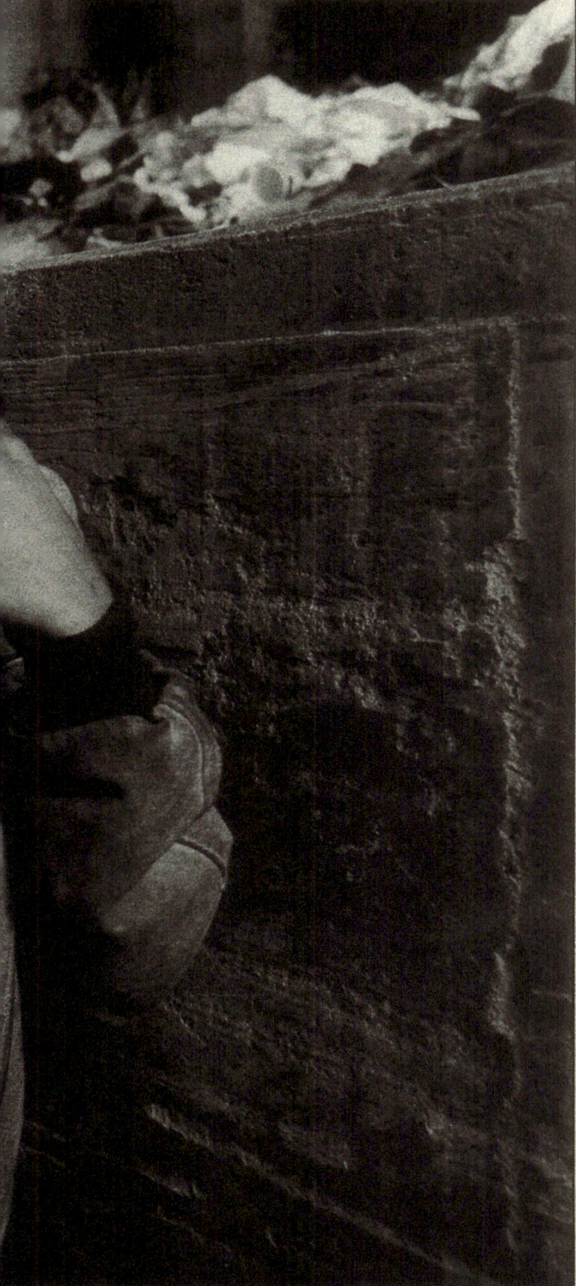

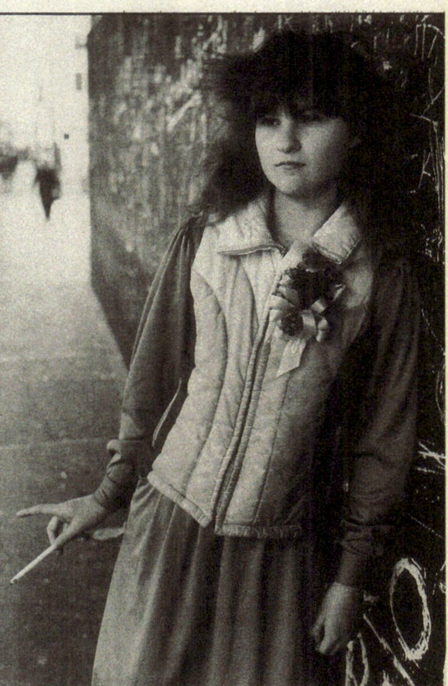

Every city in America has them. There are a thousand in Seattle alone—homeless teenagers who use only their first names to hide their identities. And more alarming than that gun in Mike's hand is what these street kids represent today: a new generation of runaway and abandoned children struggling to survive on their own. Each year more than one million American youngsters between 11 and 17 run away. More than half are girls, and the majority are never reported missing by their apparently indifferent families. These kids aren't looking for '60s-style hippie adventure. Many leave home because living there has become impossible for them. Most are fleeing turbulent households racked by conflict, violence, neglect and—in a disturbingly high percentage of cases—sexual abuse. "Some of these kids are running for damn good reasons. The most logical option they have is to get out of there," says Gordon Raley, staff director of the House Subcommittee on Human Resources, which gathers data on runaways. But a growing number are casualties of the prolonged recession. "The economy has had a tremendous impact," Raley continues. "There are a hell of a lot of kids literally kicked out and thrown away." Each year some 5,000 unidentified teenagers end up in unmarked graves, according to federal records, and another 50,000 simply disappear. No one knows what happens to them. Too young to get jobs or to receive welfare, a significant majority resort to theft, peddling drugs, and prostitution to support themselves. Father Bruce Ritter, a Catholic priest, whose Covenant House crisis centers in New York, Toronto and Houston aid thousands of kids each year, believes that 80 percent of runaways use sex to survive. "Without dealing in myth or exaggeration, there are 500,000 kids younger than seventeen involved in prostitution," says Ritter. "Nobody will dispute that. They have nothing to sell but themselves." Government programs and privately funded centers like Ritter's shelter roughly 10 percent of the chronically homeless at any given time. In Seattle, where 6,000 runaways are reported each year, there are only a single eight-bed facility, The Shelter, and a few impoverished church-run programs like the St. Dismas Center to provide help. Fending for themselves, most street kids spend the nights in abandoned buildings, unlocked cars, steam-bath cubicles, under bridges and even in cemeteries. Some pool their cash to rent cheap motel rooms, with as many as 15 sleeping on the floor. To illuminate this growing national problem and encourage more effective solutions to it, LIFE here examines these children's dangerous and pitiful lot.

Friends Rat, 16 (*far left*), and Mike, 17, have this Colt .45 only for defense, they insist, against men who try to pick them up or rob them. "I get hassled a lot," says Rat. "Mike's my protection." They picked Seattle because Mike had once lived there. Right: Laurie, 14, says she was promised $80 by a middle-aged doctor who sexually abused her but reneged on the payment. She recently left Seattle to live with a Christian group in Kent, Wash.

ost RUNAWAY KIDS EKE OUT A MEAN LIFE IN SEATTLE

Photography: Mary Ellen Mark
Text: Cheryl McCall

"Being on the streets is tough, but it's kind of a challenge," says Christy, 16, who left her suburban Seattle home five years ago when her mother moved in with a drug dealer. "Everybody here just goes day to day. A lot of us wonder where the next meal is going to come from, where we're going to sleep." To answer those needs, many of Seattle's street kids risk arrest—and worse—by becoming prostitutes, what they call "turning dates." Boys and girls, who stash their clothes in bus station lockers during the day, drift near the waterfront's Pike Street Market and wait for offers. "I've been raped eight times by dates. One held a gun on me and almost broke my arm," says Sam, 17, a professor's daughter from Idaho who ran away. "After a while, you can't handle it. I started crying all the time, having these really weird fits. I thought I was crazy. So I stopped, but then I had to start again." While boys operate independently, female prostitution is controlled by pimps, who use drugs, sex or threats to keep the girls in virtual bondage. "A girl doesn't think she can sneeze without her pimp," says Linda Reppond, executive director of the privately run Shelter. "He makes his girls dependent on drugs in order to control them. Boys do drugs to survive the humiliation of turning tricks, just to live with themselves." Tragically, trafficking in drugs is considered a step up—street kids find it less degrading than prostitution. Those are the only choices, they insist. None of these kids can go to school—even if they wanted to. They have no permanent address, and schools will not admit them. (One undersized 16-year-old, Itty Bitty, hasn't been to school since fourth grade.) Regulations ban those under 18 from adult shelters, but most of the street kids are too proud to sleep in a room full of alcoholics and bums anyway. Shadow tried it when he turned 18 this spring. "I'd rather sit in an all-night coffee shop," he says. "The government thinks if it makes it hard enough on the streets, we'll go home. But there's no place to go."

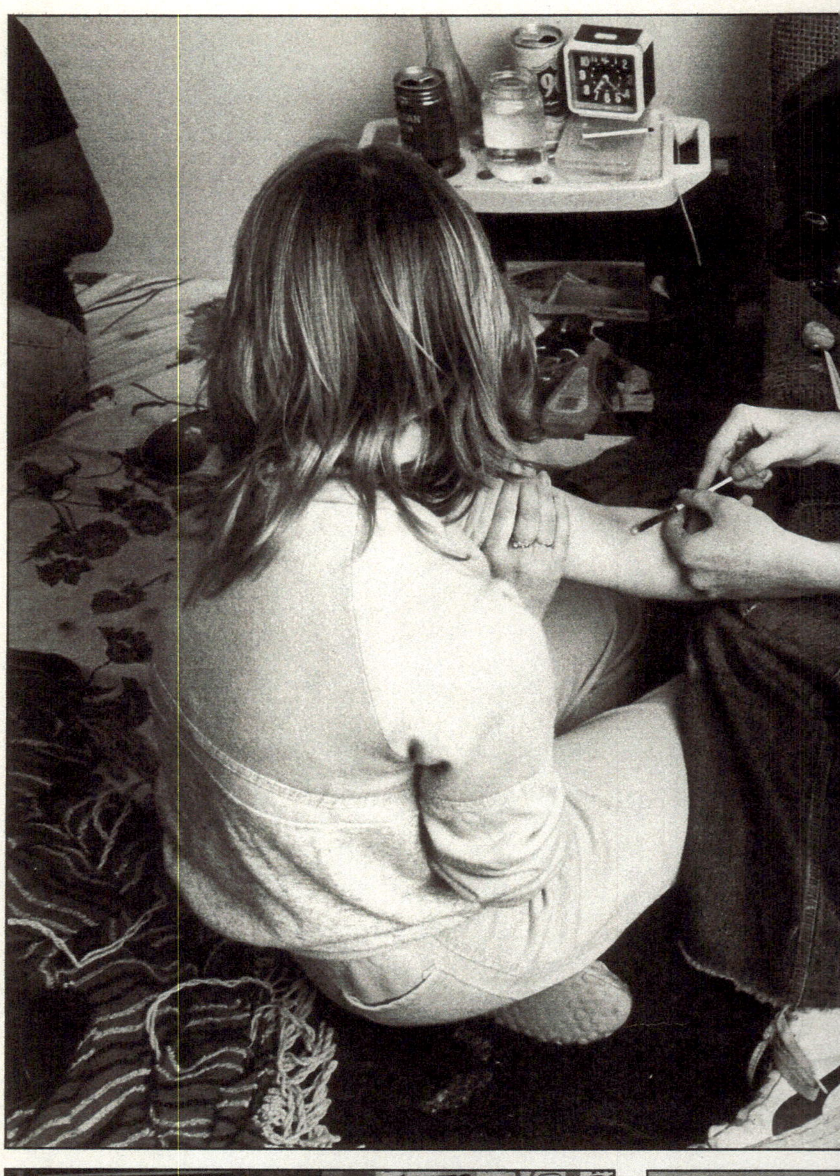

FLIRTING WITH DEATH

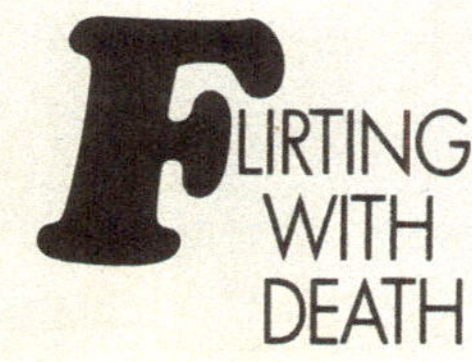

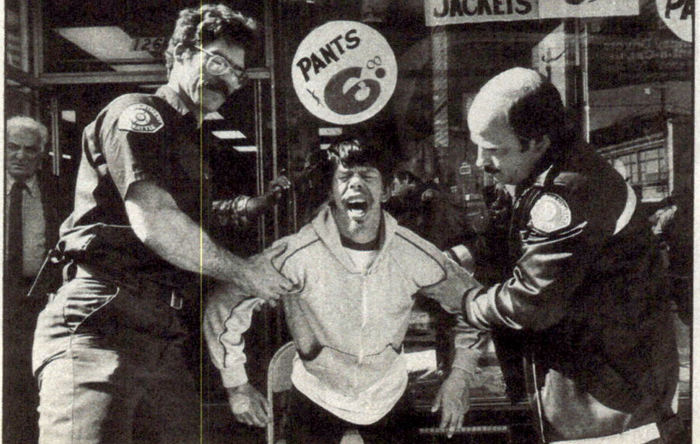

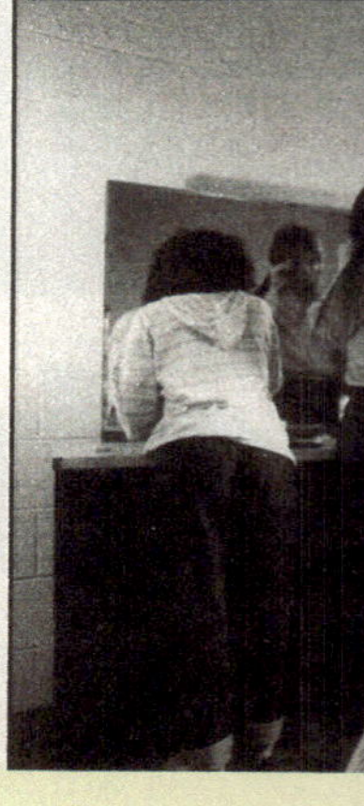

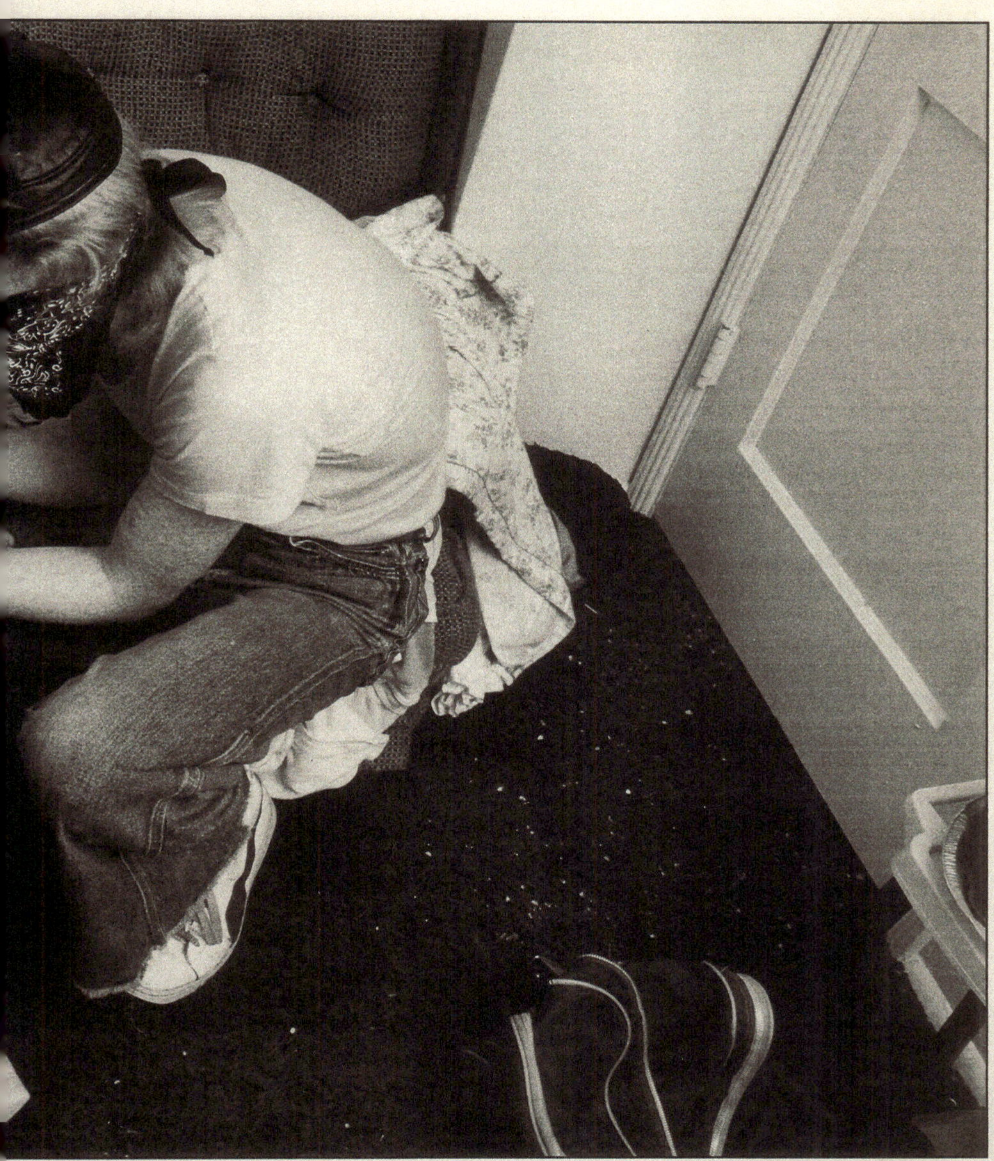

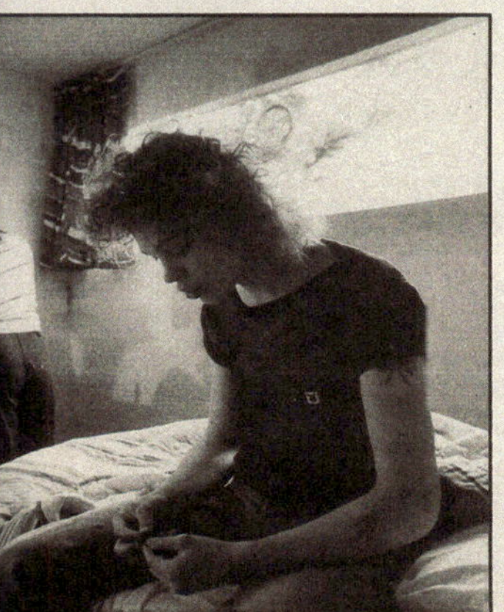

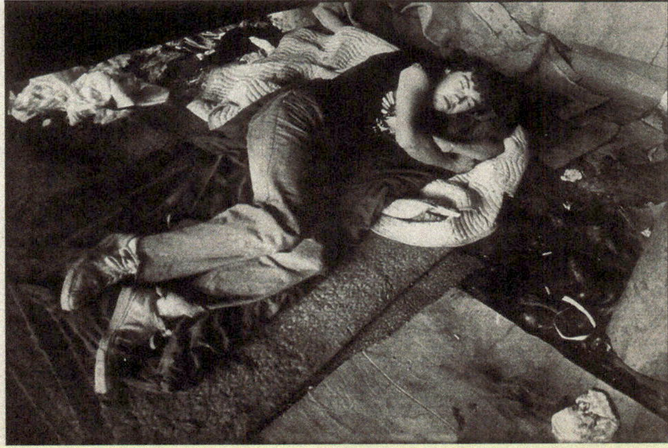

This young dealer is injecting a 14-year-old customer with MDA (methylene dioxy amphetamine) in a crash pad for runaways. At $5 a capsule, MDA is the drug of choice among Seattle street kids—though marijuana is commonest, and LSD is making a comeback. MDA users need at least five capsules to attain the desired "body rush," a violent shuddering later followed by sudden vomiting, clenching jaws and twitching eyes. The $1 "rigs" are disposable insulin syringes, but addicts dangerously reuse them as many as 50 times, honing dull needles on matchbook strips and lubricating the plungers with Vaseline. When a homeless boy *(bottom left)* collapsed in agonizing spasms, fire department medics speculated his problem was drug related and rushed him to a hospital. Center: Within an hour of leaving this motel room, the two 14-year-old girls on the right were arrested for prostitution. They call the boy on the bed their "popcorn pimp" because he is only 18. Left: James, 18, sleeps under a waterfront viaduct.

37

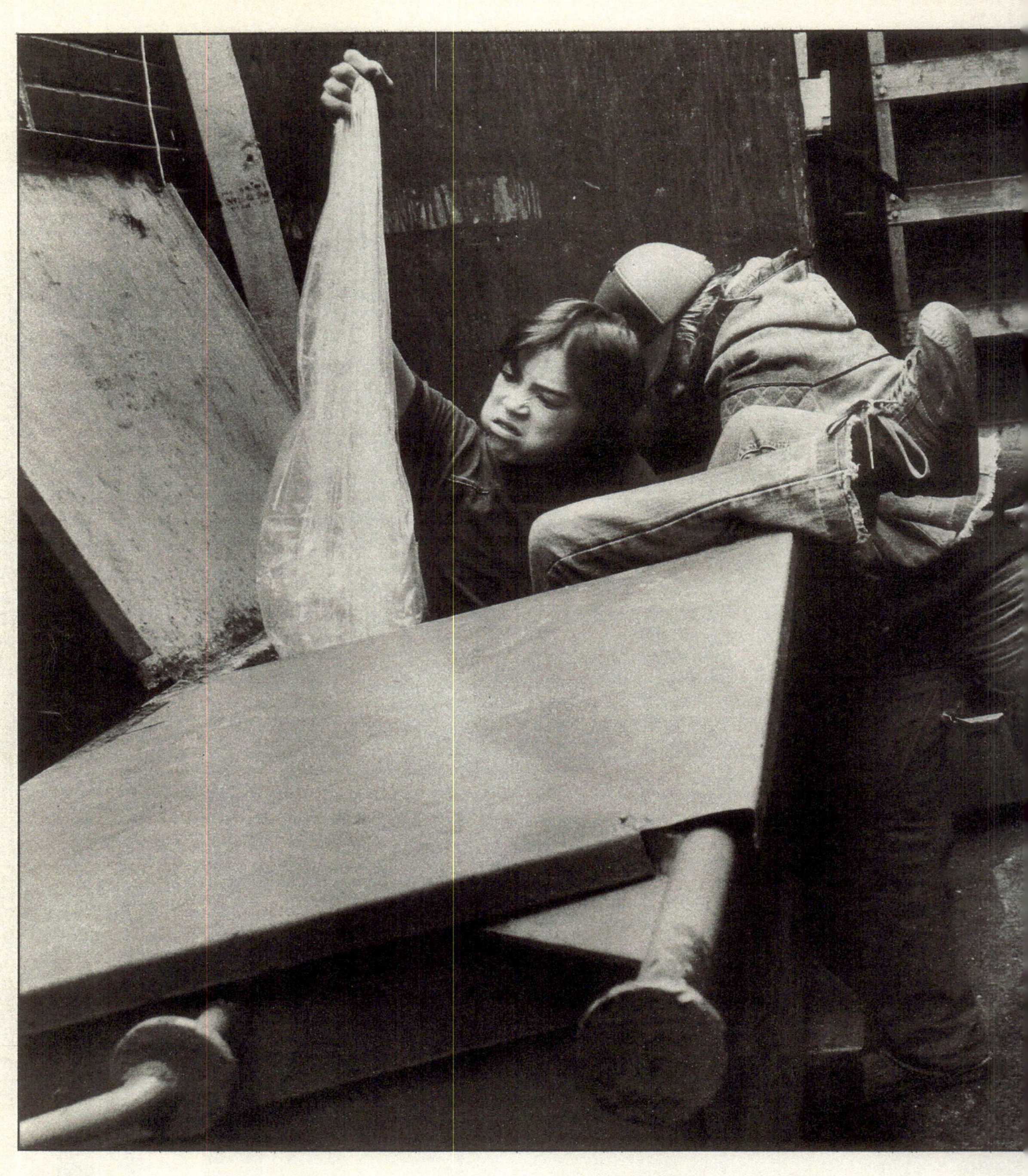

BEGGING, FORAGING IN GARBAGE,
THEY BARELY SURVIVE

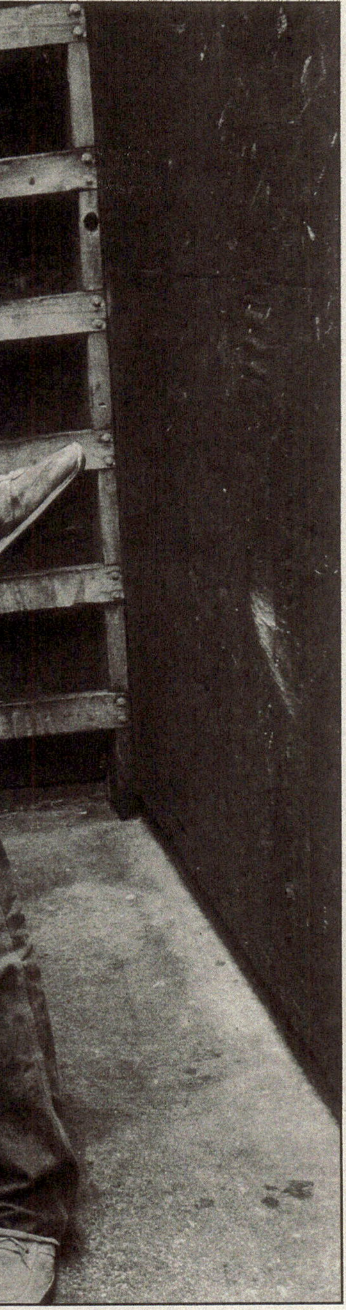

When Mike and Rat, who had lived on the same street for four years, ran away from Orangevale, Calif., last January, they met a Seattle merchant seaman who showed them the ways of the hobo: panhandling, rolling cigarettes, brushing their teeth in public rest rooms and eating $1 meals in skid row missions. Unlike many other male runaways, they have never resorted to prostitution. They sleep in a spooky, abandoned hotel that has no water or electricity, where they cleared one block-long hallway so they could roller-skate. Because the building is boarded up, they climb in at a second-story window. If police cars are parked behind the hotel at night, the boys go to a pay phone and report a nearby fight. When the duped cops take off, Mike and Rat sneak inside. Often for dinner they'll phone Shakey's and order several pizzas "with something like pineapple on them that nobody else would want." When the unclaimed food is thrown out, they grab it from the garbage bin. Mike doesn't approve of Rat's occasional shoplifting of clothes, saying, "We have enough laundry to do already." Both boys, whose parents are divorced, were excellent students. They lived with their fathers until they got into trouble with the law. Rat was caught selling marijuana in school and says his father, an aerospace technician, had warned him never to come home if that happened. "I took him seriously," says Rat. He has been in touch with his mother twice but says he stopped calling her because "she was crying and everything." Mike was charged with several counts of driving without a license after wrecking three cars. He says his father, a career Marine, threatened to send him to the state Boys' Ranch. To pay for their bus trip to Seattle, both Mike and Rat stole money from their fathers and claim they now fear them more than the authorities. "My dad literally wants to kill me," Rat believes. A more immediate threat, however, lies in the streets. After Rat was attacked by a crazed heroin addict, he sold his Pentax camera and Mike his two beloved Stratocaster guitars to buy their Colt .45. Despite this chaotic, dangerous way of life, Rat says he enjoys his freedom. Mike, however, is frankly miserable. But he knows that when he turns 18, his juvenile record will be wiped clean. "I can't wait until my birthday so I can go home again," he says.

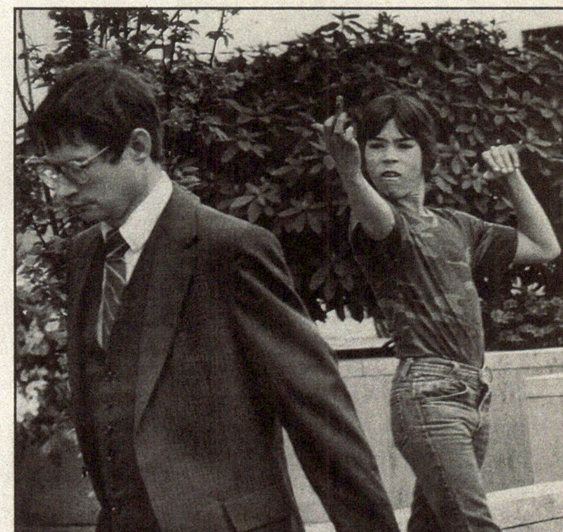

Rat gives the finger to a man who ignored his begging.

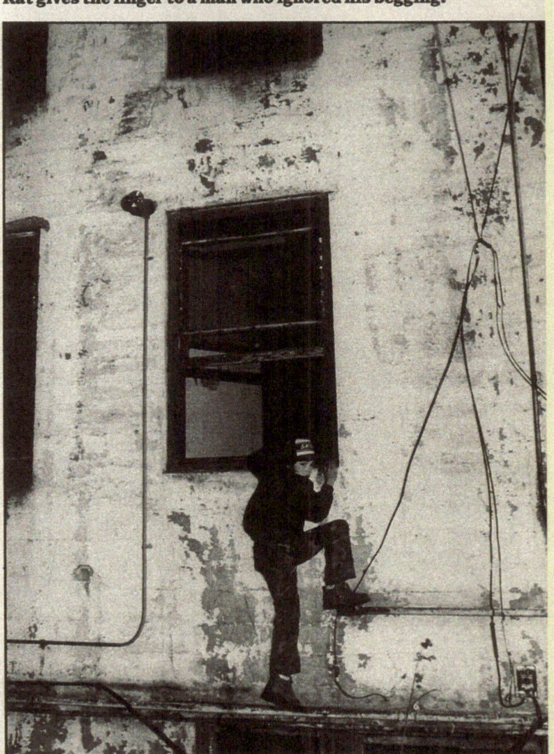

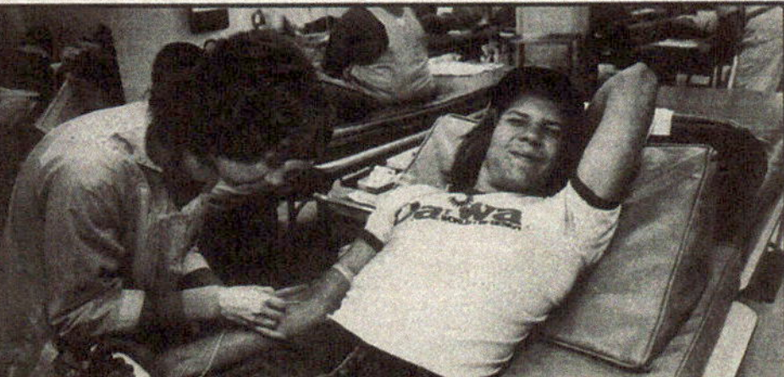

Rat and Mike call rummaging for food in trash bins behind restaurants dumpster diving.

This window is the only entry into the hotel. Left: Mike, passing for 18 with a fake I.D., earns $30 a week by selling plasma.

39

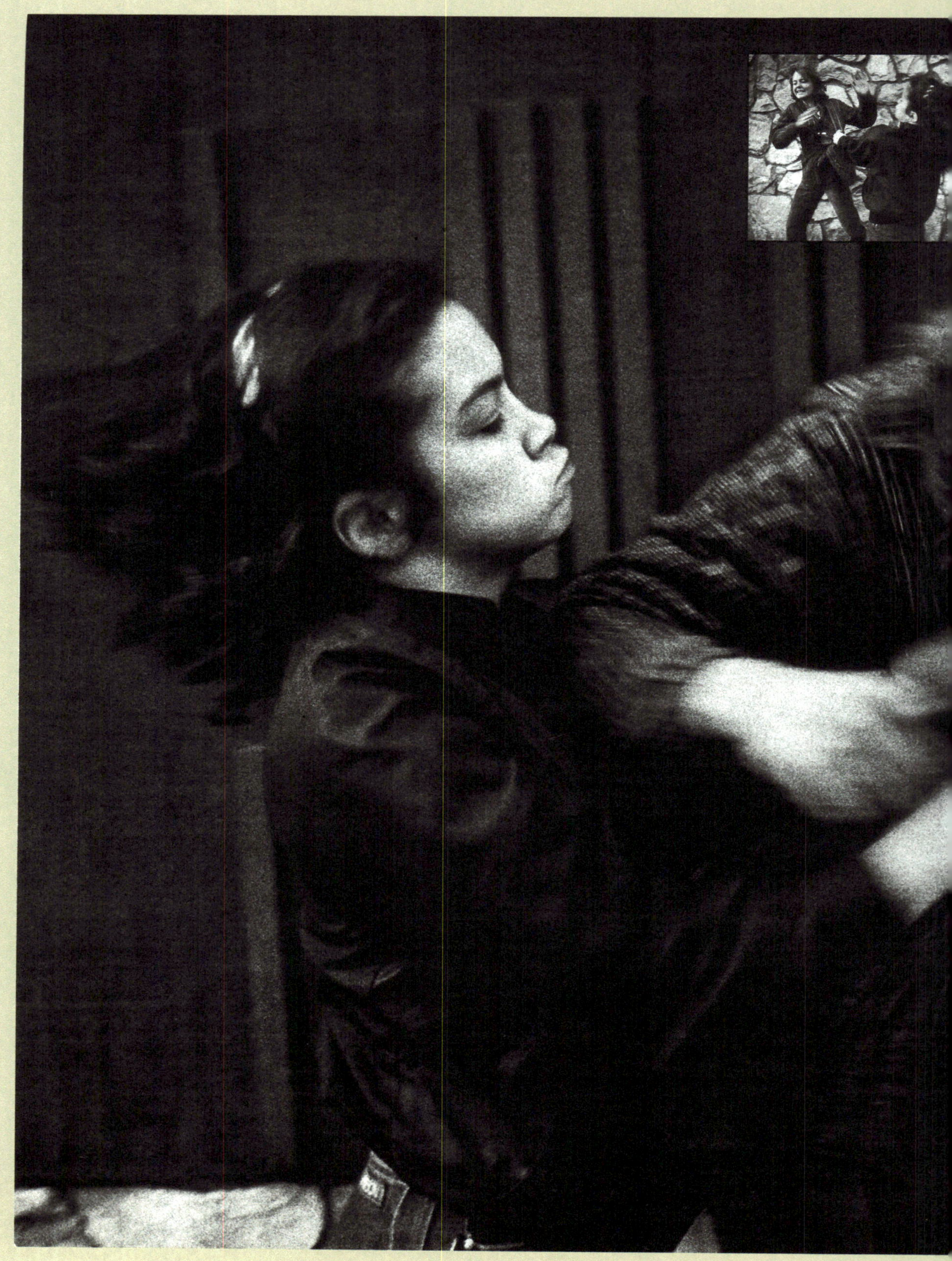

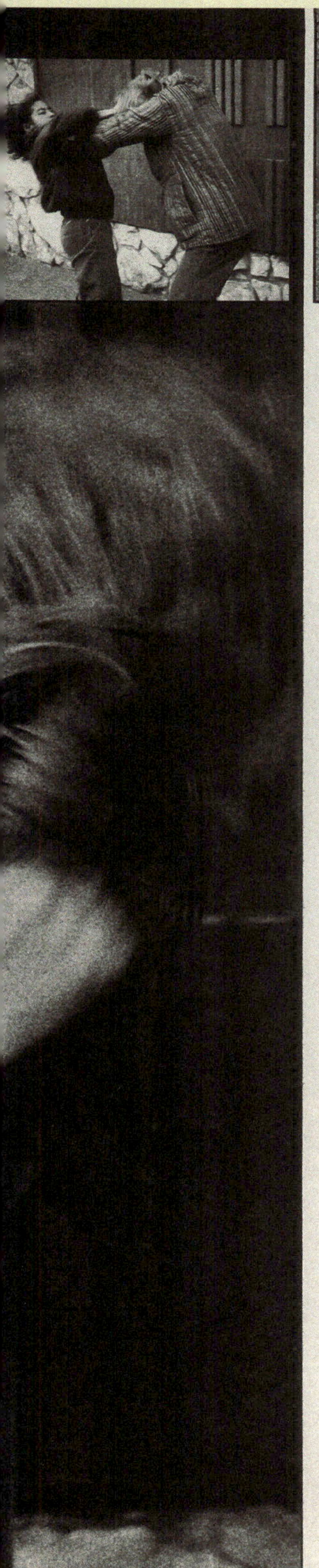
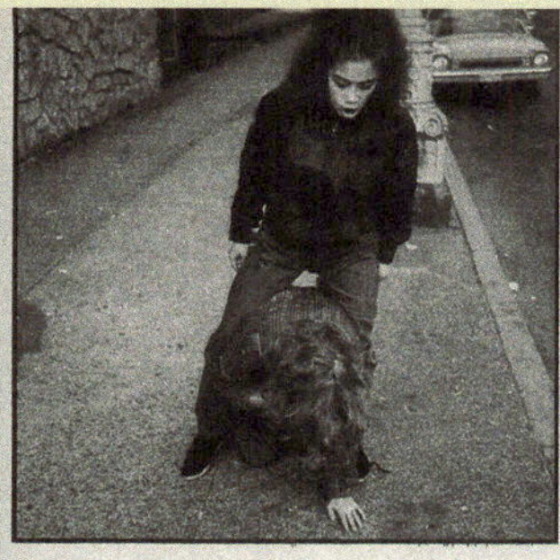
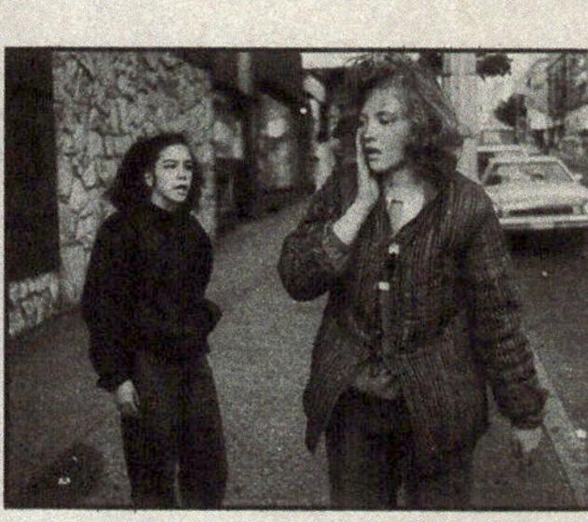

Dark-haired Patti waited until her victim's pimp was out of sight and then jumped this girl because she never returned a borrowed jacket.

Patti, 16, was arrested minutes after this brawl, cited for simple assault and released. Like many runaways, she learned violence at home and doesn't hesitate to use it—even though she's now four months pregnant—to settle all disputes. She is one of nine children, six of whom prefer the terror of the street to life in their Seattle home. "I split three-and-a-half years ago. My mom used to abuse me, and she drank a lot," says Patti. "My stepfather drinks and he made life pretty miserable. I used to get hit with things." She says she's been dragged into cars and raped seven times, once at gunpoint, but she's not tempted to return to her family. "There's no chance of it working out if I'd go back," she says flatly. Patti and her boyfriend, Munchkin, 17, used to share motel rooms with a group of kids. Then Munchkin struck a deal with a motel manager in which Patti exchanges sex with him for a room of their own each night. But they haven't yet found a solution to the $16 jaywalking and $125 littering tickets they—and all the kids—get almost daily. These are a form of police harassment, and one unpaid littering fine (the only means they have of paying is by prostitution or theft) means five nights in jail. Like teenage lovers anywhere, they can't bear to be apart. When they're broke, Patti robs weaker girls or bullies them into turning tricks and giving her the money. No one interferes. "Down here if you can't hold on to what you've got, then you don't deserve to have it," says a local drug dealer. "That's the rule." But as her pregnancy advances, Patti is becoming vulnerable. She's more hungry than she used to be and tired most of the time. She often suffers from severe stomach cramps and has swollen feet. Her only pair of jeans is too tight, and her shoes cause blisters. Sometimes, overwhelmed by it all, Patti sobs like the child she is and sucks her thumb.

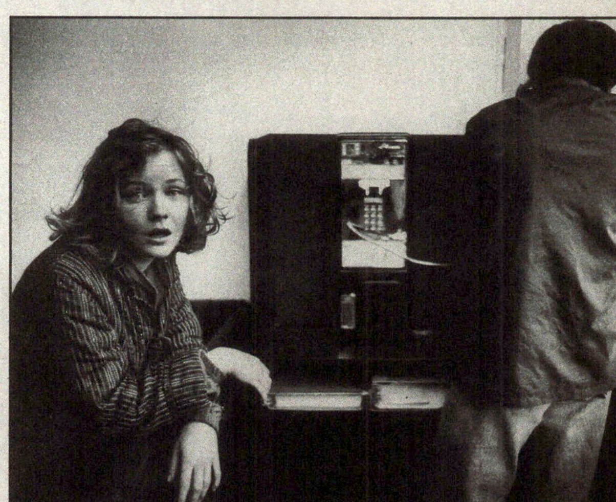

Shaken but unhurt, the girl finds her pimp. He calls the cops.

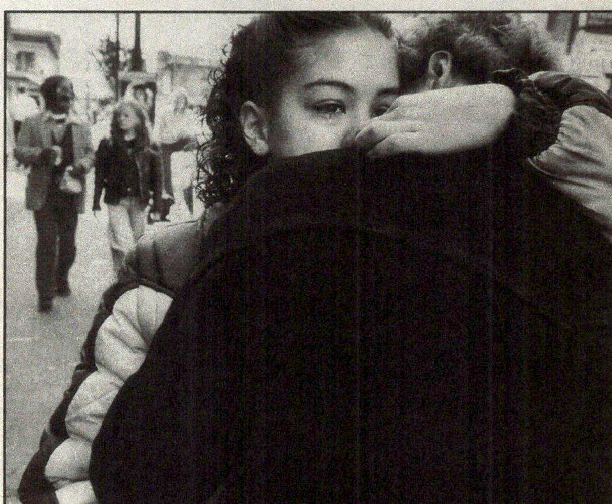

Patti's tender side is reserved for her boyfriend, Munchkin.

A GIRL WITH A GRUDGE AGAINST THE WORLD

41

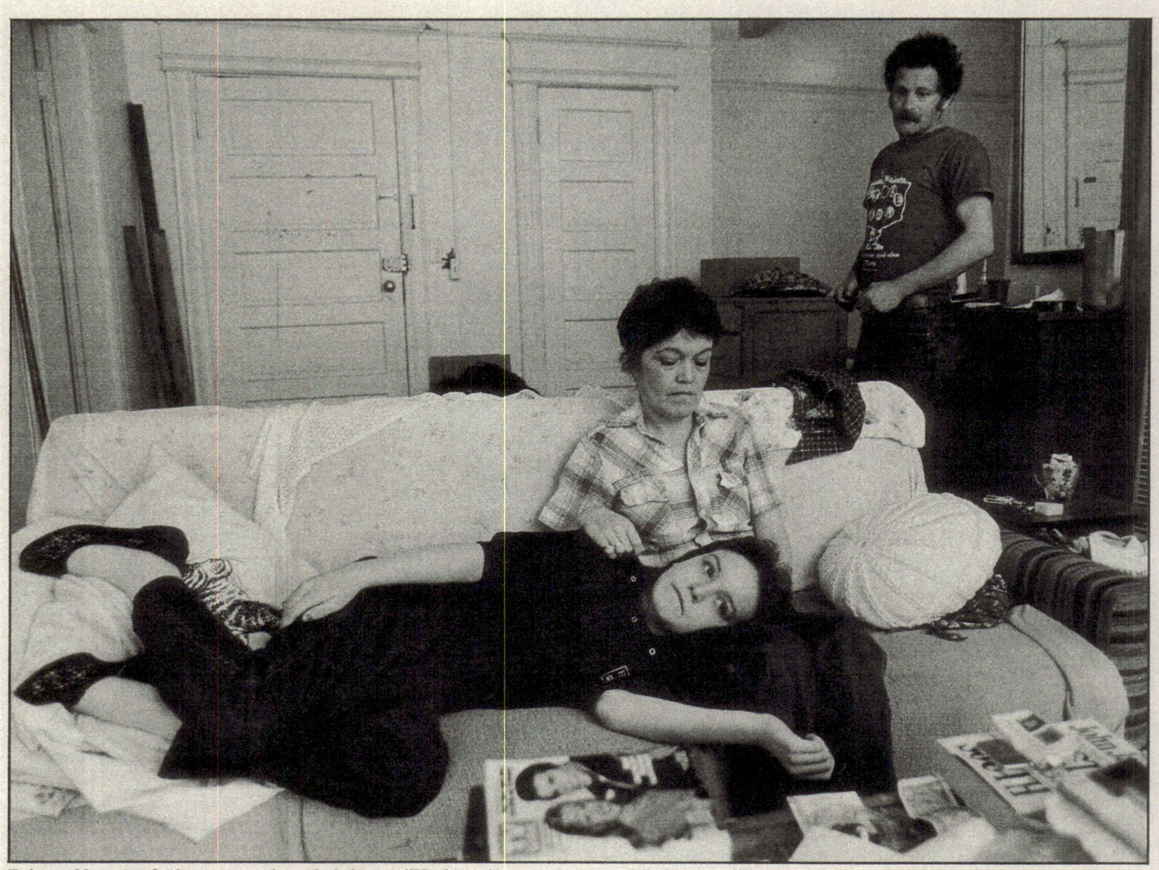

Erin and her stepfather argue when she's home. "He doesn't want me around," she says. "He wants my mom all to himself."

Erin, 14, has been arrested twice for prostitution. Her probation order states that she must live with her family, not on the streets. Home is a one-room apartment over a tavern in downtown Seattle, and her bed is the couch. Her mother and stepfather, both unemployed, spend most of their time in the bar downstairs. During the year she was on the streets, Erin was raped, was lured into posing for pornographic photographs and supported a pimp by turning tricks. She now has gonorrhea. Her story would be irredeemably bleak if no one cared. But the one positive contact she made on the streets was Teresa Kiilsgaard, 28, an outreach worker from the St. Dismas Youth Center. Kiilsgaard gives Erin advice, takes her for medical treatment and even rescued her last winter from an armed kidnapper. "I found Erin in a restaurant," says Kiilsgaard. "The guy was trying to sell her to the customers and wouldn't even let her go to the bathroom. She couldn't get away." Fortunately, programs like the Dismas Center exist in other cities too. The National Runaway Switchboard lists 7,000 agencies around the country that counsel or help youngsters in various ways, and approximately 300 shelters provide emergency housing for runaways. Congress allocated $21 million in 1983 to fund hotlines and teenage shelters but, by its own estimate, those facilities serve only 45,000 kids a year, a mere fraction of the needy. More help is required, especially in Los Angeles, where there are no shelters at all. Father Ritter's Covenant House programs have become the yardstick by which others are measured. His aim is simple: to provide as many beds as possible each night to give kids an alternative to selling themselves. In New York, he takes in 12,000 a year; the Toronto center handles 3,000 more. The Houston shelter, which opened in June, expects 5,000 this year. Ritter plans another for Boston in early 1984 because the existing facilities there, Common Life and Place Runaway House, have only 31 beds in all. Covenant Houses are staffed around the clock, ready to provide food, clothing and medical care to any youth who asks. In New York, homeless teenage mothers with their babies are also helped. "It never occurred to me when I designed our program," says Ritter, who opened his first crisis center in 1972 in New York's Times Square, "but we have a nursery now." Covenant House receives no federal funds because current guidelines restrict the number of beds in shelters to 20 and require that the facility be located outside areas of prostitution. Ritter contends that it is in the seamy neighborhoods that crisis centers are most needed. "Honest to God, in all my life, I've never met one boy or girl prostitute who didn't start out as a runaway," he says. And how can we prevent runaways? The key, Ritter says, is at home. "Kids ordinarily don't run away from warm, loving families," he says. "And those who do almost invariably return home." ♠

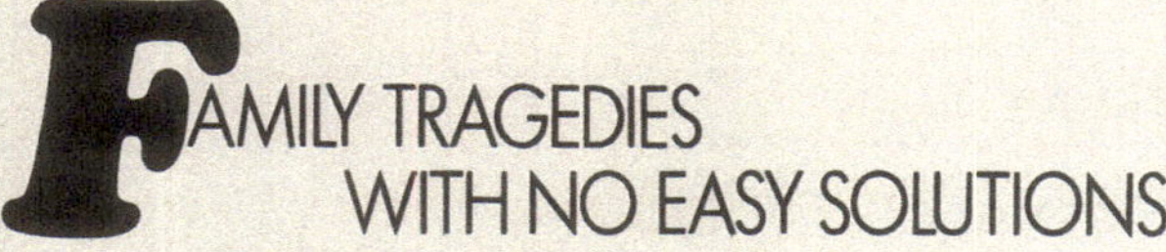

FAMILY TRAGEDIES WITH NO EASY SOLUTIONS

42

NOTES

THE LONELY CROWD (pp. 12–19)

1   S. E. Hinton, *The Outsiders* (London: Puffin, 2007), p. 50.

2   The 'outsider' is a deeply conflicted term but one used by the photographers and subjects whom this essay addresses. Although I do not use scare quotes after this point, please know that the writer treats the term with a healthy degree of ambivalence.

3   Julian Cox, 'Cashing Down the Kid from Queens', in Danny Lyon, *Message to the Future* (Fine Arts Museum of San Francisco and Yale University Press, New Haven and London, 2016), p. 21.

4   Susan Sontag, 'America, Seen through Photographs, Darkly', in *On Photography* [1977] (London: Penguin, 2008), p. 44.

5   Ibid., p. 42.

6   See Robert Genter, *Late Modernism: Art, Culture, and Politics in Cold War America* (Philadelphia and Oxford: University of Pennsylvania Press, 2010), pp. 54–89.

7   The exhibition was staged at MoMA before travelling to over thirty different countries across six continents.

8   John Szarkowski, *Arbus, Friedlander, Winogrand: New Documents, 1967* (New York: Museum of Modern Art, 2017), p. 1.

9   Patricia Bosworth, *Diane Arbus: A Biography* (London: Vintage Books, 2005), p. 23.

10 Norman Mailer, 'Brooklyn Minority Report', with photographs by Bruce Davidson, *Esquire*, June 1960, p. 129.

11 Philip Charrier, 'On Diane Arbus: Establishing a Revisionist Framework of Analysis', *History of Photography*, 36/4 (November 2012), p. 434.

12 Sandra S. Phillips, 'The Question of Belief', in Diane Arbus, *Diane Arbus: Revelations* (New York: Random House, 2003), p. 51.

13 Bruce Davidson, *Outside Inside* (Göttingen: Steidl, 2011).

14 Mark Holborn, *Beyond Japan: A Photo Theatre* (London: Barbican Art Gallery and Jonathan Cape, 1991), p. 125.

15 Cox, 'Chasing Down the Kid', p. 21.

16 Martin Parr and Gerry Badger, *The Photobook: A History*, vol. 1 (London: Phaidon, 2004), p. 260.

17 Michael Hurst and Robert Swope, eds, *Casa Susanna* (New York: Powerhouse, 2004), n.p.

18 Virginia Prince, 'Purpose of *Transvestia*', *Transvestia*, 36 (December 1965). n.p.

DIANE ARBUS (pp. 22–29)

1   Diane Arbus, note to Marvin Israel, January 1960, in Diane Arbus, *Revelations* (New York: Random House, 2003), p. 331 n.22.

2   Diane Arbus, *Diane Arbus* (Millerton, NY: Aperture, 1972), p. 1.

3   Ibid., p. 2.

4   Ibid., p. 3.

5   Diane Arbus, letter to Howard Nemerov, 10 November 1968, in *Revelations*, p. 339 n.358.

6   Susan Sontag, *On Photography* (New York: Farrar, Straus & Giroux, 1977), p. 33.

7   Arbus, *Diane Arbus*, p. 12.

BRUCE DAVIDSON (pp. 30–45)

1   Bruce Davidson, in Sean O'Hagan, 'Bruce Davidson: "I Felt I was Part of Something. That's Always Been the Instinct"', *Guardian*, 24 April 2011, available at www.theguardian.com.

2   Bruce Davidson, in *Bruce Davidson: Photographs* (New York, 1978), pp. 9–10.

3   Ibid., p. 10.

4   Ibid.

5   Ibid.

6   Davidson, in O'Hagan, 'Bruce Davidson: "I Felt I was Part of Something"'.

7   Bruce Davidson, in 'Everything is Sacred: An Interview with Bruce Davidson', *ASX*, 3 December 2011, www.americansuburbx.com.

8   Davidson, in O'Hagan, 'Bruce Davidson: "I Felt I was Part of Something"'.

9   Cited in Davidson, *Brooklyn Gang: Summer 1959* (Santa Fe, NM: Twin Palms, 1998), p. 81.

10 Ibid., p. 87.

11 Ibid., p. 93.

12 Ibid., p. 91.

DAIDŌ MORIYAMA (pp. 46–57)

1   See Steven C. Ridgely, *Japanese Counterculture: The Antiestablishment Art of Terayama Shūji* (Minneapolis, MN: University of Minnesota Press, 2010).

2   For Moriyama's work at this time in the wider context of photography history, see Simon Baker, ed., *Daidō Moriyama* (London: Tate Publishing, 2012).

3   The psychoanalytic complexities and controversies here, particularly in the Japanese context, are substantial, and this brief account deserves to be extended. See Anne Allison, *Permitted and Prohibited Desires: Mothers, Comics and Censorship in Japan* (Berkeley and Los Angeles, CA: University of California Press, 2000); Bruce Fink, *A Clinical Introduction to Lacanian Psychoanalysis: Theory and Technique* (Cambridge, MA: Harvard University Press, 1997), pp. 165–202; and Nina Cornyetz and J. Keith Vincent, *Perversion and Modern Japan: Psychoanalysis, Literature, Culture* (London and New York: Routledge, 2010). For the suggestion that Japanese counterculture, and the work of Terayama in particular, was peculiarly matricentric see Carol Fisher Sorgenfrei, *Unspeakable Acts: The Avant-garde Theatre of Terayama Shūji and Postwar Japan* (Honolulu, HI: University of Hawai'i Press, 2005)

4   Sorgenfrei, *Unspeakable Acts*, p. 74.

5   I am thinking here of the photography of Ed van der Elsken, Christer Strömholm and Robert Frank. William Klein's influence on Moriyama – especially his book *New York* (1956, published in a Japanese edition the following year) – was also decisive, as it was for other Japanese photographers. Moriyama would pursue his fixation to a euphoric end in his book *Shashin no sayōnara* (Farewell Photography) (Tokyo: Shashin Hyōron Sha, 1972).

6   Sandra Phillips, 'Stray Dog', in Daidō Moriyama, Alexandra Munroe and Sandra Phillips, *Daidō Moriyama: Stray Dog* (San Francisco, CA, and New York: SFMOMA and DAP, 1999), p. 16.

7   Jela Krečič and Slavoj Žižek, 'Ugly, Creepy, Disgusting, and Other Modes of Abjection', *Critical Inquiry*, 43/1 (2016), p. 67.

8   For an excellent, related account of this phase in Moriyama's career see Philip Charrier, 'The Making of a Hunter: Moriyama Daidō, 1966–1972', *History of Photography*, 34/3 (2010), pp. 268–90.

9   Cited in Phillips, 'Stray Dog', p. 21.

CASA SUSANNA (pp. 58–69)

1   Isabelle Bonnet, 'Les Photographies des travestis de la Casa Susanna', unpublished thesis, Université Paris 1 Panthéon-Sorbonne, Paris, 2015.

2   Virginia Prince, 'Wonderful Weekend', *Transvestia*, 12 (December 1961), pp. 14–17.

3   Katherine Cummings, *Katherine's Diary: The Story of a Transsexual* (North Charleston, NC: BookSurge Publishing, 2008), p. 155.

4   For a full examination of *Transvestia* and how it reflected the cultures of cross-dressing, see Robert S. Hill, 'As a Man I Exist; as a Woman I Live: Heterosexual Transvestism and the Contours of Gender and Sexuality in Postwar America', unpublished thesis, University of Michigan (2007), available at https://deepblue.lib.umich.edu/documents. Hill discusses the role of photographs from pp. 209 to 228.

5   Virginia Prince, 'The Life and Times of Virginia', *Transvestia*, 100 (1979), pp. 5–120.

6   See Sophie Hackett, 'Casa Susanna: Social Space', in Sophie Hackett and Jim Shedden, eds, *Outsiders: American Photography and Film, 1950s–1980s* (Toronto and New York: Art Gallery of Ontario and Skira Rizzoli, 2016), pp. 18–19, and Sophie Hackett, *What It Means to Be Seen: Photography and Queer Visibility*, exh. cat., Ryerson Image Centre (Toronto, 2014), pp. 9–23.

7   Hill, 'As a Man I Exist', p. 216.

8   Ibid., p. 382.

DANNY LYON (pp. 70–81)

1   Susan Meiselas, 'Danny Lyon', *BOMB*, 120 (Summer 2012), p. 128.

2   Danny Lyon, quoted in Tom Seymour, 'Danny Lyon: Soul of a Radical', www.bjp-online.com, 17 June 2016.

3   Danny Lyon, 'Introduction', in *The Bikeriders* (New York: Aperture, 2014), p. vii.

4   Ibid.

5   Hunter S. Thompson, 'Letter to Danny Lyon', 11 October 1966, www.phaidon.com/resource/lyon-p166.jpg, accessed 29 November 2017.

6   Sean O'Hagan, 'Danny Lyon's Inside Shots', *Observer*, 20 April 2014, www.theguardian.com.

7   James Agee, 'Preface', in James Agee and Walker Evans, *Let Us Now Praise Famous Men*, (Cambridge, MA: Riverside Press, 1960), pp. xiv–xvi.

8   Ibid.

9   Meiselas, 'Danny Lyon', p. 129.

LARRY CLARK (pp. 82–95)

1   Ralph Gibson, 'Larry Clark', *Interview Magazine*, 9 November 2010, available at www.interviewmagazine.com.
2   Larry Clark, in 'Conversations on Art with Larry Clark, Ryan McGinley, and Sylvia Wolf', Whitney Museum of American Art, public talk, 25 March 2003, transcript available at www.ryanmcginley.com.
3   Andy Grundberg, 'Subject and Style Prospects for a New Documentary', in *Crisis of the Real: Writings on Photography since 1974* (New York: Aperture, 1999), pp. 196–98.
4   'i was born in tulsa oklahoma in 1943. when i was sixteen i started shooting amphetamine. i shot with my friends everyday for three years and then left town but i've gone back through the years. once the needle goes in it never comes out. L.C'. Larry Clark, 'Preface', in *Tulsa* (New York: Lustrum, 1971), n.p.
5   Clark, in 'Conversations on Art'.
6   Larry Clark in *Darkroom*, ed. Eleanor Lewis (New York: Lustrum, 1977), p. 44.
7   Elvis Presley, 'Heartbreak Hotel', written by Tommy Durden and Mae Boren Axton (RCA Victor, 1956).

SEIJI KURATA (pp. 96–109)

1   Kurata's Ikebukuro photographs were first published as 'Kinsha: Ikebukuro Nights', in *Workshop*, 8 (1976). They were first exhibited at the Ginza Nikon Salon, Tokyo, in 1979. For his own more recent account see '1975 The City, at Summer's End', in Seiji Kurata, *Flash Up*, new edn (Tokyo: Zen Foto Gallery, 2013), n.p.
2   David E. Kaplan and Alec Dubro, *Yakuza: Japan's Criminal Underworld* (Los Angeles, CA: University of California Press, 2012).
3   Seiji Kurata, 'Camp Story Playback' (1989), reprinted in Ivan Vartanian, Akihiro Hatanaka and Yutaka Kambayashi, eds, *Setting Sun: Writings by Japanese Photographers* (New York: Aperture, 2006), p. 40.
4   In the largely male psychodrama that is Japanese photography of the late 1960s and 1970s, *Flash Up* is arguably its most masochistic text. For a reading of the psychoanalytic mechanisms involved here, see Slavoj Žižek, *The Ticklish Subject: The Absent Centre of Political Ontology* (London: Verso, 1999), pp. 369–77.
5   For a compelling ethnographic analysis of one of the more exclusive hostess clubs in Tokyo in the early 1980s see Anne Allison, *Nightwork: Sexuality, Pleasure, and Corporate Masculinity in a Tokyo Hostess Club* (Chicago, IL: University of Chicago Press, 1994).
6   Kurata, '1975 The City, at Summer's End', n.p.

IGOR PALMIN (pp. 110–123)

1   Sources: interview with Igor Palmin, 4 April 2017; interview with Sergei Bol'shakov, 8 March 2012; correspondence with Igor Tyshler, November 2017.

WALTER PFEIFFER (pp. 124–135)

1   Susan Sontag, 'Introduction', in *Peter Hujar, Portraits in Life and Death* (New York: Da Capo, 1976).
2   All subsequent quotations are from Walter Pfeiffer, interview with the author, Zurich, 22 February 2017.

CHRIS STEELE-PERKINS (pp. 136–147)

1   John Berger, 'Understanding a Photograph' [1968], in *The Look of Things* (New York: Viking, 1974), p. 180.
2   Chris Steele-Perkins and Richard Smith, *The Teds* [1979] (Stockport: Dewi Lewis, 2016), p. 7.
3   Laura Havlin, 'The Teds: Chris Steele-Perkins', www.magnumphotos.com, 21 September 2016.

PHILIPPE CHANCEL (pp. 148–159)

1   Cited in Nick Tosches, *Country: The Twisted Roots of Rock 'n' Roll* (Boston, MA: Da Capo, 1996), p. 58.
2   Philippe Chancel, cited in press release for the exhibition *Philippe Chancel: Rebel's Paris 1982*, Galerie Melanie Rio, Paris, 2016, available at www.rgalerie.com.
3   Ibid.
4   Gilles Elie Cohen, Amsterdam, 2014, cited in press release for the exhibition *Gilles Elie Cohen: Vikings and Panthers*, Addict Galerie, Paris, 2015, available at www.addictgalerie.com.

PAZ ERRÁZURIZ (pp. 160–173)

1   Paz Errázuriz in Miriam Rosen, 'Chile, 1973–2013, Conversations with Photographers 3', https://blogs.mediapart.fr, 25 September 2013.
2   Ibid.
3   Paz Errázuriz, in Ellie Howard, 'How One Woman Used Her Camera to Defy a Dictatorship', www.dazeddigital.com, 13 July 2017.
4   Quoted in Paz Errázuriz and Claudio Donoso, *La manzana de Adan / Adam's Apple* (Santiago de Chile: Zona, 1990), p. 91.

MARY ELLEN MARK (pp. 174–183)

1   Susan Sontag, *On Photography* (New York: Farrar, Straus & Giroux, 1977), p. 41.
2   Abigail Solomon-Godeau, 'Inside/Out', in *Public Information: Desire, Disaster, Document*, exh. cat., San Francisco Museum of Modern Art (San Francisco, CA, 1994), pp. 49–62.
3   Janis Bultman, 'Street Shooter: An Interview with Mary Ellen Mark', www.americansuburbx.com, 23 May 2010, originally published in *Darkroom Photography* (January–February 1987).
4   Susan Sontag, *Regarding the Pain of Others* (London: Hamish Hamilton, 2003), p. 72.

BORIS MIKHAILOV (pp. 194–201)

1   Boris Groys, *Boris Mikhailov: The Eroticism of Imperfection* (Moscow, 2015), p. 50.

PIETER HUGO (pp. 226–231)

1   Pieter Hugo, in Sean O'Hagan, 'Africa as You've Never Seen It', *Guardian*, 20 July 2008, available at www.theguardian.com.
2   Pieter Hugo, *The Hyena and Other Men* (Munich: Prestel, 2007), p. 7.
3   Hugo, in O'Hagan, 'Africa as You've Never Seen It'.
4   Ibid.
5   Ibid.

KATY GRANNAN (pp. 232–245)

1   Diane Di Prima, 'Revolutionary Letter #1', in *Revolutionary Letters* (San Francisco, CA: Last Gasp, 2007), p. 7.
2   Katy Grannan, *Model American* (New York: Aperture, 2005).
3   Katy Grannan, *The Westerns* (San Francisco, CA, and New York: Fraenkel Gallery, Greenberg Van Doren Gallery and Salon 94 Freemans, 2007).
4   Katy Grannan, *Boulevard* (San Francisco, CA: Fraenkel Gallery, and New York: Greenberg Van Doren Gallery and Salon 94 Freemans, 2011).
5   Katy Grannan, 'Foreword', in *Boulevard*, n.p.
6   Katy Grannan, The *Ninety Nine and The Nine* (San Francisco, CA: Fraenkel Gallery, and New York: Salon 94, 2011); *The Nine*, dir. Katy Grannan (2016), www.theninefilm.com, accessed 6 October 2017.
7   William Carlos Williams, 'Book I', in *Paterson* (New York: New Directions, 1963), p. 14.

TERESA MARGOLLES (pp. 246-256)

1   An ongoing project, it was shown as part of Manifesta 11 (Zurich, 2016), where Margolles dealt with the brutal murder in 2015 of one of the transgender workers featured in the work.
2   An acronym derived from Servicio Médico Forense (Forensic Medical Service).
3   See *Semefo: Lavatio Corporis*, exh. cat., Museo de Arte Contemporaneo Alvar y Carmen T. de Carrillo Gil (Mexico City, 1994).
4   Teresa Margolles, *Muerte sin fin*, April–August 2004, Museum für Moderne Kunst, Frankfurt.
5   The Biennale ran from June to November 2009; Margolles's project was curated by Cuauhtémoc Medina.
6   *Lengua* was also exhibited at the 2nd Auckland Triennial, *Public/Private, Tumatanui/Tumataiti*, in 2004.
7   Cuauhtémoc Medina, 'Zones of Tolerance: Teresa Margolles, Semefo and Beyond', *Parachute*, 104 (2001), pp. 31–52.
8   The mysterious circumstances under which the murders have been committed have given rise to much speculation. For an account of the issues see Katherine Pantaleo, 'Gendered Violence: An Analysis of the Maquiladora Murders', *International Criminal Justice Review*, 20/4 (November 2010), pp. 349–65.

SELECTED BIBLIOGRAPHY

GENERAL READING

Alcoff, Linda Martín, 'The Problem of Speaking for Others', *Cultural Critique*, 20 (Winter 1991–92), pp. 5–32

Azoulay, Ariella, *The Civil Contract of Photography* (New York: Zone, 2008)

Barthes, Roland, *Camera Lucida*, trans. Richard Howard (New York: Hill & Wang, 1980)

Berger, John, and Jean Mohr, *Another Way of Telling: A Possible Theory of Photography* (New York: Pantheon, 1982)

Dufour, Diane, et al., eds, *Provoke: Between Protest and Performance: Photography in Japan 1960/1975* (Göttingen: Steidl, 2016)

Edwards, Elizabeth, *Anthropology and Photography, 1860–1920* (New Haven, CT: Yale University Press, 1992)

Foster, Hal, 'The Artist as Ethnographer?', in Hal Foster, *The Return of the Real: Art and Theory at the End of the Century* (Cambridge, MA: MIT Press, 1996)

Garner, Gretchen, *Disappearing Witness: Change in Twentieth-century American Photography* (Baltimore, MD: Johns Hopkins University Press, 2003)

Kozloff, Max, *The Privileged Eye: Essays on Photography* (Albuquerque, NM: University of New Mexico Press, 1987)

Nicholas, Jane, 'A Debt to the Dead? Ethics, Photography, History, and the Study of Freakery', *Histoire sociale / Social History*, 47/93 (May 2014), pp. 139–55

Pinney, Christopher, *Photography and Anthropology* (London: Reaktion, 2011)

Rosler, Martha, 'In, Around, and Afterthoughts (on Documentary Photography)', in *The Context of Meaning: Critical Histories of Photography*, ed. Richard Bolton (Cambridge, MA: MIT Press, 1981), pp. 303–25

Solomon-Godeau, Abigail, 'Inside/Out', in *Public Information: Desire, Disaster, Document*, exh. cat., San Francisco Museum of Modern Art (San Francisco, CA, 1994), pp. 49–62

Sontag, Susan, *On Photography* (New York: Farrar, Straus & Giroux, 1977)

—, *Regarding the Pain of Others* (New York: Farrar, Straus & Giroux, 2003)

Tagg, John, *The Burden of Representation: Essays on Photographies and Histories* (Amherst, MA: University of Massachusetts Press, 1988)

DIANE ARBUS

Diane Arbus, *Diane Arbus*, ed. Doon Arbus and Marvin Israel (Millerton, NY: Aperture, 1972)

—, *Diane Arbus: Magazine Work*, ed. Marvin Israel and Doon Arbus, essay by Thomas W. Southall (Millerton, NY: Aperture, 1984)

—, *Diane Arbus: Revelations*, essays by Sandra S. Phillips et al. (New York: Random House, 2003)

Arbus, Doon, and Yolanda Cuomo, eds, *Diane Arbus: Untitled* (New York: Aperture, 1995)

Diane Arbus: The Libraries, exh. cat., Fraenkel Gallery (San Francisco, CA, 2004)

Gibson, Gregory, *Hubert's Freaks: The Rare-Book Dealer, the Times Square Talker, and the Lost Photos of Diane Arbus* (San Diego, CA: Harcourt, 2008)

Lee, Anthony W., and John Pultz, eds, *Diane Arbus: Family Albums* (New Haven, CT: Yale University Press, 2003)

Nemerov, Alexander, *Silent Dialogues: Diane Arbus and Howard Nemerov* (San Francisco, CA: Fraenkel Gallery, 2015)

Rosenheim, Jeff L., and Karan Rinaldo, *Diane Arbus: In the Beginning*, exh. cat., Metropolitan Museum of Art (New York, 2016)

Rubinfien, Leo, 'Where Diane Arbus Went', *Art in America* (October 2005), pp. 65–77

Sussman, Elizabeth, and Doon Arbus, *Diane Arbus: A Chronology, 1923–1971* (New York: Aperture, 2011)

CASA SUSANNA

Biegel, Hugo G., 'A Weekend in Alice's Wonderland', *Journal of Sex Research*, 5/2 (May 1969), pp. 108–22

Hurst, Michel, and Robert Swope, eds, *Casa Susanna* (New York: PowerHouse, 2005)

Transvestia [magazine], ed. Virginia Prince, Los Angeles, 1960–80

PHILIPPE CHANCEL

Chancel, Philippe, *Arirang, Corée du Nord: le plus grand spectacle du monde* (Lausanne: Favre, 2008)

—, *Datazone in Progress*, exh. cat., Jeu de Paume (Paris, 2012)

—, *Desert Spirit* (Paris: Xavier Barral, 2010)

—, *DPRK*, texts by Michel Poivert and Jonathan Fenby (London: Thames & Hudson, 2006)

—, *Workers Emirates* (Suresnes: Bernard Chauveau, 2011)

LARRY CLARK

Another Day in Paradise, dir. Larry Clark (USA: Trimark Pictures, 1998)

Bully, dir. Larry Clark (USA: Blacklist Films, 2001)

Clark, Larry, *1992* (New York: Thea Westreich, and Cologne: Gisela Capitain, 1993)

—, *Kiss the Past Hello*, texts by Dominique Baqué et al., exh. cat., Luhring Augustine and Simon Lee Gallery (New York and London, 2010)

—, *The Perfect Childhood* (Zurich: Scalo, 1993)

—, *Tulsa* (New York: Lustrum, 1971)

—, *Teenage Lust* (self-published, 1981)

Ken Park, dir. Larry Clark (USA: Kasander Film Company, 2002)

Kids, dir. Larry Clark (USA: Independent Pictures, 1995)

Van Sant, Gus, 'Larry Clark, Shockmaker', *Interview*, July 1995, pp. 42–45

BRUCE DAVIDSON

Cotton, Charlotte, 'Bruce Davidson: An Interview by Charlotte Cotton', *Aperture*, 220 (Autumn 2015), pp. 94–107

Davidson, Bruce, *Brooklyn Gang: Summer 1959* (Santa Fe, NM: Twin Palms, 1998)

—, *Central Park*, preface by Elizabeth Barlow Rogers, commentary by Marie Winn (New York: Aperture, 1995)

—, *Circus* (Göttingen: Steidl, 2007)

—, 'The Clown', *Esquire*, January 1960, pp. 71–75

—, *East 100th Street* (Cambridge, MA: Harvard University Press, 1970)

—, *England / Scotland 1960*, introduction by Alan Sillitoe (Göttingen: Steidl, 2004)

—, *Subsistence USA*, text by Carol Hill (New York: Holt, Rinehart & Winston, 1973)

—, *Subway*, afterword by Henry Geldzahler (New York: Aperture, 1986)

—, *Survey*, essays by Charlotte Cotton et al., exh. cat., Fundación Mapfre, Madrid (New York: Aperture, 2016)

—, *Time of Change: Civil Rights Photographs, 1961–1965*, foreword by John Lewis, introduction by Deborah Willis (West Hollywood, CA: St Ann's Press, 2002)

Mailer, Norman, and Bruce Davidson, 'Brooklyn Minority Report: An Inside View of the Aspirations of Embattled Youth', *Esquire*, June 1960, pp. 129–37

Tom, Patricia Vettel, 'Bad Boys: Bruce Davidson's Gang Photographs and Outlaw Masculinity', *Art Journal*, 56/2 (Summer 1997), pp. 69–74

PAZ ERRÁZURIZ

Errázuriz, Paz, *Amalia: historia de una gallina, fotolibro infantil* (Santiago: Lord Cochrane, 1973)

—, 'Forbidden Chile', *Independent Magazine*, 21 November 1990, pp. 46–52

—, *Kawesqar, los hijos de la mujer sol* (Santiago: LOM, 2003)

—, *Survey*, essays by Juan Vicente Aliaga, Gerardo Mosquera and Paulina Varas, exh. cat., Fundación Mapfre, Madrid (New York: Aperture, 2016)

—, and Claudia Donoso, *La manzana de Adán* (Santiago: Zona, 1989)

—, and Diamela Eltit, *El infarto del alma* (Santiago: Francisco Zegers, 1994)

Richard, Nelly, ed., *Poéticas de la disidencia / Poetics of Dissent: Paz Errázuriz, Lotty Rosenfeld*, essays by Diamela Eltit and Andrea Giunta (Barcelona: Ediciones Polígrafa, 2016)

JIM GOLDBERG

Goldberg, Jim, *134 Ways to Forget* (Kamakura: Super Labo, 2011)
—, *It Ended Sad, but I Love Where It Began* (Oakland, CA: These Birds Walk, 2007)
—, *The Last Son* (Kamakura: Super Labo, 2016)
—, *Open See*, texts by Amara Lakhous (Göttingen: Steidl, 2009)
—, *Polaroids from Haiti* (Paso Robles, CA: Nazraeli, 2013)
—, 'Raised by Wolves: Photographs and Documents of Runaways', *BOMB*, 53 (Autumn 1995), pp. 8–11
—, *Rich and Poor* (New York: Random House, 1985)
—, *Ruby Every Fall* (Paso Robles, CA: Nazraeli, 2016)
—, and Philip Brookman, *Raised by Wolves: Photographs and Documents of Runaways* (Zurich: Scalo, 1995)
—, and Donovan Wylie, *Candy/A Good and Spacious Land*, introduction by Pamela Franks, essays by Christopher Klatell and Laura Wexler (New Haven, CT: Yale University Press, 2017)

KATY GRANNAN

Curcio, Seth, 'The Forgotten', *British Journal of Photography*, 161/7823 (Spring 2014), pp. 24–33, available at www.bjp-online.com
Grannan, Katy, *Boulevard*, exh. cat., (San Francisco, CA: Fraenkel Gallery, and New York: Salon 94, 2011)
—, *Dream America*, text by Jeanne Greenberg Rohatyn, exh. cat., Lawrence Rubin Greenberg Van Doren Fine Art (New York, 2000)
—, *Lion King* (Paso Robles, CA: Nazraeli, 2015)
—, *Model American*, text by Jan Avgikos (New York: Aperture, 2005)
—, *The Ninety Nine and The Nine*, exh. cat., (San Francisco, CA: Fraenkel Gallery, and New York: Salon 94, 2014)
—, *The Westerns* (San Francisco, CA: Fraenkel Gallery, 2007)
—, and Hannah Hughes, *The Glint of Light on Broken Glass* (Paso Robles, CA: Nazraeli, 2016)
Miller, Sarah M., 'Katy Grannan: Central Valley', *Aperture*, 226 (Spring 2017), pp. 80–89
The Nine, dir. Katy Grannan (USA: John McNeil Studio, 2016)

PIETER HUGO

Demos, T. J., 'A Postcolonial Monstrum: The Photographs of Pieter Hugo', in T. J. Demos, *Return to the Postcolony: Specters of Colonialism in Contemporary Art* (Berlin: Sternberg, 2013), pp. 125–54
Hugo, Pieter, *The Hyena and Other Men*, text by Adetokunbo Abiola (Munich: Prestel, 2007)
—, *Messina/Musina*, short story by Stacy Hardy, interview by Joanna Lehan (Rome: Punctum, 2007)
—, *Nollywood*, texts by Chris Abani, Stacy Hardy and Zina Saro-Wiwa (Munich: Prestel, 2009)
—, *Permanent Error*, texts by Federica Angelucci and Jim Puckett (Munich: Prestel, 2011)
—, and Linda Melvern, *Rwanda 2004: Vestiges of a Genocide* (London: Oodee, 2011)
Law-viljoen, Bronwyn, 'Pieter Hugo: The Critical Zone of Engagement', *Aperture*, 186 (Spring 2007), pp. 20–29

SEIJI KURATA

Kurata, Seiji, *80s Family* (Tokyo: JICC, 1991)
—, *Flash Up* (Tokyo: Byakuya Shobo, 1980)
—, *Dai-Ajia* (Great Asia) (Tokyo: IPC, 1990)
—, *Japan* (Tokyo: Shinchosha, 1998)
—, *Foto Kyabare* (Photo Cabaret) (Tokyo: Byakuya Shobo, 1983)
—, *Kuesuto fo Erosu* (Quest for Eros) (Tokyo: Shinchosha, 1998)
—, 'Seiji Kurata Works', *Workshop*, 8 (1976)
—, *Toransu-Ajia* (Trans-Asia) (Tokyo: Ōta, 1995)

DANNY LYON

Cox, Julian, ed., *Danny Lyon: Message to the Future*, exh. cat., Fine Arts Museums of San Francisco et al. (New Haven, CT: Yale University Press, 2016)
Llanito, dir. Danny Lyon (USA: Black Beauty Video, 1971)
Los Niños Abandonados, dir. Danny Lyon (USA: Black Beauty Video, 1975)
Lyon, Danny, *The Bikeriders* (New York: Macmillan, 1968)
—, *Conversations with the Dead: Photographs of Prison Life with the Letters and Drawings of Billy McCune #122054* (New York: Henry Holt & Co., 1971)
—, *Deep Sea Diver: An American Photographer's Journey in Shanxi, China* (London: Phaidon, 2011)
—, *The Destruction of Lower Manhattan* (New York: Macmillan, 1969)
—, *Indian Nations: Pictures of American Indian Reservations in the Western United States*, introduction by Larry McMurtry (Santa Fe, NM: Twin Palms, 2002)
—, *Knave of Hearts* (Santa Fe, NM: Twin Palms, 1999)
—, *Like a Thief's Dream* (New York: PowerHouse, 2007)
—, *Memories of Myself* (London: Phaidon, 2009)
—, *Memories of the Southern Civil Rights Movement*, foreword by Julian Bond (Chapel Hill, NC: University of North Carolina Press, 1992)
—, *Pictures from the New World* (New York: Aperture, 1981)
Meiselas, Susan, 'Danny Lyon by Susan Meiselas', *BOMB*, 120 (Summer 2012), pp. 124–33
Seymour, Tom, 'Danny Lyon: Soul of a Radical', *British Journal of Photography*, 161/7830 (November 2014), pp. 42–48
Willie, dir. Danny Lyon (USA: Black Beauty Video, 1985)

TERESA MARGOLLES

Margolles, Teresa, *127 cuerpos*, texts by Patrizia Dander, Hans-Georg Lohe and Heriberto Yépez, exh. cat., Kunstverein für die Rheinlande und Westfalen (Düsseldorf, 2006)
—, *Frontera*, ed. Rein Wolfs and Letizia Ragaglia, texts by Alpha Escobedo et al. (Cologne: Walther König, 2011)
—, *Muerte sin fin*, texts by Klaus Görner and Udo Kittelmann, exh. cat., MMK (Frankfurt, 2004)
—, *Mundos*, texts by John Zeppetelli et al., exh. cat., Musée d'Art Contemporain de Montréal (Montreal, 2017)
—, *La Promesa*, ed. Ana Laura Cué Vega and Carlos Noriega Jiménez, texts by Graciela de la Torre et al., exh. cat., Universidad Nacional Autónoma de México and Museo Universitario Arte Contemporáneo (Mexico City, 2012)
—, *Sonidos de la muerte*, texts by Veronica Corchado Espinoza, exh. cat., Museo de Arte Contemporaneo de Vigo (Vigo, 2008)
—, *Teresa Margolles: We Have a Common Thread*, ed. Patrice Giasson, exh. cat., Neuberger Museum of Art and State University of New York (New York, 2015)
—, *El Testigo*, texts by Ferran Barenblit et al., exh. cat., Centro de Arte Dos de Mayo (Madrid, 2014)
—, *What Else Could We Talk About?*, texts by Cuauhtémoc Medina et al. (Barcelona: RM, 2009)

MARY ELLEN MARK

Frame, Allen, and Mary Ellen Mark, 'Mary Ellen Mark', *BOMB*, 28 (Summer 1989), pp. 44–49
Harris, Melissa, 'Mary Ellen Mark on her Photographs of Children', *Aperture*, 146 (Winter 1997), pp. 42–51
McCall, Cheryl, 'Streets of the Lost: Runaway Kids Eke Out a Mean Life in Seattle' *Life*, July 1983, pp. 35–42
Mark, Mary Ellen, *American Odyssey*, poems by Maya Angelou and La Shawndrea (New York: Aperture, 1999)
—, *A Cry for Help: Stories of Homelessness and Hope*, interviews by Victoria Kohn (New York: Simon & Schuster, 1996)
—, *Falkland Road: Prostitutes of Bombay* (New York: Alfred A. Knopf, 1981)
—, *Indian Circus*, foreword by John Irving (San Francisco, CA: Chronicle, 1993)
—, *Man and Beast: Photographs from Mexico and India* (Austin, TX: University of Texas Press, 2014)
—, *Mary Ellen Mark on the Portrait*

and the Moment, introduction by Laurie Rae Baxter (New York: Aperture, 2015)

—, Passport, interview by Eleanor Lewis (New York: Lustrum, 1974)

—, Photographs of Mother Teresa's Missions of Charity in Calcutta, introduction by David Featherstone (Carmel, CA: Friends of Photography, 1985)

—, Streetwise, foreword by Jerry Esterly, introduction by John Irving (Philadelphia, PA: University of Pennsylvania Press, 1988)

—, Tiny: Streetwise Revisited, prologue by Isabel Allende, text by John Irving and Mary Ellen Mark (New York: Aperture, 2015)

—, Twins (New York: Aperture, 2003)

—, Ward 81, introduction by Milos Forman, text by Karen Folger Jacobs (New York: Simon & Schuster, 1979)

—, and Martin Bell, 'Tiny to Erin: Photographs by Mary Ellen Mark, Interview Mary Ellen Mark and Martin Bell', Aperture, 181 (Winter 2005), pp. 24–35

Streetwise, dir. Martin Bell (USA: Bear Creek, 1984)

BORIS MIKHAILOV

Urs Stahel et al., Boris Mikhailov: A Retrospective, exh. cat., Fotomuseum Winterthur (Zurich: Scalo, 2003)

Mikhailov, Boris, Boris Mikhailov: Time Is Out of Joint, essays by Thomas Köhler et al., exh. cat., Berlinische Galerie (Berlin, 2012)

—, Case History, conversation between Ilya Kabakov and Victor Tupitsyn (Zurich: Scalo, 1999)

—, Diary, essay by Francesco Zanot (Cologne: Walther König, and Turin: Camera, Centro Italiano per La Fotografia, 2015)

—, Salt Lake, text by Friedrich Meschede (Göttingen: Steidl, 2002)

—, Tea, Coffee, Cappuccino (Cologne: Walther König, 2011)

—, Unfinished Dissertation or Discussions with Oneself, essay by Margarita Tupitsyn (Zurich: Scalo, 1999)

—, The Wedding (London: Mörel, 2010)

—, Yesterday's Sandwich (London: Phaidon, 2006)

—, and Viktor Misiano, 'Boris Mikhailov', Aperture, 220 (2015), pp. 36–49

Petrovsky, Helen, 'The Wedding', Foam, 30 (Spring 2012), pp. 181–88

Tupitsyn, Victor, 'Boris Mikhailov', Third Text, 25/3 (May 2011), pp. 291–300

DAIDŌ MORIYAMA

Moriyama, Daidō, The Complete Works, vol. 1, texts by Gerard Malanga et al. (Tokyo: Daiwa Radiator Factory, 2003)

—, The Complete Works, vol. 2, texts by Midori Matsui et al. (Tokyo: Daiwa Radiator Factory, 2004)

—, The Complete Works, vol. 3, texts by Charles Merewether et al. (Tokyo: Daiwa Radiator Factory, 2004)

—, The Complete Works, vol. 4, interviews by Takeshi Kitano and Etsuro Ishiharaby and Minoru Shimizu (Tokyo: Daiwa Radiator Factory, 2004)

—, Shashin yo sayonara (Farewell Photography) (Tokyo: Shashin Hyoronsha, 1972)

—, Karyūdo (Hunter) (Tokyo: Chuokoron-sha, 1972)

—, Nippon gekijō shashincho (Japan: A Photo Theatre), text by Shūji Terayama (Tokyo: Muromachi Shobo, 1968)

—, Zoku nippon gekijo shashincho (Japan: A Photo Theatre II) (Tokyo: Asahi Sonorama, 1978)

—, Labyrinth (Tokyo: Akio Nagasawa, and New York: Aperture, 2012)

—, Hikari to kage (Light and Shadow) (Tokyo: Tojusha, 1982)

—, Inu no kioku (Places in My Memory: Memories of a Dog) (Tokyo: Asahi Shinbunsha, 1984)

—, Platform, text by Minoru Shimizu (Tokyo: Daiwa Radiator Factory and Taka Ishii Gallery, 2002)

—, Scandalous (Tokyo: Akio Nagasawa, 2016)

—, Shinjuku (Tokyo: Getsuyosha, 2002)

—, Stray Dog, texts by Sandra S. Phillips and Alexandra Munroe, exh. cat., San Francisco Museum of Modern Art (San Francisco, CA, 1999)

—, Tales of Tono (Tokyo: Asahi Sonorama, 1976)

Schifferli, Christoph, ed., The Japanese Box (Göttingen: Steidl, 2001)

IGOR PALMIN

Fürst, Juliane, Flowers through Concrete: Explorations in the Soviet Hippieland (Oxford: Oxford University Press, 2018)

Palmin, Igor, Past Perfect, texts by Igor Palmin and Faina Balakhovskaya, interview by Vasilisa Solovyeva (Moscow: Ekaterina Cultural Foundation, 2011)

WALTER PFEIFFER

Ammann, Jean-Christophe, and Marianne Eigenheer, eds, Transformer: Aspekte der Travestie, essays by Patrick Eudeline et al., exh. cat., Kunstmuseum Luzern (Lucerne, 1974)

Nickas, Bob, 'Camera Libido: The Photography of Walter Pfeiffer', Artforum International, 41/10 (Summer 2003), pp. 170–75

O'Neill, Alistair, 'The Cult of Walter Pfeiffer', Aperture, 228 (Autumn 2017), pp. 85–94

Pfeiffer, Walter, Das Auge, die Gedanken, unentwegt wandernd, texts by Jean-François Ammann and Patrick Frey (Zurich: Patrick Frey, 1986)

—, Cherchez la femme!, texts by Martin Jaeggi and Michelle Nicol (Zurich: Patrick Frey, 2007)

—, In Love with Beauty, ed. Martin Jaeggi, Thomas Seelig and Urs Stahel, exh. cat., Fotomuseum Winterthur (Göttingen: Steidl, 2009)

—, Night and Day, ed. Markus Bosshard et al., texts by Christoph Doswald and Dorothea Strauss (Berlin: Hatje Cantz, 2007)

—, Scrapbooks, 1969–1985, ed. Martin Jaeggi (Zurich: Patrick Frey, 2012)

—, Walter Pfeiffer, 1970–1980, texts by Gerhard Johann Lischka (Frankfurt: Elke Betzel, 1980)

—, Welcome Aboard! Photographs, 1980–2000, texts by Martin Jaeggi (Zurich: Patrick Frey, 2001)

DAYANITA SINGH

Dhar, Jyoti, 'The Architecture of a Conversation: Dayanita Singh', ArtAsiaPacific, 87 (Spring 2014), pp. 68–77

Gaensheimer, Susanne, ed., La Biennale di Venezia, German Pavilion 2013: Ai Weiwei, Romuald Karmakar, Santu Mofokeng, Dayanita Singh, texts by Geoff Dyer et al., exh. cat. (Berlin, 2013)

Singh, Dayanita, Blue Book (Göttingen: Steidel, 2009)

—, Chairs, exh. cat., Isabella Stewart Gardner Museum, Boston (Göttingen: Steidl, 2005)

—, 'Dayanita Singh', Aperture, 154 (Winter 1999), pp. 12–19

—, Dream Villa (Göttingen: Steidl, 2010)

—, File Room, texts by Aveek Sen, interview by Hans Ulrich Obrist (Göttingen: Steidl, 2013)

—, Go Away Closer, texts by Geoff Dyer et al. (Göttingen: Steidl, 2007)

—, House of Love, texts by Aveek Sen (Cambridge, MA: Peabody Museum of Archaeology and Ethnology, and Santa Fe, NM: Radius Books, 2011)

—, Museum Bhavan, interviews by Aveek Sen and Gerhard Steidl (Göttingen: Steidl, 2017)

—, Museum of Chance, texts by Aveek Sen (Göttingen: Steidl, 2015)

—, Myself Mona Ahmed (Zurich: Scalo, 2001)

—, Privacy, texts by Dayanita Singh and Britta Schmitz (Göttingen: Steidl, 2004)

—, Sent a Letter (Göttingen: Steidl, 2008)

—, Zakir Hussain (Mumbai: Himalayan Books, 1986)

ALEC SOTH

Engberg, Siri, ed., From Here to There: Alec Soth's America, texts by Geoff Dyer et al., exh. cat., Walker Art Center (Minneapolis, MN, 2010)

Somewhere to Disappear, dir. Laure Flammarion and Arnaud Uyttenhove (Paris: MAS Films, 2010)

Soth, Alec, Gathered Leaves, essays by Aaron Schuman and Kate Bush (London: MACK, 2015)

—, *House of Coates*, text by Brad Zellar (St Paul, MN: Little Brown Mushroom, 2012)

—, *Niagara*, essays by Philip Brookman and Richard Ford (Göttingen: Steidl, 2006)

—, *Sleeping by the Mississippi*, texts by Patricia Hampl and Anne Wilkes Tucker (Göttingen: Steidl, 2004)

—, *Songbook* (London: MACK, 2015)

—, and Lester B. Morrison, *Broken Manual* (Göttingen: Steidl, 2010)

—, and Francesco Zanot, *Ping Pong Conversations* (Rome: Contrasto, 2013)

CHRIS STEELE-PERKINS

Steele-Perkins, Chris, *Afghanistan*, texts by André Velter and Sayd Bahodine Majrouh (London: Westzone, 2001)

—, *England, My England: A Photographer's Portrait* (Sleaford, Lincs: McNidder & Grace, 2009)

—, *Fuji: Images of Contemporary Japan* (New York: Umbrage, 2002)

—, *Northern Exposures: Rural Life in the North East*, introduction by William Varley (Newcastle upon Tyne: Northumbria University Press, 2007)

—, *The Pleasure Principle* (Manchester: Cornerhouse, 1989)

—, and Richard Smith, *The Teds* (London: Travelling Light/Exit, 1979)

CONTRIBUTORS

ORIANA BADDELEY is Dean of Research at University of the Arts London, where she is also a member of the Research Centre for Transnational Art, Identity and Nation. She has written extensively on contemporary Latin American art, including *Drawing the Line: Art and Cultural Identity in Contemporary Latin America* (co-authored with Valerie Fraser, Verso, 1989), and collaborated with Gerardo Mosquera to produce *Beyond the Fantastic: Art Criticism from Contemporary Latin America* (inIVA/MIT Press, 1996). With Toshio Watanabe and Partha Mitter she worked on the major AHRC-funded project 'Nation, Identity and Modernity: Visual Culture of India, Japan and Mexico, 1860s–1940' (2001–04).

DAVID CAMPANY is a writer, curator and artist. His books include *The Open Road: Photographic Road Trips in America* (Aperture, 2014), *Walker Evans: The Magazine Work* (Steidl, 2014), *Jeff Wall: Picture for Women* (Afterall/MIT Press, 2011) and *Photography and Cinema* (Reaktion, 2008). Recent curatorial projects include *A Handful of Dust* (various venues, 2015–19) and *Still Point of the Turning World: Between Film and Photography* (FoMu, Antwerp, 2017). He teaches at the University of Westminster, London.

TIM CLARK is a curator, writer and editor. Since 2008 he has been Editor-in-Chief at *1000 Words*. Previously he was Associate Curator at Media Space, Science Museum, London, where he worked on exhibitions including *Julia Margaret Cameron: Influence and Intimacy* (2015) and *Gathered Leaves: Photographs by Alec Soth* (2015–18). He has also organised exhibitions independently, most recently *Peter Watkins: The Unforgetting* (Webber Gallery, London, 2017) and *Rebecoming: The Other European Travellers* (Flowers Gallery, London, 2014). He co-curated Photo Oxford 2017, comprising presentations by Edgar Martins, Mariken Wessels and Martin Parr, and Sergei Vasiliev and Arkady Bronnikov from the Russian Criminal Tattoo Archive. He is also a visiting lecturer on the MA in Photography at the Nuova Accademia di Belle Arti, Milan.

LUCY DAVIES writes about art and photography for *The Telegraph*, where she is a Commissioning Editor. She has written widely on photography and art for numerous books, journals and magazines.

DUNCAN FORBES is a Researcher at the Getty Research Institute, Los Angeles, and Visiting Research Fellow at the Institute for Modern and Contemporary Culture, University of Westminster, London. His publications include *Provoke: Between Protest and Performance, Photography in Japan 1960/1975* (Steidl, 2016).

JULIANE FÜRST is Reader in Modern History at the University of Bristol. She has been researching questions of youth culture and non-conformism in the Soviet Union for many years and is the author of *Stalin's Last Generation: Soviet Post-war Youth and the Emergence of Mature Socialism* (Oxford University Press, 2010). She is currently working on a book about the Soviet hippie movement and in collaboration with the Wende Museum in Los Angeles curating an exhibition on the same topic.

SOPHIE HACKETT is Curator of Photography at the Art Gallery of Ontario (AGO) and adjunct faculty in Ryerson University's MA programme in Film and Photography Preservation and Collections Management. Her recent publications include 'Queer Looking: Joan E. Biren's Slide Shows', *Aperture* (Spring 2015), and 'Encounters in the Museum: The Experience of Photographic Objects' in the volume *The 'Public' Life of Photographs* (ed. Thierry Gervais, Ryerson Image Centre and MIT Press, 2016). Her recent curatorial projects at the AGO include *Thomas Ruff: Object Relations* and the co-curated *Outsiders: American Photography and Film, 1950s–1980s* (both 2016).

MAX HOUGHTON runs the MA in Photojournalism and Documentary Photography at London College of Communication, University of the Arts London. She edited *8 Magazine* for six years and writes regularly for the international arts press. She has curated photographic exhibitions in London, Brighton and New York. Her first book, *Firecrackers: Female Photographers Now*, co-authored with Fiona Rogers, was published by Thames & Hudson in 2017. She is also a scholarship doctoral candidate in the Faculty of Laws, University College London.

SEAN O'HAGAN is the *Guardian*'s photography and photojournalism critic and feature writer for the *Observer* newspaper. He was the winner of the 2011 J. Dudley Johnston Award from the Royal Photographic Society for 'major achievement in the field of photographic criticism'.

ALISTAIR O'NEILL is Professor of Fashion History and Theory at Central Saint Martins, University of the Arts London. He is the author of *London: After a Fashion* (Reaktion, 2007) and is a fashion curator, his most recent exhibitions being *Guy Bourdin: Image Maker* (2015) and *Isabella Blow: Fashion Galore!* (2013) at Somerset House, London. He writes for *Aperture* and *Disegno* and is preparing for an Arts and Humanities Research Council project (2018–20) on pattern-cutting with his colleague Professor Caroline Evans.

ALONA PARDO is a Curator at Barbican Art Gallery. She has curated a number of exhibitions and publications, including most recently *Richard Mosse: Incoming* (2017), *Strange and Familiar: Britain as Revealed by International Photographers* (with Martin Parr, 2016) and *Constructing Worlds: Photography and Architecture in the Modern Age* (with Elias Redstone, 2014). She has contributed widely to art magazines and books, including *Vitamin P3* (Phaidon, 2016) and *Modern Forms: A Subjective Atlas of 20th Century Architecture* by the contemporary photographer Nicolas Grospierre (Prestel, 2016).

LEO RUBINFIEN is an American photographer and writer. His books include *A Map of the East*, *Wounded Cities* (2008) and *The Ardbeg* (2010), and his photographs have been exhibited by institutions including the Metropolitan Museum of Art and the Museum of Modern Art in New York; the National Gallery of Art, Washington, DC; the San Francisco Museum of Modern Art (SFMOMA); the National Museum of Modern Art, Tokyo; and the Museo d'Arte Contemporanea, Rome. He was also Guest Curator of the exhibitions *Shomei Tomatsu: Skin of the Nation* and *Garry Winogrand* for SFMOMA and the National Gallery of Art and author of their accompanying catalogues.

AARON SCHUMAN is an artist, writer, editor and curator. He is the author of *FOLK* (NB, 2016) and has contributed essays to books including *George Rodger: Nuba and Latuka, the Colour Photographs* (Prestel, 2017) and *Alec Soth: Gathered Leaves* (MACK, 2015), among many others; he also regularly writes for

magazines such as *Aperture*, *Foam*, *Frieze*,
TIME, *Hotshoe* and the *British Journal of
Photography*. Schuman has also curated
several major exhibitions and served as Chief
Curator of Jaipur Photo 2018 and Krakow
Photomonth 2014. He is a Senior Lecturer at
the University of Brighton and Course Leader
of the MA in Photography at the University
of the West of England, Bristol.

STANLEY WOLUKAU-WANAMBWA
is a photographer, writer and former editor
of the website *The Great Leap Sideways*.
He has contributed essays to catalogues
and monographs by Vanessa Winship,
Paul Graham, Marton Perlak and George
Georgiou, guest-edited the Aperture
PhotoBook Review, and has written for
Aperture and *FOAM* magazine. He has
exhibited at Vox Populi, Philadelphia, and
at Light Work, Syracuse, where he was an
artist-in-residence in 2015, and has lectured
at Yale University, Cornell University and
The New School.

FRANCESCO ZANOT is a critic and the
Curator of Camera – Centro Italiano per
la Fotografia, Turin. He has worked on
numerous exhibitions and publications
with international photographers and
has published books dedicated to artists
including Mark Cohen, Guido Guidi, Luigi
Ghirri, Takashi Homma, Linda Fregni Nagler,
Francesco Jodice, Erik Kessels and Boris
Mikhailov. Together with Alec Soth he is the
author of the essay 'Ping Pong Conversations'
(Contrasto, 2013). He is Director of the MA
in Photography at the Nuova Academia
di Belle Arti, Milan, and has taught and
lectured in numerous academic institutions,
among them Columbia University, New
York, the École Cantonale d'Art de Lausanne,
and Università Iuav, Venice. He has been
Associate Editor of *Fantom* since its
foundation, and curated the exhibitions *Give
Me Yesterday* (2016–17) and *Stefano Graziani:
Questioning Pictures* (2017–13) at Fondazione
Prada Osservatorio, Milan.

ACKNOWLEDGEMENTS

We would like to extend our special thanks to the following individuals and institutions for their invaluable support and guidance with the exhibition research, development and realisation:

Federica Angelucci, Stevenson, Cape Town
Oriana Baddeley, University of the Arts, London
Emily Barresi, Jim Goldberg Studio, California
Alison Beckett, AGO, Ontario
Sarah Borst, Bruce Davidson Studio, New York
Elizabeth Brannan-Williams, Howard Greenberg Gallery, New York
Caroline Burghardt, Luhring Augustine, New York
David Campany
June Can, Beinecke Rare Book and Manuscript Library Yale University, New Haven, Connecticut
David Chandler
Sinazo Chiya, Stevenson, Cape Town
Tim Clark
Meagan Connolly, Bruce Davidson Studio, New York
Lucy Davies
The Diane Arbus Estate
Ola Dlugosz, Fraenkel Gallery, San Francisco
Anne Doran, *Art in America*, New York
Tiffany Edwards, Luhring Augustine, New York
Terry Etherton, Etherton Gallery, Tuscon, Arizona
Michael Famighetti, Aperture, New York
Alexandra Ferrari, Luhring Augustine, New York
Duncan Forbes, Getty Research Institute, Los Angeles
Patrick Frey, Edition Patrick Frey, Zurich
Juliane Fürst, University of Bristol
Paul Gambin, Magnum Photos, London
Sophie Hackett, AGO, Ontario
Halley Hair, Life, New York
Martin Hasselbring, Independent Magazine, London
Nicola Hederich, Galerie Peter Kilchmann, Zurich
Deslynne Hill, Stevenson, Cape Town
Ruth Hoffmann, Magnum Photos, London
Michael Hoppen, Michael Hoppen Gallery, London
Leah Horowitz, Luhring Augustine, New York
Max Houghton, London College of Communication, London
Maya Ishiwata
Lanese Jaftha, Stevenson, Cape Town

Julia Kelly-Kennedy, Simon Lee Gallery, London
Peter Kilchmann, Galerie Peter Kilchmann, Zurich
Elizabeth Koehn, Gavin Brown's enterprise, New York
Teresa Kroemer, Bruce Davidson Studio, New York
Ceri Lewis, ARTIST ROOMS, National Galleries of Scotland, Edinburgh, and Tate, London
CN Lester
Nancy Lieberman, Howard Greenberg Gallery, New York
Barbara Lisicki
Amanda Lo, Zen Foto Gallery, Tokyo
Anke Loots, Pieter Hugo Studio
Meredith Lue, Mary Ellen Mark Library/Studio, New York
Georgia Lurie, Simon Lee Gallery, London
Livia Luzzago, Sprovieri, London
Tracy Mallon-Jensen, AGO, Ontario
Karen Marks, Howard Greenberg Gallery, New York
Margherita Molinari, Sprovieri, London
Celia Montgomery, Hearst Magazine International, New York
Sohey Moriyama, Daidō Moriyama Photo Foundation, Tokyo
Gillian Murphy, The London School of Economics and Political Science, London
Sean O'Hagan
Jill Offenbeck, AGO, Ontario
Alistair O'Neill, University of the Arts, London
Yuri Palmin
Martin Parr
Mark Pearson, Zen Foto Gallery, Tokyo
John Pelosi
Bonnie Pong-Wai Ma, Zen Foto Gallery, Tokyo
Michael Prete, Howard Greenberg Gallery, New York
Gordon Read, The London School of Economics and Political Science, London
Annemarie Reichen, Galerie Peter Kilchmann, Zurich
Melanie Rio, Melanie Rio Fluency, Nantes
Alyson Rolington, ARTIST ROOMS, National Galleries of Scotland, and Tate, Edinburgh and London
Leo Rubinfien
Natalia Sacasa, Luhring Augustine, New York
Aaron Schuman
Christian Schweizer, Edition Patrick Frey, Zurich
Therese Seeholzer, Fotomuseum, Winterthur

Thomas Seelig, Fotomuseum, Winterthur
Loni Shibuyama, ONE Archives at the USC Libraries, Los Angeles
Niccolo Sprovieri, Sprovieri, London
Daphne Srinivasan, Etherton Gallery, Tuscon
Milena Stagni, Melanie Rio Fluency, Nantes
Gregor Staiger, Galerie Gregor Staiger, Zurich
Guillaume Sultana, Galerie Sultana, Paris
Chris Sutherns, Tate Images, London
William Swainger, Tate Images, London
Sandy Thomas, Sandy Thomas Advertising, Capistrano Beach
Elisa Uematsu, Taka Ishii, Tokyo
Stanley Wolukau-Wanambwa
Amy Wong, Life, New York
Sophie Wright, Magnum Photos, London
Francesco Zanot, Camera, Turin

CREDITS

Image Credits

Front cover, pp. 125, 127: Collection
Fotomuseum Winterthur

pp. 2–3, 19, 215, 217–25: © Alec Soth/
Magnum Photos

pp. 10–11, 97, 99–109, back cover: © Seiji
Kurata, courtesy of Zen Foto Gallery

pp. 13, 30, pp. 34–45: © Bruce Davidson/
Magnum Photos, courtesy Howard
Greenberg Gallery, New York

pp. 16, pp. 161–73: courtesy of the Artist
© Paz Errázuriz

pp. 23, 27–29: © Tate, London 2018, © The
Estate of Diane Arbus; Text © Art Media
Holdings, LLC, New York. Reprinted
by permission

pp. 46, 50–57: © Daidō Moriyama Photo
Foundation, Tokyo

pp. 59–69: © 2018 Art Gallery of Ontario

pp. 71–81: © Danny Lyon/Magnum Photos,
courtesy of the Artist and Gavin Brown's
enterprise, New York/Rome

pp. 83, 86–95: © Larry Clark, courtesy of the
Artist, Luhring Augustine, New York,
and Simon Lee Gallery, London/Hong
Kong

pp. 111, 114–17: © Igor Palmin, courtesy
of the Artist

pp. 118–23: © Igor Palmin, courtesy
of the Artist

pp. 128–35: © Walter Pfeiffer, courtesy
of Galerie Sultana and Galerie Gregor
Staiger, Paris and Zurich

pp. 149, 152–59: courtesy Philippe Chancel/
Melanie Rio Fluency

pp. 161, 163–71: © Chris Steele-Perkins/
Magnum Photos

pp. 174, 177–83: © Mary Ellen Mark, courtesy
Howard Greenberg Gallery, New York

pp. 185, 188–93: © Jim Goldberg/Magnum
Photos, courtesy of the Artist and Pace/
MacGill Gallery, New York

pp. 195, 197–201: courtesy the Artist and
Sprovieri, London

pp. 203, 205–13: © Dayanita Singh

pp. 227, 229–31: © Pieter Hugo, courtesy
of Stevenson, Cape Town/Johannesburg,
and Yossi Milo, New York

pp. 233, 236–45: © Katy Grannan, courtesy
the Artist and Fraenkel Gallery, San
Francisco

pp. 247, 219–56: courtesy the Artist and
Galerie Peter Kilchmann, Zurich

pp. 260–61: Beinecke Rare Book and
Manuscript Library, Yale University,
with permission of SANDY THOMAS
ADVERTISING, Capistrano Beach, CA

pp. 262–65: courtesy of ONE Archives at the
USC Libraries; with permission
of SANDY THOMAS ADVERTISING,
Capistrano Beach, CA

pp. 267–73: as originally published in *Esquire*

pp. 274–83: *Walter Pfeiffer: Scrapbooks,
1969–1985* (Edition Patrick Frey, 2012)

pp. 284–92: © The Mary Ellen Mark
Foundation/Falkland Road, Inc.;
© 1983 Time Inc. All rights reserved.
Reprinted from LIFE and published with
permission of Time Inc. Reproduction
in any manner in any language in whole
or in part without written permission is
prohibited. LIFE and the LIFE logo are
registered trademarks of Time Inc. Used
under license

Note on Language

The language used throughout this book
is the choice of each individual author.
We understand that language pertaining
to sexual identity and gender has changed
considerably over the last sixty years and
continues to evolve. Where possible, we have
ensured that any language used to describe
an individual's identity is faithful to their
own description, however we are mindful that
some of the historic terms used may now be
considered outdated.

Official copyright © 2018 Barbican
Centre, City of London.
The Authors and Artists.

First published 2018 by Prestel
Publishing Limited in association with
Barbican Art Gallery on the occasion
of the exhibition *Another Kind of Life:
Photography on the Margins*
28 February – 27 May 2018.

Barbican Art Gallery
Barbican Centre
Silk Street
London EC2Y 8DS
barbican.org.uk

EXHIBITION

Curated by Alona Pardo,
Barbican Art Gallery

Exhibition Assistants: Tatjana LeBoff,
Charlotte Flint

Research Assistant: Julie Verheye

Curatorial Intern: Harry Dougall

Exhibition Design: Casper Mueller
Kneer Ltd Architects

Exhibition Graphic Design:
Melanie Mues, Mues Design, London

PUBLICATION

Prestel Verlag, Munich · London ·
New York, a member of Verlagsgruppe
Random House GmbH, Neumarkter
Straße 28, 81673 Munich

In respect to links in the book the
Publisher expressly notes that no
illegal content was discernible on
the linked sites at the time the links
were created. The Publisher has no
influence at all over the current and
future design, content or authorship
of the linked sites. For this reason the
Publisher expressly disassociates itself
from all content on linked sites that
has been altered since the link was
created and assumes no liability for
such content.

Prestel Publishing Ltd.
14–17 Wells Street
London W1T 3PD

Prestel Publishing
900 Broadway, Suite 603
New York, NY 10003

Library of Congress Control
Number is available; British Library
Cataloguing-in-Publication Data:
a catalogue record for this book is
available from the British Library

Editorial Coordination: Lincoln Dexter

Copy-editing: Aimee Selby

Production: Andrea Cobré
and Corinna Pickart

Design: Melanie Mues,
Mues Design, London

Origination: Repro-Ludwig,
Zell am See, Austria

Printing and Binding: Kösel GmbH
& Co. KG, Germany

Paper: Profibulk, Tauro

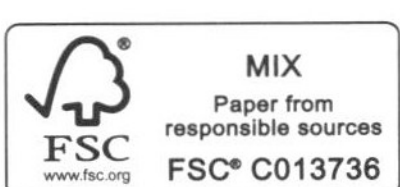

Verlagsgruppe Random House
FSC® N001967

Printed in Germany

ISBN 978-3-7913-8427-6

www.prestel.com

Front cover: Walter Pfeiffer, *Untitled*
(from *Carlo Joh*), 1973

Back cover: Seiji Kurata, *A Tattooed
Man*, rooftop of the Bungeiza Street
Building, Ikebukuro, Tokyo, 1975

pp. 2–3: Alec Soth, *USA* (from *Broken
Manual*), 2006

pp. 10–11: Seiji Kurata, *Sister Akane,
at Home, Laughing*, Honcho,
Ikebukuro, Tokyo, 1977